ENCYCLOPEDIA

OF THE

WORLD'S MINORITIES

ENCYCLOPEDIA

OF THE
WORLD'S MINORITIES

Volume 3
P–Z
INDEX

CARL SKUTSCH, EDITOR
MARTIN RYLE, CONSULTING EDITOR

ROUTLEDGE
NEW YORK AND LONDON

\-05

Published in 2005 by
Routledge
Taylor & Francis Group
270 Madison Avenue
New York, NY 10016
www.routledge-ny.com

Published in Great Britain by
Routledge
Taylor & Francis Group
2 Park Square
Milton Park, Abingdon
Oxon OX14 4RN
www.routledge.co.uk

Library of Congress Cataloging-in-Publication Data

Encyclopedia of the world's minorities / Carl Skutsch, editor; Martin Ryle, consulting editor.
    p. cm.
  Includes bibliographical references.
  ISBN 1-57958-392-X (alk. paper)
  1. Ethnic groups—Encyclopedias. 2. Minorities—Encyclopedias.
I. Skutsch, Carl.   II. Ryle, Martin (J. Martin)   III. Title.

GN495.4.E63 2005
305.8'003—dc22   2004020324

Advisory Board Members

Table of Contents

List of Entries

Thematic List of Entries

Biographies

Achebe, Chinua (Nigerian)
Adams, Gerry (Northern Ireland Catholic)
Aga Khan (Ismaili)
Ali, Muhammad (African-American)
Ambedkar, Bhimrao Ramji (Dalit)
Arafat, Yasser (Palestinian)

Bhindranwale, Jarnail Sant (India-Sikh)
Bonner, Neville Thomas (Aborigine)

Césaire, Aimé (Martiniquais)
Chavez, Cesar (Mexican-American)

Dalai Lama (Tibetan)
De Klerk, F.W. (Afrikaner)
Du Bois, W.E.B. (African-American)

Fanon, Frantz Omar (Algerian)
Farrakhan, Louis (African-American)

Gandhi, Mohandas Karamchand (India)
Garang, John (Sudanese)
Garvey, Marcus (Jamaican)
Gheorghe, Nicolae (Roma Romania)
Grant, Bernie (United Kingdom)
Guillen, Nicolas (Cuban)

Hall, Stuart (United Kingdom Afro-Caribbean)
Hamer, Fannie Lou (African-American)
Hooks, Bell (African-American)
Hume, John (Northern Ireland Catholic)

Jackson, Jesse (African-American)
James, C.L.R. (Trinidadian)
Jinnah, Muhammad Ali (Pakistani)
Jordan, Barbara (African-American)

Katari, Tupac (Aymaran)
King, Martin Luther, Jr. (African-American)

Le Pen, Jean Marie (French)
Levesque, Rene
Luthuli, Albert (South African)

Mabo, Edward (Torres Strait Islander, Australia)
Malcolm X (African-American)

Mandela, Nelson (South African)
Marcos, Subcomandante (Amerindian)
Marley, Bob (Jamaican)
Menchú, Rigoberta (Amerindian)
Morrison, Toni (African-American)
Muhammad, Elijah (African-American)

Nasser, Gamal Abdel (Egyptian)
Ngugi wa Thiong'o (Kenyan)

Ocalan, Abdullah (Kurd)

Parnell, Charles Stewart (Irish)
Peltier, Leonard (Amerindian)
Pope Shenouda III (Coptic Christian)
Prabhakaran, Vellupillai (Sri Lanka-Tamil)

Ramos-Horta, José (East Timor)
Rugova, Ibrahim (Albanian)

Saro-Wiwa, Ken (Ogoni Nigerian)
Selassie, Haile (Ethiopian)
Senghor, Leopold (Senegalese)
Silva, Benedita da (Afro-Brazilian)
Singh, Tara (Sikh)

Tiruchelvam, Neelan (Tamil-Sri Lanka)
Trimble, David (Northern Ireland)
Tutu, Desmond (South African)

Washington, Booker T. (African-American)
Wright, Richard (African-American)

Zana, Leila (Kurd)

Groups

Aborigines
Acehnese
Afar
Africans: Europe
Africans: Overview
Afrikaners
Afro-Brazilians
Afro-Caribbeans
Afro-Cubans
Afro-Latin Americans
Ahmadiyas

Nations

THEMATIC LIST OF ENTRIES

Philippines
Poland
Portugal

Qatar

Romania
Russia
Rwanda

Saint Kitts and Nevis
Saint Lucia
Samoa
San Marino
São Tomé and Príncipe
Saudi Arabia
Senegal
Seychelles
Sierra Leone
Singapore
Slovakia
Slovenia
Somalia
South Africa
Spain
Sri Lanka
Sudan
Suriname
Swaziland
Sweden
Switzerland
Syria

Taiwan
Tajikistan
Tanzania
Thailand
Togo
Turkey
Turkmenistan

Uganda
Ukraine
United Arab Emirates
United Kingdom
Uruguay
Uzbekistan

Vanuatu
Venezuela

Vietnam
Yemen
Yugoslavia

Zambia
Zimbabwe

Topics

Affirmative Action
Africa: A Continent of Minorities?
African-American Nationalism and Separatism
Afrocentricity
American Indian Movement (AIM)
Anti-Semitism
Apartheid
Assam Movement
Assimilation
Autonomy

Bilingualism

Civil War, United States
Colonialism
Creole (mixed-origin minorities)
Critical Race Theory

Diaspora
Diaspora: African
Diaspora: Chinese
Diaspora: Indian

Education Rights
Environmental Racism
Equal Opportunity
Ethnic Conflict
Exchange of Population

Federalism

Gender and Minority Status
Genocide
Globalization and Minority Cultures

Human and Minority Rights Organizations
Human Rights

Immigration
Imperialism
Indigenous Peoples

Preface

Social and political changes around the world have added an urgency to the study of minorities and minority issues. Globalization, immigration, migration, civil conflict, and ethnic tensions have brought greater public awareness to minority groups and greater academic interest to minority studies. Similarly, the international community's commitment to self-determination, cultural diversity, human differences, and the preservation of traditions has attracted the attention of the public and focused the energies of a worldwide array of scholars working in a range of subject areas.

Reflecting the interdisciplinary and international character of minority studies, the *Encyclopedia of the World's Minorities* includes the work of over 300 contributors from 40 countries specializing in areas as varied as anthropology, cultural studies, ethnography, history, international relations, linguistics, political science, and religion. These scholars work at universities and colleges as well as research centers and organizations around the globe that seek to further our understanding of minority issues and monitor the situation of minority groups. Within this community, the subject is rigorously and often contentiously argued, but the degree of interest and the intensity of debate ultimately testify to its importance. Because the study of minorities involves the difficult issues of rights, justice, equality, dignity, identity, autonomy, political liberties, and cultural freedoms, the discussions in the encyclopedia apply to many areas of public interest and student inquiry.

One of the concepts most vigorously debated by those working in minority studies is the meaning of "minority" itself. This is because the meaning does matter. In the early twentieth century, the African-American political thinker W.E.B. Du Bois declared the color line to be the defining issue of the age. From that time forward the line that demarcates a minority group, acknowledges a minority concern, or defines a minority right has had considerable consequence. The *Encyclopedia of the World's Minorities*, like minority studies itself, attempts not to finalize this definition but to present its histories and complexities.

Traditionally, a minority group has been understood to have an indigenous relationship to an area—what is called an autochthonous relationship—where it is, at a given time, numerically inferior to another group. Such a group is understood to share a cultural characteristic that one member identifies in another. This shared culture may take the form of ethnicity, race, customs, language, or religion; and it receives larger legitimacy by virtue of its long-standing presence in a region. Although this definition functions within limited contexts and is acknowledged throughout the encyclopedia, it is far from universal, because it fails to account for a surplus of historical issues and influences that we confront today.

For example, according to this orthodox definition of minority, a member of an indigenous group may enjoy a legal relationship to a nation that vastly differs from that of an immigrant, a permanent resident, or a migrant worker, all of whom may share the cultural markers of a minority group but have none of the protections. Governments that secure protections, rights, and entitlements—which may include access to employment, political processes, education, health care, the media, and the judicial system—only for recognized minorities may thereby exclude non-indigenous groups from these same privileges. The encyclopedia presents how minority studies discusses the tensions created by conferring legal privileges to indigenous minorities and withholding them from others.

Although numerical inferiority may seem a reasonable, if only intuitive, way to define minority status, it is not sufficient within minority studies. Slavery in the American South, apartheid in South Africa, and the Baathist system in Iraq—where a numerically inferior group dominated a numerically superior group—all serve to remind us that a consideration of cultural and political *non-dominance* must enter our understanding of what minority status means. Numerical superiority of one group often enforces cultural and political dominance over another group, but numbers alone do not adequately define minority or fully describe the relative influence and self-determination one group may enjoy.

In this sense, minority status has come to define a political relationship rather than an inherent or changeless attribute of a people. The discipline does not agree that minority status requires that a people share immutable characteristics that are often associated with race and ethnicity. Religion and language, for example, are not immutable identities, because they can be acquired or change, but they do figure significantly in minorities' self-identification. Recently, some scholars have argued for a definition that accounts for power and equality, in which a minority is any group that has historically been relegated to a status unequal to that of a dominant group, regardless of distinct cultural or ethnic attributes; this definition would include sexual minorities. The encyclopedia brings these issues to light, presents these arguments, and summarizes broader opinion.

The broad opinion might conclude from these debates that the most inclusive definition of a minority or minorities is preferred. Certainly there is truth in this. Nevertheless, for those attempting to create law and public policy that is responsible to an electorate, a pragmatic approach to minority issues is, however flawed, a fundamental but ever-changing reality. For example, principles such as self-determination and cultural autonomy are universally recognized (at least among democratic nations and those creating law and public policy) yet pragmatically circumscribed to prevent instability and secessionist conflicts where coexistence and integration are possible and preferred. Coexistence, intercultural communication, and civil processes are as important to minority studies as independence, difference, and diversity. Incremental progress is also a valued strategy in the discussion of minority issues. On the one hand, national laws regarding minorities are often more restrictive than international procla-mations. Thus individual nations, such as the member states of the European Community, while respecting certain basic rights for all, provide substantial protections, politically and culturally, to those minority groups officially recognized by the state. On the other hand, the United Nations uses a very broad definition of minority status and rights—one that may serve groups as they argue and agitate against political facts—but the protections that this definition *guarantees* are unhappily too few. The unhappy compromise is often a reality for the world's minorities.

Organization of the Encyclopedia

Calculations and compromises are necessary in the creation of a work that covers such a large subject. The *Encyclopedia of the World's Minorities* does not contain an entry on every minority group in every nation and region of the world. It presents for the user a thorough resource on minority studies. The information here covers the vast and diverse study of the world's minorities, introducing students to the field and providing an international perspective that enables students to pursue their own interests. To give structure to the scope of such a project, a four-pronged rationale was chosen that creates an accessible architecture for readers of the encyclopedia. This strategy organizes the encyclopedia into four clearly defined entry types: *topics, nations, groups,* and *biographies.*

Of the 562 entries in the encyclopedia, 75 **Topics entries** introduce students to the broad ideas, concepts, and concerns shared by those working on minority issues. Readers will find definitions and histories of such terms as "Autonomy," "Self-determination," and "Nationalism." Entries of this kind also include organizations and institu-tions, such as Sinn Féin, the League of Nations, and Minority Rights Group International. These entries help to familiarize students with the language of the discipline and to understand how organizations participate in the field and are discussed within it.

Nations entries (173 in total) describe the history of minorities living within national borders and so explain the political and legal apparatus that states formally create in relation to their minority populations as well as the informal conditions experienced by those groups. In nation entries the reader will find information not only about the dominant group in a country, such as the Swedes in Sweden, but about those other groups that share in the nation-state, such as the Finnish and Saami minorities in Sweden. In this respect, the encyclopedia encourages readers to think outside of categories they commonly associate with the idea of a country—to think of a nation as an assemblage of peoples and cultures rather than as a single, monolithic entity.

Groups entries, composing the largest category with a total of 251 essays, explain the history of peoples living as minorities around the world. These entries discuss whether the group is a single-nation minority or one living in multiple nations, detailing its language, religion, and political and social conditions. Each group entry also contains up-to-date population data garnered from, among other sources such as national censuses, the 2003 *World Factbook* published by the CIA for the United States Government. Group entries are of two kinds: one covers groups who, wherever they are found, live as a minority, such as the Roma (Gypsies); the other covers groups who enjoy a dominant place in a homeland but are found elsewhere as minorities, such as the Japanese. This distinction is important to recognize because the notions of identity and cultural legitimacy are so often linked with a place of origin or with a nation that the situation of stateless peoples is often ignored. Similarly, minorities seeking greater protections have often resorted to nationalism to assert political liberties.

Biographies introduce persons who figure significantly in the history of minority communities and who, through their actions or words, have articulated the larger interests of minority peoples. A total of 62 such entries include Marcus Garvey, Mahatma Gandhi, and Ngugi wa Thiong'o. Biographical entries credit an individual's importance but also reveal how leaders of minority campaigns and struggles influence one another in vastly different parts of the world, showing that a minority group identifies not always only with itself but also with other minority groups as they look to each other for guidance.

Ultimately, an encyclopedia is a wealth of integrated information that maps an area of interest and provides as many access points to that information as possible. In creating this map, the encyclopedia aims to present fact, not opinion. Its entries describe rather than persuade, explain arguments rather than take sides, present rather than resolve areas of contention. The *Encyclopedia of the World's Minorities* contains 562 **signed scholarly essays** about nations, groups, and issues around the world that, written in clear, accessible prose, create a detailed map of a complicated terrain. Each entry includes a selection of **further readings** and **cross-references** (listed in "see also" sections at the end of each entry) to other articles for those readers who wish to explore a topic in greater depth. **Blind entries** serve to guide the reader through the work. A thorough, **analytic index** provides the reader with a critical tool for accessing the work in its entirety.

Creating an encyclopedia is never a solitary undertaking. I would like to extend my appreciation to the editorial board. Their help in formulating the final table of contents was invaluable. I would especially like to thank Martin Ryle, professor of history, emeritus, the University of Virginia, Charlottesville, Virginia. His willingness to review the final manuscript in the closing months of the project was nothing short of heroic. His guidance and commitment to the encyclopedia made its publication possible. Finally, I would like to thank the hundreds of contributors whose work here will further our understanding of the world's minorities.

Notes on Contributors

Rafis Abazov, Harriman Institute, Columbia University, New York, USA.

Jon Abbink, African Studies Centre, Leiden University, The Netherlands.

Marat Akchurin, Bethesda, Maryland, USA.

Shawn Alexander, W.E.B. Du Bois Department of Afro-American Studies, University of Massachusetts at Amherst, USA.

Agron Alibali, Boston, Massachusetts, USA.

Erik Allardt, Department of Sociology, University of Helsinki, Finland.

Mehdi Parvizi Amineh, International Institute for Asian Studies, Leiden, The Netherlands.

Guy Arnold, London, United Kingdom.

Michael Azariadis, Perth, Australia.

Tuncay Babali, Department of Political Science, University of Houston, Texas, USA.

D. Shyam Babu, Rajiv Gandhi Institute for Contemporary Studies, New Delhi, India.

Michael Banton, University of Bristol, United Kingdom.

Abdoulaye Barry, University Gaston Baerger, Saint Louis, Senegal.

Trevor Batrouney, RMIT University, Balwyn, Australia.

Florian Bieber, Nationalism Studies Program, Central European University, Budapest, Hungary.

Charles Boewe, Pittsboro, North Carolina, USA.

Nadia Joanne Britton, Department of Sociological Studies, University of Sheffield, United Kingdom.

Susan Love Brown, Department of Anthropology, Florida Atlantic University, USA.

Anne Brydon, Department of Sociology and Anthropology, Wilfrid Laurier University, Waterloo, Ontario, Canada.

Marcelo Bucheli, Department of History, Stanford University, California, USA.

Debra Buchholtz, Banbury, Oxfordshire, United Kingdom.

Jeff Burke, Religious Studies Program, Lynchburg College, Virginia, USA.

Joan Manuel Cabezas Lopez, University of Barcelona, Catalonia, Spain.

Laura M. Calkins, Vietnam Archive, Texas Tech University, USA.

Gregory R. Campbell, Department of Anthropology, University of Montana at Missoula, USA.

Tim Carmichael, African Studies Center, Michigan State University, USA.

Wendy Carter, USA.

Ellis Cashmore, School of Health, Staffordshire University, Stafford, United Kingdom.

Derek Catsam, Falls Church, Virginia, USA.

Shukai R. Chaudhari, The Nepal Indigenous Development Society, Ratnanagar Tandi, Chitwan, Nepal.

Tan Chee-Beng, Department of Anthropology, The Chinese University of Hong Kong.

James Chin, School of Administrative and Political Studies, University of Papua New Guinea.

Jamsheed Choksy, Middle Eastern Studies Program, Indiana University, USA.

T. Matthew Ciolek, Research School of Asian and Pacific Studies, Australian National University.

Andrew Clark, History Department, University of North Carolina at Wilmington, USA.

Samuel Cohen, Department of English, Lehman College, City University of New York, USA.

Robert O. Collins, Department of History, University of California at Santa Barbara, USA.

Daniele Conversi, Department of Policy Studies, University of Lincolnshire, Lincoln, United Kingdom.

Allan Cooper, Department of Political Science, Otterbein College, Ohio, USA.

Susan Crate, Department of Geography, Miami University, Oxford, Ohio, USA.

Nigel Crawhall, South African San Institute/Indigenous Peoples of Africa Coordinating Committee, Cape Town, South Africa.

Kevin Curow, Bad Homburg, Germany.

Farhad Daftary, Institute of Ismali Studies, London, United Kindgom.

Loring Danforth, Department of Anthropology, Bates College, Maine, USA.

John Davies, Department of Economics, Acadia University, Wolfville, Nova Scotia, Canada.

Darién J. Davis, History Department, Middlebury College, Vermont, USA.

John H. Davis, New York, USA.

Fernand de Varennes, School of Law, Murdoch University, Perth, Australia.

Anne Decoret-Ahiha, Universitè Lyon II, France.

Neil Denslow, Independent Scholar, Dorset, United Kingdom.

Barbara Dilly, Department of Sociology and Anthropology, Creighton University, Nebraska, USA.

Elena Dingu-Kyrklund, Center of Research in International Migration and Ethnic Relations, Stockholm University, Sweden.

Audra Diptee, Department of History, University of Toronto, Ontario, Canada.

Aleksandra Djajic Horváth, Department of History and Civilization, European University Institute, Florence, Italy.

Ivana Djuric, Zagreb, Croatia.

Stephanie Hemelryk Donald, Murdoch University, Perth, Australia.

Yves Dorémieux, Anthropology Department, Center for Mongolian and Siberian Studies, University Paris X, France.

Haley Duschinski, Harvard University, Boston, Massachusetts, USA.

James Eder, Department of Anthropology, Arizona State University, USA.

Fadwa El Guindi, University of Southern California, USA.

Robyn Eversole, Centre for Regional and Rural Development, RMIT University, Hamilton, Victoria, Australia.

Brigit Farley, Department of History, Washington State University, Tri-Cities, USA.

Mariana Ferreira, Anthropology, University of Tennessee, USA.

Peter Finke, Max Planck Institute for Social Anthropology, Halle/Saale, Germany.

Sterling Fluharty, Department of History, University of Oklahoma, USA.

Bernard Formoso, Departement d'ethnologie, Universite Paris X–Nanterre, France.

Germán Freire, University of London, United Kingdom.

Victor Friedman, University of Chicago, Illinois, USA.

Hillel Frisch, Department of Political Studies, Bar-Ilan University, Ramat-Gan, Israel.

Steve Garner, School of Sociology, University of the West of England, Bristol, United Kingdom.

Erika H. Gilson, Princeton University, New Jersey, USA.

Benito Giordano, University of Manchester, United Kingdom.

Martí Grau, Barcelona, Spain.

Joseph Graves, Jr., Glendale, Arizona, USA.

Juan Carlos Gumucio, Department of Cultural Anthropology and Ethnography, Uppsala University, Sweden.

Annette Hamilton, Department of Anthropology, Macquarie University, Sydney, New South Wales, Australia.

Kevin David Harrison, Department of Linguistics, Swarthmore College, Pennsylvania, USA.

Maximilian Hartmuth, University of Vienna, Austria.

Ai Hattori, Alexandria, Virginia, USA.

Angela Haynes, Minority Rights Group, London, United Kingdom.

Dagmar Hellmann-Rajanayagam, Department of Economic and Social Science, University Erlangen-Nuremberg, Germany.

Arthur Helweg, Department of Anthropology, Western Michigan University, USA.

Kristin Henrard, Department of International and Constitutional Law, University of Groningen, The Netherlands.

J. Scott Hill, Richmond, Virginia, USA.

Jeremy Hodes, Kambah, Australia.

Krisadawan Hongladarom, Department of Linguistics, Faculty of Arts, Chulalongkorn University, Bangkok, Thailand.

Tian Hongliang, Department of Anthropology, The Chinese University of Hong Kong.

Michael Houf, Department of History, Texas A&M University–Kingsville, USA.

Jayne Ifekwunigwe, School of Social Sciences, University of East London, United Kingdom.

Rad Ilie, Cluj-Napoca, Romania.

Andrew Irving, London, United Kingdom.

Guillaume Jacques, Paris 7–Denis Diderot University, France.

Amjad Jaimoukha, Jordan Engineers Association, Royal Scientific Society, Amman, Jordan.

Annu Jalais, London School of Economics, United Kingdom.

Laksiri Jayasuriya, Department of Social Work, University of Western Australia.

Richard Jenkins, Migration and Ethnicity Research Center, University of Sheffield, United Kingdom.

Hou Jingrong, The Chinese University of Hong Kong.

Lars Karstedt, Universitat Hamburg, Germany.

Olga Kazmina, Moscow, Russia.

Ime Kerlee, Emory University, Georgia, USA.

Deepa Khosla, Department of Government and Politics, University of Maryland, USA.

Reinhard Klein-Arendt, Institute for African Studies, University of Cologne, Germany.

Laszlo Kocsis, Transylvania, Romania.

Charles C. Kolb, National Endowment for the Humanities, Washington, District of Columbia, USA.

Boris Koltchanov, Riga, Latvia.

Jill E. Korbin, Department of Anthropology, Case Western Reserve University, Ohio, USA.

Chima J. Korieh, Department of History, Central Michigan University, Michigan, USA.

Jørgen Kühl, Aabenraa, Denmark.

Olga Kul'bachevskya, Institute of Ethnology and Anthropology, Russian Academy of Sciences, Moscow, Russia.

P.R. Kumaraswamy, Jawaharlal Nehru University, New Delhi, India.

Yves Laberge, Département de sociologie, Institut Québécois des Hautes Etudes Internationales, Canada.

Andrea Laing-Marshall, Historical Department, Wycliffe College, Toronto, Ontario, Canada.

Laura Laubeova, Prague, Czech Republic.

Benjamin Lawrance, Department of History, Stanford University, California, USA.

Barbara Leigh, Institute for International Studies, Unviersity of Technology, Sydney, New South Wales, Australia.

Keith Leitich, Seattle, Washington, USA.

Rohini Lele, University of Pune, India.

David Leonard, Comparative Ethnic Studies, Washington State University, USA.

Hal Levine, Department of Anthropology, Victoria University of Wellington, New Zealand.

Jerome Lewis, Department of Anthropology, London School of Economics and Political Science, United Kingdom.

Wei Li, Department of Geography, Arizona State University, USA.

Yianna Liatsos, Department of Comparative Literature, Rutgers University, New Jersey, USA.

Peter Limb, Michigan State University, USA.

Pamela Lindell, Sacramento, California, USA.

Michael Lipson, Department of Political Science, Concordia University, Montreal, Quebec, Canada.

Miles Litvinoff, OneWorld International, London, United Kingdom.

Ludomir Lozny, Department of Anthropology, Hunter College, City University of New York, USA.

Leo Lucassen, Department of Social History, University of Amsterdam, The Netherlands.

Tamba M'bayo, Department of History, Michigan State University, USA.

Charles Macdonald, Campus St. Charles, Universite de Provence, Marseille, France.

Sarah Manapa, Biola University, California.

Richard R. Marcus, Department of Political Science, Yale University, Connecticut, USA.

Alexandra Marois.

Oliver Marshall, Centre for Brazilian Studies, Oxford University, United Kingdom.

Marco Martiniello, Belgian National Fund for Scientific Research and University of Liege, Belgium.

Bruce Matthews, Faculty of Arts, Acadia University, Wolfville, Nova Scotia, Canada.

Duncan McCargo, Institute for Politics and International Studies, University of Leeds, United Kingdom.

Pamela McElwee, Department of Anthropology, Yale University, Connecticut, USA.

John McGurk, Claremorris, Mayo, Ireland.

Eugene McLaughlin, Faculty of Social Sciences, The Open University, Milton Keynes, United Kingdom.

Joanne McLean, School of Environmental & Information Sciences, Charles Sturt University, Albury, Australia.

Manuella Meyer, Brown University, Rhode Island, United States.

Jean Michaud, Paris, France.

Paul E. Michelson, Department of History, Huntington College, Indiana, USA.

Alessandro Michelucci, Florence, Italy.

Maged Mikhail, West Covina, California, USA.

Monique Milia-Marie-Luce, Trinité, Martinique.

Ruth Murbach, Département des sciences juridiques, Université du Québec à Montréal, Canada.

Rachel Newcomb, Department of Anthropology, Princeton University, New Jersey, USA.

Beatrice Nicolini, Storia e Istituzioni dell'Africa, Università Cattolica del Sacro Cuore, Milano, Italy.

Stephan Nikolov, Sofia, Bulgaria.

Donnacha Ó Beacháin, Tbilisi, Georgia.

Denise T. Ogden, Penn State University, USA.

Jonathan Okamura, Department of Ethnic Studies, University of Hawaii, USA.

Brendan O'Leary, Convenor of the Government Department, London School of Economics, United Kingdom.

Dennis Papazian, Armenian Research Center, The University of Michigan-Dearborn, USA.

Joshua Pasternak, Routledge, New York, USA.

Doug Pennoyer, School of Intercultural Studies, Biola University, California, USA.

John Edward Phillips, Faculty of Humanities, Hirosaki University, Japan.

Anne Pitsch Santiago, University of Maryland, USA.

Hugh Poulton, London, United Kingdom.

Sabiyha Robin Prince, Columbia, Maryland, USA.

Pavel Puchkov, Moscow, Russia.

Eva Rakel, Amsterdam, The Netherlands.

Riccardo Redaelli, Milano, Italy.

Javaid Rehman, Department of Law, University of Leeds, United Kingdom.

Massimo Repetti, Genova, Liguria, Italy.

Annette Richardson, University of Alberta, Edmonton, Canada.

Edward A. Riedinger, Latin American, Spanish, and Portuguese Collection, Ohio State University Libraries, USA.

Mika Roinila, Department of Geography, State University of New York at New Paltz, USA.

Elisa Roller, Brussels, Belgium.

Victor Roudometof, Department of Social and Political Sciences, University of Cyprus, Nicosia, USA.

Helena Ruotsala, School of Cultural Studies, University of Turku, Finland.

Sue Russell, Biola University, California, USA.

P. Sahadevan, School of International Studies, Jawaharlal Nehru University, New Delhi, India.

Oscar Salemink, Department of Social and Cultural Anthropology, Vrije Universiteit Amsterdam, The Netherlands.

Amandeep Sandhu, Department of Sociology, University of Victoria, British Columbia, Canada.

L. Natalie Sandomirsky, Auburndale, Massachusetts, USA.

Christopher Saunders, Department of Historical Studies, University of Cape Town, Rondebosch, South Africa.

Richard Scaglion, Department of Anthropology, University of Pittsburgh, Pennsylvania, USA.

Antonia Yétúndé Fælárìn Schleicher, National African Language Resource Center, University of Wisconsin, USA.

Ulrike Schuerkens, Paris, France.

Richard Schur, American Studies Department, The University of Kansas, USA.

Murali Shanmugavelan, Communication for Development Programme, Panos Institute, London, United Kingdom.

Marika Sherwood, Oare, Kent, United Kingdom.

Andrei Simic, Department of Anthropology, University of Southern California, USA.

Gregory M. Simon, Department of Anthropology, University of California, San Diego, USA.

Scott Simon, Department of Sociology, University of Ottawa, Ontario, Canada.

Stefaan Smis, Faculty of Law, Vrije Universiteit Brussels, Belgium.

David Norman Smith, Department of Sociology, University of Kansas, USA.

Ingmar Söhrman, Göteborg University, Sweden.

Subhash Sonnad, Department of Sociology, Western Michigan University, USA.

Ernst Spaan, Netherlands Interdisciplinary Demographic Institute, The Hague, The Netherlands.

Sabira Ståhlberg, Varna, Bulgaria.

Erin Stapleton-Corcoran, Chicago, Illinois, USA.

Sian Sullivan, SOAS, London, United Kingdom.

Ingvar Svanberg, Department of East European Studies, Uppsala University, Sweden.

Nicola Tannenbaum, Sociology/Anthropology Department, Lehigh University, Pennsylvania, USA.

George Tarkhan-Mouravi, Tibilisi, Georgia.

Wade Tarzia, Arts & Humanities Division, Naugatuck Valley Community College, Connecticut, USA.

Philip Taylor, Department of Anthropology, The Australian National University, Canberra.

Louis Tenawa, UREDS International, Yaoundé, Cameroon.

Shanthi Thambiah, Gender Studies Program, University of Malaya, Kuala Lumpur, Malaysia.

Ewa M. Thompson, Department of German and Slavic Studies, Rice University, Texas, USA.

Patrick Thornberry, Department of International Relations, Keele University, Newcastle Under Lyme, Staffordshire, United Kingdom.

Lenora Timm, Department of Linguistics, University of California, Davis, USA.

Reeta Chowdhari Tremblay, Department of Political Science, Concordia University, Montreal, Quebec, Canada.

Frances Trix, Ann Arbor, Michigan, USA.

Linda Tie Hua Tsung, Language Center, Hong Kong University of Science & Technology, China.

Greta Uehling, University of Michigan, USA.

Saskia Van Hoyweghen, Antwerpen, Belgium.

Virginie Vate, Paris, France.

Charles Verharen, Department of Philosophy, Howard University, Washington, District of Columbia, USA.

Richard Verrone, The Vietnam Archive, Texas Tech University, USA.

Eduardo J. Ruiz Vieytez, Institute of Human Rights, University of Deusto, Bilbao, Basque Country, Spain.

Iain Walker, Orléans, France.

Charles Westin, Centre for Research in International Migration and Ethnic Relations, Stockholm University, Sweden.

Wim Willems, Institute for Migration and Ethnic Studies, University of Amsterdam, The Netherlands.

Brian Williams, Department of History, University of London, United Kingdom.

Davina Woods, Clever Women Consultants, Melbourne, Victoria, Australia.

Theodore Wright, Niskayuna, New York, USA.

P

Pacific Islanders

Capsule Summary

Location: Pacific Oceania
Total Population: 874,000 (2001)
Languages: English; Hawaiian; Samoan; Tongan; Guamanian
Religions: Indigenous; Christian

The term *Pacific Islanders* refers to a nonhomogeneous group of persons with origins in any of the original peoples of Hawaii, Guam, Samoa, or the other archipelagos of Pacific Oceania. These island groups comprise hundreds of volcanic islands and atolls separated by miles of open ocean. These distances allowed variations in language, cultural practices, and social organization patterns to develop, and these differences persist even after emigration to other countries. As a minority group within the United States, Pacific Islanders include but are not limited to Native Hawaiians, Samoans, Guamanians, Marshallese, Tongans, and Fijians.

One subgroup is known as *Micronesians*. This term, which refers to native people from the Marshall Islands and nearby island groups, came into popular use in the mid-1990s after the signing of international legal agreements known as Compacts of Free Association between the United States and three Pacific island nations (the Federated States of Micronesia, the Republic of the Marshall Islands, and the Republic of Palau). Even among Micronesians, ethnolinguistic diversity is the rule: The group includes at least 17 ethnic and cultural groups, some 20 languages, and numerous dialects.

In general, Pacific Islanders' home territories were added to the European powers' colonial empires in the late nineteenth century. As a result, most Pacific Islanders have been exposed to Westernizing influences for several generations. A process of gradual assimilation to the tastes and conventions of the dominant power has been underway for decades. Most Pacific Islanders who relocate to the United States do so in search of Western-style education and economic opportunities. For these immigrants, most of whom have arrived in the United States since the end of World War II, preservation of their native identities has been aided by their long-standing experience with Americans on their home islands. Many Pacific Islanders are comfortable moving back and forth between *pakeha*, or white, society and their native cultures. For example, many who find employment in an American-dominated context live lifestyles that are more traditional in family-dominated households.

Some Pacific Islanders have felt alienated from the larger *pakeha* society, however, and have launched a struggle to reassert native habits and customs. New communications tools, including documentary films and educational sites on the Internet, provide interested Pacific Islanders with information about traditional lifestyles, lore, and languages.

Native Hawaiians' struggle for self-assertion provides a case study of this approach. Although the Native Hawaiian population was estimated at 500,000 at the first sustained contact with whites in 1778, by the mid-1990s there were less than 240,000 Native Hawaiians living in Hawaii, where they composed about 19 percent of the state's population. In 1900, there were approximately 37,000 speakers of Hawaiian language, but by the 1990s perhaps only 8,000 Native Hawaiians were fluent in their own language. A revival of sorts is underway, however, in that several language and cultural immersion schools have opened since the mid-1980s, and the University of Hawaii offers an undergraduate degree program in Hawaiian language.

Some Native Hawaiian activists are even seeking a restoration of Hawaiian sovereignty, claiming that the Kingdom of Hawaii was overthrown in 1893 and its assets, including the islands themselves, illegally seized by the United States. Several independence groups have been formed, and in 1996 an unofficial Native-only plebiscite was held to assess interest in proposing a Native Hawaiian government for the islands. The plebiscite failed to endorse secession from the United States, but it did stoke interest in Native Hawaiian culture, art, and folkways. An unofficial Hawaiian Kingdom Government has been formed to push for greater rights for Native Hawaiians, and in 2001, it filed a complaint against the United States government with the United Nations, condemning America's occupation of the islands and demanding reparations payments.

This movement's emphasis on Hawaii's former status as an independent kingdom, however, alienates other Pacific Islanders in the United States. Activists from other Pacific Islander communities are seeking a greater alliance of interests between themselves and Native Americans, because many of them have received federal recognition of their claims as independent political authorities within their own lands. Both Pacific Islanders and Native Americans, it is argued, include many different tribes, clans, and cultural identities within their communities. The term *First Peoples* has been introduced to underscore the similarities between the two groups, each of which descends from the original occupants of lands now included within or closely affiliated with the United States.

One group of Pacific Islanders that has actively pursued emigration to the United States is the Marshallese. Most are economic migrants, but growing numbers of expectant Marshallese mothers are transferring their newborns to white Americans through adoption. Capitalizing on the Marshallese tradition of *kokojiriri*, adoption by members of the mother's extended family, native women receive medical care and cash payments from adoptive parents who believe they are rescuing Marshallese newborns from a life of poverty. By 2000, the Marshall Islands had the highest per capita adoption rate in the world. In 2003, the local government criminalized unregulated adoptions involving non-Marshallese, but potentially thousands of Marshallese children were already adopted.

Since the early 1970s, U.S. federal agencies and officials have grouped Pacific Islanders with the much larger populations of Asians and Asian-Americans for statistical and program purposes. In 1997, however, federal race data began separating Asian and Pacific Islanders into different categories. The 2000 Census allowed direct enumeration of Native Hawaiians, and revealed that Pacific Islanders residing in the United States tend to be young and to reside in metropolitan areas, most often in households with other family members, and often at or below the poverty threshold.

Pacific Islanders have particularly high rates of certain diseases, including diabetes, heart disease, and breast cancer. However, Pacific Islander women have been found to have lower blood pressure, reducing the incidence of strokes. About 21 percent of Pacific Islanders lack health insurance, compared with 16 percent of all Americans. Culturally accepted medical practices such as acupuncture and herbal treatments are often not covered by standard health insurance plans, reducing the usefulness of such coverage for Pacific Islanders.

LAURA CALKINS

See also **Hawaiians (indigenous); Marshall Islands; Micronesia; Samoa**

Further Reading

Barkan, Elliott Robert, *Asian and Pacific Islanders Migration in the United States: A Model of New Global Patterns*, Westport, Connecticut: Greenwood Press, 1993

Franks, Joel S., *Crossing Sidelines, Crossing Cultures: Sport and Asian Pacific American Cultural Citizenship*, Lanham, Maryland: University Press of American, 2000

Grieco, Elizabeth M., *The Native Hawaiian and Other Pacific Islanders Population, 2000*, Washington DC: U.S. Department of Commerce, U.S. Census Bureau, 2001

Moss, Joyce, *Peoples of the World: Asians and Pacific Islanders: The Culture, Geographical Setting, and Historical Background of 41 Asian and Pacific Island Peoples*, Detroit, Michigan: Gale, 1993

Pang, Valerie Ooka, and Li-Rong Lilly Cheng, editors, *Struggling to Be Heard: The Unmet Needs of Asian Pacific American Children*, Albany: State University of New York Press, 1998

Sandhu, Daya Singh, editor, *Asian and Pacific Islanders Americans: Issues and Concerns for Counseling and Psychotherapy*, Commack, New York: Nova Science Publishers, 1999

Sturma, Michael, *South Sea Maidens: Western Fantasy and Sexual Politics in the South Pacific*, Westport, Connecticut: Greenwood Press, 2002

Torrence, Robin, and Anne Clarke, editors, *The Archaeology of Difference: Negotiating Cross-Cultural Engagements in Oceania*, London: Routledge, 2000

Wallace, Lee, *Sexual Encounters: Pacific Texts, Modern Sexualities*, Ithaca, New York: Cornell University Press, 2003

Zane, Nolan W.S., David T. Takeuchi, Kathleen N.J. Young, editors, *Confronting Critical Health Issues of Asian and Pacific Islander Americans*, Thousand Oaks, California: Sage, 1994

Pakistan

Capsule Summary

Country Name: Islamic Republic of Pakistan
Location: Southern Asia, bordering the Arabian Sea, between India on the east and Iran and Afghanistan on the west and China in the north
Total Population: 150,694,740 (2003)
Languages: Punjabi 48 percent, Sindhi 12 percent, Siraiki (a Punjabi variant) 10 percent, Pashtu 8 percent, Urdu (official) 8 percent, Balochi 3 percent, Hindko 2 percent, Brahui 1 percent, English (official and lingua franca of Pakistani elite and most government ministries), Burushaski, and other 8 percent
Religions: Muslim 97 percent (Sunni 77 percent, Shi'a 20 percent), Christian, Hindu, and other 3 percent

The Republic of Pakistan is located in southern Asia bordering Afghanistan, China, India, and Iran. Both East Pakistan and West Pakistan, the two parts of the bifurcated south Asian country established in 1947, have sizable minority populations. That year British India was separated into the Muslim state of Pakistan (with two sections, West and East) and largely Hindu India; the partition was never satisfactorily resolved. Military clashes with India over the possession of the state of Kashmir were ongoing post-independence. A civil war in 1971 resulted in East Pakistan seceding and becoming the separate nation of Bangladesh.

Since Pakistan was split off from India as a homeland for Muslims of the Indian subcontinent, those not sharing the faith of Islam were naturally minorities. The white bar that composes approximately 10 percent of the country's national flag is said to represent these religious minorities; the green ground of the remainder is traditionally associated with Islam, while its crescent and star are ancient Islamic symbols.

After the large-scale migration of populations resulting from the partition of India, the 1961 census showed that 80.4 percent of East Pakistan's population was Muslim. The census was far from accurate, however; other accounts at about the same time estimate that Hindus made up as much as one-fourth of the population. The minorities, in descending order of numbers, were Hindus, Christians, Buddhists, and animists. The Bengali language was spoken by 98 percent of both Muslims and Hindus of East Pakistan, while most of the Christians, Buddhists, and animists, who populated the Chittagong Hill Tracts, spoke a variety of Tibeto-Burman languages and were culturally closer to the people of Burma (Myanmar) than to the Bengali speakers. In contrast to the west wing, East Pakistan had greater uniformity of culture, language, and social distinctions. However, the influx of Urdu-speaking Biharis prior to the independence of Bangladesh in 1971 gave that region, for the first time, a serious minority problem.

For the Pakistan remaining after 1971 it is convenient to consider three components: religious minorities, ethnic minorities, and linguistic minorities, though, to be sure, these are not mutually exclusive categories.

Partition saw a greater exchange of populations in West Pakistan than it did in East Pakistan. Nearly all of the Sikhs and most of the Hindus migrated to India, but most of the Christians remained, resulting in their being the largest religious minority at the time of independence. Both Catholics and Protestants, the Christians were mostly descendants of lowborn people who had been converted in past generations by missionaries. In independent Pakistan some came to occupy important positions; A.R. Cornelius (1903–1991), for example, was chief justice of the Supreme Court for 17 years.

Pakistan's two-million-strong Christian minority was dwarfed in magnitude when the Ahmadiyas (an Islamic minority sect) were declared non-Muslims in 1974, and have since suffered persecution. A problem brewing since 1953, when at least 2,000 people died in the riots following the attempt of the Jamaat-e-Islami and other religious groups to outlaw the followers of Mirza Ghulam Ahmad (1835–1908)—a central figure in Ahmadiyas' beliefs. It reached a resolution of sorts when the government of Zulfikar Ali Bhutto acceded to the wishes of the conservative *ulema* (clerics). Under the zealous Islamization policies of the government of Zia ul-Haq (1977–88), which included the infamous Hadood (punishments) ordinances of 1979, Ahmadiyas were further persecuted, resulting in their headquarters' being shifted to London, and the emigration of at least a million of their people. It is estimated that about five million remain in Pakistan. Among their celebrated figures are Muhammad Zafarullah Khan (1893–1985), Pakistan's first foreign minister, and Abdus Salam (1926–1996), its only Nobel laureate (theoretical physics, 1979). Zia's decrees, which prescribed heavy penalties for defaming Islam, have also been used against Christians.

Parsis, now numbering only about 2,500 (nearly all of whom live in Karachi), are of Zoroastrian faith. Their ancestors fled from Persia in the eighth century to escape Muslim persecution, and they came to prominence in western India in the nineteenth century through business and philanthropy. In Karachi, they pioneered in female education, since 1947 available to those of all faiths. Because of their culinary specialties, forms of worship, and practices for the disposal of the dead, Parsis may be regarded as an ethnic minority. Striking ethnic differences in the larger populations also occur between the settled agriculturists of Punjab and Sindh and the tribal people, loosely called Pathans, who inhabit a mountainous belt stretching from Chitral in the north through much of western Balochistan to the south.

Although many Pathans also follow settled, agricultural life in the fertile valleys of the North West Frontier Province, those in the hilly tribal belt beyond the reach of civil law continue to practice their own code called *pakhtunwali*, which involves generous hospitality, asylum for fugitives, and blood revenge for wrongs. Disputes are adjudicated in tribal *jirgas* (councils of elders).

At either end of the western tribal belt are other ethnic distinctions. People of African descent called Sidhis live on the Makran coast in the south. In the far north, in the Hindu Kush mountains, live the Kalash, who have retained so many of their traditional pagan rituals that they often still are referred to as Kafirs (unbelievers). Tucked away in Gilgit under the towering Karakorum Mountains, a few pockets of Buddhism still exist.

Ethnic differences are usually accompanied by language differences. Though the Pashto of the Pathans shares much vocabulary with the language of the Balochis and both are written in the same modified Arabic script as Punjabi, Sindhi is written in a form of Devanagri script and is not intelligible to Pashto speakers. Pashto has two principal dialects, and Sindhi has five. The language of the Balochis is derived from Persian. Within the area in which it is spoken (including the Makran coast) there occurs the Brahui language, which has no kinship with any other languages of Pakistan and resembles the Dravidian languages of south India. With this one exception, all the thirty-odd languages of Pakistan belong to the Indo-European family.

English continues to be the language of international affairs, and in Pakistan it is used largely in the higher reaches of government, the military, and education. Urdu is officially the national language, although it is the mother tongue only of the Mohajirs and their descendants, who have come to dominate Karachi and the larger cities of Sindh. About 30-million-strong, these immigrants from northern India brought with them a language, a culture, and what has come to be regarded in Pakistan as an ethnic identity. Their experience in Pakistan having swung between dominance over others to being dominated by others, many Mohajirs think of themselves as a persecuted minority, albeit a large one.

Pakistan remains an impoverished, underdeveloped country, with an estimated GDP per capita income of only $2,000 (2001–02). Internal political disputes, low foreign investment, and ongoing and expensive conflicts with India continue to hamper economic growth. An ongoing internal problem for Pakistan remains the multitudes of refugees from Afghanistan (who began fleeing as the result of the Soviet-Afghan War in the 1980s) flooding its borders.

CHARLES BOEWE

See also **Ahmadiyas; Afghanistan; Bangladesh;Bengalis; Bihari; Hindus; India; Mohajirs; Parsis;Punjabi; Sikhs; Zoroastrians**

Further Reading

Alavi, Hamza, "Nationhood and the Nationalities in Pakistan," in *Economy and Culture in Pakistan: Migrants and Cities in a Muslim Society*, edited by Donnan Hastings and Pnina Werbner, Basingstoke, England: Macmillan, 1990; New York: St. Martin's Press, 1991

Ali, Shaheen Sardar, and Javaid Rehman, *Indigenous Peoples and Ethnic Minorities of Pakistan: Constitutional and Legal Perspectives*, Richmond, Surrey: Curzon, 2001

Blood, Peter R., editor, *Pakistan: A Country Study*, Washington, D.C.: Library of Congress, 6th edition, 1995

Burki, Shahid Javed, *Historical Dictionary of Pakistan*, Lanham, Maryland: Scarecrow Press, 1999

Gankovskii, IUrii Vladimirovich, *The Peoples of Pakistan: An Ethnic History*, Moscow: Nauka Publishing House; Lahore: People's Publishing House, 1971

Quraeshi, Samina, *Legacy of the Indus*, New York and Tokyo: John Weatherhill, Inc., 1974

Wilber, Donald N., *Pakistan: Its People, Its Society, Its Culture*, New Haven, Connecticut: HRAF Press, 1964

Palestinian Liberation Organization

The Palestinian Liberation Organization (PLO) is an umbrella organization, set up in 1964, to represent the dispersed Palestinian people and to enable them to liberate their homeland and shape their destiny. The decision to this effect was taken at the first Arab summit in Cairo in January 1964. The PLO held its first Congress in May 1964, in the Jordanian-controlled East Jerusalem and adopted the Palestine National Covenant. Veteran Arab diplomat Ahmad Shuqeiri was made the first chairman of the PLO.

The first Palestinian Congress also set up the Palestine National Council (PNC), the PLO Executive Committee, a National Fund, and the Palestine Liberation Army (PLA). The PLO created a number of organizations to provide education, health, and relief services, and formed a quasi-government with security apparatus, a financial system, and information offices and diplomatic missions. Since 1967, the organization has strengthened its organizational, social, financial, educational, propagandist, and political activities. Its successful guerilla campaign helped consolidate its base of support among Palestinian refugees, as well as Arab peoples elsewhere. At its height, the PLO functioned inside the areas controlled by Israel, along Israel's borders and against Israeli interests around the world.

In September 1964, the second Arab summit approved the establishment of the PLA, which would be subjected to the PLO Executive Committee. The independence of the PLA remained short-lived, as units came under the auspices of the country in which they were located, and were gradually integrated into that country's army. Following the Cairo Agreement of 1994, the PLA was deployed in the Palestinian-controlled areas as the police force of the PNA.

Since its inauguration in 1964, the Palestine National Council has functioned as the Palestinian parliament in exile. The membership of the PNC was allocated to various component bodies of the PLO as well as to affiliated mass organizations representing workers, students, women, teachers, doctors, and so forth. The membership included representatives from the occupied territories as well as the Palestinian diaspora in Jordan, Syria, Lebanon, and the Gulf States. Normally, the PNC met once a year. Following the signing of the Egyptian-Israeli Peace Treaty in 1979, the PNC headquarters was moved form Cairo to Damascus.

The 1964 PLO Covenant called for the establishment of a secular and democratic Palestinian state in the whole of Palestine, as it existed under the British. The central theme of the Covenant is the elimination of Israel and its replacement by a Palestinian state established encompassing all of Palestine.

The Arab Higher Committee headed by former Jerusalem Mufti Hajj Amin al-Husseini was not in favor of creating another Palestinian body. Likewise, Jordan, which annexed the West Bank in 1951, was opposed to the formation of a separate non-territorial entity to represent the Palestinians. To mitigate this opposition, the Palestinian demand for independent statehood carefully excluded those parts of Palestine occupied by Jordan and Egypt during 1948–67. This clause became irrelevant following the Israeli occupation of the West

Bank and the Gaza Strip in 1967 and hence was excluded from the 1968 PLO Covenant. In July 1968, at the fourth PNC in Cairo, the PLO Covenant was amended and Article 9 clearly stated "Armed struggle is the only way to liberate Palestine."

While the performance of the Arab armies was dismal in the June 1967 war, the guerrilla operations were relatively successful. The fourth session of the PNC transformed the PLO from a merely political representation of the Palestinians into an umbrella organization of various military and civilian Palestinian groups, with the guerrilla groups at its core. This transformation was coupled with the PLO claiming exclusive authority to speak in the name of the Palestinians.

The *Fatah* established in 1959 has been a prominent component of the PLO, and the Popular Front for the Liberation of Palestine (PFLP) and Democratic Front for the Liberation of Palestine (DFLP) are other important components of the PLO. At the fifth session of the PNC in February 1969, the Fatah seized control of the PLO and gained the majority in the 13-member executive. Yasser Arafat, the leader of the Fatah, became the chairman and he has held the position since then. Thus, the PLO emerged as the representative of the Palestinian people in the international arena.

In 1970, a violent confrontation erupted between the PLO and the Jordanian army culminated in the Black September massacre, which saw the Jordanian army operating against Palestinian refugee camps in Jordan. The confrontation emanated from King Hussein's apprehension that the PLO would take over Jordan. At the end of the crisis, Jordan ceased to be a base for the PLO's operations against Israel and the PLO was ousted from Amman and shifted to Beirut.

Following the 1973 Arab-Israeli conflict, in June 1974 the PLO moved to the idea of establishing a Palestinian state in the occupied territories as the first step towards the total liberation of mandated Palestine.

Despite the Jordanian opposition in 1974, the Arab League recognized the PLO as the "sole and legitimate" representative of the Palestinian people. This was followed by similar recognition by a number of Third World countries. Following an address by Arafat in the United Nations (UN) General Assembly on November 22, 1974, the UN recognized the PLO as "the representative of the Palestinian people" and reaffirmed the Palestinian right to self-determination and national independence. Recognizing the right of the Palestinian refugees to return to their home and property, the UN granted observer status to the PLO and,

since then, the organization has been participating all UN deliberations concerning the Palestinians.

The absence of an independent territorial base to conduct anti-Israeli operations made PLO dependent upon Israel's neighbors for base facilities, and this in turn made it vulnerable to pressures and interests of the host countries. Most of the PLO activities against Israel emanated from the occupied territories—southern Lebanon, Jordan (until the Black September incident), Syria (until the 1975 separation of forces agreement), or Egypt (until Sadat's peace initiative in 1978). At one time or another, its guerrilla tactics against Israel put the PLO at odds with Egypt, Jordan, Lebanon, and Syria. Likewise, its financial dependence upon oil-rich Arab states made the PLO vulnerable to pressure tactics.

More than its diplomatic successes, the PLO gained international attention and recognition primarily through its guerrilla campaigns against Israel and its interests in the Middle East. Various groups affiliated with the PLO have maintained armed guerrillas who form the Palestine Liberation Army (PLA).

Following the Israeli invasion of Lebanon in June 1982, the PLO (including its commandos and PLA troops) were evacuated from Beirut and were dispersed to various Arab countries. On September 17, 1982, the Phalange militants entered the Palestinian refugee camps in Sabra and Shatilla and massacred nearly 2,000 Palestinians, including women and children. The PLO headquarters, which was moved to Tunis as part of this evacuation, was raided by Israel on October 1, 1985 leading to the death of over 70 people, with Arafat making a providential escape.

In February 1985, the PLO reached an agreement with Amman providing for political cooperation between the two and the formation of a confederation between Jordan and the Palestinian state established in the occupied territories. This understanding was opposed by a number of PLO groups and led to the formation of anti-Arafat groups backed by Syria.

The outbreak of an *intifada* (popular uprising) in the Gaza Strip in December 1987 once again brought the PLO to the forefront. Though the uprising was spontaneous and locally populated, the PLO quickly took control of the situation and became part of the Unified National Leadership of the Uprising. Capitalizing on the international attention and support, on November 15, 1988, the PNC met in Algiers for its nineteenth session and proclaimed the establishment of the state of Palestine, with Arafat as its president.

In an historical shift, it accepted UN General Assembly Resolution 181 of 1947, which recommended the partition of Palestine, renounced the use of violence to achieve the aims of the PLO, and reconciled to the idea of Palestinian self-determination in coexistence with Israel. Meanwhile, responding to the *intifada*, Jordan cut off all administrative links with the West Bank. This signaled its recognition of the PLO in determining the future status of the occupied territories and the abandonment of its erstwhile claims to the Palestinian territories.

Following these developments and Arafat's renunciation of violence, in 1988 the Reagan administration initiated a dialogue with the PLO, only to be suspended in July 1990 following an aborted terrorist attack against Israel by the Palestine Liberation Front headed by Muhammad Abbas.

The Iraqi invasion of Kuwait in August 1990 and the Palestinian endorsement of Saddam Hussein put the PLO in conflict with the prevailing Arab consensus. Oil-rich countries such as Kuwait and Saudi Arabia, the principal benefactors of the PLO, resented the Palestinian approval of the Iraqi linkage between the Kuwait crisis and the future of Palestine, and Arafat became *persona non grata* among the anti-Iraqi Arab coalition members. The sudden removal of financial support coupled with the mass expulsion of Palestinian laborers from the Gulf countries dealt a serious financial blow to the PLO.

The Iraqi defeat, the disintegration of the Soviet Union (the prime ideological supporter), and the emergence of the United States as the sole arbitrator in the post-Cold War world have significantly undermined the influence of the PLO. Following a series of negotiations with U.S. Secretary of State James Baker, the PLO backed the idea of a peaceful and negotiated settlement with Israel and agreed to attend a Middle East peace conference. Owing to Israeli opposition, it agreed to form a joint Jordanian-Palestinian delegation for the Madrid Conference inaugurated on October 30, 1991. Even though the negotiations were conducted with the Palestinians based in the occupied territories, the Tunis-based PLO leadership was very much involved in working out the modalities of Palestinian participation and the framework of negotiations. The bilateral talks between the two sides did not, however, make any progress.

Following his election as prime minister in July 1992, Labor leader Yitzhak Rabin expressed Israel's commitment to a land-for-peace policy and in January 1993, Israel lifted the official ban on contacts with the PLO. Both these moves set off secret negotiations between Israel and the PLO facilitated by Norway. On September 9, 1993, Prime Minister Yitzhak Rabin and Chairman Arafat exchanged letters of mutual recognition. On September 13, the Declaration of Principles (DOP), signed on the White House lawn in the presence of President Clinton and other international leaders, outlined the terms of reference for achieving a negotiated permanent settlement between Israel and the PLO. Both sides gradually began to implement the terms of reference. Thus, the Oslo processed was ushered in.

The DOP was transformed into a working document in May 1994, when both parties agreed to the establishment of a Palestinian Authority, delineated the geographical and functional limits of autonomy, and agreed on a framework for final status negotiations. As a result, in July 1994 the PLO and Arafat moved to the Gaza Strip from Tunis to administer the Gaza Strip and Jericho. In January 1996, a popular vote was held to elect the president of the Palestinian National Authority and 88-member Palestinian Legislative Council. Following this election, the responsibility for areas of the West Bank and Gaza ceded to Palestinian control was transferred from the PLO to the Palestinian Authority.

This, however, was unacceptable to the ten Palestinian groups, including those affiliated with the PLO, that launched a rejectionist front in Damascus and often staged protest rallies and demonstrations against the Oslo process. The most violent protest against the peace process came from the Hamas Islamic radicals, who conducted series of suicide bombing campaigns inside Israel, primarily targeting bus commuters.

Even though the Algiers declaration of 1988 signaled the abandonment of the armed struggle as a means of liberation and despite repeated commitments by Arafat, the PLO Covenant (until 1998) remained formally unchanged. On April 24, 1996, on the eve of the crucial elections in Israel, the PNC met in Gaza and passed a resolution declaring null and void "the articles [of the Covenant] that are contrary to the [September 9, 1993] letters of mutual recognition." This declaration, approved by a 504–54 vote (with 14 abstentions), was rejected by many Israelis as vague, imprecise, and insufficient. On December 10, 1998, the PNC met in the Gaza Strip and, by 81 to 7 votes (with 7 abstentions), voted to revoke the specific clauses of the Covenant referred to in Arafat's letter to Clinton, which listed those specific clauses of the PLO charter that would be modified or rescinded. The

Palestinian National Council ratified this decision on December 14, 1998. President Clinton witnessed this decision adopted by a show of hands, rather than a formal voting procedure.

P.R. KUMARASWAMY

See also **Arafat, Yasser (Palestinian); Egypt; Israel; Jordan; Syria**

Further Reading

Cobban, Helena, *The Palestinian Liberation Organization: People, Power and Politics*, New York: Cambridge University Press, 1984

Harkabi, Yehoshafat, *The Palestinian Covenant and Its Meaning*, London: Vallentine, Mitchell, 1979

Khalidi, Rashid, *Palestinian Entity: The Construction of Modern National Consciousness*, New York: Columbia University Press, 1997

Kimmerling, Baruch, and Migdal, Joel S., *Palestinians: The Making of a People*, New York: Free Press, 1993

Livingstone, Neil C., and Halevy, David, *Inside the PLO*, New York: Morrow, 1990

Miller, Aaron David, *The PLO and the Politics of Survival*, New York: Praeger, 1983

Nasser, Jamal R., *The Palestine Liberation Organization: From Armed Struggle to the Declaration of Independence*, New York: Praeger, 1991

Rubin, Barry, *Revolution Until Victory? The Politics and History of the PLO*, Cambridge, Massachusetts: Harvard University Press, 1994

Sela, Avraham, and Maoz, Moshe, editors, *The PLO and Israel: From Armed Conflict to Political Solution, 1964–1994*, New York: St. Martin's, 1997

Panama

Capsule Summary

Country Name: Panama
Location: Central America
Total Population: 3,000,000 (2004)
Minority Population: Chinese, *mestizo*, Native Indian, West Indian, white
Languages: Chinese, Caribbean Creole English, Emberá, English, Cuna, Ngäbere, Spanish, Teribe, Woun-meu
Religions: Roman Catholic, Protestant

The country of Panama is a tropical isthmus that lies on a northwest-southeast axis and connects Central America with the continent of South America. The central spine of the country is a mountain chain that at one point rises to 10,000 feet. Descending from these mountains are coastal plains along the Caribbean Sea and the Pacific Ocean. Over a narrow belt in the central part of the country, there extends a complex of lakes, rivers, and lowlands through which the Panama Canal stretches. The latter links the Caribbean and Pacific from the city of Colón to Panama City, the nation's capital.

As a land bridge connecting continents and as a waterway linking great seas, Panama contains a population that has been defined by the people passing through or settling in it. Its size is somewhat smaller than South Carolina in the United States; however, it has a mosaic of minorities to rival the most cosmopolitan of metropolises.

As an area rich in tropical vegetation and wildlife with an abundance of fresh water, Panama may at one time have had a native population greater than the number of its inhabitants today. In modern times, however, indigenous inhabitants approximate no more than 150,000 people, or about five percent of the population. The three major native groups have been the Çuna, Guaymí, and Chocó.

The first group, at one time the largest indigenous population, now composes no more than one-third of the natives. The area of the Cuna, or Kuna, has become limited to a coastal arc along the Caribbean, east of the canal zone. The Guaymí (language, Ngäbere) inhabit the northwest highlands of Panama, near the border with Costa Rica. Their remote location has allowed them to preserve their numbers and they now compose over half the native population. The Chocó (Emberá) inhabit the eastern region of Panama, near Colombia. Their number is hard to determine because they have assimilated extensively with other local cultures. Additional small Indian groups consist of speakers of Buglere, Teribe, and Woun-meu, many surviving in the remote western regions of Panama. Linguistic evidence suggests that the extensive number of Indians in Panama before the Spanish Conquest had wide regional connections to tribes in Colombia, the Caribbean, and Middle America.

The Spanish conquered the isthmus at the beginning of the sixteenth century and it became a vital link in their empire. They established the city of Panama (near the country's current capital, Panama City) on the Pacific Coast and linked it to the city of Nombre de Dios on the Caribbean by a trail known as the Camino Real. The word *Panama* was derived from an Indian expression for "place of plentiful fish." The Camino Real, which roughly preceded what would later be the route of the Panama Canal, connected the narrowest part of the isthmus, located in the middle of the region. Over this trail moved vast treasures of gold from the Inca Empire in South America to Spain.

The Spanish grip on the region was severe, devastating the native population through massacres, enslavement, and disease. Spaniards interbred with most of the remaining natives, forming a mixed or *mestizo* population that today dominates the country. The principal language of the country became, and remains, Spanish. The main religion is Roman Catholicism. At the beginning of the nineteenth century, when Spain's colonies declared independence, Panama emerged not as a separate country but as a province of Colombia.

The most significant occurrence determining the modern character of Panama's population consisted of attempts from the mid-nineteenth century onward to build fast, secure transportation across the narrowest part of the isthmus. The California gold rush prompted the building of a railroad from Panama City to Colón (Spanish for Columbus) on the Caribbean, near Nombre de Dios, that opened in 1855. The railroad brought a small contingent of American railroad contractors and a sweeping pilgrimage of prospectors from many countries. However, the only people who significantly settled in Panama and formed new elements of minority cultures were Chinese laborers and West Indian blacks who spoke Creole English. Later in the nineteenth century, French attempts to build a canal along the route of the railroad enlarged these minorities, especially those from the Caribbean.

Chinese speakers are today almost one percent of the population of Panama and others have intermarried with the *mestizo* inhabitants. Descendants of the West Indian population, who are concentrated especially around the central eastern portion of the country, are one-sixth of the population. Where they live, Creole English and the Protestant religion are dominant over the principal language and religion.

The French attempt failed, plagued by financial problems and tropical disease. At the beginning of the twentieth century, however, the United States began a successful attempt to build a canal. It encouraged Panama to declare independence from Colombia. In 1903, the United States had the government of the new country sign a treaty that ceded a ribbon of territory along the route of the first railroad and the failed French canal as an American canal zone. Overcoming the problems of tropical disease, the United States completed the Panama Canal by 1914.

The building and maintenance of the canal added further complexity to the cultural mosaic of Panama. The Canal Zone was United States territory until 1999, when it devolved to Panama. Throughout the twentieth century, therefore, the zone's American middle-class military and engineering culture was a central influence on the country. As of 2002, the GDP per capita was $6,200. The large number of Panamanians who worked for or depended on the canal adopted English as their second language. The American presence also fostered a stream of Protestant missionaries who established small Panamanian communities of mainline sects together with Pentecostals, Mormons, and Jehovah's Witness. Because of these efforts and the size of the West Indian population, Protestantism grew to encompass well over ten percent of the population. Arab-speaking and Jewish merchants also added small contingents of their languages and religions to the complex social mosaic of Panama. The complexity of minute cultural diversity along the canal cannot be underestimated. Every country that trades on the oceans and needs to traverse the Panama Canal has small delegations of commercial, shipping, or diplomatic representatives and their families in the country, meaning that at least a few dozen people from most of the nations, cultures, languages, and religions of the world reside in Panama.

EDWARD A. RIEDINGER

Further Reading

Alvarado de Ricord, Elsie, *El español de Panamá: Estudio fonético y fonológico*, Panama City: Editorial Universitaria, 1971

Bourgois, Phillipe I., *Ethnicity at Work: Divided Labor on a Central American Banana Plantation*, Johns Hopkins Studies in Atlantic Culture and History, Baltimore, Maryland: Johns Hopkins University Press, 1989

Conniff, Michael L., *Black Labor on a White Canal: Panama, 1904–1981*, Pittsburgh, Pennsylvania: University of Pittsburgh Press, 1985

Conniff, Michael L., "Afro-West Indians on the Central American Isthmus: The Case of Panama," in *Slavery and Beyond: The African Impact on Latin America and the Caribbean*, edited by Darién J. Davis, Wilmington, Delaware: SR Books, 1995

Jaén Suárez, Omar, *La población del Istmo de Panamá: Estudio de geohistoria*, Madrid: Ediciones de Cultura Hispánica, 3rd edition,1998

Meditz, Sandra W., and Dennis M. Hanratty, *Panama*, Area Handbook Series, Washington, DC: Federal Research Division, Library of Congress, 1989Langstaff, Eleanor

DeSelms, *Panama*, Oxford, England: Clio Press, revised edition 2000

Panama in Pictures, Visual Geography Series, Minneapolis, Minnesota: Lerner Publications, revised and updated edition, 1995

Pebley, Anne R., and Luis Rosero-Bixby, editors, *Demographic Diversity and change in the Central American Isthmus*, Santa Monica, California: Rand, 1997

Petras, Elizabeth McClean, *Jamaican Labor Migration: White Capital and Black Labor, 1850–1930*, Westview Special Studies on Latin America and the Caribbean, Boulder, Colorado: Westview Press, 1989

Wauchope, Robert, *Handbook of Middle American Indians*, 15 volumes, Austin: University of Texas, 1964–1975

Papua New Guinea

Capsule Summary

Country Name: Papua New Guinea
Total Population: 4.7 million
Minority Population: over 800 Melanesian and Papuan ethnolinguistic groups, Polynesians, Micronesians, and Chinese
Languages: Tok Pisin (Melanesian Pidgin, widely spoken), Hiri Motu, English, over 800 local languages
Religions: Christianity, traditional religions

Papua New Guinea (PNG) is more ethnically and linguistically diverse than any other area of its size in the world. There are over 800 languages spoken in this country roughly the size of California, and as many ethnolinguistic groups. Located in the southwestern Pacific, PNG consists of the eastern half of the island of New Guinea together with some 600 nearby islands. The islands comprise roughly 15 percent of the total land area of some 470,000 square kilometers. PNG has been an independent constitutional monarchy since 1975, with Queen Elizabeth II as titular head of state. The government is a parliamentary democracy. Christianity is the major religion. Although estimates of conversion vary widely, approximately 44 percent of the people are claimed as Protestant and 22 percent as Catholic, with the balance practicing traditional religions. The per capita GDP is slightly more than $1,000.

The physical environment of mainland PNG has contributed to its ethnic diversity. The rugged terrain makes travel difficult and limits interactions among people in many parts of the country. The central part of New Guinea is a rugged cordillera with wide alpine valley systems and many peaks over 4,000m/13,123ft. North and south of the central highlands are luxuriant lowlands drained by massive river systems, the Sepik and Ramu to the north and the Fly to the south. Situated in the wet and humid equatorial tropics, rainforests cover much of the country. PNG's plant and animal diversity mirrors that of its human population: There are 1,400 species of fish, 650 species of land birds, a dizzying array of insects, and over 10,000 species of flora.

Understanding PNG's ethnic diversity requires consideration of its prehistory. There seem to have been two major migrations into what is now PNG. Aboriginal populations of Australia and New Guinea are closely related biologically, and probably migrated from what is now Indonesia between 50,000 and 35,000 years ago (dates are contested). In contrast, a much more recent (post 3,000 BCE) migration of seafarers from Asia produced the peoples of Island Melanesia. While linguistic divisions do not map perfectly onto biological divisions, most people of the island of Melanesia today speak languages belonging to the Austronesian language family. Because of their presumed common background and relatively rapid dispersal throughout the Pacific Islands, the contemporary Austronesian peoples in PNG all have relatively similar languages and cultures. In contrast, the earlier migrants today display wide variety in culture and language resulting from more than 35,000 years of isolation, migration, and mixing. While these diverse peoples are sometimes called Papuans, many prefer the term *non-Austronesians*, because it does not suggest shared characteristics. The Austronesian-speaking peoples are sometimes called Melanesians, but because of potentially confusing regional designations, Austronesian is now preferred.

Despite their cultural diversity, a few generalizations can be made about the non-Austronesian peoples of PNG. Before contact, most of them lived in the interior of New Guinea, New Britain, and Bougainville foraging or practicing horticulture-based subsistence techniques. In contrast, the Austronesians lived primarily in coastal areas and combined fishing and maritime exploitation with horticultural techniques. Although there has been considerable migration to urban areas recently, the subsistence economy continues to be important in contemporary PNG, and these generalizations still obtain. A major ethnic divide separates the Austronesian-speaking coastal and island peoples from the diverse non-Austronesians who live in the interior of New Guinea and a few nearby islands. There are also Polynesian peoples inhabiting islands in the eastern part of the country, and some Micronesian peoples living in a few northern islands.

Although discovered by Europeans in the 1500s, New Guinea was not colonized seriously until the end of the 1800s. The Dutch settled in the western portion of the island and, in what is now PNG, Germany claimed sovereignty in the north (German New Guinea) and Britain in the south (British Papua). After World War II, during which Japan occupied northern New Guinea, Australia administered Papua and New Guinea as a mandated territory, until independence in 1975. In the northern part of the country, Melanesian Pidgin (Tok Pisin) developed as a lingua franca, whereas in the south, Hiri Motu, a pidgin based on indigenous trading languages, was spread by the colonial administration. During this period, Chinese merchants immigrated to PNG and many of their descendants remain today. After independence, however, most of the expatriate Australians who had been working in PNG returned home.

In 1989, a protracted civil war erupted on Bougainville island, where locals consider themselves to be culturally and racially distinct. Secessionists, led by the BRA (Bougainville Revolutionary Army), protested environmental destruction and the distribution of royalties from the Panguna copper mine. They eventually forced the mine to close, which sparked a bloody ten-year military confrontation. The political status of the North Solomons Province remains unsettled today.

As the foregoing illustrates, contemporary PNG's ethnic makeup is intricate due to staggering cultural diversity and the complex interplay of biological, linguistic, and political forces. There are many ways to categorize the ethnic composition of the country, and many options for self-identification. Most people strongly affiliate with family and kinship groups. Widely recognized are alliances based on language: the term *wantok* identifies a speaker of the same language or dialect. PNG is divided into 19 Provinces, together with a National Capital district, loosely organized along ethnic and cultural lines, and these too form the basis of ethnic identity. Still other identifications are based on regional units: Papuans in the south, New Guineans in the north, Highlanders in the central regions, and New Guinea Islanders. Increasing education and mobility in PNG have resulted in the formation of some tribal identities where previously there were none, and in the breakdown of still other such identifications. One thing is certain: every person in PNG is part of an ethnic minority.

RICHARD SCAGLION

Further Reading

Bellwood, Peter, James J. Fox, and Darrell Tryon, editors, *The Austronesians: Historical and Comparative Perspectives*, Canberra: Department of Anthropology, The Australian National University, 1995
Dorney, Sean, *Papua New Guinea: People, Politics and History since 1975*, Milsons Point, New South Wales: Random House Australia, 1990
Foley, William A., *The Papuan Languages of New Guinea*, Cambridge: Cambridge University Press, 1986
Hays, Terence E., editor, *Encyclopedia of World Cultures, Vol. 2, Oceania*, Boston, Massachusetts: G K Hall, 1991
Howard, Michael C., editor, *Ethnicity and Nation-Building in the Pacific*, Tokyo: The United Nations University, 1989
Ryan, Peter, editor, *Encyclopaedia of Papua and New Guinea*, Melbourne: Melbourne University Press and University of Papua New Guinea, 1972

Paraguay

Capsule Summary

Country Name: Paraguay
Location: South America
Total Population: 6,100,000 (2004)
Minority Population: *Mestizo*, Guarani, white
Languages: Guarani, Ayoreo, Chamacoco, Lengua, Sanapaná, Chulupí, Spanish, Portuguese, German, Plautdietsch
Religions: Roman Catholic, Mennonite, Protestant

Paraguay is among the poorest countries of South America, with a per capita GDP of $4,300 (2002). Warfare and military dictatorships have historically drained its resources, territory, and population. Nonetheless, the country has been unique in the maintenance of its major native culture, that of the Guarani Indians. Guarani is widely spoken and an official language of the country.

Bisected by the Paraguay River, the country is divided into two major regions. The western part consists of the arid Gran Chaco. It is the least populated area of Paraguay but has significant isolated settlements. East of the Paraguay River, rainfall increases and the climate varies from tropical to temperate. The land becomes hilly and has woodlands and grassy plains. A varied population is settled throughout this region. Marshy areas occur along the Paraguay River. The capital, Asunción, lies on the river near the southern edge of the country toward the border with Argentina.

Before the Spanish conquest, the region east of the Paraguay River formed the southern edge of a vast Indian culture that extended northward along the Atlantic coast of Brazil and down the Amazon River basin. This culture was defined by its language group, Tupi-Guarani. The Guarani were densely settled in the well-watered savannas and forests of eastern Paraguay. They outnumbered the thin trickle of Spanish colonists who entered the region during the colonial period.

Generally arriving without wives, Spanish males intermarried or mated with the native Indians, creating the *mestizo* or mixed racial population that now dominates the society. Most Paraguayans are descended from a Spanish-speaking male ancestor and Guarani-speaking female one. This lineage has made many Paraguayans bilingual, tending to speak Guarani in their home environment and Spanish in public. Guarani is the dominant language in rural areas, whereas Spanish prevails in the cities.

Guarani further held its own against Spanish because colonial natives were organized in an extensive system of Catholic missions, principally by Jesuit priests and brothers. These outposts came to exercise considerable commercial and cultural power. The Jesuits identified and codified the Tupi-Guarani language group and compiled its first texts, grammars, and dictionaries.

The hybrid nature of Paraguayan society has many singular cultural manifestations. The fine European lace produced by natives is named *nanduti*, the Guarani word for spider web. At meals, steak is eaten not with potatoes but slices of manioc. The national musical instrument of the country is not the guitar, but the harp.

By the end of the colonial period, the widespread use of Guarani and the dominance of the Roman Catholic religion had become major cultural components of Paraguayan society. Today over 90 percent of the population knows Guarani and/or Spanish and is Roman Catholic. Nonetheless, variations and additions to these dominant patterns also exist.

Through an eastern corridor of the Gran Chaco, west of the Paraguay River, pockets of other native languages continue. In the upper part of this region, there are several thousand speakers of Ayoreo and Chamacoco, which are Zamucoan languages. Below this area, in the central part of the country, are even more speakers of Lengua and Sanapaná. These are Mascoian languages. Southwest of the Mascoian area, near the border with Argentina, there are also many thousands of speakers of Chulupí, a Mataco language.

Through the southern and central portion of Paraguay are several hundred thousand speakers of German and a dialect of this langue, Plautdietsch. German immigration to Paraguay began in the late nineteenth century and increased during the twentieth. These immigrants developed small farming and commercial activities that allowed them to continue communicating in their native language. In the central Chaco, thousands of Plautdietsch-speaking Mennonites settled in rural communities. Seeking land and remote areas for the free practice of their religion, they emigrated from Russia, Canada, and the Ukraine. The Paraguayan government welcomed their settlement in the remote Chaco, allowing them considerable autonomy. National security required that the Chaco be occupied, and the Mennonites were known as successful farmers. The Mennonites are the only significant non-Catholic religious minority in Paraguay. United States missionary sects of Mormons, Baptists, Seventh-Day Adventists, and Pentecostals have established some churches.

Recent ethnic minorities that have also settled in Paraguay are Brazilians. They have moved from the southern agricultural states of Brazil into the open lands of eastern Paraguay along the Brazilian border, west of the Paraná River. Engaging in cattle ranching, they have made Portuguese and a combination of Portuguese with Spanish, known as Portanhol, common languages of several tens of thousands of speakers. The border areas of Paraguay (with Brazil and Argentina) are also a region of intense illegal commercial activity in drug trafficking, money laundering, and resale of stolen goods. Reputedly, the region also harbors Islamist cells.

Very small groups of Chinese, Korean, and Arabic-speaking minorities have settled in Paraguayan cities and towns, engaging in commercial and trade activities. There is also a colony of several generations of Japanese small-scale farmers in the country. Underpopulation due to warfare during the nineteenth and twentieth centuries has made Paraguay open to extensive immigration.

Paraguay is quite homogenous in terms of its ethnic and religious composition, with only small variations in its fundamental characteristics. The majority of the country is poor, the annual per capita gross domestic product amounting to little more than $4,000. Class

and political differences have created violent party divisions that have bifurcated national government throughout its history. The Colorado Party, although divided in factions, has long dominated, especially during the period of the dictatorship of General Alfredo Stroessner from 1954 to 1989. Numerous opposition parties challenge it, but they have not consolidated in a unified force. Due to the numerous wars in Paraguay's history, females far outnumbered males until the middle of the twentieth century. However, the gender balance of the population has now been restored.

EDWARD A. RIEDINGER

Further Reading

Ayala, José Valentín, *Gramática guarani*, Asunción, Paraguay: Centro Editorial Paraguayo, 2000

Bertoni, T. Bertoni, and J. Richard Gorham, "The People of Paraguay: Origin and Numbers," in *Paraguay: Ecological Essays* edited by J. Richard Gorham, Miami, Florida: Academy of the Arts and Sciences of the Americas, 1973, pp 109–40

Cooney, Jerry W., *Paraguay: A Bibliography of Bibliographies*, Austin, Texas: SALALM Secretariat, 1997

Hanratty, Dennis M., and Sandara W. Meditz, *Paraguay: A Country Study*, Washington, D.C.: Federal Research Division, Library of Congress, 1990

Nickson, R. Andrew, *Paraguay*, World Bibliographical Series, 84, Oxford, England: Clio Press, revised edition, 1999

Nickson, R. Andrew, and Charles J. Kolinski, *Historical Dictionary of Paraguay*, Metuchen, New Jersey: Scarecrow Press, 2nd edition, revised and enlarged, 1993

Reed, Richard K., *Prophets of Agroforestry: Guaraní Communities and Commercial Gathering*, Austin: University of Texas Press, 1991

Renshaw, John, *The Indians of the Paraguayan Chaco: Identity and Economy*, Lincoln: University of Nebraska Press, 2002

Roett, Riordan, *Paraguay: The Personalist Legacy*, Nations of Contemporary Latin America, Boulder, Colorado: Westview Press, 1991

Steward, Julian H., editor, *Handbook of South American Indians*, Washington, D.C.: U.S. Government Printing Office, 1946–1959, 7 volumes

Parnell, Charles Stewart (Irish)

The Irish leader Charles Stewart Parnell deftly forged links between the Irish at Westminster, the extremist Irish Republican Brotherhood, and the ex-Fenians in the United States and Canada. Michael Davitt, founder of the National Land League, invited Parnell to be the League's first president. In the land war between tenant farmers and their landlords in the years 1879–1882, landlordism was virtually abolished and a new system of peasant proprietorship came into being. There was such a high level of violence and outrage across Ireland that the Land League had to set up its own courts.

The British government passed a number of Coercion Acts that led to the arrest of Parnell and other Irish leaders, in October 1881, and to the suppression of the League. But the British prime minister, William Gladstone, eventually came to terms with the Home Rule Party in the Kilmainham Treaty, which released prisoners (including Parnell) and led to the Land Act of 1881, thereby initiating a policy of land reform in Ireland. Parnell saw the destruction of landlordism as merely one step to the elimination of British rule in Ireland.

In preparing his party for the general election of 1885, Parnell replaced the Land League with the National League. The election was a triumph for Parnell as he and the League won every seat outside eastern Ulster and Dublin University. He was emboldened to press on for legislative independence by constitutional means. His Irish Party held the balance of power between Liberals and Conservatives.

In England, Gladstone stated that his mission was to pacify Ireland. He had won a victory for the Liberals and he saw the justice of Parnell's call for Home Rule; he had supported it throughout his long parliamentary career. Irish Home Rule was now on Westminster's agenda. Gladstone's Home Rule Bill of 1886 roused the ire of the Conservatives, who saw the pact between Gladstone and Parnell as a betrayal of the British Empire, and of the loyal Protestants of Ireland. Gladstone's Liberals split on the issue, and the Bill was defeated.

In 1887 the *Times* of London published a series of articles under the title "Parnellism and Crime," accusing home rule advocacy leaders of complicity in murders and outrages during the land war. Forged letters implicated Parnell. Most damning was his apparent condoning of the murders of the recently appointed Chief Secretary and Under Secretary, who were sent to Ireland in May 1882. A High Court enquiry and the cross-examination of one Richard Piggott, (the forger, who later committed suicide in Madrid) exonerated Parnell, and he gained popularity, especially in Ireland.

A catastrophe in Parnell's private life destroyed him as a public figure. In November 1890, Captain William O'Shea, a home rule advocate, obtained a divorce from his wife Katharine, citing her affair with Parnell. Katherine O'Shea and Parnell had conducted a ten-year-long affair, which had produced three children. O'Shea initially turned a blind eye to the affair, hoping to further his political career and possibly not to hinder, by scandal, the future inheritance his wife was to gain from wealthy relatives.

British nonconformists, who supported Gladstone's crusade for Home Rule for Ireland as a morally just cause, now took the view that Parnell was no longer a fit person to lead the Irish Parliamentary Party. The Irish Catholic hierarchy agreed.

The effect on Parnell's political career was disastrous. He refused to step down, and the result was a serious split in the party he had built up as a powerful political force in the British House of Commons. His sudden death of a heart attack in Brighton, England on October 6, 1891—five months after his marriage to Mrs. O'Shea—hastened the rapid decline of the Irish Party in the ten years following Parnell's death.

Parnell always maintained that his own personal conduct was not involved in the political struggle, yet he was torn between his love for Kitty O'Shea and his ambitions for Ireland. Although he suffered setbacks and disappointments in his personal life, his lasting achievements as an Irish political leader remain. He raised the British public's awareness of Ireland's desire for self-government, gaining the support of Prime Minister Gladstone and his Liberal Party in the process.

Capsule Biography

Charles Stewart Parnell. Born in Avondale, Wicklow, in 1846. Home Rule M.P. for Meath in 1875. President of the Land League. In 1879, Leader of the Irish Parliamentary Party. Imprisoned from October 1881 until May 1882. Converted

Gladstone to Home Rule for Ireland. Vindicated from complicity in the Phoenix Park murders in 1889. Cited as co-respondent in the O'Shea divorce petition. Deserted by both English nonconformists, the Irish bishops, and, ultimately, by the majority of the political party he founded. Married Katharine O'Shea June 1891 and died at Brighton 14 weeks later.

Selected Works

Annual Register (1875–1891)
Hansard's Parliamentary Debates, 1875–1891

JOHN MCGURK

See also **Ireland**

Further Reading

Bew, P., *C.S. Parnell,* London,1980
Davitt, M., *The Fall of Feudalism in Ireland*, New York and London, 1904
Foster, R.F., *Charles Stewart Parnell: The Man and His Family*, London: 1976
Larkin, Emmet, *The Roman Catholic Church in Ireland and the Fall of Parnell 1888–1891*, London, 1979
Lyons, F.S.L., *Charles Stewart Parnell,* London, 1977
O'Brien, C.C., *Parnell and his Party, 1880–1890*, Oxford, 1964
O'Connor, T.P., *The Parnell Movement,* London, 1887
Parnell, Anna, *The Tale of a Great Sham*, edited by Dana Hearne, Dublin, 1986

Parsis

Capsule Summary

Name: Parsis or Parsees
Location: Minority communities worldwide; Largest communities in India, Canada, United States, England, and Pakistan; Smaller communities in Australia, South Africa, Sri Lanka, and other countries
Total population: 100,000 worldwide
Languages: Gujarati, English
Religion: Zoroastrianism/Mazdaism

Parsis (also Parsees), Persians, or Indian Zoroastrians are the descendants of émigrés who migrated to the western coast of India around the tenth century CE to escape sectarian persecution and to avoid conversion to Islam. Parsi Zoroastrian men and women traditionally refer to themselves as Mazdayasna (Mazdesn), Mazdeans or worshipers of Mazda, a term that acknowledges their veneration of the god Ahura Mazda.

Parsi immigrants gradually dispersed to towns and villages in Gujarat province, becoming farmers, carpenters, weavers, and merchants. Most public roles were restricted largely to men, domestic functions reserved for women. Education was usually trade-related and generally available to sons and less often to daughters. Each male priest ministered to a few families. Over time, such associations become hereditary. Around 1290 CE, those priests divided into five ecclesiastic groups. By the thirteenth century CE, extensive contact between Parsi and Iranian Zoroastrians had recommenced with the Iranians eventually sending texts that would educate and guide the Parsis in socioreligious matters. Pressure from Hindus compelled Parsis to make communal and ceremonial changes. Ritual sacrifice of bulls and cows was abandoned due to Hindu reverence for these animals. The Parsis came to be regarded as a caste within Hindu society. Thus, the religion became linked to ethnicity and regarded as hereditary on the Indian subcontinent, with no converts being accepted.

Contact between Parsis and Europeans began with the establishment of colonial trading houses in the seventeenth century CE. As commerce increased, so did the wealth and size of the Parsi community. In 1661 CE, the city of Bombay came under the administration of the British East India Company. There, Parsis grounded the community's fiscal success on shipbuilding and on the cotton and opium trade with China. Parsis also established themselves in textile manufacture, general commerce, and banking. The community became a mercantile arm of the British and controlled India's foreign trade for over two centuries. The community also helped found the industrial base of modern India. Parsi entrepreneurs established the iron and steel industries, hydroelectric plants, the Indian Institute of Science, and the Indian atomic energy research institute.

During the early nineteenth century, Parsis adopted secular education from the British and promoted it by founding schools for their sons and daughters. Following mores that were emerging in Europe at the time, the Parsis began encouraging educated women to take up careers in public workplaces. They also funded hospitals and philanthropic trusts for the community. All these developments spurred relocation away from the villages to large cities—especially to Bombay. Rapid urbanization began in the 1900s, reaching 94 percent by 1961 among Parsis (compared to 27 percent for Muslims, 23 percent for Christians, and 16 percent for Hindus) on the Indian subcontinent. As a result, the Parsi Zoroastrians of India developed into a highly urbanized middle class. Marriages arranged by relatives declined in frequency after the 1920s as women exercised their enhanced ability to select their own spouses. At the same time, educated women in the community began to choose careers over marriage, family, and domesticity—close to 25 percent of Parsi women remained unmarried during the 1970s and 1980s, and the community's birthrate has declined drastically. Moreover, by the late twentieth century, women's expectations had begun to exceed the reality represented by potential male partners within the community—again reinforcing the trend in declining marital and reproductive rates.

Although international dispersion occurred for a variety of socioeconomic reasons from the 1950s through the 1990s Parsis still dwell in most major cities of India, particularly Bombay (now known as Mumbai), Delhi, and Calcutta. The Parsi community presently numbers around 76,400 in India, 2,800 in Pakistan, approximately 8,000 in Canada and in the United States, 4,000 in England and Scotland, and a few thousand collectively in the other countries of Europe and in Australia. Small groups are also present in Hong Kong, Singapore, Sri Lanka, South Africa, and other Asian and African countries. Low birthrate, prohibition of the acceptance of converts, and a discouraging of intermarriage with members of other sectarian groups have contributed steadily to an overall gradual decline in demographic numbers.

Educated women, like their male counterparts, have come to play important leadership roles within the community during the past century, including editing the most widely read newsletters in North America and South Asia wherein issues of significance to societal change are debated.

JAMSHEED K. CHOKSY

See also **Zoroastrians**

Further Reading

Choksy, Jamsheed K., *Purity and Pollution in Zoroastrianism: Triumph over Evil*, Austin: University of Texas Press, 1989

Gould, Ketayun H., "Outside the Discipline, Inside the Experience: Women in Zoroastrianism," in *Religion and Women*, edited by A. Sharma, Albany: State University of New York Press, 1994, pp 139–182

Hinnells, John R., "Parsis and the British," *Journal of the K.R. Cama Oriental Institute* 46, 1978, pp 1–92

———, "Social Change and Religious Transformation Among Bombay Parsis in the Early Twentieth Century," in *Traditions in Contact and Change*, edited by P. Slater and D. Wiebe, Winnipeg: University of Manitoba Press, 1983, pp 105–125

Kulke, Eckehard, *The Parsees in India: A Minority as Agent of Social Change*, Delhi: Vikas, 1974

Langstaff, Hilary A., *Indian Parsis in the Twentieth Century*, Karachi: Informal Religious Meetings Trust Fund, 1987

Luhrmann, Tanya M., *The Good Parsi: The Fate of a Colonial Elite in a Postcolonial Society*, Cambridge, Massachusetts: Harvard University Press, 1996

Maneck, Susan S., *The Death of Ahriman: Culture, Identity, and Theological Change among the Parsis of India*, Bombay: K.R. Cama Oriental Institute, 1997

Menant, Delphine, *The Parsis,* translated by M.M. Murzban and A.D. Mango, 3 volumes, 1898, reprinted Bombay: Danai, 1994

Mistree, Khojeste P., "The Breakdown of the Zoroastrian Tradition as Viewed from a Contemporary Perspective," in *Irano-Judaica*, volume 2, edited by S. Shaked and A. Netzer, Jerusalem: Ben Zvi Institute, 1990, pp 227–254

Rose, Jennifer, "The Traditional Role of Women in the Iranian and Indian (Parsi) Zoroastrian Communities from the Nineteenth to the Twentieth Century," *Journal of the K.R. Cama Oriental Institute* 56, 1989, pp 1–103

Pashtuns (Pathans)

Capsule Summary

Name: Pathans, Pashtuns, or Pakhtuns.
Location: Afghanistan and Pakistan; small immigrant communities in the United States, Canada, and England
Total Population: 7 million in Afghanistan, 14 million in Pakistan (1998)
Languages: Pashto and Pakhto
Religion: Sunni Islam

Pashtuns, also spelled as Pushtuns, or Pakhtuns are generally called Afghans. The Hindi rendering *Pathans* is today regarded as a derogatory term employed by Indians and European colonizers. They live mainly in Afghanistan and in the North West Frontier and Baluchistan provinces of Pakistan. Pashtuns comprise approximately 50 percent of the population of Afghanistan, or about 7.5 million persons, and 10 percent of the population of Pakistan, or approximately 14 million individuals. They speak Pashto and Pakhto, two dialects of an Iranian language. Pashto became an official language of Afghanistan in 1936. Pashto/Pakhto is one of the widely used languages of Pakistan, with Pakhto predominating in the region around Peshawar and Pashto, a softer dialect, being spoken further south.

It is unclear when the Pashtuns settled in Afghanistan and Pakistan. They appear to be descendents of eastern Iranians who migrated into the region. Some of the ancestors of the Pashtuns may have been Zoroastrians, because Afghanistan and Pakistan were ruled by Zoroastrian and Iranian dynasties from the sixth century BCE to the seventh century CE. The religion of Islam reached them in the eighth and ninth centuries CE, brought by Arab and Iranian soldiers and settlers. Turkish tribes invaded and ruled the region from the tenth through sixteenth centuries CE.

Indigenous control over Afghanistan under the Durranis lasted from 1747–1772, followed by the Anglo-Afghan wars. Pashtuns regained control over Afghanistan in 1880. A constitution in 1964 granted women rights on par with those of men. The 1970s witnessed a series of *coup d'états*. A Soviet invasion of December 1979 and subsequent Russian occupation resulted in the rise of Muslim mujahidin groups. Civil war occurred after the Russian withdrawal in 1989. The fundamentalist Taliban regime in Afghanistan advocated strict Islamic law or Shari'a. Sociopolitical strife, droughts, and resulting famine have led to mass immigration eastward across a shared border into Pakistan, producing large refugee communities.

In Pakistan, which was part of the Mogul empire and then was incorporated British India (from 1857 until independence in 1947), Pashtuns now comprise approximately 70 percent of the population of the North West Frontier province. They are also present in large numbers within the province of Baluchistan, particularly the Quetta, Loralai, and Zhob districts. The Pashtun population of Pakistan witnessed a sharp increase with the arrival of about 1.2 million refugees from Afghanistan beginning in 1979 and continuing to the present day. Moving out from refugee camps along the border between the two nations, those expatriates have settled in many urbanized centers—not only Peshawar and Quetta but also in Karachi—and taken over sectors of the economy, such as trucking, previously monopolized by other ethnic groups such as the Balochis. As a result, sporadic ethnic violence has occurred between the Pashtuns and Balochis. Refugees have also migrated, via Pakistan, to England, Canada, and the United States.

The oldest literary traditions of Pashto and Pakhto are preserved in oral form. Written records may date back to the sixteenth century. Several regional and tribal dialects exist—including northwestern ones like Kabuli and central Ghilzai, northeastern ones like Afridi and northeastern Ghilzai, southwestern ones like Kandahari, and southeastern ones like Tarino and Waziri.

Pashtun/Pakhtun society is organized along hierarchical, patrilineal lines allegedly connecting tribesfolk back to an eponymous common ancestor. Affiliations to lineages and clans (*zai, khel*) are fairly fluid in practice. Major groups include the Durrani, Ghilzai, and Karlanri, each consisting of several tribes and clans. Overall, there are at least 60 tribes. Tribal genealogy determines societal rank, land use, and patterns of inheritance. Social conduct, especially for men, revolves around the concept of *pashtunwali* or *pakhtunwali*—an idealized system of hospitality, honor, and revenge used to regulate interactions and mediate disputes. This system is overseen by tribal chiefs (*khans*), a title bestowed on Pashtun leaders by Indian Mogul and Iranian Safawid rulers in the sixteenth century CE, and by tribal assemblies (*jirgas*). Blood feuds often arise between tribesmen over issues relating to personal or familial honor, especially involving women, and over the exercise of property rights, particularly grazing of livestock. Swift settlement of such feuds prevents transmission of hostilities and cycles of violence across generations within this heavily armed culture. A dance called *khatak* that arose from victory celebrations after battle is still performed by men.

Much of their society, although tribal, has become sedentary during the past century with families relying upon a combination of farming and herding. Some remain seminomadic pastoralists. In premodern and modern times, Pashtun men have routinely enlisted as soldiers—considering military service a highly honorable occupation. Others have entered mercantile professions—as rug dealers, truck drivers, and restaurateurs. Population relocation and concomitant poverty has led to a rise in drug smuggling—particularly of opium from poppies grown in Afghanistan—via Pakistan to Europe and North America.

JAMSHEED CHOKSY

See also **Afghanistan; Pakistan; Zoroastrians**

Further Reading

Bonner, Arthur, *Among the Afghans*, Durham, North Carolina: Duke University Press, 1987

Caroe, Olaf, *The Pathans 550 BC– AD 1957,* Karachi: Oxford University Press, 1958, reprinted 1983

Dupree, Louis, *Afghanistan*, Princeton: Princeton University Press, 1980

Lindholm, Charles, *Generosity and Jealousy: The Swat Pukhtun of Northern Pakistan*, New York: Oxford University Press, 1982

Marsden, Peter, *The Taliban: War, Religion, and the New Order in Afghanistan*, New York: Zed Books, 1998

McLachlan, Keith, and William Whittaker, *A Bibliography of Afghanistan*, Cambridge: Menas Press, 1983

Mills, Margaret A., *Rhetorics and Politics in Afghan Traditional Storytelling*, Philadelphia, Pennsylvania: University of Pennsylvania Press, 1991

Skjaervø, P. Oktor, "Pashto," in *Compendium linguarum Iranicarum*, edited by Rüdiger Schmitt, Wiesbaden: Ludwig Reichert Verlag, 1989, pp. 384–410

Szabo, Albert, and Thomas J. Barfield, *Afghanistan: An Atlas of Indigenous Domestic Architecture*, Austin: University of Texas Press, 1991

Palau

Capsule Summary

Country Name: The Republic of Palau
Location: Oceania, group of islands in the North Pacific Ocean, southeast of the Philippines
Total Population: 19,717 (2003)
Languages: English and Palauan official in all states except Sonsoral (Sonsoralese and English are official), Tobi (Tobi and English are official), and Angaur (Angaur, Japanese, and English are official)
Religions: Christian (Roman Catholics 49 percent, Seventh-Day Adventists, Jehovah's Witnesses, the Assembly of God, the Liebenzell Mission, and Latter-Day Saints), Modekngei religion (one-third of the population observes this religion, which is indigenous to Palau)

Located in the north Pacific Ocean in Oceania southeast of the Philippine Islands, The Republic of Palau is an island nation comprisng 16 states with just under 20,000 inhabitants. Palauans are distant relatives of the Malays of Indonesia, Melanesians of New Guinea, and Polynesians. Carbon dating of artifacts from the oldest known village sites on the Rock Islands and the terraces on Babeldaob place civilization here as early as 1000 BCE.

The first contact with Europeans came in 1783, when a British vessel was shipwrecked on a reef near Ulong, a Rock Island located between Koror and Peleliu. After this incident, a steady flow of foreign explorers came to Palau, thus opening the islands to further outside contact and influence. Foreign governance of Palau officially began when Pope Leo XIII asserted Spain's rights over the Caroline Islands in 1885, which resulted in the introduction of the Roman alphabet and the elimination of inter-village wars. In 1899, Spain sold the Caroline Islands to Germany, which began an effort to extract the islands' natural resources. Following Germany's defeat in World War I, the islands were formally passed to the Japanese under the 1919 Treaty of Versailles. The Japanese had a great influence on the Palauan culture and shifted the economy from a level of subsistence to a market economy In 1922, Koror became the administrative center for all Japanese possessions in the South Pacific. Following Japan's defeat in World War II, the Carolines, Marianas, and Marshall Islands became United Nations Trust Territories under United States administration. Palau was named as one of six island districts. On October 1, 1994, Palau gained its independence with the signing of the Compact of Free Association with the United States.

Palau's islands make up 458 square kilometers (21.74 percent arable land) with 1,519 kilometers (941.78) of coastline. Its natural resources include coconut products, marine products, and deep seabed minerals. Palau's economy is based largely on tourism, subsistence agriculture, and fishing. As of 2001, the GDP per capita was $9,000.

The government is the major employer of the work force, relying heavily on financial assistance from the United States. Palau's exports are shellfish, tuna, copra, and garments (to the United States, Japan, and Singapore) and its major imports are machinery and equipment, fuels, metals; foodstuffs (to the United States, Guam, Japan, Singapore, and Korea). Palau's sixteen states are governed by a constitutional government in free association with the United States under the Compact of Free Association entered into October 1, 1994. The government is based in the capital of Koror, and is made up of a chief of state, a bicameral Parliament elected by popular vote, and a legal system comprising a Supreme Court; National Court; and a Court of Common.

RICHARD VERRONE

See also **Malays; Melanesians**

Further Reading

Etpison, Mandy, *Palau: Portrait of Paradise*, Neco Marine Corp, 1995
Levesque, Rodrigue, *History of Micronesia: A Collection of Source Documents Mostly Palau 1783-1793* (History of Micronesia, Vol:15), Levesque Publications, 2001
Myers, Ched, and Robert Aloridpe, *Resisting the Serpent: Palau's Struggle for Self-Determination,* Fortress Press, 1990
Roff, Sue R., *Overreaching in Paradise: United States Policy in Palau Since 1945*, Denali Press, 1990

Peltier, Leonard (Amerindian)

Leonard James Peltier (Anishinabe and Lakota) is a writer and Native American activist. He is well known for speaking out against the mistreatment of Indians, and his controversial imprisonment has attracted international attention.

Leonard Peltier was born on September 12, 1944 in Grand Forks, North Dakota. His father was Leo Peltier, a mixed-blood who was three-quarters Ojibwe. His mother was Alvina Showers, the daughter of a full-blood Lakota Sioux mother. His Indian name is Gwarth-ee-lass (He Leads the People). He was raised in poverty and mostly brought up by his paternal grandparents. They frequently migrated in search of work at copper mines and logging camps. The federal government sent him 150 miles away at the age of eight to the Wahpeton Indian School in North Dakota. He was not allowed to speak his language, suffered various forms of abuse, and received only a limited education. Only later in life would he earn his general equivalency degree.

He left boarding school by the ninth grade and soon joined his father on the Turtle Mountain Reservation. There he began participating in traditional medicinal practices and dances. Before long, though, government officials arrested him for holding an illegal sun dance. This was during the late-1950s and early-1960s when the federal government was trying to assimilate Indians and terminate their legal status as tribes. As he participated in protests and demonstrations, he gained some of his earliest experience in Native resistance and activism.

As he traveled across various reservations he learned firsthand of the desperate conditions under which many Indian people lived. After moving to Seattle in the mid-1960s, he helped start an auto body shop and joined the increasing protests for Indian fishing rights in Washington State. In 1970 he joined the American Indian Movement (AIM), a group modeled after the Black Panthers, and soon rose to the ranks of leadership. He participated in AIM protests and demonstrations including the Trail of Broken Treaties in 1972. He also became quite involved in AIM's spiritual and traditional programs.

Throughout this period, the Federal Bureau of Investigation (FBI) was infiltrating and harassing AIM. This was part of a larger counterintelligence program known as COINTELPRO that aimed to disrupt and destroy militant organizations. AIM faced this pressure as it continued operations on the Pine Ridge Reservation in South Dakota after the Wounded Knee occupation of 1973. In June 1975, two FBI agents chased a young Indian named Jimmy Eagle onto a camp set up by AIM on the reservation. In the ensuing shoot-out, the FBI agents and one AIM member were killed. Four Indians were arraigned on various murder charges but Peltier was the only one ultimately convicted.

Peltier's trial took place in 1977 after his extradition from Canada. The federal government appointed a judge know for convicting Indians to the case and aggressively prosecuted Peltier, even though—as many scholars argue—the evidence was questionable. For instance, as much as 80 percent of the defense testimony was barred and (as was later learned) the FBI made false claims about the shell casing found at the murder scene. By the trial's end, Peltier had been sentenced to two life terms in prison. He has since spent most of his time behind bars at a high-security penitentiary in Marion, Illinois. His claims of innocence, and the suppressed evidence in his trials, received considerable publicity in the early 1980s and 1990s with the publication of Peter Matthiessen's bestseller, In the Spirit of Crazy Horse. In recent years, information obtained from FBI files through the Freedom of Information Act has caused some federal officials to recant their claims against Peltier. Still, he has been consistently denied parole and clemency.

Many in the world today consider Peltier a political prisoner. Some within FBI still regard him as a murderer. These challenges have not stopped him from contributing to the ongoing struggle for human rights. In the past quarter century he has established himself as an artist, author, poet, and internationally known activist. His supporters include Amnesty International, various Parliaments in Europe, 50 members of the U.S. Congress, and numerous others. He continues his fight for justice on the behalf of minority peoples everywhere.

Capsule Biography

Leonard James Peltier. Born September 12, 1944 in Grand Forks, North Dakota. Studied at Wahpeton Indian School in North Dakota. Worked in mining and logging in Montana, opened an auto body shop in Seattle, Washington, participated in the Trail of Broken Treaties in 1972, and between 1975 and 1977 was arrested and convicted for the murder of two FBI agents. Leader, American Indian Movement, 1970–1977. Prisoner in high-security penitentiary in Marion, Illinois, 1977–present.

Selected Works

Are Indians an Oppressed Minority? Leonard Peltier vs. Kevin Phillips, Minneapolis: Greenhaven Press, 1977, sound cassette
In Total Resistance, coauthored with Bobby Gene García and Robert Hugh Wilson [Standing Bear], [New York]: Leonard Peltier Support Group, 1980; abridged and revised, Kansas City, Kansas: Leonard Peltier Support House, 1986; abridged and revised, Seattle: Seattle Leonard Peltier Support Group, 1991
"No Friend of Mine," *Nation*, November 1, 1986
Leonard Peltier: My Story, National Public Radio, 1992, sound cassette
"Peltier Pleads: Please Don't Forget Me," *News From Indian Country*, September 30, 1993
"Betrayal, Hope, and the American Judicial System," *Review of Law and Social Change*, 20, no. 2 (193)
"Since I'm the Object of So Much Discussion, I Believe Its MY Turn to Speak," *News From Indian Country*, December 31, 1995
"Greetings Friends at Akwesasne Notes," *Akwesasne Notes*, March 31, 1996
Prison Writings: My Life Is My Sundance, edited by Harvey Arden, New York: St. Martin's Press, 1999, as Ecrits de Prison, Paris: Albin Michel, 2000
"In the Spirit of Crazy Horse," in *Capitalart: On the Culture of Punishment*, edited by Mariana Botey and Pilar Perez, Santa Monica, California: Smart Art Press, 2001
"Peltier Tells of Disappointment, Renewed Commitment," *Indian Country Today (Lakota Times)*, February 7, 2001
"Inipi: Sweat Lodge," in *Imprisoned Intellectuals: America's Political Prisoners Write on Life, Liberation, and Rebellion*, edited by Joy James, Lanham, Maryland: Rowman & Littlefield, 2003

STERLING FLUHARTY

See also **American Indian Movement; Amerindians**

Further Reading

Churchill, Ward, and Jim Vander Wall, *Agents of Repression: The FBI's Secret Wars Against the Black Panther Party and the American Indian Movement*, Cambridge, Massachusetts: South End Press, 2002
Churchill, Ward, "The Bloody Wake of Alcatraz: Political Repression of the American Indian Movement during the 1970s," *American Indian Culture and Research Journal*, 18, no. 4, 1994

Hogan III, Joseph C., "Guilty Until Proven Innocent: Leonard Peltier and the Sublegal System," *Boston College Law Review*, 34, no. 4, 1993

Johansen, Bruce, "Will Clinton Pardon Him? Leonard Peltier's Continuing Bid For Freedom," *Native Americas*, 14, no. 3, 1997

Kunstler, William M., "By Hook or by Crook," *Hamline Law Review*, 8, no. 3, 1985

Kunstler, William M., "Remarks on the Leonard Peltier Case," *American Indian Law Review*, 20, no. 1, 1995

Matthiessen, Peter, *In the Spirit of Crazy Horse*, New York: Viking Press, 1983; reprinted, 1992

Matthiessen, Peter, et al., "United States v. Leonard Peltier," *The New York Review of Books*, 47, no. 12, 2000

Messerschmidt, Jim, *The Trial of Leonard Peltier*, Boston: South End Press, 1983; reprinted, 1989

Privitera, John J., "Toward a Remedy for International Extradition by Fraud: The Case of Leonard Peltier," *Yale Law & Policy Review*, 2, no. 1, 1983

Sanchez, John, Mary E. Stuckey, and Richard Morris, "Rhetorical Exclusion: The Government's Case Against American Indian Activists, AIM, and Leonard Peltier," *American Indian Culture and Research Journal*, 23, no. 2, 1999

Vander Wall, Jim, "A Warrior Caged: The Continuing Struggle of Leonard Peltier," in *The State of Native America: Genocide, Colonization, and Resistance*, edited by M. Annette Jaimes, Boston, Massachusetts: South End Press, 1992

Peru

Capsule Summary

Country Name: Peru
Location: Western South America, bordering the South Pacific Ocean, between Chile and Ecuador
Total Population: 28,409,897 (2003)
Languages: Spanish (official), Quechua (minority Native American); other small groups of Native American languages
Religions: Roman Catholic (92.5 percent); Protestant (4.5 percent); various small denominations

Peru (west central South America) has three major regions. Tropical jungles feeding the Amazon basin, called the Selva (northern and eastern flanks) hold 11 percent of Peru's population. Tribal peoples live near rivers and subsist by fishing, hunting, and swidden farming in a largely traditional lifeway. Once isolated, the Selva peoples are now encroached upon by forestry and narcotics farming.

The steep Andes mountain chain has many peaks over 6,000 meters. The western side is dry, supporting few communities. High-altitude intermountain valleys fed by rivers and rains support 36 percent of Peru's population. Tropical forest grows up the eastern flank. Andean ecological zones exist in bands differing with altitude. Highest altitudes support grazing of native livestock. Lower bands support specific edible native species and Old World imports. Farmers develop trade relations across the zones or own/sharecrop small patches in each zone to form a complete subsistence, although modern land reform often damages this old, proven system. Small subsistence farms represent 70 percent of households, with the remainder being large peasant cooperatives.

The barren coast of Peru comprises rocky hills and dunes; it has a rainless yet humid climate created and moderated by the Pacific. Around 4,000 YBP simple communities developed on the coast's rich maritime environment. Fishing is still important but suffers from depletion. Other resources for society exist in the long, narrow valleys running from coast to Andes, where over half the population lives. The Andes feed these rivers all year, offering floral and faunal resources for a range of early societies. Terracing and irrigation allowed farmers to plant up steep valley sides as early as 3,000 YBP. All the early Peruvian societies and empires depended on this intensive farming. After the Spanish conquest, elite colonial families controlled irrigation water to maintain plantations with native Peruvians serving as peasant labor. The valleys now produce half of the nation's agriculture, though they comprise less than 4 percent of Peru's area.

Peru joins ancient Mesopotamia, China, India, and Central America in having developed early, indigenous, complex societies founded on intensive agriculture, forming trade ties and religious cults, and sometimes expanding militarily. The complex chiefdom of Chavin society (800–200 BCE) built large ceremonial sites and spread art style and religious ideas over a large area. Thereafter Peru saw increasingly complex societies developing urban settlements culminating in the nation state of the Inca Empire (late 1400s to 1534 CE).

Inca military expansion absorbed many ethnic groups and 50 or more languages—peoples often repressed with violence, forced transplantation, and forced language-adoption (Quechua). This produced a complex ethnic history and resentment that Spanish conquerors exacerbated. The Spanish defeated the Inca relatively rapidly by 1534, caused in part by the demoralization of virulent European disease (nearly 15 million of 16 million Peruvians died by 1800). The Spanish ruled through native lords once under Inca rule, who organized peasant labor to run Spanish enterprises.

Native social units gradually became large farming estates overseen by Spanish priests and judges. After nationhood in 1824, the "hacienda" system replaced the similar colonial rule: European-derived landlords ruled native serfs (peons) reminiscent of feudal society. Thus Peru developed a caste system where European-derived people (especially Old-World-born Spanish) held elite positions, styling themselves as conquerors long after colonial times. Mestizos (mixed Spanish and native blood) held some status positions. The caste system also included varieties of ethnic mixes: African (descendants of Spanish slaves) and Native American, Mestizo and Native American. Pure Native Americans occupied the lowest caste, enduring routine discrimination and insult. Classification within these ethnic groups decided one's residence, occupation, taxes, clothing, religion, and permission to travel.

Native American rebellions rose in the 1700s as scarce land and high taxes brought hardship. Rebellions were quelled, although some reforms resulted. Substantive improvement did not occur until extensive land reforms in 1969.

Today, Peru's ethnic makeup comprises Native Americans (45 percent, includes Quechua and Aymara), Mestizos (37 percent), White (15 percent), and African, Asian, and others (3 percent). Asians started arriving in the late nineteenth century as Chinese laborers who began as indentured servants and later entered business. Japanese immigrants (farmers and merchants) arrived beginning in the twentieth century.

Subsistence-level agriculture is still important (36 percent of labor), including small farms, corporate peasant farms, forestry, and fishing; peasant agriculture is concentrated among the highland Quechua, who combine ancient Peruvian customs with adaptation to 500 years of colonial rule. Trade and industry concentrate along the coast and coastal valleys, occupying some Native Americans but mostly European-derived people, Asians, and people of mixed ethnicity. The per capita GDP was $5,000 in 2002.

Recent Peruvian history has recurrent themes of instability, social reform, and violent change: various political parties come to power and decline in attempts to advance the nation's economy and make reforms, especially to ease Native American conditions, which continue to be difficult. The first third of the century saw a series of dictators with whom harsh politics sometimes went hand-in-hand with improved economy. The American Popular Revolutionary Alliance (APRA), formed by intellectuals in 1924, was an influential reform party for several decades. After World War II, Peru was under revolutionary rule (APRA was outlawed for a while) until 1956, when popular sentiment called for civilian rule and elections. Peru entered a phase of liberal politics and improved economy. Still, political instability resulted in indecisive elections and military juntas until 1963. The Velasco government managed some extensive reforms in the early 1970s, although another military coup in 1975 led to further attempts at reform, ending in economic disaster. At this time the leftist Shining Path guerilla movement arose in the highlands, sympathetic to Native Peruvian Americans who by this time relied much on illegal coca production for income in a broken economy. The 1990s saw the Fujimori government take power, resulting in nearly ten years of struggle with Shining Path, governmental reform, American aid, and continuing political instability, exacerbated by environmental declines affecting the economy. Underlying this recent history is an ethnic mix of descent, language, and hierarchy, along with shifts of ethnic and social identity, creating a complex social environment in which the heritage of whiteness, nativeness, colonialism, and nationhood are still central and contentious forces.

WADE TARZIA

See also **Quechua**

Further Reading

Gordon R. Willey. *An Introduction to American Archaeology: Volume Two: South America*, Englewood Cliffs, New Jersey: Prentice-Hall, 1971

Hudson, Rick A., editor, *Peru: A Country Study*, DA Pam 550-42. Area Handbook Series. Library of Congress, Federal Research Division, 4th edition, 1992

Salomon, Frank, and Stuart B. Schwartz, editors, *The Cambridge History of the Native Peoples of the Americas. Volume III, South America* (two parts), Cambridge, United Kingdom: Cambridge University Press, 1999

Poole, Deborah, editor, *Unruly Order: Violence, Power, and Cultural Identity in the High Provinces of Southern Peru*, Boulder, Colorado: Westview Press, 1994

Klarén, Peter Flindell, *Peru: Society and Nationhood in the Andes*, New York: Oxford University Press, 2000

Rosenberg, Tina, *Children of Cain: Violence and the Violent in Latin America*, New York, 1991

Stokes, Susan C., *Cultures in Conflict: Social Movements and the State in Peru*, Berkeley, California, 1995

Martínez-Alier, Juan, *Haciendas, Plantations, and Collective Farms: Agrarian Class Societies—Cuba and Peru*, London, 1977

Philippines

Capsule Summary

Country Name: The Philippines
Location: Southeastern Asia, archipelago between the Philippine Sea and the South China Sea, east of Vietnam
Total Population: 84,619,974 (2003)
Languages: Two official languages, Filipino (based on Tagalog) and English; eight major dialects, Tagalog, Cebuano, Ilocan, Hiligaynon or Ilonggo, Bicol, Waray, Pampango, and Pangasinense
Religions: Roman Catholic 83%, Protestant 9%, Muslim 5%, Buddhist and other 3%

The Philippine archipelago, composed of more than 7,000 islands, lies off the southeast coast of Asia between latitude 21°25'N and 4°23'N and longitude 116°E and 127°E. It is located below the Tropic of Cancer in the South China Sea, across from Vietnam to the West, Taiwan to the North, and Indonesia to the Southwest. It is 1,150 miles long and has a total land area of 300,000 sq km. The archipelago is divided into three sections: Luzon, the largest island, in the North, Mindanao, in the South, and the Visayas, a cluster of islands lying in-between. It has an active volcanic structure and the climate is tropical with an average year-round temperature of 27°C (82°F).

The Republic of the Philippines' 1987 constitution provides for a legislative power composed of an Upper and Lower House, an executive branch composed of a president and vice-president, and an independent judiciary branch. As of December 31, 2000, there were 16 regions, 78 provinces, 96 cities, 1,513 municipalities, and 41,943 barangays (smallest administrative units consisting of a village or a cluster of scattered hamlets) in the Philippines. As of 2002, the per capita GDP was $4,600.

A great majority—91.5 percent—of Filipinos are Christians belonging to more than 9 major ethno-linguistic groups. Around 5 percent are Muslims belonging to 10 different ethno-linguistic groups. The remaining 3 percent are upland tribal groups, or indigenous cultural communities as they are officially called.

Christian lowlanders located in Luzon are, from North to South, the Ilocano, Pangasinan, Pampangan, Tagalog, and Bicolano. The Visayas, which is the cluster of islands forming the central section of the archipelago, is occupied by the Ilongo, Waray-Waray, Cebuano, and Boholano people. Many of those, especially the Cebuano, have migrated south and are now occupying large sections of Mindanao, the southernmost part of the archipelago. In this island are found the Maranao and the Maguindanao, the two largest Muslim cultural groups, together with the Taosug, who are centrally located in the island of Jolo in the Sulu archipelago. Other Muslim groups are the Samal, Yakan, Bajau (for some), Ilanen, Sangir, Molbog, and Jama Mapun. All of them are located along the rim or in the islands of the Sulu Sea.

There are more than 100 upland tribal groups. Almost all of them are located in the mountainous interior of Northern Luzon, Mindoro, Palawan, Panay, and Mindanao. The Grand Cordillera of Northern Luzon is home to the *Igorot*, a generic name given to about ten major ethnolinguistic groups comprising the famed Ifugaos, as well as the Bontok, Kalinga, Ibaloi, Kankanay, Tinguian, Isnneg, Gaddang, and Ilongot, the latter not being Cordillera people strictly speaking. Likewise, the name *Mangyan* has been given to the various traditional cultural communities inhabiting the island of Mindoro groups, like the Iraya, Alangan,

Ratagnon, Hanunoo, and Buhid. In Mindanao also the word *Lumad* came to designate such groups as the Manobo, Bukidnon, Bagobo, Mandaya, Mansaka, Subanun, Mamanua, Bila-an, Tiruray, and T'boli. The island of Palawan is home to the Batak, the Tagbanuwa, and the Palawano (Pala'wan). Negritos (Atas, Aetas, Agtas) are found in various locations throughout the archipelago.

At the time of the discovery of the area by non-natives in the sixteenth century, the Filipinos lived in scattered groups of various levels of political integration. Muslim Sultanates were the highest form of state integration, but non-Muslim societies existed with a high degree of stratification. Recent discoveries (the Laguna copper plate bearing an inscription in an old Javanese script) have increased the span of the history of the Philippines by five centuries, at a time when the Philippines were part of a wider network of trade and exchange relations with the Indonesian archipelago and other neighboring countries, probably the Champa as well.

From the end of the sixteenth century to the end of the nineteenth century the Filipinos, with a few notable exceptions, were conquered and brought forcibly into the fold of Christianity by several religious orders who all but eradicated the native culture, especially all forms of native religious beliefs and customs.

In the eighteenth and nineteenth centuries a new class of *Mestizos*, people born from Chinese immigrants and native women, became wealthy and prominent. They formed an emerging elite, the *Ilustrados*, which ultimately inspired the Philippine Revolution and fostered a modern sense of nationhood. The American occupation of the Philippines followed until 1946, at which time the Philippines became independent.

The *Moros* are a multiethnic Muslim population located in the Sulu Archipelago and southwestern Mindanao. They are known for a long history of armed resistance against Christian and foreign domination. In the 1960s, tensions between Christian and Muslim communities increased, leading to rebellion against Martial Law declared by the Marcos administration in 1972. The leading resistance group was the Moro National Liberation Front (MNLF). The conflict

escalated from 1973 to 1975. In 1976 an agreement was signed in Tripoli between the Philippine government and the MNLF granting autonomy to the Moro region.

Under the following administrations after 1976, new armed groups and resistance movements emerged, among them the more radical MILF (Moro Independence Liberation Front), and an endemic state of war continued between Muslim armed groups and the Armed Forces of the Philippines.

The *Igorot*, also a multi-ethnic entity, are traditional indigenous communities living in the Central Cordillera of Northern Luzon. They successfully resisted Spanish domination and have retained a degree of autonomy from the central government, fighting for control of their ancestral lands against mining companies and proposed hydroelectric plants.

CHARLES MACDONALD

See also **Igorot; Negritos**

Further Reading

Corpuz, O.D., *The Roots of the Filipino Nation*, Quezon City: Aklahi Foundation Inc., 1989

Doeppers, Daniel F., and Peter Xenos, editors, *Population and History: The Demographic Origins of the Modern Philippines*, Quezon City: Ateneo de Manila University Press, 1998

Eder, James F., *On the Road to Tribal Extinction: Depopulation, Deculturation and Adaptive Well-Being among the Batak of the Philippines*, Berkeley, Los Angeles, London: University of California Press, 1987

Macdonald, Charles, "Indigenous Peoples of the Philippines: between Segregation and Integration", in *Indigenous Peoples of Asia*, edited by R.H. Barnes, A. Gray, and B. Kingsbury, Ann Arbor, Michigan: Association for Asian Studies, Inc., 1995

Macdonald, Charles J.H., and Guillermo M. Pesigan, editors, *Old Ties and New Solidarities, Studies on Philippine Communities*, Quezon City: Ateneo de Manila University Press, 2000

Steinberg, David J., *The Philippines: A Singular and a Plural Place*, Boulder, San Francisco, Oxford: Westview Press, 1994

Warren, James F., *The Sulu Zone 1768–1898: The Dynamics of External Trade, Slavery, and Ethnicity in the Transformation of a Southeast Asian Maritime State*, Quezon City: New Day Publishers, 1985

Poland

Capsule Summary

Country Name: Republic of Poland
Location: Eastern Europe, between Belarus, Ukraine, and Germany
Total Population: 38,622,660 (2003)
Languages: Polish, some German, Belarusian, Ukrainian, and Lithuanian
Religions: Roman Catholicism, Protestantism, Eastern Orthodox, Judaism, and Islam

Poland covers a large plain in Central Europe, which is about the size of New Mexico. There are several mountain ranges along the southern border of the country, and a long coastline in the north. This wide and flat stretch of land is a passageway between the eastern and western Europe. The geographic conditions played a significant role in Poland's one thousand years of political history. The capital of Poland is Warsaw, the largest city of the region.

The Polish state emerged in the Middle Ages. Historians identify its symbolic origins with an event that took place in 966 CE, the year when Prince Mesko, the most powerful chieftain of the Polanie tribe, converted to Christianity. Archaeologists recorded significant changes in the settlement pattern and population density taking place prior to the second half of the tenth century, all suggesting the existence of specific political and economic conditions for a complex society to come into being. It seems that Mesko had successfully imposed his ruling over a large area and unified several Slavic tribes into one political entity. His political domain was strengthened by the acceptance of a new religion that linked Western Slavia with the western European civilization. Mesko's son, Boleslaw Chrobry, was crowned as the first Polish king in 1025. The political changes that took place by the end of the tenth and the beginning of the eleventh century put Poland on the map of Europe.

During the formative period of the state (tenth–fourteenth centuries), Poland was marked by upheaval and uncertainty, but in the fifteenth century, under the powerful dynasty of the Jagiellons, it became one of the most potent kingdoms of medieval Europe. A century later, after creating a political and economic alliance with the Great Duchy of Lithuania, the Polish kingdom became the key part of one of the most powerful European states of the time, the Commonwealth (*Rzeczpospolita*). The Jagiellonian period was the golden age for Poland, and all other ethnic groups were incorporated into the Commonwealth. The state expanded and at its peak stretched between the Baltic and the Black seas. It was indeed an Eastern European empire, a multiethnic and multicultural state with great economic strength and strong military power, controlling most of central and eastern European politics.

The wealth and freedom of the land attracted many people. Ethnic groups that inhabited the Commonwealth included Poles, Lithuanians, Belarusians, Ukrainians, Tartars, Russians, Czechs, Slovaks, Germans, and Jews. There was also a small contingent of Hungarians, Italians, Armenians, Dutch, English, Scottish, and French colonists. Many citizens of the Commonwealth spoke several languages. Artists and professionals from around Europe worked in the Commonwealth. Dutch architects built Gdansk, while Italian architects redesigned the royal castle on the Wawel Hill in Krakow. The Italian style has become especially popular during the Renaissance. The Jagiellonian times are known for spiritual and intellectual freedom. Religious escapees from other parts of Europe found refuge in the Commonwealth. Education was a valued commodity among the Polish gentry, the precursor of the intelligentsia. The Polish elite studied mostly in Italy (Padua) and France. The first Polish university was founded in Krakow.

The Golden Age ended with the death of the last Jagiellonian king, Zygmunt II, in August 1572. After the end of the Jagiellonian dynasty, the noblemen elected the rulers of the Commonwealth. The first candidates who gathered for election in Warsaw were a Frenchman, Russian, German, Swede, and Romanian. The noblemen chose the Frenchman, Henri de Valois, to become the next ruler of the Commonwealth, but after the unexpected death of Charles IX, de Valois inherited the French throne and fled Poland. After the stormy election of 1575, the noblemen elected Stephen Batory, Duke of Transylvania, to be the next king.

The two unsuccessful contestants for the Polish crown, the Emperor Maximilian II (Habsburg) and the tsar Ivan IV (the Terrible) joined forces against the new

POLAND

ruler of the Commonwealth. The situation deteriorated with the death of Batory in 1586. Wars broke out with the Cossacks and Tartars in the East. But the devastating blow came from the North, when the once-allied kingdom of Sweden, led by king Charles X Gustavus, invaded the Commonwealth in 1655. The Swedish invasion is known in Polish history as "The Deluge," due to its devastating consequences. The Commonwealth came out of this period with territorial losses and cultural decline.

The last Polish king, Stanislaw August Poniatowski, was given no choice but to follow the design orchestrated by Russia's Catherine the Great. In consequence, the first partition of the Commonwealth by the three competing powers, Russia, Prussia, and Austria, took place in 1772, followed by the two subsequent partitions in 1793 and 1794.

The end of the eighteenth century set the scene for political drama that continued through the nineteenth and the twentieth centuries. There were some attempts to save the Commonwealth, and the most spectacular was the four-year session of the Parliament (The Great Sejm), which resulted with the first written European Constitution of May 3, 1791. The constitution was a compromise between ideas represented by republicans, radicals, and monarchists. It was a blueprint for a strong parliamentary monarchy, which gave hope that the Commonwealth could have again become a European superpower. And that perhaps was the reason why it was not acceptable to the neighboring powers, especially Russia.

After the second and the third partitions, Poland and other nations composing the Commonwealth vanished from the map of Europe for over a century, until the end of World War I, which brought new borders to Eastern Europe. After the second uprising, all Polish institutions existing in the Polish Kingdom and controlled by the Russians were abolished. A period of repression and brutality was devastating, and thousands of young people were sent to Siberia and never returned. It seems that the hardship of the second half of the nineteenth century only strengthened the cultural identity of people who identified themselves as the citizens of Poland. The country lost its territorial signature, but the nation refused to disappear. Poles lived in diaspora around the world as a people without a state.

The beginning of the twentieth century brought about new ideas and expectations for the revival of the state. World War I was considered a good chance for an independent Polish state to reemerge. Poles fought for different armies, but the most successful turned out to be General Jozef Pilsudski, who was given permission by Austria to form Polish Legions. Due to the political skills of Polish politicians, Poland regained its politically autonomous status as an independent country in 1918. The new Poland was about half the size of the Commonwealth, but remained a multiethnic society with representatives of several ethnic groups and nations (Poles, Ukrainians, Belarusians, Jews, Germans, Gypsies, Tartars, and others).

The country was slowly emerging from a long period of nonexistence. New politics, economics, arts, and sciences were developing abruptly until September 1, 1939, when the German Third Reich troops invaded Poland from the west, and seventeen days later the Soviet Red Army from the east, initating one of the most dramatic periods in modern Polish history.

Politically, the state and the nation survived. However, it emerged from the war crippled and dominated by the neighboring power, the Soviet Union. For more than forty years Poland remained a member of the communist world. The communists governed the country until 1989, when Poland had its first democratic elections since before World War II.

The newly formed government was based on the politicians who were associated with Solidarity, a trade union which was formed after a series of strikes in the summer of 1980, and later transformed into a strong civil movement. Despite its dissolution during the martial law imposed in 1981, the members kept the union alive as an underground structure. As a result of the so-called "round table talks," of 1989 between the communist government and the representatives of the civic opposition, the shift of power was arranged and a new democratic state was born.

Poland became a member of NATO, and has a good chance to join the European Union within the first decade of the twenty-first century. Poland is not only culturally part of the West, it is also a member of western political structures, and soon may join the West European Economic Union.

LUDOMIR LOZNY

Further Reading

Davies, Norman, *God's Playground, A History of Poland*, volumes 1 and 2, New York: Columbia University Press, 1982

Gieysztor, Aleksander, Stefan Kieniewicz, Emanuel Rostworowski, Janusz Tazbir, and Henryk Wereszycki, *History of Poland*, Warsaw: Polish Scientific Publishers, 2nd edition, 1979

Zamoyski, Adam, *The Polish Way: A Thousand-year History of the Poles and their Culture*, London: John Murray Ltd., 1987

Poles

Capsule summary

Locations: 38.6 million in the Republic of Poland; 9.4 million persons of Polish background in the United States; approximately 2 million ethnic Poles in countries of the former Soviet Union, primarily in Lithuania, Belarus, and Ukraine, but also in Russia, Kazakhstan and Turkmenistan; approximately 1 million in Germany, 80,000 persons of Polish background in Brazil, and a scattering throughout Europe, Australia, Canada, South Africa, and elsewhere
Total population: approximately 50 million
Language: Polish
Religions: Roman Catholic (95 percent as of 2002); small Eastern Orthodox, Protestant, Jewish communities

As a national group, the Poles underwent change from a majoritarian group in their own country to minority status in three European empires, returning to being a majority in the newly-reconstituted Poland in 1919. They left a substantial diaspora in the United States, Lithuania, Ukraine, Belarus, Germany, France, Australia, and elsewhere. The dispersal of Polish population was largely a result of the partitions of Poland in the late eighteenth century, when, in defiance of the Treaty of Westphalia, Poland was "cannibalized" by the neighboring empires of Prussia, Austria, and Russia. In 1795, Poland disappeared from the map of Europe, and these three empires acquired large Polish minorities. Polish minorities outside Poland display various degrees of assimilation, from nearly total integration and assimilation in the United States to zero assimilation in some areas of the former Soviet Union.

The Poles trace their history to the conversion of Poland to Christianity in 966, when the Polish prince Mieszko (Mesko) I married the Bohemian princess Dubrava and converted to her religion (Bohemia was already Christianized at that time). Historians interpret Mieszko's marriage as a sign of his political astuteness: By marrying Dubrava, he avoided indenturing his weak central European state to the powerful Holy Roman Empire dominated by Germany. The subsequent four centuries witnessed a continuing struggle of the Polish principality (later, a kingdom) run by the Piast dynasty against Poland's western neighbor, Germany. In Mieszko's times, the Polish state's borders coincided with Poland's present borders. However, in the twelfth century, German colonization weakened

feudal Poland demographically and territorially, while contributing to its arts and culture. The Polish population became interspersed with the German and, while many Germans eventually acquired the Polish cultural identity, others did not, thus laying the groundwork for the later German claim to Polish Silesia, Poznania, and Pomerania.

Political identity was followed by a cultural one: the numerous *Chronicles* (dating back to the twelfth century) were kept in Polish Catholic monasteries, and battle songs in the vernacular (*Bogurodzica*) began to be composed. Culturally speaking, Poland under the Piasts could be compared to western Europe under Charlemagne: not yet a cultural entity but on its way to becoming one. The Jewish immigration to Poland began in the Piast period: between 1340 and 1772, the Jews of Poland grew 75-fold, whereas gentile population grew only five-fold). The first Golden Age came in the sixteenth century, when Poland was ruled by the powerful Jagiellonian dynasty comprising present-day Lithuania, Belarus, and Ukraine. Poets Jan Kochanowski (1530–1583) and Mikolaj Sep-Szarzynski (1550–1581) composed prolific verse, drama and prose (among the numerous translations of Kochanowski's *Threnoids,* a recent one by Seamus Heaney merits attention), while political thinkers such as Andrzej Frycz-Modrzewski (1503–1572) and Stanislaw Orzechowski (1513–1566) wrote Christian-inspired treatises on how to run the *ResPublica* (thus placing Polish political thought in distinct opposition to the tradition of Niccolo Macchiavelli). The Polish Commonwealth began to be known as a place where heretics and non-Christians (Jews in particular) could find refuge (a 1575 law stipulated the freedom of religion), while the Polish noble class, comprising 10 percent of the population, acquired voting and civil rights unheard of in premodern Europe. In the eighteenth century, three-fourths of the world's Ashkenazi Jewry lived in Poland. Polish kings were elected in a manner similar to that of twentieth-century presidents, and Polish statesmen began to use the term *Res Publica* in reference to their country. Poland became a noble democracy, not unlike the Athens of antiquity. It should, however, be remembered that the system was sustained by the oppression of peasants and also of national minorities, mainly Ukrainians and Belarusians.

In the seventeenth century, the election of Polish kings became international business, and Poland's hostile neighbors, Muscovy and Prussia, did their best to affect the outcome. The mechanism of Polish royal elections proved unable to withstand outside intervention, and the result was that Poland's eighteenth century kings were already fully under the sway of the neighboring autocratic powers. This resulted in the above-mentioned partitions of Poland in 1772, 1793, and 1795. It is from that point on that the status of Poles as minorities begins.

Prussia was largely a Protestant state, and the acquisition of a large Catholic minority necessitated efforts to wipe out Catholicism (and therefore Polishness) from the state's eastern marches. The efforts to that effect intensified in mid-nineteenth century when the Prussian government assigned large sums of money for the purchase of land owned by Polish peasants. Prussia has had a reputation of having been an enlightened state that offered equal rights to minorities, but these rights did not extend to the Polish-speaking Catholics. Especially in unified Germany under Bismarck, Polish school children were routinely intimidated and beaten for speaking and praying in their native tongue, and Polish farmers were obliged to abandon family farms because of indebtedness. Several generations of such politics led to a considerable Germanization of Poznania and Silesia (Pomerania had been Germanized earlier), so that when the 1945 Yalta agreements gave these provinces to the powerless Polish state as a compensation for eastern provinces annexed by the Soviet Union, the ensuing dislocation of the German and Polish populations was bound to involve horrendous human suffering.

The largest chunk of pre-partition Poland fell into Russian hands after the Napoleonic wars. Russia acquired the city of Warsaw (in Prussian hands between 1795–1815), and it held on to it until World War I. The cultural differences between Poles accustomed to what Polish historians call "premodern democracy," and Russians whose cultural memory encoded authoritarian rule was fundamental, and it was under Russian rule that Poles suffered most as a minority. Numerous insurrections followed; the risings of 1831 and 1863 were the bloodiest and resulted in vast emigration to America and other countries. They further exacerbated Russian discrimination of Poles. Yet in the mid-nineteenth century, half of the hereditary nobility in the Russian empire was Polish. After 1863, the Polish language in the public sphere was banned, and Warsaw University professors were ordered to learn Russian. A large segment of Polish landowners and intelligentsia were dispatched to Siberia. Polish Jews were subject to discrimination by Polish Catholics and by the Russian authorities: They were a minority within the Polish minority. Poles were not allowed to hold political offices or to participate in politics. Polish industries were obliged to restructure themselves toward the Russian market, thus being effectively cut off from participation in European development. The tsarist regime skillfully played off economic antagonisms between Catholic and Jewish Poles. The damage to the economy, political culture, and social fabric was considerable, and the scars remain deep to his day.

Poles fared relatively well in the Austrian empire. As a Catholic minority, they identified with their Catholic Austrian rulers more than with the Protestant Prussians or the Eastern Orthodox Russians. They were allowed to participate in politics, and some of them achieved prominent positions in the Austrian bureaucracy (e.g., Count Agenor Goluchowski served as Minister of the Interior under Emperor Franz Josef I, and the city of Kraków became a Polish cultural center during the years of Russian oppression in Warsaw.

These political misfortunes ended in 1918 with the collapse of Prussia, Austria, and Russia. President Woodrow Wilson's support enabled Polish leader Józef Pilsudski to proclaim an independent Polish state. But German and Soviet aggression against Poland in September 1939 started World War II and reintroduced the status of Poles as a minority not only in the German and Soviet states but also worldwide, due to rapid dispersal of war refugees in western Europe and elsewhere. Polish Jews suffered the Holocaust, and the Nazis inscribed onto the Polish town of Oswiecim (Auschwitz) a history that its modest inhabitants had never envisaged. The end of World War II brought military occupation by the Soviet Union of a country renamed "People's Poland" that was nominally independent but *de facto* governed from Moscow. This situation caused further emigration to the so-called free world. The emigration abated in the 1990s. In the first decade of the twenty-first century, Poland has become home to immigrants from the former Soviet Union and Asia. At the turn of the millennium, the number of immigrants to Poland (most of them illegal) was estimated to be one million.

This turbulent history created large Polish minorities worldwide. The most numerous one is in the United States. According to the 1990 census, it numbers 9.4 million people. The largest number of Polish Americans reside in the state of New York (1.2 million), while the largest percentage of Polish Americans can be found in Wisconsin (10.3 percent). Between 1980 and 1990, the number of Polish Americans rose by 13.8 percent, whereas the total United States population increased by 9.8 percent.

Polish Jews form a separate chapter in that migratory process. The emigration of Jews from partitioned Poland has been steady since the late nineteenth century, with considerable numbers coming to the United States after World War II. However, following a premodern pattern, Polish Jews tended to identify with Jewish causes and organizations in the United States, rather than with the Polish ones, while Polish ethnic organizations tended to be overtly Catholic, thus discouraging Jewish participation. The Holocaust further separated Poles of Jewish and Catholic background. Only the post-1968 Polish-Jewish emigration has tended to seek identity both within the Jewish and Polish organizations in the United States.

The second largest Polish minority, about one million, is to be found in Germany. These are the descendants of Poles who lived under the Prussian partition in the nineteenth century, as well as descendants of those deported in World War II and immigrants from the post-1945 period. Depending on their declared origin, this minority has either enjoyed full citizenship rights or has been treated as a source of cheap labor and slated for eventual expulsion. Germany is the only country into which large numbers of Poles emigrated to produce widely differing estimates of the numbers of such immigrants. While German sources maintain that there are no more than 400,000 Poles in their country, Polish sources speak of two million. The reason for the discrepancy is the unwillingness of German legislature to grant citizenship and voting rights to those persons of non-German origin who have lived in Germany for a number of years (that concerns all minorities in Germany, not just Poles); rather, these minorities have been treated as foreigners temporarily living in Germany. Another reason is a disparity in the ways of counting: Polish sources tend to count so-called *Aussiedler* (Polish immigrants to Germany who claim German roots) as Poles, whereas German sources count them as Germans even though many of these immigrants speak Polish and are members of Polish organizations in Germany. Recent studies indicate that there are about 150,000 Poles in Berlin, 100,000 in Hamburg, and up to 200,000 in the Ruhr area. While political and social discrimination is still considerable, Poles in Germany enjoy freedom of religion. Those Roman Catholic churches that otherwise might have stood empty (such as the cathedral in Dresden or the Catholic churches in post-Protestant Bremen) resound with the Polish language on Sundays when Polish and German priests conduct services in Polish.

Brazil and other Latin American countries are home to an estimated 800,000 persons of Polish background. Poles are particularly numerous in the Brazilian state of Parana where they started arriving in the 1880s and they helped to build a modern society. In 1993, the Union of Polish Expatriate Associations and Organizations in Latin America (USOPA) was founded. In Argentina, there exists a parliamentary group called Amigos Polonia (Friends of Poland), which has made April 8 "The Day of the Polish Settler" in commemoration of accomplishments of the Polish pioneers. Throughout Latin America, there has been no discrimination against the Polish minority.

The Polish minority in Australia and New Zealand originated mainly in post-world War II immigration. Poles constitute one percent of the Australian population. They enjoy full political rights and are fully integrated but maintain their own ethnic organizations.

In contrast, the Polish minority in the Russian Federation, Lithuania, Ukraine, and Belarus, together numbering some two million people, still struggles for recognition. In these countries, the Polish minority consists of people who identify with Polish culture and whose ancestors lived in the area for centuries. In the Russian Federation, the Polish minority consists of descendants of deportees and political prisoners whom the tsarist and Soviet empires deported liberally to Siberia, Central Asia, and central Russia. Poles in Ukraine and Lithuania enjoy religious freedom, but those in the Russian Federation are subject to state-sponsored discrimination in matters religious, political, and social.

EWA M. THOMPSON

Further Reading

Bukowczyk, John J., *And My Children Did Not Know M: A History of Polish Americans*, Bloomington: Indiana University Press, 1989

Kulczycki, John J., *The Foreign Worker and the German Labor Movement: Xenophobia and Solidarity in the Coal Fields of the Ruhr, 1871–1914*, Oxford, United Kingdom, and Providence, Rhode Island: Berg Publishers, 1994

Renkiewicz, Frank, *The Poles in America, 1608–1972*, Dobbs Ferry, New York: Oceania Publishers, 1973)

Sowa, Andrzej, "South Poles," *Warsaw Voice*, May 12, No 19 (p 394), 1996

Wandycz, Piotr S., *The United States and Poland*, Cambridge, Massachusetts: Harvard University Press, 1980

Police Bias, Incidents of

The majority of police forces worldwide claim as their mandate preventing crime, bringing law breakers to justice, maintaining the peace, and protecting the community. Many pledge to discharge their duties with integrity, respect human rights obligations, treat all sections of the community equally, and deploy only minimum force. However, evidence emanating from North America, Latin America, South Africa, Indonesia, Australia, and across the European Union indicates that racial minorities are still at the forefront of discriminatory and abusive policing practices. There are a number of distinctive but interrelated allegations of racially biased police practices that divide into the over-policing of racial minorities and under-policing in relation to the specific law and order needs of these minorities.

Allegations of over-policing relate to the discriminatory use of police powers when dealing with members of racial minorities, particularly in relation to powers of surveillance, traffic stops, street frisks, arrest, detention, investigation, and resort to excessive use of force. As well as incidents of individual harassment, minority communities have complained about racial profiling of certain crime categories, saturation policing by specialist police squads, incursions on cultural and political events, as well as immigration raids. Well-publicized incidents emanating from the United States in the late 1990s dramatize how the routine policing in minority neighborhoods can tip over into extremely coercive and violent forms of social control. During the 1990s, New York City acquired a global reputation for pioneering "zero tolerance" policing practices that targeted petty crime, low level disorder, and incivility on the grounds that they were indicators of potentially serious criminal behavior. The spectacular drop in the official crime rate resulted in zero tolerance policing being exported to Europe and Australia.

However, while the crime rate plummeted the intensive policing practices associated with zero tolerance strained the already frayed relationship between the New York Police Department (NYPD) and the city's racial minorities. Two incidents provoked a nationwide discussion on the desirability of letting the police off the leash in sensitive multiracial contexts. In August 1997 it became known that Abner Louima, a Haitian immigrant, was brutalized by white police officers after an altercation outside a nightclub. As this high profile case was making its way through the courts, in February 1999 Amadou Diallo, an unarmed Guinean immigrant street vendor was shot dead by four white undercover officers from the proactive Street Crime Unit. What was particularly controversial was the fact that the police officers had fired 41 bullets, with 19 hitting the young African immigrant.

In Los Angeles, during 1999, it was established that a core group of officers of the Rampart Division of the Los Angeles Police Department (LAPD) were responsible for beating and shooting suspects, fabricating evidence, planting incriminating evidence, and rigging crime scenes in order to entrap suspects. This turned into the biggest police scandal in the history of the LAPD. The sensational revelations were extremely damaging for the police force because they struck at the heart of the force's antigang crime fighting methods in some of the city's poorest and most ethnically dense streets. The Rampart scandal revealed a new level of criminality and coined a new criminal justice concept: the gangster cop. In New York and Los Angeles the common complaint voiced was that certain communities were living in fear of the police as well as the criminals.

As a result of what they perceive to be constant harassment and discrimination, across a variety of jurisdictions, significant sections of these communities, particularly young people, have become alienated from the police. The ultimate manifestation of the near complete breakdown of the police-community relationship is the antipolice riot. Riots in the United Kingdom during the 1980s and in France during the 1990s were precipitated by what were perceived to be heavy-handed police actions in minority neighborhoods. The United States watched in shock as the most serious riot of the postwar period engulfed South Central Los Angeles, claiming 54 lives and causing millions of dollars worth of damage. Triggered by the acquittal of four white police officers for the brutal beating of Rodney King, the ferocity of the May 1992 riots indicated the depth of anger, frustration, and despair that existed in minority communities. For many respectable community leaders the verdict represented a final loss of faith by African Americans in the fairness of the criminal justice system. It also suggested that white middle-class America was willing to condone systematic police brutalization and mistreatment of minority populations.

The second facet of racially discriminatory policing relates to the alleged refusal of the police to provide an adequate response to minority community needs. Critics of the police claim that responding to the needs of residents in crime-ridden ghettos and inner cities is a lower police priority than responding to the needs of respectable neighborhoods. For the sake of maintaining public order the police have virtually abandoned certain neighborhoods. Such a "hands off" policy effectively leaves these neighborhoods in the hands of local criminals. Critics also claim to have identified a consistent pattern in the response of the police to racist crimes, that is, a lack of effective response; reluctance to prosecute; the definition of such crimes as nonracist; treating the victim as the criminal; and reacting harshly to community self-protection measures.

With the recent upsurge of right-wing extremism across the European Union and the increasing seriousness of attacks on guest workers, refugee camps, and immigrant communities, the apparent lack of police protection has become a major cause for concern. This lack of intervention stands in stark contrast to overpolicing that racial minorities claim they are normally subjected to.

In the United Kingdom, the murder of black teenager Stephen Lawrence by a gang of young white men in April 1993 propelled the issue of how the police respond to racist crime to the center of public debate. A public inquiry was established to examine why the Metropolitan Police had failed to bring the killers to justice and to make recommendations to ensure that such a miscarriage of justice did not happen in the future. The report of the inquiry chaired by Sir William Macpherson was published in a blaze of publicity in February 1999. To the consternation of the Metropolitan Police, it concluded that the police investigation was characterized by a combination of professional incompetence, institutional racism, and a failure of leadership by senior officers. As a result, United Kingdom police forces have been required to overhaul their approach to the recording, investigation, and prosecution of racist crime and to ensuring that their work practices meet the requirements of specific communities.

In the United States during the 1990s, pressure groups began to demand an effective police response to violence and intimidation directed at minority communities. As a result of prolonged campaigning, federal, state, and local authorities began to recognize the category of hate crimes. New categories of criminal behavior and corresponding sentencing guidelines were established and police forces, in certain parts of the country, established specialized investigative units to concentrate on the perpetrators of hate crime. Similar campaigns for passing hate crime legislation have also been established in Australia and Europe.

Various explanations have been forwarded to account for problematic relations between the police and racial minorities. The orthodox police position tends to deny the problem of racial harassment and discrimination. Police representatives continue to argue that the real source of the problem is the overrepresentation of certain racial groups in the criminal statistics. Thus it is argued that the criminality of certain communities results in proactive policing practices, and that there will be casualties in the "war against crime". They also point to the anti-police attitudes that are entrenched in these communities.

Complaints about harassment and discrimination are interpreted by many police officers as attempts to undermine both the efficiency of anti-police operations and force morale. As far as rank-and-file police officers are concerned that they are required by law to exercise their powers and they have the right, in the fight against crime, to use force where necessary. More enlightened senior officers would argue that the problem of racial prejudice lies with the attitudes of a minority of individual officers rather than the institution. They also acknowledge that the racist attitude of one officer can destroy the quality of service and nondiscriminatory efforts of the rest of the police force. From this perspective, the screening of applicants should be tightened, psychological testing of potential recruits improved, training in community and race relations extended, recruiting practices overhauled to ensure that the forces are representative of the communities that they serve, supervision of frontline officers intensified, and community outreach programs established.

However, research primarily from the United States and United Kingdom suggests that racially discriminatory policing is not just the prerogative of a few officers. In the aftermath of the Los Angeles riots, there were numerous news reports indicating that in certain police forces in the United States, racist attitudes were widespread among officers. The alternative explanation argues that the source of this conflictual relationship lies with the police mandate and the structural position of racial minorities. From the late 1960s, it is argued, there has been a fundamental shift as tough law and order tendencies emerged both in the United States and the United Kingdom. Those who have suffered most from this reordering of criminal justice policies have been racial minorities. They no longer have any core role to play within the new economic order and are suffering in a disproportionate manner from structural unemployment, the effects of cutbacks in welfare, and urban disinvestment. They are, for all intents and purposes, politically and socially powerless, existing on the margins of the reconstituted edifice of citizenship.

Within this context, a potent ideological connection has been made between race and crime, and this has provided the *raison d'être* for the introduction of aggressive policing tactics. Racial minorities have been criminalized and scapegoated, and white support has been mobilized for the police. Related to this perspective is the observation that police forces have used the news media to foster an image of a crisis-ridden, threatened society, in which racial minorities are responsible for an inordinate amount of predatory criminal activity. As a result, police forces have been able to demand more autonomy and resources to be able to meet the challenges of the purported crisis. The police, on this account, have actually contributed to the sense of racial crisis.

From this perspective, suggestions for improving police training and race relations courses, recruiting minority officers, and making racism a disciplinary offence will not work, because the source of the problem is structural, not individual. Racism is institutionalized in the police. The charge of *institutional racism* has been vehemently denied by police forces in the United States and United Kingdom and by various official inquiries into controversial police actions. However, in the United Kingdom, in the first years of the new century, the terms of the debate have changed as a result of the finding that institutional racism played a central role in the inability of the Metropolitan Police to bring the murders of Stephen Lawrence to justice. Police forces in the United Kingdom are now required to consider how the Macpherson report's definition of institutional racism affects their routine policies, procedures, and practices:

Institutional Racism consists of the collective failure of an organization to provide an appropriate and professional service to people because of their color, culture, or ethnic origin. It can be seen or detected in processes, attitudes, and behavior that amount to discrimination through unwitting prejudice, ignorance, thoughtlessness, and racist stereotyping, which disadvantage minority ethnic people.

Police forces in the United Kingdom have formally acknowledged the problem of institutional racism and have formally committed themselves to implementing a reform program that will enable them to become antidiscriminatory public services and to ensure that officers do not engage in inappropriate language, behavior, or perpetuate stereotypes. Critics remain skeptical about the ability and willingness of police forces to instigate the policies needed to root out racist and abusive officers and dismantle the "blue wall of silence" They argue that external pressure needs to be exercised to force change upon police forces and to monitor the functioning of reforms. In the United States, Human Rights Watch has recommended that federal aid should go only to those police departments that can demonstrate that they are taking tangible steps to respect human rights and curb police abuse. The organization also supports the creation and strengthening of civilian review agencies, establishing early warning systems to identify and track officers who are the subject of repeated complaints and creating a special prosecutor's office to pursue cases against police officers accused of criminal conduct.

EUGENE MCLAUGHLIN

See also **Racism**

Further Reading

Bowling, B., *Racist Violence*, Oxford: Clarendon Press, 1999
Cannon, L., *Official Negligence: How Rodney King and the Riots changed Los Angeles and the Los Angeles Police Department*, Boulder, Colorado: Westview Press, 1999
Cashmore, E., and E, McLaughlin, *Out of Order?: Policing Black People*, London: Routledge, 1991
Davis, M., *Ecology of Fear*, New York: Metropolitan Books, 1999

European Monitoring Centre on Racism and Xenophobia, *Annual Report*, Brussels, European Union, 1999
Human Rights Watch, *Shielded From Justice*, New York: Human Rights Watch, 1998
Macpherson, Sir W., *Report of the Inquiry into the Murder of Stephen Lawrence*, London: The Stationary Office, 1999
Miller, J.G., *Search and Destroy*, New York: Cambridge University Press, 1997
National Inquiry into Racist Violence in Australia, *Racist Violence*, Canberra: Australian Government, 1991

Political Participation

Political participation most commonly refers to the actions citizens of a country take to influence the selection of government leaders. While it is universally agreed that participation is intended to influence the government, what actions are considered legitimate is of great debate. Some scholars argue that political participation must be legal to be legitimate. Such positions advocate participation through voting and civic groups. Yet for many minorities political, economic, and social barriers significantly hamper legal routes to political participation. This has led other scholars to consider protest, violence, rebellion, and everyday forms of resistance as legitimate forms of political participation. By first looking at common legal forms of participation, we can better understand the challenges minorities face and the considerations given to extralegal forms of participation.

Political participation is the backbone of democratic governance. Government by the people is impossible if the people have no say in who or what structures govern them. Robert Dahl uses the extent of legitimate participation to define liberalization and the proportion of the population taking part in political life to define how politically inclusive a government is. Other scholars cite the right to work, the right to form and work for political parties, to petition the government, and to associate freely into groups as the core evolutionary process of democracy. When people have equal access to these rights, we can consider the country a democracy.

There are, however, significant challenges to the equality of these rights to participate. The most widely recognized challenges are socioeconomic. In a great majority of countries, the higher a person's income, the more likely he or she is to participate in the political process, and the lower a person's income, the less likely he or she is to participate in the political process. Likewise, the higher a person's education, the more likely he or she will participate in the political process, and vice versa. The poor and the uneducated do not participate because they feel disenfranchised. That is, they do not think that any of the candidates represent them. The educated tend to participate more because they feel more obligated.

The problem of motivating people of lower socioeconomic position to vote in developing societies is even more pronounced than in advanced industrial societies. The divisions between rich and poor are commonly more pronounced, access to regular information is limited, and there is a division between people who work in the industrial economy and those that work in a subsistence economy. In these cases, groups, especially political parties, commonly play a cardinal role in mobilizing popular participation. There are two conundrums, however. First, while political parties are the most critical force to the mobilization of people from low socioeconomic brackets in developing countries, in developing countries people tend to hold less of an allegiance to any one political party. Second, economic opportunities in the short to medium term favor the elite in developing societies. As a result, economic development commonly leads to an decrease in equality between groups.

As groups become disenfranchised by the lack of opportunities, their members participate less. In this way, economic development can often lead to a decrease in political participation.

Other factors also influence political participation. Postmaterialist considerations, such as how connected a person feels to his or her society, stress, health, family life, church life, and the role of the media have all proven important. In most countries men participate more than women. People of the dominant race in a country generally participate more, as do people of dominant ethnic groups and religions.

A politically charged ethnic or racial minority group is often a strong motivating factor in political participation because ethnic identity becomes a way of challenging the elite. Internal imperatives of the ethnic or racial group and external imperatives placed on the ethnic group as a whole act to motivate it. Ethnic or racial participation forms part of a larger ideological effort to reconcile ideals of equality with the reality of social and political exclusion. In some cases, such as Brazil, racial identity groups have even been used by constituent members to increase wealth, thereby doubling the groups' influence on participation. However, ethnic and racial politics is an uncertain guarantor of participation. In Guyana, for instance, participation increased due to an increase in ethnic power just to decrease when the ethnic power declined. More of an issue is that the combative nature of ethnic and racial politics often makes them a destabilizing force within a country. In Sierra Leone (1967), Nigeria (1964), Congo-Brazzaville (1959), and Zanzibar (1961) ethnic identification led to high political participation only to see the same ethnic identification lead to ethnic stratification and, ultimately, coups. The inherent volatility of ethnic and racial politics has led most proponents of democratic growth to dis courage them.

Faced with few legal options for participation, disenfranchised minority groups often turn to alternative means of participation from the informal to the extralegal. Informal participation may include collective efforts to obtain public goods, organize unemployment groups, and participation in civic association. Recent studies looking at countries as diverse as Italy, France, Ireland, Switzerland, Tanzania, Uganda, Peru, Vietnam, the Philippines, Mexico, and Trinidad and Tobago emphasize the important connection between participation in voluntary associations and participation in formal politics.

While informal participation is commonly encouraged, extralegal forms of political participation have been highly controversial. Scholars have explored the everyday forms of resistance peasants have used to combat oppressive political forces, the impact of electrical social uprisings by racial minorities, and the challenge women have presented to codified gender laws in Islamic societies. The problem is that extralegal participation undermines the existent system, challenging governance. Indeed, the control of violence is considered by many to be a fundamental charge of democratic governance.

Socioeconomic, demographic, everyday factors, civic, and extralegal factors all have proven cardinal influences on political participation. Yet, in advanced industrialized societies minority participation is often challenged. In developing societies, the problem is even graver, as the socioeconomic stratification created by development decreases, rather than increases, participation. We are therefore left to speculate as to whether political and economic gains for the world's least advantaged citizens can be made simultaneously.

RICHARD R. MARCUS

Further Reading

Andrews, George Reid, *Blacks & Whites in Sao Paulo, Brazil 1888–1988*, Madison: University of Wisconsin Press, 1991

Barker, Jonathan, *Street-Level Democracy: Political Settings at the Margins of Global Power*, West Hartford, Connecticut: Kumarian Press, 1999

Dahl, Robert A., *Polyarchy: Participation & Opposition*, New Haven, Connecticut: Yale University Press, 1971

Dietz, Henry, *Urban Poverty, Political Participation, and the State: Lima 1970–1990*, Pittsburgh, Pennsylvania: University of Pittsburgh Press, 1998

Edmondson, Ricca, editor, *The Political Context of Collective Action: Power, Argumentation, and Democracy*, London and New York: Routledge, 1997

Horowitz, Donald L., *Ethnic Groups in Conflict*, Berkeley: University of California Press, 1985

Huntington, Samuel P., and Joan M. Nelson, *No Easy Choice: Political Participation in Developing Countries*, Cambridge, Massachusetts: Harvard University, 1976

Mayo, Marjorie, *Cultures, Communities, Identities: Cultural Strategies for Participation and Empowerment*, Basingstoke: Palgrave, 2000

Migdal, Joel S., *Peasants, Politics, and Revolution: Pressures toward Political and Social Change in the Third World*, Princeton, New Jersey: Princeton University Press, 1974

Peterson, Steven A., *Political Behavior: Patterns in Everyday Life*, Newbury Park, London: Sage Publications, 1990

Scott, James C., *Weapons of the Weak: Everyday Forms of Peasant Resistance*, New Haven, Connecticut: Yale University Press, 1987

Tripp, Aili Mari, *Women & Politics in Uganda*, Madison: The University of Wisconsin Press, 2000

Verba, Sidney, Steven Kelman, Gary R. Orren, Ichiro Miyake, and Joji Watanuki, *Elites and the Idea of Equality : A Comparison of Japan, Sweden and the United States*, Cambridge and London: Harvard University Press, 1987

Verba, Sidney, Norman H. Nie, and Jae-On Kim, *Participation and Political Equality: A Seven-Nation Comparison*, London and New York: Cambridge University Press, 1978

Verba, Sidney, and Norman H. Nie, *Participation in America*, New York: Harper and Row, 1972

Pomaks

Capsule Summary

Location: Southeastern Balkan region of Europe, mostly in the territory of Bulgaria, Turkey, Greece and Macedonia; relatively small groups live in the Federal Republic of Yugoslavia, Romania, Moldova, and Albania
Total Population: 1 million
Language: Predominantly Slavic dialect
Religion: Sunni Muslim

The Pomaks, a group of people living in the southeastern European region known as the Balkans, are approximately one million strong, and primarily dwell in the territory of Bulgaria, Turkey, Greece, and Macedonia, with a small number living in Albania. Their language, Pomashka, is a Slavic dialect of the Indo-European language family that closely resembles the Bulgarian language; however, extensive Turkish and Arabic words and grammar are used in daily life. Some have adopted Macedonian or Greek as a second language. Of those living in Turkey, 94 percent are bilingual. Almost the entire Pomak population—98 percent—is Sunni Muslim. Their historic land, the Rhodope Mountains and Pirin Macedonia, was part of the Ottoman Empire. Following the Turko-Russian War of 1877–78 and Bulgarian independence in 1908, the Pomaks strongly resisted the Russian invasion and the following Bulgarian Principality's administration. The Pomak community living in today's Bulgaria is not recognized as a distinct group. During the various assimilation campaigns, the latest being 1972–73 and 1985–89, large numbers chose, without hesitation, to migrate to Turkey and live in a Muslim community rather than continue to live in Bulgaria, where they could at least speak the language.

Pomaks, a term first used in the late nineteenth century, originates from "pomagachi" and loosely translates as *helpers* or *collaborators*, referring to the voluntary assistance they provided Ottoman Turks during the conquest of their lands in the late fourteenth and early fifteenth centuries. They are the descendants of the Kumano-Pechenek Turks who, on their way from the steppes of Central Asia along the northern Black Sea route to the Balkans, stopped for some time in the Ukraine where they adopted a Slavic tongue in the eleventh century. This explains how these people were able to integrate with the conquering Ottoman *Yoruk* populations. The Pomaks' current living areas match the historic routes and settlement areas of the old Turkish tribes. Even today many towns and cities at the center of Pomak settlements are named after these tribes, examples including Kumanova in Macedonia, Kumantsi in Sofia, Kumantcha in Gotse Delchev (Nevrokop), Kumanicevo in Kesriye, Kumani Island in Vidin, Komana in Nikopol (all in Bulgaria), and Kumanitsa in Lovech.

The exact population of the Pomaks is unknown, as they are not counted in national censuses on their ethnic bases. However, according to figures as cited by Johnston in 1993, there were 270,000 Pomaks in Turkey, a figure which today is estimated to have risen to between 300,000 and 350,000 due to the continuous migration from Bulgaria and population increase. For the first time in 30 years, the Bulgarian census of 1992 considered statistics about ethnic minorities and reported the Pomak population as 143,000. This figure is far from being accurate, since most of the Pomaks in the Blagoevgrad region registered themselves as Turks, contrary to the official line of politics. In this survey, 62,000 Pomaks identified themselves as Muslims and as Turks. It is estimated that there are between 200,000 and 250,000 currently in Bulgaria. Pomaks living in Macedonia are known as the *Torbeshs*, as they maintain a strong affiliation to Turkish identity, and are estimated to be 100,000 strong. It is believed that 50,000 Pomaks reside in the Western Thrace region of Greece.

Today, identity among Pomaks is presently unstable. A characteristic feature of the Pomaks' identity is its shifting and undefined boundaries and markers. Being neither Bulgarians nor Turks, they sway in self-identification and are influenced to a great degree by the environment. In areas where Pomaks live in close contact with Bulgarians, Greeks, Macedonians, and other ethnic majorities, they tend to show affinity to the Turkish identity. Some Pomaks have attempted to construct their own identity and establish themselves as a distinct ethnic group, wherein they claim to have adopted Islam before the Ottoman conquest, making them the oldest supporters of the faith.

The Pomaks' conversion to Islam probably began in the late 1370s. The traditional view says that they did not voluntarily accept Islam, but were forced to do so. However, the references used to prove this claim are simply false. Defenders of the traditional view did not use original sources, but took information, uncritically, from other authors. One author after the other perpetuated the quotation of the source without the slightest attempt at verification. Thus, an entire literature became built on very few, and often false, sources, and unfortunately has been believed by many (for extensive discussion of this issue see Karpat and Bunnbauer).

The nationalistic Bulgarian view asserts that Pomaks are Bulgarians who were converted to Islam by force and, thus, should become Bulgarians again. During the Balkan Wars (1912–1913), Pomaks were forced to convert to Christianity. In the early 1940's, especially following the communist takeover in 1944, they were victims of a government-led name changing campaign. In 1948, communist authorities initiated programs aimed at their assimilation, including relocation to ethnic Bulgarian settlements. In the early 1970s, vigorous attempts were made to oblige Pomaks to abandon their Muslim and Arabic names and adopt Bulgarian ones. An unknown number of Pomaks who refused to accept the new names were killed or injured,

while several hundred more were interned in the notorious prison camp on Belene Island in the Danube. The most recent illustration of this historical nationalistic Bulgarian attitude is the activity of Father Boyan Saruev (former communist police chief of Smolyan, the biggest town in the Rhodope mountains), who forces the Pomaks to convert into Orthodox Christianity. However, the total number of the Christian Pomaks does not exceed one percent of the entire Pomak population in that country. Officially, they are called Bulgarian Muhammedans or Bulgarian Muslims. This intellectually created labeling of the group by the "others" is not an established term and definitely is not used by the Pomaks themselves.

There is also no empirical evidence to support the argument claiming Pomaks are descendants of the ancient Greek tribe of Thracians. Pomaks living in Greece, today, face discrimination and persecution and are often deprived of legal rights. Many have had their land taken without compensation, and freedom of movement is still restricted despite the government nullification of the long-lasting policy of the forbidden zone in Western Thrace in 1997. Generally, they cannot buy land and are unable to obtain government jobs or business licenses. Greece denies passports to Muslims, and, if a Pomak travels abroad without one, he or she is not allowed back into the country.

Today Pomaks are under great pressure and face a critical point. The young face an identity crisis, particularly in Bulgaria. A crucial problem is finding a way out of their low economic status. Economic disadvantage among Pomaks may be facilitating "Turkicization," because immigration to Turkey is perceived as one way of overcoming employment difficulties. Finally, the minority continues to live in isolation, by non-inclusion in majority activities, which can lead to dispersion of the community, this being most likely in Bulgaria and Greece.

TUNCAY BABALI

See also **Bulgaria; Turkey; Greece; Macedonia**

Further Reading

Archives of Menuhin Foundation and the World Directory of Minorities Balikci, Asen, *Pomak Identity: National Prescriptions and Native Assumptions*, Paper read to the Second Conference of the Association for Balkan Anthropology, Bucharest 20-22.9., 1997

Brunnbauer, Ulf, "Histories and Identities: Nation-state and Minority Discourses: The Case of the Bulgarian Pomaks", University of Graz, (www-gewi.kfunigraz.ac.at/csbsc/ulf/)

Poulton, Hugh, *Minorities in Southeast Europe: Inclusion and Exclusion*, London: Minority Rights Group International, 1998

In and Out of the Collective: Papers on Former Soviet Bloc Rural Communities, Edited by Bulgarian Center for Regional Cultural Studies (Sofia), Vol.1, February 1998

Karpat, K.H., editor, *The Turks of Bulgaria: The History, Culture and Political Fate of a Minority*, Istanbul: The Isis Press, 1990

McCarthy, Justin, *Death and Exile: The ethnic cleansing of Ottoman Muslims, 1821–1922*, Princeton, New Jersey: The Darwin Press, Inc., 1995

Turan, Omer, *The Turkish Minority in Bulgaria, 1878–1908*, Ankara: Turkish History Institution, 1997

"2000 Annual Report on International Religious Freedom: Bulgaria," Released by the Bureau of Democracy, Human Rights, and Labor, U.S. Department of State, September 5, 2000

Pope Shenouda III (Coptic Christian)

His Holiness Pope Shenouda III (1971–present), 117th Pope of Alexandria and Patriarch of the See of Saint Mark, was born Nazîr Gayyid Rufa'îl in 1923, in the village of Asyut, Egypt. His mother and father died when he was an infant; for the most part, he was raised by his eldest brother. After graduating from high school, Rufa'îl studied at the University of Cairo, where in 1947 he earned a BA in history and English. In the following years he served his mandatory tour of duty in the Egyptian Armed Forces and then studied at the Coptic Seminary, headed at the time by archdeacon Habib Girguis. In 1954 he entered the monastery of *al-Suryan* (the Syrians) in Wadi al-Natrun, where later that same year he was consecrated a monk and took the name Antonius al-Suryanî.

Father Antonius lived away from the monastery for a time as a hermit. In 1959, the late Patriarch Kyrillos VI (1959–1971) selected him as his personal secretary, and only a few years later, in 1962, he ordained the monk Antonius as Shenouda, General Bishop for Religious Education. As a bishop, Shenouda became known for his rhetorical skills and easily attracted thousands to his weekly public lectures, which he continues to this day. Shortly after the departure of Patriarch Kyrillos VI in 1971, Shenouda was elected his successor by lot and enthroned as Pope and Patriarch on November 14; as such, he is the head of the Coptic Orthodox Church, the largest Christian community in Egypt and the Middle East.

In Egypt, the Patriarch is the spiritual and moral leader of the Coptic community and its primary spokesman. Pope Shenouda's tenure has been one of prosperity and renewal for the Egyptian Church. He continued and expanded the Coptic Renaissance initiated by his predecessor. Under Patriarch Shenouda's leadership, this renaissance has extended even into the style of monastic dress and the creation of new and vital community services.

Through the leadership of the patriarch, the current period of renewal has been far-reaching, and is perhaps best illustrated by the revival in the monastic movement and the globalization of the Coptic Church. During the past three decades, a time in which monasticism has been in a state of decline in all churches, the Coptic Church has experienced a tremendous increase in the number of men and women seeking a monastic vocation—many of whom were inspired by the example of the patriarch and the first book he wrote, *Release of the Spirit*, which he wrote as a layman prior to entering the monastery. This phenomenon has been paralleled by an increase in the number of bishops. In the early 1970s, the Coptic Church had approximately twenty-five bishops; the number is now in excess of eighty. By increasing the number of bishops, the patriarch aims at improving the level of service church-wide.

The patriarch has likewise effectively attended to the needs of Copts living outside of Egypt. A significant number of Copts have emigrated to Western nations. Pope Shenouda accommodated them by ordaining priests to serve these scattered communities. And within the last eight years he has ordained seven bishops to serve abroad. In Africa, where the need is necessarily evangelical rather than pastoral, he has ordained two general bishops to serve the people of Kenya, the Ivory Coast, South Africa, Tanzania, the

POPE SHENOUDA III (COPTIC CHRISTIAN)

Congo, Zambia, and Zimbabwe. This is in addition to a number of bishops in western countries. For the first time, the Coptic Church is a global entity.

In addition to being the spiritual leader of a world-wide church, Patriarch Shenouda has also been a prolific writer, producing almost a hundred books and pamphlets, works ranging from exegetics and apologetics to spiritual advice. His ministry has been well served by his wit, charisma, and encyclopedic knowledge of the Scriptures.

From a socio-political perspective, the patriarch (especially since the early 1980s) has emerged as the sole advocate for the Coptic Christians of Egypt. This has not been an easy role to play, as the state has been variously tolerant and discriminatory. One of the worst periods of intolerance emerged in the early 1980s. As a rash of violence against Christians left many Copts dead, the late president of Egypt, Muhammad Anwar Sadat, began publicly accusing Pope Shenouda of having political ambitions to forge an independent Coptic state with a capital at Asyut. This took place on the heals of a renewed attempt by some factions in the Egyptian government to implement the *Shari‘a* (Islamic Law) as the foundation for the Egyptian Constitution and civil law—a change which would have been disastrous for the Coptic community. Pope Shenouda took a bold and vocal stand against these threats. President Sadat responded by arresting 150 bishops and clerics along with prominent laymen in September 1981. He then placed the patriarch under house arrest at the monastery of Anba Bishoy. Shortly thereafter, Muslim extremists assassinated Sadat, but the patriarch remained under house arrest until January of 1985. Since that episode, though relations with the state have greatly improved, at times they remain a balancing act.

Pope Shenouda has worked diligently to strengthen relations and promote mutual cooperation and understanding between the Christians and Muslims of Egypt. He often highlights the common ground that Muslims and Christians share as monotheistic religions that worship the God of Abraham. He is also quick to condemn acts of discrimination and violence committed by fanatics without projecting such actions onto the whole of the Muslim population. He repeats these themes when appropriate in his sermons and publications. The patriarch also emphasizes that the Copts, like their Muslim brothers, are loyal Egyptian citizens, stating, "Egypt is not a country we live in, but one that lives in us." Since 1986, as a gesture of national brotherhood and cooperation, he has initiated an annual *iftar* celebration at the end of the Muslim holy month of Ramadan to which he personally invites Muslim political and religious leaders.

In addition to his role in Egypt, Pope Shenouda has been globally active in numerous ecumenical meetings and consultations, especially among the Orthodox Churches. He has served as president of the *World Council of Churches,* the *Middle East Council of Churches,* and the *All-African Council of Churches.* He has been recognized throughout the world with the receipt of a number of honorary Ph.D.s and, most recently, the UNESCO Madajeet Singh Prize for the Promotion of Tolerance and Non-Violence.

Capsule Biography

Shenouda III (Nazir Gayid Rufa'îl). Born August 3, 1923 in Asyut, Egypt. BA in History and English, 1947; B.Th., Coptic Theological Seminary, Cairo, 1949; Editor, *Madâris al-Ahad* magazine, 1948–1954; Instructor at the Monastic Seminary, Hulwan, 1953–1954; consecrated a monk by the name of Antonius al-Suryanî, Wadi al-Natrun, Egypt, 1954; personal secretary to Pope Kyrillos VI, 1959–1962; ordained General Bishop for Religious Education, 1962; Chief Editor of *al-Kiraza*, the official publication of the Coptic Orthodox Patriarchate of Alexandria, 1965–present. Consecrated the 117th Pope and Patriarch of the see of Saint Mark, 1971; exiled to the Monastery of Anba Bishoy, September 5, 1981 to January 3, 1985. Awarded four honorary Ph.D. degrees; Madanjeet Singh Prize for the Promotion of Tolerance and Non-Violence awarded by the United Nations Educational, Scientific and Cultural Organization (UNESCO), 2000.

Selected Works

Release of the Spirit, articles published 1951–54, later repeatedly published as a book.
Saint Mark the Apostle and Martyr, 1975
Salvation in the Orthodox Concept, 1975
The Ten Commandments, 1977
The Law of Monogamy in Christianity, 1978
Words of Benefit, 1981
The Priesthood, 1981
Being with God, 1981
Contemplations on Epiphany, 1982
How to Begin the New Year, 1982
Adam and Eve, Cain and Abel, 1982
Spiritual Vigil, 1982
Return to God, 1982
Contemplations on Passion Week, 1983
Diabolic Warfare, 1984
The Life of Faith, 1984
The Sermon on the Mountain, 1986
Spiritual Warfare, 1986
Calmness, 1986

Characteristics of the Spiritual Path, 1987
Discipleship, 1987
Comparative Theology, 1988
Life Experiences, 1988
The Heresy of Salvation in a Moment, 1988
Purgatory, 1988
Contemplations on the Thanksgiving Prayer, 1990
Moses and Pharaoh, 1990
Tears in the Spiritual Life, 1990
Contemplations on the Resurrection, 1990
The Holy Spirit and His Work in Us, 1991
The Spiritual Person, 1991
Nature of Christ, 1991
Contemplations on the Resurrections, 1993
Fear of God, 1993
Spiritual Servant and the Spiritual Service, 1994
Our Father Who Art in Heaven, 1994
Life of Virtue and Righteousness, 1994
The Temptation on the Mountain, 1995
Fruits of the Spirit, 1996
The Two Saints Peter and Paul, 1997
Grace, 1997

God and Man, 1997
Job the Righteous, 1998
Why the Resurrection?, 1998
Thine is the Power and the Glory, 1999

MAGED S.A. MIKHAIL

See also **Coptic Christians**

Further Reading

Cragg, Kenneth, *The Arab Christian: A History in the Middle East*, Louisville: John Knox Press, 1991
Malaty, Fr., and Y. Tadros, *Introduction to the Coptic Orthodox Church*, Ontario, Canada: Saint Mary Coptic Orthodox Church, 1987, reprint Alexandria, Egypt, 1993
Meinardus, Otto F., *Two Thousand Years of Egyptian Christianity*, Cairo: American University Press, 1999
Watson, John, "Signposts to Biography – Pope Shenouda III," in *Between Desert and City: The Coptic Orthodox Church Today*, edited by Nelly van Doorn-Harding and Kari Vogt, Oslo: Novus Forlag, 1997

Population Shifts

Population shifts are a method of ethnic cleansing aimed at forcibly moving a minority population out of its ancestral land to make the region suitable for settlement by the majority or dominant population or nation. Every real or suspected member of a minority is rounded up and deported en masse to a remote region intended to serve as their final home. The aim of the displacers, or others profiting from the shift of the minority population, is to cleanse the newly seized territory of the undesired minority ethnic population, in order to form a "pure" nation-state. Population shifts are imposed by victorious states through forced peace treaties or by the central/federal government of a state. These measures are often embedded in laws and/or obscure regulations, and their enforcement is carried out by the state's army, police, or public administration.

Population shifts proved to be radical and efficient means of "solving" minority-related issues, especially during and after World War II, and are still popular among extremist politicians and other hard-line nationalists. The peace treaties made in the wake of World War I produced as many problems regarding the status of minority populations as it solved, by shifting national boundaries and creating some entirely new states.

An example case is that of the Austro-Hungarian monarchy. Its dismantling in 1919–1920 led to the creation of such states as Czechoslovakia, which had a population that was 46 percent Czech, 12 percent Slovak, 27 percent German, 9 percent Hungarian and 4 percent Ukrainian. In the case of Slovakia, 1.7 million Slovaks were awarded a territory that was inhabited by 1.9 million non-Slovaks, primarily Hungarians and Ruthenians/Ukrainians. The eastern territories of Hungary (Transylvania) were awarded to Romania, with the population breaking down as 53 percent ethnic Romanian, 47 percent Hungarian, and a significant German minority. The Voivodina region, which was awarded to Serbia, had a 1921 population that was 34.8 percent Serb, 24.4 percent Hungarian, 21 percent German, 7.7 percent Croat, 4.5 percent ethnic Romanian, and 3.9 percent Slovak and Czech. Although the population groups were located in different subregions or scattered all over the province, the Hungarians were concentrated mainly in a compact region adjacent to

the new Hungarian borders, while the Germans formed a great "island" stretching to the Banat region of
Transylvania, cut in two by the new Yugoslav/Romanian
border drawn inside former Hungarian territory. Based
on the considerable size of this ethnic island during
World War II, the Banat was designated to host a
German state.

The large population of these minority groups made
these peace treaties untenable in the long run, becoming a major point of tension between the former and
successor states. Newly created states and majority-
minority populations within those states encouraged
discrimination and resentment, as populations found
themselves newly subservient, in terms of numbers, to
majority populations, or forced into an entirely new
environment. Formerly minority populations found
themselves the majority in newly created states, or as
the result of shifted boundaries, and in some cases
relished their new status. These tensions laid the foundations for revenge, revision of the treaties, and finally
the outbreak of World War II.

The peaceful rectifications made before the war
between 1938 and 1940 were later declared void by
the victorious parties.

The most prominent case was that of the German
population, which no longer resided in Germany after
the national boundaries were redrawn after World
War II. The allied forces imposed the evacuation of the
entire ancestral German population through population
shifts. Thus, 9 million Germans from the new Polish
territories, 3 million from the Czech Republic,120,000
from Slovakia, 205,000 from Transylvania, 250,000
from Voivodina and Croatia, and 213,000 from Hungary
were shifted to Germany, while many other hundred
thousands were displaced to the Soviet Union as war
prisoners. In their places 5.5 million Poles were
moved, after 1.5 million of them were shifted from the
new parts of Western Ukraine, following the 200 km
westward push of the Polish border. Then, 1.25 million
Czechs were settled in the border zones evacuated by
the German population.

The shift of the German population was also a
method employed by the Nazis before their fall. Their
aim was to collect the smaller German minority groups
from countries which were not viewed as parts of the
future Germany, the core of the would-be great German
empire. These German populations were to be settled
in the newly annexed territories of the Reich, mainly
Poland and the Baltics, in order to increase the German
presence and influence in those regions. Thus Germans

from Basarabia, Moldavia, Romania, the Tyrol, Italy,
and Croatia were shifted to the new eastern territories.

Population shifts were most heavily employed by
Josef Stalin, in order to punish those national minorities which proved to be less loyal or even hostile to
Russia or were thought to pose such a threat. The entire
Chechen population, the whole Tatar population from
the Crimea, and the German population from the
region near the middle of the Volga River were
shifted to Siberia and Central Asia, and scattered
across the vast steppes of Kazakhstan. The new western territories annexed by Russia witnessed the massive shift of 410,000 Finns to Finland, 220,000 inhabitants of the Baltic region, and 50,000 Hungarians to
Siberia, while approximately 1 million Germans fled
from the northern half of East Prussia, evacuated
mainly by the German navy. The territory was annexed
by Russia.

The Jewish population was another target and victim of the population shifts. Although most of it was
deported to forced labor camps (later turned into
death camps), the shift of the European Jewish population was an early concern for the Nazis. They
initially hoped to shift the entire European Jewish
population to the island of Madagascar, but the plan
was aborted due to various logistical reasons, and
thus extermination ("the final solution") was adopted
as the official policy. The total number of Jewish
victims of Holocaust during World War II is estimated
at 6 million.

The Carpathian-Balkan region witnessed significant
shifts as waves of refugees created a mass exodus. The
first great wave of refugees occurred after the new
borders were drawn: 350,000 Hungarians fled beyond
the drastically shrunken new borders between 1918
and 1924, while 123,000 Bulgarians from Greece's
northern Thrakia region fled between 1918 and 1926.
Meanwhile, 250,000 Ukrainians fled from Basarabia,
which came under Romanian rule between 1918 and
1940, and 217,000 Turks, mainly from Bulgaria and
Romania, immigrated to Turkey.

In the years preceding and during World War II, as
national borders were redrawn, a new wave of refugees
swept across the region. Thus 180,000 Czechs returned
to the Czech Republic or fled abroad after Slovakia
declared its independence in 1939. Shortly after the
cessation of Basarabia to the Soviet Union, some
180,000 Romanians fled to Romania.

A much larger population of refugees was created
by the end of the War. These population shifts led to the

transformation of multiethnic states into homogeneous nation states. Major problems were left unresolved, and currently three million Hungarians (25 percent of the entire Hungarian population) and approximately 2.3 million Albanians (41 percent of the entire Albanian population) live outside their nation states, in adjacent border regions. Another ethnic minority has grown and become a significant presence; the Roman (gypsy) population in the region is estimated at 4 to 6 million.

The dissolution of Yugoslavia also led to massive waves of immigration and emigration. For example, most of the 200,000-strong Serb minority, which fled from Croatia's Knin region in 1994, was settled in Voivodina. The recent mass exodus of Albanians from Kosovo suggests that population shifts continue to persist, and present a threat to global stability.

LASZLO KOCSIS

See also **Ethnic conflict; Yugoslavia**

Portugal

Capsule Summary

Country Name: Portugal
Location: Southwest Europe, Western part of the Iberian Peninsula (92,080 sq km)
Total Population: 10,102,022 (2003)
Languages: Portuguese (official), Galician, Mirandés, Caló, Vlach
Religion: Catholic (97%).

Portugal is a unitary state with 18 districts and 2 autonomous regions. The country has been traditionally seen as homogeneous with regard to culture and ethnic composition. However some of its historical episodes, such as the early medieval fragmentation or the recent migrations from the former colonies, reveal elements of cultural and linguistic diversity within the country.

The origin of the state of Portugal is to be found in the wars against the Muslim penetration of the Iberian Peninsula in the ninth century. The kings of Asturias (a kingdom in the northern part of present-day Spain), and later the kings of Castille, conquered the northern third of today's Portugal for the Muslims. Alphonse Henriques (1128–1185) headed an independist movement which led to the birth of the kingdom of Portugal. The limits of the state were established by Alphonse III after conquering the southern region of Algarve (1249).

From the beginning of the fifteenth century, Portugal pursued expansion overseas, sparked by prince Henry the Navigator (1390–1460). Portuguese expeditions discovered Madeira (1418), the Azores (1432), and Cape Verde (1457), and traveled around the African continent, arriving in India (1498).

In the sixteenth century, Portugal's overseas empire also included large areas in southern and eastern Asia. At that time, many free peasants had to emigrate because their lands were bought by noblemen enriched with Indian trade. In 1578, the last king of the authoctonous dynasty of the Avis, Sebastian I, died in battle in northern Africa, and King Philip II of Castille inherited the country. Castilian troops proved unable to protect Portuguese colonial spheres of influence in the face of increasing Dutch and English defiance. Discontent towards union with Castille grew because of heavy taxation and economic crisis. When the Portuguese were asked to contribute with troops to the war against Catalonia (a principality also willing to withdraw from dynastic union with Castille), the nobility and the burgeoisie rose up against king Philip IV, Philip II's grandson (1640). Portugal formally recovered its independence in 1668. The new Bragança dynasty was unable to prevent the country's decline. The luxurious lifestyle of the royal court and progressive support to English commercial interests determined the country's economic underdevelopment.

During the Napoleonic wars at the begining of the nineteenth century, the royal family fled to Brazil, where ports were open to all nations. This situation prompted Brazil's declaration of independence in 1822. In 1910 a democratic republic was proclaimed, although it became rapidly authoritarian in the wake of World War I because of social unrest and the influence of Fascism. From 1932, António de Oliveira Salazar led a dictatorial government. In 1968 he was replaced by Marcelo Caetano. In the meanwhile, India had invaded the Portuguese enclaves in its territory and the African colonies revolted throughout the 1960s. The intense colonial problems marked the end of the dictatorship. On April 25, 1974, general António de Spinola, taking office as president, restored democratic freedoms and granted independence to Guinea-Bissau, Mozambique, the Cape Verde Islands, Angola, and Sao Tomé and Principe. In 1976, both the Azores (West of Portugal, population 238,000 in 1993) and the Madeira Islands (northwest coast of Africa, population 437,312 in 1993) were provided partial autonomy.

Because of its colonial past, Portugal received populations from Africa, Asia, and Latin America. In 1995, there were 103,000 people from Brazil, 100,000 from Angola and Mozambique, 31,000 from Cape Verde, 800,000 from other parts of Africa, 27,000 Arabic, 20,000 from Goa (India), and 3,000 from Timor (Indonesia) present in Portugal. But the Portuguese also experienced their own diaspora: Faced with rising domestic unemployment, many workers emigrated to other European countries during the second half of the twentieth century. In 1995, some 750,000 people in France were Portuguese-speakers (mainly Portuguese workers and/or people from the former Portuguese colonies), as were 80,000 in Belgium, 78,000 in Germany, 50,000 in Luxembourg, and 2,100 in Andorra.

Within Portugal, there are phenomena of cultural diversity deeply rooted in history. As a result of the changing limits engendered by the early medieval Christian conquests, the northeast shows two linguistic minorities. In that region, 15,000 people use the Galician language, which is close to the Portuguese language, and widely spoken in the neighboring Spanish regions of Galicia (the Entre-Minho-e-Douro and the Tras Os Montes provinces). In the southeastern part of the Tras Os Montes province, on the Spanish border, 10,000 people speak an autochthonous language, Mirandés, which probably was separated from related languages (Asturian and Leonés) in northeastern Spain at the time of the wars against the Moors. On the other hand, there are traditional Roma (Gypsy) communities in the country: Some 5,000 people use the Caló language, based on Portuguese regional dialects, while another 500 speak the Vlach language.

Due to a border controversy, we can speak of Portuguese autochthonous minorites abroad. The Spanish municipality of Olivenza (Olivença in Portuguese), situated on the left bank of the River Guadiana about 24 km (14.9 mi) south of the city of Badajoz, was under Portuguese sovreignity until the beginning of the nineteenth century. In 1801, Napoleon sought Spain's support to punish Portugal for the country's alliance with Great Britain. After some clashes, Portugal ceded the stronghold of Olivenza to Spain by signing the Treaty of Badajoz. The Treaty of Vienna, while bringing the Napoleonic wars to an end, reversed the cession and confirmed Portuguese rights over the area. When the Spanish government finally signed the treaty in 1817, it had committed itself to returning Olivenza, but this was never made effective.

Portugal never recognized Spanish de facto annexation of Olivenza, and Portuguese official maps leave the border unmarked in that area. The question has been discussed from time to time in diplomatic circles, but has never hindered good relations between Spain and Portugal, nor has it had significant echo in Portuguese public opinion.

The per capita GDP of Portugal as of 2002 was $19,400.

MARTÍ GRAU

Further Reading

Anderson, James Maxwell, *The History of Portugal*, Westport, Connecticut: Greenwood Press, 2000

Birmingham, David, *A Concise History of Portugal*, Cambridge: Cambridge University Press, 1993

Birmingham, David, *Portugal and Africa*, St. Martin's Press, 1999

Higgs, David, editor, *Portuguese Migration in Global Perspective*, Multicultural Historical Society, 1990

Kaplan, Marion, *The Portuguese: The Land and its People*, New York: Viking, 1991

Maxwell, Kenneth, and Michael H. Haltzel, editors, *Portugal: Ancient Country, Young Democracy*, Woodrow Wilson Center Press, 1990

Russell-Wood, A.J.R, *A World on the Move: The Portuguese in Africa, Asia, and America, 1415–1808*, New York: St. Martin's Press, 1993

Sapelli, Giulio, *Southern Europe After 1945: Tradition and Modernity in Portugal, Spain, Italy, Greece and Turkey*, Addison-Wesley, 1995

Saraiva, Jose H., et al., *Portugal: A Companion History*, Carcanet Press, 1998

Vincent, Mary, *Cultural Atlas of Spain and Portugal*, New York: Facts on File, 1995

Wheeler, Douglas L., *Historical Dictionary of Portugal*, London: The Scarecrow Press, 1993

Velupillai, Prabhakaran (Sri Lanka-Tamil)

Velupillai Prabhakaran, the undisputed chief of the Liberation Tigers of Tamil Eelam (LTTE), is a central figure in the Sri Lankan Tamil movement for a separate *eelam* state (the Tamil people call their nation "Tamil Eelam"). He has overseen the transformation of a non-violent struggle, led by the Tamil United Liberation Front (TULF), into a formidable militant movement under his authoritarian leadership since the late 1970s. In the process, the LTTE has emerged as one of the world's deadliest militant organizations, which has been waging a war against the Sri Lankan state for over twenty years. Prabhakaran himself has become an integral part of the militant Sri Lankan Tamil nationalism and the sub-national liberation struggle.

Born in Jaffna on November 26, 1954, in a traditional middle class family as the youngest of four children, Prabhakaran had most of his schooling in Velvettiturai, a small coastal town in northern Sri Lanka. His mother, Vallipuram Parvathi, was a deeply religious person and father Tiruvenkatam Velupillai served the Sri Lankan government as district land officer. Prabhakaran was brought up in the Hindu religious tradition under strict discipline. About himself, he said in 1986 that he was not permitted to mingle freely with outsiders and felt shy of girls. He was taught to observe personal rectitude and discipline. As a boy, he was studious and read many books at home. He received his introduction to the state of Sinhalese-Tamil relations at the age of four when he witnessed the ethnic riots of 1958. He grew up listening to stories of the brutalities then being perpetrated by the Sri Lankan Army on the Tamil people. These stories had a profound impact upon him and turned a disciplined bookish boy into a radical youth at the age of sixteen and a militant leader at eighteen.

With a radical vision for a sustained militant movement for *eelam,* he forged the LTTE from scratch in 1976, and developed it into a military phenomenon in South Asia. Prabhakaran is quintessentially a militarist who firmly believes in violence as an effective instrument of the Sri Lankan Tamils against the Sinhalese-controlled Sri Lankan state, which denied them equal rights. He is primarily a self-taught guerrilla whose dedication to the *eelam* goal is a critical factor in the perpetration of violence by the LTTE. During the long years of his life underground, he drew up the LTTE's protracted war strategy from the guerrilla tactics of Ho Chi Minh and Mao Zedong. In making the LTTE an undefeatable force, the leader has imposed stern discipline on the cadres and insisted on their sacrifice. They are warned against disloyalty to the organization and threatened with the death penalty if they betray it in any manner. The consumption of alcohol and tobacco is banned. Marriage is allowed, but loose morals are not. Violators of the moral code are severely dealt with.

Many acknowledge that the true power of the LTTE lies in the indomitable spirit of sacrifice among its ranks who, at the time of joining the organization, swear personal loyalty to their leader. It is the indifference of the members to death and their readiness to give up their lives for the supreme Tamil cause that have enabled the LTTE to remain unvanquished and apparently unconquerable. The spirit of sacrifice finds expression in suicide-attacks by the LTTE and is symbolized by the cyanide capsules strung around their necks. The suicide commandos known as Black Tigers (those who have taken the oath to carry out suicide missions) figure in the LTTE lexicon as superior men and women. Between 1980 and 2000, the LTTE carried out 168 suicide attacks against both the military and civilian targets.

The LTTE leadership has consciously nurtured the cult of martyrdom in order to achieve greater mobilization of the cadres. The last week of every November is observed as the Martyrs Week, so as to coincide with Prabhakaran's birthday. The next day is Martyrs Day (marking the first LTTE casualty on November 27, 1982). On this day, the cadres rededicate themselves to the struggle and their leader makes a commemorative speech listing the organization's policies and programs—the only rare occasions for him to communicate with his people and the world.

Prabhakaran has always considered the LTTE as the sole authentic representative of the Sri Lankan Tamils. In keeping with this self-assumed position, he has used his group's military superiority for eliminating or weakening all militant groups that have sought to share power with the LTTE or to challenge its preeminence. A number of rival militant group leaders became victims of the LTTE. The group is responsible for the deaths of prominent political leaders from both the Sinhalese and Sri Lankan Tamil communities; the long list includes President Ranasinghe Premadasa and TULF leader Amirthalingam. Chandrika Kumaratunga, the present president of Sri Lanka, escaped an assassination attempt with an eye injury in 1999. The assassination of Rajiv Gandhi, the former Indian Prime Minister, was carried out by a young LTTE female suicide bomber in 1991. Although the LTTE denied its involvement, India is convinced that the LTTE chief ordered the killing, as he wanted to avenge the Indian leader's decision to send in the Indian army (under the 1987 India-Sri Lanka peace accord), which fought a war against the LTTE during October 1987–March 1990, with the objective of implementing the accord. The Indian government wishes to put Prabhakaran on trial in the Rajiv Gandhi assassination case. His extradition is an issue between India and Sri Lanka. India, the United States, and the United Kingdom have condemned the LTTE, and its activities are also closely monitored by the governments of Canada, Malaysia, and Australia. Facing an international isolation, Prabhakaran has committed the LTTE to a peace process since February 2002. As of 2004, the peace negotiations continue.

Capsule Biography

Velupillai Prabhakaran. Born in Jaffna November 26, 1954. Youngest of four children. Schooled in in Velvettiturai. Created the Liberation Tigers of Tamil Eelam (LTTE) in 1976. Agreed to take part in a peace process, 2002.

P. SAHADEVAN

Further Reading

Sahadevan, P., "On Not Becoming a Democrat: The LTTE's Commitment to Armed Struggle," *International Studies*, New Delhi: Sage, 32, no. 3, July–September 1995
Swamy, M.R. Narayan, *Tigers of Lanka: From Boys to Guerrillas*, New Delhi: Konark, 1994

Puerto Rican-Americans

Capsule Summary

Location: United States
Total Population: 3.4 million
Languages: English, Spanish
Religion: Roman Catholic

There are almost as many Puerto Ricans living on the island of Puerto Rico as there are in the United States. The 2000 United States census revealed that there are 3.8 million inhabitants in Puerto Rico, while there are 3.4 million Puerto Ricans residing in the United States. Puerto Ricans in the United States are mainly located in the states of New York, New Jersey, Illinois, and Florida.

On November 19, 1493, Christopher Columbus took over the island of Puerto Rio on behalf of the Spanish Crown, then named *Borinquen* by the Taïnos Indians, the first inhabitants of the island. The island of Puerto Rico remained under Spanish control for over 400 years, until the Spanish-American War in 1898. On April 25, 1898, the United States declared war on Spain, and invaded the island of Puerto Rico on July 25, 1898. The Treaty of Paris on December 10, 1898, marked the victory of the United States over Spain, and the transfer of the territories of Puerto Rico, Cuba, Guam, and the Philippines. Puerto Rico then became an American territory, ruled by a military government from 1898 to 1900.

Two Organic Acts changed the situation of the island. The first Organic Act, known as the Foraker Act of May 1, 1900, established a civil government with an Executive Council and a governor of Puerto Rico appointed by the president of the United States (with the advice and consent of the Senate until 1948, the year when the first direct elections took place). The second Organic Act, also known as the Jones Act of March 2, 1917, brought few new elements. A Senate was substituted for the Executive Council.

The Puerto Ricans already had a Bill of Rights, which granted Puerto Ricans American citizenship.

But the island of Puerto Rico is an unincorporated territory, which means that the island is, on a juridical point of view, linked to the United States, but is not a full state. Puerto Ricans are American citizens, but those who live on the island do not have the right to vote in American presidential or Congressional elections. A resident Commissioner, who does not have the right to vote, represents Puerto Ricans in the United States Congress.

The United States Congress approved the present island's statute at the beginning of the 1950s, authorizing the Puerto Ricans to draft their Constitution. On July 25, 1952, Puerto Rico became *un Estado Libro Associado (ELA)*, the Commonwealth of Puerto Rico. The island has its own government, with a governor, a Senate, a House of Representatives, and a judicial branch similar to the American system with a Supreme Court and some District Appellate courts. It has autonomy for local affairs, but the United States Congress can pass judgment without appeal on the major island decisions. Congress also maintains authority on foreign affairs issues, defense, justice, monetary policies, and trade.

The statute of the island defines the relationship between Puerto Rico and the United States as: "a permanent union between the United States and Puerto Rico on the basis of common citizenship, common defense, common currency, free market, and a common loyalty to the value of democracy." Puerto Rico has been consulted several times on the statute issue since 1967. So far, they have voted against statehood.

The Puerto Rican emigration to the United States began long before the annexation of Puerto Rico by the United States. At the beginning of the twentieth century, a first wave of immigrants settled a Puerto Rican community in Hawaii. The Puerto Rican migration to Hawaii started in 1900, due to the economic and social situation in Puerto Rico and the fact that the Hawaiian Islands needed workers for their fields. It was facilitated by the federal government, which allowed the Hawaii sugar planter's association to recruit Puerto Ricans under contract. The expeditions of the years 1900–1911 created a Puerto Rican community in Hawaii and in San Francisco, where some Puerto Ricans permanently stopped en route to Hawaii.

But the larger Puerto Rican community was formed in New York City from the time of World War I. They mainly settled in East Harlem and the Navy Yard section of Brooklyn. Puerto Ricans have been settling in the United States since the nineteenth century, but it was not until after World War II that they emigrated to the United States en masse.

From that time, the Puerto Rican migration rapidly increased. In 1945, 13,573 Puerto Ricans arrived in the United States, and 39,111 arrived the year after. One factor that especially promoted this emigration was the emergence of air traffic between Puerto Rico and the United States. The economic situation in Puerto Rico and the United States played an important part in the postwar migration. The United States was experiencing a period of economic expansion, and workers were needed. During the 1940s, the Puerto Rican government engaged the island in a vast industrialization program named Operation Bootstrap. With this, Puerto Rico experienced high economic growth for a few years.

In the process, a rural society was transformed into an urban society. Industrialization led to unemployment for many agricultural workers and migration to the urban centers. The Puerto Rican government supported the migration of agricultural workers with a farm labor program, which included a contract between the worker and American employers approved by the Secretary of Labor of Puerto Rico. In 1947, it established an agency, the Migration Division of the Department of Labor, charged with helping Puerto Ricans adjust to American society. The farm program concerned thousands of seasonal Puerto Rican agricultural workers who went to work in the American fields during the offseason in Puerto Rico.

The number of Puerto Ricans in the United States kept increasing since the end of World War II. In 1960, 887,661 Puerto Ricans by birth or parentage were living in the United States; the number rose to 1.3 million in 1970, and 2.7 million by 1990. However, a very large number of Puerto Ricans have returned to Puerto Rico since the 1970s. This is due to economic changes in the United States. The rate of unemployment among Puerto Rican-Americans is double the American average. Puerto Ricans often confront discrimination when applying for a job or housing in the United States. American culture and media propagate a stereotype of Puerto Ricans as lazy criminals, as the so-called "Puerto Rican problem" was a primary topic of national discussion and debate.

The link with the island of Puerto Rico and Spanish culture can be maintained in many ways by Puerto Ricans in the United States. Puerto Rican-Americans can find newspapers about or from the island, and watch television channels and listen to radio stations that present programs in Spanish. They can also find Puerto Rican food products as *pastels* and *plátanos* in supermarket. While the link with the island is strong,

Puerto Rican-Americans have developed a cultural identity on the mainland. The Puerto Rican-American identity is pluralistic, because the group is heterogeneous. A hybrid, syncretic Puerto Rican culture also expresses itself in literature, poetry, and music.

Until the 1960s, Puerto Ricans often identified themselves with Hispanic groups. The civil rights period was a key era in the development of Puerto Rican identity. The Puerto Rican Day Parade is probably the more conspicuous example of Puerto Rican identity. The parade in the streets, especially the main parade, held on New York City's Fifth Avenue, allows Puerto Ricans to express their culture.

MONIQUE MILIA-MARIE-LUCE

Further Reading

Angelo, Corlett J., "Latino Identity and Affirmative Action," in Gracia Jorge J.E. and Pablo de Greiff, editors, *Hispanics/Latinos in the United States*, New York/London: Routledge, 2000

Carrión, Arturo Morales, *Puerto Rico, a Political and Cultural History*, W.W. Norton & Company Inc, 1983

Centro de Estudios Puertorriqueños, *Extended Roots from Hawaii to New-York*, Hunter College, City of New-York, 1998

Flores, Juan, *Divided Borders, Essays on Puerto Rican Identity*, Arte Público Press, University of Houston, 1993

Flores, Juan, *From Bomba to Hip-Hop: The Puerto Rican Culture and Latino Identity, Popular Ccultures, Everyday Lives*, New York: Columbia University Press, 2000

Glazer, Nathan, and Daniel Moynihan, *Beyond the Melting Pot: Tthe Negroes, Puerto Ricans, Jews, Italians, and Irish of New York City*, Cambridge: MIT Press, 2nd edition, 1995

Sánchez-Korrol, Virginia, *From Colonia to Community: The History of Puerto Ricans in New York City*, The University Press of California, 1983

Rodriguez, Clara E., *Puerto Ricans Bborn in the U.S.A.*, Boston: Unwin Hyman, 1989

Torre, Carlos Antonio, Hugo Rodríguez Vecchini, and William Burgos: *The Commuter Nation: Perpectives on Puerto Rican Migration*, Universidad de Puerto Rico, 1994

Punjabi

Capsule Summary

Location: Northwestern area of South Asia and diaspora communities
Total population: 94 million (2000)
Languages: Punjabi, Hindi
Religions: Hindu, Muslim, Sikh

The term *Punjabi* refers to the people who claim the geographical region of Punjab as their ethnic homeland. Punjabi is also the language spoken by Punjabis. The geographical region of Punjab is located in the northwestern area of the South Asian subcontinent. It is a butterfly shaped-region, in which one wing is in Pakistan, the other in India; the two wings meet near the Indus Valley Civilization. Thus, a Punjabi may be a Hindu, Muslim, Sikh, or other religious affiliation. A Punjab may be a citizen of India or Pakistan.

Punjabis have distinct cultural traits. The language is a unique form separated from other Asian and South Asian languages. Their harvest dance, the *bhangra*, is unique to Punjabi culture. The Punjabi have their own kinship system as well as their own folklore. Punjabis

are not an entirely homogeneous group. Punjab consists of a large alluvial plain formed by the Indus River and four major tributaries, the Jhelum, Chenab, Ravi, and Sutlej Rivers. Between each river is a *doab,* or stretch of land. The people of each *doab* have their own distinctive name and variations in their linguistic and cultural patterns. Although they are Punjabis, within that category there are subgroups of Doabans, Majans, and others.

Emigration has become a prominent behavioral pattern for Punjabis, as population pressure on the land has led to agriculture not being sufficient to maintain an entire family. Under British rule, many went into the military, but more are migrating to Europe and North America, where they are making significant contributions to the economy and lifestyle of their new home. Whether in the Punjab or elsewhere, Punjabis take pride in their belief that they are an innovative people who prosper almost anywhere, and in almost any kind of circumstances.

Punjabis trace their ancestry back to the Indus Valley and the dawn of civilization (2500–1500 BCE). They also claim to descend from the Aryan invaders, whose incursions ended the Indus Valley civilization. However, a long history of invasions and persecutions dominate Punjabi history. Located on the invasion rout into South Asia, Punjab has experienced almost continuous turbulence.

Recorded history of the region began when Darius of Persia (518 BCE) annexed Punjab and Sind. Later, Chandra Gupta annexed the region into his Indian Empire, ruled by the Mauryan dynasty. Arabs started penetrating in 712 CE. The entry of the Moghuls brought peace and prosperity to the region for 200 years. When the region went into decline between 1738 and 1747, Lahore fell to Afghan rule. During this time, Punjab was not just the meeting place for armies, it was also a meeting ground for ideas. Kabir (1440–1518), an Indian mystic and poet, attempted to unite Hindu and Muslim thought. He also preached the essential unity of all religions, and the equality of all men.

Guru Nanak (1469–1539) obtained a following, and was the first of ten gurus for what became the Sikh religious community. By the seventeenth century, the Moghul rulers saw the Sikhs as a threat to their control and began persecuting them. The Sikhs, with their distinctive symbols, especially unshorn hair, turbans, and steel bracelets, were easy targets for Moghul soldiers. By the end of the eighteenth century, however, Maharaja Ranjit Singh emerged as the ruler of Punjab, until his death in 1839. Infighting and jealousies prevented the Sikhs from rising to their former glory, and the British who took over Punjab in 1849. Sikhs were declared a martial race and they became the backbone of the Indian army.

As a reward for their loyalty, the British invested in building irrigation canals and colonies for Punjabis, so they would have a more comfortable living environment. However, discontent arose when logging and depletion of the soil caused productivity to decline. Sikh soldiers traveling abroad made contact with other countries and cultures. They learned of another avenue of economic prosperity: emigration. Thus began the era of Punjabis entering the Indian diaspora, concentrating primarily in North America, the United Kingdom, and East Africa.

Punjabis living abroad have had, and continue to take, a strong interest in their homeland, participating in its political, economic, and social institutions. Money is sent back home to relatives, and information on new seed varieties, technology, and investment capital all contribute to making both the Pakistani and Indian Punjabis the most prosperous political units of their respective countries. As one travels through Pakistani and Indian Punjab today, one will see hospitals, schools, libraries, and tractors, all built with foreign money.

When independence was granted to India and Pakistan, Punjab was divided between the two countries. Ten million people had to leave their homes and cross the border: Hindus went east to India and Muslims west to Pakistan.

Punjabis in Pakistan are generally prosperous, especially when compared to other populations and regions in Pakistan, but population growth is a major problem. The Punjab in India has been carved up, creating the states of Haryana, Himachel Pradesh, and Punjab. The 1980s was a tumultuous time for Indiaís Punjab, as Sikh militants started fighting for fair treatment from the central government. The Indian army invaded the Sikh Golden Temple in Amritsar, thus angering and alienating many Sikhs. By the time the 1990s had arrived, calm had been restored to the region.

India's Punjab is a prosperous region, proficient in agriculture and small industry. Its economy is diversified and, with the assistance of Punjabis of the South Asian Diaspora, it is becoming a more prosperous region. However, population growth continues to be a major problem for both Indian and Pakistani Punjabis.

The Punjabi language is a central Indo-Aryan language. It is very similar to western Hindi and borrows slightly from Persian, Arabic, and Sanskrit. The language has two alphabets: Lahnda, which is indigenous to the region and uses a Davenagaari script, and Gurmukhi, created by the Sikh Guru Angad (reigned 1539–1552) for Sikh scriptures. Today, Gurmukhi is more frequently used.

ARTHUR HELWEG

See also **Diaspora: India; India; Pakistan**

Further Reading

Darling, Malcolm Lyall, *The Punjabi Peasant in Prosperity and Debt*, South Asian Books, 4th edition, reprinted, 1978

Dulai, Surjit, and Arthur Helweg, editors, *Punjab in Perspectve: Proceedings of the Research Committee on Punjab Conference*, South Asia Series: Occasional Paper No. 39, East Lansing: Asian Studies Center, Michigan State University, 1987

Eglar, Zekiye, *A Punjabi Village in Pakistan*, New York: Columbia University Press, 1960

Kessinger, Tome G., *Vilayatpur, 1848–1968: Social and Economic Change in a North Indian Village*, Berkeley and Los Angeles: University of California Press, 1974

Leaf, Murray J., *Song of Hope: The Green Revolution in a Punjab Village*, New Brunswick, New Jersey: Rutgers University Press, 1974

Q

Qatar

Capsule Summary

Location: Persian Gulf, Southwest Asia
Total Population: 817,052 (July 2003)
Languages: Arabic (official), English commonly used as a second language
Religions: Islam, with Christian, Hindu, and other minorities

The State of Qatar (Dawlat Qatar in Arabic) is an independent emirate located on the west coast of the Persian (Arabian) Gulf and occupies a small desert peninsula that extends from the larger Arabian Peninsula north of eastern Saudi Arabia and the United Arab Emirates. Its territory includes an area of 4,416 square miles (11,437 square km), slightly smaller than Connecticut. Saudi Arabia and Abu Dhabi border Qatar to the south. The general topography is a low-lying, barren terrain with loose sand and pebbles and occasional limestone outcroppings; salt flats and sand dunes predominate in the south and the west coast is marked by low cliffs and hills. The climate is characteristically hot with a high relative humidity and low rainfall. Per capita GDP is $20,100 (2002 estimate).

Doha (Ad-Dawhah), Qatar's capital, is the administrative, commercial, and population center, and port located on the east coast. During the eighteenth and nineteenth centuries, the primary sources of wealth were pearling, fishing, and maritime trade. The 1986 census showed that 84 percent of the population was concentrated in Doha and in the neighboring town of Ar Rayyan. Data from 2003 suggests that 90 percent of the country's population resides in the capital and its metropolitan area. The capital, with 750,000 inhabitants, dominates the country's economy. Other major towns in Qatar include Al Wakrah (population 13,259) and Umm Said (population 6,094). Few traditional nomads remain, and less than 10 percent live in rural areas.

Qatar was settled initially by Arabic-speaking nomads who ventured from the central part of the Arabian Peninsula. Many modern-day Qataris descend from several of these migratory tribes that came to the Qatar Peninsula during the eighteenth century to escape other tribes and the harsh environments of the neighboring areas of Al-Hasra and Nejd. Ruled by the Al Thani family since the mid-1800s, Qatar transformed from a poor British protectorate noted mainly for pearling into an independent state with significant oil and natural gas revenues.

The population of Qatar before independence in 1971 must be estimated because, until oil revenues created a reason to remain on the peninsula, individuals and entire tribes migrated when the economic or security situation became insupportable. Indians were forcibly relocated in the late 1800s, leaving Qatar the only Gulf emirate without Indians until the 1950s. In 1908, a British observer estimated there were 27,000 inhabitants, of whom 6,000 were described as "foreign slaves" and 425 as Iranian boat builders. However, by

QATAR

1930 the number of Iranians had increased to 5,000, or almost 20 percent of the population, coinciding with the apogee of the pearl industry. Subsequently, the population remained relatively stable until the 1940s, when economic hardship and regional insecurity caused people to migrate to other areas, leaving Qatar with a population estimated at 16,000 in 1949.

A Qatari census in 1970 reported a population of 111,113, of whom only 45,039 (40 percent) were identified as Qatari. A tremendous demographic growth of foreign workers, including both unskilled laborers and skilled technicians, occurred in the 1970s, the direct result of petroleum exploration. As a consequence, by 1977 200,000 people lived in the country, about 65 percent of them non-Qatari. The 1992 estimate was 484,387 (with a 1992 growth rate of 3.2 percent), but by 1994 Qatar had a population of 512,779 (1994 estimate) with a growth rate of 2.6 percent. The most recent census estimate of the total population, including nonnative Qatari and other foreigners, is 817,052 (July 2003 estimate). Reflecting the significant number of migrant workers, about 67 percent of Qatar's population is male. Qatar, like the other Persian Gulf states, has not granted citizenship freely because this would necessitate sharing the new wealth with recent arrivals, and, primarily, the tribal nature of gulf society does not admit new members easily.

Qatar's ethnic groups are 40 percent Arab, 18 percent Pakistani, 18 percent Indian, and 10 percent Iranian, with all others accounting for about 14 percent of the demographic total. Economic growth in the 1970s and 1980s created an economy dependent on foreign workers, mostly from South Asia (particularly Pakistan, India, and Bangladesh) or other parts of Arabia (especially Yemen, Oman, and Saudi Arabia), as well as workers from Jordan, Palestine, Iraq, and Iran. Less than one-third of the population is composed of Qatari citizens. Although most Qatari are Arabs, some have Iranian or African ancestry. In addition, there are large foreign communities of Indians, Iranians, Pakistanis, and Egyptians, but other expatriate groups include Filipinos, Bangladeshis, Sudanese, Afghans, Sri Lankan, and Westerners (mostly British and Americans). About 3,000 U.S. citizens resided in Qatar in 1996 and more than 5,000 in 2003 (estimate). Therefore, approximately 80 percent of the population in 2003 was composed of foreign workers with temporary residence status.

Arabic is the national language, but English has become a second, common tongue. Nationally, Qatar is 95 percent Muslim and Qatari's are mainly "Wahhabi" Sunnite Muslims, but there is a small Shi'ite minority (estimated at less than 10 percent). The powerful ruling Al Thani family adheres to the same Wahhabi interpretation of Islam as the rulers of Saudi Arabia, although their interpretation is not as strict. The remaining 5 percent of the population are Christian, Hindu, Bahai, or practice other faiths.

CHARLES C. KOLB

See also **Muslims in Africa**

Further Reading

Al Noor, *Economical and Social Infrastructures in the State of Qatar*, Doha, Qatar: Al Noor Publishers, 1984
Anscombe, Frederick F., *The Ottoman Gulf: The Creation of Kuwait, Saudi Arabia, and Qatar*, New York: Columbia University Press, 1997
Ember, Melvin, and Carol Ember, editors, *Countries and Their Cultures*, New York: Macmillan Reference, under the auspices of the Human Relations Area Files (Yale University), 2001
Nyrop, Richard F., editor, *Persian Gulf States: Country Studies*, Washington, DC: U.S. Government Printing Office, 2nd edition, 1984
Winckler, Onn, *Population Growth, Migration, and Sociodemographic Policies in Qatar*, Tel Aviv: Tel Aviv University, Moshe Dayan Center for Middle Eastern and African Studies, 2000
Zahlan, Rosemarie Said, *The Creation of Qatar*, London: Croom Helm; New York: Barnes and Noble, 1979

988

Québécois

Location: Province of Québec (Canada)
Population of the Province in 1999: 7,340,000 (of which 72,430 were Amerindians)
Language Spoken at Home in 1997: 82% French; 10% English; 8% other
Religion: 95% Christian (Catholic, Protestant, Anglican); 5% other

Often called *Quebecers* in English, *Québécois*—a French language adjective from the place name *Québec*—refers to all inhabitants of the Province of Québec in eastern Canada, irrespective of their particular ethnicity. Historically, however, the French connotation associated with the term *Québécois* derives from the majority of inhabitants of the province of Québec, part of the larger group called the French Canadians (*Canadiens-français*, over 8.2 million in Canada).

Originally, inhabitants of the territory that today constitutes the Province of Québec were Amerindians belonging to the Algonkian, Iroquoian, and Inuit families. In the early seventeenth century, explorers from France established permanent settlements in the Saint-Lawrence valley (Québec City by Samuel de Champlain in 1608) and established a French colony.

Until 1763, French ancestors of today's Québécois colonized the St.Lawrence basin area. Without ever thriving, the New France colony maintained itself against the odds: low-priority support from Paris, lasting conflicts with some Amerindian groups, colonial competition with neighboring New Holland and New England, and a harsh climate.

At its height in the first half of eighteenth century, New France controlled the entire basins of the St-Lawrence, Ohio, and Missouri-Mississippi rivers, as well as nearly all the periphery of the Great Lakes, and its explorers "discovered" the Rocky Mountains. French place-names were left on an immense territory. The French set up trade networks with all Amerindian groups between the Sioux to the west and the Abénakis in the east; the Hurons and Algonquins were their main allies, the Dutch- and later English-supported Iroquois Federation, their chief foes.

Canada was the original Iroquois name of the Québec city region. By extension, it came to designate all of New France, and the local colonists came to be called *Canadiens*. After the British conquest war in 1756–1763, the "ethnonym" *Canadian* was adapted from *Canadien* to distinguish the French-speaking bulk population in the new colony from the new English masters. At the end of the eighteenth century and throughout the nineteenth century, the British colony of Canada would be strategically divided between Upper- and Lower-Canada, the lower part being roughly equivalent to today's Québec province. It was only after the establishment of Canada as an autonomous part of the British Dominion in 1867 that the term *Canadians* came to apply to all inhabitants of the whole Dominion of Canada; at that point, *Québécois* was only used to designate the inhabitants of Québec city. Eventually, Canada was also divided into provinces. What had been Lower-Canada became the Province of Québec in reference to its capital city. The French-speaking majority there prefer to call themselves French Canadians in the rest of Canada.

Assimilation of the French-speaking minority into the English-speaking majority of Canada has never been an official policy. However, it was widely believed that this cultural subgroup of Canada would naturally merge into the bulk of the Anglophone majority.

Well into the 1950s, the French-speaking majority in Québec was a rural and religious society who lived off the land as independent farmers. By the mid-nineteenth century, religion and nationalism combined to promote the *Revanche des berceaux* (revenge of the cradles) policy, which advocated large families. The policy encouraged French Canadian women to have large families—up to a dozen children—to increase their numbers relative to the Anglicans-Protestants. For decades, the average number of children per family would steadily remain higher than any other group's, close to double-digit figures. It has been estimated that the total number of French immigrants who settled in New France during the French colony's times did not exceed 10,000 individuals. More than 8 million French speakers in Canada today stem from that small group, 85 percent of whom live in Québec.

The ethnic composition of the Province of Québec in 1901 shows 80 percent with French heritage, 7 percent each for English and Irish, 4 percent for Scottish, and the remaining 2 percent a mixture of Amerindians and a few additional European and Asian origins. Today the proportion of French is 82 percent, whereas the 18 percent Anglo-Saxons of 1901 gave way to 8 percent of immigrants from various origins that adopted English as their language in Québec. The massive immigration that was responsible for the peopling of North America did not really mark Québec Province because the French language acted as a deterrent to the English-speaking and Anglophile migrants pouring in from Europe, China, and the British colonies.

It took some time before the widespread self-designation of *Canadiens-français* gave way to that of *Québécois* in the Province of Québec. Although French-speaking cultural affirmation has always been alive in Québec since the British conquest, it was in the early 1960s that politicians began to play successfully the card of a specific *Québécois* identity. From the election of Québec's Premier Jean Lesage in 1960—father of the Quiet Revolution—to the creation of the *Parti Québécois* in 1968 and eventually its first accession to power (1976–1985), the independence of Québec as a French-speaking entity has been high on the political agenda. This nationalistic affirmation has led to the declaration of French as the only official language in Québec (1977), to a first referendum on independence in 1981 (40.4 percent in favor), followed by a second one in 1995 (49.4 percent in favor). This growing assertion triggered an equally strong reaction on the part of the English-speaking minority, historically used to holding the political and economic guides of the Province and reluctant to let go of its old privileges. Whereas the majority French-speaking leaders of Québec are keen to promote the sovereignty of a French-speaking yet multicultural Québec, a radical branch of the Anglophone and a fraction of the English-speaking Amerindian minorities have brought the issue of their "forced assimilation" to the international scene, gaining a sympathetic response from some quarters. Ironically, their rhetoric is matching the one used by those who want to see Québec's sovereignty to lay their blame on the Canadian Federal government.

Parti Québécois has again been in power in Québec since 1994 and still promotes the first article of its political program, the setting up of an independent multicultural French-speaking Québec Republic. Paradoxically, since the late 1960s, among the fiercest opponents to this project are Canada's premiers from Québécois origin such as Pierre-Elliott Trudeau, Brian Mulroney, and the current premier, Jean Chrétien.

JEAN MICHAUD

See also **Canada; French; Levesque, Rene**

Further Reading

Côté, Roch, editor, *Québec 2000. Rétrospective du XXe siècle*, Montréal: Fides, 1999

Dickinson, John A., and Bryan Young, *A Short History of Quebec: A Socio-Economic Perspective*, Toronto: Copp Clark Pitman, 1988

Government of Québec's Official Website (in French, English and Spanish) <http://www.gouv.qc.ca/>

Linteau, Paul-André, René Durocher, Jean-Claude Robert, and François Ricard, *Quebec since 1930*, Toronto: Lorimer, 1991

Rioux, Marcel, *Les Québécois*, Paris: Editions du Seuil, 1979

Scowen, Reed, *A Different Vision. The English in Quebec in the 1990s*, Ontario: Don Mills; Canada: Maxwell MacMillan, 1991

Quechua

Capsule Summary

Location: Seven countries in South America; primarily Bolivia, Peru, and Ecuador
Total Population: Around eight million (estimates vary)
Language: Quechua
Religion: Primarily Roman Catholic

Ama suwa. Ama llulla. Ama quella. (Don't steal. Don't lie. Don't be lazy. —Incan proverb)

Not many people outside South America know of the Quechua (also: Quichua)— but most have heard of the Inca. The language of the Inca Empire was Quechua, or *qheshwa*. This language moved throughout the

Andean area with the Incan conquests and continued to spread, even after the arrival of the Spaniards, as an indigenous lingua franca. Now, Quechua is both a language and an ethnic identity for around eight million people in Bolivia, Peru, Ecuador, Colombia, northern Argentina and Chile, and Brazil.

The majority of native Quechua-speaking people are found in Bolivia, Peru, and Ecuador. In each of these countries, they are about a quarter of the national population—estimates vary, particularly due to the fluid nature of Quechua ethnic identity and how it is defined.

Quechua, as an ethnic identity, was born of conquest. As various local ethnic groups came under the umbrella of the Inca empire, they were exposed to Quechua, the language of their conquerors. The movement of loyal Quechua-speaking groups into newly conquered areas (for example, in southern Bolivia) hastened the spread of the language. By the time of the Spanish colonization, most of the local languages had disappeared or were well on their way to extinction. Quechua became, not just a language, but an identity based on a common language and a shared difference from the Spanish colonizers.

Despite a common identity as Quechua speakers, many Quechua today identify themselves more broadly, as *campesinos,* or peasants. The term *campesino* was adopted by highland native peoples after Bolivia's land-reforming revolution of 1952 in place of the less favored (and often derogatory) term *indio* (Indian). *Runa,* (Quechua word for "the people"), is also used as an identity marker in some areas.

The question of identity in the Andes is complex; both the Quechua and the Aymara (the other highland Andean group) are *campesinos* and share some common features of highland Andean culture. At the same time, Quechuas and Aymaras are distinct groups with separate languages. Among the Quechua themselves, distinctions among various local ethnic groups also remain in many areas. The Tarabuco, the Jalq'a, and the Calcha in Bolivia, or the Otavalos, Natabuelas, and Caranquis in Ecuador, are examples of local ethnicities which come under the Quechua umbrella.

The highland ancestors of today's Quechua were farmers and herders as well as artisans, soldiers, builders, and public servants. The engineering, road-building, and administrative feats of the Inca Empire are legendary. Under the Inca, villages paid tribute in grain, which not only supplied the empire's administrative machinery but provided a social safety net for communities struck by drought or other disaster.

Because of their sedentary and structured nature of their society, the Quechua bore the brunt of the Spaniards' colonization enterprise in South America; many people ended up as bonded labor on the Spanish crown's land grants (*encomiendas*), as tribute laborers in the silver mines of Potosí (Bolivia), and on lowland plantations. There were periodic rebellions, most notably that of Tupac Amaru in 1770.

Through the colonial rule and on through the republican period, many Quechua lived as dependents on land that had been titled to Spaniards or their descendants (whites or mixed-race *mestizos*). Quechua farmers labored on the land and returned a portion to the owner, or *patrón*; personal service to the *patrón's* family was also usually expected. In Bolivia, the 1952 revolution changed this, taking the land from many longtime landholding families and distributing it among the native Quechua who worked the land. In Peru, the agrarian reform of 1969 accomplished a similar end.

Yet, while many Quechua families now own land they work, the dividing of small plots from generation to generation has led to the phenomenon of *minifundioism*, in which many parcels are too small to support families. Also, the legacy of hundreds of years of patron-client relationships persists in many areas, where rural communities struggle with the challenge of overcoming economic hardship and creating better futures with scant resources.

Today, the Quechua are a cultured people with strong rural roots. While Quechua people have always lived in towns and cities (as artisans, tradespeople, laborers, etc.). Over the generations, these families have tended to become absorbed in the *mestizo,* Spanish-speaking culture of the national mainstream. It is in the countryside where a distinctive Quechua identity has maintained itself most strongly.

Many Quechua still move to urban areas (seasonally or permanently to seek education and work opportunities), as well as to lowland agricultural areas. Quechua *campesinos* who move to the city will usually abandon the traditional woven dress of their specific region, but many women wear a knee-length flared *pollera* skirt and blouse and retain their long braids as visible symbols of Quechua identity. The Quechua *pollera* is distinctive from both the Aymara *pollera* (which is much longer and usually worn with a shawl rather than a cardigan), and from Western dress. To a practiced eye, the style of the *pollera* can identify from which specific region the wearer comes.

While typical aspects of Quechua culture (such as traditional dress) may be abandoned when people leave their home communities, much that is Quechuan (music, foods, handicrafts, festivals, rituals, vocabulary) continues to permeate the national identity of the Andean countries. These countries are neither Spanish nor indigenous but built upon both cultures. The Quechuan identity, which itself arose from the sharing of language among many diverse local ethnicities, is still being shared: Its energetic and haunting woodwind music and its beautiful patterned textiles are becoming known internationally, even as many Quechua adopt the dress and music of other lands.

ROBYN EVERSOLE

See also **Aymara; Bolivia; Ecuador; Peru**

Further Reading

Allen, Catherine J., *The Hold Life Has: Coca and Cultural Identity in an Andean Community*, Washington: Smithsonian Institution Press, 1988

Condori Mamani, Gregorio, and Escalante G., Carmen, editors, *Andean Lives: Gregorio Condori Mamani and Asunta Quispe Huaman*, Austin: University of Texas Press, 1996

Isbell, Billie Jean, *To Defend Ourselves: Ecology and Ritual in an Andean Village*, Cornell, New York: University of Cornell Press, 1978

Meyerson, Julia, *Tambo: Life in an Andean village*, Austin: University of Texas Press, 1990

Myers, Sarah K., *Language Shift among Migrants to Lima, Peru*, Chicago: Dept. of Geography, University of Chicago, 1973

Spalding, Karen, *Huarochiri, an Andean Society under Inca and Spanish Rule*, Stanford, California: Stanford University Press, 1984

Stein, William W., *Hualcan: Life in the Highlands of Peru*, Ithaca: Cornell University Press, 1961

R

Race

Modern biologists define racial groups either as populations that have enough genetic distance between them as to be subspecies, or as hereditary lineages that have remained relatively distinct over the period of a given species existence. As such, the concept of geographical races was a central concept in the early formulation of evolutionary theories of speciation in the mid-twentieth century. It was through the development of evolutionary theories of the origin and maintenance of geographical races that the existence of races in the human species was dismissed. This began with the recognition by Charles Darwin that the naturalists of his time had defined an arbitrary number of human races. His views on human races were published in *Descent of Man* in 1871. The dismissal of human races has concluded with recent studies showing that the amount of genetic variation and genetic subdivision in modern humans in very small compared to similar species. For example, there is more genetic variation in one population of East African chimpanzees than exists in our entire species.

Biological versus Social Construction of Race

Racial definitions evolved in concert with the development of biology. Prescientific views of human variation tended to recognize physical differences between populations, but did not unambiguously recognize races or hierarchies among them. Greeks, Hebrews, and Romans did not develop well-articulated biological theories of race. Greek and Roman thinking stressed the influence of environment on physical and mental traits. Even as late as the eighteenth century European naturalists had not arrived at a consensus concerning the origin of and significance of racial differences. The Swedish naturalist Carolus von Linnaeus (1707–1778) classified humans as one species, *Homo sapiens,* and divided it into four races: Americanus, Europeus, Asiaticus, and Afer (Negro). Linneaus used emotional and cultural attributes to rank the races. He saw Americanus ruled by habit, Europeus ruled by laws and customs, Asiaticus by belief, and Afer was ruled by caprice.

It is noteworthy that eighteenth century naturalists had no consensus view of the inferiority of the Negro. Johann Friedrich Blumenbach, a student of Linneaus and the founder of modern anthropology, did not think that an objective ranking of the features of human races could be achieved. Blumenbach classified humans into five racial groups: Caucasian, Mongoloid, Malay, American, and Negro. This classification system dominated anthropological thinking until the early twentieth century.

By the mid-nineteenth century, however, the European view of the Negro and other non-European races reflected a general tone of white supremacy. This is linked to both the expansion of chattel slavery in the

Americas and the spread of European colonialism in Africa, Asia, Australia, and South America.

Probably the most important difference between the views of the eighteenth and nineteenth century naturalists is the appearance of the concept of the Negro as a separate species. This idea was particularly important in the United States, where legal challenges to the issue of slavery had been posed (for example, the Dred Scott Decision, rendered March 7, 1857). In his decision, justifying Dred Scott's return to slavery, Chief Justice Taney denies the humanness of the Negro, and states that "the Negroes had for more than a century before been regarded as beings of an inferior order . . . that they had no rights which the white man was bound to respect; and that the Negro might justly and lawfully be reduced to slavery." It was precisely this point on which Abraham Lincoln focused in his attack on slavery. Negroes were human, although inferior to whites, and the humanity of the Negro made slavery incompatible with American democracy.

Post-Darwinian Views of Race

Darwin first provided the theory required to understand human racial diversity in *On the Origin of Species by the Means of Natural Selection or the Preservation of Favored Races in the Struggle for Life,* first published in 1859. This was not intentional. He was not primarily concerned with the origin of race or diversity within the human species. He was however, concerned with the general problem of variation in biological organisms. In particular, Darwin was concerned with the nature of variations that might be important in the formation of new species. He was the first to correctly articulate the essential mechanism responsible for biological adaptation. This would lay the groundwork for subsequent investigation into the problem of which variation in a given species is the result of natural selection (and hence is adaptive) and which variation arises in populations by chance.

Darwin realized by this time that *The Origin*'s logic had important implications for the discussion concerning the origin and maintenance of diversity in the human species. He was particularly concerned with the claims of the polygenists that there were distinct species of modern humans. The polygenists claimed that the human races were in reality separate species specially created along the scale of nature. The leading theorist of polygeny was Louis Agassiz. His views were supported in America by distinguished scientists

such as Samuel Morton and popularized by Josiah Nott and George R. Gliddon.

Darwin's views on human evolution appear in *The Descent of Man and Selection in Relation to Sex,* published in 1871. He immediately recognized the weaknesses found in the racial thinking of this time; that is, naturalists could not agree on how to define races in the human species. He showed that this problem resulted from the use of inconstant characters (characteristics that are not consistently associated with each other throughout their geographic ranges). It was already known that such a procedure was faulty for taxonomic purposes outside of the human species. Darwin pointed out its absurdity by simply comparing the number of supposed human races defined by various researchers, ranging from 2 to 63.

Chapters 5 through 7 in *The Descent of Man* dealt specifically with the origin and nature of variation within the human species. Darwin was particularly concerned with dismantling the views of the polygenists who felt that the human races were actually distinct species. Therefore, his analysis tended to highlight the unity of human characteristics. Darwin starts his chapter 7, *On the Races of Man,* by emphasizing that it is necessary to analyze human varieties in the same way that a naturalist would examine variation in any other species. He had already established the principle that the mechanisms of nature, particularly natural selection, operated in the same fashion to form the human animal as well as any other. This was in contradiction to the general tendency of the nineteenth century to treat the biology of humans as unique (the result of divine purpose to separate the humans from the animals.)

Darwin then proceeded to examine the correspondence of human races to the zoological zones of Agassiz, concluding that there was some evidence for the local adaptation of humans to their various climates. Agassiz believed that human races had been created as separate species occupying different climatic zones along with other fauna and flora. However, Darwin stated that the real definition of species continuity is interfertility. This means that individuals within populations can mate and produce viable (fertile) offspring. He dismissed the weakly constructed arguments of Paul Broca concerning the supposed infertility of European settlers and Australian natives. His main argument for the interfertility of the human races derived from the data of the southern slaveholder John Bachman concerning the fertility of mulattoes. Darwin suggested that the high fertility of the mulattos in the 1854 census was inconsistent with the low fertility or even sterility predicted of true species hybrids such as the mule. From this, Darwin suggested that no valid evidence supported the notion that the human races are not interfertile. This, to Darwin, was singular proof of the biological unity of the human species.

After *The Origin* and *The Descent of Man,* naturalists began to think of human biological diversity in evolutionary terms. This did not immediately dismiss racism and racial hierarchy, particularly in anthropology. James Hunt founded the Anthropological Society of London (ASL) in 1863. This organization was devoted to the study of human biology along the polygenist paradigm. The ASL's views were vehemently racist and they championed the role of the white race, particularly the British Empire for its role in civilizing the "inferior" races of the world. The ASL was a strong advocate for Britain's support of the Confederacy during the American Civil War. Its rival society, the Ethnological Society of London (ESL), contained many of Darwin's intellectual supporters, including Herbert Spencer and Sir Francis Galton. The ESL, although convinced of European superiority, did not take an active role in calling for the enslavement and colonization of the inferior races. In addition, Darwinian theory did not preclude racism. In 1869, John Jeffries suggested that European superiority was also consistent with evolutionary mechanisms. The darker skinned races of the world were seen as primitive, whereas the Europeans represented an evolutionarily advanced state. Jeffries used the skull angle as his metric of evolutionary advancement.

The German biologist Ernst Haeckel would also develop a theory of the evolutionary history of races. Haeckel felt that each species passed through embryonic stages on its way to perfection. The Aryan race represented the pinnacle of the human species and the darker races recorded an evolutionary progression through its previous conditions.

This idea was consistent with Haeckel's general principle; ontogeny recapitulates phylogeny.

The Neo-Darwinian Synthesis and Twentieth Century Racial Anthropology

Evolutionary theory appeared without fully articulated mechanisms of heredity. The neo-Darwinian synthesis began around 1900 and was completed in the 1940s. Its main accomplishment was the incorporation of the genetic mechanisms proposed by Gregor Mendel, par-

ticulate inheritance and independent assortment, into natural selection theory. However, one of the mistakes of early neo-Darwinian thinking was a tendency to reduce complex phenotypic traits into simple Mendelian unit characters. This was particularly important in the formation of a theory of eugenics. It also had consequences for anthropology, where it took the form of confusing complex cultural developments for heritable genetic traits.

Physical anthropology at the beginning of the twentieth century focused on the clarification of racial taxonomy in the human species. For example, in 1890, Harvard professor of paleontology Nathaniel Shaler wrote that the Negro was "nearer to the anthropoid or pre-human ancestry of man," and in 1896 Edward D. Cope, professor of geology and mineralogy at the University of Pennsylvania, believed that the Negro was more apelike because of his flat nose and jaws that projected beyond the upper part of the face, the facial angle, and the deficiency of the calf of the leg and the obliquity of the pelvis. Negroes were thought to have retained the more fetal, infantile, or simian characteristics. In addition, physical anthropology was still under the influence of craniometry or the measurement of cranial capacity. The French scientists Broca and Topinard had reported that the average cranial capacity of whites was greater than that of blacks. This they expected meant that the average intelligence of blacks should be less than that of whites.

Franz Boas was one of the first twentieth century anthropologists to challenge this reasoning. Boas particularly challenged the relationship between brain weight and intellectual capacity and showed that the metric characteristics of the skull could be changed rapidly in populations by environmental conditions.

By 1930, physical anthropological reports on the classification of human populations into races showed serious anomalies. For example, Ales Hrdlicka's chapter on human races showed serious confusion over the use of physical characteristics and the delineation of racial categories. Furthermore, studies of blood protein variation would continue to erode the classical conceptions of race after the war. Biochemical techniques such as electrophoresis were now being applied to identify genetic variation in human material. For example, Linus Pauling, a physical chemist, had already begun to suspect that sickle-cell anemia was a protein polymorphism disease in 1931. Electrophoretic studies of this protein, beginning in the 1940s and continuing into the 1950s, would reveal that many forms of protein variants could be found in many of the world's populations. The analysis of protein data would have a profound impact on dismantling classical race theory. For example, Ashley Montagu's grouping of the Australoids as Negroids in his 1945 taxonomy was based on anthropometric data. This, however, was contradicted by serological data from A.S. Wiener in 1946. This study showed the complete absence of subgroup A_2 allele and R_h-negative type in the Australians and, thus, that they should be classified as "Mongolian." This difference in classification result based on the physical character one examines is an example of discordance; that is, "Negroids" and "Australoids" might share the same pigmentation or skull shape pattern, yet be entirely different in blood allele frequencies. This results from different population genetic mechanisms affecting the loci that determine these particular traits. This is the reason why earlier racial taxonomic schemes could not agree on the classification of particular populations, as described earlier by Darwin in *The Descent of Man*. Ultimately, phenotypic characters cannot be reliable indicators of evolutionary relationship. For example, sickle-cell anemia is found in a variety of human populations in conjunction with the prevalence of malaria.

Alternatively, frequencies of Alzheimer's disease or Huntington's chorea are mostly determined by genetic drift (chance events of population history.) The APP-1 gene, which is linked to a genetic predisposition for Alzheimer's disease was uncovered in a group of German immigrants to the Volga River region in Russia. This population had an unusually high frequency of Alzheimer's disease and was found to have been culturally isolated from the native Russian population. In South Africa, all cases of Huntington's chorea among the so-called white population were traced to one of the original Dutch immigrants to the cape in 1658, Jan Van Riebeeck. The frequency of the Huntington's gene in whites is 20 per million, whereas it is only 1 per million in the indigenous South Africans in 1984.

Dismantling the Race Concept in Humans

As studies of genetic variation in humans began to accumulate in the latter part of the twentieth century, it became clear that classification of populations into racial categories could not be justified. By the 1980s a significant literature had arisen on the amount of genetic diversity that actually existed within and between the populations in the human species. It was shown that in humans, the largest amount of genetic variation in our species resided at the level of the individual, not population, or race. In 1982 Nei and Roychoudhury would show that the genetic distances for protein loci between Caucasoid, Mongoloid, and Negroids were of the same order of magnitude as those for local populations in other organisms and considerably smaller than those for subspecies. Additional researchers in other studies throughout the 1980s and 1990s examined proteins, nuclear DNA, and mitochondrial DNA and continued to support this conclusion. For example, Templeton, in 1998, showed that the amount of population subdivision found globally in the human species was very small compared to other large bodied mammals with strong dispersal abilities. F_{st} statistics range between 1.0 and 0; a 1.0 indicates strong population subdivision and would be consistent with the existence of geographical races, whereas values close to 0 would be inconsistent with the existence of races. The global human value was determined to be around 0.15. Templeton also found that the human species did not contain distinct evolutionary lineages, the other criteria by which geographical races could be identified.

By the end of the decade, most molecular and physical anthropologists had arrived at the conclusion that the classical socially constructed categories of race were not valid and thus not biologically useful in the human species. The idea that there are no biological races in the human species has become the mainstream scientific view, particularly among geneticists. In 1995, research examining human genetic variation and the race concept was the subject of two symposia at the Annual Meeting of the American Association for the Advancement of Science. Both panels were composed of philosophers, anthropologists, biologists, and social scientists. In the following year, the American Association of Physical Anthropologists published a statement on the biological aspects of race that reported the same conclusion. In 1999, *Science* magazine's Genome issue devoted a section to explaining the rift between genetic reality and the "racial" categories to be used by the Office of Management and Budget (OMB) for the 2000 census. Finally, the human genome sequence was published in *Science* magazine on February 16, 2001. Analysis of the 30,000 genes reported suggests that it is not possible to use sequence information to identify an individual's race. This is probably the strongest refutation of the existence of biological races in the human species.

Conclusion

We now know that natural selection and genetic drift, acting independently of each other, on independent systems of genes, created the variability that we observe today in the human species. The selection gradients and unique population genetic events that influenced gene frequency in human evolutionary history were not correlated. This result means that characteristics like hair type, skin color, body proportions, disease resistance, or behavioral traits do not consistently match each other and cannot be used to designate racial groups. For example, Eskimos and Swedes may have highly similar cranial morphologies, and sub-Saharan Africans and Australoids may have melanic skin, yet not be closely related genetically. We also know that between-group human population genetic variation is small compared to within-group individual variation. Thus, although it is highly likely that human subpopulations will vary in a specific trait, they cannot be pigeonholed into our socially constructed racial categories. Most importantly, while we may be able to identify physical traits that we can link to specific genetic differences (such as skin pigmentation or eye color), we cannot generally link more complex traits, particularly behavioral ones to specific genes.

JOSEPH L. GRAVES, JR., AND WENDY CARTER

Further Reading

Cavalli-Sforza, L.L., P. Menozzi, and A. Piazza, *The History and Geography of Human Genes*, Princeton, New Jersey: Princeton University Press, 1994

Darwin, Charles, *The Descent of Man, and Selection in Relation to Sex*, London: J. Murray, 1871; reprint, Princeton, New Jersey: Princeton University Press, 1981

Graves, Joseph L., Jr., *The Emperor's New Clothes: Biological Theories of Race at the Millennium*, New Brunswick, New Jersey: Rutgers University Press, 2001

Montagu, Ashley, *Man's Most Dangerous Myth: The Fallacy of Race*, Walnut Creek: Alta Mira Press, 6th edition, 1997

Nei, M., and A.K. Roychoudhury, "Genetic Relationship and Evolution of Human Races," *Evolutionary Biology*, 14 (1982) Owens, K., and M. King, "Genomic Views of Human History," *Science* (1999)

Templeton, A.R., "Human Races: A Genetic and Evolutionary Perspective," *American Anthropologist*, 100, no. 3 (1998)

UNESCO, *Race and Science: The Race Question in Modern Science*, New York: Columbia University Press, 1961

Racism

Racism is racial discrimination instituted using power. It can also be described as the unequal distribution of prestige, privilege, and power based on perceived biological differences between groups. Power is the most important characteristic of this system of oppression because racists can separate, exploit, injure, or kill members of groups that they have identified as racial "others." The actions of racists are openly or implicitly justified by the belief that the victims or racial others are members of inherently inferior groups that do not merit the same consideration or treatment as the superior group or groups. Frequently, these "inferiors" are also members of minority groups.

Racism and bigotry are closely linked; however, it is inaccurate to use these terms interchangeably. Bigotry can be unrelated to institutionalized inequality and is largely attitudinal and individualized. Racism, on the other hand, emanates from entities such as the state, private industry, violent mobs, or voluntary associations. When individuals act in ways characterized as racist, not only are they utilizing power, they are also either acting as representatives of these powerful entities, whether tacitly or directly, and usually reinforcing the status quo.

Racism is popularly conceived of as a form of hate. The existence of "hate groups" in the United States, Europe, and elsewhere is one impetus for this type of characterization. While the proliferation of hate group ideology, through print media, the Internet, and other forms of mass communication, as well as the violence associated with racial supremacist groups, are forceful examples of racism, the expression of hatred is not a component to all aspects of racial inequality. For instance, when members of an "inferior" or devalued racial group pay more for goods and services because of where they live, they are discriminated against by industries that control the distribution of resources. This is an example of racism that has more to do with economic exploitation than hatred.

Racism has several other characteristics. It can be open and visible or it can be internalized to such an extent that it becomes almost invisible. This alleged disappearing of racism often occurs in societies where overtly racist behavior has fallen into public disfavor. Racism can also be obscured by other types of unequal power relations. The presence of sexism or class inequality in societies, for example, can beg the question: Are populations being discriminated against because of their race, gender, or socioeconomic status? In those instances where racism has seemingly become invisible, either because it has gone underground or because it has intermingled with other types of oppression, the perpetrators of racial inequality may no longer recognize their behavior as racist and, as a result, deny any such accusations. Where the racial domination of "inferiors" is openly discussed and displayed, racists may embrace such a label.

Race as a Social Construct That Fuels Racism

Despite the documented force of racism's ability to influence human thought and behavior, many social and natural scientists agree that race is not a verifiable, biological category (Lewontin 1987). Evolutionary science has helped us to understand that differences in human phenotype or appearance based on skin color, hair texture, and the shape of facial features are linked to Darwin's theory of natural selection and adaptation to particular conditions in various natural environments.

It is because of this discrepancy that scholars from the fields of anthropology, history, sociology, and others disciplines use to phrase "the social construction of race" to refer to the political, economic, and historical process through which racial categories have emerged over time and achieved their level of importance. Many observers of human behavior and history argue that the societal implications of the physical differences between people are of real import and not the differences in and of themselves. Those phenotypic differences particularly salient in the categorization of humans into racial groups include skin color, hair texture, and the size and shape of the body and facial features.

The discrimination of the English against the Irish people and the Nazi Holocaust support the assertion that race is a social construct and not a biological category. Germans, Irish, English, and European Jews generally share phenotypic and other characteristics, including European ancestry and a dearth of melanin. These examples often prompt people to ask, what does racism have to do with these human conflicts? Like the violent conflicts in the former Yugoslavia or in Rwanda, some observers are more likely to label these ethnic and not racial conflicts.

Regardless of any shared aspects of appearance, all the groups dominated by the Nazis were thought of as biologically inferior to the non-Jewish Germans, or Aryans. In the case of Hitler's Germany, the Nazis tortured and killed millions of women, men, and children and their armies appropriated the wealth of its victims. The role of power is apparent in the forcible removal of people from their homes, exploitation of their labor, control over their movement and social relations, and the perpetuation of physical harm or death at a moment's whim. The Nazis used ideology to convince the German people that Jews and other non-Aryans were subhuman.

Similarly, England colonized Ireland buttressed by the ideology that members of the Irish race were "lazy, naturally given to idleness, and unwilling to work for their own bread" (Takaki 1993). Ironically, similar things were said about peoples of African descent in the Unites States during their enslavement. Both cases show that racism is often replete with contradictions because although both groups were pejoratively characterized as lazy, the Irish and the Africans engaged in demanding, unremunerated labor that generated tremendous profits for the dominant group. Although the Irish were still not thought of as white upon arrival to the United States, they became absorbed into the white race by joining forces with proslavery elements to reinforce the domination of enslaved African Americans (Ignatiev 1995).

The State as a Political Purveyor of Racism

Across time and space there are many examples of states instituting racial domination. The indigenous peoples of the Americas have been the victims of a centuries-long holocaust perpetrated by the governments of Europe and the United States. This period endured long enough to see European monarchs come and go, and the advent of capitalism and the industrial revolution. In North, Central, and South America, as well as the Caribbean, the racism has taken the form of land removal, massacres, enslavement, the sexual exploitation of women, and the appropriation of indigenous skills and culture. Genocide has eliminated the great majority of Native Americans, in some instances exterminating entire ethnic groups and causing severe sociocultural dislocation for those that remain. Here, racism led the way for European settlement and the appropriation of the natural resources in the Americas. These are among the factors that have fueled the emergence of Europe and the United States as world powers.

The transatlantic trade in captured Africans is another example of both racial inequality emanating from the state and the economic rewards that can be reaped by racism. The Nazi Holocaust against European Jews, Poles, Gypsies, and other groups is another such example. Chinese immigrants to the United States were also the victims of state racism. When Chinese immigrants first migrated to the west coast of the United States, they were looked at as being very different and strange (Takaki 1993). If the story ended there, we would be discussing the confrontation of Chinese immigrants with bigotry. However, the very course of the lives of these immigrants was determined by how they were categorized and the racism they encountered upon arrival. Laws were passed that prevented the Chinese from becoming citizens or bringing their families to the United States (Zinn 1980).

The power of the state, whether it relates to control over armed forces, natural resources, mass media, or legislative prerogatives, has facilitated these forms of racial domination. Specific forms of state-sponsored racism include harsher sentencing, police brutality, and efforts to eliminate affirmative action in higher education for devalued racial groups and not the children of donors and alumni. These problems frequently target racial minorities; however, in some cases this type of domination occurs where the oppressed group is a member of the numerical majority, as under the apartheid system in South Africa.

Political racism, another way of labeling state-sponsored racism, can also be apparent in governmental approaches toward international diplomacy. The construction and implementation of trade, development, or military policies, for example, can also reflect the "racial esteem" in which states hold others. Countries held in low esteem could be the beneficiaries of unequal treatment from other, more powerful nations.

Private Industry as a Purveyor of Racism

Racist practices frequently occur in privately owned businesses and job discrimination is a common form of racism business owners engage in. Here, particular jobs are withheld from devalued races or racial groups are funneled into occupations deemed appropriate for "their kind." These practices implement a hierarchical economic structure in which its victims experience diminished income earning and wealth accumulation prospects.

In another example, banks can refuse to loan money to prospective lenders based on race. When this happens lending institutions prevent patrons from making purchases and funding educational opportunities. This type of discrimination can also deprive victims of business opportunities. All these practices can have huge ramifications for quality of life of those affected.

Real estate is another area of private industry that can engage in racist practices. One way this occurs is when members of the devalued racial group are prevented from purchasing property in areas in which they wish to live or own a business. Those discriminated against in this way may be forced into residential areas they find unsatisfactory or of less value. The availability of goods and services may also not be comparable in such areas. Racism in the real estate industry can impact the building of home equity, business opportunities, and quality of life.

Environmental racism is another form of racial inequality that comes from private industry. There are environmental injustices in the location of polluting plants within national borders or abroad. In the United States, for example, Native Americans, Latinos, African Americans, and indigenous Alaskans are disproportionately exposed to toxic contaminants in comparison with white Americans (Bullard 1997). These pollutants increase the incidence of deadly diseases and developmental retardation for exposed populations, particularly the young.

Denial of access to jobs, housing, bank loans, health care, insurance, and other goods, services, or resources severely affects quality of life and detrimentally affected the victims of racism. These forms of discrimination, working in tandem with the proliferation of stereotypical information from writers, publishers, radio broadcasters, illustrators, and the writers, producers, and directors of film and television and other mass media, can dehumanize targeted populations thereby smoothing the path to discrimination and exploitation.

Mob Violence as a Purveyor of Racism

Whereas bigotry may not be the same as racism, it can constitute the basis of it. This is apparent in the consideration of lynchings or pogroms. Mobs of people destroy property and kill or maim individuals from "inferior" groups. We see examples of this occurring across the globe and across time. Mobs have power in numbers and are often motivated and supported by ideologies emanating from the state or private industry. The idea that a group is inferior eases the path toward inflicting physical harm on men, women, or children from the devalued racial group. Thus, racism emanating from the state, private industry, nongovernmental organizations, or violent mobs often relate symbiotically.

Summary

Racism has been a destructive force in human history and is costly to all societies where it can be found. It not only takes a physical toll on its victims, it is also a detriment to their economic and psychological development. Psychosocial research has only begun to facilitate an understanding of how racial inequality causes stress and erodes hope. Stress has been linked to high blood pressure and other forms of ill health. The lack of hope can lead to self-destructive behaviors rooted in low self-esteem and lack of confidence for those who have internalized notions of their own inferiority.

Power is the most important aspect of racism. Whether emanating from the state, private industry, a violent mob, or voluntary association such as the Ku Klux Klan, racism differs from bigotry based on its institutionalized characteristics. It is not important whether racist acts are intentional or unintentional.

Racism is usually associated with ideologies of superiority and inferiority, although these notions may be unspoken or unacknowledged in numerous instances. The existence of racial inequalities may also have little to do with racial hatred or the openly expressed devaluation of a particular group. Racist practices are rooted in fear, hate, or the desire to economically exploit another population. Some racists may be direct while others act instinctively and, as a result, remain unconscious of their racist behavior.

SABIYHA ROBIN PRINCE

See also **Germany; Ireland; Race**

Further Reading

Back, Les, and John Solomos, *Theories of Race and Racism*, New York and London: Routledge Press, 2000
Bullard, Robert, editor, *Unequal Protection: Environmental Justice and Communities of Color*, Sierra Club Books, 1997
———, and Beverly Wright, *Confronting Environmental Racism: Voices from the Grassroots*, South End Press, 1993
Gossett, Race, *The History of an Idea in America*, New York: Shocken Books, 1963
Gregory, Steven, and Roger Sanjek, editors, *Race*, New Brunswick, New Jersey: Rutgers University Press, 1994
Ignatiev, Noel, *How the Irish Became White*, London and New York: Routledge, 1995
Lewontin, Richard, "Are the Races Different?" in *Anti-Racist Science Teaching*, edited by Dawn Gill and Les Levidow, London: Free Association Books, 1987
Marable, Manning, and Leith Mullings, editors, *Let Nobody Turn Us Around*, Lanham, Maryland: Rowan & Littlefield Publishers, 2000
Takaki, Ronald, *A Different Mirror: A History of Multicultural America*, Boston: Little, Brown & Co., 1993
Zinn, Howard, *A People's History of the United States*, New York: Harper Collins, 1980

Rajasthanis

Capsule Summary

Location: Rajasthan State, India
Total Population: approximately 56 million
Language: Rajasthani
Religion: mostly Hindu

Rajasthanis are the indigenous people of Rajasthan, an ethnically distinct region located in northwestern India, bordering Gujarat on the southwest, Madhya Pradesh on the southeast, Uttar Pradesh and Haryana on the northwest, Punjab on the north, and Pakistan on the west. Rajasthan consists of the sandy plains and small rocky hills of the Thar Desert in the northwest and the parched agricultural fields and grazing grounds in the semi-arid southeast. It is divided diagonally, from northeast to southwest, by the Aravalli

Hills. Rajasthanis speak one of four dialects of the Rajasthani language: Marwari (in western Rajasthan), Jaipuri or Dhundhari (in the east and southeast), Malvi (in the southeast), and Mewati (in the Alwar area), which merges into Braj Bhasa (in the Bharatpur area). Most Rajasthanis are Hindus, although there are also sizable communities of Muslims and Jains in the region.

Rajasthani History

During the period of British rule, the cluster of princely states and chiefships in this region was referred to as Rajputana, meaning "Land of the Rajputs." The dominant princely state in Rajputana was Jodhpur, located in the region of Marwar, meaning "Land of Death," a tract of sterile land covered with high sand hills and forming part of the Thar Desert. Another leading princely state was Udaipur, located in the region of Mewar, consisting of part rugged hills and part rocky plains. Other important princely states in the area included Bikaner, Marwar, Jaipur, Jaisalmer, Alwar, Dungarpur, and Dholpur, each ruled by a different princely ruler.

Rajput princes, members of the warrior-ruler caste known as Kshatriyas, gained power in the region between the seventh and thirteenth centuries and rose to ascendancy in the early sixteenth century. After key victories by the Mughul ruler Akbar in the third quarter of the sixteenth century, the Rajput princes accepted Mughul overlordship, lasting until the collapse of the Mughal Empire in the early eighteenth century. The realms then became subject to raids and assaults from Maratha chiefs. In 1818, the Rajput princes gained protection from the British Government by signing treaties that allowed the princes to retain authority over the social and economic concerns of their territories while granting colonial authorities control over foreign affairs and defense. These Rajput rulers continued to legitimize their rulerships in the princely states through caste position, clan membership, land possession, and chivalric reputation.

After India gained independence from colonial rule in 1947, these princely states and chiefships were integrated into the Indian Union in stages. The portion of Rajputana that became the state of Rajasthan consisted of 19 princely states, 2 chiefships, a small province of Ajmer-Merwara administered by the British, and several pockets of territory outside of the main boundaries of these areas. Rajasthan took its current form on November 1, 1956, with the redistribution of state borders through the States Reorganization Act. The princely rulers lost their right to titles and government-sponsored privileges in 1972. They have, however, continued to celebrate their ancestry and heritage through the formation of foundations and collectives.

Society and Culture

The Rajasthanis constitute a heterogeneous group of castes, classes, and tribes. Rajasthani society is dominated by the caste system, with Rajputs occupying the uppermost position in hierarchies of power and prestige. The word "Rajput" literally means "son (*putra*) of a king (*raja*)." Rajputs, considered a military aristocracy, are characteristically proud of their ancestry and heritage. As Lindsey Harlan (1992) describes, Rajputs in contemporary India identify themselves according to three traditional classes of their community. Royal Rajputs are direct descendents of the heads of state who once ruled independent kingdoms. Noble Rajputs are the descendents of privileged noblemen called *thakurs,* who provided military and administrative service to the royalty. Common Rajputs are the poor and powerless members of the community who, although related by blood to more aristocratic Rajputs, have taken up farming and village life. As a community, Rajputs continue to celebrate their ancestry and heritage, performing elaborate rituals on the occasions of weddings and funerals as expressions of their community identity.

The Marwaris are a merchant class of businessmen from Marwar, Mewar, and other parts of Rajasthan. Over centuries, members of this merchant class have emigrated outside of the state in large numbers, to the extent that the term *Marwari* is used colloquially to refer to any entrepreneurs, industrialists, and financiers hailing from the state of Rajasthan. Even in diaspora, they maintain strong kinship ties within their community.

The Jats, also called the Choudhary, occupy a prominent place in Rajasthani society. Traditionally known as elite landowners, in recent decades these agriculturalists have branched into professions such as military, police, and government civil service. The Gujars are cultivators, cattle breeders, and herdsmen living in the tract in the north of the Aravalli Hills, from Bikaner to Bharatpur and Jaipur regions.

Rajasthan is also home to many different tribal groups, with distinctive patterns of culture and tradition. The Bhils, one of the largest and most widely distributed tribal groups in India, live in the hilly southwest, around Banswara, Chittaurgarh, and Dungarpur. The Minas (Mewatis), Meos, Banjaras, and Gadia Lohars inhabit the northeastern districts of Alwar, Jaipur, Bharatpur, and Dholpur. The Grasias and Kathodis live in the Mewar region, the Sahariyas live in a small section of the Kota district, and the Rabari cattle-breeders live in the Marwar region.

Hinduism is the primary religion of Rajasthanis, particularly among members of the ruling class, although Islam expanded significantly in the region through Muslim conquests and invasions beginning in the late twelfth century. Jainism is particularly strong among members of the elite landowning and trading castes, with exquisite temples at Mt. Abu, Jaipur, Chittaurgarh, and Jaisalmer, and important pilgrimage sites at Ranakpur, Delwara, Mahavirji, and Nakodaji. There are small populations of Christians and Sikhs in the state.

HALEY DUSCHINSKI

See also **Gujaratis; India; Sikhs**

Further Reading

Balzani, Marzia, *Modern Indian Kingship: Tradition, Legitimacy, and Power in Rajasthan*, Santa Fe, New Mexico: School of American Research Press, 2003

Gold, Ann Grodzins, *Fruitful Journeys: The Ways of Rajasthani Pilgrims*, Berkeley: University of California Press, 1990

Gold, Ann Grodzins, and Bhoju Ram Gujar, *In Times of Trees and Sorrows: Nature, Power, and Memory in Rajasthan*, Durham, North Carolina: Duke University Press, 2002

Harlan, Lindsey, *Religion and Rajput Women: The Ethic of Protection in Contemporary Narratives*, Berkeley: University of California Press, 1992

Kasturi, Malavika, *Embattled Identities: Rajput Lineages and the Colonial State in Nineteenth-Century North India*, Oxford: Oxford University Press, 2002

Rudolph, Susanna Hoeber, and Lloyd I. Rudolph, "Rajputana under British Paramountcy," *Journal of Modern History*, 38, no. 2 (1966)

Unnithan-Kumar, Maya, *Identity, Gender and Poverty: New Perspectives on Caste and Tribe in Rajasthan*, Providence, Rhode Island: Berghahn Books, 1998

Vidal, Denis, *Violence and Truth: A Rajasthani Kingdom Confronts Colonial Authority*, Oxford: Oxford University Press, 1997

Ramos-Horta, José (East Timor)

Until 1975 East Timor was an eastern Asian outpost of the Portuguese empire. It occupied the eastern half of the island of Timor, Portugal having settled the area five centuries before. Surrounded by the Moslem-dominated islands of Indonesia, East Timor evolved as a Catholic country. The Teturn were the main ethnic group, interbreeding with the Portuguese. The name for all East Timorese ethnic groups as a whole was Maubere. In most recent times, the East Timorese have come primarily to speak Teturn, the principal local tongue mixed with Portuguese vocabulary. They have rejected any Indonesian language or Portuguese per se.

As the Portuguese empire disintegrated in the early 1970s, Indonesia resolved to occupy East Timor. It conducted a brutal invasion of the area in 1975, murdering tens of thousands of the inhabitants, subordinating the area to military rule, and settling Indonesian civilians in it. That the East Timorese would ever free themselves from this brutal occupation seemed virtu-

ally hopeless. However, a handful of their leaders resolved to reverse this desperate situation.

Key among these figures was the journalist and diplomat, Jose Ramos-Horta (surname may also appear without hyphen, as Ramos Horta). Displaying tireless self-sacrifice and living most of his life in exile, he worked with steadfast pacifism to free his country first from the Portuguese and then from the Indonesians. In 1999, his objective was almost miraculously achieved when Indonesia finally withdrew. For his nonviolent pursuit of this goal, in 1996 he received the Nobel Peace Prize, together with the East Timor Catholic bishop, the Rev. Carlos Felipe Belo. The award gave international sanction and support for East Timorese independence.

On returning from exile to East Timor, Ramos-Horta argued that East Timor should win independence through peaceful means. Others opposed him, maintaining that independence could only be achieved through armed resistance. They operated a guerilla movement within East Timor. He, however, remained committed to the idea of resolving international problems through peaceful, diplomatic means.

Increasingly Ramos-Horta noted the need of minorities and disadvantaged peoples to know more about diplomacy and peaceful international conflict resolution. He left his United Nations (UN) post in 1985, becoming special representative abroad of the Conselho Nacional da Resistencia Maubere (NCRM, National Council of Maubere Resistence). This council consolidated all political forces and currents in East Timor, including the armed resistance movement, headed by Xananá Gusmão (Sha-nah-NAH Goos-MOWHN). The council maintained, however, that an independent Republic of East Timor would not keep a standing army.

In 1989, Ramos-Horta established a diplomacy training program for minorities at the University of New South Wales, and moved to Sydney, Australia. A close neighbor of East Timor and a developed country with a western culture, Australia came to be of key international support for him. His tireless efforts for human rights and the peaceful resolution of international problems began to bring him increasing international recognition and support.

The breakup of the dictatorial regime of Gen. Suharto in Indonesia allowed the East Timorese to vote in a 1999 referendum for separation from Indonesia. Withdrawing Indonesian troops ransacked, raped, and killed their way out of East Timor. The new country was desperately poor. Because of its impoverished condition, it obtained temporary UN administration, and survived economically from international donations. Returning to East Timor, Ramos-Horta became Foreign Minister in the UN executive cabinet. At the end of 2001, the East Timorese voted for a constituent assembly to prepare the country for full independence.

Capsule Biography

Jose Ramos-Horta was born in Dili, the capital of East Timor, on December 26, 1947. Both his Portuguese grandfather and father were exiled by Portugal for political reasons. His father arrived in East Timor in 1936, marrying a local woman. They had 11 children, four of whom died resisting the Indonesian invasion. Ramos-Horta's primary school education occurred at the Catholic mission school in Soibada. He returned to Dili for his secondary education, completing it at the Liceu Dr. Machado. From 1969 to 1974, he pursued a career as a journalist, expressing opposition to Portuguese colonial rule and any Indonesian intervention. He was exiled in 1970 to Mozambique, in southeast Africa, then also a Portuguese colony. He married a Mozambique judge, and they had one son, born in 1977. His awards include an honorary doctorate from Antioch and also one from a Catholic university in Brazil. A college of Oxford University made him a Fellow. In 1993 he received the Norwegian Thorolf Rafto Human Rights Award. In 1996 he received a Dutch award for his work for unrepresented nations and peoples, the Portuguese Order of Freedom, and, finally, the Nobel Peace Prize. With the Nobel Prize, the relentless efforts of Ramos-Horta obtained international resonance.

Selected Works

Funu: The Unfinished Saga of East Timor, 1987

EDWARD A. RIEDINGER

See also **East Timor**

Further Reading

Dunn, James, *Timor: A People Betrayed*, Milton, Queensland: Jacaranda Press, 1983

Hainsworth, Paul, and Stephen McCloskey, editors, *The East Timor Question: The Struggle for Independence from Indonesia*, London: I. B. Tauris, 2000

Nobel Peace Prize, 1996. http://www.nobel.se/peace/laureates/1996/index.html *Towards a Peaceful Solution in East Timor*, Sydney: East Timor Relief Association, 1996

Rasha'ida

Capsule Summary

Location: Eritrea, Sudan
Total Population: approximately 60,000
Language: Arabic
Religion: Islam

Little is known about the society and way of life of the Rasha'ida, who are found in the Eritrean-Sudanese border area. They descend from Arab nomadic pastoralists who crossed over from what is now Saudi Arabia, probably for political reasons, and moved to the coastal areas south of the Sudanese port city of Suakin in the first half of the nineteenth century (the year usually cited is 1846). Later, in the time of the Mahdi disturbances in Sudan in the 1880s, they moved into northern Ethiopia up to Massawa (now in Eritrea). The Rasha'ida did not assimilate into other groups but successfully recreated their society and way of life as independent camel-herding pastoralists in the semi-arid zones of their new homeland. In Eritrea they are the only group who speak Arabic (in a Bedouin dialect) as their mother tongue, but few are literate. The Eritrean independence war from 1962 to 1991 led to a large number of Rasha'ida taking refuge in Sudan. During the armed conflict in the 1980s between the two Eritrean liberation movements, the predominantly Muslim Eritrean Liberation Front (ELF) and the highland Christian-dominated Eritrean People's Liberation Movement (EPLF), the Rasha'ida were on the side of the latter.

Rasha'ida social organization is strongly patrilineal. They are divided in three main clans: the Zinenu, the Baratiq, and the Barasa. One group, the Jahidin, settled as fishermen on some islands of the Dahlak Archipelago near the Eritrean coast, but appear to have returned to Arabia. Rasha'ida have preferential patrilateral cousin marriage, that is, a man marrying a daughter of one of his father's brothers. This results in marital unions largely within their own group (endogamy). Rasha'ida women veil the lower nose and mouth in all contacts with outsiders, and sometimes wear a silver-colored, mask-like face-cover, or *arusi*. A longer type mask, extending down to the waist, is called the *burga*. The women of the Rasha'ida are immediately recognizable by their richly embroidered and colorful gowns. The men usually wear white cotton robes and turbans. Rasha'ida women are also well-known for their production of the typical silver jewelry, which they sell mostly in the Kassala market.

Rasha'ida still are predominantly transhumant camel herders, moving between rainy-season and dry-season pastures. An average well-off Rasha'ida household may have from 40 to 60 camels. They breed racing camels for export to Saudi Arabia and the Gulf States, as well as a sturdy, smaller type of camel used for transport and milk production. This type is known for its tenacity in times of drought and its relatively high milk yield. Both types of camel are the result of long (cross-) breeding by Rasha'ida experts, who also have a great indigenous knowledge of camel diseases and their treatment. The Rasha'ida recognize family lines and seven-generation pedigrees of good racing camels. The surplus camel milk is made into butter (*zibde*) and ghee (*zamin*) or into boiled, coagulated sour milk (*madhur*), with a long storage time. Some other livestock, like sheep and goats, are also kept if environmental conditions allow. The second mainstay of the Rasha'ida diet, next to camel milk, is sorghum. In Sudan, Rasha'ida were employed in large-scale mechanized sorghum cultivation schemes. The sorghum fields provide additional, postharvest fodder (stalks) for the camels in the period of scarcity in April-May. In some areas Rasha'ida are cultivators only, while others are also involved in profitable trade.

When on the move, the Rasha'ida pastoralists live in cloth or goatskin tents, but they also have small villages with huts of wattle and daub. Small groups of Rasha'ida have moved to cities like Kassala, Gedaref, Asmara, and Massawa, where some have taken up trade or a variety of other occupations, for example, truck driver. Others, however, subsist on the margins and live in poverty. Rasha'ida are accustomed to and still maintain a high level of mobility. Trade and the camel export business frequently bring many of them to Saudi Arabia, where they have kinship links.

The Rasha'ida try to maintain their social cohesion and close-knit society, but herding life both in Sudan and in Eritrea is made increasingly difficult because of climatic and other problems, for example, tensions with their Beja neighbors. Although camel husbandry does no notable ecological damage and is sustainable in the long run, the Eritrean government is stimulating the sedentarization of Rasha'ida in the Semhar region, intending to provide primary education, health care, and so on, as well as improve tax collection among them. In the past two decades, few studies were made on Rasha'ida society, but in Sudan as well as in Eritrea—where they are one of the nine recognized "nationalities"—they are tiny minority groups with a precarious position.

JON ABBINK

See also **Eritrea; Sudan**

Further Reading

Köhler-Rollefson, I., B. Musa, and M. Fadl, "The Camel Pastoral System of the Southern Rashaida in Eastern Sudan," *Nomadic Peoples*, 29 (1991)

Rastafari

Location: Caribbean, Europe, and United States, primarily, with smaller presence elsewhere
Total Population: approximately 2 million worldwide; an estimated 60 percent of Jamaicans identify themselves as Rastafarians
Language: Jamaican-English patois
Religion: Rastafarian

Rastafari are followers of Rastafarianism, a religious movement that emerged from Jamaica in the 1930s. Originally an early twentieth century cult where followers gathered at meeting places in expectation that ships would arrive to take them to Africa, in the 1970s and 1980s, Rastafari eventually developed into a global movement, with devotees from African-descended people everywhere. White people, Asians, and Arabs comprise minorities within the movement.

The fundamental tenets of Rastafarianism state that Haile Selassie (Ras Tafari), the late emperor of Ethiopia, is God (a living messiah) and that he will arrange for all black people from throughout the African diaspora to return to their ancestral homeland, Africa. They believe that they (and the black race, in general) descended from the ancient king of Israel, David. The particular interpretation of these beliefs differs widely, and each Rasta, or "Rastaman" as followers are called, regardless of gender, assimilates and applies his or her own personal interpretation. Beyond the multifarious versions of doctrine, however, there is an underlying political impulse that unifies all followers. The belief that white imperial rule continues to enslave people of African origin or descent, not in a physical sense,

translates to what Rastas term a kind of "mental slavery." Rastafari understand themselves to be involved constantly in a struggle against Babylon (as white postcolonial rule, in every manifestation, is called) and, for many, only the restoration of an independent unified Africa will bring an end to their exile.

History

The Rastafari first appeared in Jamaica in 1930, shortly after the demise of Marcus Garvey's Universal Negro Improvement Association, which was organized around the ambition to take black people to settle in Africa. Garvey's slogan was "Africa for the Africans," and he campaigned in the Caribbean and North America, buying steamship lines and organizing migration programs for his members (who, at one point, may have exceeded 1 million). Although Garvey's mission went unfulfilled, the myth surrounding him became appreciably bigger than the man himself.

Word circulated in Jamaica that Garvey had prophesied "Look to Africa when a black king shall be crowned, for the day of deliverance is near." Although Garvey may have made this statement, it is almost certain that he did not intend it to refer to the rise of Prince Ras Tafari, who, in 1930, became emperor of Ethiopia and took the official title of Haile Selassie I. Garvey had by then slipped from prominence—his most active period was in the early 1920s—although his words were granted new meaning when several Jamaican Garveyites (as his acolytes were known) proclaimed that Haile Selassie was the black king of whom Garvey spoke and that the "day of deliverance" meant the exodus to Africa.

Although Garvey had criticized Haile Selassie's political rule of his people and deplored his capitulation after Italy's invasion of Ethiopia in 1935, during his most influential period, Garvey had made Biblical allusions, often citing the Book of Revelation as a foretelling of the destiny of black people. He also used "Ethiopia" synonymously with his vision of an arcadian "Africa," a continent freed of European colonial interference.

Garvey wrote in volume one of his *Philosophy and Opinions* that the "Negroes believe in the God of Ethiopia, the everlasting God." His conception of a black God was also significant; he implored his followers to destroy images of white Christs and Madonnas and replace them with black versions.

Garvey warned his followers that "No one knows when the hour of Africa's redemption cometh, It is in the wind, It is coming. One day, like a storm, it will be here." But he refused to endorse the messianic interpretation of his teachings, preferring the pragmatic tasks of building steamships bound for Africa. Revisionists insisted that Ras Tafari (Haile Selassie) was king, God, and redeemer and would soon arrange for a miraculous transportation of black people to Ethiopia. Rastafari congregated at ports, waited at airfields, and organized their lives around the expectation that the millennium would, as they put it, soon come.

Today Rastafarianism is not a highly organized religion. Most Rastas do not identify with any sect or denomination, though there are two primary groups within the religion: the Bobos and the 12 Tribes of Israel. Rastafari emblems include the colors of red, black, and green, which were Garvey's colors, probably taken from those of the Ethiopian national flag. Dreadlocks are also cultivated. Photographs of Masai warriors that circulated among Rastas in the 1930s apparently inspired the long, twisted coils of hair that became the most dramatic visual symbol of Rastafari. Rastas also make liturgical use of *ganja*, a form of marijuana that grows freely in the Caribbean. They smoke the drug as a sacramental rite during the often-elaborate ceremonies that were introduced, originally to induce the apocalypse; this practice continues to the present day, one of the most important rituals being the *Nyabinghi*. (Nyabinghi refers to island-wide religious gatherings of Rastas where communicants "praise Jah" and "chant down Babylon.") Rastas still view *ganja* as imbued with sacred properties.

Haile Selassie was revered as Jah (the form of "Jehovah" used in Bibles prior to the King James version, which Rastas reject as a European corruption), and his image adorned various kinds of artwork in prints, posters, and so on. The emperor's 1966 visit to Jamaica was a tumultuous affair, with Rastas gathering expectantly to greet him. Haile Selassie refused to acknowledge the status he commanded with Rastas, although he never denied that he was the "God of Ethiopia" to whom Garvey alluded. He also invited a party of Rastafari to Ethiopia to discuss a settlement. After the visit of a congregation, a small Rastafarian settlement was established in Ethiopia.

Globalization

The expansion of Rastafari from a Caribbean cult to a global movement began in the 1970s and its catalyst was the late Bob Marley, the reggae musician whose albums bore titles such as *Rastaman Vibration* (1976) and *Exodus* (1977). Marley not only used his music to spread the postulates of the Rastafari, he also, perhaps unwittingly, made the Rastafarian image fashionable. A commanding figure with a mane of locks and stunning stage presence, Marley became internationally renowned as both a musician and a performer. His fame triggered an intense public interest in his beliefs, and during the mid-1970s, young black people in the major cities of England and the United States began assuming that this was the discursive process by which Rastafarian worldviews were discussed and disseminated. Marley's personality and music provided a crucial (if not wholly accurate) mechanism through which the Rastafari movement grew.

Rastafari blended unwittingly with the spirit of rebellion that stirred British cities in the early 1980s, and the political critique of Babylon struck a chord with black youths who singled out the police as their principal oppressors. The police came to signify Babylon in the eyes of Rastas.

Haile Selassie's death in 1975 did little to sway or diminish the movement. Rastafari either refused to believe what they called the "lies of Babylon" or they insisted that their deity had assumed a spiritual form. The movement's growth slowed in the late 1980s, and its impact is now regarded with historical, rather than contemporary, interest. Although the Rastafarian philosophy may be seen as exotic, the critical interpretation of colonialism in its subtext was a potent device in sharpening awareness of the global condition of black people as well as their shared history. Rastafarians still face some discrimination, but they achieved a major victory by being granted consultative status at the United Nations in 1996.

ELLIS CASHMORE

See also **Garvey, Marcus (Jamaican); Jamaica; Selassie, Hailie (Ethiopian)**

Further Reading

Cashmore, Ernest Ellis, *The Rastafarians*, London: Minority Rights Group, 1984; updated edition, 1992

Chevannes, Barry, editor, *Rastafari and Other African-Caribbean Worldviews*, London: Macmillan, 1995; New Brunswick, New Jersey: Rutgers University Press, 1998
Garvey, Marcus, *Philosophy and Opinions*, 3 vols, edited by Amy Jacques Garvey, 1923; 1925; London: Frank Cass, 1967
Mulvaney, Rebekah Michele, *Rastafari and Reggae: A Dictionary and Sourcebook*, New York: Greenwood Press, 1990

Refugees

Although the problem of refugees did not begin in twentieth century, it certainly became for the first time an issue of international concern. The first twentieth century refugee movements saw displaced Armenians flee Turkish genocide, cross border movement between ethnic Turks and Greeks in the 1920s, and Russians fleeing the revolution of 1917. The latter resulted in the first international effort to establish the legal status of refugees. Under the auspices of the League of Nations, Dr. Fridtjof Nansen, the first High Commissioner for Refugees, developed the first international identity paper known as the Nansen Passport, which gave refugees of specific categories possession of legal and juridical status under the High Commissioner, who acted for them in a quasi-consular capacity. Although legal status is of great importance to refugees, there are also many other requirements that a refugee has, including the basic needs of food and shelter and, later, the need for developmental aid of social and material assistance to which he or she is legally entitled as part of their guarantee of human rights.

Definition

The most problematic part of any discussion of refugees is actually defining the refugee in terms of international law and eligibility for assistance. No single consensus definition employed by all nations or international instruments exists. The most widespread accepted one is the United Nations 1951 Convention and 1967 Protocol relating to the status of refugees. According to the 1951 Convention, a person is a refugee:

> [a]s a result of events occurring before 1 January 1951 and owing to well-founded fear of being persecuted for reasons of race, religion, nationality, membership of a particulars social group or political opinion, is outside the country of his nationality and is unable or, owing to such fear, is unwilling to avail himself of the protection of that country; or who, not having a nationality and being outside the country of his former habitual residence as a result of such events, is unable or, owing to such fear, is unwilling to return to it.

Because many refugees in the Cold War period were produced after the cutoff date, the 1967 protocol removes the clause "before 1 January 1951" to be more inclusive.

Nonetheless, in many cases, it becomes difficult to distinguish between refugees and migrants. Technically, refugees flee to save their lives, while migrants seek to improve their economic prospects. This distinction becomes quite tenuous when citizens flee countries where poverty and violence are direct consequences of the political system. The key difference remains persecution: a deliberate act of the government against individuals. Therefore, victims of general insecurity, oppression, or systematic economic deprivation find themselves excluded. From the perspective of international law, the main characteristics of a refugee are that they are outside of the home country and do not have the protection of their country of origin.

While the United Nations High Commissioner for Refugee (UNHCR) is charged with making this determination, the 1951 Convention and 1967 Protocol are not the only tools through which the UNHCR can aid displaced persons. The UNHCR can also extend his "Good Offices" to virtually any group. It has been on that basis that the UNHCR granted assistance to new refugees in Africa and Asia. This development took place to permit the High Commissioner to aid groups who did not clearly come within the statute's definition or for whom the HC did not want to make a statute eligibility determination.

Perhaps the most progressive international instrument was produced by the Organization of African Unity (OAU), which broadened the definition of a refugee in 1969. Not only were those who had a "well founded fear of persecution" included, but also persons who, "owing to external aggression, occupation, foreign domination or events seriously disturbing public order in either part or the whole of his country of origin or nationality, is compelled to leave his place of habitual residence in order to seek refuge in another place outside his country of origin or nationality." Most nations, at least in Africa and Asia, follow this definition, albeit informally.

Causes

The predominant cause of refugee displacement has traditionally been warfare. This proved especially true during the Cold War, as foreign intervention extended the length of a conflict and subsequently the time and characteristics of refugee flows. Refugees also flee military coups, massive human rights violations, political instability, and lack of government protection in their countries. Frequently, however, refugee movements are triggered by governments as a move to reduce or even eliminate targeted classes or ethnicities within a nation's borders or even to affect the political climate of neighboring countries. Increasingly, these displaced persons do not fall within the definitions of the 1951 Convention and the 1967 Protocol. These nonconvention refugees represent larger problems for the international community than Convention refugees because they have little legal standing in terms of international law. In the last few decades, most of the world's refugees and displaced people centered in the poorest parts of the world in Africa and Asia and have moved from one third world country to another: Sudanese, Somalis, and Ethiopians, Uganda, Kenya, and Yemen; Mozambicans to Malawi; Liberians in West Africa; and Burmese in Bangladesh. Though many of these refugees are often pawns or victims in relations between states, that is not to say they are always passive political actors. Some consider themselves freedom fighters attempting to recapture their homeland, destabilize the current regime, or form a separate nation, as has been the case for Cubans and Eritreans.

Reception

Refugees frequently receive a mixed welcome in their host nations. Some, like Rwandan Tutsi and other African refugees, are cultural and economic minorities who can assimilate into and find safety among related groups in neighboring countries. Despite this cultural affinity, many governments grow unwilling to admit refugees whose presence, in turn, threatens to disrupt the existing order of racial, religious, and ethnic balance as well as potentially diminish national security. Therefore, the host or potential host nation to the refugees has limits. Even without the potential for increased tension, limits to a country's capacity for reception still exist. This capacity is based upon the performance of its economy and ability to absorb displaced populations into its workforce, the host population's adaptability to multicultural change, and the confidence of governments in the ability of the new arrivals to adjust to life in their new country (especially in the case of European governments).

Many nations throughout the twentieth century made the assumption that international action for refugees need only be temporary. Refugees would, in time, either be repatriated to their home county or assimilated and eventually naturalized by the host nation. The former of the two potential results initiated significant debate in the immediate post–World War II period, until the United Nations agreed that repatriation must take place on a voluntary basis. Article 33 of the 1951 Convention spelled out the principle of nonrefoulement or the prohibition of expulsion:

> No contracting state shall expel or return ("refouler") a refugee in any manner whatsoever to the frontiers of territories where his life or freedom would be threatened on account of the race, religion, nationality, membership of a particular social group or political opinion.

Unable to expel unwanted, but already admitted refugees, governments then take steps to prevent further increases in population. This is usually accomplished by denying entrance to refugees (even if the nation is a member of the convention) by labeling all unwanted migrants as economic refugees without the legal protections afforded by the UN instrument.

Many governments have welcomed refugees deemed potential economic assets. Most notably during the Cold War, where among European refugees were people with valuable technical skills who could be put to work immediately and Western European nations desired the additional manpower for reconstruction and repopulation. Cold War refugees were also used as political statements. For the United States, the majority of refugees entering the country came from communist countries "voting with their feet" against communism and embracing Western society. In the post–Cold War period, though, that has usually not been the case.

UNHCR and Other Agencies

The twentieth century saw many agencies, official and voluntary, seek to aid the plight of refugees. None have been more important or instrumental than the United Nations High Commission for Refugees (UNHCR). From its founding in 1949, the UNHCR grew from a nonoperational agency to one with programs in housing, vocational and professional training, resettlement, and integration. The UNHCR also performs a variety of activities with governments or voluntary agencies such as certifying the eligibility of refugees, intervention on behalf of individuals for whom recognition, asylum, or nonrefoulement is concerned, providing some material assistance, and citing and condemning violations of human rights and international law. The UNHCR, though, has no power to compel nations to provide refugees with even minimal standards of treatment, which reduces the High Commissioner's tools to moral persuasion and diplomatic pressure. Fortunately, the UNHCR does not act alone. UNHCR is aided greatly by voluntary agencies such as the Red Cross, World Council of Churches, International YMCA/YWCA, and Doctors Without Borders, to name a few, who aid displaced persons and provide assistance to all refugees including those who do not fall under the mandate of official international bodies.

Continued Problems

Refugees remain an international concern of great proportions. While governments and voluntary agencies continue to seek better solutions to aid refugees, global and regional circumstances continue to create more displaced persons. By the end of the 1990s, the number of refugees had risen to the 20 million mark. These refugees have much the same needs as those at the beginning of the twentieth century: asylum, immediate aid, developmental aid, and legal protection.

Worldwide, the annual cost of refugee aid programs only amounts to US$7 billion, only a fraction of what is needed and a net reduction in spending per refugee over the last 20 years. In 1980 the UNHCR spent approximately $60 for each refugee under its care and protection. This figure had fallen to $38 per refugee by 1990. A Third World refugee then received around five cents a day during the last decade. This sum covers a host of necessities such as food, water, shelter, transport, logistical support, and medium- to long-term development assistance. Significantly, aid packages face substantial barriers in making these meager funds available to those who need the help the most. In civil war conditions, especially on the African continent, it can be virtually impossible for aid to reach refugees. Once there, problems still exist as humanitarian agencies can be subjected to harassment, co-opted by rebel groups, or expelled by unfriendly governments or opposition groups.

Whether in a resettlement camp or outside the auspices of the UNHCR or other international aid agencies, the conditions of refugees continue to be of concern and a major problem. Historian Judy Mayotte phrased it well in describing the perils of the refugees: "The vast majority of those who flee do not get into rickety boats and risk pirate attacks, or cross steep, snow-covered mountains, or willingly live under burlap, behind barbed-wire, or in 6 × 8 foot spaces stacked three high and twelve or more deep unless they are fleeing for their lives." In those camps, many languish for years. Indeed, the majority of today's refugees have lived in camps at least five years and in many cases for much longer. The inability of the international community to overcome the conditions of the refugee camps or provide an alternative is "one of the greatest failures of the international humanitarian and political systems."

More and more, governments throughout the world have become less tolerant of refugees and are closing their borders to them, feeling that there is no space for immigrants of any kind. As places of entry close to refugees, legal protection becomes paramount. Lacking legal status, which not only includes travel documents, but also education, employment, property, or access to courts, the most generous aid packages will not achieve satisfactory temporary measures, much less a permanent solution.

MICHAEL HOUF

See also **Tutsi; United Nations and Minorities**

Further Reading

Holborn, Louise, *Refugees: A Problem of Our Time*, Metuchen
New Jersey: The Scarecrow Press, 1975

Loescher, Gil, *Beyond Charity: International Cooperation and
the Global Refugee Crisis*, Oxford: Oxford University Press,
1993

Mayotte, Judy, *Disposable People? The Plight of Refugees*,
Maryknoll, New York: Orbis Books, 1992

Washington DC, *World Watch Papers*

Religion Versus Ethnicity

Religion and ethnicity are complex phenomena. The opposition "religion versus ethnicity" shows that these notions intersect with each other, influence each other but do not completely correlate. This opposition reflects several problems, that is, the correlation between ethnic and religious affiliation, the integrative and disintegrative role of religion in ethnic processes, the role of religion in ethnic conflicts, and the peacemaking process.

It is also crucial that the importance of ethnic or religious affiliation was different in various historic periods. In the Middle Ages religion played such a big role in the life of society that religious affiliation was more meaningful than ethnic one. It was more difficult to overcome religious borders than the ethnic ones. Thus, a deeper crevasse was between Muslim and Christian worlds, Eastern and Western Christianity, than between Catholicism and Protestantism. In later periods ethnic self-consciousness arose and in most cases became more significant for people. Although, even in modern history, religious identity sometimes is more strong. Thus, British India was partitioned into India (mainly Hindu) and Pakistan (Muslim) as independent states in 1947. A characteristic feature of the modern era is that many countries are getting more and more religiously heterogeneous. Simultaneously, religious tolerance (first of all, in the United States and European countries) is gradually replacing religious hostility. However, confrontation on religious grounds remains the cause (at least outwardly) of some contemporary ethnic conflicts (for example, in Sudan, Sri Lanka, Northern Ireland, etc.).

Correlation between Religion and Ethnicity at Present

In general, at present religious and ethnic affiliations do not tightly correlate with each other. Although

there are ethnic groups that are mainly monoreligious (Poles and Portuguese—Catholics, Greeks—Orthodox, Jews—adherents of Judaism, Persians—Shi'a Muslims, etc.), even among them religious homogeneity is not absolutely complete. More often it is possible to speak about a dominant religion of such-and-such people. In these cases one denomination prevails, but there are also more or less numerous religious minorities. For example, among Russians the overwhelming majority are Orthodox but there are different groups of "old believers," Baptists, Pentecostals, and others; the majority of Hungarians are Catholics, although a quarter of them are Reformed; the main denomination of English people is Anglicanism, but there are also Methodists, Catholics, Baptists, and others among them. Finally, there are multireligious peoples, like Germans (Lutherans, Catholics, Reformed, etc.) and, of course, Americans (Catholics, Baptists, Methodists, Pentecostals, Lutherans, Mormons, Presbyterians, Episcopalians, etc.). In addition, among many peoples (first of all, in Europe, America, and Communist countries of Asia) there are nonreligious and those indifferent to religion. On the other hand, most denominations have representatives of different ethnic groups among their adherents (for example, Roman Catholics are Italians, Poles, Spaniards, Brazilians, Mexicans, and many others; Orthodox are Russians, Romanians, Greeks, Serbs, Bulgarians, and others; Lutherans are Germans, Swedes, Finns, and others).

Religious Affiliation as a Factor of Ethnic Identity

Though there is no strict correlation between religion and ethnicity, ethnic and religious identities are often connected with each other, and religious affiliation may be a strong factor of ethnic identity. The studying of the role of the religious affiliation in ethnic identity can be based on the multidimensional approach to religion and the thesis that religiousness is a composite phenomenon. Using this framework it is obvious that along with others there is a cultural dimension of religion. Mainly through this dimension religion influences the ethnic identity of people. On the one hand, religious practice usually absorbs ethnic particularities of culture (this problem always faces religious organizations in their missionary activity, when they have to adapt to local cultures and conditions). But, on the contrary, religion itself influences ethnic culture, which is reflected in folklore, literature, architecture, and music. Some religious prescriptions determine specific features of the mode of life, labor ethics, moral norms, and so on. Religious faith can also reveal people's deepest sources of cultural values. It is also important that religious tradition is always conservative. It is the same during the centuries despite transformations of social systems and changes of political regimes. It makes religion a repository of common memory of nation or ethnic community or some other group. The ethnization of religion also means the increase of its popularity among the representatives of a certain ethnic group. That is why religious identification is often significant even for those who do not practice but associate themselves with some denomination just out of tradition. Sometimes, religion can play a role of a "marker" of ethnic identity. It is what is visible and what sets one group apart from another.

Integrative and Disintegrative Role of Religion in Ethnic Processes

The role of the religious factor in ethnic identity is the most obvious for ethnic minorities that differ from surrounding population in their religious affiliation. This religious "unlikeness" reinforces ethnic self-consciousness and often becomes the main component in ethnic identity. In such cases ethnic self-consciousness is focused on the religious affiliation. Religious affiliation helps such groups to prevent assimilation and remain a community. For example, in the 1990s it happened that the Lutheran Church became for the Ingrian Finns (a small ethnic group living mainly in northwest Russia) not only a religious organization but also a cultural center consolidating them. It was due to two main reasons. First, in the situation in which many Ingrian Finns were scattered throughout the country, the native language was forgotten by younger people, and many elements of the traditional culture were lost, the religious affiliation became the main marker differentiating them from the surrounding population. Second, the Church of Ingria has traditionally paid much attention to ethnic culture and has been an "ethnic church." The church has contributed to the rebirth of national feelings of Ingrian Finns, the strengthening of their identity, and the growth of interest in Finnish culture and language. The Ingrian Finns are very dedicated to their church. The degree of their religiosity is considerably higher than among Finns in Finland. Moreover, the feeling of belonging to the community leads even nonbelievers to the church, primarily during the great holidays. The church leaders see one of their most vital aims as preserving Ingrian Finns as a distinct ethnic group with its own history and culture. To promote this, the church often organizes courses in the Finnish language, folklore festivals, and so on. Now, adherence to the Evangelical Lutheran Church of Ingria is the basis of the ethnic identity of the Ingrian Finns. In Russia, for most, their religious affiliation is a more important indicator of their ethnic identity than knowledge of the Finnish language or Finnish rituals and traditions. Interestingly, after moving to Finland (the rate of emigration of Ingrian Finns is very high) they are not as religious as they were in Russia. Belonging to the Lutheran Church is no more a "marker" of their ethnic identity. They mostly need other things (such as better command of Finnish) to become "real" Finns and to integrate into the Finnish nation. This does not mean the transformation of religious convictions but rather has cultural grounds and can also prove that, in Russia, belonging to the Lutheran Church is a strong indicator of the ethnic identity of Ingrian Finns.

Common religious affiliation can integrate neighboring peoples and promote their common self-consciousness and cultural similarity. This is the case of Moro settled in Philippines. Moro is a common name for such ethnic communities, as Maguindanao, Iranun, Maranao, Yakan, Tausug, and Sama, which profess Islam (appeared there in the fourteenth century). They live on Mindanao and some neighboring small islands, speak related languages, and are very close in their traditional culture. They are aware of their closeness and oppose themselves as a single entity to all other Philippine peoples. Moro pursue war against the government of the Philippines and a claim for independence. A similar case is represented by Naga in northeast India. These are different ethnic groups (Sema, Lotha, Angami, Mao, Konyak, Ao, Tanghul, etc.), but common history and religious affiliation (they are Baptists) led to the formation of common self-consciousness. Now Naga are on the way to integrating into one ethnic community. There is also a low-level guerilla campaign for Naga independence.

The integrative role of religion is most important in crisis periods (war, occupation, etc.). The history of many people (Greeks, Bulgarians, Armenians, and others) who underwent foreign control testifies that the preservation of traditional religion prevents ethnic assimilation and helps to retain state independence.

Religion can also play a disintegrative role in ethnic processes. For example, a religious factor was rather significant in the formation of Serbs and Montenegrins (Orthodox), Croats (Roman Catholics), and Bosnians (Muslims) from the Serbo-Croatian linguistic and cultural community. Religious diversity split the Punjabi linguistic community. Muslim Punjabis, Sikh Punjabis, and Hindu Punjabis tend to retain separate ethnicity, moreover, rather than have complicated relations with each other. Religious affiliation (along with belonging to the different states) led to the separation of Hindu Bengalis (settled in India) and Muslim Bengalis (settled in Bangladesh).

When some small group differs with its religious affiliation from the rest of the population speaking the same language, it can also lead to the formation of a separate group with its own ethnic self-consciousness. This is the case with Kriashens. The word *Kriashens* is a corrupted form of Russian *kreshchenye,* which means "baptized." Kriashens are mainly the descendants of the Tatar-speaking group baptized in the sixteenth century under Ivan the Terrible. They were converted to Orthodoxy either from Islam or from paganism. At first Kriashens's self-consciousness was only religious. But in the late nineteenth century an idea arose that the Kriashens were a separate ethnic group, although in that period they were usually known as "Baptized Tatars" or "Christians of the Tatar origin." But already in the early twentieth century there was a strong tendency among them to identify themselves not only as a religious group but also as a separate ethnic group. In fact, religious unlikeness led to the Kriashens starting to differ from the rest of Tatars in their dialect, traditional culture, sometimes social position, and political orientation. During the 1920 and 1926 population censuses, Kriashens were counted as a separate ethnic group. Later their status as a separate group was denied because atheism was proclaimed in the Union of Soviet Socialist Republics (USSR); any religious differentiation was neglected and the most obvious feature that differentiated Kriashens from the rest of Tatars was religious affiliation. But even under such conditions they were not integrated with Muslim Tatars although they both spoke the Tatar language. In the 1990s, when the role of religion increased in Russian society, the Kriashens became more consolidated and their own ethnic self-consciousness became more meaningful for them. They became very active in attempts to restore their status as a separate ethnic community.

Religion in Ethnic Conflicts

Since ethnic and religious identities are closely connected in the popular mind, the role of religion may be very significant in ethnic conflicts and wars. Hence, there is an opportunity that, in such cases, religion can be used by both peacemakers and nationalistic extremists. In particular, the peacemaking potential of religion in conflict resolution is used by the World Conference on Religion and Peace. Also, under the initiative of the Russian Orthodox Church, an Interreligious Peace Forum was held in Moscow in November 2000. It gathered the leaders of many denominations. They were unanimous that religious leaders can (better than others) promote resolution of ethnic conflicts and establishment of peace and tolerance in Russia. Unfortunately, in the contemporary world there are examples of religious extremism as well, and thus, because of religious solidarity, mercenaries travel from one Muslim country in conflict to another (for example, to Tajikistan, and earlier to Bosnia and Kosovo).

Thus, the manifestation can be different but it is clear that religion and ethnicity are tightly intertwined with each other. Hence, comparative ethnographic and religious exploration is crucial for gaining a more in-depth understanding of personal and social identity, as well as the essence of ethnic and religious movements.

OLGA KAZMINA

See also **specific religions**

Further Reading

Bowden, Henry W., and Paul Ch. Kemeny, editors, *American Church History: A Reader*, Nashville, Tennessee: Abingdon Press, 1998

Glock, Charles Y., *Religion in Sociological Perspective Essays in the Empirical Study of Religion*, Belmont, California: Wadsworth, 1973

Glock, Charles Y., and Rodney Stark, *Religion and Society in Tension*, Chicago: Rand McNally, 1969

Johnstone, Patrick, editor, *Operation World*, Grand Rapids, Michigan: Zondervan Publishing House, 1993

Stark, Rodney, and William S. Bainbridge, *The Future of Religion: Secularization, Revival and Cult Formation*, Berkeley, Los Angeles, London: University of California Press, 1985

Казьмина, Ольга, "Интегрирующая и дезинтегрирующая роль религии и этнические процессы в современной России" (The Integrative and Disintegratve Role of Religion and Ethnic Processes in Contemporary Russia), *Ab Imperio*, 2 (2000)

Мчедлов, Михаил, Юрий Аверьянов, Владимир Басилов, et al., editors, *Религии народов современной России. Словарь (Religions of the Peoples of Contemporary Russia)*, Москва: Республика, 1999

Пучков, Павел, "О соотношении конфессиональной и этнической общностей" (On the Correlation of Religious and Ethnic Communities), *Советская этнография*, 6 (1973)

Пучков, Павел, "Интегрирующая и дезинтегрирующая роль религии в этническом процессе" (The Integrative and Disintegratve Role of Religion in the Ethnic Process), in *Расы и народы*, edited by Брук, Соломон, Арутюнов Сергей, et al., выпуск 21, Москва: Наука, 1991

Тишков, Валерий, Павел Пучков, et al., editors, *Народы и религии мира: Энциклопедия (Peoples and Religions of the World: Encyclopedia)*, Москва: Большая Российская Энциклопедия, 1998

Religious Nationalism

In Europe religious nationalism goes back to the Reformation. It intensified in the nineteenth century, owing largely to the imperialism of the large European nations trying to suppress the smaller ones. While religious nationalism has somewhat abated after the fall of communism (Yugoslavia being a notable exception), Islamic nationalism has surged forward, propelled partly by the destructive legacy of colonialism in Asia, Africa, and the Middle East.

It is customary to trace the rise of modern nationalism to the French Revolution, when a kingless people proclaimed itself sovereign. However, religious nationalism goes back to Martin Luther rather than to the French Revolution. In simple terms, religious nationalism designates a national identity defined virtually exclusively by religion. Modern religious nationalism arose when Martin Luther broke off from the Catholic Church and initiated an era of religious diversity in Europe. Until then, European nationalisms were dormant, neutralized as it were by the communality of religion. Except for the Jews, all Europeans were Roman Catholics. The rise of Protestantism gave rise to the law of *cuius regio, eius religio*, or "the religion of the principality is defined by its ruler." Thus religious nationalism was born.

While religion has been a characteristic feature of peoples and geographical areas throughout history, in the nineteenth century it became a constitutive and sometimes indispensable part of national identity. At that time, owing to the development of literacy and rapid population increases, nationalism experienced a tumultuous growth. The European middle classes increasingly sought identity through participation in "imagined communities" sharing the same language, history, and religion. Many European countries favored one religion above all others: thus, the English favored the Church of England, the Prussians, Lutheranism, and Spaniards, Catholicism. But in conditions of national sovereignty and relative prosperity, extreme forms of religious nationalism did not develop in Western Europe. Not so in Central and Eastern Europe, where nations with diverse histories lived "cheek by jowl," and where religiously based nationalisms intensified accordingly. The voracious imperial appetites of the European powers were largely to blame. After the absorption of the Polish-Lithuanian

Commonwealth (a self-proclaimed "republic" in which Christianity, Judaism, and Islam coexisted in relative harmony) Russia, Austria, and Prussia acquired large minorities that did not share the religion of the majority. Russia, an Eastern Orthodox country, acquired a four million-strong Catholic minority consisting of Poles and Ukrainians; Prussia, a Protestant country, likewise acquired a Polish Catholic minority; and Austria, a Catholic country, ventured east with an acquisition of the "Uniate" (Byzantine Catholic) Ukrainian minority. Superimposed on this religious patchwork was a large Jewish minority that the Russians pushed westward, into the so-called Pale of Settlement situated in Eastern Poland, Ukraine, and Belarus. Economic competition, linguistic incompatibility, and denominational differences deteriorated into a frantic search for national identity by means of religion. Religious differences hardened, and confession began to be identified with nationality. Those who professed Judaism were increasingly seen as being of Jewish nationality; Catholicism became associated with Polishness; Eastern Orthodoxy, with Russianness; Byzantine Catholicism, with the Ukrainian national identity.

The Romantic philosophers such as J.G. Herder contributed to these developments. Herder expressed the much-quoted opinion that each nation has its own unique characteristics, and that the Slavs are a race of the future. Herder's ideas were appropriated by the so-called Slavophiles in Russia who extolled Russian national identity and proclaimed the superiority of Eastern Orthodoxy over Roman Catholicism. In Fyodor Dostoevsky's *The Brothers Karamazov,* this religious nationalism is brilliantly presented in the musings of the *Russian* monk, Father Zosima. In the twenty-first century, Russian nationalism remains strongly linked to Eastern Orthodoxy even though, according to polls, one-third of Russians declare themselves to be atheists.

It is not accidental either that Zionism was born in Central and Eastern Europe, and that the leading Zionists had Eastern European roots. Likewise, after the Grand Master of the Teutonic Knights, Albrecht von Hohenzollern, converted to Protestantism in the sixteenth century, the foundation for the Prussian Protestant identity was established, and Prussia increasingly began to be seen as distinct from the Western German principalities that were strongly Catholic. Similarly, Polish nationalism (which developed partly as a response to the partitions of Poland) became linked with the Roman Catholic Church. In conditions of partition, the only link between the Austrian, Russian, and Prussian parts of Poland was the Church that supported the use of the Polish language in religious services and in literature. Ukrainian nationalism was fostered by the Austrian authorities as a means of weakening Polish presence in Western Ukraine. Ukrainians were resentful of the Polish nobles who owned Ukrainian lands while culturally and religiously identifying with Poland rather than with Ukraine. After the 1596 Brest Union, Western Ukrainians identified with the "Uniate" Ukrainian Catholicism, different in ritual and practice from Roman Catholicism.

While Central and Eastern Europe are centers of religiously based nationalisms, other parts of the world followed suit in the twentieth century. Decolonization was followed by a growth of national awareness; and, of course, decolonization itself resulted partly from the growth of nationalist identity in Asia, Africa, and Latin America. While in Latin America the colonizers (Spain and Portugal) shared religious identity with the colonized, in Asia and Africa religious otherness was sometimes cultivated as a means of liberation. Islam in particular has become a tool by means of which separation from the former colonial masters was sought in Indonesia and in Central Asia, and even in the Philippines where the majority of population is Christian. The Islamic countries of Asia flaunted their religion as proof that they were "different" from their white masters and therefore should be independent of the European powers. A similar situation existed in India with regard to Hinduism, and in China with regard to Taoism and Buddhism. In the twenty-first century, many third-world nations define themselves in terms of religious nationalism. Depending on the degree of democracy in a country, other denominations are tolerated or persecuted. In India, democratic institutions have been adopted and all denominations are permitted to coexist, although being an Indian continues to be associated with Hinduism and rioting against "Western" religions is not uncommon. In Saudi Arabia and in several other Middle Eastern countries only one religion is allowed. Saudi Arabia is a country in which not even a sign of another religion can be displayed in public. In the twenty-first century, the most religiously intolerant countries tend to be Islamic, from Asia and Africa to the Middle East. However, in Iraq even under Saddam Hussein other denominations were tolerated to the point of accepting a Christian, Tariq Mikhail Aziz, as Deputy Prime Minister. As for Israel, while all denominations are tolerated there, civil and religious legislation favors the Jews.

Communism tried to eradicate the association between nation and religion, with mixed results. While ostensibly the Chinese are atheists, strong social customs of Taoism are present even under the present repressive regime. Largely, religious nationalism tends to weaken in conditions of democracy and prosperity. Given the remoteness of prosperity in many parts of the world, religious nationalisms are likely to continue to flourish in the foreseeable future, with the accompanying tendency toward political instability and regional separatism.

EWA M. THOMPSON

See also **Nationalism**

Further Reading

Baron, Salo W., *Modern Nationalism and Religion* [1947], New York: Meridian, 1960
Davies, Norman, *God's Playground: A History of Poland*, New York: Columbia University Press, 1984
Hastings, Adrian, *The Construction of Nationhood: Ethnicity, Religion and Nationalism*, Cambridge, United Kingdom: Cambridge University Press, 1997
Herder, J.G., *Ideen zur Philosophie der Geschichte der Menscheit* [1784–91] (English translation by Frank Manuel, *Reflections on the Philosophy of the History of Mankind*), Chicago: University of Chicago Press, 1968
Thompson, Ewa M., "Nationalism, Imperialism, Identity: Second Thoughts," *Modern Age*, 40, no. 3 (Summer 1998)

Religious Separatism

Religious separatism is one of the main varieties of separatism. Separatism is usually understood as movements aimed at the separation of a certain part of the state and the founding of a new state or an autonomous region of this territory. In the case of religious separatism, the emphasis is on the religious differences between the population of the territory seeking to separate and the population of the major part of the state. Religious separatism is often tightly connected with ethnic separatism; hence, it is sometimes difficult to divide these varieties of separatism from each other.

In the twentieth century, despite the secularization of society, conflicts on religious grounds continued as did religious persecutions. In 1915 and later, the Christian population of the Ottoman Empire (Armenians, Greeks, and Assyrians) was subjected to barbarian persecution that resulted in the deaths of more than a million people. Such religious conflict and persecution against particular categories of believers have been the basis for religious separatism.

In the mid-twentieth century, the tendency toward religious separatism was clearly manifested in the division of former British India into two independent states—predominantly Hindu and Muslim. This division, on which Muslim leaders insisted, was accompanied with harsh conflicts between Hindus and Muslims, mass floods of refugees, and mutual massacres. It cost the lives of hundreds of thousands people from each side. Later separatist movements continued on the South Asian subcontinent, caused by both religious and ethnic motives.

Thus, Pakistan was split into two states, following ethnic, not religious, affiliation. The Bengali population of East Bengal suffered from discrimination, launched an armed struggle that was supported by India, finally broke all the ties with the western part of the country, and proclaimed independence in 1971. However, in the 1970s in the newly created state, separatist forces appeared in the so-called Chittagong Hill Tracts. There separatism had a clear-cut religious aspect. Unlike the mostly Muslim population of Bangladesh, the Chakma, the main ethnic minority of the country who are settled in the Chittagong Hill Tracts, profess Buddhism.

India, after independence, also faced separatist tendencies, the most serious of them of a religious nature. These are the movements for the separation of Punjab and Jammu and Kashmir.

The separation of Punjab is connected with the Sikhs. Sikhism is a religion formed in the late fifteenth and early sixteenth centuries in a Hindu milieu. To a certain degree, it is a synthesis of Hinduism and Islam. For a long time, confrontation with Muslims was typical for Sikhs, caused by their long-lived wars with Muslim rulers as well as with Muslim conquerors (Afghans). When questions arose about Britain leaving the South Asian subcontinent, the Sikh leaders called for the creation of an independent state of Sikhistan or Khalistan. Muslim leaders urged the territories of Punjab, populated with Sikhs, to pass to Pakistan. As a result of clashes between Muslims on the one side and Sikhs and Hindus on the other side, hundreds of thousands people died and millions had to escape. Since the creation of a buffer state between India and Pakistan was not in British plans, Sikhs had to choose between incorporating into either India or Pakistan. They chose India. However, in the Indian state of Punjab, Sikhs were not the majority—Hindus were. Sikh leaders insisted on changing the state's borders, and central authorities met their claims. After that, Sikhs were the majority in Punjab, but the conditions of the new division did not completely satisfy them. In particular, they did not like that the common capital city, Chandigarh, was built for both Punjab and the mostly Hindu state of Haryana. Sikhs were also unsatisfied with the system of supplying water resources. At first, politicians that held moderate positions prevailed in Sikh leadership, but then more radical figures gained more and more influence. They claimed to create the independent state of Khalistan. Sikh militants settled down in the Golden Temple of Amritsar. Indian authorities stormed the temple, which Sikhs perceived as defilement. The resultant hate led to the death of Indira Gandhi, Indian prime minister, in 1984, killed by her Sikh bodyguards. This, in turn, caused massacres of Sikhs, resulting in some 3,000 deaths. Though the situation became more stable over time, the secessionist movement is still popular among Sikhs.

The religious character of separatism is also absolutely evident in the Indian state of Jammu and Kashmir. It is the only Indian state where Muslims are the majority. Its incorporation into India during the division of the former British India is because at that time it was a principality, wherein the decision of where to incorporate was in the jurisdiction of the rulers. Kashmir's maharaja was not Muslim but Hindu. Many of the Muslim leaders of Kashmir, supported by Pakistan, insist on the necessity of changing the situation. This circumstance is aggravated by the actions of terrorists who endanger the local population and frighten away foreign tourists who previously contributed significant revenue to the state. Among the partisans of separation of Jammu and Kashmir from India, though, there is no mutual understanding concerning the future of the state. Some see it as a part of Pakistan, others suppose that it must become an independent state, and still others just claim larger autonomy of the state within India.

Friction between the Muslim and Hindu populations of Jammu and Kashmir has recently increased by new troubles between neighboring Muslim and Buddhist communities settled in the northern part of the state. The Buddhist community is represented by Tibetan-speaking Ladakhs, who do not insist on the founding of an independent state, but demand the separation of Ladakh from Jammu and Kashmir and the recognition of its status as a union territory subject to the Indian central authorities.

Among other separatist movements in India (Tamil, Assamese, Nepali, Santal, Gond, and others), the features of religious separatism are probably most typical in the Naga movement. Naga live in northeastern India. Despite significant linguistic and cultural differences, they were aware of themselves as a unified entity. To a great degree it is due to their religious homogeneity: the overwhelming majority of Naga are Baptists. In 1947 when the independence of India and Pakistan was proclaimed, a political organization of these people— the Naga National Council—unilaterally declared the independence of its country. However, nobody recognized this act. After negotiations between India and Naga's leaders failed in 1956, guerilla war erupted. With some respite it continues although Nagaland became a state in 1963.

Religious separatism is also clearly manifested in some countries of southeastern Asia, primarily Indonesia and the Philippines. In Indonesia, at different times, several separatist movements have arisen that included a religious aspect to their ideology. Some of these movements represent interests of Muslim ethnic groups who thought that the central authorities pursued a too secular policy, not sufficiently oriented to the Muslim majority. There were movements among the Sundanese, the second largest people of Indonesia (late 1940s to the early 1960s), and among the Achehnese (1990s). On the other hand, some movements also had religious grounds but appeared within the local Christian (mainly Calvinist) population because of the domination of Muslims in the state's leadership. Primarily, this is the type of separatism among the population of the South Moluccas, where the Republik Maluku Selatan was proclaimed but then soon crushed by the Indonesian military forces.

Religious character was even more evident in a separatist movement in the south of the Philippines where the Moro National Liberation Front (*Moro* means "Muslims") launched intense rebel activity supported by Libya. This organization united the representatives of many ethnic groups settled in the southern part of the Philippines: Maguindanao, Ilanon, Maranao (Lanao),

Yakan, Tausug, Samal, Bajau, Sangir, and Mapun. According to different estimates, these peoples are four to eight percent of the total population of the country. The Moro have a long tradition of struggling. For three centuries they struggled against Spaniards who captured the Philippines; then for more than 30 years they fought with Americans; and finally since the 1960s they have struggled against the Philippine government.

In Myanmar there are many separatist movements (Karen, Shan, Kachin, and others), although some features of religious separatism (along with ethnic separatism) are probably manifested only among the Kachin, two-thirds of whom profess Christianity.

In the countries of eastern Asia there are separatist tendencies among China's national minorities such as the Uighur and Tibetans. But these separatist tendencies have primarily political and ethnic grounds, and only then religious ones (Uighur are Muslims, and Tibetans are Buddhists-Lamaists).

The largest and the most widely known separatist movement in southwestern Asia is the movement for independence of Kurdistan. Evidently, though, it has no religious basis and is completely caused by the aspirations of the largest world minority, as the Kurds sometimes call themselves, to create an independent state on their ethnic territory, located in the borders of Turkey, Iran, Iraq, and Syria.

It is evident, however, that Turkish separatism on Cyprus has a religious character along with an ethnic one. The overwhelming majority of the population are Orthodox Greeks. Turks, professing Islam, make up only 18 percent. In 1974, the northern part of the island was occupied by the Turkish troops, and in 1983 the Turkish Republic of Northern Cyprus was declared. However, no state, except for Turkey, recognized it.

A religious character is even more clearly manifested in separatist tendencies of Hazara, located in the central part of Afghanistan. Although Muslim, like the rest of Afghanistan's population, they adhere to a Shi'a faith. Hence, they always felt prejudice from both the authorities and the surrounding Sunni population. At present, they struggle against the Taliban, together with other forces, and at the same time, they try to ensure better conditions for their future. Admittedly, different political leaders of Hazarajat view the future of their people in different ways. Some are ready to be satisfied with autonomy on their ethnic territory; others want to proclaim an independent state in Hazarajat; and, finally, still others wish to join their motherland to Shi'a and a much more prosperous Iran even though the territory of Hazarajat is not immediately adjacent to the border of this country.

In Tajikistan, neighboring Afghanistan, religious separatism exists among so-called Pamir's peoples. In the Mountain Badakhshan Autonomous Region there are nine Pamir peoples: Yazgulyams, Roshani, Khufs, Bartangi, Oroshors, Shugni, Badzhui, Ishkashimi, and Vakhi. Among them, only most of the Yazgulyams are Sunni Muslims. The rest of them are adherents of Ismailism, a radical form of Shi'a Islam. Although the Mountain Badakhshan Autonomous Region is still considered part of Tajikistan, there is no real control by Tajik authorities over this region. It is self-governed and enjoys great financial assistance from the Ismaili leader Aga-khan. Regardless of further development, there is no doubt that some intention to separation of this region of Tajikistan will remain.

In Africa there are several countries where confrontation between Christian and Muslim populations exist, but primarily in the Republic of the Sudan. The north of this country is populated with Arab Muslims, Nubian, and other peoples converted to Islam (Beja, Fur, and Masalit). The Muslim population comprises approximately 70 percent of the total population of the country. Most of the population settled in the southern part of the country is either Christian (20 percent) or Animist (10 percent). For several decades, guerilla war between the North and South has continued in the Republic of the Sudan.

The North/South problem, though not as harsh as in Sudan, is faced by two additional African countries: the Republic of Chad and Nigeria, the largest African country. In Chad, Muslims are 45 percent of the population (these are Arabs, Tubu, Daza, Kanembu, and so on, settled in the north of Chad), and Christians are 35 percent (some of Sara, Gulay, and other peoples). In Nigeria, Muslims, dominating in the North (Hausa, Fulani, Kanuri, and others), are 40 percent of the total population, while Christians, prevailing in the southern part of the country (most of Yoruba, Igbo, Ibibio, and others), make up about 50 percent. The rivalry and confrontation between these two main religious groups sometimes leads to deadly clashes. There are also tensions in relations between Muslims and Christians in Ethiopia, Eritrea, Tanzania, Côte d'Ivoire, and other countries.

In Europe, where religious separatism occurred often in the past, now there are no clear-cut claims for separation just because of religious differences. In the first part of the twentieth century, as a result of religious separatism, six Ulster counties (where Presbyterians and Anglicans prevailed and Catholics were a minority) were separated from Ireland. In the late twentieth century, religious factors played a significant role in the disintegration of Yugoslavia. Several peoples, actually speaking the same language but professing different religions—Orthodoxy (Serbs and Montenegrins), Catholicism (Croat), and Islam (so-called Muslim Slavs), were divided politically.

PAVEL PUCHKOV

Further Reading

Barrett, David B., editor, *World Christian Encyclopedia: A Comparative Study of Churches and Religions in the Modern World*, Nairobi a.o.: Oxford University Press, 1982

Barrett, David B., editor, *World Christian Encyclopedia: A Comparative Survey of Churches and Religions AD 30–AD 2200*, New York: Oxford University Press, 2001

Gurr, Ted Robert, *Minorities at Risk: A Global View of Ethnopolitical Conflicts*, Washington, DC: United States Institute of Peace Press, 1993

Johnstone, Patrick, *Operation World*, Grand Rapids, Michigan: Zondervan Publishing House, 5th edition, 1993

Litvinov, Miles, editor, *World Directory of Minorities*, London: Minority Rights Group International, 1997

O'Brien, Joanne, and Martin Palmer, *The State of Religion Atlas*, New York, a.o.: Simon & Schuster, 1993

Pučkov, Pavel Ivanovič, *Le religioni nel mondo d'oggi*, Milano: Teti editore, 1978

Shorter Encyclopaedia of Islam, Leyden and London: E.J. Brill and Luzac, 1961

The Troubles: The Background to the Question of Northern Ireland, London: Thames Futura, 1980

Казьмина, Ольга Евгеньевна, и Павел Иванович Пучков, *Основы этнодемографии*, Москва: Издательство "Наука," 1994 (Kazmina, Olga Yevgenyevna, and Pavel Ivanovich Puchkov, *Fundamentals of Ethnodemography*, Moscow: Nauka Press, 1994)

Puchkov, Pavel Ivanovich, and Olga Yevgenyevna Kazmina, *Religions of the Contemporary World*, Moscow: Russian Academy of Education University Press, 1998

Roma (Gypsies)

Capsule Summary

Location: The Roma are traditionally nomadic people found in most European countries and, in smaller numbers, in the Americas. The largest concentrations have been in Romania, Slovakia, Hungary, and Moldova

Total Population: 5 million (as estimated in the late 1990s, but other estimates range as high as 10 million)

Language: Romany

Religions: Christians, Muslims

History and Myths

The history of the Roma (also called Rom or Gypsies) is clouded by myth. The Gypsies are said to have left their original homeland, India, around the year 1000 and to have slowly migrated westward through Persia and Armenia, reaching Byzantium and Greece by the end of the eleventh century. They stayed for some time in the Balkans and then moved to western Europe at the beginning of the fourteenth century. There they wandered from town to town claiming to be pilgrims from Egypt; the word *Gypsies* is derived from "Egyptians." At first they were welcomed and given alms, but soon this attitude changed, and increasingly the Gypsies came to be regarded as beggars, parasites, and outright criminals. From about 1500 onward, their nomadic lifestyle, which was considered antisocial, seems to have led to an increasing number of clashes with the authorities, so that a negative spiral of criminalization and repression developed. In the first half of the eighteenth century, this situation had been exacerbated to the point where Gypsies were hunted down and attempts were made to exterminate the group.

Since about the 1970s, the stereotype of Gypsies as parasites and criminals has gradually been replaced by an image of this people as nomadic, anarchistic victims of sedentary modernization; however, the focus on repression and on the Gypsies' discordant relationship with sedentary society has persisted. Only relatively recently have social historians offered an alternative to this predominantly ethnocultural explanation. These scholars implicitly or explicitly integrate the story of the Gypsies into changing attitudes toward poverty, vagrancy, and banditry.

It is true that there has always been some degree of tension and trouble in the relationship between Gypsies and the majority, and that at times the majority—especially as represented by central authorities—has been overtly hostile toward Gypsies and other itinerant or traveling groups. In Europe since the Middle Ages, Gypsies have encountered deep-rooted prejudice, rejection, racial discrimination, and even persecution. During the Nazi period, especially the years of World War II, at least 220,000 Gypsies died or were killed in concentration camps. Moreover, there seem to have been mass murders of the Gypsy populations in the Ukraine, the Crimea, Croatia, Serbia, and other warring regions, though we can only speculate about the numbers killed. It is logical that these deadly episodes have come to be emphasized by Gypsy intellectual leaders in the political fight for international recognition of the Gypsies as a nation. Still, identity formation during the postwar era has addressed only slavery, war, and persecution—the more general animosity between host societies and the "travelers" seems to have been simply accepted as a historical given.

Recent studies indicate that the overall image of the Gypsies is seriously inaccurate. First, with regard to the historic social and economic position of Gypsies and other itinerant groups in western Europe, it is evident that there have never been "Gypsy occupations" as such: all the occupations associated with Gypsies in the literature on these groups were also practiced by non-Gypsies. Second, even itinerancy was not peculiar to Gypsies: tens of thousands of people were itinerants without being looked on as Gypsies. Third, characteristics such as the family as working unit, mobility, and self-employment were general phenomena and cannot be explained by reference to a "Gypsy culture." However, the specific combination of "Gypsy occupations," self-employment, and traveling with one's family was significant in that people in western Europe who chose such a way of life were very likely to be labeled "Gypsies" (or something similar) by the authorities. From the fifteenth century on, this definition was so powerful that it was very difficult for certain people to avoid being identified as Gypsies, and the identification could easily lead to the development of ethnicity. People who were categorized in this way began to feel that they were different from others and so began to cultivate their own way of life and the symbols attached to it.

The question of ethnicity and group formation is inextricably bound up with Gypsy occupations, because the economic choice of an itinerant profession with the family and an overtly itinerant life resulted in stigmatization. Cultural characteristics such as dress and language seem to have been less important in this respect. The stigmatization can be explained partly by

the mistrust toward itinerant occupations in general. Most accusations against Gypsies were similar to those against hawkers, entertainers, and craftsmen who left their families at home. These ideas were reinforced from time to time by sedentary economic organizations such as the guilds, which tried to defend their privileges and monopoly. However, stigmatization never led to the disappearance of itinerant professions. Notwithstanding their distrust, many authorities realized that itinerancy fulfilled a necessary economic function, and they therefore restricted themselves to opposing the alleged abuses.

These abuses were especially associated with people who took their families with them. Invariably, this category is put forward as an example of people who took undue advantage of the legal possibilities for itinerant occupations. The only way to escape being labeled, and stigmatized, as a "Gypsy" was to stress one's distinctive character as a member of a professional group. Showmen were the most successful in this respect; but beginning in the early twentieth century the same process can be discerned in German organizations of hawkers, who managed to be excluded from stigmatization in all the western European countries: by organizing and lobbying, hawkers convinced officialdom that they were honest businessmen who could not be compared to the "dishonest" Gypsies. Thus, the restrictive and discriminatory policies toward Gypsies did not make their economic activities impossible. Also, although Gypsies did not play a key role in certain economic sectors, their work cannot be dismissed as parasitic or as begging in disguise. Even the most repressive authorities occasionally admitted that Gypsies could be useful and in some instances—such as seasonal work—indispensable. In fact, economically Gypsies can be compared to the lower and middle classes. There were Gypsy beggars and criminals, but most Gypsies earned a modest living, and some, such as coppersmiths and horse-dealers, were quite successful.

Furthermore, itinerant occupations in general and Gypsy occupations in particular could survive only if they adapted to changing economic conditions. The widespread ideas that industrialization caused the decline of itinerant occupations and that Gypsies always held onto their traditional occupations can both be dismissed. The process of industrialization and modernization was by no means uniform, and it had divergent effects. Industrialization may have made many itinerant and traditional occupations obsolete, but other occupations emerged in their place, and presumed "Gypsies" as well as non-Gypsies reacted accordingly. Not until after World War II do we find that in many countries Gypsies were forced into a fairly hopeless social and economic position. Explicit legislation—for example, the Caravan Act of 1968 in the Netherlands—made traveling virtually impossible; such laws, combined with strong anti-Gypsy sentiments in society at large, resulted in a dead-end street for Gypsies. Gypsies and others were deprived of their itinerant occupations, discriminated against in the regular labor market, and unable to escape their own group and the stigma associated with it; and it became very difficult for many of them to cope with this economic situation.

Traveling Groups in Western Europe

As already noted, traveling groups served a useful social and economic function in western Europe but were nevertheless confronted with repressive policies from the fourteenth century on. This had to do with the authorities' habitual practice of making distinctions, within the migrant population, between the "good" and the "bad" or the "honest" and the "dishonest"—or, as the Polish historian Geremek (1991) put it, between migrants with and without an excuse. One key to understanding the situation is the development of the system of poor relief in western Europe. Beginning in the fifteenth century, such aid was restricted to the local poor; simultaneously, poor immigrants were denied citizenship, and as a result, the category of vagrants and Gypsies was created. In excluding aliens, this system of relief had far-reaching effects on traveling groups, who not only were stigmatized but, rightfully or not, were expected to be reduced to beggary. In the nineteenth century poor relief was linked to the place where one lived, but this final transition could no longer change a great deal for traveling groups. On the contrary, every municipality then ran the risk of becoming liable for their support—a risk that motivated authorities, more strongly than ever, to prevent travelers from staying, let alone settling.

However, to explain the persistent stigmatization of traveling groups in the nineteenth and twentieth centuries, especially in Germany and France, poor relief must be linked with the process of state formation. From the end of the eighteenth century on, internal migration in western Europe increased. Owing to the continuing commercialization of the agricultural sector and the unevenness of industrialization, jobs became less secure and mobility increased. In agriculture year-long contracts were replaced by irregular demand, and in industry much work (such as construction) was still seasonal and some (such as factory work) was often temporary as well. This instability in the labor market caused many workers to move continually from place to place. Not surprisingly, in view of the traditional ideas about migration and mobility, the authorities became increasingly concerned about this migration. Even though migration may have been the rule, as it was in preindustrial Europe, the norm still was sedentarism. There was widespread fear that a great mass of rootless, wandering paupers would develop.

Apart from political disturbances, this fear of the mobile poor, especially those who were labeled vagrants, seems to have been a major reason for professionalizing the police in France and Great Britain. Vagabonds were depicted as the prototype of the criminal, because of their supposed refusal to work and to accumulate possessions. The police in the German states also focused on vagabonds, as can be seen in the emerging police journals, which gave considerable attention to harmful tramps (*gemeinschädliche Umhertreiber*). Although most tramps did not commit serious crimes, the state police tried to exercise constant supervision and control by sharing detailed information about them among the local police forces. The ideas and practices of police executives were directly influenced by the increase in population and by migratory trends.

The monitoring of itinerant groups was reinforced by the specialization of police forces that took place in the late nineteenth century as part of a general bureaucratization accompanying state formation in western Europe. Special branches were established for the surveillance of "social problems" such as prostitutes, aliens, vagrants, and—in some countries—Gypsies. The sections that occupied themselves with these categories were strongly influenced by the generally negative image of traveling groups; and these sections were able to gain some autonomy and some power to define problems according to their own perceptions and in their own interest, if only to justify their existence. In the late nineteenth century and the early twentieth, the main objectives of the policies concerning traveling groups were sedentarism, regular work, and—in the case of foreigners—expulsion. As a result, there was more and more emphasis on distinguishing between nationals and foreigners and between "normal" and antisocial citizens.

Ottoman and Hapsburg Rule

The Ottoman and Hapsburg empires seem to have been quite different from regimes in western Europe with regard to the treatment of Gypsies. Both empires were multiethnic, although the Ottoman Empire offered a better social environment for the stable, harmonious coexistence of diverse ethnic groups.

The presence of Gypsies in Bulgaria probably predated the invasion of the Ottoman army in the second half of the fourteenth century. In addition, though, many Gypsies entered the Balkans as part of that army (as servants and craftsmen) and then became sedentary people settled in Bulgarian lands or nomadic people based there. In the archives of the central government and local administration, they are called *chingene*, *chingane*, *chigan*, or *kibti*. Although a growing number of them became Muslims, especially from the seventeenth century on, they had to pay a head tax (*haradzh*) regardless of their faith. Only blacksmiths in the service of the army, who lived in fortresses, were exempted; they had a special status and belonged to a special Gypsy *sandzhak*, a nonterritorial administrative unit.

Most Gypsies settled; only a minority were wandering groups. Both categories were distributed over different special tax units (*dzhemaats*). Some of them gave up their traditional itinerant occupations and turned to farming. Most, however, continued in itinerant trades (of which there were a great variety), especially as blacksmiths and musicians but also as tinkers, goldsmiths, shoers, sieve makers, tailors, and servants. The fundamental division of the population was into the faithful (Muslims) and *raya* (mostly Christian), but Gypsies were given a special ambiguous status: they seem to have been categorized according to their ethnic roots and idiosyncratic religious practices.

The position of Gypsies seems to have been more favorable in the Ottoman Empire than in the Hapsburg Empire or in western Europe—a conclusion supported by the fact that throughout the early modern period numerous runaway Gypsy slaves migrated to Ottoman lands from the neighboring vassal principalities of Wallachia and Moldavia. The relatively favorable position of the Gypsies under Ottoman rule may be because many of them were sedentary; but those who continued their nomadic way of life also seem to have been left in peace and not to have been regarded as a threat to a well-ordered society. Another factor was the Ottoman system of flexible administrative units (*dzhemaat*). Also, itinerant Gypsies were by no means the only nomadic group; pastoral tribes such as the Yörüks were actually much more numerous. Although they posed administrative problems to the authorities, they constituted an integral part of the sedentary society and fulfilled certain functions without which the society would not have been able to survive. The Ottoman state realized this and gave each clan a *yurt*, summer and winter pasture lands that had fixed limits recorded in the imperial registers.

Thus, the diverging treatment of Gypsies in southeastern and western Europe is explained not only by differences in the approach to ethnic and other minorities but also by the fact that Gypsies could be fitted into the state administrative system as members of a well-defined unit—and also because they did not pose a threat to the general principles of the poor relief system. Moreover, although western Europeans feared "masterless men," this fear may have been less pronounced in the Ottoman Empire, where the state tried to address a shortage of man power by raiding the nonoccupied part of Balkans and other foreign territories for slaves.

International Romani Union

In general, the situation of Gypsies as a group did not improve during the postwar period in western or eastern Europe. The only important change was the development of a social movement with nationalistic aspirations, led by intellectuals who stressed a common need for emancipation. Some important work in the field of Gypsy studies comprises the Gypsies' social aims; their political ambitions, particularly for recognition as a global people; and their current struggle for recognition of their history during the Nazi period. Certain leading scholars in this area themselves wish to be associated with the International Romani Union, which can be described as a movement of Romani nationalism. This is actually a very mild form of nationalism: cultural, antiterritorial, and looking to Gandhi and Fanon for inspiration. The movement developed in opposition to earlier discourse in European states and among European scholars about the nature of "true Gypsies," and it can be described as a sociopolitical reaction against anti-Gypsy attitudes and policies. Members of the movement see the history of Gypsies in Europe as a tale of two genocides: the first in the sixteenth century, when "anticommercial nomadism" began; the second in the twentieth century, when that kind of life vanished. In between, an overall Gypsy identity would have come into being, although it is emphasized that by the late nineteenth century western

European Gypsies often hardly knew there were Gypsies in other countries—for instance, in eastern Europe. Gypsies at this time tended to insist that only their own immediate associates were "true Gypsies"; all others were half-breeds or imitations. On the other hand, if they were dealing with *gaje* (non-Gypsies)—whom they believed to be prejudiced against Gypsies—they might well have found it more convenient to insist that in fact they were only traveling traders, who should not be persecuted as though they were "Gypsies."

Romani nationalists of the 1960s wanted to eradicate both internal scapegoating and external stigmatizing by society in general; they explicitly sought to transcend divisions among traveling groups, which they considered tribal. Their way of institutionalizing the culture involved accepting the variety of Gypsy or traveler ethnicities and overlooking historical differences. This social strategy could succeed because of a general assumption that claims to ethnic homogeneity are self-validating. In other words, "We are one, because they say we are one. So let's unite." Ultimately, present or past cultural similarities need not be decisive; what is decisive is the common experience of racism, persecution, and genocide—an experience that historically did happen to all the so-called Gypsy groups. We are then talking about an antiracist movement. In the social engineering of this movement, reality does not always correspond with political truth. What the spokespeople want is a consensus that a common national identity has to be formed, to serve as a foundation for common institutions that will be sufficiently strong and sufficiently legitimate to represent a Romani people internationally. Presumably such institutions could then receive collective reparations (similar to those paid to Israel), from states like Germany deemed to be the successors of regimes that pursued genocide against the Gypsies. The spokespersons and activists consider that this is the only way to reach their goals, because international institutions, such as the United Nations, recognize no other platform, or no other source of pleas, for the human rights of minorities. But bodies such as the International Romani Union are continually frustrated by factionalism: the real differences in interests and ideology among Romani politicians have thus far precluded any financially secure institutional base to which it would be politically possible to pay collective reparations. The Pentecostal Romani churches are notably better organized than the Romani political organizations and are financed by their own members.

To a certain extent, Romani spokespeople manipulate history to achieve emancipatory political goals. This strategy, which is common in ethnopolitics, combines the idiom of nineteenth-century nationalism with that of modern antiracism. It is in a sense a reaction against the way scholars and policy makers pursued political goals in the past. Still, there were actual historical attempts to "civilize" traveling groups by isolating them; there was forced assimilation, in colonies, in camps, or by putting a stop to traveling in caravans; and during the Nazi regime Gypsies were sterilized, deported, and sent to concentration camps. Furthermore, in the postwar period—especially in eastern Europe—the socioeconomic position of Gypsy groups remained far from prosperous, if not deplorable. Not one government seemed to be prepared to counter the general feeling of the public, which was chiefly dismissive, by undertaking reforms, nor did there seem to be any group of Gypsies willing to mobilize for nationalistic goals. Consequently, there is a considerable chance that the plea for tolerance toward groups on the margins of society will eventually return, together with a reminder of past and present persecutions. But an emphasis on the contrasts between Gypsies and the rest of society can be dangerous: applying the idiom of nineteenth-century nationalists and folklorists and adapting it to modern times by including a diaspora from a homeland (in this case, India) could give malevolent minds an argument against the idea of a nation within a nation.

Beyond the Diaspora

However, the farther one goes back into time, the more difficult it is to find convincing evidence for the existence of self-proclaimed Gypsy groups sharing a common past, an origin, or even a sense of ethnicity. From the fifteenth century on, various explanations circulated regarding the origin of people who traveled in groups and had itinerant occupations. They were classified as conglomerations of antisocial vagrants on the edge of society; as heathens, in other words non-Christians; as Egyptians, because of their association with magic and sorcery; and as Jews who had been in hiding during severe persecutions.

A shift in scholarship was brought about by a book on Gypsies written by the German historian Grellmann in 1783. Mainly based on rudimentary linguistic comparisons, he claimed that Gypsies had moved away from northern India—specifically, Hindustan—four centuries earlier. He also analyzed traits that he considered characteristic of Indians and indeed of all eastern peoples. Grellmann's highly speculative and associative argument led him to identify Gypsies as descendants of the lowest class of Indians, the pariahs, also known as Sudras. These people supposedly had fled their homeland during a war of conquest waged in the beginning of the fourteenth century by Timur, who was bent on bringing Islam into India by fire and sword. What happened to the Sudras afterward remained unclear. Grellmann thought that their most likely route was through Arabia, Egypt, and Turkey, but because there was no factual evidence, he felt that another pattern of emigration was equally possible.

This new interpretation of the Gypsies' diaspora was very successful, not least because it was in accord with the ethnonationalist discourse of the time. Grellmann's book was translated into several languages, and the Gypsies' link with India was considered firmly established from then on. In the next two centuries, outsiders continued to study the origin of the Gypsies; however, no one systematically tried to learn if the Gypsies themselves were aware of any myths, stories, or other oral traditions that might indicate a faraway homeland. Moreover, there are no written sources that might offer solutions. But this did not prevent Gypsies or their representatives from using the presumed Indian homeland to support ethnonational claims. In 1971, the World Romani Congress was held in London. This initiative was backed by the prime minister of the Indian Punjab, the supposed homeland of the Gypsies, who in the same year created the Indian Institute of Romani Studies; still, in the decades that followed, no concrete evidence for a link to India was found. Angus Fraser (1992) refrains from taking a stand in the contemporary debate on language and origin; rather, he offers an array of possibilities from which his readers are free to choose, though there is almost no firm empirical basis for any of the prevailing beliefs.

Language would seem to be the best guide to origins; but in the end, it fails. Because historical records are almost nonexistent, there is ample room for speculation. Fraser's extensive reading of the available literature on the subject brings him to the conclusion that as long as it remains impossible to narrow the possible choices of times and places, disputes will persist as to exactly who—in terms of caste, occupation, and ethnic origin—left the Indian subcontinent a thousand years or more ago, and whether or not these people left as a single group. Some scholars have claimed on linguistic grounds that on first entering Persian territory, the Gypsies must have been a single race speaking a single language. Others have produced contrary linguistic evidence and argued that the morphological, lexical, and phonological differences between European, Armenian, and Asian Romani might be more easily explained if there had been more than one exodus or if there was already some differentiation within the language at the time of the exodus. As far as Fraser is concerned, the latter standpoint appears the more persuasive.

To repeat, though, there are no conclusive answers about the Gypsies' origin; and it also bears repeating that this lack does not seem to bother Gypsy intellectuals and political leaders. At the time of this writing, the Web site of the International Romani Union, with representatives from 26 countries, explicitly asked for recognition of Gypsies as a people and even as a nation. The leaders of this mainly eastern European movement no longer accepted the name "Gypsies"; they preferred the more proper designation "Roma," noting, however, that not all Gypsies or nomadic peoples are Roma. They considered themselves descendants of the ancient warrior class of northern India, particularly the Punjab; they also considered that their own language, religion, and customs made them identifiable as such and could be directly linked to those of the modern Punjabi. Thus, the pariah ancestors postulated by Grellmann had been transformed into non-Aryan warriors. In effect, the concepts and data that best suit the aspirations of a pan-nationalistic movement are given the status of "truth." Historical knowledge (or lack of historical knowledge) and political aims have become intertwined in the minds of the leaders of these parties and social movements.

It should be noted that the claims and aspirations of self-proclaimed Gypsy leaders have not necessarily trickled down to the people they represent. In one relatively recent anthropological study of the Vlach Gypsies in Hungary, the author states that for the ordinary Gypsy in an unofficial ghetto on the edge of an eastern European village or town, the maneuvers of Gypsy intellectuals on the national and international stages rarely meant much, at least as yet. According to this author, Romani political parties sometimes seem to expend more effort on establishing their credibility among non-Gypsy authorities than among their own constituents. He says that in a survey of 10,000 Hungarian Gypsies, 90 percent of the respondents were unable to name even one Gypsy political party. After years of fieldwork, he concludes that the Gypsies he studied had no homeland to dream of and no original territory to reclaim. What made them special was that they were nevertheless quite happy. They did not share the obsession with origins. This author agrees with the earlier findings of the English anthropologist Judith Okely (1983), with regard to Gypsy travelers in England, that the idea of Indian origins unnecessarily "exoticizes" the Gypsies and ignores their own view of themselves. In other words, most nonintellectual Roma do not seem to care where their ancestors came from. With the exception of the educated Gypsy intellectuals who run the Roma political parties, in Hungary and eastern Europe the Roma do not seen to have an ethnic identity. For them, identity is constructed and constantly remade in the present, relative to significant others; it is not something inherited from the past.

Linguistic research may point toward India as a possible origin of at least a part of the contemporary Gypsy population; but this does not mean that Gypsies today are aware of a homeland that they left or from which they were expelled, or of the traumatic consequences of a diaspora. They evidently have no collective cherished memory of an ancestral home, no developed or documented myth of such a home, and no hope of an eventual return to it. Furthermore, there is no political or social movement for a return, even though the contemporary Gypsy intelligentsia has, since the last quarter of the twentieth century, have emphasized the tie with India. Apparently, they claim this tie to provide a historical foundation for their nationalism: the myth of an Indian genesis is bound up with nationalistic aims and is not meant to imply a right to return to India.

It is true that many so-called Gypsy groups shared an itinerant lifestyle in the past, that there was ethnic awareness and solidarity within subgroups, and that members of a subgroup were connected by a common culture, etiquette, and relationships. Another general trait that still exists today is an emphasis on the difference between "us" (Gypsies) and "them" (non-Gypsies). However, there is hardly any evidence of close ties in the past between the various groups labeled "Gypsies," "Rom," or the like by the state. Hungarian, German, and English Gypsy groups, for instance, hardly ever seemed to be aware of each other's existence; still less did they have any sort of common group ideology. Evidently, the awareness of a collective fate developed in reaction to the Nazis'

persecution and murder of Gypsies, and the experience under the Nazis was the binding principle. Political leaders stress that consciousness of a common language and culture plays a role, but the extent to which this is true remains uncertain. The recent history of Gypsy nationalism, an antiracist movement, is certainly becoming better known to non-Gypsies. However, the nationalists have been far less successful in mobilizing grassroots support.

WIM WILLEMS AND LEO LUCASSEN

See also **Hungary; Moldova; Romania; Slovakia; Spain**

Further Reading

Acton, Thomas, *Authenticity, Expertise, Scholarship, and Politics: Conflicting Goals in Romani Studies*, Inaugural Lecture Romani Studies, Greenwich University Press, 1998

Fraser, Angus, *The Gypsies*, Oxford and Cambridge, Massachusetts: Blackwell, 1992 (See also later editions.)

Fricke, Thomas, *Zigeuner im Zeitalter des Absolutismus: Bilanz einer einseitigen Überlieferung*, Pfaffenweiler: Centaurus, 1996

Geremek, B., *Les fils de Cain: L'image des pauvres et des vagabonds dans la littérature européenne du XVe au XVIIe siècle*, Paris: Flammarion, 1991

Hancock, Ian, Siobhan Dowd, and Rajko Djuri, editors, *The Roads of the Roma, A PEN Anthology of "Gypsy Writers,"* Hertfordshire, 1998

Lucassen, Leo, *Zigeuner: Die Geschichte eines polizeilichen Ordnungsbegriffes in Deutschland, 1700–1945*, Köln and Weimar: Böhlau-Verlag, 1996

Lucassen, Leo, Wim Willems, and Annemarie Cottaar, *Gypsies and Other Itinerant Groups: A Socio-Historical Approach*, London and New York: Macmillan and St. Martin's Press, 1998

Marushiakova, Elena, and Vesselin Popov, *Gypsies (Roma) in Bulgaria*, Frankfurt am Main, 1997

Mayall, David, *Gypsy-Travellers in Nineteenth-Century Society*, Cambridge: Cambridge University Press, 1988

Okely, Judith, *The Traveller-Gypsies*, Cambridge: Cambridge University Press, 1983

Rao, Aparna, editor, *The Other Nomads: Peripatetic Minorities in Cross-Cultural Perspective*, Köln: Böhlau Verlag, 1986

Stewart, Michael, *The Time of the Gypsies*, Oxford: Oxford University Press, 1997

Willems, Wim, *In Search of the True Gypsy: From Enlightenment to Final Solution*, translated from the Dutch by Don Bloch, London and Portland, Oregon: Frank Cass, 1997

Romania

Capsule Summary

Location: southeastern central Europe

Population: 22,271,839 (July 2003). Romanians (89.4%); Hungarians (7.1%); Gypsies (1.8%); Germans (0.5%); Ukrainians (0.3%); Lippovan-Russians (0.2%); Turks (0.1%); Jews, Albanians, Armenians, Bulgarians, Italians, and others (0.4%). Some 10 million Romanians live abroad in neighboring countries (e.g., Moldavia, the former Yugoslavia, Hungary, and Greece) and in western Europe, the United States, Canada, Australia, Israel, South America, and elsewhere

Language: Romanian (official language), which is a Romance language

Religions: Orthodox (87%); Catholic (5%); Protestant (3.5%); Greek-Catholic (1%); Neoprotestant (Baptist, Unitarian, etc.); Muslim; Jewish-Judaic

Per Capita GDP: $7,600 (2002)

The formation of the Romanian people can be traced back to the second millennium BCE, when the territory bordered by the Carpathians, the Danube, and the Black Sea was inhabited by an Indo-European people, the Thracians. Beginning in the sixth century BCE, Greek sources mentioned this territory, known as Dacia, and its stable population (Getas in Greek, Dacians in Latin). The Greek historian Herodotus considered the Geto-Dacians the "bravest and the fairest of the Thracians." After the Roman Empire expanded to the Danube, the battles for Dacia began. Dacia was conquered after two wars (101–102 and 105–106, commemorated on Traian's Column in Rome) and remained part of the Roman Empire for almost 200 years, during which Latin became the official and the spoken language of the Geto-Dacians. There were Christians in Dacia in the second century, and the population adopted Christianity especially after 313, when Constantine I made it the religion of the Roman Empire. The Roman period is still reflected in the name Romania.

From the third century to the thirteenth, migratory peoples—Huns, Gepidac, Avars, Slavs, Petchenegs, Cumans, and others heading toward western Europe—invaded the territory of the Daco-Romans. These migrations delayed the consolidation and unification of the area. In the late ninth century, Hungarians settled in Pannonia and set up a kingdom there from which they began a political and military expansion; by 1200 they ruled all of Transylvania. (The states that were part of Transylvania—Glad, Menumorut, and Gelu—are mentioned in sources as early as the tenth century.) After the waves of migration ended, the independent states of Wallachia and Moldavia were formed; later, the Catholic kingdoms of Poland and Hungary would attack them. After the conquest of Constantinople by the Turks (1453), the Ottoman Empire along the Danube tried to dominate and rule the three Romanian principalities.

Thus, from the fourteenth century until the end of World War I (1918), the Romanians were forcibly divided into the three principalities of Transylvania, Wallachia, and Moldavia. These principalities remained connected, since the Romanians (their principal inhabitants) had a common language and religion; and they were never abolished as states—they maintained their internal autonomy and culture. However, they never became one state: In 1600 Mihai the Brave tried to unify them; his attempt was short-lived, though it became a symbol of Romanian unity.

From the early eighteenth century until the mid-nineteenth, three empires—the Ottoman, the czarist, and the Hapsburg—contended for the territories inhabited by Romanians. In consequence, Austria annexed a part of Wallachia (Oltenia, 1718–1739) and the northern part of Moldavia (Bucovina, 1775–1918); and Russia occupied the eastern part of Moldavia (Bessarabia, 1812–1918). Also, the armies of the three empires defeated the revolution of 1848, in which the Romanian states were involved.

In 1859, the modern Romanian national state was constituted when Alexandru Ioan Cuza (r. 1859–1866) was elected as the single ruler of Wallachia and Moldavia. The new state was named Romania in 1862. In 1866 Romania became a constitutional monarchy under the German prince Carol I of Hohenzollern-Sigmarinen. In 1877, Romania won its independence fighting on the side of Russia against the Ottoman Empire. Romania entered World War I in 1916 on the side of the entente consisting of France, England, and Russia. At the end of the war, the territories populated mostly by Romanians—Bucovina, Bessarabia, and Transylvania—became unified with Romania, which was recognized as a national state by the Treaty of Versailles. Between the two World Wars, Romania developed an advanced market economy: Bucharest was called "little Paris"; and another important city, Timioara, where an anticommunist revolution would take place in 1989, was called "little Vienna."

During World War II, Romania lost some territory. Under the Ribbentropp-Molotov Pact (1940), Bessarabia and northern Bucovina were annexed by the Soviet Union; under the Dictate of Vienna, northwestern Transylvania became part of Hungary (which was then a fascist state) and southern Dobrudja (the Cadrilater) became part of Bulgaria. In 1940, King Carol I abdicated and Romania came under the rule of General (later Marshal) Ion Antonescu, who fought on the side of Germany against the Soviet Union to regain Bessarabia and northern Bucovina. On August 23, 1944, Antonescu was arrested, by order of King Mihai I. Romania then switched sides and fought against Germany.

The peace treaty concluded in Paris in 1947 canceled the Dictate of Vienna but sanctioned the Soviet Union's annexation of Bessarabia (which since 1991 has formed the Republic of Moldavia) and northern Bucovina; also, the Cadrilater remained part of Bulgaria. During the war, the Soviet Union had sent tanks—and a communist regime—to Romania. On December 30, 1947, King Mihai I was obliged to abdicate, and Romania (like the other countries occupied by the Soviet Union) became a "people's republic." In 1965, when the leader of the Communist Party in Romania was Nicolae Ceausescu, Romanian communism was "nationalized," although without abandoning Marxist-Leninist doctrine. After 1971, a more Asian type of communism was established.

In December 1989 there was an anticommunist revolution in Romania, and Ceausescu and his wife Elena were executed. Romania then became more European; and as of this writing it was making efforts at integration with the European Union (EU) and the North Atlantic Treaty Organization (NATO). According to its constitution, Romania is a unitary national (nonfederal) state.

Traditionally, various ethnic groups (Hungarians, Gypsies, Germans, Izeklers, Jews, Swabians, Turks, Tartars, and others) have coexisted in Romania, which has developed a general attitude of tolerance and multiculturalism. In fact, the Romanians—who have evidently resolved the issue of the rights of national minorities—might well be taken as a model by European countries that are still confronting problems of nationalistic fragmentation.

ILIE RAD

See also **Roma (Gypsies); Hungarians**

Further Reading

Castellan, George, *A History of the Romanians*, New York, 1989

Deletant, Andrea, and Dennis Deletant, *Romania*, World Bibliographical Series, Volume 59, Denver, Oxford, and Santa Barbara, 1985

Giurescu, Dinu C., *Illustrated History of Romanian People*, Bucharest, 1981

Hitchins, Keith, *The Romanians (1774–1866)*, Oxford, 1996

Iorga, Nicolae, *Histoire des Roumains et de la romanite orientale*, 10 volumes, Bucharest, 1937–1945

Oțetea, Andrei, editor, *The History of the Romanian People*, New York, 1974; London, 1985

Pop, Ioan Aurel, *Romanians and Romania*, Bucharest, 1998

Seton-Watson, R.W., *A History of the Romanians from Roman Times to the Completion of Unity*, Cambridge, 1934; Hamdon, 1963

Romansh

Capsule Summary

Location: Grisons (Grischun) in southeastern Switzerland
Total Population: 65.000
Language: Romansh or Rhaeto-romance (five different dialects and one standardized written language), a Romance language like French, Italian, and Spanish

History

The Romansh language originates from the Latin spoken by the Roman soldiers who conquered the territory at the beginning the first century CE. The Roman cultural and linguistic influence was thorough. When Germanic tribes later invaded central Grisons, they separated the different Romansh-speaking groups and slowly made German predominate.

Independent local authorities and Austrian nobles competed in dominating the country, but in the late Middle Ages the people of Grisons united in three leagues to keep their independence against foreign threats. The capital Chur became predominantly German speaking as a consequence of a terrible fire in 1464. The reconstruction was carried out by German-speaking artisans who then stayed and dominated the town afterwards. This was a hard blow to the Romansh language, which then became just the language of the countryside.

The population in the southeast became Protestant, whereas the northeast Romansh speakers are Catholics. This confessional division of the Romansh speakers has until recently been a hindrance to linguistic or political unification of the Romansh-speaking groups.

In 1794 the Three Leagues decided that German together with Italian and "the two varieties of Romansh, Sursilvan and Ladin" were recognized as official languages, but when the Grisons in 1803 became part of the Helvetian (Swiss) Confederacy, Romansh became a minority language without official status until Mussolini argued that Romansh was an Italian dialect and thus Grisons ought to be ceded to Italy. In a referendum in 1938, Romansh was made a national language, which gave it official status within the canton but not outside.

Society

In 1996 Romansh was finally made a partly official language that could be used for written communication with national authorities as well as local ones. The government undertook language political measures, granted economic subsidies, and signed the European Charter for Regional and Minority Languages and the European Convention for the Protection of National Minorities. This change of status had considerable positive consequences, but the real outcome is still questionable.

There is no unified literary standard language. Instead there are five different dialects. Only 36,000 of the 65,000 Romansh-speaking people live in the canton and use Romansh, and the those outside mostly use other languages in their daily life.

In the Rhine Valley people speak the closely related dialects, Sursilvan (20,000 speakers) and Sutsilvan (1,500). In the southeast, in Oberengadin, people speak Puter (3,500), and further east, in Unterengadin, Vallader (6,000). These two are sometimes called Engadin or Ladin. In central Grisons there is a bridge dialect, Surmiran (3,500). The rest of the Romansh speakers in Grisons live in Chur. The dialects are mutually understandable. Almost all Romansh speakers are bilingual, with German as the second language. The percentage of Romansh speakers in Switzerland has been slowly decreasing, from 1.1 percent in 1880 to 0.8 percent in 1983, but the real number of speakers has increased (from 46,430 in 1880 to about 65,000 in 1999). In Grisons the number of Romansh speakers has stayed at about 36,000 people during the last century, but due to the rapid increase in numbers of German speakers and, to a lesser extent, Italian speakers, which both have doubled, the percentage of Romansh speakers has decreased from 40 percent to 23 percent.

In 1919 a Romansh cultural and linguistic society called *Lia Rumantscha* was created. Its main objectives are to coordinate the work of associated societies, represent the Romansh people, organize the teaching of Romansh in the *scolettas* (Romansh Kindergartens), promote Romansh culture, elaborate dictionaries, publish books, and translate official documents into

Romansh. The symbolic and real value of having an officially recognized organization is of great importance to the Romansh speakers.

There have been several attempts to create a unified language. They all failed until the Lia in 1978 decided to make a new effort, and in 1982 they presented the outlines of Rumantsch Grischun, which was not based on any dialect but on a statistical method, that is, the lowest common denominator between the dialects. This new language was to be used for administrative purposes, while the different dialects were to remain the literary and school standards for every region. At first, many protested against this artificial new standard, but at the same time the number of official publications and signs in Romansh in Grisons have increased more than 20 times, which has improved the prestige and the use of the language.

Romansh is taught at school in the first six classes, but after that only two to three hours per week. Romansh may be the only language used at school until German is introduced in the fourth grade, or the school may be German speaking with a few weekly hours in Romansh. The local authorities decide for every village to what degree Romansh shall be taught. A local majority can thus promote or reduce the teaching of Romansh. A certain Romansh resignation to German is sometimes noticeable. While German is a compulsory language at school in all Romansh-speaking areas, Romansh is not necessarily taught in German schools in the same areas, and now there is a concern that German schools offering both French or Italian and English might successfully compete with the Romansh schools and undermine the Romansh schooling that mostly have to offer German and one of the other official languages.

Outside the Romansh-speaking area, the language is totally excluded. The local decision is based on the linguistic territorial principle, that is, Romansh can only be taught in areas where the language traditionally has been used, which means that there does not exist any possibility to learn Romansh outside the traditional Romansh territory—not even for Romansh-speakers who move within the canton. In Chur there is a training college with a section for Romansh teachers, but there is no university in Grisons, and only at the universities of Fribourg and Zurich are there professors of Romansh. The language is also taught at the university level in Bern, Geneva, and Sant Gallen.

Even the military accepted the linguistic situation; there exist four Romansh companies, and military manuals have been translated into Romansh.

In 1997 the four Romansh newspapers were merged into one daily paper, *La Quotidiana,* with articles in all six linguistic varieties. Since 1924 there have been radio transmissions in Romansh, although they were not made regular until 1943. Today there is a daily ten-minute-long nationwide news program. In Grisons the daily transmissions are now, since 1987, four hours long. Earlier the radio transmissions were scarce. TV programs in Romansh are few—only a couple of hours per week. The radio program *Radioscola* has had a great importance in educating Romansh speakers of all ages.

To sum up, the words of the Romansh poet Peder Lansel are still valid: "Ni Talians, ni Tudais-chs, Rumantschs vulains restar" (Not Italians, nor Germans, we want to remain Romanshs).

INGMAR SÖHRMAN

See also **Switzerland**

Further Reading

Billigmeier, Robert H., *A Crisis in Swiss Pluralism*, Den Haag: Mouton Publishers, 1979

Catrina, Werner, *Die Rätoromanen: Zwischen Resignation und Aufbruch*, Zürich: Orell Füssli, 1983

Gregor, Douglas Bartlett, *Romontsch, Language and Literature*, Cambridge: The Oleander Press, 1982

Haiman, John, and Paula Beninca, *The Rhaeto-Romance Languages*, London and New York: Routledge, 1992

Mützenberg, Gabriel, *Destin de la langue et de la littérature rhéto-romanes*, Lausanne: L'âge d'homme, 1974

Rugova, Ibrahim (Albanian)

Ibrahim Rugova was the dominant political personality of the Kosovo Albanian community throughout the 1990s. Both as president of the largest party in Kosovo, the Democratic League of Kosovo, and as president of the unrecognized "Republic of Kosovo," Rugova has been largely identified with the peaceful resistance of the Albanian population in Kosovo against the repressive policies of Yugoslavia/Serbia under the leadership of Slobodan Milošević.

Rugova assumed a political function only in the late 1980s. He studied literature at the University of Priština and at the École des Hautes Études in Paris. Rugova began his professional career as a literary critic and professor of literature at the University of Priština. His position as president of the Kosovo Writers Union initiated his political activities in the late 1980s.

In the context of increasing pressure from the Serbian government under the leadership of Slobodan Milošević to revoke the autonomy of Kosovo within both Serbia and Yugoslavia and rising tensions between Serbs and Albanians, the writers union, as did its counterparts in other parts of Yugoslavia, engaged in political debates. Rugova was one of the cosignatories of an Appeal of 215 intellectuals against revoking the autonomy of the province. In response, Rugova was expelled from the League of Communists. As president of the writers union, he was one of the first public figures to call for the independence of Kosovo. Although he did not belong to the original founders, the Democratic League of Kosovo (LDK), he was made president of the party due to his prominence as president of the writers union. The party quickly established itself after its foundation in December 1989 as the most important party of the Kosovo Albanians and marginalized all other political forces. It structure resembled a national movement, encompassing a broad political spectrum united by the aim of representing Kosovo Albanian interests. As cofounder and president of the party, Rugova soon eclipsed Kosovo Albanian functionaries from the League of Communists as the dominant politician.

The political program of Rugova and the Democratic League consists of four pillars: (a) independence for Kosovo, (b) nonviolent resistance to Serbian rule, (c) boycott of all Serbian and Yugoslav institutions, and (d) state and institution building in Kosovo.

In July 1990 the assembly of Kosovo, dominated by the League of Communists, under the leadership of Rugova declared Kosovo a republic. Subsequently the assembly was suppressed by Serbian authorities. The assembly met again in July 1990 in Kačanik/Kaçanik to pass the constitution for the "Republic of Kosovo." The choice for independence by Rugova and the LDK was confirmed in a referendum in September 1991 in which the Albanian population in Kosovo participated: The results showed that 99.8 percent of the voters endorsed independence. At clandestine elections in May 1992, declared illegal—but not disrupted—by the Serbian authorities, the Democratic League won the parliamentary elections overwhelmingly with 76 percent of the vote. Rugova's role as leading politicians among the Kosovo Albanian community was confirmed with an endorsement by 99.8 percent of the valid votes as president of the Republic of Kosovo.

In the following years Rugova and the LDK build up a network of parallel institutions in Kosovo, ranging from schools and a university to health care and other public services. This institution-building effort was both a response to the expulsion of Albanians from the official structures controlled by the Serbian authorities and an attempt to build a separate Kosovo state. The LDK and other parties boycotted all Yugoslavian institutions, including all the elections in Serbia and Yugoslavia. Although the international community looked favorably upon the peaceful resistance propagated by Rugova, his aim to achieve independence for Kosovo received only little international support. Only Albania under President Berisha recognized the Republic of Kosovo, without much impact on the reality in Kosovo itself.

After years of tense, yet relatively stabile, parallel systems in Kosovo, the first direct discussions between Rugova and Miloevi took place in 1996. These negotiations led to an agreement on the formal reestablishment of Albanian schooling. The agreement was, however, never fully implemented. In the same year Rugova came under increasing pressure from the Student Union of the University of Priština (UPSUP), which demanded a more active, yet still peaceful, resistance to the Serbian authorities and the Kosovo Liberation Army (UÇK), which sought to counter the oppressive Serbian rule with violence. The criticism of Rugova from the mostly urban student movement and the UÇK in many rural communities diminished his predominance on the political scene in Kosovo and seemed to defeat his policy of mixing passive nonviolence and maximalist demands for independence.

The second underground parliamentary and presidential elections in March 1998 were overshadowed by the harsh repression of the UÇK in Drenica by Serbian security forces. Several Albanian parties and candidates withdrew from the elections, leading to a renewed victory of Rugova, which did, however, lack the legitimacy of the first elections in 1992.

The increased fighting between the Kosovo Liberation Army and Serbian forces affected mostly the Albanian civilians, many being forced to flee their homes. In light of this development, the influence of Rugova over events diminished rapidly. In the peace talks in Rambouillet and Paris in February and March 1999 Rugova had to concede the leadership of the Kosovo Albanian delegation to Hasim Thaçi, one of the political leaders of the UÇK. The failure of the talks and the (hesitant) support of the Albanian delegation, including Rugova, for the American-proposed peace plan triggered the massive NATO intervention into the conflict.

With the beginning of the NATO bombing of Yugoslavia and the expulsion of approximately 1 million Albanians from Kosovo, the political options pursued by Rugova seemed defeated. Rugova himself was held under house arrest by the Serbian government and was taken to Belgrade for several—much publicized—meetings with Slobodan Milošević, which further undermined his already shaken credibility. Although he was able to leave for Western Europe later in the war, the political developments in Kosovo were determined by the political leadership of the UÇK, which appointed mayors, directors, and other officials upon the entry of NATO into Kosovo in June and July 1999. The previous institutional network and the political dominance of the LDK was thus greatly reduced and Rugova returned to Kosovo only belatedly.

In the years following the war, with Kosovo under UN administration, Rugova and the LDK managed to reestablish themselves. Corruption and links to organized crime, as well at the radical political agenda of

most political forces emerging from the UÇK, reduced their support among the population. The achievement of de facto independence and the departure of Serbian forces (followed by the expulsion of most Serbs living in Kosovo) eliminated the threat to the Albanian population, which gave rise to the UÇK. The renewed political predominance of the LDK and Rugova was confirmed at the local elections in October 2000, in which the party won more than 50 percent of the vote, far ahead of other parties.

Rugova's political style combines intellectual and frequently wavering behavior with the role of an unchallengable leader. This has exposed him to criticism by both intellectuals and more radical political figures. Since the war in 1999 Ibrahim Rugova no longer exercises the same dominance of the political scene in Kosovo as before; he nevertheless manages to remain the most important representative of the Kosovo Albanian population.

Capsule Biography

Ibrahim Rugova. Born December 2, 1944, in Cercë/Crnce, Kosovo (Yugoslavia). Studied at a public school in Peć/Peja, 1967; University of Priština, 1971, M.A.; École des Hautes Études en Sciences Socials, Paris, 1977; Specialization; University of Priština, 1984, PhD Journalist; Literary Critic; Researcher, Albanological Institute, Priština; Professor of Literature, University of Priština; President of the Kosovo Writers Association; President of the Democratic League of Kosovo, 1989 to current; President of the (unrecognized) Republic of Kosova, 1992-1999. Currently living in Priština, Kosovo (Yugoslavia). Awards: Peace and Freedom Award (Denmark), 1995.

Selected Works

"Kahe dhe Premisa të Kritikës letrare Shqiptare, 1504–1983" [Directions and Premises of Albanian Literary Critique 1504–1983], PhD dissertation, University of Priština, 1984; published 1985
Refuzimi Estetik [The Esthetic Refuse], 1987
Pavarësia dhe Demokracia [Independence and Democracy. Interviews and Articles], 1991
La Question du Kosovo: Entretien avec Marie-Françoise Allain et Xavier Galmiche [The Kosvo-Question: Discussions with Marie-Françoise Allain and Xavier Galmiche], 1994
FLORIAN BIEBER

See also **Albania**

Further Reading

Carlen, Jean-Yves, Stève Duchêne, and Joël Ehrhart, *Ibrahim Rugova: "Le frêle colosse du Kosovo"* [Ibrahim Rugova: The Frail Colossus of Kosovo], Paris: Desclée de Brouwer (Témoins d'humanité), 1999

Clarke, Howard, *Civil Resistance in Kosovo*, London and Sterling, Virginia: Pluto Press, 2000

Judah, Tim, *Kosovo: War and Revenge,* New Haven and London: Yale University Press, 2000

Maliqi, Shkelzen, "The Albanian Movement in Kosova," in *Yugoslavia and After: A Study in Fragmentation, Despair and Rebirth*, edited by David D. Dyker, and Ivan Vejvoda, London and New York: Longman, 1996

Maliqi, Shkëlzen, *Kosova: Separate Worlds. Reflections and Analyses 1989–1998*, Priština: MM; Peja/Peć: Dukagjini, 1998

Mertus, Julie, *Kosovo: How Myths and Truths Started a War*, Berkeley: University of California Press, 1999

Troebst, Stefan, *Conflict in Kosovo: Failure of Prevention? An Analytical Documentation, 1992–1998*, ECMI Working Paper 1, May 1998

Vickers, Miranda, *Between Serb and Albanian: A History of Kosovo*, New York: Columbia University Press, 1998

Russia

Capsule Summary

Name: Russia, or Russian Federation
Location: eastern Europe and northern Asia
Total Population: 144,526,278 (July 2003 estimate)
Minority Populations: approximately 18 million (12 % of the total population)
Languages: Russian and approximately 130 other languages (Tatar, Ukrainian, Chuvash, Bashkir, etc.)
Religious Denominations: Eastern Orthodox (majority), Sunni Muslim, Protestant (Baptist, Pentecostal, Lutheran, Seventh-day Adventist, etc.), Lamaist Buddhist, Catholic, Jew, Animist, and others

Russia is the largest (by its territory) state of the world. It is located in eastern Europe and northern Asia. Its area is more than 17 million square kilometers (6.6 million square miles). Its per capita GDP is $9,700 (2002 estimate). Russia is a federative republic. Its subjects are 21 republics (Adygheya, Altai, Bashkortostan, Buryatia, Chechen, Chuvash, Daghestan, Ingushetia, Kabardino-Balkar, Kalmykia, Karachay-Cherkess, Karelia, Komi, Mari El, Mordovia, Sakha [Yakutia], North Ossetia-Alania, Tatarstan, Tyva, Udmurt, and Khakassia), one autonomous region (Jewish), ten autonomous districts (Aga Buryat, Chukchi, Komi-Permyak, Koryak, Nenets, Taimyr [Dolgano-Nenets], Ust-Orda Buryat, Khanty-Mansi, Evenki, and Yamalo-Nenets), six areas, 49 regions, and two cities of federal jurisdiction.

According to the *Tale of Bygone Years*, the oldest Russian chronicle, Russian statehood appeared in 862, when prince Rurik started ruling in Novgorod, one of the Russian cities. Soon the old Russian state united most lands populated with Eastern Slavic tribes. How-ever, increased feudal fragmentation led to the situation where the unity of old Russian lands became, in significant degree, nominal. As a result, Russia could not put up strong resistance to the Mongol invasion in the thirteenth century. It had to pay tribute to the Mongol khans although Russia kept control over its internal affairs. The defeat of Mongol-Tatars by the Russian troops during the *Kulikovo* battle in 1380 crucially weakened the yoke, and 100 years later the yoke was removed entirely.

Nevertheless, Russia continued to have feudal units, faintly linked with each other. The strongest of them were called great principalities. In the rivalry among all these state formations, the Great Principality of Moscow won. Gradually it became the consolidating center of all Eastern Slavic regions. In the fourteenth to sixteenth centuries the Russian centralized state had been formed around Moscow. It united the northern part of the territory populated with Eastern Slavs, as well as some regions in the east (Volga Region, Urals, and Siberia). Out of a mainly monoethnic state it became a polyethnic state. During the seventeenth and eighteenth centuries, the major part of the Ukraine and all of Belorussia were incorporated into Russia (before, these territories had belonged to Poland and Lithuania). By the early twentieth century Russia was a powerful state, quickly developing both politically and economically.

The failures of Russia during World War I helped Communists (who were materially provisioned by Germany, which was fighting against Russia) to seize power via the October coup. The cruel terror launched by the new authorities led to the destruction of millions

RUSSIA

of people. Ill-advised agricultural policy led to famine in the country. It also took millions of lives. As a result, by the beginning of World War II, Russia was weakened and not well prepared. This led to very extensive human losses during the war. However, Russia together with the allied countries won this war. At the end of the war and afterward, the authorities continued to pursue the policy of repression. Whole peoples were exiled to areas with hard living conditions. The postwar decades even more clearly showed the economic nonefficiency and political bankruptcy of the Russian system. In the late 1980s the leaders of the country had to pursue reforms, although among the political leaders there still were those who were against any transformations. Their attempt at a coup d'etat in 1991 failed and resulted in the collapse of the totalitarian regime.

Ethnic Composition of Population and Linguistic Situation

It is difficult to define the exact number of minorities living in Russia. In the last (1989) census of the population 128 peoples were identified. However, 17 of these national groups are numerically very small in the territory of Russia (numbering 700 or fewer persons each). Moreover, they do not belong to the native population. Hence, it is possible to not count them while determining the total number of peoples residing in Russia. In addition, because of certain circumstances one group was identified under two names in the census. This is the case of Mountain Jews and Tats. At the same time, 34 ethnoses living almost only in Russia were not separately identified in the census and were included within the composition of larger peoples (all these peoples should be counted during the 2002 census). Thus, with a certain degree of convention, it is possible to consider that there are 144 peoples living in Russia.

For the purpose of systematization, the peoples of Russia will be united in language families and groups according to their linguistic affiliation.

The Indo-European language family is the most widespread in Russia (practically all over the country). The largest within it is the Slavic group, to which belong Russians (119.9 million people or 81.5 percent of the total population of the country), Ukrainians (4.4 million, 3 percent), Byelorussians (1.2 million, 0.8 percent), Poles (95,000), Bulgarians (33,000), Czechs (4,000), and Serbs (1,600). In the Germanic

group of the same family can be placed Germans (842,000, 0.6 percent) and conventionally (because of their former speaking language, Yiddish) Ashkenazi Jews (537,000, 0.4 percent). To the Armenian group of the Indo-European family belong Armenians (532,000, 0.4 percent); to the Iranian—Ossetes (402,000, 0.3 percent), Tajiks (38,000), Mountain Jews—Dag Chufuti (31,000), Kurds (5,000), Persians (3,000), Central Asian Jews (1,400), and Afghans (1,000); to the Romance—Moldavians (173,000, 0.1 percent), Romanians (6,000), Spaniards (2,000), and Cubans (1,600); to the Indo-Aryan—Gypsies (153,000, 0.1 percent); to the Baltic—Lithuanians (70,000) and Latvians (47,000); to the Greek—Greeks (92,000).

The second largest is the Altaic family. The peoples speaking the languages of this family live predominantly in the Volga and Urals regions, Northern Caucasus, and in Siberia. The Altaic family is represented primarily by its Turkic group, which unites Tatars (more than five million, 3.4 percent of the total population), Chuvashes (1.8 million, 1.2 percent), Bashkirs (1.3 million, 0.9 percent), Kazakhs (636,000, 0.4 percent), Yakuts (380,000, 0.3 percent), Azerbaijani (336,000, 0.2 percent), Kryashens (300,000, 0.2 percent), Kumyks (277,000, 0.2 percent), Tuva (206,000, 0.1 percent), Siberian Tatars (190,000, 0.1 percent), Karachays (150,000, 0,1 percent), Uzbeks (127,000), Khakas (78,000), Balkars (78,000), Nogai (74,000), Altaians (48,000), Kirghiz (42,000), Turkmen (40,000), Crimean Tatars (21,000), Shors (16,000), Nagaibaks (11,000), Gagauz (10,000), Turks (10,000), Kumandins (10,000), Dolgans (7,000), Karakalpaks (6,000), Talangits (5,000), Uighurs (3,000), Tubalar (3,000), Teleuts (1,700), Chelkans (1,000), Tofalar (700), and Chulyms (700). To the Mongolian group of the Altaic family belong Buryats (415,000, 0.3 percent), Kalmyks (166,000, 0.1 percent), Khalkh-Mongols (2,000), and Soyots (2,000); to the Korean group—Koreans (107,000); to the Tungus-Manchu group—Evenki (30,000), Evens (17,000), Nanai (12,000), Olcha (3,000), Udihe (2,000), Oroches (700), Negidals (600), Oroks (400), and conventionally Tazes (200). The latter are Udihe in origin but assimilated with Chinese, switched to the Chinese language, then later to Russian.

The peoples speaking the languages of the Uralic-Yukaghir family are mainly settled in the Volga region, the north of the European part of Russia, and in Siberia. This family is represented in Russia by its three groups. To the Finno-Ugric group belong Mordvinians

1032

(1.1 million, 0.7 percent of the total population), Udmurts (715,000, 0.5 percent), Mari (644,000, 0.4 percent), Komi (336,000, 0.2 percent), Komi-Permyaks (147,000, 0.1 percent), Karelians (125,000), Finns (47,000), Estonians (46,000), Khanty (22,000), Vepses (12,000), Vesermyans (10,000), Mansi (8,000), Hungarians (6,000), Saami (1,800), Izhors (400), and Votians (200); to the Samoyed group—Nenets (34,000), Selkups (4,000), Nganasans (1,300), and Enets (200); to the Yukaghir group—Yukaghirs (1,100) and conventionally (because they lost their native language close to Yukaghir and switched to other languages) Chuvans (1,400).

Another large language family in Russia is the North Caucasian family. To the Abkhaz-Adyghe group belong Kabardians (386,000, 0.3 percent of the total population), Adyghe (113,000), Cherkess (51,000), Abaza (33,000), Shapsugs (10,000), and a small group of Abkhaz living in Russia (7,000); to the Nakh-Daghestan group belong Chechens (899,000, 0.6 percent), Avars (464,000, 0.3 percent), Dargwa (320,000, 0.2 percent), Lezgi (257,000, 0.2 percent), Ingushes (215,000, 0.1 percent), Laks (106,000), Tabasarans (94,000), Kaitaks (30,000), Andi (20,000), Rutuls (20,000), Aguls (18,000), Tsez (12,000), Bezhta (10,000), Chamalal (7,000), Tsakhurs (6,000), Akhvakh (6,000), Bagulal (6,000), Karata (5,000), Tindi (5,000), Botlikh (3,000), Godoberi (3,000), Kubachi (3,000), Udi (1,100), Khvarshi (1,000), Archi (1,000), Hunzib (800), and Hinukh (400).

In some cities of Russia the representatives of the Kartvelian family—Georgians (131,000)—live. In the same family are also placed Georgian Jews (1,200 in Russia).

The Chukotko-Kamchatkan and Eskimo-Aleut, numerically small, language families are restricted to the territory of the extreme northeast of the country. The first includes Chukchi (15,000), Kamchadals (9,000; now speak Russian), Koryaks (6,000), Alutors (3,000), Itelmens (2,000), and Kereks (100); the second includes Eskimos (1,700) and Aleuts (600). The Yeniseian family is even smaller. It embraces Kets, settled by Yenisei River (1,100) and Yughs (there remained only 15 of them, and only two or three persons can speak the native language). Nivkhs (5,000) speak an isolated language.

There are also in Russia the representatives of some nonindigenous peoples speaking the languages of other families. These are Assyrians (10,000) and Arabs (3,000), belonging to the Semitic language family, Chinese (5,000)—the Sino-Tibetan family, and Vietnamese (2,000)—the Austro-Asiatic family.

As mentioned above, 34 peoples were not identified in the 1989 census. The so-called Ando-Tsez peoples (Andi, Botlikh, Godoberi, Karata, Akhvakh, Bagulal, Chamalal, Tindi, Khvarshi, Tsez, Hinukh, Bezhta, and Hunzib) as well as Archi were included within the composition of Avars; Kaitaks and Kubachi were numbered among Dargwa; Shapsugs—among the Adyghe; Votians and Kamchadals—among Russians; Vesermyans—among Udmurts; Kryashens, Nagaibaks, and Siberian Tatars—among Tatars; Talangits, Teleuts, Kumandins, Chelkans, and Tubalar—among Altaians; Chulyms—among either Tatars or Khakas; Yughs—among Kets; Soyots—among Buryats; Alutors and Kereks—among Koryaks. Tazes were included into the combined group of "other peoples."

It is necessary to have in mind that the data on the numbers of peoples are mainly based on the 1989 census, whereas the number of some communities and their proportion in the total population of the country have considerably changed during the more than ten years after the census. It is connected with the differences in the birth rates, which are very high among North-Caucasian peoples, and also with the moving to Russia of many legal and illegal immigrants. There has been a significant increase of emigres from the Trans-Caucasus countries (Armenians, Azerbaijani, and Georgians), as well as from Afghanistan, China, and Vietnam. On the contrary, the numbers of Germans, Jews, Greeks, and Finns have greatly decreased due to emigration.

The status of national minorities can be affiliated with the peoples who do not have republics or national-territorial formations and with the parts of the peoples who have states or national-territorial formations but live outside them. In total, approximately 18 million people (12 percent of the population) can be included in the category of national minorities. As to the total of non-Russian population of the Russian Federation, it comprises 27 million (18 percent).

The number of languages in Russia is close to the number of minorities living there, because the overwhelming majority of peoples, in more or less equal degree, preserved their original languages. If the languages of some numerically very small nonindigenous peoples, numbering only a few hundred or even dozens of people in Russia, are not counted, some 130 languages are still in use in the country. Approximately 80 of them have written forms.

Thus, the number of languages in Russia is a little less than the number of peoples. This is because sometimes two or more peoples speak the same language and there are also several peoples who lost their languages. For example, both Kabardians and Cherkess speak one and the same Kabardian-Cherkess language, Adyghe and Shapsugs speak the Adyghe language, Karachays and Balkars speak the Karachay-Balkar language, Tatars, Siberian Tatars (the latter consider themselves as a separate people, different from the Volga Tatars), Kryashens, and Nagaibaks speak the Tatar language. Vesermyans now speak the Udmurt language. Soyots in the late nineteenth century switched from their original Turkic Soyot language to the Buryat language. Previously Chuvans spoke the language related to Yukaghir, but then they switched to either the Chukchi or the Russian language. As was noted, Tazes first went through language assimilation with the Chinese, but now are gradually switching from Chinese to Russian. A small group of Yughs actually lost its language and now they speak Russian. Russian is a native language for Kamchadals, who are Russian-Itelmen mestizos who consider themselves a separate people. As to the languages of Kaitaks and Kubachi, many linguists suppose that these are the dialects of the Dargwa language and others consider them to be two different languages. The same is true about the language of the Central Asian Jews: it is identified either as the dialect of Tajik or as a separate language.

The degree of the preservation of their native languages differs greatly among different peoples. Whereas in total 94.6 percent of the population indicated the language of their nationality as their native tongue, this index among Russians is 99.96 percent. This index is also high among many Caucasian people (98.8 among Chechens, 98.2 among Ingushes, 97.7 among Karachays, 97.6 among Kabardians, and so on), as well as among Tuva (98.4), Yakuts (94.0), and Kalmyks (93.1). On the other hand, this index is only 8.9 percent among Jews, 15.1 percent among Poles, 36.2 among Byelorussians, 36.5 percent among Koreans, 41.8 among Germans, 42.8 among Ukrainians, 44.5 among Greeks, and 48.6 among Karelians. This index is also low among many northern people: 16.8 percent among Oroches, 18.8 among Itelmens, 23.3 among Nivkhs, 24.3 among Udihe, and so on. Only 27.6 percent of all non-Russian populations of Russia consider Russian to be their native language. In addition, 60.4 percent of the non-Russian population do not consider Russian to be their native

language but are fluent in it. Thus, 88 percent of the non-Russian population have a good command of Russian, but this increases to 97.7 percent for the total population.

Religious Composition of Population

Russia is not only a multiethnic country, it is also multireligious. Different religions, as well as their trends, divisions, church organizations, and sects, are represented there. However, the leading position belongs to Orthodox Christianity. In 988, on the initiative of Great Prince Vladimir, there was baptism of Russians. Since that time Eastern Christianity became the main religion on the territory of Russia. Despite the 70-year persecution against religion and primarily against Orthodoxy launched after the 1917 October coup (during these repressions millions of believers were annihilated, and almost all church leadership and dozens of thousands of clergy were shot), the Russian Orthodox Church continues to be the most influential institution among believers. According to some estimates, about half of the population considers itself to be Orthodox. The adherents of Orthodoxy are the majority of believers among Russians, Karelians, Votians, Izhors, Vepses, Saami, Komi, Komi-Permyaks, Udmurts, Vesermyans, Mordvinians, Chuvashes, Kryashens, Nagaibaks, Gypsies, Khanty, Mansi, Kumandins, Chelkans, Chulyms, Shors, Khakas, Kets, Yakuts, Nanai, Oroches, Yukaghirs, Itelmens, Kamchadals, Aleuts, as well as those Russian Byelorussians, Moldavians, Bulgarians, Gagauz, Greeks, most of Ossetes, Mari, Nenets, Selkups, Teleuts, Tubalar, Tofalar, Dolgans, Evenki, Evens, Oroks, and Chuvans; those Russian Ukrainians, Georgians and Abkhaz; significant groups of Kalmyks, Western Buryats, Altaians, Talangits, Enets, Negidals, Koryaks, Alutors, a few Kabardians, Nivkhs, and Chukchi.

In the seventeenth century, old believers separated from the Russian Orthodox Church. Now they comprise more than two million. The vast majority of them are ethnic Russians. They are divided into "priestly old believers" and "priestless old believers."

In the seventeenth century and later the sects of so-called Spiritual Christians (Khlysty, Scoptsy, Dukhobors, Molokans, and others) broke away from the Russian Orthodox Church. In their teaching they went far from traditional Christianity. The number of the adherents of these sects (mostly ethnic Russians) is quite small.

The second division of Christianity—Catholicism—is less represented in Russia. About 500,000 people profess it (including 300,000 adherents of the Latin rite and 200,000 adherents of the Byzantine rite). The followers of Latin rite are Poles, Lithuanians, some Germans, and Latvians living in Russia. The Byzantine rite is typical for some Ukrainians settled in Russia.

More than one million people in Russia profess Protestantism. Protestant denominations are represented by Baptism and Pentecostalism (among Russians, Ukrainians, Germans, and others), Lutheranism (among Germans, Latvians, and Finns), Adventism (among Russians and others), Mennonite faith (among Germans), and others. Marginal Protestant denominations have also spread in Russia. There are Jehovah's Witnesses, Moonies, and Mormons in small numbers in Russia.

Another division of Christianity—the Monophysite faith—is represented in Russia by the Armenian Apostolic Church, uniting the majority of Armenians settled in the country.

Nearly one-tenth of Russia's population professes Islam. Most of Russia's Muslims are Sunnis. These are the overwhelming majority of Tatars, Bashkirs, Siberian Tatars, Kazakhs, and other representatives of Central Asia who settled in Russia, Adyghe, Shapsugs, Kabardians, Cherkess, Karachays, Balkars, Chechens, Ingushes, Avars, Ando-Tsez peoples, Archi, Dargwa, Kaitaks, Kubachi, Laks, Tabasarans, Lezgi, Kumyks, and Nogai; some Ossetes and Georgians (Adzhars), Abkhaz, and Azerbaijani, settled in Russia. The majority of Azerbaijani living in the country are Shi'a Muslims.

Buddhism has spread in Russia among the Tuva, a major part of the Kalmyks and Soyots, as well as among Eastern Buryats and represented by the Lamaist trend.

The adherents of Judaism are religious Russian Jews.

Animism still exists in Russia among some Mari, a small number of Chuvashes and Udmurts, as well as among some peoples of Siberia and the Far East (the overwhelming majority of Nganasans, Udihe, Kereks, Eskimos, most Enets, Talangits, Negidals, Chukchi, Koryaks, Alutors, Nivkhs, significant groups of Nenets, Tofalar, Dolgans, Western Buryats, Soyots, Evenki, and Evens).

In the early twentieth century Burkhanism (a syncretic religion) appeared among Altaians (Altai-kizhi)—one of the Siberian peoples.

Some nontraditional-for-Russia religions have come to Russia recently. These include the neo-Hinduist sect Hare Krishna, Church of Scientology, Baha'i faith, and others.

PAVEL PUCHKOV

See also **Russians**

Further Reading

Александров, Вадим Александрович, и др., редакторы, *Народы Европейской части СССР, т. I*, Москва: Издательство "Наука", 1964 (Aleksandrov, Vadim Aleksandrovich, a.o., editors *Peoples of the European Part of the USSR, Volume I*, Moscow: Nauka Press, 1964

Белицер, Вера Николаевна, и др., редакторы, *Народы Европейской части СССР, т. II*, Москва: Издательство "Наука," 1964 (Belitser, Vera Nikolaevna, a.o., editors, *Peoples of the European Part of the USSR, Volume. II*, Moscow: Nauka Press, 1964)

Казьмина, Ольга Евгеньевна, и Павел Иванович Пучков, *Основы этнодемографии*, Москва: Издательство "Наука," 1994 (Kazmina, Olga Yevgenyevna, and Pavel Ivanovich Puchkov, *Fundamentals of Ethnodemography*, Moscow: Nauka Press, 1994)

Косвен, Марк Осипович, и др., редакторы, *Народы Кавказа, т. I*, Москва: Издательство Академии наук СССР, 1960 (Kosven, Mark Osipovich, a.o., editors, *Peoples of Caucasus, Volume. I*, Moscow: USSR Academy of Sciences Press, 1960)

Левин, Максим Григорьевич, и Леонид Павлович Потапов, редакторы, *Народы Сибири*, Москва и Ленинград: Издательство Академии наук СССР, 1956 (Levin, Maksim Grigoryevich, and Leonid Pavlovich Potapov, editors, *Peoples of Siberia*, Moscow and Leningrad: USSR Academy of Sciences Press, 1956)

Пучков, Павел Иванович, "Религиозный состав населения России," в *Народы России: энциклопедия*, под редакцией Валерия Александровича Тишкова и др., Москва: Издательство Большая Российская Энциклопедия, 1994 (Puchkov, Pavel Ivanovich, "Religious Structure of the Population of Russia," in *Peoples of Russia: Encyclopedia*, edited by Valeri Aleksandrovich Tishkov, a.o., Moscow: Great Russian Encyclopedia Press. 1994)

Тишков, Валерий Александрович, Павел Иванович Пучков и др., редакторы, *Народы и религии мира: энциклопедия*, Москва: Издательство "Большая Российская Энциклопедия", 1998 (Tishkov, Valeri Aleksandrovich, Pavel Ivanovich Puchkov, a.o., editors, *Peoples and Religions of the World: Encyclopedia*, Moscow: Great Russian Encyclopedia Press, 1998)

Токарев, Сергей Александрович, *Этнография народов СССР*, Москва: Издательство Московского университета, 1958 (Tokarev, Sergey Aleksandrovich, *Ethnography of the Peoples of the USSR*, Moscow: Moscow University Press, 1958)

Толстов, Сергей Павлович, Николай Николаевич Чебоксаров и Кирилл Васильевич Чистов, редакторы, *Очерки общей этногрфии: Европейская часть СССР*, Москва: Издательство "Наука", 1968 (Tolstov, Sergei Pavlovich, Nikolai Nikolaevich Cheboksarov, and Kirill Vasilyevich Chistov, editors, *Essays of General Ethnography: European Part of the USSR*, Moscow: Nauka Press, 1968)

Толстов, Сергей Павлович, Максим Григорьевич Левин и Николай Николаевич Чебоксаров, редакторы, *Очерки общей этнографии: Азиатская часть СССР*, Москва: Издательство Академии наук СССР, 1960 (Tolstov, Sergei Pavlovich, Maksim Grigoryevich Levin, and Nikolai Nikolaevich Cheboksarov, editors, *Essays of General Ethnography: Asian Part of the USSR*, Moscow: USSR Academy of Sciences Press, 1960)

Grimes, Barbara E., editor, *Ethnologue: Languages of the World*, Dallas, Texas: Summer Institute of Linguistics, Inc., 13th edition, 1996

Kazmina, Olga Yevgenyevna, and Pavel Ivanovich Puchkov, "Ethnodemographic Processes in the Russian Federation," *Anthropology & Archeology of Eurasia*, 34, no. 4 (1995)

Litvinoff, Miles, *World Directory of Minorities*, London: Minority Rights Group International, 2nd edition, 1997

Russians

Capsule Summary

Location: northern Asia (that part west of the Urals is included with Europe), bordering the Arctic Ocean, between Europe and the North Pacific Ocean

Total Population: 144,526, 278. Substantial minority populations found in Estonia (28% of population, approximately 400,000), Latvia (29%/600,000), Kazakhstan (30%, five million) and Ukraine (17%, eight million)

Language: Russian

Religions: Orthodox (80%), Muslim, and Roman Catholic

The most populous of all the Slavic peoples, Russians have played a changing role in the Eurasian lands since 988. They constituted a majority in Kievan and Muscovite Russia, after which they became the ruling group in the far-flung possessions of Imperial Russia and the Soviet Union. In the nineteenth and early twentieth centuries, sizable contingents departed and formed Russian enclaves in Europe, America, and Asia. After the USSR's 1991 collapse, Russians became a majority in the new Russia and a somewhat beleaguered minority in neighboring states.

Russian history dates to 862, when warring Slavic tribes summoned a Scandinavian prince, Rurik, to rule them. Rurik's successors established themselves in Kiev, where they forged ties with the Byzantine Empire. Prince Vladimir strengthened the relationship in 988 when he accepted Byzantine Christianity (Orthodoxy), which became a fundamental part of Russian national identity.

Kievan Russia registered many successes, but was eventually undermined by power struggles among Vladimir's successors. The appearance in 1240 of the Mongols, a ruthless fighting machine from the east, found Kiev ill prepared to resist.

Invasion, Fragmentation, and Resurgence, 1240–1700

The Mongol invasion had a great impact on the Russian state. It demolished Kievan Russia, fracturing it into small fiefdoms or appanages. The entire southwest passed from Russian control and the country's center of gravity shifted north of the occupied areas, to Vladimir-Suzdal'. There Prince Andrei Bogoliubskii built fortresses, towns, and churches, including Russian Orthodoxy's temporary headquarters.

But it was an outpost called Moscow that became the capital of post-Kievan Russia. Located on high ground, Moscow was convenient to major rivers and trade routes, and it enjoyed good leadership. Prince Ivan Kalita won from the Mongols the right to collect the tribute throughout the region, permitting him to amass funds with which to ransom Russian princes and territories. Kalita convinced the head of the Russian church, Metropolitan Peter, to move his headquarters to Moscow in 1326, where they laid the foundations for the Kremlin. Ivan's successor, Dmitrii Donskoi, bolstered Moscow's prestige with a military victory over the Mongols at Kulikovo in September 1380.

Half a century later, Ivan III came to power. His claim to the throne was immensely strengthened by the fall of the Byzantine Empire to the Ottoman Turks in 1453, which left Moscow as the only unconquered Orthodox capital. In 1472, Ivan married the niece of the last Byzantine emperor and added the Byzantine double eagle to his personal standard. Like the Byzantines, Ivan had territorial ambitions beyond Muscovy. Money, inheritance, and coercion enabled him to conquer Iaroslavl', Rostov, Dmitrov, and Uglich by 1500. He ended Novgorod's independence and took Tver' by 1485. Intrigues with the rival Crimean Tatars helped him inflict a serious defeat on the Mongols in the late 1400s. Crowned with another of Ivan's achievements, the magnificent Kremlin complex, Russia was clearly on the rise.

Ivan IV, "*Groznyi* (terrible)," improved upon his predecessor's conquests when he defeated a Mongol army and annexed its territory. Russian armies routed the Kazan' Khanate in 1552, an event commemorated in St. Basil's Cathedral in Moscow, and later took the Astrakhan Khanate. These campaigns and the conquest of Siberia, which brought in thousands of non-Russians, marked the beginning of multiethnic statehood for Russia.

Ivan IV's triumphs abroad were accompanied by upheaval at home. He used his private army, the *oprichniki*, to wage a bloody war on his domestic opponents. The military campaigns took their toll on the population, which found its freedom increasingly limited. The Tsar himself fatally wounded the dynasty when he killed his son Ivan in November 1581, making his frail son Fedor his heir.

Fedor died childless in 1598. Ivan IV's respected adviser, Boris Godunov, became Tsar but was plagued by a series of natural disasters and the appearance of a pretender. After Boris died in 1605, the discontented rallied to other pretenders. Poland and Lithuania invaded the country and chaos ensued. In 1612, a national militia assembled to expel the invaders and arrange the accession of a new dynasty in the person of 16-year-old Michael Romanov in 1613.

The first Romanovs were preoccupied with the aftermath of civil war and invasion. Yet this era also saw the continued expansion of the Muscovite state. The cradle of Russian statehood, the Kievan lands, had been dominated by Lithuania and Poland since the thirteenth century. By the early seventeenth century, however, religious conflict and a series of internal disputes caused civil unrest there. Polish attempts to put down the disturbances only worsened the situation, leading to a move for union with Russia. In the 1654 Treaty of Pereiaslavl', much of Ukraine was returned to Rus', with guarantees of autonomy from the Tsar. Ukrainians shared a common ethnic origin with Russians, but centuries of life in Lithuania and Poland had resulted in cultural and religious divergence.

An odd domestic conflict soon demonstrated that expansion was not universally popular. A prominent Orthodox cleric, Nikon, declared that inaccuracies had made their way into Russian church books over time, an intolerable circumstance in a state that was staking claim to religious and political leadership. He met determined opposition from the archpriest Avvakum, who insisted that the church that survived the fall of the Byzantime Empire could have no such deficiencies. This dispute soon spread throughout the country and the followers of Avvakum known as "old believers" for their belief in the uniqueness of Russia as reflected in the pre-Nikon church. Avvakum was executed, and Nikon became Patriarch and saw his view officially adapted. This conflict proved durable and damaging, however, ultimately forcing many Russians to leave Russia in search of opportunities to maintain their vision of the Orthodox faith.

The New Empire

Peter I had no doubts about the state's direction upon his accession in 1696. He inherited a land expanded yet vulnerable, lacking the means to defend its gains against adversaries in the north and south. The Tsar combined realism with ambition in addressing these weaknesses, beginning with a long tour of Holland and England in search of expertise in practical enterprises such as shipbuilding and medicine in 1697. Proclaiming "I am a student and I seek teachers," Peter apprenticed himself to master craftsmen and recruited top talent to Russia. Immediate results of the trip included the founding of a naval academy to provide home-grown expertise for the new Russian navy.

A modern, seafaring state required an accessible port and a new capital, both of which materialized in St. Petersburg, founded in 1703.

The new city required a new worldview and new people. Peter enlisted the nobility in state service as a condition of their privileges. He forced them to resettle in Petersburg, where they would be clean-shaven, dressed in the European style and "liberated" from old mores.

Peter simultaneously extended Russia's influence abroad. He was victorious in the northern war with Sweden, adding new Baltic territory in the 1721 Treaty of Nystadt. His campaigns against the Ottoman Turks yielded early victories before suffering reversals, but he had signaled that Russia would contest the Ottomans. By Peter's death in 1725, Russia had become an empire and a world power.

Peter's true heir emerged half a century later in Catherine II. Like her predecessor, Catherine had an ambitious domestic agenda, including the recruitment of foreigners, in this case German colonists for the central and southern Volga regions. These "Volga Germans" proved to be a great boon for Russian agriculture. However, Catherine's greatest achievements came in advancing the Russian Empire. She used a personal relationship with the Polish ruler, Stanislaw Poniatowski, to leverage changes advantageous to Russia in Polish policy. After Poles rebelled against them, she sent Russian troops to "restore order." When the Ottoman Empire declared war on Russia in the midst of the Polish crisis in 1768, she responded in kind.

Victory was swift but disconcerting for Austria and Prussia, whose rulers feared an imbalance of power among the three states. To appease them, Catherine agreed to a partition, each power taking Polish territory for itself. Russian Poland included some four million Jews, who soon were restricted to living outside the major cities, in the so-called Pale of Settlement.

Catherine subsequently drove a hard bargain with the Ottomans, winning in the 1774 Treaty of Kuchuk Kainardji the right to intervene on behalf of Orthodox Christians in the Ottoman possessions. This helped her to annex the Crimea and bring thousands of Crimean Tatars into the empire. The empress failed to realize her "Greek Project," the destruction of the Ottomans and resurrection of Byzantium. But she succeeded in key imperial tasks such as extending the empire, neutralizing Poland, and incorporating millions of non-Russians.

Imperial Zenith and the Beginnings of Decline, 1796–1856

Catherine was succeeded by her son, Paul, whose reign ended tragically in 1801. Alexander I declared that he would pursue the goals of his grandmother, Catherine. Like Catherine, Alexander had ambitious domestic plans, but saw his regime shaped by events abroad. After brief agreement with Napoleon, the Tsar found himself rallying his people to fight a "patriotic war" against the French invaders in 1812. Emerging victorious from a bloody, scorched-earth struggle, Alexander triumphantly hosted the negotiations for the Peace of Paris, which restored the status quo in Europe.

Before the Napoleonic invasion, the Russian government used favorable circumstances to acquire more non-Russian peoples and territories, including Georgia, a Christian nation in the Caucasus long besieged by Muslim neighbors. Agreement with the Ottoman Empire in 1812 included control of Romanian-majority Bessarabia, and a brief war with Sweden in 1809–10 brought Finland into Russia. In his tenure, Alexander had further expanded Russia's borders and immensely strengthened Russia's position in the world.

Alexander's successor, Nicholas I, came to power in the midst of the 1825 Decembrist revolt, a demonstration by Russian officers in favor of a constitutional regime. Proclaiming his fealty to the principles of autocracy, Orthodoxy, and nationalism, he punished the rebels severely. In central Europe, where the danger of revolutionary change was clear, Nicholas applied his credo religiously. When Russia's Poles rebelled in 1830, the Tsar put them down and joined other monarchs against revolutionary movements elsewhere on the continent. In 1849, he sent Russian forces to help the Habsburg Monarchy to crush the Hungarian rebellion.

In southeast Europe and the Caucasus, Nicholas proved less consistent in defense of the status quo. His armies violated the integrity of the Persian Empire, to incorporate thousands of Christian Armenians in the 1820s, setting the stage for years of conflict with native Caucasian tribes. Invoking Kuchuk Kainardji, the Tsar fought the Ottoman Empire, to rescue Greek rebels in 1828–29. In 1854 Nicholas contemplated the destruction of the Ottoman government in a dispute over Orthodox privileges in the Holy Land. This perceived attempt to dominate southeast Europe brought down the wrath of the European powers and a war in Crimea, which Russia lost badly.

Reform, Reaction, Crisis 1856–1917

Nicholas died during the war and his son, Alexander II, negotiated the peace, which abrogated the Kuchuk Kainardji Treaty. Alexander withdrew from European affairs temporarily, turning his imperial focus east. Between 1856 and 1881, Russian armies conquered large swatches of Central Asia, incorporating thousands of Muslims into the empire. Alexander also took advantage of internal disarray in China to improve his position in the Far East.

But domestic concerns preoccupied this tsar. Alexander knew that internal weaknesses contributed to the Crimean debacle. If Russia hoped to remain a great power, it would have to modernize its armed forces, which required the creation of a system of reserves. Since unhappy serfs with weapons could wreak havoc on the estates, Alexander ended the institution of serfdom in 1860.

As part of these reforms, Tsar Alexander turned his attention to the status of Russia's ethnic and religious minorities. Before his reign, Russian Jews had faced restrictions and non-Russians were, at best, an afterthought. By 1870, however, it was clear that national sentiments were a force to be reckoned with, having helped to unify Germany and divide Austria. Alexander seemed determined that Russia's minorities become a source of strength rather than discord. Declaring as his goal the "fusion of this people with the indigenous population," the Tsar ended many discriminatory measures against Russian Jews. In Finland and the Baltics, he allowed the use of the local language for official purposes.

This attempt at inclusiveness did not extend to Poland, which staged another revolt in 1863.

Alexander's reforms came too late for those impatient for change. Members of the revolutionary group "People's Will" had already decided to replace the tsarist government with a utopian socialist regime. After several unsuccessful attempts, they assassinated the Tsar on March 1, 1881.

The murder failed to destroy the tsarist system. Instead, it brought to power Alexander III, who concluded that his father's reforms had endangered the empire and changed course. This tsar believed that the Russian rulers must eradicate rather than grant concessions on local differences. In Poland, Ukraine, and the Baltic, the use of local languages was deemed subversive, leading to the absurd case of students taking Polish literature courses but in Russian translation. Alexander III imposed drastic new restrictions on Jews, for example, limiting their enrollment in schools, and stood by while mobs targeted Jews and their livelihoods for attack. These policies were the catalyst for the first major emigration from Russia, as Jews left by the tens of thousands to resettle in the United States.

Alexander III's son, Nicholas II, followed his father's example. Dismissing calls for reform, he attempted to combine economic modernization with reactionary administrative policies, including Russification. The consequences were often fatal, as in Ukraine where citizens who were unable to read Russian language signs died from drinking cholera-infested water. However, Nicholas encountered difficulties his father had not. In 1904, a Russo-Japanese conflict over disputed Far East territory led to a war that Russia lost disastrously. A wave of disturbances followed. In the Russian cities, strikers demanded political change. In Warsaw, Riga, and non-Russian areas, protesters directed their ire against Russia and Russian policies that denied them their language and culture.

Although Nicholas eventually granted a constitutional regime, he remained reactionary in his policies toward ethnic and religious minorities. The results were predictable: Jews and non-Russians, notably Leon Trotskii and Felix Dzerzinskii, numbered among the most committed members of a growing revolutionary movement by 1914.

After the Japanese defeat, Nicholas was drawn into Serbia's cold war with Austria-Hungary, which led ultimately to the assassination of Archduke Franz Ferdinand in Sarajevo in 1914. When the Tsar took the decision to defend Serbia, the stage was set for an ill-prepared Russia to enter a major European conflict.

War and Revolution, 1917–1924

Within weeks of entering the war, the Russian government was in serious trouble. Uncomprehending troops, incompetent leadership, and chronic shortages of such essentials as ammunition and winter clothing exposed the country's weaknesses. Nicholas worsened the situation by taking personal command of the army in 1915, making the unpopular Tsarina Alexandra and her confidant, Rasputin, the public face of the Russian government. By March 1917, battlefield losses and domestic shortages led to disturbances that forced the abdication of the Romanov dynasty. The succeeding Provisional Government, headed by Alexander Kerenskii, promised action on popular issues like land reform after the convocation of a Constituent Assembly. However, it was weakened by public weariness with the war and challenged by Vladimir Il'ich Lenin and an invigorated revolutionary movement. It could not manage the war or the growing impatience of the populace and gave way to Lenin and the Bolsheviks on November 7, 1917.

It was apparent to many Russians—those of noble birth, intellectuals, businessmen, even some peasants—that they could not remain in the new state. Some fought the Bolsheviks in the White Army. Most fled abroad eventually—about 300,000 to France and Germany, 200,000 to the Baltic countries, 150,000 to the Balkans, and 150,000 to China. Nearly 30,000 citizens went to the United States, among them ousted Provisional Government chairman Kerenskii.

Taking advantage of the Bolshevik government's perilous circumstances—civil war, foreign intervention, famine—many non-Russians escaped as well. The 1918 Treaty of Brest-Litovsk, which the Bolshevik government negotiated as a means of exiting the war, brought the loss of Finland, Estonia, Lithuania, Latvia, and part of Poland, which became independent states.

Bolshevik policy toward the remaining non-Russians promised a clear break with the past. It rejected Russification and called for each group to opt for national independence or join the new state, where a People's Commissariat for Nationalities would help manage the transition. Inevitably, however, as the Bolsheviks extended their rule throughout the country, all the non-Russian areas came under the influence of a reconstituted empire: the Soviet Union. Even though the new state made no mention of Russia or Russians, a small, predominantly Russian group again governed a large non-Russian constituency.

The Stalin Era, 1928–1953

After their victory in the civil war, the Soviet leaders initiated a New Economic Policy (NEP), a retreat from the draconian policies of its first years designed to bring economic recovery from years of turmoil. Russians and non-Russians alike enjoyed a period of relative cultural freedom, including use of local languages in school. This interval was short-lived. The NEP coincided with the last illness and premature death of Lenin and a struggle for the party leadership among Lenin's colleagues. The Georgian, J.V. Stalin, emerged victorious by 1928.

Stalin's victory had a dramatic impact on all citizens of the USSR. His goal was nothing less than the transformation of the Soviet Union into a first-rank industrial power. All citizens became soldiers in the war to achieve it. In the first five-year plan, many found themselves drafted into labor armies in remote industrial cities, like Magnitogorsk. To guarantee the food supply for workers, Soviet officials transformed the countryside into a network of collective farms, a severe and sometimes fatal trial for peasant farmers. Wherever they were, Soviet citizens experienced the abrupt disappearance of beliefs and practices not directly associated with life before Stalin. Russians witnessed the widespread destruction of churches and monasteries, the main repository of their culture and identity since 988. In central Asia, women were forced out of the veil and into the factory. In one of the most notorious events of the Stalin era, some two million Ukrainian peasants lost their land and their lives. Everywhere, citizens were obliged to embrace a Stalinist culture, featuring adoration of the Soviet leader, the primacy of the Russian language, and a new pantheon of heroes and holidays. Those who protested were arrested and punished for "bourgeois nationalism"; new Soviet people were supposed to focus exclusively on the good of the collective.

In 1934, the assassination of the Leningrad party chief, Sergei Kirov, gave Stalin additional means of enforcing his vision. Hundreds of Bolshevik officials were arrested and charged with complicity in the murder. Interrogations and trials produced more arrests, triggering a reign of terror in which millions were shot or imprisoned. All nationalities felt the consequences; the entire leadership of the Turkmen Republic was purged. Now individuals loyal to Stalin, most of them Russians, would administer the republics.

In the midst of this domestic drama, a foreign threat materialized in Nazi Germany. Adolf Hitler declared himself Europe's savior from Soviet Communism and openly coveted Soviet lands for German colonization. At first, Stalin sought anti-Hitler alliances with France and Britain. Eventually, however, the two dictators found each other. Hitler needed Stalin's neutrality in Germany's planned invasion of Poland; Stalin's price was half of Poland and Hitler's blessing for the retaking of the Baltic states and Bessarabia. Both parties received satisfaction in the Nazi-Soviet nonaggression pact of August 1939. Accordingly, after the Nazis attacked Poland on September 1, 1939, the Soviet Army took eastern Polish territory, followed in 1940 by Estonia, Latvia, Lithuania, and Bessarabia. The Soviet administrators initiated purges of the native leadership, clergy, and others opposed to the USSR. In the Baltic states, nearly half of the native population was deported to Siberia, to make way for resettlement of Russians there. Meanwhile, Stalin tried unsuccessfully to recapture Finland in the "Winter War" of 1940.

In spite of their agreement, Hitler double-crossed Stalin and invaded the USSR on June 22, 1941. Refusing to believe an attack was imminent despite evidence to the contrary, Stalin had left the western border vulnerable, and German progress was swift. As they marched toward Moscow, German troops often received warm welcomes from citizens who had suffered from Bolshevik rule. Some collaborated with the Nazi forces in anti-Jewish outrages, such as the infamous Babi Yar massacre of September 1941, since some Jews had figured prominently in the Bolshevik revolution.

As before, all Soviet citizens reckoned with Stalin, who typically favored coercion and scapegoating in the prosecution of the war. Generals unable to bring immediate victory were shot, and soldiers in the battle for Stalingrad fought knowing that NKVD blocking units would shoot them if they retreated. Many non-Russians were singled out for special punishments. The descendants of Catherine II's Volga Germans paid for Hitler's sins in their August 1941 deportation to Central Asia and Siberia. The Chechen and Ingushi peoples and the Crimean Tatars suffered the same fate, after Red Army defeats in the Caucasus in 1941–42.

After the war, notwithstanding the tragic repatriation of some two million Russians to the USSR—where Stalin had them shot or imprisoned—about 50,000 made their way to the United States, settling on the East Coast and entering a wide variety of professions. At home many Soviet citizens hoped for a new postwar beginning. They were disappointed.

While publicly hailing the triumph, Stalin imprisoned those returning from German captivity and conducted reprisals against Ukrainians, Balts, and others accused of collaboration with the enemy. The beginnings of the Cold War triggered a campaign against "cosmopolitans," which quickly came to mean Jews. By the 1950s, Stalin had became obsessed with perceived Jewish plots inside the Kremlin. In late 1952, he ordered the arrest of Jewish doctors and allegedly planned mass arrests of Jews throughout the country. Only his death in March 1953 spared the country that ordeal.

From Stalin to Chernenko, 1953–1985

Nikita Sergeevich Khrushchev eventually emerged as Stalin's successor. He attempted to mitigate the effects of Stalinism, to safeguard the Soviet leadership and restore a measure of normality. After signaling a change of policy with the release of selected labor camp inmates, Khrushchev openly condemned Stalin at the twentieth Communist Party Congress. He castigated his predecessor for his cult of personality, illegal imprisonments, and lack of preparedness for war. The speech had a dramatic effect outside the USSR, leading to disturbances in Poland, Hungary, and East Germany. An armed intervention in Hungary demonstrated that while Khrushchev had condemned Stalinism, he would not diminish the Soviet presence in Eastern Europe.

Undoubtedly, Khrushchev's de-Stalinization had positive effects on the Soviet people. Millions of the unjustly accused were released and rehabilitated. From the standpoint of aggrieved nationalities, the legacy was mixed. In allowing their return home, Khrushchev redressed wrongs done to the Chechen and Ingushi people in 1944, but German and Baltic peoples received no such courtesy. Khrushchev dealt a blow to Russians and their culture in a renewed antireligious campaign in the early 1960s.

Today, Khrushchev is remembered positively, as the man who helped defuse the Cuban crisis. In October 1964, his colleagues believed he had damaged the USSR's prestige abroad and endangered the Communist Party at home, hence his ouster in October 1964. Khrushchev's successor, L.I. Brezhnev, ended an era of liberalization by staging a show trial of two writers, Yuli Daniel and Andrei Siniavskii, on charges of anti-Soviet agitation. There were indications even of a Stalinist revival. However, the Khrushchev era had emboldened some citizens, who proved unwilling to retreat to frightened silence. Devotees of Russian culture organized to restore old churches; writers condemned the demise of traditional Russian values in fiction known as "Village Prose." Ukrainians quoted Lenin's nationality policy in oblique protest of their fate in the USSR, and in many non-Russian areas, citizens pointedly explored native music and folk culture. The boldest moves came from Soviet Jews, who began asking for exit visas from the USSR after its embrace of the Arab States in the 1967 war with Israel. Some 400,000 sought to leave for Israel. Many ended up in the United States.

Brezhnev and his successors, Yuri Andropov and Konstantin Chernenko, responded to these developments by expelling Solzhenitsyn, putting prominent dissenters on trial and trapping many would-be Jewish émigrés by refusing them visas. They never resorted to mass terror, however; in fact, they avoided vigorous action, except to send Russian troops to "restore order" after an anti-Communist coup in Afghanistan in 1978. The country sank into stagnation.

M.S. Gorbachev and the End of the USSR, 1985–91

Realizing that the country was in a perilous condition, M.S. Gorbachev launched a program of reform upon coming to power in 1985. "Uskorenie," or quickening of tempo, was designed to revive the economy by getting citizens to work harder. The 1986 Chernobyl disaster demonstrated the need for criticism and transparency, leading to Gorbachev's policy of glasnost' or openness. Uskorenie and glasnost' combined in "perestroika" or general restructuring. Ideally, citizens would be empowered to improve conditions in the country by embracing elements of market economics, such as small private businesses, and demanding accountability from their bosses and leaders. But some refused to follow the script. Non-Russians demanded not economic change, but redress of past grievances or independence. There were deadly clashes between Soviet troops and citizens in Georgia and Lithuania in 1989 and 1991 and persistent Azerbaijani-Armenian conflict over the disputed territory of Nagorno-Karabakh. Russians asserted their own prerogatives in electing as president of the Russian republic B.N. Yeltsin, a frequent critic of Gorbachev. Despite domestic travails, Gorbachev pressed on with measures to improve the economy and ensure the viability of the state, negotiating arms reduction with the United States, ending the Afghan war, and allowing the east European satellites a peaceful exit from the Soviet orbit.

RUSSIANS

By 1990, Gorbachev knew that maintaining the traditional Soviet Union would likely be impossible without coercion. Thus, he proposed a new political arrangement that would allow the republics maximum autonomy without granting outright independence. This came partly out of concern for Russians living in Lithuania, Latvia, and Estonia, who feared retribution for the sins of past Soviet leaders. Although key provisions were still unsettled, the so-called Union Treaty was in final preparation by 1991.

In mid-August, with Gorbachev away on vacation, colleagues who opposed the treaty and the general direction of the country decided to oust their leader. They mobilized Soviet army units in Moscow and appeared on TV to announce a change of government. However, Yeltsin rallied outraged Muscovites, who barricaded themselves in and around the Russian Parliament, appealing to soldiers to support their elected government over the unelected coup plotters. In the end, Yeltsin and the opponents of the coup carried the day. When Gorbachev returned to Moscow, he tried to revive the Union Treaty, but Yeltsin was secretly negotiating with the leaders of Ukraine and Belarus', to replace the USSR with a loose confederation of former Soviet states. They announced the agreement that produced the Commonwealth of Independent States—minus Georgia and the Baltic States—on December 8, 1991, declaring "the USSR, as a subject of international law and geopolitical reality, ceases to exist." Some Russians now lived in their own state, but friends and relatives outside the new borders faced life in foreign countries, the "near abroad."

Since 1991, Russians have traveled divergent paths. Those with sufficient ambition or means went abroad, many ending up in the United States, where they constitute a vibrant new minority in cities across the country. In New York, for example, they have created a parallel Russian universe of restaurants, clubs, and media. In Russia proper, citizens have risen and fallen with the fortunes of their new state, whose most acute long-term challenge involves negotiating a settlement with rebellious Chechens after 12 years of war, ethnic cleansing, and suicide bombings. Life for Russians in the near abroad, especially Estonia and Latvia, has been problematic, because they are viewed either as remnants of an unhappy past or a fifth column through which neighboring Russia can continue to influence events. The new governments have made proficiency

in the local language a citizenship requirement, a hardship for Russians since Estonian and Latvian are inordinately difficult and time-consuming to learn. Language can be essential for political candidates, so Russians lack the means to defend their interests, though in Estonia all residents may vote in local elections. Employers have tended to hire their own, too, so that Russians have not fared well economically. These circumstances alarm some political scientists, who describe the Russian minority issue in the Baltics as potentially the most dangerous in Europe.

Today Russians' long-term prospects look nominally better. Estonia and Latvia have fresh incentive to implement generous integration policies, because their admission to the European Union depends upon good faith efforts in that area. However, language remains the price of admission to full citizenship, and while human rights advocates have lauded grassroots efforts in Estonia to improve proficiency, full participation in civic life remains elusive for many Russians. If language remains nonnegotiable, integration experts recommend the creation of an ombudsman, or some similar mechanism, for the resolution of Russian grievances and problems. In any case, it is safe to say that the eventual enfranchisement of Russians will pay dividends, both in the image of the two states abroad and in detente with their Russian neighbor.

It is difficult to draw any long-term conclusions about Russians in the new millennium. One can say with certainty that whether they are in the majority, in the Russian state, or members of Russian enclaves abroad, they will remain a force to be reckoned with.

BRIGIT FARLEY

See also **Russia**

Further Reading

Figes, Orlando, *A People's Tragedy: The Russian Revolution, 1891–1924*, London: J. Cape, 1996
Hosking, Geoffrey, *Russia: People and Empire 1552–1917*, Cambridge: Harvard University Press, 1997
Hughes, Lindsey, *Russia in the Age of Peter the Great*, New Haven: Yale University Press, 1998
Martin, Janet, *Medieval Russia, 980–1584*, New York: Cambridge University Press, 1995
Raeff, Marc, *Russia Abroad: A Cultural History of the Russian Emigration 1919–1939*, New York: Oxford University Press, 1990
Remnick, David, *Lenin's Tomb: The Last Days of the Soviet Empire*, New York: Vintage Books, 1994

Rwanda

Capsule Summary

Country Name: Republic of Rwanda (Rwandese Republic)
Location: central Africa (bordering Congo, Uganda, Tanzania, and Burundi)
Total Population: 7,810,056 (July 2003 estimate)
Ethnic Populations: Hutu (Bahutu), 85%; Tutsi (Batutsi), 14%; Twa (Batwa), <1%
Languages: Kinyarwanda (official) universal Bantu vernacular, French (official), English (official), and Kiswahili (Swahili) used in commercial centers
Religions: Roman Catholic, 56.5%; Protestant, 26%; Adventist, 11.1%; Muslim, 4.6%; indigenous beliefs, 0.1%; none, 1.7% (2001)

The Republic of Rwanda, known as the "Land of a Thousand Hills," is located just south of the equator in east-central Africa. At 26,340 square kilometers (approximately 10,169.93 square miles), it is slightly smaller than Maryland and borders Burundi, Democratic Republic of the Congo, Tanzania, and Uganda. This beautiful, mountainous country is one of the most densely populated countries in Africa, and the vast majority of the population lives as subsistence agriculturalists. Its major exports are coffee and tea, and deforestation and soil erosion are major problems. Since 1994, the government has been engaged in major infrastructure projects, and as a result, the road system is quite good, by African standards. One of the world's poorest countries that is almost entirely dependent upon agriculture, Rwanda's GDP per capita income was just $1,200 in 2002.

Rwanda is a country with a troubled history of ethnic violence and genocide, particularly since the independence era. The deliberate killing of the Tutsi ethnic group, in an effort to eliminate them completely, has been attempted on more than one occasion by the majority Hutus since 1959. Rwanda and neighboring Burundi are two of the few African states whose borders were not arbitrarily created by the colonists at the Berlin Conference of 1884–85. Prior to colonization, each was an independent Tutsi kingdom. During precolonial times, Tutsi and Hutu were more fluid categories based on occupation with Tutsis living as pastoralists and Hutus as agriculturalists. In fact, although the Tutsis were dominant and formed the warrior-aristocracy, Hutus could become Tutsis by gaining wealth while Tutsis who fell on hard times could become Hutus (Dravis 1996). The Twa are the original inhabitants of the forests of Rwanda, Uganda, and Congo. They make up less than 1 percent of Rwanda's population and have played a minimal role in the economy and political system.

History

Germany was the first European power to colonize Rwanda (1899), but it turned over the territory to Belgium in 1917, following its defeat in World War I. It was under Belgian colonial rule that ethnic divisions became defined and the categorization of Tutsi and Hutu became more rigid. In the 1930s, the Belgian colonial government issued identity cards that included rigidly defined ethnic affiliations in an effort to more easily control the people. The Belgians also sought to centralize control over Rwanda by instituting a uniform system of rule that eliminated pockets of autonomy, some of which were Hutu controlled, that had existed under the traditional Tutsi kingdom. The Belgian government was particularly neglectful of the people under its colonial administrations. Rwandans were not provided much education, nor was the infrastructure or a viable economy developed under the colonial government.

The rigid view of unchanging ethnic identity came to be adopted by Hutu extremists who initiated and directed the Genocide of 1994. As David Newbury points out, this view is based on "a biological model of social classifications" that is seriously called into question by the historical facts (Newbury 1997, 213). In fact, Hutus and Tutsis have long shared a common culture, religion, and language, and prior to colonization, conflicts that occurred were about the process of state formation and power, and more often occurred within ethnic groups than between them (Newbury 1997, 213).

In the mid-1950s, the Belgian colonial administration reversed its policy of supporting the Tutsi hierarchy and began to support the Hutu majority who demanded a more democratic system of governance. Tutsi elites began agitating for immediate independence and the Hutu elites sided with the Belgians in demanding a transition period in which educated Hutu leaders would take power followed by full independence. From 1959 to 1961, Hutu leaders carried out a mass-killing of the Tutsi in which 20,000 to 100,000 were killed and after which thousands fled. By 1964, 300,000 Rwandan refugees were registered with the UN High Commissioner for Refugees in Uganda, Burundi, Tanzania, and Congo (Kimonyo, 2000). It was the children and grandchildren of these refugees who returned to Rwanda after the 1994 genocide to reclaim the government.

Independence

Rwanda's first president was Grégoire Kayibanda, and his government was dominated by Hutus from the central and southern regions of the country. A massacre of Hutus in neighboring Burundi in which some 100,000 to 300,000 Hutus were killed triggered a slaughter of Tutsis in 1972–73 in Rwanda. To restore peace, the Rwandan military took over the government in 1973. Unlike Rwanda, independence in Burundi did not lead to a transition of power from the Tutsis to the Hutus. The Tutsi elites in Burundi managed to maintain power through force, and this circumstance was a constant factor in shaping Rwandan politics over the past four decades. Burundi was seen as a threatening example of what might happen in Rwanda if the Hutu elites allowed the Tutsis to gain power. The July 1973 coup in Rwanda brought Major General Juvenal Habyarimana to power. From this time until the end of the genocide in 1994, the government was dominated by Northern Hutus, particularly from the Gisenyi region. The main political actors, known as the *akazu* ("household") were Habyarimana, his wife Agathe and her brothers, and a handful of trusted advisers. Over time, not only did Habyarimana's closed style of rule alienate the Tutsis, it also alienated Hutu elites from other regions.

During the mid-late 1980s, two factors contributed to the weakening of the Habyarimana regime. First, the economy began to decline due to a deterioration in terms of trade and a decrease in external economic aid. Second, external forces began to press African regimes, in general, for greater openness and increased political participation for the population. On top of these pressures, Habyarimana was threatened by an invasion of Tutsi rebels from neighboring Uganda in 1990.

Masses of Tutsis fled Rwanda after the 1959 Hutu revolution and the 1973 massacres, and they were discouraged from returning home by the Habyarimana regime. A new generation of Rwandans, some of mixed Rwandan and other parentage, grew up in neighboring Uganda, Tanzania, Burundi, and Congo. Many of the exiled Rwandans in Uganda were instrumental in the fight against the dictatorships of Idi Amin and Milton Obote during the 1970s and 1980s. Some Tutsi soldiers, like current Rwandan President Paul Kagame, came to be highly ranked within the Ugandan military after Yoweri Museveni took power in 1986. After some years in favor in the Ugandan military, Rwandan Tutsi soldiers began to be resented by their Ugandan counterparts. In addition, the economy of Uganda was faltering, so Ugandans were growing discontented with the large Rwandan population living there. These factors, combined with the repressive rule of the Habyarimana regime, contributed to the establishment of the Rwandan Patriotic Front (RPF) in 1987 and its invasion of Rwanda in October 1990. The initial invasion by the RPF was repulsed by the Rwandan army (Armed Forces of Rwanda, FAR) with assistance from troops from Zaire and monetary assistance from France and Belgium. Over the course of the following two years, the RPF was able to continue launching invasions into Rwanda. The insurgency was serious enough for the Habyarimana government to eventually agree to peace talks with the rebels. Between August 1993 and January 1994, the government and RPF agreed to two power-sharing arrangements. The RPF was to gain a certain number of cabinet positions within the government and integrate its soldiers into the FAR. Extremist Hutus within the government of Rwanda were vehemently opposed to any power-sharing arrangement with the RPF, and clashes broke out between different factions of the government.

Genocide

In April 1994, the plane carrying President Habyarimana and Burundian President Ntaryamira was shot down over Kigali. Most analysts blame Rwandan Hutu extremists for the assassination of the presidents. What is clear is that the assassination of the presidents was the signal to Hutus extremists (*Interahamwe,* or those who fight together) to begin their genocidal campaign against the Tutsis and moderate Hutus of Rwanda. In just 100 days, between 500,000 and 800,000 Rwandans were killed. The genocide was highly organized by a core group of Hutu extremists who spread their message of hate and vengeance via leaflets, the radio, and word of mouth. Neighbors were exhorted to kill neighbors, husbands to kill their in-laws, and children to kill their teachers or vice versa. Some people were forced to kill or be killed by the leaders of the genocide, while others adopted the Hutu power ideology as their own and believed they must kill in order to survive. Most people were killed using simple tools such as machetes, though there were also incidents of grenades being launched into churches harboring people or people sheltered in schools being burned alive. No community was left untouched by the genocide. Up to 80% of the Rwandan Tutsis living in the country at the time were wiped out. Untold numbers of Hutus were also killed.

The international community was very reluctant to stop the Rwandan genocide through military intervention. At the time of the Arusha accords in August 1993, the UN had agreed to send a number of troops to Rwanda to oversee the implementation of the peace agreement. Twenty-five hundred UN troops were deployed in November 1993 with a mandate that did not include peace making or the ability to intervene to stop attacks by either side in the conflict. Hence, the force was ineffective when the genocide was launched in April 1994. Western countries pulled their citizens out of the country but did nothing to stop the slaughter of Rwandans. The U.S. government was reluctant to call the massacre a genocide because by law it would have been required to intervene, and it was reluctant to do so after the failed intervention in Somalia just six months before in which 17 US soldiers were killed and 75 injured. The French and Belgians had long been supportive of the Habyarimana regime and did nothing to stop the genocide once it had begun. The UN did not give its peace keepers in Rwanda an expanded mandate after the killings began even though UN leaders knew ahead of time that the genocide had been planned. The failure of the international community has since been acknowledged by nearly every government and international organization that failed to act.

The genocide was halted in July 1994 by the RPF. They captured several of the leaders of the genocide, but many also fled to neighboring Zaire. In addition, approximately two million Hutus also fled Rwanda after the RPF put a halt to the killing. Many feared revenge attacks by the RPF, and many others had actually taken part in the genocide. The refugee flow to Zaire (now the Democratic Republic of Congo) soon became a humanitarian emergency and the international community responded with aid and assistance. The refugees remained in Zaire, many against their will threatened by Hutu militias, until late 1996. Between mid-1994 and late 1996, the Hutu extremists

who had fled Rwanda continued to launch invasions into the country, especially in the northwest, from the relative safety of the refugee camps. In September 1996, a rebellion was launched in eastern Zaire after the local governor ordered Congolese Tutsis out of the country. It was only after this rebellion began that the Rwandan refugees began to return home, largely because Rwandan forces began attacking the refugee camps looking for Rwandan Interahamwe and ex-FAR. For the most part, the refugees who returned to Rwanda were not subject to revenge attacks by the Rwandan government, though countless thousands were killed in the fighting in eastern Zaire.

The insurgency within Rwanda was quashed by the end of 1998, and the country has not had open conflict since that time. Unfortunately, the threat of ethnic conflict in Rwanda remains strong. First, extremist Hutus continue to promote an ideology of hatred. They are mainly based in eastern Congo where they are currently being supported by the Congolese government. Rwanda and Uganda both have troops in eastern Congo for security reasons. They are unlikely to pull out until the Congolese government stops supporting rebel groups who want to topple their respective governments. Congo, for its part, is supported by Angola and Zimbabwe. Angola has legitimate security reasons for its participation in the Congo civil war and Zimbabwe has received economic benefits from allying itself with the government. The conflict is unlikely to be resolved soon, though the assassination of Laurent Kabila in January 2001 might help the peace process along. Kabila was largely responsible for blocking the Congo peace process.

In early 2001, Rwanda itself remained relatively peaceful, and the government had instituted several measures to ensure peace and stability within its borders. Although the government is unlikely to allow popular participation in general elections, it is trying to promote unity and reconciliation within its borders. One of its greatest challenges is bringing to justice more than 120,000 genocide suspects who are currently in Rwandan jails. Those accused of masterminding the genocide are being tried under the established justice system. However, the established institutions do not have the capacity to handle the entire caseload of suspects, so the government has adopted laws to create *gacaca* courts. These courts are based on a traditional system of justice that allows the local communities to determine the guilt or innocence of persons accused of crimes. The process of trying the genocide suspects in these community-based courts had not yet begun in early 2001. The trial of genocide suspects will likely put great pressure on Rwanda's civil society, and whether justice, as perceived by both sides in the conflict, is carried out will largely determine the stability and reconciliation of the country.

ANNE PITSCH

See also **Congo; Genocide; Tutsi; Twa; Uganda**

Further Reading

Dravis, Michael, "Tutsi and Hutu in Rwanda," working paper of the *Minorities at Risk Project*, directed by Dr. Ted Robert Gurr, University of Maryland, 1996 (update 1998). http://www.bsos.umd.edu/cidcm/mar/rwanda.htm

Gourevitch, Philip, *We Wish to Inform You that Tomorrow We Will Be Killed with Our Families: Stories from Rwanda*, New York: Farrar, Straus, and Giroux, 1998

Kimonyo, Jean Paul, "Causes of the Rwandan Genocide and Beyond" (conference paper), *Conflict and Peace-Making in the Great Lakes Region*, Entebbe, Uganda: 2000 (paper available from the Center for Conflict Management at the National University of Rwanda)

Lemarchand, Rene, *Rwanda and Burundi*, New York: Praeger Publishers, 1970

Newbury, Catherine, *The Cohesion of Oppression: Clientship and Ethnicity in Rwanda, 1860–1960*, New York: Columbia University Press, 1988

Newbury, David, "Irredentist Rwanda: Ethnic and Territorial Frontiers in Central Africa," *Africa Today*, 44, no. 2 (1997)

Uvin, Peter, *Development, Aid and Conflict: Reflections from Rwanda*, Helsinki, Finland: United Nations University World Institute for Development Economics Research, 1996

Uvin, Peter, "Ethnicity and Power in Burundi and Rwanda," *Comparative Politics*, 31, no. 3 (April 1999)

S

Saami

Capsule Summary

Location: Northern Scandinavia, northern Finland, Kola Peninsula
Total Population: Approximately 60,000
Languages: Saami (several dialects) and language of respective majority populations
Religions: Lutheran (Laestadian, a Protestant Free Church), Orthodox

The Saami people are an indigenous ethnic minority inhabiting the mountains and forest regions of northern Scandinavia, northern Finland, and the Kola Peninsula. To the outside world they were previously known as *Lapps*, a name given to them by early Scandinavian colonists and spread internationally. Today this is seen as a depreciative term. In the few existing medieval texts that mention the Saami, they are referred to as *Finns* or *Fenni*, as in the name of the Norwegian province *Finnmark*. (This term should not be confused with the same word *Finns* denoting Finnish-speakers of Finland.) *Saami* is the self-referential word of the Saami people in their own language, and it is now the accepted designation of this people in the four states between which Sápmi, the Saami homeland, is divided. The Saami of Kola and the Inari region in Finland are sometimes referred to as *Skolt Saami*. The Saami total approximately 60,000 persons divided between the states of Norway (35,000), Sweden (17,000), Finland (6,000), and Russia (2,000). Numbers vary in different sources depending on definitions of who is recognized as Saami. For many years the official Swedish position was that only groups and families engaged in reindeer herding were entitled to Saami rights and hence Saami identity. Numbers are greater when self-identification is employed. Quite a few people with Saami forebears have assimilated into the majority population and the economic activities of mainstream society but may nevertheless identify themselves culturally as Saami.

Language and Religion

The Saami language embraces several dialects, some of which are so different from one another that linguists regard them as different languages rather than as dialects of one common language. Major divisions are South Saami (spoken in the southern regions of the Saami homeland in Sweden and adjacent Norwegian areas), North or Central Saami (spoken in Norway, northern Sweden, and northwestern Finland), and East Saami (spoken in the Inari region and Kola). Each division includes a number of subdialects. Speakers of a South Saami dialect will understand neighboring South Saami dialects, but normally not North Saami speakers, or dialects prevalent in the eastern Saami settlement area, and vice versa. Today 75 percent of the Saami people are North Saami speakers. Saami is a Finno-Ugric language placed under the umbrella of Uralic languages. Though Saami is related to Finnish, and has been influenced by Finnish, differences of vocabulary and grammar do not permit mutual understanding. As an ethnic minority in all four states controlling the Saami homeland, everyone masters the majority language of one's respective country. Loans from regional majority languages explain some of the dialectical diversity. Missionaries in the seventeenth century were the first to develop a written version of the Saami language. The New Testament was published in Saami in 1755. However, it was not until 2000 that Saami was recognized as a national heritage language in Sweden.

The Saami of the Nordic countries are Protestants. It was not until the Reformation that missions set out to Christianize the Saami people. In particular the teachings of L.L. Laestadius had great impact on the Saami in the nineteenth century. Today a majority of the Norwegian and Swedish Saami belong to congregations of the Free Church founded by Laestadius. The Kola Saami, on the other hand, assimilated into the Russian Orthodox Church. Knowledge of pre-Christian religiosity is based on documentation of early missionaries. Beliefs centered on the forces of nature and survival in a harsh climate. Spirits of the forefathers would protect animals, plants, and young children and bring good luck in hunting. The bear was a holy animal. This veneration of ancestors and nature had many elements in common with shamanist beliefs present among minority peoples of northern Russia. The *nåjd* (the Saami shaman) served as an intermediary between the real world of everyday life and the spiritual world of ancestors. Parts of this cosmology have found cultural expression in songs *(joiks),* stories, and artifacts.

Origins

The Saami seek recognition as an indigenous people of northern Scandinavia and Kola and align themselves as a Fourth World Nation, together with Native Americans, Aborigines, Maori, and Inuit. This is a troublesome demand to the regional states because it raises controversial issues of land rights and land usage. The states have generally been unwilling to endorse the Saami claim as a First Nation with specific entitlements. However, archaeology and genetics appear to support the Saami cause. Archaeological findings demonstrate that people inhabited coastal lands on the Arctic Ocean as far back as 10,000 BCE when the rest of northern Europe was covered by inland ice. Genetically the Saami reveal some atypical traits that can only be explained as the result of a prolonged period of isolation from other prehistoric peoples. The Saami may therefore trace their genetic

heritage to these early settlers. An alternative theory based on comparative linguistic analyses contends that Saami originated from a people in the Ural region. At some stage these presumed ancestors settled around the Gulf of Finland. They were driven north to their present habitat in Sápmi as Finnish tribes entered.

The accepted view today combines these two explanations. A people living in isolation north of the ice sheet for several thousands of years accounts for the uniquely distinct genetic characteristics of the Saami. As the ice sheet melted contacts established with speakers of a Finnish-Ugric language further east. The Saami then trace their origins both to the settlers north of the inland ice as well as to Finno-Ugric speaking people entering the present settlement area.

Economy

Little is known about Saami history before the fourteenth century when more regular contacts with the Scandinavian Crowns developed and when Swedish and Norwegian peasants colonized river valleys and coastal districts in the north. Tacitus mentions *Fenni* in a text from 98 CE, and occasional references occur in later medieval texts. The Saami used the land for hunting and fishing, combining this with small-scale agriculture. The reindeer, or Caribou in North America, is an indigenous animal of the Arctic region and of central importance to Saami economy. Wild reindeer were hunted but the animal was also domesticated; ancestors of the Saami were probably involved in this domestication. Reindeer produced meat, milk, skins, and fur and were also used as draft animals. As wild reindeer migrated from summer pastures in the mountains to the winter pastures of the lowland forests, the Saami moved freely through the territory because national boundaries did not exist in practice. The national borders between Norway, Sweden, and Russia in the Arctic area were not determined until the eighteenth and early nineteenth centuries. Reindeer herding, believed to have started in the fifteenth century, was historically practiced in mountain regions as far south as central Sweden and southern Norway. Herding is land extensive due to the seasonal migration patterns. Today it is undertaken with the use of modern means of communication and equipment (snow cats, helicopters, cellular phones). However, only a minority of the Saami are reindeer herders. Saami living on the Arctic coast have fishing as their main source of livelihood. The Kola Saami are primarily engaged in small-scale agriculture and fishing. Herding has mainly been undertaken by

Saami of Norway and Sweden, but is always supplemented by other sources of income. Today the tourist industry is gaining in economic importance.

State Control

The Swedish Crown took an interest in the Arctic North of Scandinavia in the early fourteenth century to appropriate the prosperous commerce in skins and furs from Finnish and Russian traders and to check Russian advances in the Arctic north. The Scandinavian Crowns imposed taxes on the Saami in the early seventeenth century and administrative structures were established that affected Saami society and land use. The state achieved control over trade, herding, and land use, and opened up the northern inlands for colonization and economic exploitation. The Scandinavian nation states forming during the nineteenth century had little sympathy for Saami needs of cultural distinctiveness. Education was only available in majority languages. Saami cultural traditions were thought of as remnants of a heathen past doomed to die. The authorities regarded reindeer herding as an economic activity among others, not as a livelihood supporting a unique culture. Thus Saami were defined as persons engaged in herding, and in that capacity entitled to certain customary and hereditary rights to land use. If not utilized this right would be forfeited for future descendents. A remarkable provision was that herders were prohibited to combine this economic activity with agricultural pursuits.

Throughout the twentieth century herding clashed with the economic interests of the regional states in mining, forestry, hydroelectric schemes, railways, and road transports. The Swedish authorities were particularly insensitive to Saami needs for special rights as an indigenous people. In Norway on the other hand a general understanding of the Saami position has improved over the past 30 years. This came about after clashes in the 1970s between the Saami of the Alta region and the Oslo government about a dam on the Alta River. The dam was built but the government was forced to recognize Saami rights. The central problem for the Saami of Sweden remains the lack of recognition in practice of their traditional right to use land for herding. There is a reindeer herding act, and a 1989 amendment to this act, which guarantees the Saami the right to use land for grazing of their herds, and for moving herds from summer to winter pastures. But interests of farmers, hunters, the forest industry, the mining industry, and hydroelectric schemes conflict with the interests of the Saami. Farmers and foresters are entitled to full compensation for damage caused to plantations and seedlings by the reindeer. However, bureaucracy is involved and to land owners things would be simpler without reindeer herding at all. Inevitably there is tension. Basically the Saami are not interested in land ownership as such but of land use according to rights sanctioned by traditional usage. The legal problem is the lack of historical documents testifying to this right.

The so-called *Taxed mountains case* of 1966–1981 in Sweden was about Saami claim to ownership of land in the province of Jämtland. The evidence attesting to this claim were documents proving that the Saami had paid tax to the Swedish Crown in the seventeenth century for this land. The district court in Jämtland ruled in favour of the Saami cause. However the case was contested through all instances. The High Court of Appeal ruled that evidence was insufficient to establish historical ownership of land, offering the interpretation that it was rather a leasehold arrangement. Surprisingly, the fact of having paid taxes on land has been sufficient evidence in other cases to establish land ownership. Another blow to the Swedish Saami was being dispossessed of their exclusive right to hunt small game in the mountain region and the land above the cultivation zone. To the Saami this was yet another example of great symbolic importance where the Swedish state encroached upon traditional rights.

During the Cold War the small *Skolt* Saami population of Kola was out of touch with the larger Saami communities in the Nordic countries and under heavy pressure to assimilate into mainstream Soviet society. After the fall of the Soviet Union in 1991 contacts with other Saami centers resumed and cultural exchange programs developed.

CHARLES WESTIN

See also **Finland; Finns; Norway**

Further Reading

Beach, Hugh, *Reindeer-Herd Management in Transition: The Case of Tuorpon Saameby in Northern Sweden*, Stockholm: Almqvist & Wiksell, 1980

Hannum, Hurst, *Autonomy, Sovereignty and Self-Determination: The Accommodation of Conflicting Rights*, Phildelphia: University of Pennsylvania Press, 1996

Jahreskog, Birgitta, editor, *The Sami National Minority in Sweden*, Stockholm: Almqvist & Wiksell, 1982

Oosten, Karich, and Cornelius Remie, *Arctic Identities: Continuity and Change in Inuit and Saami Societies*, Leiden: CNWS publications, 1999

Sammallahti, Pekka, *The Saami Languages: An Introduction*, Kárásjohka: Davvi girji, 1998

Saint Kitts and Nevis

Capsule Summary

Country Name: Federation of St. Kitts and Nevis
Location: Islands in the northern section of the eastern Caribbean Sea, about one third of the way from Puerto Rico to Trinidad and Tobago
Total Population: 38,763 (2003)
Language: English
Religion: Christian (Anglican, Protestant, Roman Catholic)

Located in the northern section of the eastern Caribbean Sea directly south of Anguilla, west of Antigua and Barbuda, and approximately 1,300 miles southeast of Miami, Florida, United States, the twin-island nation of Federation of Saint Kitts and Nevis was Britain's first colony in the West Indies with the founding of a settlement in 1623. St. Kitts and Nevis were first settled by Arawak and Carib Indians moving up through the islands from South America between 5,000 and 7,000 years ago. When Christopher Columbus arrived in 1493, both islands had long been occupied by well-established Indian communities. By the early seventeenth century, the inhabitants of Nevis had disappeared. They were victims of Spanish attacks, European diseases, and war between the rival European countries in the Caribbean.

Columbus named the larger of the two islands St. Christopher, in honor of the patron saint of travelers, and British sailors shortened it to St. Kitts. Nevis derived its name from the Spanish phrase *Nuestro Senora del las Nieves* ("Our Lady of the Snows") because of a white cloud surrounding the island's single peak that early Spanish travelers viewed. Both St. Kitts and Nevis are volcanic islands, which is responsible for their unpredictable geologic history, their lush tropical vegetation, and their central mountains, the largest of which is St. Kitts' central peak, a 3,792-foot extinct volcano. The Carib inhabitants knew their island as *Liamuiga*, or "fertile land," a reference to the island's rich volcanic soil.

The islands make up 261 square kilometers or 100 square miles (Saint Kitts 168 sq km [66 sq mi]; Nevis 93 sq km [36 sq mi]) with 135 km (84 mi) of coastline. The inhabitants of the islands speak English, are predominantly members of the Anglican Church, and have a 97 percent literacy rate. The islands' government is a constitutional monarchy with a British-style parliament, with it s capital at Basseterre on St. Kitts. The chief of state is the reigning monarch in Great Britain, with an appointed Governor General and Prime Minister. Great Britain granted St. Kitts and Nevis formal independence on September 19, 1983. Sugar was the traditional mainstay of the islands' economy until the 1970s and the crop still dominates the agricultural sector. Today tourism, export-oriented manufacturing, and offshore banking have assumed larger roles in the economy, with tourism now the chief source of the islands' revenue. The gross domestic product (GDP) per capita as of 2002 was $8,800.

RICHARD VERRONE

Further Reading

Hackett, Kieran J., *Of Nevis Lighters and Lightermen: The Sailing Lighters of St. Kitts and Nevis*, Writers Collective, 2003

Hanley, Gweneth, *Caribbean Social Studies for St Kitts & Nevis (Caribbean Social Studies)*, Macmillan Education, 2001

Hubbard, Vincent K., *Swords Ships and Sugar: A History of Nevis*, Premiere Editions International, 2002

Kozleski, Lisa, and James D. Henderson, *The Leeward Islands: Anguilla, St. Martin, St. Barts, St. Eustatius, Guadeloupe, St. Kitts and Nevis, Antigua and Barbuda, and Montserrat*, Mason Crest Publishers, 2003

Lelllouch, Deborah, *Nevis: Queen of the Caribbean*, Hummingbird Productions, 2000

Michael, Annette W., *Sugar is All: Caribbean Short Stories and Poems from St. Kitts and Nevis*, Morris Publishers, 2001

Permentor, Paris, and John Bigley, *Antigua, Barbuda St. Kitts & Nevis Alive*, Hunter Publishing, 2001

Richardson, Bonham C., *Caribbean Migrants: Environment and Human Survival on St. Kitts and Nevis*, University of Tennessee Press, 1983

Saint Lucia

Capsule Summary

Country Name: Saint Lucia
Location: The Caribbean Sea and North Atlantic Ocean, north of St. Vincent, south of Martinique
Total Population: 162,157 (July 2003)
Ethnic Populations: black (90%), mixed (6%), East Indian (3%), white (1%)
Languages: English (official), French patois
Religions: Roman Catholic (90%), Anglican (3%), other Protestant (7%)

Saint Lucia is an island country that is part of the Windward Islands of the Lesser Antilles located midway down the Eastern Caribbean chain, between Martinique and St. Vincent, and north of Barbados. The island is 27 miles long and 14 miles wide with a population of approximately 163,000.

St. Lucia was first settled by Arawak Indians around 200 CE. By 800, their culture had been superseded by that of the Caribs. These early Amerindian cultures called the island *Iouanalao* and *Hewanorra*, meaning "Island of the Iguanas." The Europeans discovered St. Lucia in 1504 when Juan de la Cosa made a landing there. It had been believed that Columbus had discovered St. Lucia in 1502, but recent evidence suggests that he only sailed close to the island. A permanent European presence was established in the area of the island in the 1550s by Francois le Clerc. The Dutch arrived around 1600 and established a fortified base at Vieux Fort. The French arrived by 1650 and purchased the island for the French West India Company. The island's first European settlements and towns were French, beginning with Soufriere in 1746. By 1780, 12 settlements and a large number of sugar plantations had been established. The British captured St. Lucia from the French in 1814, after the island had changed possession 14 times between the two countries. St. Lucia remained under the British crown until it became independent within the British Commonwealth in 1979.

The island is 616 square kilometers (238 square miles), with 606 kilometers (377 miles) of coastline. The inhabitants of the islands speak English (the official language) and French, are predominantly Roman Catholic, and have a 67 percent literacy rate. The islands' government is a British-style parliamentary democracy with it s capital at Castries. The chief of state is the reigning monarch in Great Britain, with an appointed Governor General and Prime Minister. St. Lucia has been able to attract foreign business and investment in recent decades, especially in its offshore banking and tourism industries. The manufacturing sector is the most diverse in the Eastern Caribbean area. The country's chief export is bananas (41 percent), and food and manufactured goods are the primary imports. The gross domestic product (GDP) per capita as of 2002 was $5,400.

RICHARD VERRONE

Further Reading

Bell, Brian, *Insight Compact Guide St. Lucia*, Insight Guides, 2004

Brownlie, Alison, *Heart of the Caribbean: Landscape of St Lucia*, Hodder & Stoughton Children's Division, 2001

Hall, A.T., and Peter Adrien, *Metayage: Capitalism and Peasant Development in St Lucia 1840–1957*, University Press of the West Indies, 1996

Henshall, Janet, "St. Lucia," in *World Bibliographic Series, 185, ABC-CLIO*, 1996

Luntta, Karl, *The Rough Guide to St Lucia*, 2nd edition, Rough Guides, 2003

Orr, Tamara B., *The Windward Islands: St. Lucia, St. Vincent and the Grenadines, Grenada, Martinique, & Dominica*, Mason Crest Publishers, 2003

Sturge, John, *The West Indies in 1837: Being the Journal of a Visit to Antigua, Montserrat, Dominica, St. Lucia, Barbados, and Jamaica*, reprint edition, International Specialized Book Services, 1968

Sullivan, Lynne M., *Martinique, Guadeloupe, Dominica & St. Lucia Alive!* Hunter Publishing, 1999

Sakha (Yakut)

Capsule Summary

Location: The Sakha Republic, Northeastern Siberia, Russia
Total Population: approximately 350,000
Language: Sakha (Yakut)
Religion: Shamanism

The Sakha (Yakut) are an ethnic group inhabiting the Sakha Republic of northeastern Siberia, Russia. Their exact origin continues to be a subject of much debate. The most popular contemporary theory asserts that the Sakha are a relatively young ethnicity which formed when their Turkish ancestors transmigrated from Lake Baikal in southern Siberia to the present area, approximately 500 years ago, and intermingled with the local Evenk, Even and Mongols. The Sakha language is a Turkic language with many borrowed Mongolian and Evenk words. Although Russian Orthodoxy was introduced in the late nineteenth century, most Sakha agreed to be baptized in order to alleviate their fur tribute, rather than for true spiritual conversion. Most contemporary Sakha who profess to religion practice the traditional shamanic belief of their ancestors.

The Sakha Republic covers approximately 3 million square kilometers (1.2 million square miles) and occupies one-fifth of the Russian federation. The total population is about 1 million inhabitants. Recent census statistics describe the Republic's ethnic composition as 33 percent Sakha, 48 percent Russian, 10 percent Tungus, 5 percent Ukrainian, and 4 percent other. The Sakha are considered the dominant indigenous group of the Republic due to having numbers far surpassing the other groups including Evenks, Evens, Yukagir, and Chukchi.

The Sakha inhabit one of the most extreme climates in the world. Summer temperatures have been recorded as high as 31°C (87.8°F) and winter lows at –70°C (–94°F).

The Republic is also extreme with regard to mineral wealth. An old Sakha legend relays this well: "When the Gods were flying over the earth to give out the mineral wealth among the lands, when they got over the Sakha Republic, it was so cold that they froze and their trunk of riches spilled out all over the Republic." Every element in the periodic table can be found in the Republic. There are also extensive gas, oil, and coal reserves within the Republic's boundaries.

The Sakha, traditionally horse and cattle breeders, largely inhabit the agricultural areas of the Republic, which include the central and Vilyui regions. The lush hayfields of these areas are what initially attracted the migrating Turkic ancestors in the first place. The Sakha are presently the northernmost keepers of horses and cattle in the world, which is no small feat. Cows must be kept in barns for the long nine-month subarctic winters. Each cow and new calf requires two tons of hay for fodder to sustain them. This makes for an intensive summer season, marked by cutting, stacking, and storing hay over the short two-month season before the first snows fall in September.

In addition to horse and cattle breeding, a small percentage of Sakha, inhabiting the arctic regions of the Republic and living among Evenk and Even, practice reindeer herding. These Sakha are often referred to as *northern Sakha*. Whether horse and cattle breeders or reindeer herders, all contemporary rural Sakha also rely heavily on forage through hunting, fishing, and gathering wild food stuffs.

The Sakha have a rich and diverse folklore. One of their best known works is the epic poem, the *Olonkho*, traditionally performed by a master storyteller over the course of several evenings. The Sakha also perform improvisatory singing, either solo, called *tyuk*, or in the context of the circle dance, called *ohyokhai*. Other genres include *chabirghakh*, a rap-like composition which weaves together story and jokes, traditionally in competition to see which performer can rap faster. The main traditional instrument of the Sakha is the *khomus* or Jew's harp, which is played largely with emphasis on rhythms and imitations of nature sounds. Lastly, the Sakha have a diverse number of traditional games, the most popular of which include *mas tardihii* or the stick pull; *kylyy, ystanga,* and *kuobakh*, three forms of hopping; *khapsagi* or traditional wrestling; *khaamiska*, a game of dexterity with small wooden blocks played somewhat like jacks; and *oybonton yylahin*, a game of individual balance. To the present day the main holiday of the Sakha is the *yhyakh* festival, which takes place on the days around the summer solstice. The festival originated as the Sakhas' plea to the myriad of benevolent sky deities for all the right conditions of sun, rain, and warmth to bring about plentiful hay, herds, and food stuffs. The white shaman enacts the ceremony, offering *kumiss* and other sacrificial foods to the sky deities. The festival then continues into a communal prayer fueled by the improvisatory singing of the *ohyokhai* dance. This is followed by traditional games, *Olonkho*, singing, and, culminating the festival, *at suruute*, horse races. To this day the Sakha who attend y*hyakh* believe that without this summer gaiety and ritual they would lack the necessary energy to complete the intense and all important work of the summer— harvesting sufficient hay to see their herds through another long subarctic winter.

When the Sakhas' Turkic ancestors migrated north from the shores of Lake Baikal, they had to adapt their horse and cattle practices to the northern climate. Their settlement pattern, up until the early twentieth century, was one of living in extended clan groupings scattered across the lush grasslands and taiga forest areas.

Russians Cossacks, sent on the empire's decree to find new lands to explore and annex, began arriving in Yakutsk in the early 1600s. In 1632 the Russian government established a fortress on the Lena River, in the place of present-day Yakutsk, which marked the incorporation of the Republic into the Russian state. Despite this status, the Russian state practiced nonintervention up until the end of the nineteenth century, with the only imposition being *yasak* or fur tribute. This nonintervention served to preserve the Sakha customs and native authority. Since the mid-seventeenth century the Republic's area has been a place of exile, a prison without walls, a gulag, for all three generations of Russian revolutionaries—from the Decembrists to the Bolsheviks.

The Republic was officially named the *Yakut Autnonomous Soviet Socialist Republic* in 1922, but there was much protest and fighting after that. The leaders of the Sakha nationalist movement were repressed and later executed due to their "bourgeois nationalism." Since the fall of the Soviet empire and the renewed Sakha nationalism of the early 1990s, their names have been reified.

During the Soviet period (1917–1991) the traditional Sakha clan settlements scattered across the landscape were gradually consolidated during the process of collectivization beginning in the late 1920s and culminating with the establishment of agro-industrial state farm complexes in the late 1950s and early 1960s. As a result, ancestral homesteads were left abandoned to be invaded by the surrounding forests and later, the lands adjoining them were turned under for use as agricultural fields for the state farm system. With the formation of the state farm systems, the Sakha entered the ranks of the working class, a significant change from their former collective enterprises in which they shared the annual products of their labors. Now with a paycheck every two weeks and village stores well-stocked with consumer goods, the Sakha, like their "comrades" across the Union of Soviet Socialist Republics (USSR), enjoyed a working-class consumer life. Villages were abuzz with activity, homes had televisions and new furniture, and government subsidies continued to keep the operational aspects of these agro-farms alive and thriving. Residents also enjoyed the many perks of the Socialist systems, including free health care, free education, and many social services never dreamed of before that time, including delivery of free water and firewood.

The main force that drove this "consumer life" was the exploitation of the Republic's vast mineral wealth. Gold, diamonds, and coal were the forefront of attention and the exploitation of these resources brought many "outsiders," including Russians, Ukrainians, Belarusians, and the like, to work in the industrial centers. The rural areas were considered the manufacturing centers of foodstuffs to feed these nascent mining initiatives.

Since the fall of the Soviet Union in 1991, rural areas have lost their government support and most state farms have folded, leaving the local authorities in charge of the allocation of shares of the farm resources to the people. Misappropriation and inequity has been the rule in such dealings, leaving the majority of the rural populations impoverished. At the same time, the fall of the Soviet system was the beginning of sovereignty for the Sakha Republic. Although on the legal front this sovereign status is superceded by Russian federal law, it has allowed the Republic many previously unknown concessions as regards the Republic's main wealth, its mineral reserves. The Republic's sovereign status has also been the stronghold of ethnic identity and cultural revival, which has brought about renewal of Sakha language, cultural traditions, and shamanistic practices.

SUSAN CRATE

See also **Siberian Indigenous Peoples**

SAKHA (YAKUT)

Further Reading

Fedorova, Y.N., *Nasileniye Yakutii: Proshloye i Nastoyashiye (The Population of Yakutia: Before and Now)*, Novosibirsk: Nayuka, 1998

Jordan, Bella, and Terry Jordan-Bychkova, *Siberian Village: Land and Life in the Sakha Republic*, Minneapolis: University of Minnesota Press, 2001

Ksentofontov, G.V., *Uraankhai Sakhalar: Ocherki po Drevni Istorii Yakutov (The Uraankhai Sakha: Sketches of the Ancient Yakut History)*, Yakutsk: National Publishers, 1992

Maak, R.K., *Vilyuiski Okrug* [The Vilyui Okrug], Moscow: Yana, 1994

Okladkinov, A.P., *Yakutia before Its Incorporation into the Russian State*, Montreal: McGill-Queen's University Press, 1970

Seroshevski, V.L., *Yakutii: Opit Etnograficheskovo Issledovaniye* [The Yakut: Knowledge from Ethnographic Research], Moscow: Rosspen, 1993

Tichotsky, John, *Russia's Diamond Colony: The Republic of Sakha*, Amsterdam: Harwood Academic Publishers, 2000

Samoa

Capsule Summary

Country Name: Independent State of Samoa
Location: Oceania, group of islands in the South Pacific Ocean, about half of the way from Hawaii to New Zealand
Total Population: 178,173 (2003)
Languages: Samoan (Polynesian); English
Religions: Christian 99.7% (about one-half of population associated with the London Missionary Society; includes Congregational, Roman Catholic, Methodist, Latter-Day Saints, Seventh-Day Adventist)

The Samoan archipelago lies northeast of New Zealand in the Western Polynesian sector of the South Pacific. Archaeological evidence points to human occupation of these islands by at least 1000 BCE, with a society making pole and thatch buildings and pottery in place by around 100 BCE. By 1000 CE stone implements and permanent structures were in use. Even at this stage social organization focused upon patriarchal village councils composed of *matai*, or chieftains of local kinship groups. These leaders' inherited titles commanded deference and conferred authority to resolve local disputes. The village *fono,*, or councils were the keystone of local authority.

In the 1870s the European powers and the United States became active in Western Polynesia. In the western half of the archipelago, European planters began to develop plantations for the commercial production of coconuts and copra. The U.S. government sought a coal storage depot for its naval and merchant fleets engaged in trade with Japan, China, and Southeast Asia. Indigenous crop production and barter arrange-

ments were disrupted by these developments, and political rivalries between tribal clans were stoked by foreign meddling. Western battleships began making frequent visits to the islands in the 1880s.

In 1899, following the pattern employed in the division of Africa, diplomatic representatives of Britain, Germany, and the United States convened to discuss the future of Western Polynesia. The three powers partitioned the archipelago, with Germany seizing power over the larger western sector, known as Western Samoa, and the United States taking control of the eastern end of the island chain.

The U.S. sector, known as American Samoa, includes Tutuila Island and six smaller islands, and at the time of partition had a population of 6,000. It was placed under the control of the U.S. Navy, which developed coaling facilities at Tutuila's Pago Pago bay, a natural deepwater harbor. As naval and merchant vessels shifted from coal to diesel fuel in the 1910s, U.S. interest in the islands waned. *Fono* and other aspects of traditional Samoan culture were left largely undisturbed. The *matai* retained their authority over local affairs, and communal land ownership remained intact. By 1940 the population of American Samoa had grown to about 13,000.

During World War II American Samoa suddenly became a strategically important outpost for U.S. forces battling Japanese expansionism in the South Pacific. Airfields, roads, and storage and training facilities were built on Tutuila, and large numbers of Samoans became involved in a cash economy for the first time.

The local self-defense force, the *fitafita*, was expanded, and performed a variety of observation and guard duties. When the war ended, economic dislocations were widespread. U.S. policy permitted *fitafita* members an opportunity to enter the U.S. Navy. Although hundreds did so, unemployment remained one of American Samoa's most serious postwar problems.

In the 1950s American Samoa's relations with the United States changed. The U.S. Department of the Interior assumed authority over its affairs, and the traditional *fono* system was modified to create a bicameral legislature with powers to enact local regulations. A constitution was promulgated in 1960. Nonetheless, unlike other territories added to the United States in this period, American Samoa remained an unincorporated territory without full representation in the U.S. Congress.

During the 1960s federal aid and development programs were implemented in American Samoa. Remote islands were supplied with electricity and telephone service and new schools were built. Food stamps and school lunch programs began to alter traditional food consumption patterns, and Westernized tastes caused a decline in local agricultural production. Other Western influences were introduced through radio and television. Modern industry, particularly commercial fishing and fish processing, was introduced. By 1980, 90 percent of American Samoa's exports were canned tuna, virtually all of it bound for the U.S. market.

Local laws began to reflect the intensifying Samoan nationalism. Immigration was restricted and limits were put on foreign investment and landholding. Some 92 percent of the population lives on Tutuila, concentrated around Pago Pago. To escape overcrowding and poverty many young Samoans move to the United States, particularly Hawaii, California, and Washington. Half of the high school graduates each year go to the West Coast, either to attend college or to find employment. Many of these youth never return to American Samoa, but instead regularly remit cash to family members who remain behind.

By 2003 the population of American Samoa reached 70,260. Large numbers of resident aliens add to the population, with many economic migrants arriving from Tonga and Western Samoa to work in the canning plants. With family links to citizens of American Samoa, many eventually gain residency there, which in turn enables them to move to the United States. The gross domestic product (GDP) per capita of American Samoa was $8,000 as of 2000, while the GDP of Samoa overall was $5,600 as of 2002.

Western Samoa was part of Germany's colonial empire between 1899 and 1914. As part of its contribution to World War I, New Zealand occupied the islands. Western Samoa later became a League of Nations mandate territory administered by New Zealand. In the late 1920s a short-lived anticolonial movement developed. A riot in December 1929 left 13 people dead, and Samoans decided to pursue nonviolent protests against foreign rule, including civil disobedience and nonpayment of taxes.

After World War II New Zealand decided upon a strategic plan for decolonization of its territories in the Pacific, and Western Samoa became an independent state in January 1962. As in colonial days, its chief exports are still coconuts and derivative products. By 2001 Western Samoa had a population of 180,000 people on a total land area of 2,900 square kilometers (1,120 square miles). To address overcrowding the government actively encourages emigration of young people, expecting these migrants will remit cash to family members still in the country. Many go to American Samoa, but others move to New Zealand, which by treaty accepts 1,100 Samoan immigrants annually. In periods of economic expansion in New Zealand, many times this number are admitted as "guest workers." It is believed that thousands of these temporary visitors overstay their visas and merge into New Zealand's underground economy.

LAURA CALKINS

See also **Pacific Islanders**

Further Reading

Drozdow-St. Christian, Douglas, *Elusive Fragments: Making Power, Propriety & Health in Samoa*, Durham, North Carolina: Carolina Academic Press, 2002

Duranti, Alessandro, *From Grammar to Politics: Linguistic Anthropology in a Western Samoan Village*, Berkeley, California: University of California Press, 1994

Field, Michael, *Mau: Samoa's Struggle for Freedom*, Auckland: Palynesian Press, 1991

Hempenstall, Peter, *Pacific Islanders under German Rule: A Study in the Meaning of Colonial Resistance*, Canberra: Australian National University Press, 1978

Hooper, Antony, et al., editors, *Class and Culture in the South Pacific*, Auckland and Suva: University of Auckland and the Institute of Pacific Studies, University of the South Pacific, 1978

Mageo, Jeannette Marie, *Theorizing Self in Samoa: Emotions, Genders, and Sexualities*, Ann Arbor: University of Michigan Press, 1998

Maiava, Susas, *A Clash of Paradigms: Intervention, Response, and Development in the South Pacific*, Burlington, Vermont: Ashgate, 2001

Mead, Margaret, *Coming of Age in Samoa*, New York: William Morrow, 1928

Meleisea, Malama, *The Making of Modern Samoa: Traditional Authority and Colonial Administration in the History of Western Samoa*, Suva: University of the South Pacific, 1987

O'Meara, Tim, *Samoa Planters: Tradition and Economic Development in Polynesia*, Ft. Worth, Texas: Holt, Rinehart & Winston, 1990

Rutherford, N., and A.J. Hempenstall, *Protest and Dissent in the Colonial Pacific*, Suva: University of the South Pacific, 1984

Smith, Bernard, *European Vision and the South Pacific*, Melbourne: Oxford University Press, 1989

San (Bushmen)

Capsule Summary

Location: Southern Africa (Namibia; Botswana; Angola; South Africa; Zambia; Zimbabwe)
Total Population: 100,000; 68,000 in Angola (2002); 30,000 in Botswana (2000); 54,000 in Namibia (2000)
Languages: Khomani and other San dialects
Religions: Ancestor Worship (Animism)

There are an estimated 100,000 San people in Southern Africa. They are a minority in each of the six countries where they live: Namibia, Botswana, Angola, South Africa, Zambia, and Zimbabwe. The group has no collective name for themselves in any of their many languages. The term *San* is considered derogatory as it was applied to the group by their ethnic relatives and historic rivals the Khoi. The term *Bushmen* is preferred.

The majority of San live in Namibia and Botswana, mostly in the arid Kalahari region, with only small populations in neighboring countries. The San consist of many different ethnic groups descended from the aboriginal *homo sapiens* population that has inhabited Southern Africa for more than 120,000 years. By contrast, black, Bantu language-speakers only arrived in the region some 3,000 years ago. There is a substantial economic and power imbalance between marginalized San people and the more powerful and better resourced dominant black and white populations.

Contrary to outside assumptions, the San are not one ethnic group. Today, there are distinct cultural communities using over 35 Khosian languages from three completely unrelated language families (Ju, Khoe, and !Ui-Taa) plus several isolated language varieties in East Africa. San languages are distinguished by their frequent use of click sounds. These are produced by snapping the tongue back from various parts of the mouth. The most common symbols for the four major clicks shown here are: !, |, ‡, and ||, which are alveo-palatal, dental, palatal, and lateral respectively.

The appropriate term for the whole group of identities is a topic that is still under debate. Settlers referred to hunter-gatherers as *Boesjesman* in Dutch, or *Boesman* in contemporary Afrikaans. Bantu language-speaking farmers referred to hunter-gatherers as *Abatwa, Batwa, Basarwa,* or *Baroa* depending on the territory. All of these terms have become heavily stigmatized over time. European anthropologists coined the term *San* in the 1930s. The word allegedly comes from a Khoe dialect term meaning "to gather," although it also has the implication of poverty and servitude. The term *Khoesan* is applied to the language grouping but is itself a misnomer; mixing economic, cultural, and linguistic categories into one inaccurate label. Today many groups identify with the term *San*, though *Bushman, Boesman* and *Basarwa* are still common within some communities. Activists prefer that communities be referred to by their own ethnolinguistic identities, such as *!Xû, Bukakhwe, !Xóõ, G|wi, Bukakhwe, G||ana, Khwe, Naro, Ju|'hoansi, ‡Khomani,* and *Hai||om*. There are generic words for *San* in San languages, such as *Ncoakhwe (N|qoakhoe), Tsasi* and *N||n‡e* but these have not caught on.

The other non-San identified groups within the Khoesan language families include the Khoekhoe (also called *Nama*), the Damara (non-San hunter-gatherers), the Hadzabe and the Sandawe both of East Africa.

Though San and Khoekhoe people have the same genetic origin, in contemporary history they usually distinguish between those cultures that lived by hunting and gathering (i.e., San) and those who lived by pastoralism (i.e. Khoekhoe).

Throughout the region, San people experience serious and continuous forms of discrimination, marginalization, and, in some cases physical abuse by dominant ethic groups. Generally, San people are smaller than their black, Bantu-speaking neighbors and European settlers. In some cases San are lighter skinned than other African groups. Dominant groups hold these visible distinctions as icons of inferiority. The expansion of the colonial economy forced hunter-gatherers into relationships of servitude to the wealthier cattle and sheep-herding cultures around them. From the colonial point of view San people were nonentities. San were considered to be economically unproductive, living a purely subsistence and sustainable lifestyle. The colonial tradition of legal invisibility has carried through to all of the postcolonial governments, where San rights to land are mostly ignored based on the fact that the San are *transhumant* (i.e., those who migrate within a territory) and do not own land in a legally recognized sense. Cultural and linguistic rights are considered unnecessary and absurd by authorities.

In South Africa, the impact of colonial incursions and conflict with African neighbors (Khoe and Bantu) led to an almost complete extermination and assimilation of all San peoples. There were over a dozen San ethnolinguistic groups recorded by settlers in the 1700s in South Africa. Today there is only one surviving group, with a few descendants from another group scattered on farms in the east of the country. The new South African government has made efforts to redress the past violence by providing the ‡Khomani San community with land in the southern Kalahari, and providing land for the !Xû and Khwe communities near Kimberley who were displaced to South Africa from Namibia and Angola after they had been forced to serve the South African Defence Force in its war against Namibian independence.

In Botswana and Namibia, the main human rights concerns revolve around the rapidly eroding land and natural resource base of San communities, their low status and enforced servitude to more dominant groups, anti-environmental policies that are destroying wild life and livelihoods, and the abuse and marginalization of San children in the educational systems.

Several serious land rights crises are related to the status of National Parks on traditional San territory. Thousands of people have been displaced by the creation of Etosha National Park in Namibia, and more recently by the exclusion of San from the Central Kalahari Game Reserve (CKGR) in Botswana. Though the Government of Botswana denies using force or coercion, there is evidence of coercion and bad faith in the removal of thousands of people out of CKGR into inadequate relocation camps at New Xade and other sites.

The recent political crisis in the Caprivi Strip has impacted negatively on local San people. The strip of Namibian land that runs across the top of Botswana to the Zambezi River has been the site of serious political disturbances for two years now. Some local chiefs claim that they are being ignored by the government in Windhoek and are calling for secession. The San were not involved in the secessionist movement but were apparently victimized during a state crackdown on dissent in 1999. Two thousand Khwe people fled across the border into Botswana. In April 2002 the governments of Botswana and Namibia signed an agreement with the United Nations High Commissioner for Refugees (UNHCR) outlining the details of a repatriation plan for these refugees.

The constitution of Botswana is based on the principle that all citizens are ethnically Batswana, speakers of the only official language, Setswana. In reality Botswana, like its neighbors, is a multiethnic and multilingual country. Though the San suffer very specific discrimination, speakers of other languages such as Kalanga and Nama also experience animosity from the state and the dominant culture. Community efforts in western Botswana have led to one San language, Naro, being standardized and introduced into schools.

Namibia acknowledges its multilingual identity but has taken few steps to deal with the educational crisis facing San children. Of the six or more distinct Khoesan languages spoken by indigenous Namibians, only two are standardized and offered in school. Khoekhoegowap, the language of the Nama and Damara people is offered right through to University. Ju|'hoansi, the largest San language is only offered in primary schools and only as a result of community efforts.

The situation of Khwe people in Zambia is dire, with many suffering from hunger and malnutrition. There is little or no access to state resources such as clean water or education. The Government of Zambia does not count Khwe people in its census or include them in National Education policy. The San people of Western Zimbabwe have been displaced from their traditional territory and live in isolation and extreme poverty. Their language and traditional knowledge is rapidly dying out. The Government of Zimbabwe ignores their existence entirely.

All San peoples are at serious risk from the Human Immodeficiency Virus (HIV) and the accompanying Acquired Immune Deficiency Syndrome (AIDS). Botswana has one of the highest incidences of AIDS per capita in the world. Typically, poor, marginalized, and displaced peoples are at high risk for HIV infections. As with smallpox in the eighteenth century, AIDS is becoming a new form of genocide in the twenty-first century for indigenous peoples.

Heritage rights are emerging as a new area of contestation. The ancestors of present-day San peoples covered Southern Africa with some of the finest rock art in the world. The images painted with natural dyes inside caves, on cliffs, and engraved into rocks number in the tens of thousands across the whole region. They represent a high level of artistic achievement as well as recount the images of a highly sophisticated cosmology.

San people are known for their trance dancing traditions, which are shared throughout their many cultures. According to San elders and anthropologists, shaman healers use the dance to tap ancestral and supernatural sources of power to effect healing in the community. Shamans are known to be able to take the form of animals and can astral travel during trance states. Ancestors communicate healing songs to shamans during dreams. These songs are then modified and used in healing rituals within the community. European settlers felt greatly threatened by these supernatural powers and the trance dances were suppressed and stigmatized as unchristian and heathen. Much of the rock art of Southern Africa portrays these sacred images including in places where the original people have been driven to extinction. The technology and skill of rock art painting died out over 100 years ago. Governments in the region are moving to conserve rock art sights and then exploit them for tourism. San communities are asking to be involved in the conservation and interpretation of these sites, as well as to benefit from the profits arising from their commercialization. Two examples are the expulsion of the San from Tsodilo Hills in Botswana, and the marginalization of the ‖Xegwi from the creation of National Heritage Site at Cathedral Peaks in the Drakensberg Mountains of South Africa.

Since 1991, San communities have become increasingly organized and are attempting to defend their rights and change public perceptions about their cultures and human rights. The most important initiative has been the formation of the Working Group of Indigenous Minorities of Southern Africa (WIMSA). WIMSA is a council made up of San leadership from different communities in Namibia, Botswana, and South Africa. WIMSA has been actively involved in the building alliances with indigenous peoples around the world, and participating in the United Nations Decade of the World's Indigenous Peoples. As of 2001, San throughout the region were busy establishing elected national San Councils that they hoped would have an advocacy impact at national level and provide development assistance to impoverished communities.

Major institutions working for San empowerment include the South African San Institute (SASI) operating out of South Africa, Legal Assistance Centre in Namibia, and the Kuru Development Trust (KDT) and Ditshwanelo both based in Botswana.

Recently both the International Labour Office (ILO) and the Africa-Caribbean-Pacific parliamentary group have sponsored reviews of civil and human rights of San people in Southern Africa. President Mbeki of South Africa has made it clear that he supports the cultural and land aspirations of San people, and sees them as inherent elements of the "African Renaissance."

The preference of San activists has been to associate themselves with the Indigenous Peoples rights movement rather than the Minority rights movement and related United Nations process. The concept of minority rights is unpopular in Africa, and has been associated with the interests of White Nationalist groups. Indigenous Peoples rights include principles of protecting access to natural resources and the right to protect valuable and threatened indigenous knowledge systems relating to ancient hunter-gatherer economic and cultural systems. The nature of discrimination against the San does not arise from their numerical inferiority, indeed there are hundreds of other ethnic groups across the region, but rather that they are considered to be primitive and less than human by their neighbors. This prejudice is related to their aboriginality and economic and cultural systems.

NIGEL CRAWHALL

See also **Angola; Botswana; Namibia; South Africa; Zambia; Zimbabwe**

Further Reading

Barnard, Alan, *Hunters and Herders of Southern Africa: A Comparative Ethnography of the Khoisan Peoples*, Cambridge University Press: Cambridge, 1992

International Labour Office (ILO), *Indigenous Peoples of South Africa: Current Trends, Project for the Rights of Indigenous and Tribal Peoples*, ILO: Geneva, 1999

Leroux, Willemien, *Torn Apart: San Children as Change Agents in a Process of Acculturation: A Report on the Educational Situation of San Children in Southern Africa*, WIMSA and KDT: Windhoek, Namibia, 1999

Working Group of Indigenous Minorities of Southern Africa, *Report on Activities* (sequential annual reports), April 1996 to March 1997; April 1997 to March 1998; April 1998 to March 1999; April 1999 to March 2000, WIMSA: Windhoek, Namibia

San Marino

Capsule Summary

Country Name: Republic of San Marino
Location: Southern Europe, an enclave in central Italy
Total Population: 28,119 (2003)
Language: Italian
Religion: Roman Catholic

The Republic of San Marino is a landlocked country in north-central Italy and one of the smallest countries and oldest republics in the world. The total area of the state is 24 square miles (62 square kilometers, or one-third the size of Washington DC). It has a Mediterranean climate with mild to cool winters and warm and sunny summers. The terrain is composed of mostly rugged mountains, the Apennines. The highest point is Monte Titano (2477 feet; 755 meters). The capital is San Marino, and the largest city is Serravalle.

San Marino is believed to have been founded by a stonemason, St. Marinus of Dalmatia (present-day Croatia), who established a community of religious followers and gave the country its name circa 301 CE. By the mid-fifth century, a settlement had formed and with the exception of a few short periods San Marino has maintained its independence, partly due to its relatively inaccessible location and its poverty. In 1631 the Papacy recognized the republic's independence. Italy and San Marino signed a treaty of economic cooperation in 1862 solidifying the two countries political, economic, and cultural relationships. Volunteers from San Marino fought for Italy in World Wars I and II; Allied aircraft bombed the republic in 1944. San Marino fell under the sway of Italian Fascism, and from 1947 to 1957 the republic was ruled by a Communist-socialist coalition government.

The post-WWII era introduced several social and political changes. A left-wing coalition led by the Communists ruled from 1978 to 1986, at which time the Communists joined with the Christian Democrats to form a new government. In 1960 women were given the right to vote, and in 1973 they were granted the right to hold public office. The Communist party changed its name in 1990 to the Democratic Progressive party and continued in coalition with the Christian Democrats. San Marino became a member of the United Nations in 1992 and has been has been governed by a centrist Christian Democratic-Socialist party coalition since 1993.

Its executive branch consists of two co-chiefs of state elected every six months by the parliament, the Great and General Council. The government, known as the Congress of State, is elected by the parliament every five years. The head of the government, who is the Secretary for Foreign and Political Affairs, is also elected every five years by the parliament. The legislative branch consists of a 60-seat unicameral Grand and General Council elected by popular vote every five years. The Judicial branch is known as the Council of Twelve. The key political parties are Communist, Ideas in Movement, National Alliance, Party of Democrats, San Marino Christian Democratic Party, San Marino Popular Alliance of Democrats, San Marino Socialist party, and Socialists for Reform.

San Marino's population of approximately 28,119 consists of two ethnic groups, the Sammarinese majority, who are a mixture of Mediterranean, Alpine, Adriatic, and Nordic ethnic groups and represent 84 percent of the population, and the Italians who account for 16 percent of the population. There are no marked ethnic or racial divisions in the republic. Virtually all of the republic's inhabitants speak Italian and are Roman Catholic. About half of San Marino citizens reside abroad, mainly in Italy, the United States, and France. However, recently the country has begun to receive a modest number of immigrants, no longer exclusively from neighboring Italy but from other nations. Integration of minorities, therefore, is a relatively new experience for San Marino, and its government will likely be challenged to establish laws and programs for dealing with the integration of peoples from different ethnic, linguistic, religious, and cultural backgrounds into society. Social and political trends continue to closely follow those of Italy.

San Marino's key industries are tourism, banking, textiles, electronics, ceramics, cement, and wine. The tourist sector contributes over 50 percent of the gross domestic product (GDP). The GDP per capita income was $34,600 in 2001. Agriculture also contributes strongly to the economy; 74 percent of land is cultivated and 22 percent are pastures. Export commodities are mostly building stone, lime, wood, chestnuts, wheat, wine, baked goods, hides, and ceramics; among imported commodities are a variety of consumer manufactured goods and food. The euro is the official currency.

LUDOMIR LOZNY

See also **Italians**

Further Reading

Carrick, Noel, *San Marino*, Chelsea House, New York, 1988

Edwards, Adrian, and Chris Michaelides, *San Marino*, Clio Press 1996

Spadolini, Giovanni, *San Marino: L'idea della repubblica: Con documenti inediti dell'archivio de Pasquale Villari*, Firenze: Le Monnier 1989

São Tomé and Príncipe

Capsule Summary

Country Name: Democratic Republic of São Tomé and Príncipe
Location: Western Africa, islands in the Gulf of Guinea, straddling the Equator, west of Gabon
Total Population: 175,883 (2003)
Ethnic Populations: *mestico, angolares* (descendants of Angolan slaves), *forros* (descendants of freed slaves), *servicais* (contract laborers from Angola, Mozambique, and Cape Verde), *tongas* (children of *servicais* born on the islands), Europeans (primarily Portuguese)
Languages: Portuguese (official); Guinea Crioulo (majority) with dialects of São Tomense; Angolar (Ngola) and Principense
Religions: Christian 80% (Roman Catholic, Evangelical Protestant, Seventh-Day Adventist) and Catholic-Afro Spiritist Syncretism

The country of São Tomé and Príncipe is a consolidation of two groups of Atlantic islands, their size roughly equivalent to greater metropolitan Washington DC. São Tomé is the largest and lies the farthest south and west, 200 miles (322 kilometers) from Libreville, Gabon. Near it are the islets of Cabras and Rolas. Príncipe lies the farthest north and is 175 miles (282 kilometers) west of Equatorial Guinea. Near it are the islets of Bombom, Caroço, and the Tinhosas. São Tomé and Príncipe lie 100 miles (161 kilometers) apart on a southwest-northeast axis. Their total area is somewhat larger than that of New York City.

The islands had no native population when the Portuguese claimed them at the end of the fifteenth century, as Portugal made its pioneering voyages of discovery down the coast of Africa. Virtually all inhabitants of São Tomé and Príncipe came as African slaves to be traded to other colonies or to supply labor for the major agricultural cycles that occurred on the islands: sugar, followed by coffee, and, into this century, cocoa. Slave trading occurred into the nineteenth century. The islands were an entrepôt and processing center for human cargo brought from the West African mainland.

The ethnic and linguistic groupings of the population are due to these historical settlement and commercial patterns. The dominant *mestiço* group is a mixed race, resulting from interbreeding among Portuguese, some other Europeans, and Africans. The latter were brought from a radius in the African interior extending down the coasts of the Bights of Benin and Biafra, the Congo region, and down to Angola. The *angolares* are a small group on the southern coast of São Tomé descended from Angolan survivors of shipwreck several centuries ago and whose livelihood is fishing.

Forros are descendants of slaves freed in the nineteenth century. *Serviçais* are the descendants of contract laborers who came from other Portuguese colonies in Africa, such as Cape Verde, Angola, and Mozambique; and *tongas* are their native-born offspring. A small population of Portuguese and a few other Europeans continue in the country since it became independent in 1975.

Urban inhabitants appear a relatively large number with more than a fourth of the country's population concentrated in the capital city, São Tomé. However, the history of the country is rural, rooted in an export agricultural economy, most recently based on the cultivation of cocoa. The agricultural economy and society are poor. Soils are exhausted and eroded. This situation is somewhat similar to that of Cape Verde, another former Portuguese colony that is an island country off the coast of Africa. Per capita gross domestic product (GDP) is $1,200 (2002.).

The language of the country is predominantly the Guinean version of *crioulo*. This is Portuguese mixed with base African languages from the surrounding regions, mostly western Bantu. The dominant dialect is São Tomense. It is used by most inhabitants of São Tomé, the island with the largest population, and may have approximately 100,000 native speakers or second-language users. Angolar (also Ngola) *crioulo* is spoken by the Angolan-descended group on São Tomé, whose base African language is probably KiMbundu Bantu. Principense occurs on Príncipe, but its use is dying out.

Portuguese colonization implanted the Catholic religion. More than three-fourths of São Tomé and Príncipe is Catholic. However, as throughout the Portuguese empire, this religion intermixed with native beliefs, creating a creole syncretism of African spiritist religion and Catholicism. Over the last century Protestant missionary advances have challenged the dominance of Catholicism. There are now significant minorities of Evangelicals and Pentecostals.

The population growth is over three percent annually, so that almost half the population is under 14. About another half of the population is in the range of 15 to 64 years. Those over 65 are a tiny minority. Nearly three-fourths of the 15 or older population is literate; illiteracy is in the minority.

EDWARD A. RIEDINGER

Further Reading

Carmen, Raff, and Miguel Sobrado,"In Angola, Guinea Bissau and São Tomé e Príncipe," *A Future for the Excluded: Job Creation and Income Generation for the Poor*, London: Zed, 2000

Chabal, Patrick, and David Birmingham, *A History of Postcolonial Lusophone Africa*, Bloomington, Indiana: University Press, 2002

Girardo, Lorenzino, *The Angolar Creole Portuguese of São Tomé: Its Grammar and Sociolinguistic History*, LINCOM Studies in Pidgin and Creole Languages, no. 1; Munich: LINCOM Europa, 1998

Gowan, Susan Jean, and Elna Schoeman, "Portuguese Guinea/Guinea Bissau, Cape Verde, São Tomé e Príncipe, Portuguese-Speaking Africa as a Whole," *Portuguese-Speaking Africa, 1900–1979: A Select Bibliography*, 3, Braamfontein, South Africa: South African Institute of International Affairs, 1982–83

Hodges, Tony, *São Tomé and Príncipe: From Plantation Colony to Microstate*, Boulder, Colorado: Westview Press, 1988

Lorenzion, Gerardo, *The Angolar Creole Portuguese of São Tomé: Its Grammar and Sociolinguistic History*, Munich: LINCOM Europa, 1998

Seibert, Gerhard, *Comrades, Clients, and Cousins: Colonialism, Socialism, and Democratization in São Tomé and Príncipe*, Leiden, The Netherlands: Research School of Asian, African, and Amerindian Studies, Leiden University, 1999

Shaw, Caroline S., "São Tomé and Príncipe," in *World Bibliographical Series*, 187, Oxford, England and Santa Barbara, California: Clio Press, 1994

Saro-wiwa, Ken (Nigerian)

Ken Saro-Wiwa was a prominent Nigerian writer and human rights-environmental activist, a leader of the Ogoni minority. Ogoni territory covers 404 square miles (1046 square kilometers) in the northeast of the fertile, oil-rich Niger Delta and is inhabited by 500,000 people with a population density of 15, 000 per square mile. Traditionally, Ogoni were farmers and fishermen. British colonial invasion in 1901 deprived them of their independence and arbitrarily placed their land in the division of Opobo and then, after 1947, under the Ogoni Native Authority. After national independence in 1960, the federal Nigerian state brought together nearly 300 distinct peoples but power was concentrated among the three major ethnic groups, Yoruba, Hausa, and Igbo. Ogoni were grouped in the Eastern Region with Igbo. Postcolonial economics and national politics dominated by coups favored elites and did not resolve deep problems that became acute for marginalized minorities such as the Ogoni. These problems drove Saro-Wiwa into politics.

The early life of Saro-Wiwa was notable for his literary prowess. His academic career was interrupted by civil war. When the Eastern Region declared unilateral independence in 1967, he was working at the University of Nigeria, Nsukka, in the East. He opposed the Igbo military's secessionism, in part due to what he perceived as Igbo domination of minorities, and was employed by the federal government first as administrator of the oil port of Bonny and then in the Rivers State Cabinet as commissioner of Works, Land, and Transport, of Education, and of Information and Home Affairs from 1968 to 1973, when he was dismissed after urging Ogoni autonomy.

Saro-Wiwa then concentrated on business and writing. His success in retail and real estate allowed him to establish the Saros publishing house. He became a popular columnist, writing for newspapers and magazines such as *Vanguard, Daily Times*, and *Punch*. He emerged as a major writer with his antiwar novel *Sozaboy* (1985), set in the Biafran war. The novel, subtitled "a novel in rotten English," creatively mixed Creole and English, reflecting his frustration with the domination of minority vernacular languages such as his own Khana. He wrote and produced the popular television series *Basi and Co*. from the mid-1980s until it was suppressed by the military in 1992.

Saro-Wiwa's shift to political activism is seen in his autobiographical *On a Darkling Plain* (1989). In November 1990, with other leaders, he founded the Movement for the Survival of the Ogoni People (MOSOP), an umbrella body of Ogoni civic organizations. At the heart of Ogoni complaints was oil.

Massive, high-quality oil reserves in Ogoniland had been exploited by Royal Dutch Shell since 1958. Oil dominated national income (providing more than 80 percent of federal revenue) but very little (1.5 percent) returned to the Delta and, as the Nigerian constitution had no provision for minority or mineral rights, the Ogoni got no royalties. There was minimal investment in the region by government or companies, with chronic neglect of water resources, hospitals, housing, and schools and a lack of electricity.

Unregulated oil exploitation brought severe pollution. Once fertile land was polluted annually by 2.3 billion cubic meters of oil, with 3,000 spills between 1976 and 1991. Constant gas flaring emitted 35 million tons of carbon dioxide and 12 million tons of methane annually. Saro-Wiwa described the impact: water, farmlands, and atmosphere poisoned, intense hydocarbon vapors, methane, carbon monoxide and dioxide emitted by gas "flared 24 hours a day for 33 years in very close proximity to human habitation," acid rain, oil blow-outs, pipelines across farms. People suffered endemic diseases; mangrove forests, animals, and fish all died; and the land was rendered infertile.

In 1990, Ogoni leaders submitted a Bill of Rights to the Nigerian President, urging autonomy, representation, fair return from resources, development of minority languages, and environmental protection. It was ignored. In November 1992, MOSOP told oil companies they must pay reparations for devastated land or leave. After pressure on oil workers, Shell temporarily withdrew staff. In 1993 (the U.N. Year of Indigenous People) there were large-scale, peaceful demonstrations. On January 4 (now Ogoni Day) 1993, some 300,000 Ogonis held a massive protest. In April, peaceful protests against pipe-laying by a U.S. contractor across Ogoni farms were met by bullets from

Nigerian troops. In response to worldwide campaigns to expose Shell's duplicity, the company requested protection and the military formed a task force to eliminate MOSOP. Occupation followed, with Ogoni police replaced with officers from different ethnic groups. In November, General Sani Abacha seized power and even more brutal repression ensued, with over 1,000 killed and thousands made homeless.

Saro-Wiwa was imprisoned in 1993, described in his *A Month and a Day* (1995). In May 1994 he was again arrested on the pretext he had allegedly incited youth to murder four local politicians. In October 1995 he and eight codefendants were sentenced to death by a military tribunal widely denounced as a show trial. They were all executed on November 10; acid was poured on his body. The dictatorship faced wide international condemnation and was suspended from the Commonwealth.

Saro-Wiwa adopted a view of "indigenous colonialism" akin to the theory of internal colonialism. In *Genocide in Nigeria* (1992) he argued that the Ogoni are an exploited minority, their appeals ignored by majorities. He spoke of the danger of "the extinction of our nation." He also had a wider vision of a united, democratic Nigeria in which all minorities had rights. His closing statement to the Military Tribunal before his execution sums up his views: "Appalled by the denigrating poverty of my people, . . . distressed by their political marginalization and economic strangulation, angered by the devastation of their land, . . . anxious to preserve their right to life and to a decent living, and determined to usher to this country as a whole a fair and just democratic system which protects everyone and every ethnic group . . . I have devoted . . . my very life."

Since democratization in 1998, political organization among minorities has been freer but the community has received no reparations and pollution and repressive acts continue. On January 4, 1999, two dozen protestors involved in an oil strike were killed. Saro-Wiwa's funeral, five years after his death, was emblematic of unresolved minority problems: authorities refused to deliver his bones to his family, and the funeral held in his home village went ahead without his remains.

The significance of Saro-Wiwa is immense. His relentless battle for justice shamed governments and oil companies. His fight against repression and environmental devastation inspired other oppressed minorities such as the Ijaw, Uzere, and Irri, as well as oil

workers, to take action on these issues. His writings highlighted the position of minorities, their culture, and dilemmas. His brutal death focused national and international attention on the plight of the Ogoni and repression in Nigeria. The failure—in the face of brutal repression and multinational interests—of the movements he led suggests that the problems of minorities in Nigeria are likely to continue.

Biography

Kenule (Ken) Beeson Saro-Wiwa. Born Bori, Ogoni, Nigeria, October 10, 1941. Educated at Government College, Umuahia (1954–1961), and University College, Ibadan (1962–1966). Graduated in English. Briefly taught at Government College, Umuahia, Stella Maris College, Port Harcourt, University of Lagos, and University of Nigeria, Nsukka. Administrator of Bonny, 1967–70. Commissioner of Works, Land, and Transport, Education, and Information and Home Affairs, Rivers State, 1968–1973. Director, National Directorate for Social Mobilisation, 1987. Founder, later president, Movement for the Survival of the Ogoni People, 1993–1995. President, Ethnic Minorities Rights Organisation of Africa. Vice-Chairperson, Unrepresented Nations' Peoples Organisation. Arrested four times and imprisoned, 1993. Adopted by Amnesty International as a Prisoner of Conscience. Arrested, convicted by military tribunal, 1995. Awards: Commonwealth Writers Prize for African Literature, 1987; Fonlon-Nichols Prize for excellence in creative writing, 1994; Right Livelihood Award, 1994; Goldman Environmental Prize for Africa, 1995; Noma Award for Publishing (Honorable Mention), 2000. Executed November 10, 1995, Port Harcourt, Nigeria.

Selected Works

Basi and Company: A Modern African Folktale, 1977
Songs in a Time of War, 1985
Sozaboy, 1985
A Forest of Flowers: Short Stories, 1986
On a Darkling Plain: An Account of the Nigerian Civil War, 1989
Similia: Essays on Anomic Nigeria, 1991
The Singing Anthill: Ogoni Folk Tales, 1991
Genocide in Nigeria: The Ogoni Tragedy, 1992
A Month and a Day: A Detention Diary, 1995 [posthumous]

PETER LIMB

See also **Autonomy; Human Rights, Ethnic Conflict; Nigeria; Self-Determination**

Further Reading

Comfort, Susan, "Struggle in Ogoniland: Ken Saro-Wiwa and the Cultural Politics of Environmental Justice," in *The Environmental Justice Reader: Politics, Poetics, & Pedagogy*, edited by Joni Adamson, Mei Mei Evans, and Rachel Stein, Tucson, Arizona: University of Arizona Press, 2002

Eshiet, Imo Ubokudom, Onookomne Okome, and Felix Akpan, editors, *Ken Saro-Wiwa and the Discourse of Ethnic Minorities in Nigeria*, Calabar: University of Calabar Press, 1999

Killam, Douglas, and Ruth Rowe, editors, "Ken Saro-Wiwa," in *The Companion to African Literature*, Bloomington: Indiana University Press, 2000

McLuckie, Craig W., and Aubrey McPhail, editors, *Ken Saro-Wiwa: Writer and Political Activist*. Boulder, Colorado: Lynne Rienner Publishers, 2000

Na'allah, Abdul Rasheed, *Ogoni's Agonies: Ken Saro-Wiwa and the Crisis in Nigeria*, Trenton, New Jersey: Africa World Press, 1998

Okome, Onookome, editor, *Before I am Hanged: Ken Saro-Wiwa, Literature, Politics, and Dissent*, Trenton, New Jersey: Africa World Press, 2000

Olorode, Omotoye, et al., editors, *Ken Saro-Wiwa and the Crisis of the Nigerian State*, Lagos: Committee for the Defence of Human Rights, 1998

Wiwa, Ken, *In the Shadow of a Saint*, New York: Doubleday, 2000

Saudi Arabia

Capsule Summary

Country Name: Kingdom of Saudi Arabia
Location: Middle East, bordering the Persian Gulf and the Red Sea, north of Yemen
Total Population: 24,293,844 (includes 5,576,076 non-nationals) (2003)
Ethnic Populations: Arab (90%), Afro-Asian (10%)
Languages: Arabic (official), some English
Religion: Islam (mostly Sunni Muslim with a Shi'ite minority)

The Kingdom of Saudi Arabia (in Arabic *Al-Mamlakah Al-'Arabiyah As-Sa'udiyah*) is a nation with an area of approximately 868,000 square miles (2,248,000 square kilometers), occupying nearly four-fifths of the Arabian Peninsula. About one-fifth the size of the United States, it is bordered by Jordan, Iraq, and Kuwait on the north; by the Persian (Arabian) Gulf, Qatar, the United Arab Emirates, and Oman on the east; by a part of Oman on the southeast; by Yemen on the south and southwest; and by the Red Sea and the Gulf of Aqaba on the west. Portions of the borders with Oman, Yemen, and the United Arab Emirates are ill-defined or disputed. A territory of 2,200 square miles (5698 square kilometers) along the Gulf coast was shared by Kuwait and Saudi Arabia as a neutral zone until 1969, when a political boundary was established.

There are five ecological zones. These are the village farmer-populated Western Highlands, which borders the Red Sea (the arid northern half is called the *Hejaz* and the southern portion, which receives monsoon rains, is the *Asir*); the Central Plateau or Najil

inhabited by nomadic herders; the thinly populated Northern Deserts; the populated Eastern Highlands or Hasa bordering the Persian (Arabian) Gulf; and Rub al Khali (the 250,000 square mile (647,500 square kilometer) "Empty Quarter," which is uninhabited except for some nomads). More than 25 percent of the population resides on 1 percent of the land. The gross domestic product (GDP) per capita was $11,400 as of 2002.

Saudi Arabia is a Muslim and an Arab state, so that both attributes are a fundamental influence on the kingdom's foreign relations. Makkah (Mecca) and Medina, the holiest cities of Islam, are located in the western part of the country and have provided Saudi Arabia with external contacts since the sixth century. Islam obliges all Muslims to make the *Hajj* (pilgrimage) to Mecca, and the number of pilgrims currently exceeds 2.8 million per year (about half from Arab countries and half from African and Asian countries).

Saudi Arabia is named for the house of Sa'ud, the founding and ruling dynasty that dates from the fourteenth century. Ottoman Turks controlled the peninsula from 1891 and the Sa'ud family was exiled from 1906 to 1932. Since the 1930s, petroleum exploration and refining introduced significant social and economic changes because of the influx of millions of foreign skilled and unskilled workers and by the employment of Saudis in nontraditional jobs. This extraordinary socioeconomic change altered neither the government nor the centrality of religion. Until the 1960s, most of the population was still nomadic or seminomadic but due to economic and urban growth, more than 95 percent of the population is now settled. In addition, Saudi students study abroad, mostly in the United States and Europe.

Politically, Saudi Arabia comprises 13 provinces; Riyadh, the national capital, is located in the east-central portion of the nation. The major populated areas are in the central Hejaz, in Asir, in central Najd, and near the Persian Gulf. The largest cities include Riyadh (4.9 million inhabitants, 2003), Jiddah, Mecca, At-Ta'if, Medina, Ad-Dammam, Al-Hufuf, Tabuk, Buraydah, Al-Mubarraz, Khamis Mushayt, Al-Khubar, Najran, Ha'il, Jizan, and Abha.

Saudi Arabia's population is estimated to be nearly 25 million including about 6.4 million resident foreigners; these figure are double the demographic profile of 1986. Presently, Arabs comprise 90 percent of the population, and Afro-Asians less than 10 percent. Ethnically, most Saudis are Arab but others are of mixed ethnic origin, descended from Turks, Iranians, Indonesians, Indians, Africans, and others, a majority of whom immigrated as pilgrims, stayed, and currently reside in the Hijaz region along the Red Sea coast.

Initially, most of the foreign petroleum workers were Arab, such as Yemenis, Egyptians, Palestinians, Syrians, and Iraqis. However, increasing numbers of non-Arab Muslims such as Pakistanis have been employed, as have large numbers of non-Muslim South Koreans and Filipinos who are hired in group contracts for specified periods. Arabs from nearby countries (especially Yemen, Oman, Jordan, Iraq, and Iran) are employed in the kingdom, and there are significant numbers of Asian expatriates (mostly from India, Pakistan, Bangladesh, Indonesia, and the Philippines). In 2003, there were fewer than 100,000 Westerners (mostly American and European technicians, specialists, or military) living in Saudi Arabia. Because of a long history of regionalism and tribal autonomy, social and linguistic variations have

developed among the Saudis. Significant external influence from black Africa is evident along the Red Sea coast, while influences from Iran, Pakistan, and India are notable in the east.

Saudis speak Arabic, a Semitic language that originated in Arabia. Saudi Arabia's native population is almost entirely Sunni Muslim, adhering to traditionalist or orthodox views called the *Wahhabism* in the West. This puritanical interpretation of Sunni faith is named after Muhammad ibn 'Abd al-Wahhab (1703–1792). About 4 percent of the population, concentrated chiefly at the oases of Al-Hasa and Al-Qatif, are Shi'ites who adhere to Shi'ism, the second major branch of Islam. The public worship and display of non-Muslim faiths is prohibited.

CHARLES C. KOLB

See also **India; Iran; Pakistan; Muslims: Sunni in Shi'a Countries; Muslims: Shi'a in Sunni Countries**

Further Reading

Anscombe, Frederick F., *The Ottoman Gulf: The Creation of Kuwait, Saudi Arabia, and Qatar*, New York: Columbia University Press, 1997

Champion, Daryl, *The Paradoxical Kingdom: Saudi Arabia and the Momentum of Reform*, New York: Columbia University Press, 2003

Ember, Melvin, and Carol Ember, editors, *Countries and Their Cultures*, New York: Macmillan Reference, under the auspices of the Human Relations Area Files (Yale University), 2001

Kupershoek, P.M., *Arabia of the Bedouins*, London: Saqi, 2001

Lancaster, William, *The Rwala Bedouin Today*, 2nd edition, Prospect Heights, Illinois: Waveland Press, 1997

Lecker, Michael, *Jews and Arabs in Pre- and Early Islamic Arabia*, Aldershot, U and Brookfield, Vermont: Ashgate, 1998

Nyrop, Richard F.editor, *Saudi Arabia: A Country Study*, 4th edition, Washington, DC: U.S. Government Printing Office, 1984

Shaw, John A., and David E. Long, *Saudi Arabian Modernization: The Impact of Change on Stability*, Washington, DC: Georgetown University, Center for Strategic and International Studies, 1982

Scotland, *See* Scots

Scots

Capsule Summary

Location: United Kingdom, emigrants in United States, Canada, and Australia
Total Population: 5,054,800 in Scotland, approximately 28,000,000 claim Scottish ancestry worldwide
Languages: English (official), Scottish Gaelic, and Scots
Religion: Presbyterian

The term *Scots* refers to an ancient kingdom of Scotland, the people of the Scottish nation, or a linguistic group, dependent upon its context. The most widely used definition of *Scots* is that of a group of people—past, present, and future—who claim Scotland as their homeland. However, the term Scots may also refer to the descendent of fifth-century settlers to Scotland originating from Northern Ireland, or *Scots* may be a linguistic category, referring to people who speak the Scots language. Regardless, the complexity of the term *Scots* reflects Scotland's long history of struggle for autonomy from a series of invaders—including the Romans, Vikings, and English—all the while working to realize its own expansionist and colonialist agenda. In 1707 the Act of Union united Scotland with England and consequently, Scotland and its people have struggled to forge a national identity distinct and separate from Britain.

History

The first settlers in Scotland date to at least 4000 BCE. These Stone Age hunter-gatherers, most of whom settled along the west coast of Scotland, are believed to have come from the European mainland. However, no written record of the early Scots exists, and most knowledge of these people is obtained from archaeological ruins and physical relics. The first written record of the people of Scotland was penned by the Roman historian Tacticus during the first Roman invasions in Scotland around the year 79. During the next three centuries Roman emperors continued to assert their domination upon Scotland, but were met by great resistance by native Scottish tribal groups. The Roman Empire fell in 410, resulting in the withdrawal of Roman forces in Britain. These Roman conquests left little enduring impact upon Scotland or her people.

By 600 Scotland was populated by four groups—the Picts, the Scots, the Britons, and the Angles. The Picts, or "painted ones," were descendents of the first settlers in Scotland. The Britons—a group closely related to the Welsh—came from southern Britain in the first century BCE. The Scots, a Gaelic-speaking group originally from Northern Ireland, arrived in Scotland in the fifth century. The Angles, or Anglo Saxons, were a Germanic-speaking people from across the North Sea that settled Scotland from the fifth century on. Christianity was brought to Scotland with the Scots and during the next few centuries Scotland was converted to Christianity in the form of Celtic Catholicism. However, religious unification did not equate to immediate political solidarity—each kingdom sought to expand its kingdom and increase its power, resulting in fierce battling for several centuries.

In the late eighth century Vikings began invading Scotland, and by the tenth century they had established settlements on the western and northern islands of Scotland. Battles with the Vikings led to increasing need for fortification of the Scottish kingdoms, particularly the kingdom of the Picts. Using the need for solidarity among the Scottish kingdoms as a means of gaining personal power, and taking advantage of the weakened Pictish kingdom, in 843 Kenneth MacAlpin—known previously as King Kenneth of the Scots—successfully seized the title of King Kenneth I of the Scots and Picts and unified the kingdoms of the Scots and Picts into the kingdom of Alba. Alba survived throughout Viking onslaughts but internal strife continually threatened the Scots-Pictish kingdom, as assumption of the throne was often gained through violence and treachery.

In 1066 Normans from France gained control of England and replaced the Anglo-Saxon kingdoms with a single English state. After the Norman conquest of England, numerous English citizens settled in the Scottish Lowlands, where their presence fostered the development of Anglo-Norman practices and customs such as feudalism and Roman Catholicism. For the next two centuries, the English aspired to overtake Scotland, but Scotland resisted English domination. However, close and convoluted familial relationships between Scottish and English royal families strengthened England's claim to Scotland and foreshadowed the events that would later befall Scotland.

Hostilities between England and Scotland abated during the early thirteenth century, only to appear again when Scotland found itself with no apparent heir to the throne in 1290. A number of individuals made their claim. Scotland turned to Edward I of England to anoint the new king of Scotland. Although he elected John Balliol as King of Scotland, he did so with the stipulation that the new king accept him as overlord of Scotland. Balliol reneged upon this agreement in 1295, entering into an alliance with France that would last for 250 years. As a consequence of this "auld alliance," Edward I crossed the Scottish border in 1296, defeated the Scots army in a bloody battle, stripped Balliol of the crown, and proclaimed himself king of Scotland, signaling the unification of England and Scotland.

Edward I's actions led to the Scottish Wars of Independence. Scottish insurrection groups led by William Wallace fought against Edward I and executed a victorious attack against England in 1297, only to be crushed at the Battle of Falkirk in 1298. In 1304 all Scottish nobles were forced to give homage to Edward I and Wallace was executed in 1305. The Scots were more successful in 1314 when, led by Robert Bruce, they defeated the English forces at the Battle of Bannockburn. This victory led to the drafting of the Declaration of Arbroath by the Scottish Parliament in 1320, which proclaimed Scotland's independence from England.

Although Scotland gained independence from England, this victory did not signal a cease to the conflict between England and Scotland. At this time Scotland was also plagued with administrative chaos as weak kings, Highland chiefs, Lowland feudal barons, and papal clergy fought tirelessly to gain control and power within Scotland. This chaos continued for centuries, creating at times a climate of lawlessness, political instability, and violence. As the fourteenth century came to a close, the House of Stuart—a royal family often plagued with misfortune, and relentless attacks by Britain—began its four-century reign of Scotland. Further complicating the state of affairs in Scotland was the Protestant Reformation, a movement that began in the sixteenth century as a series of attempts to reform the Catholic Church, but ended in division and the establishment of several other Christian churches.

The Protestant Reformation took hold in Scotland because it had been largely a Catholic country for a number of centuries, yet many Scottish leaders had resented the Catholic Church's power. The Reformation came to an apex in Scotland when the Scottish Parliament abolished papal authority and adopted a reformed Confession of Faith. Ruling Scotland at that time was Mary, Queen of Scots, herself a Catholic of the House of Stuart. She refused to ratify this legislation and as a result was forced to abdicate the throne to her son James VI, reared a Protestant. She was later executed as a Catholic threat to the Protestant English throne.

Scotland's transference of royal power from a Catholic Queen to a Protestant King had even greater significance to Scotland when in 1603 the crown of England was passed to James VI. He took the title James I of England while simultaneously holding the Scottish crown, ruling Scotland and England as separate kingdoms, joined by one crown. Although his reign was relatively successful, James VI struggled at times to appease the Presbyterian majority and Catholic subjects, the latter who waged several rebellions during his reign.

Charles I (son of James VI) was not as diplomatic in his reign of both countries, and his lack of understanding of the Scottish people caused him to become alienated from his subjects. His lack of political savvy as king of either the British or Scottish monarchies, evident in the English Civil War of 1642–1648, led in part to his surrender to the Scots and later execution in 1649. The Scottish military became very active in English politics at this time and as a result, in 1654 Oliver Cromwell, leader of the British parliamentary forces, defeated Charles II of Scotland and forced the Scots to unite with England. Scotland agreed to the Act of Union of 1707 primarily as a political maneuver executed to increase Scotland's role with parliamentary affairs, to improve Scottish trade and industry, and to promote peace between Scotland and England,. This union marked Scotland's inclusion in the United Kingdom of Great Britain. The Scottish Parliament was dissolved, but Scotland retained separate churches (Presbyterian) and laws.

For approximately forty years after the union, political unrest ensued in Scotland as loyalists to the House of Stuart—particularly Scottish Highlanders—fought to restore the Stuart dynasty, resulting in the unsuccessful Jacobite Rebellions of 1715 and 1745. The latter part of the eighteenth century marked a shift from preoccupation with political matters to other areas of intellectual enquiry. In this period, called the "Scottish Enlightenment," David Hume won world fame in philosophy and history, Joseph Black in science, John Millar in social theory , Robert Adam in architecture, and Adam Smith in political economy. Poets and writers of the time, such as Robert Burns and Robert Fergusson, revealed a tendency in their works to resist the union and assimilation with English culture by reviving Scottish vernacular culture and mythology of the past. However, outright criticism or political activism against the crown was not prevalent in the late eighteenth or early nineteenth centuries.

The early nineteenth century witnessed the Industrial Revolution in Scotland, with advances in industry and manufacturing technology such as textiles, coalmining, iron production, and shipbuilding. Industry boomed prior to World War I, only to be followed by dire economic conditions postwar. This economic hardship was instrumental in the formation of The Scottish Nationalist Party in 1934. The formation of this political party signaled the slow movement towards home rule in Scotland, as well as the overall growth of Scottish Nationalistic sentiments among her people. However, Scottish nationalism's role in political activism did not gain momentum until the 1960s. In 1997 the Scots passed a referendum that allowed them to establish a Scottish parliament—the first since 1707—which first convened in 1999.

Society and Culture

Scotland is one of the four regions that comprise the United Kingdom—the other regions being England, Northern Ireland, and Wales. Scotland is located in the northern third of the island of Great Britain. The current population of Scotland is approximately 5 million or one-tenth the total population of the

United Kingdom. Approximately three-fourths the population of Scotland resides in urban communities, in particular, the cities of Edinburgh (Scotland's capital) and Glasgow.

Scotland has two major land regions: the Highlands and the Lowlands. The Highlands cover the northern two-thirds of Scotland and are extremely mountainous. The Highlands are sparsely populated. This in part reflects the Highland Clearances of the late 1700s to mid-1800s, during which tens of thousands of men, women and children were evicted—most of whose families had resided on their property for many generations—from their homes in the Highlands to make way for large-scale sheep farming. They were resettled on parcels of land, most of which were usually too small and of such poor agricultural quality that subsistence farming proved impossible. The Highland Clearances created destitution and starvation for many Highland Scots and as a result large numbers opted to relocate to the Lowlands of Scotland and England, while others emigrated to Australia, Canada, and America, locales where Scotland had already established Scottish colonies.

About three-fourths of the population of Scotland lives in the Lowlands of central Scotland, although the region makes up only one-sixth of Scotland. The Lowlands have historically been the most economically vital region of Scotland, as it contains the most agriculturally productive lands. In the nineteenth and twentieth centuries coal was heavily mined in the Lowlands, and today the region remains central to Scotland's economy.

There are three main languages in usage in modern-day Scotland. English is the main language of the majority of Scots and is the official language of Scotland, but there are two additional languages spoken by minority populations in Scotland—Scottish Gaelic and Scots. Roughly-speaking, Scottish Gaelic-speakers are more prevalent in the Highlands, while Scots-speakers have historically resided in the Lowlands. Gaelic was the main national language of Scotland from the tenth century but began to decrease in usage with the coming of the Anglo-Normans in the twelfth century. Usage of Gaelic has receded since the destruction of the clan system in the 1700s. Today about 80,000 Scots speak Scottish Gaelic, primarily in the Hebridean islands and in pockets of the western mainland. *An Comunn Gaidhealach* was founded in 1891 in an attempt to preserve Gaelic language, literature, art, and music and the organization remains active today.

Scots, also known as *Lowland Scots* or *Lallan Scots*, is a vernacular language that originated as a dialect of Old English. Scots came to Scotland with the Anglo Normans in the twelfth century and has its own vocabulary, cadence, and accent. Although most Scots speak and write English, the fusion of Scots and English into a single common language happened relatively recently. Scots was the national language of the Stuart dynasty, functioning as the language of royalty until the union of the crowns in 1603. Both Scottish Gaelic and Scots function more strongly as spoken languages than as literary languages.

It has been said that following the Act of Union of 1707 the histories of Britain and Scotland merged, thereby erasing much of their differences. However, Scotland's cultural history in the last three centuries is much more complex and reflects its struggle to maintain an autonomous cultural identity while simultaneously functioning as a viable economic and political player within the United Kingdom. Although Scotland did not have an autonomous political identity for several hundred years, the Scots created and fostered a Scottish identity distinct and separate from England primarily through the maintenance and (at times) invention of Scottish cultural traditions. These include the promotion of the Scottish Gaelic and Scots languages, enacted most clearly through language revival movements and support of literature written in the two languages; the romanticizing and mythologizing of past ways of life in the Gaelic Highlands; the sponsorship of literature and historical scholarship centered on the Scottish experience; and the maintenance of Scottish religious practices, holidays, festivals, and family customs. Additionally, diasporic communities of Scots in North America, England, and Australia, most of whom left Scotland hundreds of years ago, continue to forge bonds of "Scots-ness"—many bridging immense geographic distances—by embracing, preserving, and reinventing Scottish cultural practices and traditions abroad today.

ERIN STAPLETON-CORCORAN

See also **Ireland; United Kingdom; Wales**

Further Reading

Broun, Dauvit, R.J. Finlay, and Michael Lynch, editors, *Image and Identity: The Making and Re-Making of Scotland through the Ages*, Edinburgh: John Donald Publishers, 1998

Devine, T.M, *The Scottish Nation*, New York: Penguin Putnam, 1999

Fisher, Andrew, *A Traveller's History of Scotland*, New York: Interlink Books, 2002

Harris, Nathaniel, *Heritage of Scotland: A Cultural History of Scotland and its People*, New York: Checkmark Books, 2000

Menzies, Gordon, *The Scottish Nation,* Edinburgh: Edinburgh University Press, 2002

———, *Who Are the Scots?* Edinburgh: Edinburgh University Press, 2002

Strathern, Andrew, and Pamela J. Stuart, *Minorities and Memories: Survivals and Extinctions in Scotland and Western Europe*, Durham, North Carolina: Carolina Academic Press, 2001

Trevor-Roper, Hugh, "The Invention of Tradition: The Highland Tradition of Scotland," in *The Invention of Tradition*, edited by Eric Hobsbawm and Terence Ranger, Great Britain: Cambridge University Press, 1983

Secession

Secession can be described as an act or a process by which a part of a state withdraws from that state to become independent. It is associated with the right to self-determination and for this purpose labeled *secessionary self-determination* to distinguish it from other manners by which a people can exercise its right to self-determination. Self-determination is defined as free choice of one's own acts or states without external compulsion, or determination by the people of a territorial unit of their own political future without coercion from powers outside that region.

While self-determination was accepted as a right under international law during the second half of the twentieth century, its roots can be traced back to the various theories on nationalism developed during the eighteenth but mainly the nineteenth century. The American Declaration of Independence already proclaimed self-determination as a moral right: "[I]t becomes necessary for one people to dissolve the political bands which have connected them with another; . . . it is the Right of the People to alter it and to institute new Government . . . [to affect] their Safety and Happiness." However, it was during the coming of age of the national movements in Europe during the mid-nineteenth century that the slogan was postulated that every nation be allowed the freedom to choose its political status, that every nation was entitled to form a state and every state to include just one nation. This doctrine led to unification processes throughout the European continent. However, the opposite feature of this doctrine was that states which could not convince their inhabitants that they belonged to the same nation and thus constituted a nation state, were to disappear while new independent state entities would be formed through the secession of constituent parts of the former state.

At the present, the world counts more than 4,000 population groups that could be identified as nations. If all these nations would invoke these theories on nationalism in order to secede, a great number of states would cease to exist, but also the world community would be unable to function under the premises of the current understandings in international relations. This explains that international law as well as international politics have considerably restricted the possibility to appeal to secession as a means to exercise self-determination.

When looking at the international instruments on self-determination with which secession is generally associated, one can state that international law limits the possibility to appeal to secession by referring to the principle of national unity and territorial integrity recognized in a number of international instruments, without, however, fully outlawing secession. The Charter of the United Nations (UN Charter) recognizes in general terms the principle of self-determination but equally refers to the principle of territorial integrity. This principle of territorial integrity is construed in the UN Charter as an obligation binding on states and not the secessionary groups operating within a state. This means that, according to the original meaning of the UN Charter, secession is, with the exception of the intervention by another state, considered as a political issue for which international law remains neutral.

When the Charter provisions on self-determination were specified by the General Assembly of the United Nations during the decolonization era, pronouncements on self-determination were inextricably followed by a territorial integrity clause. Not all these clauses are, however, as strict as the clause contained in General Assembly Resolution 1514 (XV) of December 14, 1960, which mentions that "any attempt aimed at the partial or total disruption of the national unity and the territorial integrity of a country is incompatible with the purposes and principles of the Charter." General Assembly Resolution 2625 (XXV) of October 24, 1970, however, requires for the principle of national unity and territorial integrity to be applicable that the state in question possesses a government "representing the whole people belonging to the territory without distinction as to race, creed, or color." The 1993 Vienna Declaration and Program of Action adopted by the United Nations Conference on Human Rights even speaks of "any distinction" and not only racial or religious discrimination. Some commentators interpret these clauses as suggesting that secession is allowed under international law on the condition that (minority) groups fighting for their independence are driven by the lack of representation and are not supported by external powers. Of course, a state threatened by a secession movement can use all lawful means to combat it. Other commentators refer to the same wording of the clauses to suggest a narrow reading. The clauses in fact speak of "the whole people" instead of "all the distinct peoples." This leads these commentators to conclude that these instruments did not allow for groups within a state to claim a right of secession, because it is the people of the state as a whole which is entitled to react against minority rule, rather that the distinct minorities or groups within a state.

State practice has been too scarce to prove either of such views. With the end of the Cold War and the subsequent collapse of the Soviet Union in 1991, the dismantling of the Socialist Federal Republic of Yugoslavia, and the successful secession of Eritrea from Ethiopia in 1993, secessionary self-determination has again shaken the conscience of international law. Indeed, most of those involved in the disunifying or dismantling processes in these countries have frequently endeavored to legitimize their struggle using self-determination vocabulary. These precedents have again pointed to the lacunae in the international law of self-determination and have forced the international community to show its most creative side in order to find solutions to developments that were previously regarded as purely political, at most domestic, legal questions. The collapse of the

Soviet Union in 1991 and the splitting of Yugoslavia were indeed too quickly considered as dissolutions, a term employed for a process in which all constituent parts of the state agreed to extinguish the state and form new entities.

Thus international instruments considerably limit the possibility to appeal to secessionary self-determination. However, when secessionary movements do not violate the principle of national unity and territorial integrity, international law takes a very neutral position and leaves the field for national law or international politics. In such case, it is currently very likely that the international community will accept a newly formed state entity if the secessionary process that led to the separation can be labeled "remedial secession." In other words, if it repairs a past injustice, that is, when a distinct people has a legitimate claim to territory that was wrongfully annexed by another state (e.g., the Baltic states), or is a reaction against a present repression when a distinct people or minority is systematically repressed within an existing state and denied equal opportunity to participate in the political process or subjected to ongoing gross violations of human rights. This is, however, international politics and therefore all cases are not necessarily treated in like manner. In the current state of affairs, secession is often regarded as an *ultimum remedium,* or a solution of last resort, when all other options to live together in one state entity have failed.

STEPHAAN SMIS

See also **Eritrea; Yugoslavia**

Further Reading

Brilmayer, Lea, "Secession and Self-Determination: A Territorial Interpretation," *Yale Journal of International Law*, 19 (1991)

Buchheit, Lee C., *Secession: The Legitimacy of Self-Determination*, New Haven: Yale University Press, 1978

Cassese, Antonio, *Self-Determination of Peoples. A Legal Reappraisal*, Cambridge: Cambridge University Press, 1995

Heraclides, Alexis, *Self-Determination of Minorities in International Politics*, London: Frank Cass, 1991

Musgrave, Thomas D., *Self-Determination and National Minorities*, Oxford: Clarendon Press, 1998

Tomuschat, Christian, editor, *Modern Law of Self-Determination*, Dordrecht: Martinus Nijhoff Publishers, 1993

Selassie, Haile (Ethiopian)

Haile Selassie I (1892–1975), became emperor of Ethiopia (formerly Abyssinia) in 1930. He modernized Ethiopia in the 1920s and 1930s by moving it into the contemporary political scene.

Selassie was born on July 13, 1894, as Lij Taffari Makonnen at Enjersa Goro, near Harrar. He was the son of Ras Makonnen Wolde Michael, a member of the Solomonic Dynasty, cousin and the chief advisor to Emperor Menelik II, who had defeated the Italians at the Battle of Sadowa in 1895. His mother was Woizero Yeshimebet Ali AbaJiffar. He was ordained as a priest, serving in St. Michael's Church in Harrar. He was later home educated by French Capuchin monks. He excelled in the French, German, English, Amharic, Tigrigna, and Oromign languages as well as in world history, geography, and philosophy. Selassie also became a well-versed scholar in the Ge-ez language.

Selassie was given governorships of the Sidamo, and later Harer, provinces by Menelik II. His progressive policies, centered on redistributing the power held by the local nobility, and establishing a centralized government and a civil service, made him popular. The younger generation in Ethiopia saw him as a symbol of change. Menelik's successor on the throne, his grandson Lij Yasu, was unpredictable and unpopular with the Christian majority because he was closely associated with Islam. Selassie led the resistance against Lij Yasu, who was deposed in 1916 and replaced by Menelik's daughter Zauditu, who became empress in 1917. Selassie was appointed as regent and heir apparent, as a female ruler was considered unbecoming.

As regent, Selassie nearly single-handedly achieved Ethiopia's admission to the League of Nations in 1923. His visits to major European capital cities garnered significant attention, as no other Ethiopian ruler had traveled abroad before. Zaudatu died on November 2, 1930, and Selassie became emperor, taking the name Haile Selassie.

In 1931, Selassie promulgated a new written constitution that increased central government authority. He established schools throughout the country, reinforced police powers, outlawed slavery, built roads and hospitals, and repealed outdated taxation. He adapted Ethiopia to the world's economy for the first time by exporting coffee, which brought in considerable revenue. Improved communication aided his reforms.

When Fascist Italy invaded Ethiopia in 1935, Selassie went into exile in England. Selassie turned to the League of Nations for assistance. The British liberated Ethiopia in 1941, and Selassie regained his throne. He instigated reforms in social, educational, and economic areas. He modernized the administration of Ethiopian government and society on a gradual basis. However, he retained his absolute power and played his ministers against one other, so that none would be powerful enough to stage a coup d'etat. Consequently the country stagnated. While he was visiting South America in 1960, rebels seized power, but Selassie returned and quelled the uprising which had failed due to lack of planning and popular support. The uprising ocurred due to the declining economy and the poor standard of living endured by the majority of Ethiopians.

Selassie realized the importance of African unity at a time of emerging independent African nation states. He was instrumental in establishing the Organization of African Unity in 1963. The headquarters of the OAU were built in Addis Ababa.

Selassie did not designate a successor after his three sons predeceased him. Civil war broke out between Eritrean nationalists and Ethiopians. Famine due to drought overwhelmed the country. Selassie in his advanced age and increasing senility was unable to handle these overwhelming problems.

A military takeover by the Coordinating Committee (Derg) of the Armed Forces, Police, and Territorial Army in 1974 resulted in Selassie's dethronement. The monarchy was dismantled and Selassie was deposed on September 12, 1974. Selassie was imprisoned in his palace. A socialist regime replaced the monarchy. The military government allegedly had Selassie murdered on August 25, 1975, in Addis Ababa.

Selassie's influence expanded outside of Ethiopia even after his death. He inspired later activists such as Martin Luther King Jr. and Nelson Mandela. He is considered God by followers of the Rastafarian religion. Selassie was buried near a latrine after his death. After the regime that overthrew him was itself overthrown, in 1991, Selassie's remains were moved to a mausoleum that also held the remains of other rulers, including Menelik II. He was reburied in the Holy Trinity Cathedral, as he wished, in November 2000.

Biography

Haile Selassie I. Born July 23, 1894, as Lij Taffari Makonnen at Enjersa Goro, near Harrar. Married Wayzaro Menen in 1911. Named emperor on November 2, 1930, taking the name Haile Selassie. Went into exile in England upon Italy's invasion of Ethiopia in 1935. Regained his throne in 1941, after Great Britain liberated Ethiopia. Dethroned September 12, 1974. Allegedly murdered by the government on August 25, 1975, in Addis Ababa.

Selected Works

My Life and Ehtiopia's Progress, 1892–1937: The Autobiography of Emperor Haile Selassie I, edited and translated by E. Ullendorf, 1976

ANNETTE RICHARDSON

See also **Ethiopia; Rastafari**

Further Reading

Getachew, Inirias, *Beyond the Throne: The Enduring Legacy of Emperor Haile Selassie*, Addis Ababa: Shama Books, 2001
Legum, Colin, *The Fall of Haile Selassie's Empire*, London: R. Collins, 1975
Locot, Hans Wilhelm, *The Mission: The Life, Reign and Character of Haile Selassie*, New York: St. Martin's Press, 1989
Marcus, Harold G, *Haile Selassie I: The Formative Years, 1892–1936*, Los Angeles: UC Press, 1987
Mosely, Leonard, *Haile Selassie: The Conquering Lion*, Eglewood Cliffs, New Jersey: Prentice Hall, 1965

Self-Determination

Self-determination is the principle that states that peoples should be self-governing. It constitutes the basis of calls for independent statehood for groups including the Basques, Chechens, Kosovars, Kurds, Palestinians, Tibetans, and Québecois. International legal bodies have designated self-determination as a right, but its precise status in international law remains contested. The concept has both internal and external dimensions. The external aspect refers to political independence and freedom from outside oppression and interference. The internal aspect entails democratic self-government. There is considerable ambiguity regarding the meaning and implications of self-determination, especially with regard to the questions of how to define the peoples to whom the principle applies, and whether and under what conditions self-determination implies a right to secession or statehood.

The concept of national self-determination arose with the assertion of popular sovereignty in the American and French revolutions. It has bases in nationalism, liberalism, and socialism. Both Lenin and Stalin argued for national self-determination as a means of advancing the socialist cause. President Woodrow Wilson, in his Fourteen Points speech to the U.S. Congress on January 8, 1918, and in later speeches, advocated national self-determination as a basis for postwar international order. Critics, including Wilson's Secretary of State, feared the principle would instead undermine stability by encouraging challenges to existing borders, and Wilson later expressed regret that his advocacy had raised the hopes of peoples whose desire for independence could not be satisfied without endangering international peace and stability. Reflecting the dilemma of reconciling the principle of self-determination with the maintenance of international order and stability, responses by the international community to claims of national self-determination from Wilson's day forward have often reflected state interest rather than principle.

In the post-World War II context, self-determination became closely associated with the process of decolonization, and its application was largely limited to the independence of former colonies. Thus, during the era of decolonization, the self to whom the principle of self-determination applied was defined in territorial rather than in ethnic terms. These peoples often comprised ethnically heterogeneous groups combined within arbitrarily drawn colonial boundaries. Emphasis was placed on the external rather than internal dimension of self-determination, in part due to fear of newly independent states fragmenting into tribal and ethnic parts.

The principle of self-determination took on new prominence with the end of the Cold War, as first the Soviet empire, and then the Soviet Union itself, dissolved. Former Soviet satellite states acquired internal self-determination, and former Soviet republics their independence. In Germany and Czechoslovakia, borders were redrawn to combine or divide states, in the name of national self-determination. The protracted and violent breakup of Yugoslavia involved claims of self-determination based on ethnicity. In Quebec, the secessionist movement peacefully sought separation from Canada through the political process. In contrast to the era of decolonization, post-Cold War self-determination claims by ethnic and cultural minorities within existing states have been more prevalent, and more problematic. The proliferation of post-Cold War secessionist movements raised the question of whether changes in international relations—in particular globalization and shifts in the nature of armed conflict—had reduced the minimum size for a state to be viable, making secession more feasible. However, in response to post-Cold War calls for ethnic self-determination, arrangements for increased autonomy and self-governance within existing states have increasingly been promoted as an alternative to independent statehood for ethnic and minority groups.

Self-determination is both a right and a principle in international law, but its precise content and legal status is contested. Legal experts continue to debate whether the right of self-determination constitutes a peremptory norm (*jus cogens*) in international law, which would override agreements contrary to the norm. Also, uncertainty persists regarding the definition of a people (i.e., colonies, federal units, or any collectively defined people), and what, precisely, a right to self-determination entails: a right to secession, or merely a right to arrangements for autonomy and democratic rights within existing boundaries.

Article 1(2) of the United Nations Charter makes reference to "the principle of equal rights and self-determination of peoples," but as a basis for maintaining peace, not as a right. The UN General Assembly subsequently elevated the principle of self-determination to the status of a right in its 1960 Declaration on the Granting of Independence to Colonial Countries and Peoples [Resolution 1514 (XV)] and 1970 Declaration on Friendly Relations [Resolution 2625 (XXV)]. Both of the 1966 UN Covenants on Human Rights (the Covenant on Civil and Political Rights, and the Covenant on Economic, Social, and Cultural Rights) declare, in their common Article 1 that "All peoples have the right of self-determination." The International Court of Justice has declared self-determination to be a right in customary international law that all states are bound to respect. The 1975 Helsinki Final Act and 1981 African Charter on Human and Peoples' Rights also declare the existence of a right to self-determination.

The right to self-determination is generally conditioned upon the maintenance of territorial integrity, with limited exceptions. The 1970 Declaration on Friendly Relations and later UN Declarations limit the right to self-determination by enjoining interference with the territorial integrity of states that represent their citizens without discrimination. This implies that systematic discrimination reduces the force of the principle of territorial integrity relative to the self-determination claims of a persecuted minority. Thus, some prominent legal experts have argued that self-determination should be considered to imply a right to secession (only) in extreme cases of internal repression. Furthermore, many experts argue that self-determination provides a legal basis for secession only along preexisting boundaries of federal subunits. But the view that self-determination does not imply a right

to secession necessarily points to a greater emphasis on internal self-determination. Self-determination can thereby be held to require respect for minority rights, possibly including autonomous self-governance, rather than secession. Ultimately, however, both what constitutes a relevant people, and the consequences that follow from the right to self-determination, remain contested. These ambiguities confound the principle of self-determination both legally and politically.

MICHAEL LIPSON

See also **Basques; Chechens; Kurds; Québecois; Tibetans; United Nations and Minorities**

Further Reading

Bayefsky, Anne, *Self-Determination in International Law: Quebec and Lessons Learned*, Boston and London: Kluwer Law International, 2000

Buchanan, Allen, "Self-Determination and the Right to Secede," *Journal of International Affairs*, 45, no. 2 (1992)

Cassese, Antonio, *Self-Determination of Peoples: A Legal Reappraisal*, Cambridge: Cambridge University Press, 1995

Danspeckgruber, Wolfgang, editor, *The Self-Determination of Peoples: Community, Nation, and State in an Interdependent World*, Boulder: Lynne Rienner, 2002

Freeman, Michael, "The Right to Self-Determination in International Politics: Six Theories in Search of a Policy," *Review of International Studies*, 25, no. 3 (1999)

Hannum, Hurst, *Autonomy, Sovereignty, and Self-Determination: The Accommodation of Conflicting Rights*, Philadelphia: University of Pennsylvania Press, 1990; revised edition, 1996

Heraclides, Alexis, *The Self-Determination of Minorities in International Politics*, London: Frank Cass, 1991

Knop, Karen, *Diversity and Self-Determination in International Law*, Cambridge: Cambridge University Press, 2002

Kovács, Mária M., "Standards of Self-Determination and Standards of Minority-Rights in the Post-Communist Era: A Historical Perspective," *Nations and Nationalism*, 9, no. 3 (2003)

Pomerance, Michla, *Self-Determination in Law and Practice: The New Doctrine in the United Nations*, Boston and London: Martinus Nijhoff, 1982

Tamir, Yael, "The Right to Self-Determination," *Social Research*, 58, no. 3 (Fall 1991)

Semang

Capsule Summary

Location: Northern Peninsular Malaysia and extreme southern Thailand
Total Population: approximately 3,000
Languages: several Aslian (Mon-Khmer) languages
Religions: indigenous religions

The term *Semang* refers to a category of aboriginal people (*Orang Asli* in Malay) living in the lowland tropical rainforest of northern Peninsular Malaysia and extreme southern Thailand. The Semang comprise at least seven small culturally and linguistically distinct groups, including the Kensiu (population 224) of eastern Kedah state in Malaysia and southern Thailand; Kintak (235) and Lanoh (359) of northwestern Perak; Jahai (1,049) of northeastern Perak and northwestern Kelantan; Mendriq (145) of central Kelantan; Batek (960) of southern Kelantan, western Trengganu, and northern Pahang; and Maniq (also called Tonga or Mos; about 200) of southern Thailand. The total Semang population in Malaysia (officially 2,972) makes them a miniscule minority in a nation of over 22 million. The Semang of Thailand form an even smaller minority.

Semang are distinguished from the other broad categories of Malayan aborigines (Senoi and Aboriginal Malays) by their physical appearance, languages, and economic systems. Semang are typically small and dark-skinned with black, woolly hair. They are sometimes called *Negritos* (Spanish for "little blacks") in official and scholarly parlance. All but one of the Semang groups speak languages in the Northern Aslian division of the Mon-Khmer language family. Until recently, Semang lived by hunting and gathering and collecting forest products for trade, unlike most other Orang Asli, who practice various types of agriculture. Most Semang follow their own religions, though a few have recently become Muslims.

The Semang probably descended from the hunter-gatherers who produced the Hoabinhian stone tools that were used in the Malay peninsula from about 10,000 to 3,000 years ago. After the arrival of agriculture, probably introduced by immigrants from the north, some Hoabinhians adopted swidden ("slash-and-burn") farming, while others—the ancestral Semang—continued hunting and gathering, augmented by trade with their agricultural neighbors. After Malay-speakers from modern-day Indonesia settled along the coastal plains and larger rivers, Semang began collecting forest products, such as rattan and resin, to trade to them. As the Malay population increased, however, Malay relations with Semang and other Orang Asli soured. In the eighteenth and nineteenth centuries Malay slave raiders decimated the Orang Asli population, driving survivors into the interior. The British colonial government outlawed slavery in the late nineteenth century, but otherwise left the Orang Asli to their own devices. After World War II, the colonial government established a department of aborigines to win Orang Asli loyalty away from Communist insurgents based in Orang Asli areas. After Malayan independence in 1957, the government charged the department—now called the Department of Aboriginal Affairs (*Jabatan Hal Ehwal Orang Asli*)—with providing education, health care, and economic development to Orang Asli.

Until recently, most Semang hunted and gathered and traded rainforest products, much like their ancestors. Staple foods included wild tubers, seasonal fruits, nuts, bamboo shoots, and honey. They hunted arboreal game—mainly monkeys, squirrels, and birds—with bamboo blowpipes and poisoned darts, and smoked and dug burrowing animals out of holes. Some Semang also hunted with bows and arrows, though this practice died out in the twentieth century. People fished with natural poisons and spears, and traded hooks, lines, and nets. They obtained rice, flour, metal tools, cloth, tobacco, and other goods from Malay and Chinese traders in return for forest products, and they worked for outsiders as opportunities arose—for example, helping Malays harvest their rice in return for a small share of the crop. Most groups occasionally planted a few crops, and some groups, such as the Mendriq, became skilled farmers. Both men and women engaged in all these economic activities, although men did most of the blowpipe hunting and rattan collecting. Semang strongly emphasize the obligation to share food, especially meat, to ensure that no one goes hungry.

Hunting and gathering Semang lived in temporary camps consisting of a cluster of small thatched lean-to shelters, each housing a married couple and their small children, a group of adolescent boys or girls, or an unmarried adult. Most camps contained two to twenty shelters, housing up to 60 people, and lasted from one night to six weeks, depending on how long the supply of food and trade goods endured. When resources ran out, people moved and set up a new camp.

The basic unit of Semang society was the conjugal family—a husband, wife, and their young children. Families were autonomous. For example, when camps broke up, couples decided whether to move with the group, form new groups, or join other camps. Leadership was very weak; people might listen to respected camp members, but they were under no obligation to accept their advice.

Semang religions center on numerous superhuman beings. One is a fearsome thunder god who sends violent storms to topple trees on people who have broken taboos, for example, by mocking certain animals. Offenders may cut their shins and throw a mixture of blood and water to the thunder god and the earth deity to assuage their anger. Shamans communicate with superhuman beings through dreams or trances to obtain curing songs and medicines. At the beginning of the fruit season, camp members may hold singing sessions to ask the superhumans for abundant fruit. Semang believe that the dead go to a paradise, usually pictured as an island at the western horizon.

Some groups bury the dead in trees to facilitate their journey to the afterworld.

Since the early 1960s, the Malaysian government has pressured the Semang to settle down as subsistence and cash crop farmers, although it has not provided them with secure titles to the land on which they are supposed to live. Government and private agencies have also worked to convert them to Islam, the religion of the dominant Malays. Today most Semang live in poverty in government-sponsored resettlement villages, some as nominal Muslims. However, those retaining access to rainforest continue to hunt and gather and collect trade goods at least some of the time.

KIRK ENDICOTT

See also **Malaysia; Orang Asli; Thailand**

Further Reading

Endicott, Kirk, *Batek Negrito Religion*, Oxford: Clarendon Press, 1979
Evans, I.H.N., *The Negritos of Malaya*, Cambridge: Cambridge University Press, 1937
Lye, Tuck-Po, *Changing Pathways: Forest Degradation and the Batek of Pahang, Malaysia*, Lanham, Maryland: Lexington Books, 2004
Schebesta, Paul, *Among the Forest Dwarfs of Malaya*, London: Hutchinson, 1928
———, *Die Negrito Asiens: Wirtschaft und Soziolgie*, Vienna and Mödling, 1954
———, *Die Negrito Asiens: Religion und Mythologie*, Vienna and Mödling, 1957

Senegal

Capsule Summary

Country Name: Republic of Senegal
Location: West Africa, on the Atlantic coast
Total Population: 10,580,307 (July 2003)
Ethnic Populations: Wolof (43.3%), Pular (23.8%), Serer (14.7%), Jola (3.7%), Mandinka (3%), Soninke (1.1%), European and Lebanese (1%), other (9.4%)
Languages: French (official), Wolof, Pulaar, Jola (Joola or Diola), Mandinka (secondary)
Religions: Muslim (94%), indigenous beliefs (1%), Christian (5%) (mostly Roman Catholic)

Senegal is a presidential republic located in Western Africa, bordering the North Atlantic Ocean, between Guinea-Bissau and Mauritania. The economy is predominantly agricultural and heavily dependent on groundnut cultivation and foreign aid. The gross national product (GNP) per capita income was $1,500 in 2002. Seventy percent of the labor force is employed in agriculture (peanuts, millet, corn, rice, cotton, cattle, and fish). Other industries include fish processing, phosphate mining, fertilizer production, and petroleum refining. The Human Development Indicator (HDI) ranks Senegal 155 out of 174 countries. Twenty-one percent of the population lives in Dakar, the capital and chief port; 54 percent of the population lived below poverty level in 2002.

Senegal comprises two main Muslim Sufi brotherhoods, the Tidjanyya and the Mouridyya, which exert a major influence on cultural, economic, and political life. The Qadiriyya and the Layen brotherhoods are present but less important. The Mouridiyya brotherhood was founded in the 1880s by Sheik Amadu Bamba and preaches hard work as a means to salvation. The Roman Catholic minority (10 percent) exist mostly among Serere-Siin and Diola (Joola) groups. Senegal is a secular state with religious freedom despite its largely Muslim population.

History

Senegal's regional history has been preserved in Arabic documents and in oral epic poems that are recited by bards (griots). Recorded history dates from the eighth to the eleventh centuries, when the area was part of the empire of Ghana and then the Tekrour empire in the ninth and eleventh centuries. The Djolof kingdom arose and flourished during the thirteenth and fourteenth centuries in the area between the Senegal River and modern-day Dakar. The Portuguese were the first Europeans to explore the coast in 1455 and they traded in the kingdom of Senegal until the sixteenth century, when they were forced out by the Dutch, British, and French. The first French settlement at St. Louis was established in 1658. During the nineteenth century, the French gradually established control over the Senegal river basin.

Under French colonial rule Senegal inherited a legacy of democratic principles evidenced by a variety of political forces that emerged during the 1950s, including a strong trade union movement, Islamic sects, and the presence of Marxism. The Senegalese had received a form of French citizenship in the nineteenth century and were since that time represented in the French national assembly. The Union Progressiste Sénégalaise (UPS), founded in 1958 by Léopold Sedar Senghor, a popular poet and intellectual, arose as that leader's vision of local and regional traditional interests in combination with socialist ideas of collectivism and egalitarianism. Senghor married the support of foreign and local business interests, Islamic leaders, and

socialists in his successful political reign, which lasted 30 years. In 1958 Senegal became a self-governing member of the French Community, and then a member of the Mali Federation with Soudan (now Mali) from 1959 to 1960, before seceded from the federation to become an independent state in August 1960.

Dakar, once the administrative center of French West Africa and now the capital of Senegal, emerged as an active nexus for African politics. Under Senghor, who maintained strong allegiances and ties to French culture and politics, Senegalese foreign policy at time was geared towards the encouragement of French private investment and French use of military facilities in Senegal. Senegal followed a moderate political course under his presidency, which ended in 1980 when he stepped down in the wake of economic recession, giving the reigns to Abdou Diouf, who served for 19 years.

During the 1980s, political party activity intensified, and border conflicts emerged among Senegal and its neighbors—the Gambia, Guinea-Bissau, Mauritania, Guinea, and Mali. In April 1989 a border conflict regarding livestock grazing rights erupted between two Senegalese and some Mauritanian farmers. This resulted in the deaths of the two Senegalese, causing a crisis that fuelled long-standing ethnic and economic rivalries. What began as a disagreement turned into a war endangering citizens of both countries. Mauritania nationals, most residing in Dakar, were attacked by Senegalese nationals and vice versa. Mauritania deported Wolof, Tukulor, and Senegalese Fulani residing in that country. The Moor population in Senegal decreased from 300,000 (1988) to 5,000 (1993). It was believed that several hundred people, mostly Senegalese, lost their lives; and the conflicts did not end until an agreement between the two countries was finally reached in 1994.

A rebel separatist movement in the southern Casamance region, mobilized by the Mouvement des forces démocratiques de la Casamance (MFDC, or Movement for the Democratic Forces of Casamance) also emerged in the late 1980s as a violent struggle that lasted into the 1990s. Largely composed of the ethnic groups Diola (Joola-Fogny and Joola-Kasa), the MFDC asserted that the Casamance region ought to be considered autonomous and that France had favored such an arrangement during the colonial era. Casamance nationalism was based on regional and religious identity—Casamance is animist and Christian and comprised a diverse ethnic population of Diola, Fulani, and Mandinke, as opposed to the majority of Senegal, which was and is Muslim. Ongoing and often violent clashes between the Senegalese government and separatist rebels severely affected the country's tourist industry, negatively impacting an already strained economy. At the end of 1993 France declared that Casamance had not existed as an autonomous territory prior to colonial period, and that they had neither demanded nor considered independence for the region at the time of decolonization. Abdoulaye Wade (of the Socialist Party) has been president since April 2000.

Groups and Minorities

The over 50 ethnic groups of Senegal today live in relative peace and harmony, despite their diversity and differences in economic advancement. The chief ethnic groups are the Wolof (43.3 percent) who live on the coast and in the area around Dakar and the Thiès; the Serer (14.7 percent), a major group in the Gambia; the Fulani Fulfulde (Peulh or Fula) (23.8 percent) who are scattered throughout the northeastern region, in the Senegal River Valley and also (Fulacunda) in the Upper Casamance region; and the Diola (Jola or Joola) (9 percent), the majority of whom inhabit the Casamance region. There are other minor ethnic groups, each with their own culture and language. These include the Tukulor (Toucouleur) of the central Senegal river valley; the Lebou, living on the peninsula of Cap-Vert; the Mandinka, the Niominka, the Soninke, the Bassari, and the Bambara. Other minority cultures include the Moors (Maures or Naar), the Lebanese, and the French. Linguistically, the Wolof have become dominant, and their language is the most widely spoken language in Senegal.

The number of languages listed for Senegal is 42, and the national languages are Fulfulde, Wolof, Soninke, Serere, Joola-Fogny, and Malinke. Secondary languages are Jola-Fogny, Wolof, or Pulaar. All the ethnic groups speak African vernacular languages which in turn are divided into dialects. Only 12 percent are literate in the official language of French.

The Tukolor, the Haalpulaar, the Fulbe Jeeri, and the Fulacunda languages are separate Fulbe subgroups with separate dialects. Bunndu is a Fula geopolitical state composed of a mixture of Tukulor and Fulbe Jeeri. Fuuta Tooro was a major Tukulor geopolitical state. Herdsmen Fulbe Jeeri (350,000) live in Jeeri, a region in which a large number of diverse lineages still follow a seminomadic life.

The Fuuta Jalon (Fullo Fuuta, Futa Fula) are looked upon as outsiders in Senegal, where they represent 1.5 percent of the population. They travel from Guinea to work seasonally in Casamance, eastern Senegal, and Dakar. The Soninké (Marka, Sarakolé) number 150,000 and live along the Senegal River, principally north and south of Bakel. In Southeast and South Senegal, the ensemble Wamei-Konyagi (14,000), Budik (5,400), Badyara (6,500), and Basari (6,500) belongs to the Tenda group. In general, women intermarry with men from Fulbe and other groups and children become part of the Fulbe group.

The Bambara (or Bamana) live in Eastern Senegal (55,000); the Malinke (258,500) and the Mandinka (Manding, Mande) (445,500) and the related group the Jahanka (21,900), who speak a language related to Malinke and Mandinka, using Arabic characters to write it, live in the central southern and southeastern regions.

In Casamance, the Diola (Joola) group comprises two subgroups: the Jola-Fogny (Dyola, Joola) number 210,000 in the area surrounding the city of Bignona and southeast of Ziguinchor. The Jola-Kasa (or Casa) (30,000) have a language related to Jola-Fogny, but distinct from it. The Bainouk (or Elomay) (20,700), the Balanta (78,100) and the Mandyak (70,200) also live between the Casamance and the Geba-Cacheu rivers.

East and southeast of Dakar, the Serer group comprises three subgroups: the Serere-Sine (they call themselves *Sereer*) (848,000) in the Saloum Valley; the Serere-Noon (they call themselves *Noon*) (25,000) in the area surrounding Thiès and in Thiès; their dialect—the Noon—is very different from Serere-Sine. The Serer-Safen (they call themselves *Safi*) (35,400) in the southwest of and near Thiès. Their dialect, Safi-Safi, is used in trade.

Other smaller groups are the Mankanya (19,400); the Ndut (21,200) in the west central and northwest of Thiès. The Gusilay (16,700) who live in the Ziguinchor area; the Kerak (10,000) in southwestern Senegal; the Palor (they call themselves *Waro*) (7,100) in the west central, west southwest of Thiès; the Karon (6,500) in southwestern Senegal along the coast; the Kassonke (6,000); the Bandial (5,000) along the Casamance River, and in the Ziguinchor-Oussouye area; the Mlomp (or Gulompaay) (3,500) mainly north of the Casamance River; the Kwatay (3,500) south of the mouth of the Casamance River; the Lehar (2,800), north of Thiès in west central Senegal, call themselves *Lala*.

MASSIMO REPETTI

See also **Diola (Joola); Senghor, Leopold (Senegalese)**

Further Reading

Barbier-Wiesser, François-George, editor, *Comprendre la Casamance*, Paris: Karthala, 1994

Charbit, Yves, and Salif Ndiaye, editors, *La population du Sénégal*, Paris: DPS-CERPAA, 1994

Colvin, Lucie Gallistel, *The Uprooted of the Western Sahel. Migrant's Quest for Cash in the Senegambia*, New York: Praeger, 1981

Cruise O'Brien, Donald, *The Mourides of Senegal. The Political and Economic Organization of an Islamic Brotherhood*, Oxford: Claredon Press, 1971

Diop, Momar Coumba, *Sénégal. Trajectoire d'un Etat*, Paris: Karthala, and Dakar: Codesria, 1992

Diouf, Makhtiar, *Sénégal, les ethnies et la nation*, Paris: L'Harmattan, 1994

Gouvernement du Sénégal, *Recensement Général de la Population et Habitat*, Dakar: Bureau du Recensement, 1988

Magassouba, Moriba, *L'islam au Sénégal—Demain les Mollahs?* Paris, Karthala, 1985

Nolan, Riall W., *Bassari Migrations: The Quiet Revolution*, London: Westview Press, 1986

Tracy, David S., *Arts and Politics in Senegal (1960–1996)*, Trenton: Africa World Press Inc, 1998

Van Chi-Bonnardel, Régine, *Atlas National du Sénégal*, Paris: IGN, 1977

Senghor, Léopold (Senegalese)

The first president of the Republic of Senegal in West Africa from 1960 to 1980, a poet and statesman, Léopold Sédar Senghor emerged as one of Africa's outstanding intellectual and political figures of the twentieth century. A Roman Catholic and Serer (an ethnic group believed to have migrated to central Senegal from the North in the tenth to thirteenth centuries), he led a predominantly Muslim and Wolof nation.

Senghor was born October 9, 1906, in Joal, a coastal town in central Senegal. His father, a wealthy merchant of noble descent, was a Serer Catholic. His mother was a Peul (Fulani Muslim), one of a pastoral and nomadic people; Senghor was raised as a Catholic in predominantly Muslim Senegal. The country was dominated by the Wolof ethnic group, making Senghor essentially a "double minority." He was also a major political figure not to come from the Four Communes of Senegal (Goree, Saint-Louis, Dakar, and Rufisque), the communities in which French citizenship rights were partially extended to African inhabitants. He attended the Ngazobil Catholic Mission School and prepared for the priesthood at Libermann Seminary in Dakar but he transferred to the Public Secondary School in Dakar (later Lycee Van Vollenhoven). In 1928, he went to France to study at the Lycee Louis le Grand where one of his classmates was Georges Pompidou, later president of France.

Senghor was one of the originators of the concept of *négritude*, understood as the literary and artistic expression of the black African experience in the twentieth century. Cultivated namely in Paris in the 1930s among French and black intellectuals, historically the concept has been described as a reaction against French colonialism and a proponent of African culture, especially the notions of beauty, harmony, and nostalgia for the past. Artists and writers who were practitioners and supporters of *négritude,* including Frantz Fanon, Léon Damas, and Aimé Césaire, profoundly influenced African identity in the French-speaking black world. Inspired by the romantic vision of Africa in Harlem Renaissance authors, early European ethnographers, and the French poets Rimbaud, Mallarmé, and Baudelaire, Senghor began to produce poetry that embraced and in part launched the concept of *négritude*. He contrasted the African experience with the rationalism, mechanization, capitalism, materialism, bourgeois values, individualism, and decrepitude of the West. Senghor became one of the first Africans to express discontent with the French colonial policy of assimilation, although he retained an intense and lifelong admiration for French culture, especially in the fields of language, literature, and philosophy. He married a Frenchwoman and spent considerable time in France.

In 1935 he became the first African to pass the competitive *agrégation* examination for teachers after obtaining his French citizenship. The following year he was drafted into the French army. After military service, he taught in Tours and outside of Paris. At the start of World War II, he was again called to serve. After being captured and nearly killed by German troops, he spent two years as a prisoner of war and upon his release in 1942, he returned to teaching near Paris and worked with the French resistance.

With the end of the war, Senghor's literary career reached fruition with the publication of his first volume of poetry in 1945, *Chants d'Ombre*, a compilation of poems dealing with the themes of exile and nostalgia, in part inspired by the philosopher Henri Bergson. In 1945, he entered politics and was elected a deputy to the French Assembly with the support of the French Socialist Party (SFIO). After breaking with Lamine Guèye, who was allied with the socialist party, in 1948, Senghor formed the Bloc Démocratique Sénégalais (BDS), a political party that promoted a strain of African socialism based on traditional village cooperation and collectivism, religious faith, and a new nationalism. That same year, he and Alioune Diop, a Senegalese intellectual living in Paris, launched *Presence Africaine*, a Paris cultural journal devoted to the promotion of African culture and *négritude* whose advisory board members included Jean-Paul Sartre, André Gide, and Albert Camus. A year later he was appointed professor at the Ecole nationale d'Outre-Mer.

When given the choice in 1958 to vote for autonomy or continued association with France, Senghor argued strongly for autonomy and yet continued close ties with France. But in 1960 as the French ended colonial rule in West Africa, Senghor negotiated independence for the Mali Federation (Senegal and French Soudan, later Mali). The federation quickly fell apart and Senghor declared Senegal an independent republic. Complete independence was achieved upon dissolution of federation with Mali on August 20, 1960. He was elected president and he appointed Mamadou Dia as Prime Minister. Senghor quickly nationalized peanut marketing, initiated rural cooperatives, and instituted a national system of agricultural credit, extension services, and cooperative administration. He also carefully courted powerful Muslim leaders.

In 1962, a constitutional crisis erupted and Dia and his top allies were arrested and imprisoned for treason. The constitution was rewritten to provide for a single, strong executive, and Senghor ruled with an iron hand for the next eight years. Opposition parties were eliminated through banning or absorption, and freedom of the press and association were severely limited. Senghor

overcame political unrest in 1963 and student riots in 1968 by force. He was reelected president unopposed in 1963, 1968, and 1973. His secure political position allowed him free reign to promote African culture. The Festival of Negro Arts in Dakar in 1966 crowned his promotion of *négritude*. He helped establish various regional development associations, winning him respect as an elder statesman. However, Senegal's economic base did not expand under his presidency, the national debt increased, and infrastructure deteriorated. The Senegalese peasants, however, never wavered in their admiration for Senghor. His political philosophy was one that examined and embraced African socialism, which was not, to Senghor, a wholly Western concept. He believed that socialism shared with African cultures the notion of sharing and universality throughout history.

In 1970, Senghor felt confident enough to reintroduce the position of prime minister and appointed Abdou Diouf, an obscure young technocrat. Two opposition parties were legalized in the 1970s but Senghor still won the 1978 election in a landslide. He changed the name of his BDS political party from the Union Progressiste Sénégalaise (UPS) to the Parti Socialiste (PS or Socialist Party). The 1970s were a particularly difficult period for the Senegalese economy with a major drought in the mid-1970s and declining prices and demand for peanuts, the country's only real export. Many of the socialist policies promoted by Senghor were clearly not working. Even large amounts of international assistance, especially from France, did not improve economic conditions. Senghor appeared increasingly distant and aloof from politics as Diouf assumed the administration of daily government and international affairs.

Senghor continued to write poetry. In 1974 he won the Apollonaire Prize for Poetry and he published volumes of poetry in 1979 and 1980. On December 31, 1980, Senghor resigned in favor of Diouf who ruled the country for the next twenty years. Senghor thus became the first African leader installed at independence to resign voluntarily.

In 1983 he was the first African elected to the Académie Française . He continued to pursue his career as one of Africa's most respected statesmen, remaining on the international scene for many years being involved with the Socialist International and the Palestine Liberation Organization. In 1988 he published a philosophical memoir, *Ce que je crois* ("What I Believe") and continued to publish poetry in the 1990s.

Biography

Leopold Sedar Senghor. Born October 9, 1906, in Joal, Senegal, West Africa. Attended Catholic mission school of Ngazobil; continued studies at Libermann Seminary and Lycée Van Vollenhoven, finishing secondary-school education in 1928. Moved to Paris, graduated from Lycée Louis-le-grand, 1931. Granted French citizenship, 1932; served in regiment of colonial infantry, obtained *agrégation* degree in grammar, Paris, 1935; taught at Lycée Descartes in Tours, Lycée Marcelin Berthelot (Paris), 1935–1942; served in French army, captured by Germans, spent 18 months in a prisoner of war camp. Appointed professor, African languages, École Nationale de la France d'Outre-Mer, 1944; Member of French Assembly, 1945–1958. Founding co-editor of cultural journal, *Presence Africaine,* 1948. Established political party, *Bloc democratie senegalais,* 1948. Married in 1948 Ginette Eboué, had two children, divorced; President of the Mali Federation (dissolved), 1960. President of the Republic of Senegal, 1960–1980. Winner, Apollonaire Prize for Poetry, 1974. Elected to the Académie Française, 1983. Died in France December 20, 2001.

Selected Works

Chants d'Ombre, 1945
Hosties noires, 1948
Ethiopiques, 1956
Nation et voie africaine du socialisme, 1961
Nocturnes, 1961
Pierre Teilhard de Chardin et la politique africaine, 1962
Selected Poems, 1964
Negritude et Humanisme, 1964
Prose and Poetry, 1965
Les fondements de l'Africanite ou Negritude et Arabicite, 1967
Poemes, 1977
Elegies majeures, 1979
La poesie de l'action, 1980
Ce que je crois, 1988
Oeuvre politique, 1990

ANDREW F. CLARK

See also **Césaire, Aimé (Martiniquais); Diola (Joola); Fanon, Frantz Omar (Algerian); Senegal**

Further Reading

Ba, Sylvia, *The Concept of Negritude in the Poetry of Leopold Senghor,* Princeton: University Press, 1973
Collins, Grace, *Trumpet for His People: Leopold Sedar Senghor of Senegal,* New York: Sights Productions, 1995
Klubach, William, *Leopold Sedar Senghor: From Politics to Poetry,* New York: Peter Lang, 1997
Markovitz, Irving, *Leopold Sedar Senghor and the Politics of Negritude,* New York: Atheneum, 1969
Spleth, Janice, *Leopold Sedar Senghor,* New York: Macmillan, 1985
Vaillant, Janet, *Black, French and African: A Life of Leopold Sedar Senghor,* Cambridge: Harvard University Press, 1990

Serbia and Montenegro, *See* **Serbs; Montenegrins; Yugoslavia**

Serbs

Capsule Summary

Location: Serbia and Montenegro Republic, Bosnia and Herzegovina (mainly in the Serbian Republic–*Republika Srpska*); several zones in eastern Croatia and the Dalmatian hinterland (Knin city); northern areas of Macedonia, southwestern Romania (mainly around the city of Timişoara); United States; Canada; Western Europe; Australia
Total Population: 12 million
Language: Serbo-Croatian
Religion: Orthodox Christian

Origins

The whole region north of the Black Sea was inhabited in the early centuries CE by a mixture of tribes which included Slavs and Sarmatians (Iranian nomads). The Sarmatians gained political dominance over the other tribes, and it seems likely that some of the Slav tribes thus acquired an Iranian-speaking ruling elite. Ptolemy, writing in the second century, located the *Serboi* among the Sarmatian tribes north of the Caucasus. Most scholars believe that Serbs were Slavic tribes with Iranian ruling castes, or that they were originally Iranian tribes which had acquired Slavic subjects. By the early seventh century, the Serbs had established a kingdom (*White Serbia*) in central Europe, in the modern Czech Republic. From there, they migrated down toward the western Balkans. This Slav substratum has absorbed the remnants of a population whose ancestors may originally have been Illirians, Celts, Romans, individuals from all parts of the Roman Empire, Goths, Alans, Huns, and Avars.

The Serbs settled in an area corresponding to modern southwestern Serbia, and gradually extended their rule into the territories of Duklje (Montenegro) and Hum (Herzegovina). The Serb population was organized on a traditional tribal basis: extended families were united as clans, and clans as tribes (*plemena*). The territory of a tribe, called a *zupa*, was ruled by a territorial chief. They were pagans, worshipping a variety of gods. In the ninth century, Serb tribes organized themselves as an independent state in the frontier of the Byzantine empire. Between the years 867 and 874, Serbs converted en mass to Byzantine Christianity (today, Christian Orthodoxy).

In the Middle Ages

In 1077 the *knez* (prince) from Zeta (contemporary Montenegro) became the first Serb king, Michael. But in 1196, Serbs were subsumed once again into the Byzantine political realm. In 1217, Stefan Prvovjencani obtained his royal crown from the pope, and St. Sava received permission to establish an autocephalous Serbian Orthodox archbishopric (1219).

In 1389, the Serbs were defeated in battle against the Ottoman Empire. Kosovo was lost to the Ottomans, and the medieval Serbian kingdom came to an end. The loss was a massive blow, and is a key event in Serbian history. After the defeat of the Serbian kingdom, a large number of Serbs migrated to present-day Vojvodina, the centers of which were Novi Sad and Sremki Karlovci.

In the Seventeenth through Nineteenth Centuries: Nationhood and Nationalism

With the arrival of this large number of Serb refugees, the Serb community formed the majority of the population of so-called Ottoman Hungary by the seventeenth century. This state included the territory between the rivers Sava et Drava, and Danube and Tisza. In 1691, the Austrian emperor Leopold I guaranteed to the Serbs religious freedom and the right to self-administer their own Church. However, a large portion of the Serbian peasantry was oppressed by the Magyar (Hungarian) nobility. At the same time, a small class of traders and scholars grew, to form the nucleus of a Serbian petite bourgeoisie. This bourgeoisie founded a Serbian high school in Karlowitz (1790) and, afterwards, in Novi Sad (1810).

From the eighteenth century until 1881, the Habsburg Empire, operating out of Austria, created a military frontier (*boina krajina*). This became the territory where people who traced their ancestors to the Southern Serbs or the *Vlach* fully adopted the Serb identity (as articulated by the Orthodox faith). The process of Orthodoxy becoming a key element of the Serbian identity was completed after the Serbian uprising and the establishment of the autonomous Serbian principality. At the time of the foundation of this political system, Belgrade (*Beograd*, "The White City") was only a modest village near the Austrian fort of Kalemegdan, and the predominantly Muslim city of Uzice (population 20,000).

In 1690, after the Patriarchate of the Serbian church proved disloyal to the Ottomans during the Vienna War, the first migration of Serbs to southern Hungary took place. Though the main Serb populations were concentrated in the region south of the Sava and Danube rivers during the Ottoman rule, these massive migrations allowed the Serbs to transplant the Ottoman *millet* system (based in the autonomy of the ethnoreligious communities) to the Habsburg Monarchy. This was a great instrument for the spread of a Serb national identity in the western Balkans. During the eighteenth century, a Serbian high culture flourished within the Habsburg Empire. When another war between the Austrians and the Turks began in 1788, the Habsburg military authorities created a military corps in which several future Serb leaders were trained, including Karageorge. He was the *Vrhovi vod* ("Supreme Driver") of a revolutionary Serb army that conquered Belgrade from the Turks in November 1806, and created an embryonic Serbian state from 1804.

After several violent conflicts, Belgrade was reconquered by the Ottomans in 1813. Nevertheless, this brief Serbian state was the reference point for nineteenth century Serbian nationalism, which regarded this briefly independent Serbian state as the heir of the Serb medieval kingdom.

In April 1815, a second Serb uprising occurred, led by Milos Obrenovic. Eight months later, Obrenovic was appointed governor of a Serbian autonomous region within the Ottoman Empire. In 1830, Obrenovic received the title of hereditary prince of Serbia, and Serbia became an Ottoman autonomous principality, a quasi-independent state that undertook a modernization of its structures, including the education system.

In 1842, Milos Obrenovic was forced to flee to Austria, and Aleksandr Karageorgevic, son of the military hero Karageorge, was elected as the new prince of Serbia. The new government centralized the state administration and created a regular army. In 1859 Obrenovic returned to power.

In this same period, Vuk Stefanovic Karadzic, the Serbian poet and language reformer, broadened the definition of Serbdom to include all those who spoke the Stokavian dialect of the Serbo-Croatian language, regardless of religion. The Serb nation, therefore, was not exclusively Orthodox. Ilija Garasanin, Serbia's minister of the interior from 1862 to 1865, agreed with this linguistic nationalism, creating in 1844 the concept of the *Nacertanije* ("Great Project"), which aimed to embrace in the same political project all the peoples speaking Serbo-Croatian. The first political act of the *Nacertanije* was the Serbo-Turk wars (in 1876 and 1877), which paved the way for eventual Serbian independence in 1878 (confirmed by the Berlin Treaty)—an independence, moreover, that included the annexation of the formerly Ottoman regions of Nis, Vranje, Pirot and Toplica by the Serbian state. The administration of Bosnia-Herzegovina, however, was awarded to Vienna, a move which took some of the momentum away from the *Nacertanije,* and encouraged the Serbian state to more fully focus its attentions on Macedonia and Kosovo.

In 1903 Peter I, another king of the Karageorgevic dynasty, came to the throne. He ruled Serbia until 1921. At the beginning of the twentieth century several secret associations were formed, including the National Defense and *Ujedinjenje ili Smert* ("Union or Death"). These associations were not endemic to the Serbian kingdom; they were prevalent throughout the western Balkan region. A primary goal at the time was to unite all Serbian peoples into a larger Serbian state that would include all the countries that some of the former Serbian nationalists considered as rightfully belonging to one Serbian nation. This would include Croats, Bosnians, Montenegrins, and Macedonians.

After the end of World War I and the defeat of the Ottoman Empire, the *Kingdom of Serbs, Croats and Slovenians* was created on December 1 of 1918, known as *Yugoslavia* ("The State of the Southern Slavs") since 1929.

Before WWI, Serbia was a parliamentary democracy. But the new administration of the newly formed nation was increasingly authoritarian. Ethnic pressures remained prevalent. Tension escalated until, in 1928, the Montenegrin Serb radical nationalist Punisa Racic shot and killed three Croat deputies in Parliament. Months later, King Alexander closed down Parliament, canceled the Constitution, and proclaimed his personal dictatorship.

After the Yugoslavian King Alexander was killed in Marseille (1934), Dimitrije Ljotic, a former minister to the king, founded the *Zbor* ("Assembly") movement, an ultra-nationalist and violent Serb Fascist association that had more than 30,000 members in 1938. King Paul, cousin of Alexander, signed a pact with Nazi Germany in March 1941. This pact was considered an act of treason by the Serbs. Peter II, son of Alexander, was appointed the new king, and the Serb masses took to the streets in protest. Nevertheless, the Nazi army invaded Yugoslavia, setting up a fascist Croatian puppet government responsible for the murder of hundreds of thousands Serbs, Jews, and Roma (Gypsies).

Several resistance groups and armies sprung up in response to Nazi rule. In northern Bosnia, after the capitulation of the Yugoslav government (April 17, 1941), a group of Serb officials joined by Colonel Draza Mihailovic formed a militia in the mountains of Ravna Gora, in the tradition of the *Chetniks* of the nineteenth century, a name that comes from the word *cheta* ("troop"). These Chetniks clashed with the army of the communist resistance leader, Josip Broz' (better known, later, as Tito), and were deeply monarchist, nationalistic, anti-Croats, and devout followers of Orthodox Christianity.

The collaboration of Serb civilians with the Chetniks (or Tito's forces) was the reason given by the Nazis for the massacre they carried out in the city of Kragujevac, in which 7,000 people, including hundreds of children with their teachers, were killed.

Ethnic hatred was exacerbated by the Nazis. Serbs were killed by fascist *Ustashi* (Croatian militias) and, in turn, the *Chetniks* massacred Muslims and Croats. Approximately 350, 000 Serbs were killed between 1941 and 1944.

After World War II, a communist government was set up, led by Josip Broz (Tito). Yugoslavia became a federal state, and the Serbs scattered through seven of these eight republics and autonomous provinces (Bosnia-Herzegovina, Croatia, Montenegro, Serbia proper, Vojvodina, Kosovo, and Macedonia). The multinational character of this regime was illustrated by the ethnic stock of its principal rulers: Tito (Croat), Edvard Kardelj (Eslovenian), Aleksandar Rankovic (Serb) and Milovan Djilas (Montenegrin). Each republic had its own Communist Party, and the Federal Communist Party (known later as the League of Yugoslavian Communist) was the federation of each different national-based party.

President Tito died in May 1980 with no clear successor. In the years from 1986 to 1989 there developed a social movement known as the *Serb Cultural Revolution* which was started in 1986 through the publication of a *Memorandum* edited by the Serb Academy of Sciences. This report aimed to show the causes of the poor and stagnant economic and cultural situation in Yugoslavia, while criticizing the breakdown of the state into so many republics and provinces by the Constitution of 1974, as well as the plight of the Serbs in Kosovo and Croatia. Future leaders—notably, Slobodan Milosevic—would be inspired by this work.

Society

The most important institution of traditional Serbian society was the *zadruga*, an extended family composed of ten to twenty small families, related by blood, who lived and worked together, jointly owned property, and recognized the authority of a single patriarch. The extended family most often included four generations of men, their wives, and their children. Once a girl married, she would leave the *zadruga* of her parents for that of her husband. No member of the *zadruga* had any personal property other than clothes or the women's dowries.

Traditional Serbian society was strongly patriarchal. The *zadruga* leader, called the "old man" or the "lord of the house," had absolute power over his family and was treated with the utmost respect. He was considered the wisest because he had lived the longest. His duties included managing the purchase and sale of all household property; division of labor among *zadruga* members; and settling personal disputes. Older men within the household could offer advice, but the "old man" had the final word. Obligatory signs of familial respect included rising whenever he appeared and eating only after he had begun and before he had finished his meal. The "old man's" wife (or the senior woman if he were widowed) had similar authority over traditional women's activities such as tending the garden, observing holiday rituals, and sewing. The senior woman commanded similar respect from *zadruga* members, but she was never allowed to interfere in functions designated for men.

When a *zadruga* broke up (normally because it became too large for easy management), property was divided equally among its members. Before the twentieth century, many villages were formed as outgrowths of an enlarged *zadruga*. The largest of the extended family organizations in Serbia and other territories with Serbian population, began breaking up in the 1840s. At that time, the Ottoman Empire instituted new inheritance laws that did not take *zadruga* property patterns into account. A second stage of fragmentation occurred as the expectation of automatic integration into the extended family gradually weakened in younger generations: sons began leaving the *zadruga* at the death of the "old man," and newly arrived wives failed to adjust to the traditional system. As a result of such pressures, smaller households began to proliferate in the nineteenth century.

The *zadruga* breakup accelerated after Yugoslavia gained its independence and began instituting Western-style laws that gave women equal inheritance rights, although in many parts of Serbia women did not begin demanding their legal inheritance until well into the twentieth century. The disintegration of large family holdings gradually led to the impoverishment of the peasants as land ownership became more fragmented and scattered with each generation. Furthermore, even after extended families broke up, many peasants continued to work cooperatively.

The familial system sometimes extended to include godparents and adopted brothers and sisters, unrelated individuals enjoying the same status as close relatives. Godparenthood included another set of traditional relationships that knit village society together. Godparents kept close ties with their godchildren throughout their lives, and the godparent/godchild relationship could be transferred from generation to generation. Godparents were treated with the utmost respect and had an important role in all important events in a godchild's life, beginning with baptism. The familial relationship was so strong that a taboo developed against the marriage of children related to the same family through godparenthood. Historically, *zadruga* membership could include 100 or more persons. Various adult members specialize in economic activity in a variety of ecological settings: hunting and trapping in high mountains, herding in mountain valleys, farming and trading in the lowlands. With that organization, members hedge against economic failure by diversifying, but enjoy the production efficiencies of labor specialization.

The *zadruga* was a useful institution under traditional conditions: it provided a pool of labor to cover all necessities (illness, war-time service, etc.). In mountainous regions, the *zadruga,* extended family household, continues to carry influence. Also, family ties descending from male ancestors receive great attention. A common ancestor, last name, and patron saint identify many. Some rural men are able to accurately recite several hundred living and deceased relatives extending over some eight to ten generations.

In addition, ties by blood brotherhood (*pobratimstvo*) and godfatherhood (*kumstvo*) are important in some regions. The *kumstvo* (from *kum,* "godfather") relationship created an intricate web of social relations that were far away from the ethnic divisions, and implied, for example, social (not biological) parenthood between families from Serb ancestry with other families from Rumanian or Muslim origins. For example, in eastern Serbia, in the 1950s, Serbs received *kumstvo* from Rumanians and Gypsies. *Kumstvo* was a means of avoiding interethnic conflicts. In the 1960s the *kumstvo* institution was still flourishing in some mountain regions of southern Serbia. *Kumstvo* was by its very nature an intergroup exchange and contributed to the structure of the larger society. In Serbia, reciprocal *kumstvo* were regarded as permissible, as are multiple ties of *kumstvo* (even encompassing more than 20 different family groups). To give *kumstvo* was equivalent to being a sponsor, and to receive *kumstvo* meant to agree to be sponsor and carry out the activities of the relationship. The most striking exchange of *kumstvo* for a nonmaterial good is that for pardon for manslaughter or homicide. This social mechanism was essential for atonement for homicide and settlement of blood feuds.

Under the highly unsettled conditions of the great migration, during which the Serbs retreated from the Turks or flowed back into liberated areas, and within the context of the constant feuding which were characteristic of some mountains regions until recently, kinship ties were of crucial importance. And ties of *kumstvo* served to extend the network of trust, particularly when a small and weak group moved into a new region. A newly arrived *zadruga* would thus commonly offer a child for baptism to a resident *zadruga*, and in fact had to select some group from the area as *kum* if the migration had been long. *Kumstvo* was often offered to arrange settlement.

Today: The Diaspora

The Serb diaspora is highly concentrated in Australia, where several Orthodox parishes and different associations such as the *Tasmanian-Serbian Association* are located, most in Queensland, Sidney, and Melbourne. New Zealand is also home to some Serb communities. In 1973, the Serbian Orthodox Diocese of Australia and New Zealand was formed with a residing bishop in St. Sava's Monastery in Elaine, Victoria.

The 996 Canadian census recorded 40,200 Serbs in Canada (mainly in Vancouver and Ottawa). Canada has a Serbian Orthodox Diocese. In the United States there is the Western American Diocese of the Serbian Orthodox Church. One of the more important Serb associations in the United States is the Serbian Unity Congress. In the United States the Serb diaspora is concentrated in Arizona, Florida, Ohio, New England, Georgia and, especially, California, Illinois and Indiana. In the United Kingdom the diaspora is represented as well, and the Serbian Orthodox Church is present in different cities, including London, Birmingham, and Oxford. There is also a significant Serbian diaspora in Sweden and in Switzerland. There is a population of approximately 6,000 to 7,000 Serbs in Russia today.

Romania is home to more than 50,000 Serbs. They have parliamentary representation by means of the party, the Union of Serbs in Romania. The Serbian National Church is also present. The Serbs of Hungary were originally largely immigrants escaping the Turkish threat in the sixteenth and seventeenth centuries, settling mostly in southern Hungary. Those Serbs had religious autonomy, although they were suspicious of the Hungarian influence. Their leaders, including Metropolitan Rajacic, had supported the Hungarian independence movement. There are some 5,000 Serbs in Hungary living primarily in the southern region of Backa or the Banat. Until the beginning of the twentieth century, some Serb settlements reached even to Budapest, and Szent Endre (St. Andrew) was soon to become a cultural center of the Serbs in Hungary. Today, there are some Serbs that arrived recently as refugees to Hungary. They are scattered in camps on the outskirts of Budapest and in areas on the border with Serbia. Their spokesman, Vidan Ivanovic, says that together with their families, there are about 1,300 Serbs in these camps. Ivanovic said he fled after he was called up to serve in the army. In Austria, especially in the metropolitan area of Viena, there are also some Serb communities, as there are in Greece, the Netherlands, and France.

National Minorities

While most of Croatia's Serbs live in urban centers, just over one quarter are scattered in villages and towns, mostly in lightly populated parts of the central mountain belt, in Lika and Banija, and in northern Dalmatia. These zones constitute the frontier belt were the Serbs settled between the sixteenth and the eighteenth centuries.

At least 400,000 Serbs fled Croatia at the end of the war in Yugoslavia in 1995. Some sources suggest that even higher numbers of Serbs fled Croatia, 1.2 million being one significant example. The homes of approximately 20,000 Serbians were set on fire and destroyed during the war in the years between 1991 and 1995, most especially during the great Croatian offensive of May through August in 1995.

In July 1997, in Zagreb, on the premises of the Serb cultural society called *Prosvjeta* (SKD), the Serb National Council (SNV) was founded. The leader of the main Serbian party in Croatia and president of the SNV, Milorad Pupovac, has insisted that Serbs living in Croatia should be given proportional representation in the parliament to ensure they do not lose political influence. In May 2003 there was increasing discussion regarding the legal status of the properties lost by the Serbs that fled the region during the war (today, the Croatian region of Eslavonia). The origin of these problems can be traced to 1996, when the Croatian Parliament denied the payment of restitutions to the expulsed Serbs. But in recent declarations, the Croat Justice Minister, Ingrid Anticevic-Marinovic, has promised to overturn the decision of 1996. In October 2002, Milorad Pupovac, the President of the National Serbian Council in Croatia, noted that, in the wake of the war and Slobodan Milosevic's reign of political terror and turmoil, the Serb minority in Croatia requires guaranteed legal protection of their cultural and national preferences and status.

In the northern Serbian province of Vojvodina, several political parties have arose representing positions across the political spectrum. For example, one party is dedicated to the rights of the Hungarian minority. There is also the Serbian Radical Party (SRS), a firmly nationalistic party. This polarization explains the tense atmosphere that exists in the postwar, postcommunist former Yugoslavia.

In the wake of the civil war in the former Yugoslavia, there is an autonomous Serbian Republic (*Republika Srpska*) centered in the city of Banja Luka. This Serbian Bosnian entity was created in Banja Luka in March 1992, and it is officially recognized as the political system of the Bosnian Serbs after the Dayton Peace Agreement (1995). In 2000, a U.S. Committee for Refugees mission in Bosnia remarked that reconciliation showed some signs of taking hold between Serbs and other ethnic groups (Croats and Muslims).

The *Republika Srpska* has no intermediate tier of government between its central institutions and the municipalities; here the entity level performs tasks that belong to the cantons in the Federation. The Constitution grants municipalities self-rule in all matters delegated to them by the Serbian political entity. The legislative framework for local democracy was originally established by the 1994 law on territorial organization and local self-government, which was amended in 1996 and 1997. This provided for the territory's division into 64 municipalities and two cities governed by special laws (Serb Sarajevo, comprising six municipalities, and Banja Luka) A new law on local self-government was passed in November 1999 to address a number of problems, such as disputes as to jurisdiction between local and central government departments.

With concerns over physical security receding, significantly larger numbers of displaced persons returned to their homes during the year 2000 to areas where they constitute a minority. In many cases, the successful implementation of Bosnia's property laws enabled them to reclaim their homes. Notwithstanding these positive developments, questions lingered regarding the sustainability of so-called minority returns and reconciliation between the former warring parties. The overwhelming majority of the returnees continued to be elderly people returning to rural areas where they posed little challenge to the political control of the majority group. With chronically high unemployment, economic prospects for many returnees, particularly in *Republika Serpska*, the Bosnian Serb entity, remained bleak.

In modern-day Macedonia (official name: Former Yugoslav Republic of Macedonia) the Serb minority (around 40,000 persons) inhabits the northern fringe, near the border with Serbia. Their most important political representation is provided by the Democratic Serbian Party (DPS).

During the war in Kosovo, around 200,000 Serbs fled the region. There, Serbs are politically represented by the Serb National Council of Kosovo and Metohija. On its fourteenth meeting, held on December 21, 2002, in Gracanica Monastery, the Serb National Council discussed the security situation and its strategy for survival and the return of displaced Serbs to Kosovo and Metohija.

In the Serbian republic of Serbia and Montenegro, political violence was still present until recently, as illustrated by the murder of the Prime Minister, Zoran Djindjic, on March 12, 2003. In Bosnia-Herzegovina, some reconciliation processes between Serbs and the other ethnic communities of the country continue. As an example, the Serbian president of Bosnia was present at the July 11, 2003, commemoration of the Srebenica massacre against Muslims.

JOAN MANUEL CABEZAS LÓPEZ

See also **Bosnia and Herzegovina; Croatia; Croats; Macedonia; Macedonians; Montenegrins; Slovenia; Yugoslavia**

Further Reading

Banac, Ivo, *The National Question in Yugoslavia. Origins, History, Politics*, Ithaca: Cornell University Press, 1984

Gakobich, Robert, and Milan M. Radovich, compilers, *Serbs in the United States and Canada: A Comprehensive Bibliography*, 2nd edition, University of Minnesota, 1992

Garde, Paul, *Vie et mort de la Yougoslavie*, Paris: Fayard, 1991

Gimbutas, Marija, *The Slavs*, New York: Praeger, 1970

Jelavich, Charles, *South Slav Nationalisms. Textbooks and Yugoslav Union before 1914*, Columbus: Ohio University Press, 1990

Judah, Timothy, *The Serbs: History, Myth, and the Destruction of Yugoslavia*, New Haven, Connecticut: Yale University Press, 2000

Malcolm, Noel, *Bosnia. A Short History*, London: MacMillan, 1994

Sexuality

Sexuality (Latin *sexus*: the quality of being either female or male) denotes the social, (including the legal) implications of sexual behavior, that is, the attitudes, practices, and concerns related to sex. An interdisciplinary science that focuses on sex and sexuality is called sexology. There seems to be a great variety of sexual practices and customs across cultures and epochs. Levels of sexual tolerance and ways of defining and managing socially disfavored sexual behavior differ cross-culturally to a great extent. There are a number of cultures characterized by a much higher level of sexual permissiveness than Western culture. Aspects of sexuality such as homosexuality, premarital sex, prostitution, rape, public nudity, contraception, infanticide, abortion, polygamy, pornography, and child sexual abuse are among those that are most present in sexuality debates today. The following brief overview of the history of sexuality and the Western development of sexology reflects the variety of methods employed to manage sexuality in different eras,
also providing an insight in attitudes towards sexual/gender groups considered inferior, primarily homosexuals and women.

Antiquity and the Middle Ages

Classical Greek physicians and philosophers, such as Hippocrates, Aristotle, Plato, and Galen, were already studying and discussing human sexual behavior, ethics, education, and politics, as well as reproduction and therapy for sexual dysfunctions. Greek ideas remained influential until the nineteenth century, when the development of science generated the appearance of different ideas about sex and sexual behavior. In antiquity sexuality was not only a subject of physiological research, but figured prominently in art as well. *Ars Amatoria* (circa 1 BCE), the work of the famous Roman poet Ovid, for example, instructed on the art of seduction and lovemaking, as did the *Kama Sutra*, written by the Indian scholar Mallanga Vatsayana.

The sexological knowledge of antiquity was preserved and further developed by Arabic and Jewish scholars, including Ibn Sina (Avicenna), Ar-Razi (Rhases), Ibn Ruschd (Avveroes), and Maimonides. For example, Aristotle's idea of the inferiority of female generative power in relation to the male was dominant in the Western ideology of sexuality for centuries and was brought back in the eleventh century to medieval Europe by the Arabic scholar Ibn Sina (Avicenna). It was then adopted by St. Albertus Magnus and further elaborated by his pupil St. Thomas Aquinas in the thirteenth century. The ascetic approach, originating from Plato who in his later works doubted the benefit of sexual pleasure and attempted to distinguish between procreative and sterile sex, combined with a concern about deviant sexuality scattered through the *Old Testament*, served as the basis of the Christian approach to sexuality that began with *Paul's Epistle to the Romans*, continuing through the works of St. Augustine and culminating in the works of Aquinas. The Judeo-Christian norm of heterosexual marriage as a prerequisite for sexual intercourse with the only aim of procreation and the stigmatization of other forms of sexuality as sinful would resonate through public discourses until the twentieth century.

The Middle Ages in other parts of the world witnessed the appearance of works such as the Chinese handbook on sex *Su-Nui-Jing* or *The Perfumed Garden*, a love manual written by the Tunisian Sheikh Nefzaoui, who dedicated one of the chapters to homosexual love. The chapter was later left out of the French translation and is today lost.

The Italian Renaissance testified to the birth of new knowledge of human anatomy and therefore new insights into the nature and features of human sexuality. Leonardo da Vinci was among the first to describe some internal sex organs. His pioneering work was later carried on by other European anatomists who made new discoveries. Regnier de Graaf discovered female ejaculation and the Graafian follicles, Gabrielle Faloppio described the oviducts today called Fallopian tubes, Bartholin's glands were named after Caspar Berthelsen (Bartholinus), while William Cowper found Cowper's glands.

The Enlightenment

The eighteenth century saw an abundance of research on sexuality in general as well as a couple of prominent works that referred to some of its specific aspects. In 1760 *Onanism*, a very influential book about the purported dangers of masturbation, was written by a physician named Samuel Tissot. His ideas would resonate through the literature on adolescent sexual education until the beginning of the twentieth century. This was the birth of the fear of masturbatory insanity. A great crusade against masturbation, based on the correlation between masturbation and deviance, was fought by a number of educators in that and the following century.

However, this period testified also to the appearance of the Marquis de Sade's *The 120 Days of Sodom* (1787), a masturbation fantasy secretly written during his imprisonment in the Bastille on charges of immorality. Toward the end of the century, two important books were published: Mary Wollstonecraft's *Vindication of the Rights of Woman* (1792), in which she exposed the ideological character of the widespread patriarchal belief in the "natural" role of women that served as the basis for their legal and social discrimination, and Thomas Malthus's *Essay on the Principle of Population* (1798), which would open the way for the discussions of the dangers of overpopulation and would later result in a number of neomalthusian campaigns for contraception.

Nineteenth Century

The 19th century was marked by several important discoveries related to human sexuality as well as the first organized campaigns for the legal and social equality of women. It is the age in which the egg cell was discovered (1827), as well as the vulcanization of rubber that made possible the mass production of condoms (1844). In contrast to Wilhelm von Humboldt's neutral classification of human sexual behavior according to its four possible objects (self, other sex, same sex, and animal [1826–1827]), Heinrich Kaan's *Psychopathia sexualis* (1843) connected sexual behavior to diseases of the mind, paving thus a route for the use of medieval theological terms such as "perversion" or "deviation" when discussing nonprocreative sex, and thus paving the way for the so-called medicalization of sin. The French physician B.A. Morel further elaborated the concept of degeneration, which would remain one of the key concepts in medical and sociopolitical debates about sexuality until the beginning of the twentieth century.

The first book to represent male homosexuality as a natural expression of a "female soul in a male body" was written by the German lawyer Karl-Heinrich Ulrichs, who named the phenomenon *uranism*, and the individuals characterized by it *uranians* (1863). The Hungarian writer Károly Mária Kertbeny (Benkert), who coined the term *homosexuality* (1869), later carried on Ulrichs's plea against the Prussian law against "unnatural vice." In the same year, John Stuart Mill published his book *The Subjection of Women* (1869), in which he pleaded for the legal and social equality of the sexes. In 1870 the first medical history of same-sex erotic attraction was published in the journal *Archive für Psychiatrie und Nervenkrankheiten.* In a short time a number of similar medical histories appeared, representing the homosexual desire as a psychiatric illness. The first trace of moral relativism appeared a couple of years later, in the work of the Italian physician and anthropologist Paolo Matengazza, whose *Trilogia dell' amore* abounded in cross-cultural observations (1872–1885).

Sexuality Research from 1896 to 1936

The basis of sexology that had appeared through the work of Richard von Kraft-Ebing (*Psychopathia sexualis*, 1886) was further elaborated by the next generation of researchers such as Havelock Ellis, Sigmund Freud, and Magnus Hirschfeld. A final demand for establishing a new science that would focus on sexuality would come in 1907 from the Berlin physician Iwan Bloch, who in his study *The Sexual Life of Our Time,* pointed out the necessity of establishing sexology—a discipline that would include both the natural and cultural sciences.

Sexology developed along two lines, one mostly interested in the nature and consequences of sexual behavior and attitudes explored through psychiatric case studies or laboratory experiments (Kraft-Ebing, Freud), and the other more empirical and activist, focused both on collecting data about various everyday sexual practices and on the struggle for law reforms regarding sexuality (Ellis, Hirschfeld). The latter held the sexuality ideology of Judeo-Christian civilization to be an important obstacle to the understanding of sexuality and to the reform of laws and social practices regulating it.

So in 1897 Magnus Hirschfeld, the Berlin physician, founded the world's first gay rights organization, the Scientific Humanitarian Committee, the goal of which was to fight for the abolishment of the German antihomosexual law that punished sexual contact between men. Hirschfeld soon began his statistical surveys on homosexuality, which were ended by legal action shortly thereafter. In 1914 Magnus Hirschfeld's study *Homosexuality in Men and Women* appeared. Five years later he opened the first Institute for Sexology in Berlin and in 1928 founded the *World League for Sexual Reform.* The League called for the legal and social equality of the sexes, reform of sex legislation, as well as the right to contraception and sex education. On May 6, 1933, the Nazis closed Hirschfeld's Institute for Sexology in Berlin and its library was publicly burned four days later.

Anthropological works that appeared during this period, such as Bronislaw Malinowski's study *The Sexual Life of Savages in North-Western Melanesia* (1929) and later the work of Margaret Mead and others provided important insights into different sexual practices characteristic of non-Western societies. Margaret Mead compared sex roles among three New Guinea groups, showing that sex roles were not inborn but a product of learning, opening thus a new and important perspective in Western research of sexuality.

In the 1940s the French judge in Bangkok, René Guyon, attacked the sexual policies of the League of Nations as repressive, only to repeat his criticism in 1951, when he attacked the United Nations for betraying the idea of sexual rights in their Universal Declaration of Human Rights.

Modern Developments

Modern sex research appeared with the work of Alfred C. Kinsey, a zoologist at Indiana University in Bloomington, Indiana, in the United States, who started his mainly sociological studies of human sexual behavior around 1938 and founded the Institute for Sex Research shortly after the end of World War II. Kinsey created the scale from one to six for defining a person's homosexual to heterosexual behavior. The period that followed witnessed great changes in approaches to human sexuality: the discovery of the first hormonal contraceptive (1951) that would become widely available at the beginning of the 1960s, as well as the appearance of homosexual liberation organizations such as the first American gay liberation organization *The Mattachine Society* (1951) and the first lesbian emancipation organization in the United States called *The Daughters of Bilitis* (1957).

In 1949 Simone de Beauvoir published her socio-cultural and historical study *The Second Sex*, arguing for the end of the discrimination of women. The book became a monumental work of literature for feminist movement worldwide. The American medical psychologist John Money introduced the important distinction between sex and gender that would give a huge further impetus for the research of human sexuality (1955).

The sexual revolution, which was soon to follow, brought about a gradual improvement of political, social, and legal attitudes to homosexuals. However, only 1973 did the American Psychiatric Association remove the diagnosis *homosexuality* from its *Diagnostic and Statistical Manual*. Since the 1960s there has been an enormous expansion of research into sex and gender, with an ever-growing number of articles and books. This research has been greatly influenced by feminism as well as by the appearance of HIV/AIDS in the 1980s. The last two decades of the twentieth century produced a great disciplinary variety in the study of gender and sexuality: cultural studies, postmodern psychoanalytic theory, feminist scholarship, and developmental research have contributed to enlarging knowledge on different aspects and forms of sexuality. Thus has Queer Studies (homosexuality, bisexuality, and transsexuality/transgenderism), previously present only in academic discussions of "deviance" and "sexual dysfunction," become an established subject field in academia. In 1978 the International Lesbian and Gay Association (ILGA) was established. Today it includes more than 350 member organizations all over the world.

ALEKSANDRA DJAJIC HORVÁTH

See also **Gender and Minority Status; Homosexuality and Minority Status**

Further Reading

Beemyn, Brett, and Mickey Eliason, editors, *Queer Studies: A Lesbian, Gay, Bisexual and Transgender Anthology*, New York: New York University Press, 1996

Brettell, Caroline B., and Caroline Sargent, editors, *Gender in Cross-Cultural Perspective*, Englewood Cliffs, New Jersey: Prentice-Hall, 1993; 2nd edition, 1996; 3rd edition, 2001

Bullough, Vern L., and Bonnie Bullough, editors, *Human Sexuality: An Encyclopedia*, New York and London: Garland Publishing, 1994

Dynes, Wayne F., editor, *Encyclopedia of Homosexuality*, New York: Garland Publishing, 1990

Francoeur, Robert T., and Raymond J. Noonan, editors, *The Continuum Complete International Encyclopedia of Sexuality*, New York: Continuum, 2004

Herd, Gilbert, editor, *Third Sex, Third Gender: Beyond Sexual Dimorphism in Culture and History*, New York: Zone Books, 1993

Seychelles

Capsule Summary

Country Name: Republic of Seychelles
Location: Eastern Africa, group of islands in the Indian Ocean, northeast of Madagascar
Total Population: 80,469 (2003)
Languages: Seselwa (Creole), English, French (all official)
Religions: Roman Catholic (90%), Protestant (Anglican) (8%), Muslim (2%), Hindu, etc.

The Republic of Seychelles is a group of islands located in the Indian Ocean, northeast of Madagascar and approximately 1,600 km (994 mi) east of mainland Africa. With a land area of 455 sq km (176 sq mi), it has a tropical marine climate with 40 granitic and about 50 coralline islands. The capital is Victoria, situated on Mahé, the largest of the islands.

Before European contact, the area was likely the trading grounds of visiting Arabs, over 1000 years ago.

The islands' location would have made them ideal for early seafaring peoples including the Phoenicians and Indonesians. The first settlers were fifteen Europeans from *Isle de France* (Mauritius) and *Isle de Bourbon* (Isle de la Reunion), seven slaves, five South Indians, and one black woman. However, there is no doubt that pre-European seafarers (Arabs, Persians, Indians, and Chinese) visited the Islands.

As the islands were not home to any one indigenous population, present-day Seychellois are composed of immigrants, mostly of French, African, Indian, and Chinese descent. The principal ethnic majority (89 percent of the population) are the Creoles, who are of mixed Asian or African and European descent. Other ethnic minorities include Indians, Chinese, and a small number of French descendants. A French Creole language (Seselwa), the language of 94 percent of the nation, was adopted as the first official language in 1981. English is the second language and French the third, all of them officially recognized. Most Seychellois are Christians, primarily Roman Catholics.

In 1756, Seychelles became a French colony under the name of *Séchelles*, named for Jean de Moreau of Séchelles, Minister of Finance under the kingdom of Louis XV. During the nineteenth century, the English gave the area the name of *Seychelles*. Seychelles remained an English colony from 1903 until 1976, when the archipelago gained independence, becoming the Republic of Seychelles.

During the Napoleonic War period (1769–1820) the Seychelles were regarded as a strategic acquisition as the British fought to contain French expansion. After Napoleon Bonaparte's defeat at the Battle of Waterloo, the French were forced to give up the islands, although because Britain did not maintain a permanently stationed force, control changed seven times in 13 years. The 1814 Treaty of Paris confirmed British rule. After the abolition of slavery in 1835, the British Navy stopped the slave ships in the area and released their cargo on the archipelago, thus increasing the African population of the island, so much so that in 1860 they represented 50 percent of the entire population, estimated at that time to be approximately 5000 (Valdam 1983).

A small number of South Indian (Parsis and Gujaratis) merchants also arrived from Mauritius (in about 1850) and from India (in 1895). In 1898 the British brought Indian laborers (mainly from Madras) to the Seychelles to build roads. The last people to arrive were Chinese merchants. At first they came from Mauritius, but later arrived from Canton (Mainland China) and Hong Kong.

The Seychelles became a British crown colony in 1903. By 1963, political parties had developed in the colony. The following year, two new parties, the Seychelles Democratic Party (SDP) led by James Mancham, and the Seychelles People's Unity Party (SPUP) led by France-Albert René, replaced existing parties. Independence from the UK was attained on June 29, 1976, under a coalition government lead by Mancham. Although the coalition appeared to operate smoothly, political divisions between the two parties continued, and one year later Mancham's government was overthrown. Prime Minister René led a successful coup and imposed a one-party socialist state. After 16 years of single-party rule and with pressure from within and the donor countries, he allowed opposition

parties in 1991. Socialist rule was brought to a close with a new constitution and free, democratic elections in 1993, which he won with his party, the Seychelles People's Progressive Front (SPPF). Presently other parties include the Democratic Party (DP), the Mouvement Seychellois pour la Democratie, and the Seychelles National Party (SNP, formerly the United Opposition or UO). René (who is both the chief of state and head of government) has remained president since 1977; the next elections will be held in 2006.

From the outset, the democratic government made the rehabilitation of the Creole language culture one of its objectives. The first action in that direction was the decision to make the Seselwa the first official language in 1981 and its introduction in the formal educational system as the medium of instruction with a national literacy drive. Seselwa developed from dialects of southwest France spoken by the original settlers; it is primarily a French vocabulary with a few Malagasy, Bantu, English, and Hindi words.

This policy stimulated the written Creole literary production which was extremely limited; an orthography of the language was completed only in 1981. English remains the language of government and commerce, and French, while discouraged as a remnant of colonialism, retains prestige among older residents of the Seychelles and is the language of the Roman Catholic Church. The government also encouraged the development and the modernization of Creole music, dance, and theatre since the 1980s.

According to a 2001 Human Rights Report issued by the U.S. Department of State, the René government, whose party dominates the legislature, continued to wield power virtually unchecked. Although human rights were generally respected, security forces occasionally arbitrarily arrested and detained citizens. Moreover the government failed to investigate or punish those involved in the violations of citizens' human rights during a law enforcement crackdown in 1998. Discrimination against foreign workers also remained problematic.

The Seychelles' economy has increased substantially since independence, with leading growth in the tourist sector, which employs about 30 percent of the labor force and provides more than 70 percent of hard currency earnings. However, the government has been concerned to reduce the dependence on tourism by promoting the development of farming, fishing, and small-scale manufacturing. For example, tourism suffered after 1991–1992 due largely to the Gulf War, and again following the September 11, 2001, terrorist attacks on the United States. The gross domestic product (GDP) per capita income in 2002 was $7,800.

ABDOULAYE BARRY

See also **Gujaratis; Mauritius; Mauritania; Parsis**

Further Reading

Banks, L., *The Seychelles*, Mauritius: E. Baker, 1840
Benedict, B., *People of the Seychelles*. London: HMSO, 1966
Fanda, Marcus, *The Seychelles: Unquiet Island*, Boulder, Colorado: Westview Press, 1982
"Human Rights Reports for 2000: Seychelles," *US Department of State*, February 2001. http://www.humanrights-usa.net/reports/seychelles.html
Koechlin, Bernard, *Les Seychelles et l'Ocean Indien*, Paris: Harmattan, 1984
Lee, Christopher, *Seychelles: Political Castaways*, London: Elm Tree Books, 1976
Valdam, Albert, *Le Creole: Structure, statut et origine*, Port-au-Prince: Gaston Plancoon, 1983
Webb, A.W.T., *Story of Seychelles*, Seychelles, 1964

Shan

Capsule Summary

Location: Burma (Myanmar) in the Shan State; Thailand in Maehongson Province, China in Yunnan
Total Population: approximately 5 million; 4 million in Burma and 1 million in Thailand and China
Languages: Shan (Tai Long) and other assorted Tai languages
Religion: Theravada Buddhist

Shan are an ethnic group living in Northern Burma, northwestern Thailand, and in Yunnan in Southern China. Shan are both linguistically and culturally related to Thai and Laotians, as well as the Dai peoples in China and North Vietnam. Shan are minority populations in Burma, Thailand, and China; each national government has its own minority policies. The majority of Shan live in Burma and that is where being Shan is most problematic.

No one knows where the Tai peoples first lived; they appeared initially in what is now China. In the thirteenth century, Thai peoples moved south into what is now Burma, Thailand, Laos, and Vietnam, establishing numerous small states. Occasionally Shan ruled southern Burma but by the fourteenth century, the Burmese regained control of lower Burma. Shan ruled numerous small states between central Burma and southern China. The domain of larger states included a large number of villages scattered over broad territories as well as small states that recognized their sovereignty. There were also numerous small states with domains that might include only a few villages. This multitude of Shan states never formed a unified Shan kingdom. The states often had subordinate political relationships with each other and with the rulers of Burma and China; it was acceptable and politically expedient to acknowledge all the more powerful states as overlords.

Political relationships among various Shan states and with the Burmese and Chinese waxed and waned; at times a particular Shan state was powerful, at times Chinese power extended into the area, and, at other times, the Burmese were powerful, able to dominate most of the Shan states. The Burmese played the larger Shan states off each other so that these states were not a threat to the Burmese crown while the Shan states attempted to play the larger powers off each other in order to maintain their autonomy. These were political rather than ethnic maneuvers; states dealing with states rather than Burmese dealing with Shan.

The British established control over Burma in 1886. The British saw themselves as the successors to the Burmese king and to all the territory the king controlled. Like other Western powers, the British worked to create a Burmese state that reflected European ideas of what a state is and how it worked. One basic assumption was that each ethnic or national group should have its own separate territory; where ethnic groups mixed, they worked to separate them. Lower Burma was ruled directly as a province of India. In the north, however, the British made particular relationships with each Shan prince and ruled indirectly, placing a British official to deal with external matters and guiding the princes in internal matters. These individual relations were changed in 1922 when the British created the Federated Shan States, producing, for the first time, a unified Shan polity. The outcome of the British colonial process was to create a sense of national ethnic and political identity within the diverse populations of Burma. Some Burmese see this British separation of the Shan States from lower Burma as the cause of ethnic conflicts between Burmese and Shan. However, this divide and conquer pattern had a long history within the region. What was different with the British policy was the separation in ethnic rather than political terms.

World War II only increased ethnic divisiveness within Burma. The Burmese independence movement sided with the Japanese and formed the Burmese Independence Army (BIA). Many of the minority groups fought along side the British while most Shan princes attempted to remain neutral. When it became clear that the Japanese were losing, Aung San, the leader of the BIA, switched to the British side. As a result, in 1947, Aung San and his political party worked with the British to establish the terms of Burmese independence. One key element for the new Union of Burma was the Panglong agreement of 1947 between Aung San and Shan and other minority groups. Based on the Panglong agreement, the 1947 constitution allowed the Shan states (and the Karenni state) the right to secede after a ten year period of joining the Union.

Aung San and members of his cabinet were assassinated before independence; a number of ethnic and political groups were in rebellion; and the Communists won in China in 1949 causing the nationalists Chinese to flee from southern China into Northern Burma. These events meant that the constitution was never fully implemented and that Burmese military were active in the Shan State. As a consequence of this turmoil and weak political leadership, the Burmese army and its leaders acquired more power. They became a caretaker government in 1958, returned control to a democratically elected government in 1960,

and then in 1962, took control of the government again. The military, led by General Ne Win, has remained in power until today.

Most Shan leaders, while unhappy with the Burmese government and the actions of the Burmese army within the Shan State, did not join any of the active rebellions. However, they worked to reform the Burmese constitution in order to make Burma into a federated state, as was proposed in the Panglong Agreement. The military coup in 1962 ended all this. The constitution was revoked, Shan leaders were arrested, and, at least two of them died while under military arrest.

Since then there have been a number of Shan armies fighting the Burmese government: these include the Shan State Army (SSA), the Shan United Revolutionary Army, and the Shan United Army. The SSA has been in existence the longest—the Shan army currently fighting the Burmese government is the SSA—but who makes up the army and its leadership has changed through time. It is difficult to sort out the armies, their alliances with other Shan and minority armies, and their sources of funds. These armies have taxed the local populations, taxed trade between Burma and Thailand, and provided protection for trade caravans. They have also been involved in the drug trade. The political goals of these armies have ranged from an independent democratically ruled Shan State to a true federated Burmese state that respects the rights of all the peoples who inhabit Burma.

NICOLA TANNENBAUM

See also **China; Dai (Tai); Myanmar; Thailand**

Further Reading

Elliott, Patricia, *The White Umbrella*, Bangkok: Post Books, 1999
Mangrai, Sao Saimong, *The Shan States and the British Annexation*, Ithaca and New York: Cornell Southeast Asia Data Paper 57, 1965
Smith, Martin, *Burma: Insurgency and the Politics of Ethnicity*, 2nd edition, New York: Zed Books, 1999
Yawnghwe, Chao Tzang, *The Shan of Burma: Memoirs of an Exile*, Singapore: Institute of Southeast Asian Studies, 1987

Shor

Capsule Summary

Location: Kemerovo Administrative Region, (South Central Siberia), Russian Federation
Total Population: 12,585 (1989)
Languages: Shor; Russian
Religion: Orthodox Christian; formerly animist

The Shor are an indigenous people of Siberia who inhabit forested regions in the foothills of the northern Altai mountain range of southern Siberia. Traditionally hunters and gatherers of the vast Siberian boreal forests, many Shor now live mixed among the Russian population in an urban, industrialized setting in the *Kuzbass*, Russia's largest coal producing region.

The Shor belong linguistically to the large and dispersed family of Turkic peoples and have ethnic ancestry linking them to other, non-Turkic Siberian peoples, most likely Ob-Ugrian and Yeniseyan peoples. They have mixed in recent decades with the Russian-speaking population of Siberia and are becoming increasingly Russified. The Soviet census of 1979 counted 15,000 Shor, including 9,760 mother tongue speakers (61 percent). By 1989, the census found a reduced number of 12,585. In 1998, the Shor themselves estimated their numbers to be only a few thousand, in the absence of any official count. There are reportedly only three small villages in Kemerovo district where the Shor are still concentrated as a majority population.

The current number of fluent speakers of Shor is probably under 1,000, and the language is severely endangered. Even in villages where the Shor form a majority, children are no longer acquiring Shor as their mother tongue. This fact is greatly regretted by the older generation, yet they also express a desire for their children to speak Russian in order to succeed. Given the current demographic situation, the language is likely to disappear within a generation or two. As the language goes, the rich oral traditions of the Shor will likely be forgotten. These include myths, songs, and stories connected with the bear cult, hunting, shamanism, and an animistic world view.

The Shor were traditionally hunters, fishers, and gatherers, who practiced agriculture and animal domestication to a much lesser degree. As with all Siberian peoples, hunting would have been a highly ritualized activity for the Shor, due to its connections to forest places and to animals—especially the bear—regarded as having spiritual significance. Spoils of hunting were shared among an extended kinship collective, as a way of counterbalancing the risk that an individual hunter might find no game on a particular outing. Men hunted in the winter, spending many days or weeks hiking or skiing through the forests. Hunting provided not only meat, a primary source of food, but also valuable furs. A portion of furs was paid in tribute to more powerful neighboring groups. In early times these would have included the Mongols, and after the seventeenthcentury, primarily Russians.

As Siberia was colonized by the Russians from the seventeenth century onwards, the Shor became scattered in small pockets amongst the larger population. As recently as the 1920s the Shor lacked any unifying ethnic identity, and identified more closely with traditional clan groupings (known as *söök*). Knowledge of one's clan membership was necessary to avoid marrying within the clan, which was forbidden.

The Shor lacked any standardized language, writing system, or cohesive political identity until the twentieth century. In the later half of the twentieth century the Shor were given a standard literary language, based on the *Mras* dialect, with elements of *Shor* dialect and *Chulym* dialect. For a brief period, the standard language came to be used in native-language schools and in over 100 published books. This brief flowering of a Shor literary culture was followed by a period of severe repression of culture and language. During 1937 to 1945, Shor language schools were shut down and in 1942 the Shor language newspaper called *Kyzl Shor* ("The Red Shor") ceased publication. Subsequently, the Shor stopped using their language for publishing, public functions, or school instruction, and used it only as a home language.

In the modern era, not only the Shor language, but the Shor people themselves have been politically marginalized. They never truly wielded administrative control over their own lands and people. As a token gesture towards the Shor minority, the Soviet state established a Shor National Region, called *Gornaya* ("mountain") *Shoria*, in 1929. The indigenous Shor population may have composed a majority at the time of creation of this national administrative unit. But a rapid influx of Russian and other immigrant settlers during the early years of the Soviet industrialization drive quickly reduced them to a minority in their own titular region. The Shor National Region was ultimately disbanded in 1939, and the land ceded to Kemerovo province.

It was not until the era of *perestroika* that some Shor felt free to express their linguistic and cultural identity once again. With help from Russian and other scholars, they undertook a revival of the literary language and began using it in publishing, pedagogy, and other social functions. A language association was founded, and in 1988, a chair of Shor Language and Literature was created at the State Pedagogical Institute in Novokuznetsk, the provincial capital. This institute offers teacher training in the Shor language and literature. Within a year of its founding, teachers of various subjects who were themselves Shor began to teach Shor in some small village schools. Still, progress towards self-determination and ethnic

autonomy has been quite modest. Attempts at reviving the Shor literary language show only minimal prospects for success, as the generation of Shor under the age of 30 has already become fully monolingual Russian-speakers.

The Shor still have official state recognition as a "small-numbering" minority people of Russia, which allows them certain rights of participation in cultural and political groups and activities. But these small concessions cannot in any way counter the enormous social pressures causing the Shor to become fully Russified in culture and language, and thereby to lose their language and ethnic identity. Like most indigenous Siberian peoples, the Shor now face the likely prospect of full assimilation into the dominant Russian culture in the near future.

K. DAVID HARRISON

See also **Siberian Indigenous Peoples**

Further Reading

Forsyth, J., *A History of the Peoples of Siberia*. Cambridge: Cambridge University Press, 1992

Siberian Indigenous Peoples

Capsule Summary

Location: Siberia (Russia)
Total Population: Northern minorities, 200,000 people (26 peoples according to the official registration), with Yakuts, Buriats, Komis, Tuvans, 1,500,000 people
Languages: four linguistic groups (Uralic, Altaic, Paleoasiatic, Eskaleut)
Religions: Shamanism (animism), with later and partial conversion to Buddhism or Orthodoxy depending on the region and the peoples

Siberia contains more than 30 indigenous peoples. Of these, 26 were officially registered in 1925–1926 as *Northern minorities*, belonging to different linguistic families. They are spread over four ecological areas: tundra, forest-tundra, taiga, and steppe, on a territory covering 65 percent of Russia. Most of them are located in subarctic and arctic areas.

Important groups like Buriats and Yakuts are not classified as "minorities."

Traditionally, Siberian indigenous peoples were fishers, hunters, or herders, and reindeer (wild or domesticated) played a central role in the life of many of them. The traditional way of life remains alive in many regions, but so-called modern occupations have recently appeared.

In Siberian societies, the transmission of membership to the familial group is patrilineal and the rule of residence is patrilocal, often neolocal today. Some peoples used to be polygynes, mostly among herders (for instance, among Chukchees).

As early as the founding of Kievian Russia in the tenth century CE, Slavic populations demonstrated the desire to expand throughout the area. The turning point occurred when Ivan IV the Terrible (1533–1584) conquered Astrakhan and Kazan in the southeast. Ivan wanted Russia to gain new territories and access to the sea, and for himself to become the "monarch of all Siberia."

From that moment, Cossacks and fur traders went further east through Siberia. By the seventeenth century, the conquest was achieved, mostly thanks to an infiltration process. Nevertheless, it led to military actions in some regions, for instance, in the Kamchatkan and Chukotkan territories. Wars against Koryaks and Chukchees began in 1690, and the indigenous groups were defeated. Relationships between indigenes and incomers were mainly based on trade. In the meantime, indigenes were subjected to the *yasak,* a tax to be paid in furs to the czar.

Siberia became a land of exile and labor camps. Indigenes were constantly in relationships with a population who had been rejected by the Russian society. Nevertheless, the monographs and literature written by the nineteenth-century intelligentsia banished to these regions for political reasons, such as Vladimir Bogoraz or Vladimir Il'ich Iokhel'son (Jochelson), constitute today the most illuminating documents about native peoples.

The contact with the Russian population led to various changes in the life of indigenous peoples. First, it facilitated the spread of formerly unknown diseases that gravely affected the demography of many groups. Trade with Russians promoted conversion in the natives' ways of life: some hunters and fishermen shifted partly to fur hunting and trapping in order to exchange more products; other hunters adopted herding and some herders developed their herds. Although several peoples lost part of their territory (such as the Koryaks, Itelmens, Enets, Eskimos, and the Yukaghirs), others extended theirs (for example, the Nenets, Chukchees, Evenks, and Evens). Smaller groups found themselves included in larger ones. The contact with incomers led also to Russification, a process of assimilation whereby indigenous populations were converted to Russian culture and religion. The Itelmens for instance were almost totally assimilated by the nineteenth century. Newcomers often did not respect the indigenes' rights and ways of life. To escape these conflicting relationships, many peoples retreated in the tundra or in the taiga.

After the 1917 Revolution, the problems of the North-Siberian population worsened. If, at first, the Committee of the North (founded in 1923 and including scientists familiar with Northern regions, such as Bogoraz) aimed at gradually integrating indigenes in the Soviet society while respecting their way of life, later on, the Soviet policy tended to assimilate them as quickly as possible. At the beginning of the 1930s, sovietization intensified. When the Committee had created a Latin transcription of the indigenous languages, in 1937 it was decided to transcribe it to Cyrillic without consulting any specialist. The Committee of the North was dissolved in 1935, and several of its members were arrested.

The language and the culture of the Soviet Union, according to Stalinist ideology, must be Russian: shamans were considered enemies and sent to gulags (labor camps); children were sent to boarding schools where they were to lose their traditional way of life and language. Reindeers were collectivized and the supposedly rich herders were branded as *kulaks* (bourgeois peasants) and arrested. Hunters were settled and the whole economy (herding, fishing, and hunting) was collectivized and organized in *sovkhozes* (state farms).

Newcomers arrived in large numbers in the 1950s and the Siberian peoples became a minority on their own land. For instance, in 1989, in the Chukotka autonomous region, the indigenes (including Chukchees, Koryaks, and other peoples) amounted to only 9.7 percent of the population.

In the 1970s, several villages, arbitrarily deemed "without future prospects," were closed and their inhabitants relocated in different places, sometimes where they were unable to live on their traditional economy (for instance in Novoe-Chaplino, in Chukotka, where Eskimos could no longer hunt sea mammals).

At the beginning of the twenty-first century, Siberian peoples are facing great difficulties as the result of the loss of indigenous languages and cultures. In the social and economic context, indigenes are most of the time subjected to constant and sometimes inconsistent changes. In Chukotka, after *perestroika,* reindeers were partly privatized and then nationalized again. Unemployment and alcoholism remain a central part of contemporary life. At the same time, people are going back to their traditional life and knowledge because it is the only way to survive.

But native peoples are also facing an ecological disaster: industrial development and exploitation of underground resources including gas and oil exploration. Drilling has destroyed the natural environment and prevented indigenes, whose livelihood and religion is closely connected to nature, from their traditional ways of subsistence. For instance, Udege people have seen the forest where they used to live destroyed. Khanty were the first to protest against the ecological problems of their territory where petrol and gas were exploited without their inclusion or consent. Ecological and social problems have serious consequences on the natives' health: life expectancy is much shorter for indigenes than for majority Russians.

Another central problem is the question of identity. At the age of 16, every young person living in Russia receives a passport in which his or her nationality is listed: he or she is a citizen of Russia while belonging to a defined ethnic group. However nationality does not take into consideration mixed heritage, in particular different linguistic and cultural legacies. Furthermore, the nationality written on a passport sometimes does not fit with the indigenous self-name: Chukchees are registered as *Čukči* in Russian, although their ethnonym is *lyg'oravetl'an*. As a consequence, this policy created artificial distinctions within the same populations: for instance, Itelmens were called *Kamchadals* by Russians and their self-name (*Itenmi* misquoted as *Itelmen*) was not officially recognized in documents before 1927. Presently both appellations still exist and confuse the definition of this people's identity.

Indigenous languages, unofficially forbidden at the end of the 1950s, are again presently taught in schools. Nevertheless, other subjects are all in Russian. However, providing native peoples with schooling enabled an indigenous intelligentsia to emerge, who has earned the right to fight for native rights. Siberian indigenous peoples are hence trying to revive their culture. Organizations appeared to defend indigenes' rights, such as RAIPON (Russian Association of Indigenous Peoples of the North), founded in 1990 and today comprising 34 regional associations of Northern minorities, and L'auravetl'an (from the self-name of the Chukchee people), founded in 1996, a national information center on indigenous issues connecting native peoples scattered in a very large territory.

Siberian indigenous peoples can be classified by different linguistic groups. Four major indigenous peoples are the Uralic, the Altaic, the Paleoasiatic, and Eskaleuts. Each group has its particular culture and way of life, although there is a common background.

Uralic Peoples

These include the Ob-Ugrian and the Samoyeds. Of the Ob-Ugrian, the population is divided among the Khantys (or Ostyaks, 22,551 people) and the Mansys (or Voguls, 8,461) according to the RAIPON's latest data and the last census (1989). The Ob-Ugrian groups live in Northwest Siberia, in the Autonomous Region of Khanty-Mansi and Yamalo-Nenets, Tomsk Region. Their religion is shamanism (animism) and some have converted to the Russian Orthodox faith. Their traditional economy includes hunting, fishing, and reindeer herding. Of the second group, the Samoyeds, the population includes the Nenets (34,646), Enets (209), Nganassans (1,278), and Selkups (3,612).

They reside in Northwest and West Siberia, the Yamal Peninsula, Nenets Autonomous Area, Yamalo-Nenets and Khanty-Mansi Autonomous Region (Nenets), Taimyr Peninsula, Taimyr Autonomous Area (Enets and Nganassans), and the Ob Region (Selkups). They also practice shamanism (animism), and their traditional economy comprises reindeer herding (Nenets), wild reindeer hunting, fishing, and reindeer herding (Enets and Nganassans).

Altaic Peoples

These include the Tunguso-Mandchus, Turcs, and the Mongols. Within the Tunguso-Mandchus group, the population includes Evenks (30,163), Evens or Lamuts (17,199), Nanays (12,023), Ulchis (3,233), Udeges (2,011), Orochis (1,200), Negidals (642), and Orokis (190). The Tunguso-Manchus are scattered throughout Siberia, in the Yamalo-Nenets, Dolgano-Nenets and Evenk Autonomous Regions, the Republic of Sakha-Yakutia, the Republic of Buriatia, Area of Amur, Sakhalin, Irkutsk, and Chita, Territory of Khabarovsk and Primorie (Northeastern China). In Northeastern Siberia they reside in the Khabarovsk territory, Magadan Region, Chukotka and Kamchatka (Evens). In Southeastern Siberia they live in the territory of Khabarovsk and Primorie (Nanays, Udeges, Orochis); Khabarovsk Territory (Ulchis, Negidals); and the Sakhalin Island Region (Orokis). The religion of the Altaic peoples is shamanism (animism), with some numbers practicing the Russian Orthodox faith (for example the Negidals). Their traditional economy includes hunting, fishing, and reindeer herding.

Among the Turcs, the total population includes the Dolgans (6,929) and Yakuts (380,200), who reside in North and Central Siberia (the Dolgano-Nenets Autonomous Area and the Republic of Sakha-Yakutia). Their religion is also shamanism (animism), and these peoples maintain traditional economies of wild reindeer hunting (Dolgans), hunting, fishing, cattle and horse herding (Yakuts).

The Mongols comprise a total population of Tuvans (or Tyvans, 206,200) and Buriats (421,000). They reside in South Siberia in the Republic of Tuva, Mongolia, China (Tyvans), and the Republic of Buriatia (Buriats). They practice shamanism (animism) as well as Buddhism. Traditional economies include reindeer herding and hunting and cattle, sheep, and horse herding.

Paleoasiatic Peoples

These include the Luorawetlan and other Paleoasiatic groups. Included in the Luorawetlan group are the Chukchees (15,184), Koryaks (9,242), Itelmens or Kamchadals (2,481), and Kereks (100). They reside in Northeastern Siberia, Kamchatka (Koryaks, Itelmens in the south), Chukotka (Chuckchees, Koryaks in the south) and part of Northern Yakutia (Chukchees). They practice shamanism (animism), and some, such as the Itelmans and the Koryaks, have been partially converted to Russian Orthodoxy.

Traditional economies include fishing, sea mammal hunting, and reindeer herding.

Other Paleoasiatic peoples from disparate regions include the Kets (1,113), Yukaghirs (1,142), and Nivkhs or Giliaks (4,673). They are located in West Siberia, the Khanty-Mansi Autonomous Region, Turukhansk Area of Krasnoyarsk Region (Kets); Northeastern Siberia: Chukotka and Yakutia (Yukaghirs), Southeastern Siberia: Khabarovsk and Sakhalin Area (Nivkhs). Also

practitioners of shamanism (animism), the traditional economies of such peoples includes hunting and fishing (Kets, Nivkhs), and reindeer hunting and herding (Yukaghirs).

Eskaleuts

Among the fourth group, the Eskaleuts, the total population includes Eskimos or Yupigit (1,719), who reside in Northeastern Siberia, along the seashore of Chukotka. They practice shamanism (animism) and sea mammal hunting.

VIRGINIE VATE

See also **Buriats; Mongols; Russians; Sakha (Yakut)**

Further Readings

Bogoraz W., *The Chukchee,* The Jesup North Pacific Expedition, New York, G.E. Stechert, Leiden, E.J. Brill, AMS Press, 1904 (1975)

Czaplicka M.A., *Aboriginal Siberia: A Study in Social Anthropology*, Clarendon Press, Oxford, 1914 (1969)

Funk, D., and L. Sillanpää, editors, *The Small Indigenous Nations of Northern Russia: A Guide for Researchers*, Abo Akademi University: Social Science Research Unit, publication no. 29, 1999

"RAIPON" (Russian Association of Indigenous Peoples of the North), <http://www.raipon.org>

Tiškov, V.A., editor, *Narody Rossii, enciklopediia*, naučnoe izdatel'stvo (Bol'šaia Rossijskaia Enciklopediia), Moscow, 1994

Vakhtin N., "Native Peoples of the Russian Far North," in *Polar Peoples: Self Determination and Development*, London: Minority Rights Publications, 1994

Sierra Leone

Capsule Summary

Country Name: Republic of Sierra Leone
Location: Western Africa, bordering the North Atlantic Ocean, between Guinea and Liberia
Total Population: 5,732,681 (2003)
Languages: English (official, regular use limited to literate minority), Mende (principal vernacular in the south), Temne (principal vernacular in the north), Krio (English-based Creole, spoken by the descendants of freed Jamaican slaves who were settled in the Freetown area, a lingua franca and a first language for 10% of the population but understood by 95%)
Religions: Muslim (60%), indigenous beliefs (30%), Christian (10%)

The Republic of Sierra Leone is located on the west coast of Africa, with its western peninsula projecting into the Atlantic Ocean. It is bordered to the north and northeast by Guinea and to the south and southeast by

Liberia. Sierra Leone has a population of 5,732,681 (2003) comprising 17 main ethnic groups including Creoles, descendants of freed slaves who first arrived from Nova Scotia in 1787. Although Creoles count for less than 2 percent of the population, they form a significant minority in the country's sociopolitical configuration.

The Mende and Temne are the two largest ethnic groups, each accounting for about 30 percent of the total population. Other groups include the Limba, Lokko, Kisi, Kono, Koranko, and Yalunka. A former British colony and member of the Commonwealth of Nations, Sierra Leone attained independence in 1961. In 1991, a civil war broke out when armed fighters of the Revolutionary United Front (RUF) led by Corporal Foday Sankoh began fighting against the government, then headed by Major General Joseph Saidu Momoh. Despite the war, in 1996 Sierra Leone held multiparty elections for president and parliament. Ahmed Tejan Kabbah and the Sierra Leone People's Party won the elections, and he became president. Sierra Leone's gross domestic product (GDP) per capita was $500 in 2002.

History

The history of Sierra Leone before Portuguese explorers and traders visited the coastal areas during the fifteenth century has not yet been fully researched by archeologists and historians. From mid-fifteenth century on, European trading ships anchored in the Rokel estuary because it was an important source of fresh water and wood for those en route to India. European goods like clothes and weapons were exchanged for gold and ivory until the 1550s when slaves became an important commodity, after plantations in the Americas were opened.

Sierra Leone was affected by the Mane invasion during the mid-sixteenth century. The Mane were a marauding group of fierce warriors displaced as a result of the collapse of the Mali Empire. They entered Sierra Leone from Liberia and succeeded in conquering ethnic groups along the coast such as the Temne and Bullom. The Mane however were less successful in their attempt to move northward and conquer the Limba, Yalunka, and Susu. New ethnic groups were created as a result of the Mane onslaught. The Mende, who entered Sierra Leone from Liberia in the eighteenth century, were descendants of the Mane. They established major polities in the southern part of the country.

In 1787, about 400 freed blacks from Nova Scotia were settled in the area of present-day Freetown (capital)

under the auspices of antislavery philanthropists like Granville Sharp. In subsequent years the initial settlers were joined by the Maroons from Jamaica, the "Black Poor" from England, and *recaptives* or slaves set free by a British naval squadron, which intercepted slave ships along the West African coast in the early 1800s.

Between 1896, when the British declared a protectorate over the interior of Sierra Leone, and 1961, Sierra Leone gradually moved toward independence. The first prime minister of independent Sierra Leone was Sir Milton Margai. When Sir Milton died in 1964 his younger brother, Sir Albert Margai, succeeded him. Following the indecisive 1967 elections, a group of army officers took over the government and suspended the Constitution. After the military government was overthrown in 1968, the opposition leader Siaka Stevens, leader of the All People's Congress (APC), became prime minister.

In 1971, Stevens became president under a new Constitution. Sierra Leone became a one-party state after a new Constitution was adopted in 1978, which made the APC the only legal political party. After Stevens retired in 1985 he handed over power to his handpicked successor, the head of the Sierra Leone Army, Major General Joseph Saidu Momoh.

Since 1991, civil war between the government and the Revolutionary United Front (RUF) has resulted in tens of thousands of deaths and the displacement of more than 2 million people (well over one-third of the population), many of whom are now refugees in neighboring countries. A United Nations peacekeeping force as well as support from the World Bank and the international community demobilized the RUF and Civil Defense Forces (CDF) combatants. In April 1992, Momoh was overthrown by a group of young soldiers led by Captain Valentine Strasser. Strasser was then ousted in a palace coup by his second in command Julius Maada Bio in January 1996. This paved the way for presidential and parliamentary elections in February of that same year, which were won by Kabbah again and the Sierra Leone People's Party (SLPP).

Society and Ethnicity

Of the 17 ethnic groups composing Sierra Leone's population, the Mende (30 percent) and Temne (30 percent) are the largest. The Mende occupy the southern half of the country whereas the Temne are found mostly in the central and northern part. The third largest group is the Limba, also found in the northern section of the country. Other relatively smaller groups include the Kono, Kuranko, Loko, Madingo, Susu, Vai, and Yalunka who, like the Mende, belong to the Mande language group. The Gola, Kissi, Krim, and Sherbro, who are linguistically affiliated to the Temne, belong to the Mel language group.

The Creoles, descendants of freed slaves mostly found in Freetown peninsula, speak Krio, a lingua franca in Sierra Leone, mainly derived from English. The Creoles were the most Westernized and educated group during the 19th century and early 20th century. They formed a small but powerful minority for much of the colonial period. However after independence they became less visible in politics even though they continued to dominate the civil service and other professional fields like law and medicine for some time. The Lebanese community in Sierra Leone is also a tiny minority, which plays an influential role in the country's economic activities.

Sierra Leone has extensive mineral resources including diamonds, bauxite, and rutile. At the same time, it is one of the world's ten poorest nations, according to the UN. During the country's ten-year civil war, which started in 1991, the rebel movement, RUF, and its supporters used diamond revenues to buy arms and sustain the war against the government. An estimated 50,000 Sierra Leoneans have been killed and others displaced and forced into refugee camps in neighboring countries like Guinea and Liberia. While the UN peacekeeping presence ended the civil war, rebel gang fighting, ethnic rivalries, illegal diamond trading, refugees, and corruption continue to be a problem. The country's next presidential and parliamentary elections will be held in May 2007, as both the international community and local leaders and organizations seek solutions for a lasting peace.

TAMBA M'BAYO

See also **Creole (mixed-origin minorities)**

Further Reading

Allie, Joe, *A New History of Sierra Leone*, London: Macmillan, 1990
Binns, Margaret, and Tony Binns, *Sierra Leone*, Santa Barbara, California: Clio Press, 1992
Cartwright, John, *Political Leadership in Sierra Leone*, Toronto: University of Toronto Press, 1978
Conteh-Morgan, Earl, and Mac Dixon-Fyle, *Sierra Leone at the End of the Twentieth Century: History, Politics and Society*, New York: Peter Lang, 1999
Fyfe, Christopher, *Sierra Leone Inheritance*, London: Oxford University Press, 1964
———, *A Short History of Sierra Leone*, London: Longman, 1979
Fyle, Cecil M., *The History of Sierra Leone: A Concise Introduction*, London: Evans, 1981

Sikhs

Capsule Summary

Location: Homeland of Punjab, a butterfly shaped region that bridges India and Pakistan and includes Harayana; other populations scattered around the globe, primarily in former British colonies and North America
Total Population: ranges from 18 to 20 million
Languages: Gurumukhi (language of the scriptures), Punjabi
Religion: Sikhism

The Sikhs are a religious community highly respected for their aggressive, innovative, and militaristic behavior. They are perhaps the most mobile and versatile people in the whole of India.

The Sikhs are visible because of the distinctive symbols they wear: a turban and the *5 Ks*. The *5 Ks* include *kes*, uncut hair which is usually covered by a turban and symbolizes strength and sainthood; *karha*, a steel bracelet on the right wrist which, if not protected, is very vulnerable in combat; *kirpan,* a sword*; kangha,* a comb in the hair, disorderly hair symbolizes madness; and *kachha*, specially designed under shorts to promote freedom of movement and remind the wearer to use his life giving fluids properly. These symbols combined communicate the Sikh ideal, a soldier-saint brotherhood that upholds and respects women.

Numbering between 18 and 20 million world wide, Sikhs live in scattered communities, with 500,000 in Britain, 225,000 in Canada and 100,000 in the United States. They also have sizable communities in Malaysia, Singapore, Hong Kong, and East Africa. They, like many other South Asians followed the British colonial flag.

Punjab, the Sikh homeland is a butterfly-shaped region that bridges India and Pakistan. Some of the Sikh holy places are in Pakistani Punjab, and their access to them was limited, until the last decade, when Pakistan felt that the political, social, and economic position of the Sikhs in India created an opportunity to gain Sikh political support in India and abroad. They then granted Sikhs greater freedom to visit their holy places.

Sikhism is the youngest of India's monotheistic religions. It was born in the Punjab which is located on the invasion route into India and a place where Muslims and Hindus lived side by side. Guru Nanak (1469–1539), the founder of the Sikhs was born and died in the Punjab although he traveled much in between. He taught that "There is no Hindu; there is no Mussalman," which was acknowledging that in the eyes of the divine, all are equal. This central truth has to be appreciated if humanity is to surmount the barriers that divide people. At the age of eleven, he refused donning the sacred thread of the twice-born castes and preached what is another tenet of the Sikhs, the abolition of caste and the equality of man. He set forth the concept of one god, a the belief that could eliminate social strife by helping people overcome their prejudices. Worshiping the one god, an amorphous deity, as well as being part of the world, not withdrawing like the sages, became central to Guru Nanak's teachings and the belief system of the Sikhs.

This new faith incorporated various tribes and castes of Punjab, especially the Jats, who were rural agriculturalists and were very courageous in times of political turmoil and upheaval. Thus, for Sikhs, worship is central, whether at home or in the *gurdwara*, the building designated for Sikh ceremonies and social events. There is a common kitchen that serves all regardless of caste or other social position.

The peace, love, and worship preached by Guru Nanak was not to be. Successor after successor followed their founder as the faith grew so fast that the Mogul rulers perceived it as a threat. As a result, some Sikh Gurus were captured and brutally tortured, and their followers were also martyred.

It was during this time of persecution that Guru Gobind Singh (1666–1707), their tenth and last Guru proclaimed the *Adi Granth*, or *Guru Granth Sahib*, Sikh scriptures, to be their Guru after his death. He transformed his followers into a soldier-saint brotherhood called the *Khalsa*, which literally means "army of the pure." He gave them the mission to "uphold right in every place and destroy sin and evil; that right may triumph, that good may live and tyranny be uprooted from the land." He gave his followers the moral justification for warfare in preaching that, "when all other means fail, it is righteous to draw the sword." With that ideology he instructed Sikhs to wear the *5 Ks*, which symbolize righteous militancy. Other tenets included a ban on tobacco and the institution of common titles: women were to be a *Kaur*, which means "princess" and men were to titled *Singh*, which means "lion." He also instituted *Amrit*, a baptism ceremony. All Sikhs do not adhere to the code of conduct or wear the symbols, but they are considered Sikhs by many because of their devotion, participation, and respect for the Sikh gurus.

Guru Gobind Singh was martyred, and open rebellion broke out as bands of Sikh guerrillas hastened the collapse of the Mogul administration while keeping Afghans at bay. Thus, Sikh history of this time is a cycle of rulers and invaders slaughtering and Sikhs avenging so that at times it seemed that rivers of Sikh blood flowed through the Punjab. The fortunes of the Sikhs ebbed and flowed. First, under Banda Singh Bhahadur, a follower of Gobind Singh, but not a guru, who was so feared that the Muslims of Northern India declared a Holy War against him. After Banda was captured, tortured, and publicly beheaded, the Sikhs seemed crushed, but capable leadership and the Sikhs, along with the other incursions taking place in the Punjab, drove the Muslim governors to impotence. Gradually, the Sikhs evolved into twelve *misls* or militias headed by prominent leaders. Initially, they were military brotherhoods of a democratic type. Every soldier had a say in the deliberations and booty was shared equally with the officers. Twice a year, in the spring and autumn, there was a general assembly in Amritsar to discuss past successes and failures and plan for the future. Misls did not remain democratic. As the Sikhs became land holders, leadership became hereditary and leaders began fighting among themselves.

Into this vacuum stepped Maharajah Ranjit Singh (1780–1839) who led the Sikhs into a period of glory by the end of the century. Maharajah Ranjit Singh established a Sikh kingdom under his rulership. He was a master of diplomacy and of dividing his enemies. He modernized the Sikh army. He hired French, Italian, German, Irish, and Greek soldiers to drill his troops. He set up foundries in Lahore to make canon balls and trained Muslim gunners to man the canons. Maharajah Ranjit Singh did not place any faith in the loyalty of the foreigners and he was right, they deserted later.

Maharajah Ranjit Singh is the most popular hero in Sikh history. He was not a handsome man. He was stricken with smallpox, which deprived him of one eye. He was small dark and ugly. But he lead the Sikh people to their destiny. He united the warring misls into the Khalsa. He expanded the basis of his state from the sacred to the secular; he placed Muslims in positions of trust without discrimination. He was humble, courteous, and never lost his humble touch. He led his armies by fighting in the forefront, risking his life like any common solder.

Disunity and intrigue among the ruling families followed Maharajah Ranjit Singh's death and the region was annexed by the British in 1849. The continued military activity of the Sikhs along with their tradition of military readiness made them ideal members for the modern armies of India and Great Britain.

As a result of this turbulent history, martyrdom, survival in the wake of persecution, and fighting for what is just, are prominent themes in Sikh culture.

Recognizing the militaristic qualities of the Sikhs, the English classified them as a martial race and incorporated them into the Indian Army. Their loyalty to the crown was crucial for the British to maintain control in South Asia and the Sikhs were handsomely rewarded with land grants and preferences in the Armed Forces. They also served admirably in both World War I and World War II, not only in Asia, but also in the European theater.

In spite of their militaristic tradition, they did not lose their ability to get the soil to yield a bountiful harvest. They were crucial in the development of the canal colonies of the Northwest Frontier. And partly due to the skill of the Sikh farmer, Punjab is considered the breadbasket of India. Sikh military experience acquainted them with opportunities throughout the Empire and they took advantage of them by emigrating. For example, many Sikhs who served in Hong Kong under the British flag returned there.

Starting in the late 1800s, Sikh identity became stronger and more exclusive as a result of the Singh Sabha movement. These groups emphasized their separateness from the Hindus in theology, ritual, social practice, and politics. The movement was culminated in a nonviolent campaign (1920–1925) to wrest control of gurdwaras and shrines from British-supported managers, who were often Hindu, and have Sikhs responsible for their own shrines. Their wish was granted; since 1925, the Sikh Gurdwara Protection Committee (a central management committee) has supervised the shrines and played a role in Sikh politics.

In spite of their loyalty to the Crown, the suffering of the Sikhs was not to end. In 1947, the Sikh homeland, the Punjab, was partitioned between India and Pakistan, many were left destitute and resources were taxed. When news of opportunities abroad reached them through friends, relatives, and travel agents, many decided to take advantage of them, and England was a primary destination for Sikh emigration. Sikhs had previously entered Canada at the turn of the century and numbered 5,000 by 1907. In 1914, however, in the famed Kamagata Maru incident, a shipload of Sikhs were denied entry, thus maintaining the color bar for Canadian immigration.

Some crossed over into the United States and, after enduring the brunt of violence in the state of Washington, followed the railroads south to settle around Stockton and Yuba City, California. Like other Asians and South Asians, they suffered as a result of discriminatory laws and social violence. Sikhs were often called *rag heads* or the *turban tide*. The Hindu conspiracy trial was one such incident where Sikhs, and other people from India were tried for conspiracy—a move instigated by British intelligence to eliminate the *Gadr* or freedom movement for Indian independence that was centered in San Francisco.

Sikhs do not emphasize conversion, but starting in the 1970s under the leadership of Harbajan Singh, a group of western converts called *gora* or "white" Sikhs have developed. Although they are active in local gurdwaras in North America, they also have their own organization. They were not initially recognized by the wider Sikh community but now they are accepted.

Economic problems in the Punjab along with frustrations related to their minority status contributed to increased Sikh militancy in the 1970s, and a movement for *Khalistan*, a separate Sikh State. In 1984, Indian troops attacked the Golden Temple, the holiest of Sikh shrines, to eliminate the Sikh militants there. Political chaos in the Punjab followed, which led to Prime Minister Indira Gandhi being assassinated by one of her Sikh body guards. This led to widespread atrocities, especially in Delhi where Sikhs were systematically tortured and killed. The Punjab especially became a battleground between Sikh militants and government forces with monetary and diplomatic support coming from the overseas Sikh community. Starting in the 1990s, peace was gradually restored and Sikhs continue to provide leadership in public institutions and their professions, whether in the Punjab or overseas.

ARTHUR HELWEG

See also **India; Pakistan; Punjabi; Singh, Tara (Sikh)**

Further Reading

Barrier, N. Gerald, and Verne A. Dusenbery, editors, *The Sikh Diaspora: Migration and the Experience beyond Punjab*, Delhi: Chanakya Publications, 1989
Helweg, Arthur W., *Sikhs in England*, 2nd edition, New Delhi: Oxford University Press, 1976
Singh, Khushwant, *The Sikhs Today*, 3rd edition, New Delhi: Orient Longman, 1985
O'Connell, Joseph T., editor, *Sikh History and Religion in the Twentieth Century*, Toronto: Centre for South Asian Studies, University of Toronto, 1988
Singh, Pashura, and N. Gerald Barrier, *Sikh Identity: Continuity and Change*, New Delhi: Manohar, 1999
Singh, Patwant, *The Sikhs*, New York: Alfred A. Knopf, 2000

Silva, Benedita Da (Afro-Brazilian)

For most of Brazilian history, to be black and female has been to be subordinate in a vast, narrowly hierarchical society. That a black female might one day be elected to the Brazilian Senate, the stronghold of the dominant elite, has always been highly unlikely. However, in 1994 Benedita da Silva was the first to achieve this extraordinary political accomplishment.

Popularly referred to as Bené, da Silva was born in a *favela* (shanty community) in Rio de Janeiro in 1943. As a young woman she became increasingly active in a group for neighborhood improvements although she never attended high school. She became a community leader at a significant moment in Brazilian history. In 1964, a reactionary military regime had taken power, suppressing leftist parties and movements, and repressing labor organizations. However, rampant inflation and massive unemployment in the following decade eroded military authority. As of 1979 the regime decided to allow a gradual opening of society and eventual return to civilian, democratic government.

At this time a Worker's Party (Partido Trabalhista in Portuguese, known by its initials, P.T.) came into existence at the instigation of metalworkers in the industrial metropolis of São Paulo. The military allowed local municipal elections to occur in 1982. As a rising community leader with solid local support, da Silva became the P.T. candidate for a seat on the city council in Rio de Janeiro. Winning with the largest number of votes, the extraordinary victory of a *favela* resident received national attention as well as ridicule.

A poor black woman in public office was an anomaly in the Brazilian government. However, da Silva pursued her platform of improving working and living conditions for the poor. In 1986 she was elected as the P.T. candidate for Congress and reelected in 1990. At that time she lived between Chapéu Mangueira and the new federal capital, Brasília. She pursued a program of legislation for women's rights, worker's safety and benefits, Indian rights, street children, agrarian reform, and environmental protection. She participated in the writing of the new constitution for Brazil during 1987–1988.

Her first political defeat came in 1992 when she lost her bid to become mayor of Rio de Janeiro. In 1994 she was elected, by more than two million votes, to the Brazilian senate. Four years later she left the senate to become lieutenant governor of the state of Rio de Janeiro on a ticket that brought together a coalition of leftist parties. She became governor when the incumbent resigned before the end of his term to run in the presidential election of 2002. Increasingly she has been able to advocate her program on an international stage, lecturing and participating in conferences in the United States, Europe, Asia, and Africa.

Biography

Benedita da Silva, born in Rio de Janeiro, March 11, 1943, one of 13 children, only eight of whom survived. Married the first of three husbands in 1958; had four children (two died shortly after birth). Initially practiced spiritism (indigenous religion), participated in Catholic renewal movement of base ecclesiastical communities; since the late1960s has adhered to Protestantism, first Evangelical, and then Pentecostal. Worked as a domestic, factory worker, and janitor; obtained a state government job and then became a nurse's aid. Earned high school equivalency degree (1980) and went to university, majoring in social work.

EDWARD A. RIEDINGER

See also **Afro-Brazilians; Brazil**

Further Reading

Andrew, George Reid, "Brazilian Racial Democracy, 1900–90: An American Counterpoint," *Journal of Contemporary History*, 31, no. 3 (1996)

Aquilera, Luis, "The Challenge to the Brazilian Left: A Conversation with Benedita da Silva," *Dollars and Sense*, no. 217 (May 1, 1998)

Benjamin, Medea, Maísa Mendonça, and Benedita da Silva, *Benedita da Silva: An Afro-Brazilian Woman's Story of Politics and Love*, Oakland, California: Food First Book, 1997

Benjamin, Medea, and Maísa Mendonça, "Benedita da Silva: Community Activist and Senator, Brazil," *NACLA Report on the Americas*, 31, no. 1 (1997)

Burdick, John, "What is the Color of the Holy Spirit?: Pentecostalism and Black Identity in Brazil," *Latin American Research Review*, 34, no. 2 (1999)

Hanchard, Michael George, *Racial Politics in Contemporary Brazil*, Durham, North Carolina: Duke University Press, 1999

Mendonça, Maísa, and Vicente Franco, *Nasci mulher negra* [I Was Born a Black Woman], videocassette, color, 44 mins., San Francisco: Global Productions, 2000

Sindhis

Capsule Summary

Location: Sindh (Pakistan)
Total Population: 30 to 40 million
Language: Sindhi
Religion: Predominantly Muslims

Sindhis are the indigenous people of the Sindh, a province of Pakistan. Controversy surrounds the number of ethnic and linguistic groups within the province of Sindh. Pakistan's population census no longer provides information on ethnic, linguistic, or racial background of its citizens. According to the most recent dicentennial census that was conducted in 1998, out of the total Pakistani population of 130.6 million, the population of Sindh is 30 million (around 23 percent of the total population). Sindhi nationalists question the results of the 1998 census, claiming that this census considerably underrepresents their numerical strength. The vast majority of Sindhis are Muslims. The Sindhis have their own language called *Sindhi*.

History

Sindhis represent an ancient culture and civilization. Their history goes back at least 5,000 years. The region of Sindh historically enjoyed a considerable degree of autonomy which allowed it to establish its own culture and traditions. The Sindhi language also developed with substantial written literature around which a distinct identity could form and flourish. Sindh has been home to many invaders including the Arabs, the Ghaznis, the Moghuls, and the British. In the expansion of Islam towards South Asia, Sindh became the first region to be conquered by the Arabs in 711 CE. Modern-day Sindh is bordered by Punjab in the north, the Arabian sea and Rann of Kutch to the south, India to the east, and the Baluchistan province of Pakistan to the west. Sindh is the third largest of Pakistan's four provinces with an area of approximately 140,908 square kilometers (54,407 square miles). Indigenous Sindhis have serious grievances against the persistent migration of other groups, primarily the Urdu-speaking Muhajirs, but also in more recent years, the Punjabis and the Pukhtuns.

Independence

The partition of British India (August 1947) resulted in substantial changes in the ethnic composition of the people of Sindh. Nearly 1 million Muslims from India came to settle largely in the urban cities of Karachi and Hyderabad, while an equal number of Hindus and Sikhs fled to India. The term *Muhajirs* represents the descendants of those Indian Muslims who migrated to Sindh after the partition. At the time of their arrival in Sindh, the Muhajirs were welcomed wholeheartedly by the indigenous Sindhis. However, the Muhajirs were better educated and politically astute and soon began to dominate Pakistan's political system. In the first few years of Pakistan's existence, the country's political scene was dominated by the Muhajir politicians. In the influential federal and provincial civil services, the Muhajirs also established a predominant hold. Karachi, the new federal capital, which by 1951 was to have a majority of Muhajir population, was taken away from Sindh province and placed under federal administrative control. The consequences were enormous, resulting in the abolition of Sindhi within Karachi's federal offices and the replacement of Urdu-speaking office workers, the closure of the Sindhi Department at the University of Karachi, and a ban on Sindhi in University examinations in Karachi. The Sindhis were left at a disadvantage. No comparisons could be drawn between them and the Muhajirs and their Sindhi hosts, since language, culture, politics, and society were all very different.

During the 1950s the province of Sindh faced another wave of migrants, which involved Pukhtuns (from the North-West Frontier Province of Pakistan) and more significantly the Punjabis (from the province of Punjab). By the time of Pakistan's first military coup in 1958 while Muhajir domination came to an end the Punjabis had begun to take control of the State and provincial affairs. Although the coup leader, President Ayub Khan was himself a Pakhtun, nearly 80 percent of the military hailed from the province of Punjab (the most populous province of Pakistan). The increasing dominance of the Punjabis was reflected in the 1960s through the transfer of the Federal Capital to Islamabad (Punjab) and by the increasing hold of the Punjabis in affairs of all the provinces including Sindh. Some relief and support was provided during the brief period of the Prime Minister Bhutto (1972–1977), an indigenous Sindhi. During Bhutto's government several indigenous Sindhis were appointed or promoted to high offices within the national and provincial governments. To improve the Sindhi representation within the civil service, a lateral entry program was introduced. To help increase the number of indigenous Sindhis,

11.4 percent of the seats were reserved for them in the federal bureaucracy.

The brief period of reprieve and vindication of the rights of Sindhis came to an abrupt end with another military coup. In July 1977, General Zia-ul-Haq, a Punjabi, toppled the elected civilian government and imposed martial law within the State. Bhutto was arrested, tried, and executed in 1979 on charges of murdering a political opponent. The case against Bhutto had been established on largely circumstantial evidence and his appeal against conviction was dismissed by a 3:2 split decision in the Supreme Court— a verdict based along ethnic lines with the three Punjabi judges dismissing his appeal. The execution of the Sindhi Prime Minister was perceived by Sindhi nationalists as a direct assault on the Sindhi nation. Sindhis agitated against the military rule and in favor of restoring democracy. The military responded by repression— a state of affairs which continued until the assassination of General Zia-ul-Haq in August 1988. After Zia's assassination, democracy returned to Pakistan and Zulfiqar Ali Bhutto's daughter, Benazir Bhutto was elected as Pakistan's first woman Prime Minister in December 1988. She was dismissed in 1990 but was reelected in the general elections of 1993 only to be dismissed again in 1996. During her brief spells in government, she attempted to address some of the complaints put forward by the Sindhis. A number of Sindhis were included in the Federal cabinet. Efforts were made to promote the Sindhi language and Sindhi were given preferential treatment in civil services and institutions of higher education.

These efforts however were not sustained enough to have brought a permanent change in the position of Sindhis. Sindhis continue to have substantial grievances. Their biggest fear is submersion and marginalization since even within their own province they continue to be politically, economically, and numerically dominated by outsiders. To improve their position, Sindhis demand a complete ban on future settlements. Similarly, the Sindhis insist on restrictions to be placed on the sale of properties and the allotment of businesses to those not domiciled in Sindh. Sindhis demand greater provincial autonomy and less interference from Islamabad. The Sindhis want to replace Urdu, the national and provincial language, with their own Sindhi language. The Sindhis also want to have the existing quota system expanded so that they receive a greater share of jobs in the provincial services and positions in institutions of higher education.

JAVAID REHMAN

1105

See also **Pakistan; Punjabi**

Futher Reading

Ali, Shaheen Sardar, and Javaid Rehman, *Indigenous Peoples and Ethnic Minorities of Pakistan: Constitutional and Legal Perspectives*, London: Curzon Press 2001

Rahman, Mushtaqur, *Land and Life of Sindh: Pakistan*, Lahore: Ferozsons Publishers, 1993

Rehman, Javaid, "Self-Determination, State-Building and the Muhajirs: An International Legal Perspective of the Role of the Indian Muslim Refugees in the Constitutional Developments of Pakistan," *Contemporary South Asia*, 3, no. 2 (1994)

Rehman, Javaid, and Nikhil Roy, "South-Asia," in *World Directory of Minorities*, edited by Miles Litvinoff, Patrick Thornberry, et al., London: Minority Rights Group, 1997

Rehman, Javaid, *The Weakness in the International Protection of Minority Rights*, The Hague: Kluwer Law International 2000

Wright, Theodor, Jr., "Center–Periphery Relations and Ethnic Conflict in Pakistan: Sindhis, Muhajirs and Punjabis," in *Comparative Politics*, 23, no.3 (1991)

Singapore

Capsule Summary

Location: South East Asia, surrounded by Malaysia and Indonesia
Total Population: 4,608,595 (July 2003); Chinese (76.8%), Malays (13.9%), Indians (7.9%), other ethnic groups (1.4%)
Languages: Four official languages: English (administrative language), Malay (national language), Chinese (Mandarin), Tamil
Religions: Buddhism (42.5%), Taoism (8.5%), Islam (14.9%), Christianity (14.6%), Hinduism (4.0%), other religions (e.g. Judaism, Zoroastrianism) (0.6%), no religion (14.8%)

Singapore was founded in 1819 by Sir Stamford Raffles. His intent was to open a port under British flag in order to circumvent Dutch and Spanish commercial monopolies in Indonesia and the Philippines. Singapore was chosen for its strategic location—all ships between India and China had to pass through it.

At the time of its founding, Singapore was inhabited by a small number of Malay and Orang Laut (seafarers) fishing peoples and about 30 Chinese planters and traders. As Singapore grew as an entreport, it attracted an influx of Chinese migrants from mainland China. In 1963 Singapore joined the federation of Malaysia, but two years later it was expelled when the ruling People's Action Party (PAP) challenged Malay political supremacy. Singapore became an independent state in 1965.

Singapore is a republic with a Westminster parliamentary system of government. It has often been called a one-party state since it has been ruled by the PAP since independence. The opposition is weak and are not a serious threat to the PAP dominance. The concept of human rights is not recognized, rather "Asian values" based on community over individual rights is encouraged.

Ethnic issues are sensitive issues, and it is government policy to maintain the Chinese population at a constant 76 percent, thus leading to many calling Singapore "a Chinese island in a Malay sea" given that it is bordered by two much larger Malay countries. Singapore is a fully industrialized state, achieving this status in less than three generations, earning the nickname "Tiger" economy. Per capita gross domestic product (GDP) is $25,200 (2002 estimate).

Indians

The Indians first came in the late eighteenth century. Often Indian men came alone to work to support families back in India. Indian women and complete Indian families were rare before World War II. About two-thirds of the Indian population are Tamils from southeastern India's Tamil Nadu state; a small number came from Jaffna peninsula in Sri Lanka. Other significant Indian groups are: Malayalis (8 percent); Punjabis, mostly Sikh (8 percent); and Gujaratis (1 percent). This diversity is reflected by religious affiliation; an estimated 50 to 60 percent are Hindu, 20 to 30 percent Muslim, 10 to 12 percent Christian, 7 percent Sikh, and

1 percent Buddhist. Although Tamil is one of the republic's four official languages (along with English, Malay, and Mandarin), recent surveys show that more Indians claimed to understand Malay (97 percent) than Tamil (79 percent). The Muslim-Indian tended to intermarry with Malays (who are Muslims) at a fairly high rate and to be absorbed into the Malay community, continuing a centuries-old process of assimilation of Indian males to Malay society. There are significant differences within the community in terms of occupational and education attainment. The untouchables for the most part did unskilled or semiskilled labor, while the Jaffna Tamils and the Chettia caste, who were traditionally moneylenders and merchants, were often professionals and wealthy businessmen.

Although caste is outlawed, the older generation still regard caste as important, especially when it comes to marriages. It is common for upper-caste Indians to "recruit" wives of a similar caste back in India for their sons. Significant issues for the Indian community included securing residence status for spouses from arranged marriages in India, and entrance for the Indian families of men who had worked in Singapore and for the Brahman priests who were necessary for Hindu religious life. Politically, the Indian community is well represented in the government and the current president is the second Indian to occupy the post.

Malays

The Malay came from peninsular Malaya, Sumatra, Java, and the other islands of the Indonesian archipelago. From the mid-nineteenth century to post World War II years, many Javanese migrated to Singapore, attracted both by urban wages offering a higher living standard and population pressures in Java. It has been estimated that 60 percent of the community traced their origins to Java and an additional 15 to 20 percent to Bawean Island in the Java Sea north of the city of Surabaya. The British colonialists had considered the Malays as the indigenous people, simple farmers and fishermen who were Islamic; they preferentially recruited the Malays to the police, the armed forces, and unskilled positions in the public service. In 1961 more than half of Singapore's Malays depended on employment in the public sector.

After independence, the Chinese-dominated government regarded the Malay preponderance in the police and armed forces as a potential threat as the PAP government saw itself as a tiny Chinese enclave squeezed between two much larger Malay neighbors (Malaysia and Indonesia). The number of Malays in the security services were reduced. A program to resettle the Malays from their *kampungs* (ethnic enclaves/villages) into government built high-rise flats and bring them into the mainstream economy was instituted. By the 1980s, a large proportion of Malay women were working outside the home, having fewer children, and instituting divorces—all major social changes. The changes also brought undesirable changes. The Malays conspicuously occupied the lower rungs of society; with the lowest level of educational attainment among all the major ethnic group, the Malays were concentrated at the low end of the occupational hierarchy and had the lowest average earnings. The 2000 census showed only 6.9 percent of all professional and administrative and managerial personnel were Malays. Many still do not finish high school and the numbers entering universities are dismal, despite the fact that any Malay entering university is virtually assured of a government scholarship.

In sharp contrast to neighboring Malaysia with its compulsory policies of affirmative action for the Malay majority, Singapore's government insists on the meritocracy system. The government blamed the poor achievement of the Malay community as a "cultural deficit" or their supposed "rural" attitudes. Government help is thus limited to "self-help" organizations run by Malay foundations or associations such as Mendaki (Majlis Pendidikan Anak-anak Islam or Council for the Education of Muslim Children).

Unlike the Indians, the ordinary Malays feel that the Chinese-dominated government looked down upon them and subtly discriminates against them. Certain key positions in the armed forces are still unofficially closed to Malays as their loyalty is suspect. Since almost all Singaporean Malays have family ties in Indonesia and Malaysia, the government fears that their loyalty to the island republic may be less than complete should conflict erupt between Singapore and her immediate neighbors. In successive elections, the Malays have voted against the PAP, reinforcing the government view that the Malays are not "patriotic" enough.

Government Action on Minority Rights

The Constitution provides for a Presidential Council for Minority Rights, tasked to draw attention to any legislation which, in its opinion, discriminates against any racial or religious community. The council also investigates these matters if referred to it by Parliament or the Government. The present council consists of a chairman and 14 members. The President appoints all council members on the advice of the Cabinet.

The government also tries to maintain racial harmony by deliberate policies such as compulsory military service for all males, an education system that uses English as the medium of instruction (Malay Chinese, English, and Tamil are all official languages), and housing policy that breaks up ethnic enclaves. The idea is to create the "Singapore" identity. Racial tolerance is couched in terms of national survival and identity. Multi-culturalism is strongly promoted (along with self-discipline, austerity, and respect for authority) as a matter of national identity.

JAMES CHIN

See also **Malays; Sikhs; Tamils**

Further Reading

Alatas, Syed Hussein, Khoo Kay Kim, and Kwa Chong Guan, *Malays/Muslims and the History of Singapore*, Singapore: Centre for Research on Islamic & Malay Affairs, 1998

Li, Tania, *Malays in Singapore: Culture, Economy, and Ideology*, Singapore: Oxford University Press, 1990

Pugalenthi, Sr., *Indian Pioneers of Singapore*, Singapore: VJ Times International, 1998

Rahim, Lily Zubaidah, *The Singapore Dilemma: The Political and Educational Marginality of the Malay Community*, Kuala Lumpur: Oxford University Press, 1998

Siddique, Sharon, and Nirmala Shotam-Gore, *Singapore's Little India, Past, Present, and Future*, 2nd edition, Singapore: Institute of Southeast Asian Studies, 1990

Walker, Anthony R., *New Place, Old Ways: Essays on Indian Society and Culture in Modern Singapore*, Delhi: Hindustan Pub. Corp., 1994

Singh, Tara (Sikh)

Tara Singh, also known as Master Tara Singh, was born into a Hindu family in the Malhotra subcaste of the Khatris. Although Singh kept the Hindu name of Nanak Chand for the first 17 years of his life, he converted to Sikhism in 1902. Founded circa 1500 by Guru Nānak in India as a progressive monotheistic religion based on the rejection of idolatry and caste, Sikhism's followers were Sikhs (seekers of truth). Singh's conversion to Sikhism resulted from attending the meetings of the Singh Sabha movement. A Sikh reform movement, Singh Sabha began in response to the decline of the Sikh faith in face of the increased activities of Christian missionaries and the Arya Samaj (a Hindu religious organization).

While his father's influence and the pro-British stance of the Singh Sabha movement made Singh a supporter of the British in his younger days, his political outlook changed when he became a student at Khalsa College, Amritsar, in 1903. By the time Singh graduated in 1907, he had decided to devote his life to the Sikh religion and community. As such he offered his services at a nominal rate to the Sikh community in Layallpur, provided it agreed to open a Sikh high school. The community agreed, and Singh became the head master of the school, thus earning the honorific title of *Master*.

Singh became an important figure in the Sikh politics at the time of the Gurdwara Reform movement in the early 1920s. Many of the old and historical *gurdwaras* (prayer palaces) were under the control of the *Mahants*—professional priests who usurped the offerings and income for their personal use. The reform movement aimed to free the *gurdwaras* from the control of priests and force them to comply with popular control. Singh was arrested at the Guru ka Bagh (the garden of the Guru) during a protest meeting against the *mahant* of a nearby *gurdwara*. He also joined the militant, anti-British Babar Akali movement in the period of its inception in 1921. When the Shiromani Gurdwara Prabhandhak Committee (SGPC) was formed to manage the Sikh shrines, Singh became a member initially, then a vice president and eventually the president in 1930 while he was still in jail.

Beginning in the 1920s, Singh took part in various Akali party mobilizations that often brought him in conflict with the authorities. When the Congress party launched the civil disobedience movement in 1930, Singh supported it and went to jail for his opposition to the colonial British government. He was charged with sedition and on trial for three years. It is a measure of his dissention that, from 1930 to 1967, Singh was arrested 14 times. In the 1930s and 1940s, Singh led several militant agitations in support of Akali claims. While some of these agitations were aimed at the colonial British government and others at the Unionist government, Singh always advocated on behalf of the Sikhs, who in turn rallied behind him.

During World War II Singh supported the British effort in face of the objections by the Indian nationalists; for him the goal was to secure political protection and advancement for the Sikhs and their causes. But at the same time, Singh joined the Quit India movement, a coalition of Indians who wanted the colonial British authority to leave India and return to Britain. When negotiations for independence began, Singh vehemently opposed any division (partition) of India. Then, as a move to frustrate the Muslim demands of a separate state (Pakistan) and as a move to consolidate the gains for the Sikh community, Singh broached the idea of Azad Punjab.

Also known as *Sikhistan* and *Khalistan*, Azad Punjab was the name given to the idea of the partition of the Punjab into two parts—one dominated by a Hindu and Sikh majority, and another dominated by a Muslim majority. While the name Azad Punjab was first mentioned in a resolution of the All India Akali Conference at Dahela Kalan on July 24, 1942, it was only on December 2, 1942, that Singh advocated the partition of the Punjab into two separate provinces. According to Singh's idea of partition, Azad Punjab was to comprise the following areas: Ambala, Jullunder, and Lahore Divisions; Lyallpur district out of Multan Division; and some portions of both the Montgomery and Multan Divisions. Singh wanted to maintain the 40, 40, and 20 balance of Hindu, Muslim, and Sikh percentages in the Azad Punjab.

However, after the partition of India in 1947, the Punjab in India resulted with a Hindu majority and Sikh minority. After independence Singh led the movement for Punjabi Suba: the idea that a Sikh majority state with the Sikh language, Punjabi, as its only official language was needed to protect the minority Sikhs from the overwhelming Hindu presence in India. When, at the instigation of the Arya Samaj (a Hindu religious reform movement in Bombay), the Hindus in the Punjab opted for Hindi as their first language in the national census, the Sikhs protested. But when, in 1957, the national government declared Punjab to be a bilingual state, with both Punjabi and Hindi as official languages, Singh mobilized the population in support of a Punjabi Suba, a Punjabi-speaking state.

On August 15, 1961, Singh began a fast until death at the *Harimandir Sahib* (the Golden Temple) in Amritsar, in order to force the Indian Prime Minister at the time, Jawaharlal Nehru, to accept the Sikh demand for a Punjabi state. Singh vowed that he would not break his fast if his demands were not accepted. But when Nehru responded with a personal letter promising to investigate the Sikh demands, Singh broke his fast after 43 days. Singh's failure to carry out his promise of fasting until death inspired the wrath of the Sikh people, and he was called before a council of *panj pyaras* (five Sikhs selected by the community to render decisions reflecting the will of the community) and punished for his actions. This incident destroyed the political career of Singh, but he did live to see the creation of a Punjabi Suba in 1966.

Biography

Tara Singh. Born June 24, 1885, in Harial, Rawalpindi, India (now in Pakistan). Studied at Public School in Rawalpindi; Khalsa College, Amritsar, B.A., 1907; Teacher Training College, Lahore, Teaching Diploma, 1908. Taught at Khalsa High School, Lyallpur, 1908–1920. Died in Chandigarh, India, November 22, 1967.

Selected Works

Meri Yaad
Meera Safarnama, 1969

AMANDEEP SANDHU

See also **Bhindranwale, Jarnail Sant (India-Sikh); Sikhs**

Further Reading

Bhullar, Rajwant, "Master Tara Singh and Struggle for Sikh Representation, 1920–47," *Panjab Past and Present* (Patiala), 24, no.1 (1990)
Brar, J., "Master Tara Singh and the Demand for Sikh Homeland," *Panjab Past and Present* (Patiala), 21, no.2 (1987)
Dhami, M., *Minority Leaders Image of the Indian Political System: An Exploratory Study of the Attitudes of Akali Leaders*, New Delhi: Sterling Publishers 1975
Kaur, Kuldip, *Akali Dal in Punjab Politics: Splits and Mergers*, New Delhi: Deep and Deep Publications, 1999
Lamba, Krishan, *Dynamics of the Punjabi Suba Movement*, New Delhi: Deep and Deep Publications, 1999
Sarhadi, Ajit, "Master Tara Singh and Sikh identity," *Punjab Journal of Politics* (Amritsar), 10, no.2 (1986)

Sinn Féin

Sinn Féin is an Irish Republican political party. It has transformed itself from its origins as the political wing of the Irish Republican Army to a party that urges peaceful and democratic means to unite Ireland.

The term *Sinn Féin* means "We Ourselves" in the ancient Gaelic language. The party was founded in 1905 by pacifist Arthur Griffith (1872–1922) who published *The United Irishmen*. He propounded passive resistance to British policies. Sinn Féin languished as a small party until it was mistakenly credited for instigating the Easter Rising, protesting British rule, that had been organized by Michael Collins (1890–1922) of the Irish Republican Brotherhood (IRB). The Easter Rising was suppressed by the British with more than 1,300 deaths. In response, the largely Catholic populace elected a majority of 73 Sinn Féin members to Parliament in 1918, Eamon de Valera (1882–1975) became Sinn Féin's president. However the members refused to take their seats. Instead, the members established their own Irish Assembly in Dublin, named it the *Dáil Eirean* and declared Irish independence from Britain. Sinn Féin founded the Irish Republican Army in 1919 as its unofficial military force.

In 1920 Britain and Collins, as *Dáil's* representative, concluded talks and compromised by splitting Ireland into two areas; the six counties in the northeast became Northern Ireland with a British Protestant majority and a minority of Catholics while the rest of Ireland was largely Catholic with a minority of Protestants. The Government of Ireland Act in 1920 was a political and social compromise. Consequently, Sinn Féin split into two factions: one led by Collins and Griffith who were protreaty and were supported by the Irish people, and the antitreaty faction led by deValera and including some members of the IRA who wanted a united Ireland and refused fidelity to King George V. Collins headed the army of the Irish Free State while DeValera headed a group called the Irregulars. Griffith disagreed with the physical force exuded by the IRA. Although Collins was Commander of the IRA and Minister of Finance while deValera was on a fundraising tour in the United State, real power lay with the IRA's 15,000 members who were led by hard line Republican Cathal Brugha (1874–1922).

During The Anglo Irish War from 1919 to 1921 guerilla warfare was the mainstay of IRA policy.

Both the Irish and the British committed atrocities during events that followed partition. The IRA killed the British while the British killed the Irish. The British Black and Tans military irregulars suppressed the nationalist groups led by Collins and the Irish people sided with the nonmilitant wing of Sinn Féin. A cease-fire was arranged in 1921 and the *Dáil* finally passed the treaty on January 7, 1922. The British supported the Free State government, quelled opposition, and killed Brugha by bombing the IRA headquarters. Homes were burned, 77 antitreaty followers were executed, and 11,000 were arrested. The IRA lost its moorings when deValera put a stop to resistance. The IRA had Collins killed in 1922. The Irregulars were defeated. On May 24, 1923, the Civil War was over after more 4,000 Irish had been killed.

In 1927, deValera and other antitreaty supporters split from the Republicans. He established the *Fianna Fail* party, becoming prime minister in 1932, and Sinn Féin nearly perished. Ireland became independent in 1948 but the British banned civil rights demonstrations and instituted internment. Protests occurred when it was discovered that more than 90 percent of the detainees were Catholics. By then the IRA had become Marxist oriented, ultimately losing the support of the Catholic minority.

Extremely poor social conditions led the Irish Catholics to fight in The Troubles from 1969 to 1972 with massive Republican support. The Northern Irish Catholics minority deemed they were considered unequal to the Protestants; they wanted equality with them as was their right as British citizens. Their civil rights movement began in 1968. They demanded improved housing, employment, and the right to vote as British citizens in British territory. The poor Catholics who did not pay taxes could not vote so "One man, one vote" became the slogan. Sinn Féin and the IRA became involved. The IRA split into two factions: the Official IRA and the violence-oriented Provisional IRA which resulted in the appearance of the British Ulster Volunteer Force.

Disparate groups believed contrasting things. Some Protestants agreed with Catholic demands while other Protestants disagreed and split into factions. The Battle of the Bogside on August 12, 1969, was a turning point. The Catholic majority in Londonderry peacefully demanded change. The British responded with unnecessary violence. Protesters saw the British army as the enemy trying to destroy them and saw the burnings in Belfast in 1969 as evidence. The Catholics used violence and the rump of the IRA was resurrected. The watershed was Bloody Sunday II on January 30, 1972, when illegal marchers approached British troops in Derry. The troops overreacted and 14 marchers were killed. This unified the Catholics across Ireland. World opinion sided with the Catholics. Northern Ireland's Parliament was suspended. The IRA received large numbers of recruits. Direct rule was introduced by the British in 1972 and the IRA remained violent. Sinn Féin meanwhile was a propaganda tool for the IRA; it raised the necessary funds and spoke for the IRA.

Meanwhile the Marxist Sinn Féin faction became the Workers Party and the other faction supported the provisional IRA. By this time Sinn Féin consisted of second- and third-generation members. One of these people was the intelligent Gerry Adams, leader of Sinn Féin since 1983, who made it a Republican political party determined to use electoralism rather than violence. Sinn Féin decided to take its seats in the *Dáil* in 1986. Adams altered IRA tactics and the militants were no longer in charge of policy. In August 1994 the IRA ceased its military operations after lengthy negotiations. Intermittent violence by the IRA thereafter brought it dishonor. Peace talks resumed and another cease-fire was declared in 1997. Peace talks resumed. A final peace agreement was reached after the people of both Northern Ireland and Ireland supported the peace agreement in a referendum held in May 1998. Sinn Féin members were elected to the *Dáil* and the IRA was disarmed.

Sinn Féin has endured the vagaries of volatile Irish politics. The party that began as a nationalist movement has evolved into a respectable Republican party that won the long fight to be democratically elected.

ANNETTE RICHARDSON

See also **Adams, Gerry (Northern Ireland Catholic); Catholics in Northern Ireland; Irish Republican Army; Northern Ireland**

Further Reading

Adams, Gerry, *Before the Dawn: An Autobiography*, New York: William Morrow & Co., 1997
Davis, Richard P., *Arthur Griffith and Non-Violent Sinn Féin*, Dublin: Anvil Books, 1974
Dillon, Martin, *The Dirty War*, London: Routlledge, 1990
Laffan, Michael, *The Resurrection of Ireland: The Sinn Féin Party, 1916–1923*, Cambridge: Cambridge University Press, 1999
Mackay, James, *Michael Collins: A Life*, Edinburgh: Mainstream Publishing, 1996
Taylor, Peter, *Provos: The IRA and Sinn Féin*, London: Bloomsbury, 1997

Slavery

Slavery is a bundle of social, political, and economic relationships in which persons were owned, dominated, and controlled by others. An essentialist definition of the slave by Nieboer is "a man who is the property of another, politically and socially at a lower level than the mass of the people, and performing compulsory labor" (Nieboer, *Slavery as an Industrial System*, 1910). Such ownership rights gave the master control over the labor and services of the slave. In many slave-holding societies, slaves were regarded as property. They could be bought, sold, and inherited like any other property. As such, slaves lacked both social and legal rights. They were socially and symbolically dead within the social structure in which they existed. Slaves were usually considered somehow different than their owners. They might belong to a different race, religion, nationality, or ethnic background. Focusing on such differences denied legal and other rights to slaves. Slavery is often characterized by loss of free will and the use of violence as a means of control and domination. Slaves were not often in a minority. If any protection was afforded the slave, it was chiefly as the property of his or her master who often had the power of life and death over the slave. Slaves constituted a significant portion of the population in many slave-holding societies. But the processes and means of obtaining slaves varied among slave-holding cultures and were important determinants of the demographics.

Historical Perspective

The practice of slavery is coeval with human existence and was a widespread phenomenon. Until the nineteenth and twentieth centuries when slavery was legally abolished in different parts of the world, this ubiquitous institution was widely accepted. Historically, traces of slavery are visible in every age and in every nation. Slavery existed in different forms and varying degrees in classical Europe, the Orient, Africa, and pre-Columbus America. Most of the ancient civilizations including Sumerians, Babylonians, and Egyptians practiced some form of slavery. Slavery was a well-developed institution in classical Rome. Slavery existed in ancient Greece, pre-literate China, Japan, and the ancient Near East. The Jews, the Greeks, the Romans, and the ancient Germans recognized and practiced slavery. The establishment of the Western and Northern Barbarians on the ruins of the Roman Empire, led to the extension of slavery in the newly settled areas. The barbaric codes, like the Roman, regarded slavery as an ordinary condition of humankind.

The conditions of slaves and slavery varied considerably. Slaves performed many different functions but the conditions of their existence were similar in societies with large slave populations. Slavery may have arisen from the economic use of war captives as in the ancient civilizations. The victors in battle often enslaved the losers. In ancient Egypt and Mesopotamia, slaves were captured aliens who were mainly used in domestic work for the upper classes. Slavery may have developed with the rise of private property. According to Marx, the development of ancient slave systems (Greco-Roman) was an organic accessory of the land and development of property. There is a legalistic exposition to the development of slavery. In Neo-Babylonian times (612–539 BCE) foreign slaves might have been used as agricultural labor (Orlando Peterson, 72). Over time, other reasons have been used to justify slavery.

Ancient Greece

Slavery played a major role in the political economy of ancient Greece. Palatine (palace) slavery seems to have existed in pre-Homeric times. From about 750 BCE, slavery expanded in response to the rise of a nobility and an agricultural economy. There were many different ways in which a person could become a slave in ancient Greece. Slaves were made of war captives, victims of piracy, and pawns who could not repay debts. Some were born into slavery as children of slaves. But the success of the Greek at wars increased the number of slaves.

Slavery in ancient Greece was mainly urban and industrial in character. The life of slaves varied greatly. Slaves were treated differently depending upon their purpose and duty. Urban slaves were treated more humanely. A household servant often had a fairly good situation. They were often treated almost as part of the family and were allowed to take part in the family rituals and sacrifices. Slaves worked throughout Greek society from wealthy households to sacred temples, farms, and mines. They worked as factory workers, shopkeepers, and as ship's crewmembers. Slaves in the mines suffered through terrible working conditions. The life of a mineworker or ship's crewmember was a life of misery and danger. These people usually did not live long because of the dangerous conditions of their work. Those forced into these conditions were often criminals condemned to death.

Greek law gave slave owners almost complete power over their slaves. The laws allowed any type of punishment except death. Slaves had no rights in courts of law. A slave could buy his own freedom or receive it as a gift for outstanding service. There were limits to what a slave could do. An ex-slave could almost never become a Greek citizen. They could not enter the Gymnasium or the Public Assembly. They could not use their own names, but were assigned names by their master.

Greek society was highly stratified in terms of class, race, and gender. The segregation of male and female roles within ancient Greece was justified by philosophical claims of the natural superiority of males. Slave women were at a disadvantage in Greek society because of their sex. Male slaves were assigned to agricultural and industrial work. Female slaves were assigned a variety of domestic duties, including shopping, fetching water, cooking, serving food, cleaning, child care, and wool working in wealthy households. Female slaves were often subjected to sexual exploitation.

Any children born of master-servant liaisons were disposed of because female slaves were prohibited from rearing children. Slave girls also performed unofficial services. Slave women were included in some religious affairs and could be initiated to the Eleusinian Mysteries, which celebrated the myth of Persephone. Thus, the fate of a Greek slave girl was determined by circumstance and more or less rested in the hands of her owners.

Romans

Slavery was a prevailing feature of all Mediterranean countries in antiquity, but the Romans had more slaves and depended on them more than any other people. In Rome's early years, most Romans worked their own small farms. The Punic Wars (264–146 BCE) changed Roman society dramatically. The war increased the number of slaves and the growth of Roman slavery. As Rome expanded and conquered its foreign neighbors, the slave population grew. These slaves were put to work in large plantations, which replaced the traditional agrarian system. These changes made the Roman Republic a slave-based society. The largest numbers of slaves were in Italy. In Rome there were great numbers in the imperial household and in the civil service. Rich individuals also had large numbers of slaves as a status symbol and for work. It is estimated that around two million slaves out of a population of about six million at the time of Augustus lived in Rome and Italy. The practice of slavery became more common in the city of Rome. Here the slave population grew to be a third of the total population by 31 BCE.

Roman law treated slaves brutally. Many laws concerning slavery were developed to deal with the status and treatment of slave. Slaves could not possess property, enter into contracts, or marry. If a slave owner died violently within his own house, his slaves could be executed because they had not prevented his death. However, a slave was permitted to buy his freedom and become a Roman citizen. Such brutal treatment infuriated the slaves. Since slaves usually greatly outnumbered their owners, revolts were very frequent. Spartacus led one of the most famous slave revolts. His army of 90,000 defeated two Roman armies before he was killed in battle and thousands of his soldiers captured and crucified. Over time, Roman slaves shouldered more responsibilities in agriculture, the home, and the government. Free Romans assumed that slaves could accomplish any service. Thus, they excused themselves from practical concerns and the need to learn practical skills. Some historians believe that this attitude led to the fall of Rome and gave rise to serfdom in the Middle Ages in Europe.

Asia

Slavery had existed in parts of Asia for thousands of years. As one of the world's oldest civilizations, China had a long history of slavery. Slaves were made of war captives and kidnap victims. People also sold their wives, children, or themselves into slavery to satisfy debts. Slaves worked as household servants, in agriculture, construction, and as government bureaucrats. Slaves could be adopted by their masters and, in some cases, inherited wealth from their masters. Wang Mang abolished slavery in China in 17 CE, but it was restored when he lost power six years later. Slavery was not officially abolished until 1910.

Slavery existed in ancient India as early as 100 BCE. By 500 BCE slavery was fully established. Laws regulated the lives of slaves, most of whom performed agricultural labor. The Muslim conquest in the twelfth and thirteenth century increased the importance of slaves in administration and the army. By 1841, India had about 8 million slaves. Slavery was abolition in India in the nineteenth century although it persisted in different forms in the twentieth century. Slavery was a major institution in Thailand where the slave population was about 25 percent of the population in the mid-nineteenth century. In Burma, household slavery was more benign except in the case of the pagoda slaves. Pagoda slaves were considered unclean and were greatly despised (Patterson, 72). Slavery was important in Malaysia before European contact where slaves provided domestic service. Slavery was of minor importance in Japan and may have been largely employed in agriculture. In Korea, however, slavery was a very important institution. War captives were enslaved and executed a variety of tasks. Slavery gained importance when war captives began to be distributed to the nobility as booty. The slave population was significant in the development of large agricultural estates owned by the nobility. The urban middle class also owned large numbers of slaves. The institution of slavery continued to be important in Korea until the Japanese conquest in 1905.

Africa

Slavery was well-developed in some African societies before the Portuguese reached the coast of West Africa

1113

in the middle of the fifteenth century. But the conditions of slaves and the nature of slavery varied greatly. Kinship structures, economic conditions, political systems, and institutions influenced the nature of African slavery. These factors also determined the system of incorporation into the world of the freeborn. Slaves were used by some of the empires in Africa in production prior to European contact. In other areas, they were used as domestic help. Typically, slaves were made of war captives, criminals, and people in debt. But slaves were often incorporated into the new community or kin group.

In some African societies, slavery was not always confused with the notion of superiority and inferiority. On the contrary, it was common for African owners to adopt slave children or to marry slave women. Such slave women became full members of the family. This was because wealth was measured in people in many African societies. In some instances slaves of talent accumulated property and achieved very high status. Kings sent slaves to govern provinces while some occupied important positions in courts. But between enslavement and incorporation into a new community, the slave had neither rights nor any social identity (Klein, 2). Slavery was not a lifetime status—people might be born free, made slaves for a period, and then be free again for the rest of their lives. Slavery in Africa was a punishment but slaves typically had some rights. They could marry, own property, and inherit from their owners. They could own their own slaves. The children of slaves were not regarded as the property of their owners but were often free and did not generally inherit the status of their parents.

Capitalism played a major role in the transformation of African slavery. The difference between pre-Atlantic slavery in Africa and the Atlantic slave trade emerged from the profit motives of the Europeans and the social structure of African slavery. Plantation slavery developed in eastern Africa in the nineteenth century. The African rulers of Zanzibar relied on slave labor just as white plantation owners of the American South did. During the nineteenth century, African slaves composed up to 90 percent of the island's population. Slaves worked on the island's clove plantations. This fueled the demand for new slaves, driving a vigorous slave trade that brought Africans from East and Central Africa. Growing British influence in the 1860s and 1870s led to the end of slavery in Zanzibar. In parts of West Africa, large-scale use of slaves in agriculture did not emerge until the transition from slave trade to commodity trade in the nineteenth century.

Islam and Slavery

Slaves were widely used in the Islamic societies until the early periods of the twentieth century. Islam permitted enslaving war captives but it prohibited enslaving other Muslims. Those faithful to foreign religions could live as protected persons, *dhimmis*, under Muslim rule (as long as they maintained payment of taxes called *Kharaj* and *Jizya*). However, the spread of the Islamic Empire resulted in a much harsher interpretation of the law. A *dhimmis* could be enslaved if he was unable to pay the taxes. Islam also permitted the sexual propagation of slaves to generate more slaves for their owner.

Slaves were obtained through purchase, conquest, and as tribute from vassal states. Children of slaves were also slaves. Eunuchs fetched higher prices than other males. This encouraged the castration of slaves. The majority of these slaves came from Europe and Africa. Black Africans were transported to the Islamic Empire across the Sahara and up the coast of East Africa to the Persian Gulf. This trade had been well-entrenched for over 600 years before the Europeans arrived and had contributed to the expansion of Islam across North Africa. During the time of the Ottoman Empire, the majority of slaves were obtained by raiding in Africa. Russian expansion had put an end to the source of female and male slaves from the Caucasians. The women were highly priced in the harem, and the men in the military. Military slaves were favored in Islamic slavery. By the ninth century slave armies were in use across the whole of the Islamic Empire. The early slave armies tended to be white, taken from Russia and Eastern Europe. The first independent Muslim ruler of Egypt relied on black (Nubian) and white (Mamaluks) slaves for military service. In North Africa black slaves from Nubia and Sudan were extensively used in the army in Tunisia and Morocco.

The Qur'an prescribed a humanitarian approach to slavery. Islamic law required owners to treat slaves well and provide medical treatment, but slaves had no right to be heard in court or own property. They could only marry with the permission of their owner. Conversion to Islam did not automatically give a slave freedom nor confer freedom to their children. Highly educated slaves and those in the military could win their freedom, but those used for basic duties rarely achieved freedom. Mortality rates were high and still significant as late as the nineteenth century in North Africa.

New World Slavery

Europeans had experimented with plantation slavery in the Mediterranean islands prior to the expansion into the New World. Italian merchants produced sugar in Cyprus, Sicily, Crete, and Rhodes using slave labor from a variety of sources, including Greece, Turkey, and Bulgaria. The Portuguese began to explore the Atlantic islands in the fifteenth century where they developed sugar plantations based on the Mediterranean model. From the sixteenth century on, the Portuguese established sugar plantations on the Islands of Sao Tome and Principe with slave labor drawn from the West African mainland. Thus the use of African slaves spread from the Mediterranean to islands off the coast of West Africa. In the sixteenth century, Sao Tome became the largest single producer of sugar for the European market. These initial experiments owned and run by European overseers and manned by African slave labor, formed the blue print for the plantations in the Americas and the Caribbean.

Portuguese explorers reached Brazil in 1500. The establishment of sugar plantation in Perambuco marked the beginning of the New World plantation slavery. Europeans began enslaving Africans in the fifteenth century after the attempt to enslave Indians failed. The attempt by the Dutch to capture this region failed and they moved to the Caribbean islands, where they established their own plantations. When Spanish and Portuguese sea captains began to explore the Americas they took some African servants with them. Some of these Africans proved to be excellent explorers. European colonization and exploitation of the New World followed swiftly upon Columbus's voyage of discovery of 1492. After the arrival of the Europeans there was a sharp decline in the local population of most of the islands in the Caribbean Sea. This created the problem of labor needed to exploit the natural resources of these islands. The Europeans came up with a solution by the enslavement of Africa. Africans were immune to many tropical diseases and survived better than the Native American population. They were also cheaper to obtain than Europeans or people from other areas.

The Atlantic slave trade was different from earlier forms of slavery in several respects. It was the first form of slavery that was solely motivated by commercial incentives. The African slave trade was a capitalist invention. The large-scale capitalist mode of production, which required cheap labor, triggered the African slave trade. It was capitalism that introduced chattel slavery and the enslavement of Africans on a colossal scale. Slaves became profitable after the discovery of the New World and the subsequent insatiable demand for workers on the plantations.

In the seventeenth and eighteenth centuries, Caribbean sugar plantations satisfied Europe's hunger for sugar. Cultivating sugar in the heat and humidity of the tropics was hard and miserable work. It was the demand for sugar and the development of the small Atlantic islands that gave the New World slavery its character. It has been estimated that over a million people lived in Cuba before the arrival of the Europeans. Twenty-five years later only 2,000 people were left. Large numbers had been killed, while others died of starvation, disease, suicide, or from the consequences of being forced to work long hours in the gold mines. Planters brought Africans to the islands instead.

The Europeans tapped into the existing trade networks. An estimated 15 million Africans were transported to the Americas between the middle of the fifteenth century to the middle of the nineteenth century. To maximize their profits slave ships often carried twice their maximum capacity from Africa to the Americas. It has been estimated that only about half of the slaves taken from Africa reached the Americas. A large number of slaves died on the journey from diseases and the horrible conditions during the Middle passage. Chained together by their hands and feet, the slaves had little room to move. Others committed suicide. Many of the slaves were crippled for life as a consequence of the way they were chained up on the ship.

Slaves were initially made up of war captives, criminals, and debtors. The demand for slaves in the Americas required new ways to enslave Africans. Soon slave traders turned to kidnapping and armed raids. These methods provided steady supply of Africans to the slave market in the Americas. The need for more slaves increased warfare as Africans traded guns for slaves. British merchants eventually dominated the market for over 100 years. They built coastal forts in Africa where they kept the captured Africans until the arrival of the slave ships. The merchants obtained the slaves from African chiefs in exchange for goods from Europe. British slave traders shipped huge numbers of Africans to English, French, and Spanish colonies in the Americas. They made enormous profits, and much of this wealth later helped to finance the Industrial Revolution.

Slaves were extensively utilized in Spanish America. Spain's colonies in Latin America had an enormous need for labor. Their gold and silver mines needed workers. Their plantations and cattle ranches needed field hands. The Spanish first enslaved Native Americans, but the Indians suffered terribly from European diseases and miserable working conditions. With massive decline in the Native American population, Spain, like other Europeans, looked elsewhere for labor. They began importing Africans. The Spanish imported millions of Africans—more than the British and Americans brought to the United States.

Portuguese colonists in Brazil needed slaves for their sugar plantations and gold and silver mines. At first, they enslaved the Indians of Brazil. The Indians suffered greatly under the miserable conditions of slavery. The Portuguese turned to Africans. By the nineteenth century, Brazil had about 2 million slaves—half of the country's entire population. Brazil became one of the greatest slave-holding nations in the New World. Many Brazilian plantation owners lived in distant cities and left overseers in charge of the plantations. Overseers had no financial reason to keep slaves healthy, and often treated them brutally. The average life span for a slave in Brazil was about seven years. The Brazilian slave trade did not end until the 1850s and the slaves were not freed until 1888.

In the seventeenth century Europeans began to establish settlements in the Americas. Forms of servitude akin to slavery were already practiced in Virginia's tobacco fields. Indentured servants served longer and subjected to more rigorous punishment and traded as commodities. The division of the land into smaller units under private ownership led to the emergence of the plantation system. Starting in Virginia the system spread to the New England colonies. Plantation crops such as tobacco, rice, sugar and cotton were labor intensive. European immigrants had gone to America to own their own land and were reluctant to work for others. Indentured servants and convicts from Britain were not enough to satisfy the demand for labor. Planters therefore began to purchase slaves.

Unlike the other parts of the Americas, the 13 English colonies in mainland North America received fewer slaves. This was because sugar dominated plantations and slavery elsewhere in the colonial Americas. In colonial North America, tobacco plantations dominated the Chesapeake region, particularly Virginia and Maryland. Rice plantations were in South Carolina and Georgia. These employed the most Africans. The presence of Africans began to increase from the 1670s. The Dutch began to supply increased numbers of Africans to Virginia. Twenty African slaves were brought to Jamestown, Virginia, in 1619. At first these came from the West Indies but by the late eighteenth century they came directly from Africa. The conversion to slavery had important advantages over indentured servitude. The master had absolute control over the time or work he could command from his slaves. Masters could also increase their production capacity by putting more slave men, women, and children to work.

A series of complex colonial laws began to relegate the status of Africans and their descendants to slavery in the United States. The legal recognition of slavery formed the basis of racial separation. Thus race and racial stereotypes and the insistence on the supremacy of whites created the tenacious contest of American slavery. Various slave laws and mechanisms were used to control slaves. These included the forced separation of parents and children, the sexual exploitation of slave women, and the branding of slaves. Conditions in the plantations were bad. Slaves were in the fields from sunrise to sunset and at harvest time they worked eighteen-hour days. Women worked the same hours as the men and pregnant women were expected to continue until their children was born. The death rate among slaves was high. To replace their losses, planters encouraged the slaves to have children. Child bearing started around the age of 13, and by 20 women slaves would be expected to have four or five children. Young women were often advertised for sale as "good breeding stock". The United States outlawed the transatlantic slave trade in 1808, but the domestic slave trade and illegal importation continued for several decades.

Slave Life and Rebellions

For many decades, African slaves lived in drudgery. Slaves were forced into a lifetime of servitude. Gradually, slaves lost their rights and became mere property. The law gave masters total power over slaves, including the right to kill their slaves. Working conditions were terrible. Field slaves worked from dawn to dusk six days a week, with a brief break at midday. They ate very little food. These conditions drove up the death rate. About one-third of Africans died within three years of arrival in the West Indies. To maintain the slave population, more Africans were imported. It was cheaper for many slave owners to work their slaves to death and replace them with new imports.

On large plantations this power was delegated to overseers. These men were under considerable pressure from the plantation owners to maximize profits.

They did this by bullying the slaves into increasing productivity. The punishments used against slaves judged to be under-performing included whipping. Sometimes slave owners mutilated and branded their slaves as an example for others. Slave owners in Virginia smoked slaves by putting them in tobacco smokehouses. But the treatment of slaves varied with different slave systems, and so did the forms of resistance.

Enslaved Africans did not accept their situation. Rebellions were frequent and they often mutinied onboard slave ships. Many slaves aboard the ships often sacrificed their own lives by jumping overboard. In the New World, slaves revolted and resisted in different ways. Slaves ran away from the plantations. They formed maroon communities throughout the Caribbean and Latin America. The resistance to slavery is demonstrated time and time again in the successful and unsuccessful attempts to escape from bondage. But harsh discipline crushed most of them. The owners' equal determination to protect their investment is demonstrated by their assiduousness in pursuing runaway slaves. Advertisements on flyers or in newspapers aided bounty hunters and kidnappers, as well as bona fide law enforcement officers, who worked together to return escapees to their owners. States with large numbers of slaves introduced their own slave codes. The main idea behind these codes was to keep the slaves under the tight control of their owners. The death penalty was introduced for a whole range of offences. Slaves could be executed for murder, rape, burglary, arson, and assault upon a white person. Plantation owners believed that severe punishment would deter slaves rebellions.

But punishment did not often stop escapes and revolts. The revolt on the French colony of Saint Domingue (now Haiti) in the 1790s succeeded. The slaves under Toussaint L'Ouverture defeated the French and established the Republic of Haiti—the world's first black republic. In the United States, Nat Turner, a slave owned by Joseph Travis of Southampton, Virginia, believed that he had been chosen by God to lead a slave rebellion. On August 21, 1831, Turner and seven fellow slaves murdered Travis and his family. Over the next two days, Turner's band killed around 60 white people in Virginia. Turner had hoped that his action would cause a massive slave uprising but only 75 joined his rebellion. Over 3,000 members of the state militia were sent to deal with Turner's gang, and they were soon defeated. In retaliation, more than a hundred slaves were killed. Turner was captured six weeks later and

executed. In the United States, slaves escaped from the American south into Canada and other safe havens in the United States.

Abolition

Abolitionist movements were rare in the history of slavery because there were few critiques before the nineteenth century. There was no moral and economic rationale for the abolition of slavery until the nineteenth and twentieth century. Advocates against slavery did not exist because such moral authorities as the church found justifications for slavery. However, several factors account for the abolition of slavery in the nineteenth century. There were those who saw slavery as morally wrong. Only when the British public turned against slavery did Britain try to end, or abolish it in Europe and the Americas. Intellectual and political factors combined with the declining fortunes of the trade to make the abolition of slavery inevitable. Some people in Britain began protesting slavery in the late 1700s. Many still defended slavery, saying that abolition would ruin the British economy. Efforts to abolish slavery failed in Parliament until abolitionists exposed the horrors of the slave trade. These reports fueled public distaste for the institution. Slavery within England was outlawed in 1772. In 1807, the Abolition Act ended the British slave trade. And in 1833, the Emancipation Act abolished slavery in all British colonies. The success of the slave revolts in the French colony of Saint Dominique compelled France to abolish slavery in its remaining colonial territories in 1848. The Spanish American colonies followed by abolishing slavery between 1823 and 1886.

Contemporary Forms of Slavery

The nature of slavery has changed historically, but it continued in different forms into the twentieth century. After the communist revolution in China, the government established concentration camps called *laogai*. Most of the people imprisoned there were political prisoners. People in these camps were forced to work as slave laborers. In the 1920s and 1930s, young girls (*mui tsai*) were traded and enslaved as prostitutes. Nazi Germany enslaved millions of people. Forced labor slavery began in 1942. They sent communists, socialists, Jews, Gypsies, gays, and prostitutes to concentration camps. Prisoners were worked to death in chemical and rocket factories. Those too weak to work were killed. The slave camps were part of a larger Nazi effort to exterminate millions of Jews and other people. Slavery continues in some form today, especially in the developing countries of the world. In some parts of Asia, children are sold into bondage or forced to work against their will. Young men and women are forced into prostitution. Many people from the developing countries are lured to the West under different guises where they end up working under conditions of slavery in households, factories, and as prostitutes.

CHIMA J. KORIEH

See also **Brazil; Colonialism; Civil War, United States; Cuba; Haiti; Race**

Further Reading

Bradley, K.R., *Slaves and Masters in the Roman Empire*, New York: Oxford University Press, 1987

Coniff, Michael L., and Thomas J. Davis, *Africans in the Americas: A History of the Black Diaspora*, New York: St. Martin's Press, 1994

Engerman, Stanley, Seymour Drescher, and Robert Paquette, editors, *A Historical Guide to World Slavery*, New York: Oxford University Press, 1998

Finlay, Moses I., editor, *Classical Slavery*, London and Totowa, New Jersey: Frank. Cass, 1987

Kopytoff, Igor, "Slavery," *Annual Review of Anthropology*, 11 (1982)

Klein, Martin, *Slavery and Colonial Rule in French West Africa*, Cambridge: Cambridge University Press, 1998

Maine, H.S., *Ancient Law: Its Connection with the Early History of Society and Its Relation to Modern Ideas*, London: Murray, 1861

Miller, Joseph C., *Slavery and Slaving in World History: A Bibliography, 1900–1991*, Millwood, New York: Kraus International Publications, 1993

Morgan, L.H., *Ancient Society, or Researches in the Lines of Human Progress from Slavery through Barbarism to Civilization*, New York: Kerr, 1877

Nieboer, H.J., *Slavery as an Industrial System*, 2nd edition, Hague: Nijhoff, 1910

Northrup David, editor, *The Atlantic Slave Trade*, 2nd edition, Boston: Houghton Mifflin Company, 2002

Patterson, Orlando, *Slavery and Social Death: A Comparative Study*, Cambridge, Massachusetts: Harvard University Press, 1982

Watson, Alan, *Roman Slave Law*, Baltimore: Johns Hopkins University Press, 1987

Williams, Eric, *Capitalism and Slavery*, The University of Carolina Press, 1972

Slovakia

Capsule Summary

Country name: Slovak Republic
Location: Eastern Europe, bordered by the Czech Republic, Poland, Ukraine, Hungary, and Austria.
Total Population: 5,430,033 (July 2003)
Ethnic Populations: Slovak (85.7%); Hungarian (10.6%); Roma (1.6%) (the 1992 census figures underreport the Gypsy/Romany community, which is about 500,000); Czech, Moravian, Silesian (1.1%); Ruthenian and Ukrainian (0.6%); German (0.1%); Polish (0.1%); other (0.2%) (1996)
Languages: Slovak (official), Czech, Hungarian, Polish, and Ukrainian
Religions: Roman Catholic (60.3%), atheist (9.7%), Protestant (8.4%), Orthodox (4.1%), other (17.5%)

The Slovak Republic is a new East European democracy that gained its political independence in 1993, in the aftermath of the 1989 Velvet Revolution in former Czechoslovakia. The history of the Slovak people encompasses a millennium—one thousand years of struggle for cultural survival. Although the country has not been on the map of Europe, the Slovaks were there for centuries.

Like in all East European nation-states, the population of modern Slovakia is multiethnic. The Slovaks dominate, but among several minority groups the ethnic Hungarians are the most numerous, followed by the Roma people (Gypsies), Czechs, Ukrainians, Germans, Moravians, and Poles.

The Slovakian landscape is predominantly mountainous with the highest elevations reaching over 8,000 feet. The capital of Slovakia is Bratislava. It is located in the southwestern outskirts of the country, on the Danube River. The country is landlocked.

History

Slovaks are western Slavs. They stem from the Slavic people who probably migrated to Eastern and Central

Europe from the Euro-Asian frontier sometime during the fifth and sixth centuries CE. Their origin remains a mystery and the subject of anthropological and historical debates. The Slavic farmers who settled between the Danube and the Carpathian Mountains adapted well to the local ecological conditions. They organized and maintained the first Slavic-ruled state known as the Great Moravian Kingdom of the ninth and tenth centuries CE. The Kingdom became most powerful under the reign of Svatopluk of Nitra at the end of the ninth century. At its peak the Great Moravian Kingdom controlled areas beyond the Carpathians to the north and most of the territory later known as Czechoslovakia.

The Kingdom was threatened primarily by the Magyars (Hungarians), non-Slavic nomads, who settled in the region in the eighth century CE, and invaded the northern plains of the Danube Basin, cutting off the Slovak lands from the rest of the Great Moravian Kingdom. After the battle of Bratislava in 907, the victorious Hungarians established their ruling over the eastern portion of the Great Moravian Kingdom, the region predominantly settled by Slovaks. This was the beginning of a thousand-year struggle of the Slovak people to regain their political independence. For a millennium the territories populated by Slovaks have been incorporated in various non-Slavic states, namely Hungarian and Austrian. Eventually, in the beginning of the twentieth century, after World War I, Slovakia has became a part of a Czech-dominated state called Czecho-Slovakia (later Czechoslovakia), and finally, in 1993, gained political independence. Regardless of the prolonged lack of political representation, the Slovaks have survived as an ethnic group culturally distinct from the Czech and other Slavic populations of the region.

Society and Culture

The majority of Slovak citizens (69 percent) practice Roman Catholicism; the second-largest group are Protestants (9 percent). About 2,300 Jews remain of the estimated pre-World War II population of 120,000. The official state language is Slovak, a Slavic language, but Hungarian is also widely spoken in the south and enjoys a co-official status in some regions.

Cultural influence from Western Europe on the Slovak territories is ancient. The Hungarian kingdom in Eastern Europe that dominated for some time was a multiethnic state. At the top of the social hierarchy were the Hungarian nobility and the Slovak landowners,

followed by foreigners (among them Germans and Jews, who settled in Nitra in the twelfth century CE and only some of whom owned land), and the peasants (predominantly Slovaks, who did not own land). Although politically insignificant, peasants were free to migrate. At the bottom of the social structure were prisoners of war (slaves), the property of nobility.

Some influential noble Slovak families gain power during the thirteenth and fourteenth centuries and created an oligarchy that in fact ruled Slovakia. The end of the fourteenth and the fifteenth centuries witnessed more foreign influence forcing social changes, which materialized in rapid urbanization. Louis I granted several privileges to the Slovak inhabitants of the kingdom, including equality in their voting privileges with the German colonists and Hungarians. The multiethnic towns were obliged to accept bilingualism.

In the beginning of the fifteenth century Slovakia was a scene of social unrest, which erupted all over Europe due to economic and political instability during the fourteenth century. The crisis also involved the Church, and neighboring Bohemia became the center of religious upheaval, which erupted with the Jan Hus revolt. Hussites were present in Slovakia but their influence seemed to have been rather limited. The spread of Reformation ideas in the fifteenth century had introduced new ways of thinking about politics, economy, and social issues. The most significant outcome of the Reformation and Counter-Reformation was the acceptance of cultural richness and diversity.

The Turkish occupation of the Hungarian Plains in the sixteenth century caused an influx of the Hungarians to the Slovak area, including Hungarian aristocracy, who had profoundly influenced the Slovak social structure and contributed to the urbanization of many Slovak towns. By the end of the sixteenth century there were 150 towns in Slovakia with over 1,000 guilds.

While the sixteenth and early seventeenth centuries were intellectually challenging, the end of the seventeenth and the beginning of the eighteenth century were marked by social unrest and rebellions against the Austrian Habsburgs. The Habsburg rule (1526 to 1830) profoundly impacted the Hungarization (or Magyarization) of Slovakia by slowing it down and favoring the German-influenced culture. German replaced Latin as the language of administration and schooling for example.

The eighteenth century was the origin of the nationalistic movement, which materialized a century later as a part of widespread pan-Slavic consciousness. The Slovak language was gaining popularity outside the household, in administration and the educational system. Slovak script developed as a combination of local dialects impacted by the Czech language orthography. Although the Slovaks had been part of the Hungarian state for centuries, the end of the eighteenth century witnessed the beginning of the national awakening, which slowly materialized into the early twentieth century.

For Slovaks, nationalism was problematic because as a collection of disparate ethnicities, the people did not necessarily share a national past. Their empire had been in fact a multiethnic and multicultural political entity. The Slovak leaders realized however that the most efficacious approach towards political independence was to create a national consciousness. A number of social circles emerged in Slovakia to promote these ideas and oppose Hungarian assimilation and cultural dominance in 1848–1849.

In 1867 the Habsburg lands in central Europe were reconstituted as the dual monarchy of Austria-Hungary. As early as 1861 education in secondary Catholic schools began using the Slovak language. In 1863 an institution of Slovak culture, the so-called *Matica slovenska*, opened to become the center of education, and national identity, which the authorities closed in 1875. The Memorandum of the Slovak Nation was the most significant document produced by the Slovak leaders in the nineteenth century; it illuminated basic principles about Slovak cultural and political autonomy within the Empire. Politically, they wanted to create a North Hungarian Slovak District, where the Slovak language would be the official language of administration. The economic and political turmoil of the second half of the nineteenth century caused a massive immigration from Slovakia (approximately 30,000 immigrants annually).

The two regions, Czechia and Slovakia, merged into one political unit on October 28, 1918, creating Czechoslovakia and officially ending almost a thousand years of Hungarian supremacy over Slovaks. The merge, however did not create a free Slovak state. The breakup of the Austro-Hungarian Empire in 1918 gave the Slovaks hope for creating their political representation but the lack of political leadership, administrative structure, and political center was troublesome. Therefore the idea of merging with the Czechs was amplified and Slovaks have been incorporated once again into a political structure controlled by others. The first year of semi-independence was a struggle for political recognition. For a short time Eastern Slovakia was under Soviet rule. Despite the steps undertaken by Slovak politicians towards greater autonomy, their attempts failed.

During the First Czechoslovak Republic the emphasis was on building a Czechoslovak nation. The Slovak territories were modernized and industrialized, but the region also suffered several economic hardships. Since the beginning of the 1920s cultural life and education flourished. Universities, the national theater, and the national philharmonic orchestra were founded in Bratislava. Almost 200 Slovak-language newspapers and journals were published and Slovak national autonomy overwhelmingly emerged in the 1930s.

The first Slovak republic existed from 1939 until the end of World War II in Europe in 1945. Slovaks gained independence at the time of peace but the existence of independent Slovakia was tied to wartime. The fate of the newly born state depended on the interplay between ideology and politics of the time. The new country was not recognized by the United States and France, and Great Britain withdrew their support, primarily because the Slovak government had signed a treaty with Nazi Germany despite protests among Slovak intellectuals in the Democratic and Communist parties. On March 14, 1939, Slovakia declared its independence and became another state in Central Europe under control of the Third Reich and later communist rule.

Neighbors such as the Czechs, Hungarians, Austrians, and Russians have always dominated Slovaks. The recent independence came in January 1993 as a consequence of the splitting in East Europe and the fall of the Soviet Union in 1991. The Velvet Revolution of 1989–1990 established democratic government in Czechoslovakia, but it took another three years until the second Slovak Republic was proclaimed. The Slovaks and the Czechs agreed to a peaceful separation on January 1, 1993. Slovakia was invited to join NATO and the EU in 2002. Ethnic tensions have not, despite democracy, ended in Slovakia. The Roma minority have in recent years faced discrimination and human rights abuses at the hands of the government. Roma have been forced into slums, segregated areas on the outskirts of cities, usually with poor housing conditions.

The economy has grown 3 percent in 2002 and enjoys a higher per capita gross domestic product (GDP) than other transitional countries in Western Europe. The 2002 estimate for per capita GDP was $19,200.

LUDOMIR LOZNY

See also **Germans; Poles; Roma (Gypsies); Slovaks; Ukrainians**

Further Reading

Dvornik, Francis, The *Making of Central and Eastern Europe*, Gulf Breeze: Academic International Press, 1974

Kirschbaum, Stanislav J., *A History of Slovakia. The Struggle for Survival*, New York: St. Martin's Griffin Press, 1995
Turnock, David, *Eastern Europe: A Historical Geography 1815–1945*, London: Routledge, 1988

Slovaks

Capsule Summary

Location: North Carpathian region of Europe, mostly in the territory of Slovakia
Total Population: approximately 4.5 million
Language: Slovak
Religions: Roman Catholic, Evangelical Protestantism

The Slovak nation is a young one, having proclaimed its independence from Czechoslovakia on January 1, 1993. Approximately 85 percent (4.5 million) of the population of Slovakia are Slovaks; in addition there are small minority groups scattered across the territory of the former Austro-Hungarian Empire. Minorities live chiefly in the Czech Republic (3.5 percent of the population), the Vojvodina autonomous province of Serbia (3.16 percent), the Carpathian region of Ukraine (0.59 percent), Croatia (0.12 percent), Hungary (0.07 percent, mainly in Bekes county), and in Romania (0.25 percent). In all these regions they have been settled since the eighteenth century, when the Ottoman Turks were driven out from Hungary. Other small scattered groups of Slovaks reside in the Vienna region of Austria, 0.06 percent in Serbia proper, 0.01 percent in Montenegro and others in the Southern border region of Poland.

Slovak society is relatively divided along religious, historical, and language lines. The Czech language dominated since the fourteenth century and was adopted by Slovak priests and teachers as the language of literature. Protestantism emerged from the influence of the Czech Hussites, and the Catholic masses looked with suspicion on the evangelical leaders of the 1848–1849 revolution. Until the eighteenth century, the Slovak people lived in harmony within the Hungarian majority and the Hungarian successes in the battles against the Turks were considered the Slovaks' as well.

Later the dialect from the Western Trnava region, used by Catholics, was called literary Slovak, but the evangelicals protested it and gradually this became Czech as well, due to the region's proximity to Moravia. The Czechs did not consider the Slovak a nation and deemed their language as primitive. The present-day Slovak language is closely related to the Polish and Czech languages. Slovak is similar to Czech especially in written form (because the Slovak literary language has taken over Czech spelling), but differs from it both phonetically and grammatically. Struggles between the Czechs and the Slovaks did not change until the 1840s, when linguist and philosopher Ludovit Stur (1815–1856), became the chief figure of the Slovak movement. Today a significant portion of the Slovak people are nationalist, considering national dominance a priority before social, cultural, and economic development. The only criteria needed to claim Slovak identity is to speak the language.

The rise of Slovakian nationalism in the late nineteenth and early twentieth centuries arose as a product of centuries of domination by Hungarians, Czechs, Germans and finally Soviet rule. The first Slovak republic existed from 1939 until the end of World War II in Europe in 1945, when it fell under control of Nazi Germany. On August 29, 1944, 60,000 Slovak underground troops rebelled against the Nazis in what became known as the Slovak National Uprising. Although they did little to stop the superior Nazi forces, such an act of resistance became an important historical landmark for the Slovaks and further cemented national consicousness. The Slovaks considered the 1968 Soviet invasion of Slovakia, Moravia, and much of Bohemia as the victory of their communist leaders over the Czechs, enabling Slovaks to occupy important offices in Prague, which fueled even more the Czechs' hatred of them. The Slovak national ideology considered every non-Slovak as an alien and the foreign entrepreneurs, other values, and languages as dangerous. The emergence of the Slovak National Party and the racist Stur Society (named for the nationalist that persecuted ethnic minorities) were manifestations of nationalism and growing tensions.

The 1970s were also characterized by the development of a Slovak-influenced dissident movement that rose in reaction to the aforementioned movements. On January 1, 1977, more than 250 human rights activists signed a manifesto called *Charter 77*, criticizing the government for failing to support human rights. Charter 77 was an informal civic initiative or group in Czechoslovakia active from 1977 to 1992 that opposed Communist normalization, particularly in the 1980s. Reactions against the members of the group—who were characterized as "antistate, antisocialist, and demogogues"—was severe and included loss of citizenship, detention, trial, and imprisonment. Václav Havel (later to be the first president of the Czech republic) was active in the group and also later tried for subversion.

Slovaks celebrated the end of Soviet rule in 1989 and the creation of an independent state, Slovakia, in 1993 as a parliamentary democracy.

LAZLO KOCSIS

See also **Czech Republic; Slovakia**

Further Reading

Daniel, David P., and Milan Strhan, compilers, Slovakia and the Slovaks: A Concise Encyclopedia, Bratislava: Encyclopedical Institute of the Slovak Academy of Sciences: Goldpress Publishers, 1994

Johnson, Owen V., *Slovakia, 1918–1938: Education and the Making of a Nation*, Boulder: East European Monographs and New York: Columbia University Press, 1985

Mikus, Joseph A., *Slovakia and the Slovaks*, Washington: Three Continents Press, 1977

———, *Slovakia: A Political and Constitutional History: With Documents*, Bratislava: Academic Press: Slovak Academic Press, 1995

Slovenia

Capsule Summary

Country Name: *Republika Slovenija* (Republic of Slovenia)
Location: Southeastern Europe between Austria and Croatia
Total Population: 1,935,677 (2003)
Ethnic Populations: Slovene (88%), Croat (3%), Serb (2%), Bosniak (1%), Yugoslav (0.6%), Hungarian (0.4%), other (5%) (1991)
Languages: Slovenian (91%), Serbo-Croatian (6%), other (3%)
Religions: Roman Catholic, Lutheran, Muslim, and others

Slovenia is located in southeastern Europe, bordering Austria in the north, Italy in the west, Croatia in the south and southeast, and Hungary in the northeast. The country has a land area of 20,273 square kilometers (7,819 square miles) and it was one of the smallest parts of the former Socialist Federal Republic of Yugoslavia (SFRY).

The population of Slovenia is estimated at about 1,935,700, up from 1,913,355 (according to the 1991 census). It is predominantly urban with around 70 percent of the people living in cities and towns. The country's capital city, Ljubljana (*Laibach* in German), is home to 340,000 people (2004), or 15 percent of the population. Slovenia has a population growth rate of 0.14 percent, and it is estimated that the population could cross the two million line within the next five years. Slovenia has a high population density, standing at around 98 people per square kilometer (255 people per square mile).

Slovenia is a unitary republic, and its form of government is a parliamentary republic. The government declared its independence from Yugoslavia on June 25, 1991. The country adopted its new Constitution on December 23, 1991, but it was changed several times, especially in the view of the accession to the European Union. The *Drzavni Zbor* (Parliament) is a unicameral 90-member national legislative body. The president is the head of state and elected by popular vote for a five-year term. The president nominates the prime minister, usually the leader of the majority coalition, who must be approved by the *Drzavni Zbor*. A number of political parties, ranging from radical nationalist groups to democrats, have been active in the country. The Slovenian Constitution reserves representation of minorities in the Parliament and in the local councils. Slovenia did not experience a civil war or civil strife as other parts of Yugoslavia did after the break up the SFRY, despite some tensions between the Slovenian majority and ethnic minorities. In the late 1990s there was an inflow of illegal migrants from the Middle East, Pakistan, Albania, and some other countries to Slovenia, as they used Slovenian territory as a transit route on the way to the European Union. However, most of them remained in the country temporarily, and they did not settle on its territory.

Slovenia is a multiethnic country. Ethnic Slovenians, who are ethnically and linguistically close to other south Europe's Slavic groups, make up 88 percent of the country's population. Ethnic Croatians make up the largest minority of around 3 percent of the population, while ethnic Serbs make up 2 percent, Bosnians make up 1 percent, Hungarians make up 0.4 percent, and various other groups together make up the remaining 5.6 percent of the population. The population of the country remained stable for the last 30 to 40 years, although in the 1990s there was considerable increase in the size of the Albanian, Turkish, and some other communities. The current ethnic structure was formed during the nineteenth and twentieth centuries, when Slovenia was a part of the Austrian-Hungarian Empire. After its collapse Slovenia was incorporated into Yugoslavia. World War II left a deep dividing mark in the country, as some Slovenians supported anti-Nazi resistance, while the others—called *domobranci*—collaborated with the Nazis. After the war, the new Communist government persecuted *domobranci*, sometimes executing them without a trial. A much-heated debate about the war legacy and treatment of the partisans and *domobranci* resurfaced in the 2000s and was in the center of the public attention and press for a while.

Slovenian language uses the Latin alphabet, unlike some other Slavic languages, for example, Serbian, Macedonian, and others. The language policy was not a central issue in political debates in the 1990s.

By the late twentieth century Slovenia was one of the most developed regions of the SFRY.

In the 1990s, Slovenians, like people in many other former Communist countries, witnessed the strength-ening of the Catholic Church in the country. The majority of Slovenians (70 percent) belong to the Roman Catholic background, while most of the Serbs belong to the Orthodox Church. Despite the growth of religious practice and the influence of the churches, religion does not play an important role in the political life. There are also many other small religious communities whose religious practices are generally tolerated.

Slovenia underwent major transitional changes with the inflow of the foreign direct investments and assistance provided by Austria, Germany, and some multilateral organizations, such as the European Bank for Reconstruction and Development. The government successfully conducted mass-privatization, price liberalization, and currency reforms. The Slovenian government privatized most of the enterprises in the industrial and agricultural sectors between 1991 and 1999. Slovenia introduced its currency, the *Tolar*, in 1992. The exchange rate of the Slovenian *Tolar* was fluctuating freely throughout the 1990s.

Slovenian's gross domestic product (GDP) per capita is among the highest in the former socialist countries (in purchasing power parity), at around $19,200 (2002). These reforms brought macroeconomic stability and significant rise in the living standards. The unemployment rate remained relatively high at over 11 percent of the labor force, affecting rural people, women with children, and the Roma community. The Roma community still remains one of the most vulnerable economically ethnic minorities in the country. In 2003 the United Nations Development Programme (UNDP) put Slovenia in 29th place in its Human Development Index (HDI). It is, behind Hong Kong, Barbados, Singapore, and Dominica, but ahead of the Republic of Korea, Brunei, and the Czech Republic.

RAFIS ABAZOV

See also **Croats; Serbs; Yugoslavs (Southern Slavs)**

Further Reading

Bekó, Jani, *Foreign Trade Flows and Economic Activity in Slovenia: Causality Patterns from a Transition Episode*, Budapest: Hungarian Academy of Sciences, Institute for World Economics, 2002

Havlik, Peter, *Trade and Cost Competitiveness in the Czech Republic, Hungary, Poland, and Slovenia*, Washington, DC: World Bank, 2000

Heenan, Patrick, and Monique Lamontagne, editors, *The Central & East European Handbook*, Chicago: Glenlake Pub., 2000

International Monetary Fund, *Republic of Slovenia: Statistical Appendix*. Prepared by P. Antolin-Nicolás, P. Dyczewski, and D. Tzanninis, Washington, DC: International Monetary Fund, 2003

Jesih, Boris, et al., *Ethnic Minorities in Slovenia*, 2nd edition, Ljubljana: Institute for Ethnic Studies, 1994

Komac, Miran, *Protection of Ethnic Communities in the Republic of Slovenia: Vademecum*, Ljubljana: Institute for Ethnic Studies, 1999

Monitoring the EU Accession Process: Minority Protection: Country Reports, Bulgaria, Czech Republic, Estonia, *Hungary, Latvia, Lithuania, Poland, Romania, Slovakia, Slovenia*, Budapest: Central European University Press, 2001

Petersen, Roger, *Resistance and Rebellion: Lessons from Eastern Europe (Studies in Rationality and Social Change)*, Cambridge: Cambridge University Press, 2001

Review of Agricultural Policies: Slovenia, Paris: Organisation for Economic Co-operation and Development (OECD), 2001

Somalia

Capsule Summary

Country Name: Somali Democratic Republic
Location: Eastern Africa
Total Population: 8,025,190 (July 2003)
Ethnic Population: Gosha, Shebelle, Boni, Boon, Dabarre, Garre, Tunni, Jiidu, Maay, Mushungulu, Oromo, Bajuni, Mwini
Languages: Somali (official), Southern Oromo, KiMushungulu, Maay, Boni, Boon, Dabarre, Jiidu, Garre, KiSwahili, Tunni, Arabic, Italian, and English
Religions: Sunni Muslim, with a few Animists and Christians

Somalia is located in northeastern Africa, in the southern region of the so-called Horn of Africa, near the Arabian peninsula coasts. The country is extremely poor with a $600 per capita income in 2002. Although the official form of government is a democratic republic, clan rivalries and oppositions threaten any real stability. Currently there is no permanent national government, only a transitional, parliamentary national government.

Between 1885 and the 1920s the territory of modern Somalia was progressively invaded by British and Italian colonial troops. In 1960 both Somali regions were unified and took their independence as a single state. Somalia, as it appears on maps, existed only since 1960. Properly speaking, the process of construction of the Somali nation started in the 1960s and broke up in the late 1980s, when the region came under the control of competing militias controlled by different clans' leaders. Since 1991, there have been more than a dozen efforts at national reconciliation, however, none of these have been successful. Various groupings of Somali factions have sought to control the national territory (or portions thereof) and have fought small wars with one another. Various international attempts to end the chaos and loss of life—including interventions led by the United States (UNITAF), and the United Nations Operation in Somalia (UNOSOM) occurred. War ended in March of 1994, but the fighting continued until June. In February 1995, the ONU troops fled Somalia; the country has since remained immersed in a constant atmosphere of violence and pillage.

Somali was the name of a people long before the current state of Somalia. The Somali language belonged to the lowland branch of the East Cushitic languages, and originated in the southern part of the country around the tenth century.

As an ethnic category, *Somali* is not clearly delineated. Certain groups have increasingly come to see themselves as Somali in the course of Islamization. There are also transitional linguistic and cultural areas between Oromo and Somalis in which groups may define themselves more as one or the other depending on what happens to be politically opportune.

Cultural History

During the centuries between the tenth and the second century BCE, different peoples occupied the area now called Somalia. At the far north lived groups of Eastern Cushites, the Ahmar-Dharoor peoples. The coastal and river areas in the south were inhabited by Southern Cushites. Towards the south, inland, were located the Proto-Somali peoples. The cultural transformation of the river regions (to 500 CE) lead to the formation of several clusters of Bantu communities in these zones. Between 500 and 900 the ongoing expansion and differentiation of the former peoples of Somalia was connected with the spread of camel-raising and the commerce. In the tenth century a new era of sea-going commerce commenced.

Between 1000 and 1400, Islam commenced to be taken inland beyond its initial points of entry via trade streams.

Islam had become the most common religion in Somalia by the fifteenth century. In the southern region, the Ajuraan imamate of the fifteenth and sixteenth centuries brought large areas under a single rule. Commerce spread increasingly inland, strengthening the ties between different southern regions and between towns and the interior. Afterwards, until the nineteenth century, an increasingly complex interpenetration of different peoples (Maay-speaking communities, Darood groups, etc.) took shape. Swahili, in its Bajuni and Mwini dialects, continued to be important along the southern coasts. And in the nineteenth century, the slave trade from East Africa brought an additional component of Bantu-speaking people into the mix. That complex heritage is still in place today.

Chief Minority Groups

The problems faced by minority groups in Somalia existed prior to the armed conflict that continues in parts of Somalia following the overthrow of the dictator Siyad Barre in 1991, and the collapse of Somalia's government. These problems have arisen as a result of cultural values that segregate and exclude the minority groups from dominant clan societies. These minority groups are considered inferior, without full rights; hence their low social, economic, and political status.

The Mushungulu are around 50,000 persons that live in Southern Somalia. Descended from Bantu fugitive slaves who escaped from their Somali masters in the Middle Shabeelle region around 1840. In northeast Tanzania, they were called Zigula. Nowadays, they are Muslim, but some of them still believe in their traditional animist religion. The Gosha ethnic community emerged in the 1870s, when several groups from slave origins were united under the same ethnic label (*Gosha*, that is to say, "the forest" in Somali language). Originally, they were groups both from southeastern Africa ancestry (Yao, Nyasa, etc.) and from Oromo heritage. A solid group identity has not been actively forged by the Gosha because of the variety of backgrounds. Most of Mwini and Bajuni fled to Kenya during the civil war. In this cruel war, a lot of people for other minorities (especially Gosha and Mushungulu) were massacred by different militias.

A separate political consciousness may be developing among all minority communities in southern Somalia as a result of the brutality and abuses that they have suffered during the civil war. The ties of affiliation that some of these groups felt to their Somali clans may be overridden by the lack of protection these clans provided during the years of violence. The state's protection is even farther away from these communities—they have no trust in a historically corrupted and weak state.

JOAN MANUEL CABEZAS LÓPEZ

See also **Somalis**

Further Reading

Ahmed, Ali Jimale, editor, *The Invention of Somalia*, Lawrenceville, New Jersey: The Red Sea Press, 1995

Cassanelli, Lee V., "Social Construction on the Somali Frontier: Bantu Former Slave Communities in the Nineteenth Century," in *The African Frontier. The Reproduction of Traditional African Societies*, edited by Igor Kopytoff, Bloomington: Indiana University Press, 1989

Gurdon, Charles, editor, *The Horn of Africa*, London: UCL Press, 1996

Lewis, I.M., *A Modern History of Somaliland: From Nation to State*, London and New York: Longman, 1980

Schlee, Günther, *Regularity in Chaos: The Politics of Difference in the Recent History of Somalia*, Halle, Germany: Max Planck Institut for Social Anthropology, 2001

Somalis

Capsule Summary

Location: Somalia, Somaliland, Djibouti, Ethiopia, Kenya
Total Population: about 11 million
Language: Somali (many dialects)
Religion: Islam (99%)

The Somali are an important people in the Horn of Africa, living in at least five contiguous countries. They form the majority in their homelands Somalia, a state that collapsed in 1991, and Somaliland, the former British colony self-governing since 1991, and in Djibouti, a small state on the Red Sea where the other 40 percent of the population is located. In Ethiopia and Kenya, the Somali are quite important minorities. In Ethiopia there is an autonomous *Somali National Regional State*, one of the largest territories in federal Ethiopia. In both Kenya and Ethiopia there is recurrent political unrest in Somali regions and regular clampdowns by state authorities occur in times of unrest. In Djibouti, the *Issa* Somali are the dominant group (They include the current president as well as his predecessor).

The Somali are traditionally camel pastoralists (still about 60 percent of the population today) with a mobile and dynamic life style, developed in harsh, semi-arid regions. Many are also engaged in trade, fishery, agriculture, and the urban service sector (or what remains of it after many years of civil war). In major towns, like Beledweyn, Kismayo, and Baidoa, but especially Mogadishu, armed militias of certain clan-based war lords emerged in the 1990s. They originated in part from resistance movements against the military dictatorship of then president Mohammed Siyad Barre, but degenerated into robbery, preying upon the urban population and extorting protection money.

The Somali have been one of the major political players in the Horn of Africa and also a frequent factor of regional instability and conflict. In the early sixteenth century Somali warriors formed the core of an Islamic army that tried to conquer and extinguish the Christian Ethiopian highland state. The central Somali state that was founded in 1960 collapsed in 1991 with the demise of the Siyad Barre dictatorship.

Somalis share a language, a faith (Islam), and a way of life, but are internally deeply divided on the basis of clan identity, territory, and occupational status. Indeed, clan identity seems to be the primary defining factor in the social and political life of the Somalis. Patrilineal kinship or *tol* is the element through which Somalis define clan allegiance, lineage membership, and personal identity. Clans (and the overarching clan-families) have traditional alliances to share pasture and water sources as well as to give mutual support in situations of dispute or conflict. There are also adoption relations (*sheegad*), whereby members of a clan choose to become attached to another, more powerful clan and can reach prominence in it. This principle of adoption also extends into neighboring ethnic groups. Smaller, less powerful clans usually have a relationship of alliance and protection with a larger one.

The Somali have six large clan families: the Dir, Hawiye, Isaaq, Darood, Digil, and Rahanwein. These families subdivide on the basis of segmentation into clans (*qolo* or *qabila*), subclans, and lineages. Genealogical consciousness is highly developed among Somalis, who often know their pedigrees up to the fourteenth ancestor. The first four groups are collectively known as *Samaale*, the other two as *Sab*. The Sab, who account for about 20 percent of the population, are predominantly agriculturalists and live in southern Somalia along the two great rivers, the Shebelle and the Juba. As they differ in language from the other Somali groups, have a different history, and tend to be looked down on by the pastoral Somali, the Sab often feel like a minority. The Sab, however, share a clan-based sociopolitical structure with other Somalis. In the coastal cities there has emerged a mixed culture of Swahili, Arabs, and others, who, strictly speaking, are outside the clan system. The same applies to the occupational caste groups, like Midgan, Yibir, and Tumaal, who are mostly hunters, blacksmiths, traditional magicians, and tanners.

Somali sociopolitical organization is strongly patrilineal and male-dominated. Somali pastoral family units (*qois*) live in camps or hamlets and cooperate with other units to form a *rer*, a territorial unit on the basis of a dominant lineage or clan segment. Male elders and religious leaders are respected and form a mediatory force in conflicts and disputes, which are frequent. There are chiefs (*ugaz*, *garad*, or *bogor*), but these have little authority. Clan councils (*shir*) are an important forum for democratic community debate. Women have a vital social and economic role and serve also as a connecting and often mediating force between clans (of their husbands and of their fathers and brothers).

The form of Islam adhered to by Somali is of the Sunni tradition, and many males are members of Sufi brotherhoods, especially the Qadiriyya and Salihiyya. Due to enduring clan rivalries, great differences in the numerical and economic strength of clans, and an economy and way of life based on transhumant camel pastoralism, Somali society is inherently unstable and does not lend itself easily to durable state formation. Many observers, starting with the British pioneer traveler-explorer R. Burton in the mid-nineteenth century, commented on the fierce independence and egalitarian ethos of the Somali, as expressed in their readiness to use force for defense of the herds and of their personal honor. The Somali are also noted for a very highly developed culture of verbal and literary expression, and pride themselves in poetic and rhetoric feats.

It should be noted that Somali society is not ethnically homogenous, as many past authors have presented it. There was a substantial minority (approximately half a million) of Bantu-speaking people in the south, known under various names such as *WaGosha, Boni, Jareer, WaZigua,* or *Mushunguli.* These groups differed in language, culture, and physical traits from the Somali and were cultivators, craftsmen, or fishermen. Many were also used as slaves, and thus subject to discrimination and abuse by Somali. Others converted to Islam to escape slavery and assimilated into Somali society, becoming adoptees or members of a clan. Nevertheless, social integration and intermarriage remained quite limited. In the course of the Somali civil wars since 1988, many Bantus were the victim of devastating violence and fled to Kenya or to the islands near the Somali coast. Most of them have now emigrated, with a substantial number being accepted in 2002 by the United States as refugee immigrants.

In the 1990s, civil war, endemic violence, and state collapse led to a tragic decline of the Somali sociopolitical order. Largely as a result of the enduring violence, a few hundred thousand Somalis migrated to North America (especially Canada), the Gulf States, and Europe, as refugees or for family and economic reasons. Many have made successful careers in their new countries, and send remittances back to their country of origin. Somali migrants also maintain family ties and political links there, thus forming a typical transnational community.

JON ABBINK

See also **Somalia**

Further Reading

Abbink, Jon G., "Dervishes, Moryaan and Freedom Fighters: Cycles of Rebellion and the Fragmentation of Somali Society, 1900–2000," in *Rethinking Resistance: Revolt and Violence in African History*, edited by J. Abbink, K. van Walraven, and M. de Bruijn, Leiden: E.J. Brill, 2003

Brons, Maria, Martin Doornbos, and M.A. Mohamed Salih, "The Somali Ethiopians: The Quest for Alternative Futures," *Eastern Africa Social Science Research Review*,11, no. 2 (1995)

Burton, Richard F., *First Footsteps in East Africa*, London: Dent, 1856

Cassanelli, Lee V., *The Shaping of Somali Society: Restructuring the History of a Pastoral People 1600–1900*, Philadelphia: University of Pennsylvania Press, 1982

Compagnon, Daniel, "Somali Armed Units: The Interplay of Political Entrepreneurship and Clan-Based Factions," in *African Guerrillas*, edited by C. Clapham, Oxford: James Currey, and Bloomington: Indiana University Press, 1998

Helander, Bernard, "Power and Poverty in Southern Somalia," in *The Poor Are Not Us*, edited by D. Anderson and V. Broch-Due, Oxford: James Currey, 1999

Lewis, Ioan M., *Blood and Bone: The Call of Kinship in Somali Society*, Lawrenceville, New Jersey: Red Sea Press, 1994

Luling, Virginia W., "The Other Somali—Minority Groups in Traditional Somali Society," in *Proceedings of the Second International Congress of Somali Studies*, 3, edited by Th. Labahn, Hamburg: Buske, 1983

———, *Somali Sultanate: The Geledi City-State over 150 Years*, London: Haan Associates and Piscataway, New Jersey: Transaction Publishers, 2002

Prunier, Gérard, "Segmentarité et violence dans l'espace somali, 1840–1992," *Cahiers d'Etudes Africaines*, 146, no. XXXVII-2 (1997)

Turton, E.R. "Somali Resistance to Colonial Rule and the Development of Somali Political Activity in Kenya, 1893–1960," *Journal of African History*, 13, no. 1 (1973)

Songhai-Zerma

Capsule Summary

Location: Mali (near Niger river), southwestern Niger, northeastern Burkina Faso, some oasis of southern Morocco and Algeria, and northern territories of Benin
Total Population: around 3 million
Languages: Different languages of the Songhai-Zerma branch of the Nilo-Saharian family
Religions: Mainly Muslim, but with a high degree of former traditional beliefs

The label *Songhai-Zerma languages* refers to four big languages or dialectal sets: (1) the properly speaking Songhai (also Songhay), that is subdivided in some differentiated speeches: Western Songhai (Tombmata, Jenné, Timbuktú, Araouan), Central Songhai (Tinié, Maransé, Kaado) and Oriental Songhai (Gao, Gabero, Kel Alkaseybaten, Bamba); (2) the Zerma, spoken in the southern areas of the Songhai cultural region, downstream from the river Níger; (3) the Dendi language, an idiomatic set placed southward of the Zerma area; and (4) the Tadaksahak, a variety of the Songhai's languages that is still spoken in the south of Morocco (Tafilalt), in the southwest of Algeria, and in the southern curbing of the Sahara (in the states of Mali and Niger). In spite of this large plurality of languages and groups, the Songhai-Zerma peoples have a clearly distinctive ethnic consciousness and constitute a large cultural complex with a differentiated history and their own sense of belonging.

History

The exact origin of the Songhai-Zerma peoples is very difficult to discern. In spite of this, it seems to be commendable that the principal, original nucleus of the Songhai ethnic conglomerate was in the former city of Kukya. This important nucleus of population worked as a point of attraction of human groups proceeding from lands in the south, in the zone of the Dendi (north of modern Benin) and fused with the autonomous populations. It is probable that Kukya constituted, through a certainly long period, a symbolic capital and a religious center of the Songhai world. In the same period, the condition of political and commercial capital became condensed upstream from the Niger, concretely in Gao city.

On the other hand, the conduction of the political directives of this social formation was, apparently, in the hands of the Jaas, a social group that constituted a Songhai fraction crossbred of Lemta Berbers, probably founded about the seventh century. At the beginning of the eleventh century, the Jaas converted to the Islamic faith, but this does not seem to have extended to the Songhai in a massive way. About the twelfth century, when Gao happened to be the capital of the Songhai state, this political system already was occupying both shores of the river Niger between Dendi and Gao's region. In the last decade of the thirteenth century, the mandinga armies conquered the Songhai kingdom. In 1325 they placed a mesquite in Gao.

The Songhai dynasty of the Sonni constituted the most important nobility group of warriors. Founded in the thirteenth century, only a hundred years after they declared their independence from the Mandinga empire, the Songhai's new leader, Sonni Ali, managed to conquer the cities of Timbuktú and Jenné, and to repel the Mossi armies (from modern Burkina Faso). After the death of Sonni Ali (1492) the elites of Gao's empire engaged in a fierce struggle for political

primacy. The more Islamized sectors won and founded the new Askia dynasty, which was defeated by Moroccan troops in 1591. In 1660, the downfall of the Moroccan authority was complete; ten years later the Bambara king of Segu, Biton Kulibaly, seized Timbuktu. In 1680, the Tuareg Ulimiden, from the region of the Adrar of Iffoghas (in the Sahara), invaded Gao, the former capital, and they did the same with Timbuktu in 1787. Later, between the end of the eighteenth century and the beginning of the nineteenth, there came a shift in the invasions that led to the end of the Peul, after which French troops came to the Songhai countries.

Society and Ethnic Plurality

The Songhai societies preserved a strong animistic component in its religious structure. This deep influence is clearly shown by the persistence of dances of possession, worship rituals, geniuses (holey) power, the social belief in witchcraft, the divinatory arts and talismans, as well as in the existence of diverse divinities, among whom Hake Dikko (divinity of the river) and Dongo (god of the beam) are the most significant.

The cultural Songhai background originally arose from the collision between immigrated elements and autochthonous communities like the Gurmanche, Do, Koromba, Cii, and the immigrant communities that were created by the Songhai identity matrix: Tuareg, Bella, Arabs Hassaniyya, Soninke, Mandinga, Hausa, Diawara, and others.

An interesting Songhai group, the Arma, constitute a small social community whose members are the distant descendants of Moroccan and Andalusian soldiers who occupied Timbuktu at the end of the sixteenth century. Another small subgroup inhabiting the Tabelbala's oasis (south of Algeria) are the Korandje or Tadaksahak ("sons of Isaac"), who probably descended from former slaves imported by the Moroccan sultans in the seventeenth century. Other Songhai groups are the fishermen Sorko, Korongoy, and Bozo; the Kurtey and Wogo (hybrids of Sorko and urban Songhai); the Gow (hunters); the peasants Zerma of southwestern Niger; the Maransé of Burkina Faso; and the Dendi of northern Benin.

In present-day Mali, an antigovernment riot involved Tuareg and the Songhai militia, the Mouvement Patriotique Ganda Koy (MPGK). Nevertheless, on November 11, 1994, the Tuareg and the MPGK signed an agreement of high place the fire that does not turn out to be a guarantee with a view to the cessation from this one bloody ethnic polarisation that marked the everyday political reality of the African states that tried to transplant the Western model of Nation-State.

JOAN MANUEL CABEZAS LÓPEZ

Further Reading

Harrison, Byron, Annette Harrison, and Michael J. Rueck, *Southern Songhay Speech Varieties in Niger. A Sociolinguistic Survey of the Zarma, Songhay, Kurtey, Wogo, and Dendi Peoples of Niger*, Niamey: Summer Institute of Linguistics, 1997
Hunwick, J.O., "Religion and State in the Songhay Empire, 1464–1591," in *Islam in Tropical Africa*, edited by I.M. Lewis, Oxford: Oxford University Press, 1966
Rouch, Jean, *Les Songhay*, Paris: Presses Universitaires de France, 1954

Soninke

Capsule Summary

Location: West Africa, primarily in Senegal, Mauritania and Mali
Total Population: approximately 1 million
Language: Soninke
Religion: Muslim

The Soninke, also known as the Sarakole, Serawoolies, and Saracolet, are an ethnic group living in the Sahelian region of West Africa, primarily along the upper Senegal River in eastern Senegal, northwestern Mali, and southeastern Mauritania. They have also dispersed to other neighboring West African countries, such as Burkina Faso, the Gambia, Cote d'Ivoire, Guinea-Bissau, and Guinea-Conakry. The Soninke are a small minority in all these countries. Because of their dispersal and intermarriage, the Soninke are often not clearly distinguishable from other neighboring ethnic groups and an estimate of 1 million is highly speculative. The Soninke are Muslims and are particularly noted in the region for their skills as itinerant traders and sailors. Since the 1960s, many adult male Soninke have migrated to France. In some Soninke villages in the Senegal River region, there are very few young men between the ages of 20 and 50 since they work and reside permanently in France and only return to the region periodically to visit their families. The Soninke language is part of the Mande group of the Niger-Congo family. Increasingly, however, many Soninke have abandoned their language for those of other groups, especially Wolof in Senegal and Bambara and in Mali. Many Soninke have intermarried with other ethnic groups and can be considered Soninke in name only.

The Soninke founded and ruled the empire of ancient Ghana, called *Wagadu* in indigenous oral traditions, the first known major state in the Western Sudan. The empire, with an economy based on agriculture and trans-Saharan trade, particularly in gold and salt, flourished in the Sahelian region south of the Sahara Desert from about the sixth through the eleventh centuries. The Soninke were the first in the Western Sudan to establish trading links with Arab-Berber merchants from North Africa, and they were also among the first to become itinerant traders in West Africa. Many smaller states and chiefdoms paid tribute to the Ghana Empire, which stretched from the Atlantic Ocean to the Niger River. The capital at Kumbi-Saleh, in southern Mauritania, contained numerous mosques and several different quarters, including an Arab quarter, as well as the king's court. The empire's decline in the late eleventh century caused a Soninke diaspora, particularly of Muslim clerics and merchants. The majority of Soninke, however, remained in the transitional zone between the Sahara desert and the Sudanic belt.

The Soninke were an important minority in the Mande-dominated empire of ancient Mali, which succeeded ancient Ghana as the most important state in the Western Sudan in the thirteenth and fourteenth centuries. With the decline of Mali, several small Soninke states, including Gajaaga, Gidimaka, and Jara, regained their independence which they maintained until the nineteenth century. Predominantly agriculturalists, the

Soninke also engaged extensively and profitably in commerce, benefiting from the symbiotic relationship between the desert and savanna economies and the proximity of the Senegal River. The Soninke converted relatively early to Islam; in some places, the word *Saracolet* became synonymous with *marabout*, or "religious teacher." The Soninke, though sharing the tripartite social division of free-born, artisan, and slave descent common to neighboring peoples, contained a separate category of mercenaries and warriors who captured the slaves used by merchants and agriculturalists. During precolonial times, as many as one-third of the Soninke population may have been slaves. The Soninke constituted a significant and integral component of the greater Mande formation that, along with the Fulani, dominated the middle and upper Senegal and Niger River valleys before the arrival of the French in the nineteenth century.

During the colonial period, many Soninke were engaged in the gum arabic trade on the Senegal River. In addition, many Soninke were hired by the French as sailors, or *laptops*, on naval and trading vessels. These Soninke sailors established a diaspora all along the Senegal River. The colonial authorities often promoted French-speaking Soninke to prominent political positions in the upper Senegal region and ruled through them. Many Soninke volunteered or were drafted into French military service and fought overseas in World War I and World War II. Some Soninke remained in France after the war. With independence for most of the region in 1960, a steady flow of Soninke migrants from West Africa to France began, until the Soninke formed three-quarters of the West African migrant worker population in France. In rural areas along the Senegal River valley, from 20 to 70 percent of the active male population of Soninke villages may be absent, leaving women, old men, and hired workers to tend their fields and herds. Absences that tended to last two to four years on the average are now increasingly, despite French opposition, becoming much longer and often permanent. Remittances from France allow families left behind to have concrete housing and consumer goods in greater quantities than their neighbors, but the monies are not being reinvested in the economic development of the Soninke heartland in Mauritania, Mali, and Senegal, an area especially hard hit by drought and growing desertification. Other Soninke have migrated to urban areas of West Africa where they are engaged in petty commerce and other trading.

Soninke agricultural communities are organized around the elder male members who wield considerable authority. The tripartite social division of free-born, artisan, and slave has been maintained, even in the Soninke diaspora in France, although today there is some intermarriage among the social groups and the distinctions are not as sharply drawn. Islam continues to play a critical role among both rural and urban Soninke.

ANDREW F. CLARK

See also **Mali, Mauritania, Senegal**

Further Reading

Colvin, Lucie, et al., editors, *The Uprooted of the Western Sahel: The Migrants' Quest for Cash in the Senegambia*, New York: Praeger, 1981
Curtin, Philip, *Economic Change in Precolonial Africa: Senegambia in the Era of the Slave Trade*, Madison: University of Wisconsin, 1975
Manchuelle, Francois, *Willing Migrants: Soninke Labor Diasporas, 1848–1960*, Athens: Ohio University Press, 1997
———, "Slavery, Emancipation and Labor Migration in West Africa: The Case of the Soninke," *Journal of African History*, 30 (1989)
Nwanunobi, C.O., *Soninke*, New York: Rosen, 1996
Pollet, Eric, and Grace Winter, *La societe soninke*, Brussels: Universite de Bruxelles, 1971

Sorbs

Capsule Summary

Location: Middle Europe, South East Germany alongside the border with Poland

Total Population: approximately 60,000
Language: Lusatian Sorbian (in two forms: Upper and Lower)
Religions: Catholicism (Upper), Lutheran (Upper and Lower)

The Sorbs are an ethnic group in Germany, around the Spree (*Sprjewja*) river, southward from Berlin and eastward from Dresden alongside the border with Poland. They are divided into two language subgroups: Upper (province Saxony, vicinity of the town of Bautzen—*Budyšin* in Sorbian), and Lower (province Brandenburg, around Cottbus [*Chośebuz*]). In 1880 there had been 166,000 people speaking one of the two forms of Sorbian, immediately after World War II there were about 100,000, and currently there are approximately 40,000 in Saxony and 20,000 in Brandenburg. Thus, according to the most pessimistic assessment, after 50 to 100 years this will be a dead language after having survived the harshest times of abuses and maltreatment. Sorbian belongs to the West Slavic subfamily of the Slavic language group. Upper Sorbian—closer to the Czech (stress always on the first syllable)—is the main basis of the literary language; Lower is closer to the Polish. Sorbian morphology has preserved some archaic features that have disappeared from other Slavic languages: dual number in the names and verbs, aorist and imperfect forms. Many words are borrowed from German, which has also influenced spelling and pronunciation.

History

The Sorbs were an important part of the Baltoslavic tribes. Their ancestors moved 1,500 years ago from the Northern Carpathian Mountains to settle during the fifth through seventh centuries CE in the region between the rivers Elbe/Saale in the West and Oder, as well as its tributaries Bóbr and Kwisa in the East. Their name comes from the place Lusatia (*Łužica*), where a necropolis and an ancient settlement has been discovered. Sorbs were subject of intensified Germanization and assimilation especially during the tenth through the thirteenth centuries, but managed to preserve their cultural and everyday life traditions and customs. Major vocations were agriculture and farming, and secondary vocations were fishing and hunting. From early times metal ore output and processing were also developed. In order to prevent German assaults they used to inhabit remote sites, surrounded by wooden bulwarks and other fortification facilities. Sorbs' cultural impact and trade reached as far as to the Lower Danube—the lands of Ancient Thrace.

Though there are many earlier examples, mainly translated from Latin Christian scripts, original pieces of Sorbian writings (*pismowstwo*) emerged in the sixteenth century. The poet and protestant vicar Handrij Zejler (1804–1872) initiated the first literary movement, which later evolved into the cultural-publishing society *Maćica Serbska*, established in 1847 in Budyšin. Jakub Bart, self-called *Ćišinski* (1856–1909), a poet and priest, led the Youth Sorbs' Movement against the Germanization, and improved the system of literary sorts. An important role here played the Sorbian cultural organization *Domowina* ("Homeland," founded in 1912).

During the Nazi regime in Germany Sorbian culture and identity became a subject of fierce prosecution and repression. Sorbs' limited cultural autonomy was established after 1945 in the frames of the later German Democratic Republic with the adoption of the *Sorbengsetz* (Sorbian Law) in 1948, and a specific article in the country's Constitution. Funded by the provincial governments there exist two museums, community cultural centers, folk songs' and dance ensemble, *Domowina* society, German-Sorbian Theatre, Research Institute, Publishing House, an Upper Sorbian daily *Serbske Nowiny* (Sorbian News), as well as the Lower Lusatian weekly magazine *Nowy Casnik* (New Magazine), monthly Lutheran journal *Pomhaj Bóh* (Help me, my God), and Catholic monthly magazine for teachers and children *Katolski Posol* (Catholic Envoy).

Sorbian Society

Sorbs' destiny proved that both with state support, or with repression, assimilation of this smallest Slavic people ever continues, and there is seemingly no measure to stop it. War and rapid industrialization in the German Democratic Republic (GDR) ignited mass migration: local people spread to many other places all over the country, while many Germans came to find jobs at the local mines and plants. Today migration is due to the high unemployment in the area, which exceeds 20 percent after all major enterprises there (with the sole exception of coal mines) went bankrupt. Current provincial constitutions of both lands—Saxony and Brandenburg—provide ample rights: to preserve their ingenuity, to develop Lusatian culture, to be taught at their maternity languages, and to use them for official purposes. Both Federal and local governments grant generous funding of Sorbs, which is relatively constant—32 million Deutsche Mark (DM) since 1992.

Sorbian is actually spoken only in the rural areas of the Upper Lusatia, where Catholic people live. Radio Budyšin (MDR) broadcasts in Upper Sorbian 3 hours daily, and Radio Chośebuz (ORB) broadcasts 2 hours daily. In the Lower Lusatia only elder people use native language, while young people prefer to communicate in German. Younger generations of Sorbs more and more are abandoning their ethnicity's customs, considering them as something obsolete and out of fashion, and tend to behave as their fellow Germans. Mixed marriages increase. This leads to a loss of connections with an individual's own background and culture. The local Branderburger TV station (ORB) has broadcast only in Lower Sorbian once monthly since 1992, and from September 2001 starts the responsible Saxony TV station (MDR). A project exists to open strictly bilingual kindergartens and elementary schools all over Lusatia. Some of the most pessimistic prospects for the future of the Sorbian culture and customs see them being preserved only in local ethnographic reservations, pressure groups, museums, and folk ensembles. This situation could hardly save an old Slavic national culture and two of the Western Slavic languages from dying.

STEPHAN E. NIKOLOV

Further Reading

Barker, Peter, *Slavs in Germany—the Sorbian Minority and the German State since 1945*, Lewiston-Queenston-Lampeter, 2000

Kasper, Martin, editor, *Language and Culture of the Lusatian Sorbs throughout Their History*, Berlin, 1987

Pastor, Thomas, *Die rechtliche Stellung der Sorben in Deutschland*, Bautzen, 1997

Pech, Edmund, *Die Sorbenpolitik der DDR 1949–1970. Anspruch und Wirklichkeit*, Bautzen, 1999

Scholze, Dietrich, editor, *Die Sorben in Deutschland: Sieben Kapitel Kulturgeschichte*, Bautzen, 1993

Šatava, Leoš, *Národnostní menšiny v Evropě: Encyklopedická příručka*, Praha, 1994

South Africa

Capsule Summary

Location: Southern tip of Africa
Total Population: 42,768,678 (July 2003)
Languages: 11 official languages, including Afrikaans, English, Ndebele, Pedi, Sotho, Swazi, Tsonga, Tswana, Venda, Xhosa, Zulu
Religions: Christian, Muslim, Hindu, indigenous beliefs and animist

After decades of racial policies, political infighting, extreme violence and worldwide isolation, South Africa enjoyed a metamorphosis from a racially biased white minority governed country to universally elected black majority rule in 1994.

South Africa is a naturally resource-rich, geographically varied, industrialized country situated at the southern tip of the African continent. It covers 1,219,090 square kilometers or 470,693 square miles. It is bordered by the Atlantic and Indian Oceans, Mozambique, Swaziland, Zimbabwe, and Botswana. Lesotho is an autonomous state within South Africa.

The Khoisan peoples, the Khoikhoi, and the San and the Bantu, largely Xhosa and Zulu are South Africa's indigenous peoples. White encroachment began when the powerful Dutch East India Company brought white European settlers to Cape Town in 1652; they imported slaves from South East Asia as their labor force. Many settlers became *Boers*, a Dutch word for "farmer." More settlers were enticed by free passage; they came from Germany, France, and the Netherlands quickly taking over the best farming land. White contact resulted in decimation with Khoikhoi and San peoples contracting smallpox, being killed by the whites, or becoming servants to Boers. Dutch was the original white language but slowly changed by adopting vocabulary from fellow whites, slaves, and black servants; it became the Afrikaans language. The Xhosa had lost their land to the whites by 1770 despite a century long struggle. The British occupied Cape Colony in 1814 and gained control with new British settlement causing greater land loss for the Xhosa.

The Boers, also known as Afrikaners, disagreed with having English as the formal language and with granting equal rights to the Khoikoi and to slaves. The abolition of slavery added to Boer discontentment.

Consequently, thousands of Boers left Cape Colony in 1836, making a lengthy journey known as the Great Trek to find a new homeland. They occupied lands belonging to the Zulus, vanquishing them in the subsequent territorial wars and creating Natal, the Transvaal, and the Orange Free State. In 1843 the British annexed Natal but Transvaal and the Orange Free Sate were recognized as independent.

Gold and diamond discoveries in Kimberley in 1867 and Witwatersrand in 1895 caused great friction, especially after Britain annexed the areas. The First Boer War against the British was fought in 1881; the Boers won. The newly arrived foreigners (*uitlanders*) were constrained from political rights by the Boers. Tensions mounted and in 1899 the Boers declared war on the British empire. The bitterly fought Second Boer War ended in the Boers surrendering in 1902; their territories were declared British colonies.

In 1910, the Transvaal, the Orange Free State, the Cape Colony, and Natal, were granted self-government by the British and formed the Union of South Africa, based on The Government of South Africa Act of 1909. The white minority gained majority power in the Constitution despite objections by people like Indian lawyer Mohandas Gandhi who used civil disobedience tactics to gain some rights for the Indian population. He inspired the establishment of the South African Native National Congress (SANNC) in 1912, later to become the African National Congress.

The white National Party was founded in 1914 by Boer general James Barry Munnik Hertzog to promote Afrikaner supremacy. Under Hertzog's racially motivated policies, blacks were removed from the cities and lost voting rights while jobs opened up for poor Afrikaners. The Labour Party joined the Afrikaners and they won the 1924 election. South Africa gained independence in 1931. Hertzog lost power in 1939 to South Africa's second prime minister, Boer General Jan Smuts.

The National Party (NP) was reorganized by Daniel Francois Malan, a fierce Afrikaner nationalist. Gaining power in 1948, the NP initiated the racially discriminatory apartheid policies that exacerbated the segregation endured by nonwhites. Groups were categorized as white, (the minority), Colored, Indians, and Blacks (who made up the majority of the population) ostensibly to prevent a civil war between the black ethnic groups. A huge bureaucracy was established to maintain this policy. The 1950 Population Registration Act categorized groups, The Mixed Marriages Act disallowed mixed marriages and made sexual relations between whites and blacks a crime, and the Group Area Act prevented nonwhite ownership of lands or leases. The 1954 Resettlement of Natives Act removed the Colored in the Cape from white neighborhoods. Ten tribal homelands were established.

Vehement opposition arose. The ANC protested by using strikes, boycotts, and rallies to voice their concerns; they were quashed by the government. The ANC split in 1959 when members left due to the ANC's alliances with white liberals. The former members created the Pan-Africanist Congress (PAC) which worked toward an all black government. Some blacks who walked in public without the required passes were shot by police in Sharpeville. The ANC and the PAC were banned in 1960. South Africa was declared a Republic on May 31, 1961.

NP prime minister Henry Verwoerd, an extreme racist who had supported the Nazis in World War II, won 122 seats in the 166 seat Parliament in 1966 but was assassinated shortly thereafter. His successor, NP Balthazar J. Vorster, pursued reconciliation with the British. The NP ranks split over the issue. In 1976, blacks in Soweto rioted to protest apartheid policies. Vorster lost power in 1978 due to a financial scandal and was succeeded by Pieter Willem Botha who pursued cautious reforms to end apartheid.

The Constitution was revised in 1984 with a three-house Parliament, one each for whites, Coloreds, and Asians, but none for blacks. The dismantling of apartheid began when numerous racial restrictions were repealed but suffrage was withheld from blacks. Clashes between the Xhosa-based ANC and the largely Zulu Inkatha Freedom Party and the ensuing violence and thousands of deaths caused great international consternation. A state of emergency was declared in1985 and remained in effect until 1990. In 1986 many states throughout the world enacted economic sanctions on South Africa. Botha's government repealed more apartheid laws in 1986. Namibia gained independence from South Africa in 1990.

Botha's successor NP Frederik Willem de Klerk realized that South Africa would fall into the abyss of civil war and thus hastened the pace of reform. He lifted the bans of the ANC and PAC. DeKlerk freed Nelson Mandela who had been imprisoned since 1964; they negotiated mutually satisfactory political changes. By 1991 the last of the apartheid laws were repealed.

An interim Constitution was promulgated in 1993. Universal rights were enshrined in a bill of rights that allowed freedom of opinion, belief, religion, express, the press, and political activities as well as rights to health care, food, water, education, and adequate housing. The first South African universal elections were held in 1994. Nelson Mandela and the ANC won the election and he became the first black president of South Africa. He served in that position until l999 when another ANC member Thabo Mbeki won the election.

South Africa's journey to racial equality is a story of hatred, tenacity, reconciliation, and renewal. Ultimately human rights triumphed and everyone now has a voice.

ANNETTE RICHARDSON

See also **Apartheid; De Klerk, F.W. (Afrikaner); Mandela, Nelson (South African)**

Further Reading

Beck, Roger, *The History of South Africa*, Westport, Connecticut: Greenwood Press, 2000

Davenport, T.R.H., *South Africa: A Modern History*, 4th edition, Toronto: University of Toronto Press, 1991

Davis, Stephen, *Apartheid's Rebels: Inside South Africa's Hidden War*, New Haven, Connecticut: Yale University Press, 1988

Mandela, Nelson, *Long Walk to Freedom*, Boston: Little, Brown and Company, 1995

Pakenham, Thomas, *The Boer War*, London: Weidenfeld and Nicolson, 1979

Thompson, Leonard M., *A History of South Africa*, revised edition, New Haven: Yale University Press, 1996

South Asian Americans (India, Pakistan, Bangladesh)

Capsule Summary

Location: United States
Total Population: 1.25 million
Languages: English, Hindi, Urdu, and other languages of South Asia
Religions: Hindu, Muslim, Jain, Sikh, Christian, and other religions of South Asia

South Asian Americans are a rapidly growing community that is making significant contributions to the United States, while helping their place of origin. South Asian Americans are people who immigrate to the United States but claim South Asia, primarily India, Pakistan, or Bangladesh, as their homeland. Before the region obtained independence from Britain in 1947, these countries were part of India. The Partition of 1947 created two sovereign states, those of the Republic of India and Pakistan. Bangladesh later broke away from Pakistan in 1971. South Asian immigration to the United States has been primarily from India, but recently, Pakistani and Bangladeshi influx has reached noticeable proportions. The three communities share much in history and culture and thus can be treated as a unit. Ethnic identity is always changing and as more Pakistanis and Bangladeshis enter the United States,

it is likely they will stress their distinctiveness from other South Asian Americans.

Immigrants have always strengthened the cultural development of the United States. However with the implementation of Public Law 89–236 (effective 1968), which removed national origins as a factor for immigration, the United States has benefited immensely from the contributions of the over 1.2 million members of the South Asian community. As of 1998, five percent of all the physicians in the United States obtained their primary medical degree in India, which saved millions of dollars in education costs per medical person. Thirty percent of all hotels and motels in the United States are owned by Asian Indians, which revived a dying "mom and pop" motel industry. Their median family income in the United States is 25 percent higher than for all U.S. households. Sixty-five percent of Asian Indian males hold managerial, professional, or technical jobs while 80 percent hold college degrees.

As a community, Asian Americans have enriched American culture, brought technological innovation, substantially contributed to the intellectual base, and increased U.S. economic wealth. However, India has greatly benefited from its overseas community, with billions of dollars of remittances and novel innovations. For example, India hosts the new "silicon valley," located in Hyderabad, where computer software is developed and marketed worldwide at a much lower price than software produced in the United States that is of comparable quality. It was developed and is being managed largely by emigrants and returnees. As one travels through high-emigration regions, especially Punjab, Gujarat, and Kerala, one sees modern architecture built with overseas capital, modern tractors, machinery, wells, hybrid seeds, and factories—all of which came from abroad, were bought with overseas money, or were the result of emigrant work and ideas. India's medical facilities, public works, and medical personnel were all financed by that region's overseas contingent. In this period of rapid globalization, a transnational perspective allows for a larger picture of immigrant behavior that is characterized by vast cultural interaction between the host country and the emigrant country.

Emigration from South Asia has been a dominant behavioral pattern since the Indus Valley Civilization (2500–1700 BCE). The impact of early forays is still evident today in Central and East Asia where Indian mythology, dance, and theater are still prominent. Movement from Western India to Africa dates back to the second century BCE. Although a flourishing trade existed, permanent settlements did not develop. Small-scale movement changed to mass emigration as Indians provided cheap labor for Britain's colonies after slavery was outlawed. Some sold themselves into indenture, which was in essence a new system of slavery. What resulted was a 10 million Indian diaspora scattered throughout the former British Empire, but concentrated where there were labor intensive economies, especially plantation systems, namely Mauritius, Fiji, Trinidad, and East Africa. Since India obtained independence, destinations for Indian emigrants have included North America, Australia, and the Middle East.

Initially Asian Indians came to the United States as sea captains and traders in the 1790s, actively pursuing trade between India and North America, and a few came as indentured laborers. In 1900, there were about 2,000 resident Indians: 500 being merchants, several dozen religious teachers, and some medical professionals.

Asian Indian immigration increased rapidly after 1905. Six thousand entered the West Coast between 1907 and 1917, another 3,000 were barred. Most were from the region of Punjab, a butterfly-shaped area bridging India and Pakistan. Many were adherents to the Sikh faith and noticeable because of their turbans and unshorn hair. Hindus and Muslims were prominent but not so distinctly visible.

As Indian immigration increased, anti-Asian violence, which was common on the West Coast, began targeting Asian Indians. Also discriminatory interpretations were used and laws promoting inequality were passed, such as though prohibiting Asians from owning land and being eligible for U.S. citizenship. In fact, the Immigration Act of 1917 is referred as the "Indian Exclusion Act." In this hostile environment, along with the 1930s Depression, several thousand chose to return to India. Thus, the 1940 census showed only 2,405 Indians living in the United States, and most of them around Yuba City, California. Since the immigration of Asian Indians was barred and laws prohibited Asian Indians from owning land, some married Mexican women, which gave rise to a new ethnic group, the Punjabi-Mexican community.

After the World War II, legalization gave Asian Indians the right to citizenship, which permitted them to own land, and a quota for immigration (100 could enter each year) was established, which allowed family reunification. Between 1948 and 1965, 6,474 Asian Indians entered the United States as immigrants.

Partly due to the national mood during the Civil Rights Movement, the Immigration and Nationality Act of 1965 removed the national origins clause in U.S. immigration legislation. Preference was given to highly educated and skilled individuals. India had a ready pool of such talent and they took advantage of the new legislation and the mass movement from India to America began. By 1975, Asian Indians numbered 175,000; by 1980 they were 387,223; and by 1990 they numbered 815,447. In 1997, Asian Indians numbered 1.215 million and were entering the United States at a rate of 850 per week, ranking third in countries providing immigrants. Also in 1997, Michigan, Pennsylvania, New Hampshire, Ohio, West Virginia, New Jersey, Mississippi, and Delaware all had one thing in common—the largest number of foreign-born immigrants in those countries have India as their country of origin.

Initial prominent immigration starting at the turn of the century was primarily uneducated Punjabi villagers of the Sikh faith. Many had initially entered Vancouver, British Columbia in Canada. Facing discrimination and hostility, they crossed into the United States to work in the lumbering enterprise around Bellingham and Everett, Washington. Experiencing violence and discrimination there also, they worked on the railroads and followed them down to the San Joquine and El Centro Valleys around Stockton and Yuba City, California. These agrarian regions fit with the agricultural background of those from India and the early history of the South Asian Americans is the story of those in California. Ties with their homeland were maintained as they sent money back to India and participated in the Ghadr Party, an organization prominent in the early part of the twentieth century promoting India obtaining independence from Britain. There were a few scattered individuals but the center of the community remained in California. Facing discrimination, not being allowed to bring spouses, and declining economic opportunities caused South Asian men to leave, which caused the community to decrease in size until the passage of the Luce-Cellar Bill in 1948 made some immigration and family reunification possible. After that, South Asian American numbers slowly increased.

Since 1968, things changed drastically and South Asian immigration became numerous and dominated by the highly educated, well trained professionals. Post-1968 South Asian Americans now fall structurally into three distinct segments: (1) initial immigrants, (2) second wave immigrants, and (3) third wave or sponsored immigrants. *Initial immigrants* are those who came in the 1960s, were dominated by a cohort of highly educated men, and worked as doctors, scientists, and academics who migrated for better educational and professional opportunities. Generally their wives had little more than a high school education and did not work outside the home. Today their children are in college, marrying, and starting families. Their concerns revolve around retirement and their children's marriages, hopefully to a person from their home region, not a white or a South Asian American—the latter likely to be spoiled by American influence.

These initial immigrants, like those that follow them, like their privacy. Thus they do not form residential enclaves. The telephone, automobile, and good roads enable them to have the best of both worlds—privacy and membership in the South Asian American social network. The telephone plus frequent flights enable these and those that follow to be involved in family and community affairs in India as if they were living there, which also makes them subject to the norms and strictures of the community in their homeland. Living into two communities, can, in fact, create conflicts for immigrants who find themselves simultaneously confronted with the different social, cultural, political, and economic realities of the United States and India.

When they initially arrived, the goal was to return to India with their fortune early enough so their children would not be "corrupted" by American ways. Usually, however, the return was postponed so that the youngsters did not want to leave their friends in the United States. Returning for retirement was also a consideration but leaving the children and grandchildren, even for India, was too large a price to pay.

In 1987, gangs of youths calling themselves *Dot Busters* (*dot* refers to the *bindi* mark worn by Hindu women on their forehead) attacked Asian Indians in Jersey City, New Jersey. For the first time, the East Coast community had to deal with external racism, internal division, and to how to deal with the situation. Even now, a consensus has not been reached and the external hostility is still there.

The *second wave immigrants* came to the United States in the 1970s. Like the initial segment, they too were highly educated professionals. Unlike their compatriots in the initial segment, their wives were highly educated and worked outside the home. Today their children are college-bound teenagers, and their chief concerns include facilitating this education. The *third wave* or *sponsored segment* are those immigrants sponsored by established family members. They are generally less well-educated and more likely to work in the motel industry, own and run small grocery stores, gas stations, and other small business ventures. Their concerns revolve around establishing themselves in a successful business.

South Asian Americans have been able to organize for specific causes and to exert political pressure. They cooperate with the Pan-Asian movement over such issues as immigration legislation, gaining fair treatment in university admissions, or eliminating the glass ceiling, while at the same time working for local or civic causes.

ARTHUR HELWEG

See also **Bangladesh; Diaspora: Hindus; India; Pakistan; Sikhs**

Further Reading

Helweg, Arthur W., and Usha M. Helweg, *An Immigrant Success Story: East Indians in North America*, Philadelphia: University of Pennsylvania Press, 1990

La Brack, Bruce, *The Sikhs of Northern California 1904–1975: A Socio-Historic Study*, New York: AMS Press, 1988

————, "South Asians," in *A Nation of Peoples: A Sourcebook on America's Multicultural Heritage*, edited by Ellott Robert Barkan, Westport, London: Greenwood Press, 1999

Leonard, Karen Isaksen, *South Asian Americans*, Westport, London: Greenwood Press

Rangaswamy, Padma, *Namaste America: India Immigrants in an American Metropolis*, University Park: Pennsylvania State University Press, 2000

Tinker, Hugh, *The Banyan Tree: Overseas Emigrants from India, Pakistan, and Bangladesh*, Oxford and New York: Oxford University Press, 1977

South Asians in Asia and The Pacific

Capsule Summary

Location: West Asia and the Pacific
Total Population: 5.33 million
Languages: English, Hindi, Urdu, and others
Religions: Hindu, Muslim, Christian, and Sikh

Of the 10 million people of the South Asian diaspora, about 5.6 million reside in the Asia Pacific region. They originate primarily from India, Pakistan, and Bangladesh. Before gaining independence from Britain in 1947, the entire region was considered India. The Partition of 1947 created from this region two discrete sovereign states, India and Pakistan. Bangladesh later obtained independence from Pakistan in 1971.

After slavery was abolished in the British colonies in the early nineteenth century, cheap labor was needed especially in areas dominated by plantation economies or labor-intensive technologies such as sugar and cocoa plantations, coal mines, and estates. In India, at that time, there were overcrowded agricultural districts where crop failure plunged entire villages into near starvation. Also, individuals left for personal reasons, such as displeasing a village elder, having a family quarrel, or being wanted by the authorities. During this time, emigration was stimulated by the desire to leave India more than the desire to go elsewhere. Agents near the ports of embarkation, especially Madras and Calcutta, used dubious methods of recruitment. Consequently, the Tamil and Telugu districts of the Madras Presidency in the south and Bihar's Chhota Nagpur and the United Provinces in the north were primary areas of recruitment. Their destinations in the Pacific were primarily Mauritius, the first country to receive indentured workers, starting in 1834, then South Africa in 1860, and Fiji in 1879. Movement to East Africa started in 1895, the Middle East or West Asia in 1972, and Malaysia in 1900. Most entered as indentured cheap laborers to replace the slaves who had just been freed. They left India with the goal of returning, but only about a third did and they arrived home penniless and almost all in poor health.

Conditions for emigrants going to and living in the Caribbean were similar to those going to or living in Mauritius, South Africa, or Fiji. Villagers in the interior were particularly vulnerable to dubious methods used in recruitment. They were also easier to control, partly because of their ignorance and partly due to the deculturalization process. Once recruited, many laborers had to travel hundreds of miles on foot to reach a port of embarkation, which took up to 30 or 40 days. They would then have to wait, sometimes as long as three weeks, in a depot full of strangers who spoke a different language and had different customs. The recruits wore convict-type clothing, had to often eat strange food, learn a new language, and live in conditions similar to those of their slave predecessors. During the voyage, they were also treated like their slave predecessors, living in overcrowded and filthy conditions where sickness was rampant and the death rate in one passage was as high as 38 percent. Upon landing, the arrivals were marched to their camps, which were usually old slave quarters.

The workers had few rights, which were generally ignored. Health care was poor, living conditions abysmal, working conditions primitive, pay low, and fines and targets unrealistically high. Because of fines and deductions, workers at the end of their indenture ended up owing money rather than keeping any. Suicide rates were, not surprisingly, high. In the mid-1870s, the rate was 46 per million in Madras and 54 per million in the UP; but, by comparison, it was 640 per million in Natal and 780 in Fiji, which climbed to 831 in 1810. The workers also were relatively isolated culturally because it was primarily a male population who could not visit their homeland due to lack of money and difficult traveling conditions. Thus, maintaining their culture was difficult at best; however, some of their music, food, language, religion, and celebrations were retained.

Movement to East Africa was different than movement to Malaya. For East Africa, significant immigration began in the late nineteenth century and virtually all were "free passengers." They were mostly from Gujarat and Punjab. They also were able to keep close contact with their homeland. Because of these close ties, those from Gujarat and Punjab were often considered an alien element. This was possible because their settlements had closer proximity to South Asia and transportation was more comfortable, faster, and efficient. Thus, for these people, spouses were brought from the homeland and communications and travel to and from South Asia was more common, resulting in a stronger maintenance of the culture of their homeland.

In Malaysa, the South Asian community was primarily Tamils from Madras. Those that worked on plantations, called *plantation Indians*, were considered by the British managers as industrious and docile in their acceptance of conditions, most living for the day when they would return to their village in India. After World War II, South Asians became politically active. The Indians realized their future was in being educated and in business, roles they have actively pursued, especially in Singapore where they are more recognized as a distinct component of Singapore's multiethnic society.

Post-1950 emigrees went to Britain and Australia and many left East Africa for Britain and India. By the 1970s, the emigration stream from South Asia had changed from unskilled, uneducated, rural villagers to highly educated professionals, technicians, engineers, doctors, and academics. Some went to Australia, but the oil-rich Gulf States were the largest recipients. Many went initially as temporary workers but the South Asian contingent remains high. In the 1990s, a South Asian community began developing in Japan, composed primarily of unskilled people. Many have remained by overstaying their visa and others have married Japanese spouses.

The South Asian diaspora of today has one major difference from its predecessors: contact with the homeland is much more extensive. Magazines, newspapers, and videotapes from South Asia are distributed worldwide, and travel back and forth to the homeland is easier and more affordable. Thus visits by politicians, government representatives, and performing artists are quite common, and the age-old dream of maintaining one's culture abroad is being realized.

ARTHUR HELWEG

Further Reading

Clarke, Colin, Ceri Peach, and Steven Vertovec, editors, *South Asians Overseas: Migration and Ethnicity*, Cambridge and New York: Cambridge University Press, 1990

Patel, Dhiru, "South Asian Diasporas," http://www.himalmag.com/99Dec/diaspora.html.

Tinker, Hugh, *The Banyan Tree: Overseas Emigrants from India, Pakistan and Bangladesh*, Oxford, New York, Delhi, and Karachi: Oxford University Press, 1977

———, *A New System of Slavery: The Export of Indian Labour Overseas 1830–1920*, London, New York, and Bombay: Oxford University Press

Vertovec, Steven, editor, *Aspects of the South Asian Diaspora, Oxford University Press Papers on India, 2, Part 2*, Delhi, Bombay, Calcutta, and Madras: Oxford University Press, 1991

South Asians in Europe

Capsule Summary

Location: United Kingdom, Netherlands, France, Germany
Total Population: approximately 1.5 million
Languages: Hindi, Urdu, Punjabi, Gujarati, Bangla
Religions: Muslim, Hindu, Sikh, Buddhist, Christian, Jain, Parsi

Southern Asia is also known as the Indian subcontinent and includes Bangladesh, India, Pakistan, and Sri Lanka. The Southern Asian presence in Europe is mainly the result of the continuing development of the world capitalist economy and the rebuilding of shattered national economies following World War II. The Southern Asian population of Europe is estimated at 1.5 million, a substantial 85 percent of which is settled in the United Kingdom. At the beginning of the twenty-first century, Southern Asians constituted just over three percent of this country's total population. The other main receiving countries for migrants from Southern Asia are The Netherlands, France, and Germany which together account for a further 12 percent of Europe's Southern Asian population. There is a much smaller Southern Asian population in a number of other European countries, most notably Spain, Portugal, and Sweden.

Southern Asians in Europe are a diverse group according to country of origin, religion, language, and culture. The majority came from peasant farming families but a minority had urban origins with commercial skills and/or professional qualifications. Over half of Britain's Southern Asian population is of Indian origin, approximately one-third originates from Pakistan and one-tenth from Bangladesh. It is drawn from three areas of the subcontinent: Punjab which covers the border between India and Pakistan in the northwest, from which two-thirds of British Southern Asians originate, Gujarat on the western coast, from which one-quarter originate, and Sylhet District in the northeast of Bangladesh. These are by no means the poorest areas, reflecting that economic migration is an entrepreneurial activity requiring some premigration financial outlay. It is estimated that just under half of Southern Asians in Britain are Muslim, 27 percent are Hindu, and 20 percent are Sikh. A small minority follows a number of other religions including Buddhism and Christianity. These figures disguise significant heterogeneity among followers of each religion. Languages spoken include Hindi, Urdu, Punjabi, Gujarati, and Bangla, often with dialects that are specific to the individual's region of origin. Cultural traditions and practices vary according to country and region of origin as well as caste, sect, and kinship-group membership.

History

The first Southern Asians to travel to Europe came as sailors, students, and emissaries at the height of the British Empire. Throughout the twentieth century, a far greater number traveled freely to Europe as economic migrants and engaged in various unskilled, skilled, professional, and entrepreneurial occupations. The tradition of migration from Southern Asia developed from the late nineteenth century on and was initially related to the deprivation that arose from attempting to sustain a large population on a limited amount of fertile land. The main concentration of European Southern Asians in the United Kingdom is a legacy of Britain's extensive imperial involvement on the Indian subcontinent. Until immigration controls gradually put a stop to it, Southern Asians were entitled to travel freely to the United Kingdom as members of the British Empire and, later, the Commonwealth. The countries of the Indian subcontinent gained independence from Britain in the years following World War II. The departing British initially encouraged immigration to Britain because Southern Asia was seen as a cheap and plentiful source of labor at a time of high demand. The peak period of immigration from India and Pakistan was 1955 to 1964 and for Bangladesh it was much later in the early 1980s. During the late 1960s and early 1970s, a small number of Southern Asians also settled in the United Kingdom as political refugees from East Africa. They became known as *twice migrants* because many had lived in Africa for generations but were forced to leave due to the Africanization policies of the Kenyan and Ugandan governments. Their presence in East Africa and their flight to the United Kingdom was another legacy of Britain's colonial involvement in Africa and India.

The spatial distribution of the United Kingdom's Southern Asian population reflects the destinations of the early migrants who settled in major centers of industry where they were most likely to find employment. The main receiving centers for the immigrants were Greater London, the West Midlands, Greater Manchester, the mill towns of Lancashire and West Yorkshire, the East Midlands, and Glasgow. Most found employment in various forms of manufacturing industry, such as textiles and engineering, which offered poor conditions of employment including low rates of pay and unsociable working hours.

With the exception of twice migrants who mainly arrived as complete family units, Southern Asians generally followed a pattern of chain migration. Individual men usually came alone to find work and lived together often in over-crowded conditions in shared houses. This enabled them to send part of their earnings to members of their extended family who had sponsored the migration by providing the airfare and regarded it as an investment. Migration was not usually intended to be permanent as many men expected to return to Southern Asia after successfully increasing their family's capital and, as a result, its standing in the local social hierarchy. Migration was not therefore an individual activity as their continued membership of and responsibilities to the extended family were paramount. However, during the 1960s and early 1970s, a series of immigration acts in the United Kingdom gradually reduced the men's rights and status and helped to encourage chain migration as many Southern Asians chose family reunification whilst it remained an option. During this period, wives and children arrived in substantial numbers from the subcontinent.

The presence of women in an immigrant community generally indicates that the migration is permanent, and Southern Asians were no exception in this respect. By the mid-1970s, they had established thriving communities in cities and towns across the United Kingdom (and other parts of Europe to a much lesser extent). The pattern of chain migration followed by Southern Asians facilitated the development of spatially and culturally distinct communities because many kin and fellow villagers settled in the same part of a European town or city. Although this helped to make Europe a home away from home, the majority cherished what is usually referred to as a *myth of return* as they still perceived Southern Asia as their real home and intended to go back. However, there was a gradual realization that they had grown accustomed to a standard of living that could not be matched, or at least sustained, if they returned and their children, who had been born and/or brought up in Europe did not usually wish to leave.

Society

The myth of return has gradually subsided, mainly because relative prosperity and global developments in communications have enabled Southern Asians to maintain extensive ties with Southern Asia. They send money to relatives on the subcontinent, invest in the local economy by purchasing property, land, and businesses, and sustain close kinship networks, often through arranged marriages. Cheap and efficient air travel has increased the regularity and length of visits and has enabled the first generation of migrants to visit with their European-born and/or reared offspring. Overall, improvements in communications have ensured that there is a constant, substantial two-way flow of goods, information, and people helping to sustain intercontinental ties.

Permanent migration to Europe has led to greater emphasis on retaining cultural traditions and practices. The first generation of Southern Asian migrants has developed diverse and imaginative ways to re-create

their familiar cultural and religious world and pass it on to younger generations. For example, the extended family has remained the norm among them but the types of housing available in Europe initially hindered its physical reproduction. They have addressed this by acquiring more than one property on the same street and, in some cases, people who are related have bought most or all of the properties on one street. Southern Asians also rapidly established places of worship close to where they lived. They initially transformed existing buildings but an increasing number of mosques and temples are built due to a combination of donations from local Southern Asians and religious organizations overseas. Places of worship have become the symbolic and practical focal points of local communities and are used for a diverse range of formal and informal educational, political, and social activities. In particular, life-cycle rituals such as those associated with birth, marriage, and death can be properly carried out according to religious tenets and cultural traditions. Specialist fabric, food, hardware, home entertainment, and jewelry shops are an integral part of most neighborhoods as a result of Southern Asian entrepreneurial activity, some of which have developed into national and international businesses.

Southern Asians usually define themselves either as *Asian* or according to their specific country of origin. This disguises that religious affiliation is a very important source of common identity among migrants and that their everyday experiences are mainly centered on much narrower loyalties of caste, sect, and kinship group. In fact, caste remains a dominant feature of social organization among Southern Asians in Europe and kinship networks remain caste-specific. At its most basic level, caste refers to the reciprocal responsibilities of a group of people with common interests. Southern Asians who do not follow the Hindu religion reject the principle of caste as, for example, Muslims and Sikhs condemn it on theological grounds. However, in rural communities of different religions on the subcontinent, the hereditary ascribing of occupation reinforces caste-like divisions and further group closure occurs from the preference for arranged marriages between cousins. As immigrants, caste-like loyalties have proved a very effective means of gaining access to jobs and housing, receiving financial and emotional support particularly in times of difficulty and mobilizing collectively to gain scare resources in the wider society.

The strength of community, caste, and kinship ties has been extremely valuable in challenging and overcoming the various forms of disadvantage and discrimination that

Southern Asians have faced. They were initially expected to assimilate into the majority culture and society so it has taken many years for local and national governments to recognize and begin to address their specific cultural needs and interests. For example, the religiously and culturally based dietary and dress requirements of Southern Asian children have gradually been accommodated in European schools. The tenacity with which Southern Asians have protected and continuously reproduced their cultural traditions has resulted in a tendency for them to be seen, and to see themselves, as outsiders in European societies despite having full citizenship. This has been compounded by their experiences of racial discrimination, harassment, and attacks. However, by the end of the twentieth century most children of Southern Asian origin in the United Kingdom had been born there. This means that during the twenty-first century a rapidly increasing percentage of Europe's Southern Asian population will regard Europe as home and know no other. There is much evidence that the second generation is successfully forging a place in European society whilst maintaining the religion and culture of their parents. For example, the majority wish to have an arranged marriage despite the different social norms of the wider society. Rates of intermarriage therefore remain very low although they are slowly increasing.

It is said that Southern Asians face a "Jewish" future in Europe because they have increasingly entered white-collar, professional, entrepreneurial and self-employed occupations and are achieving high levels of educational attainment and home ownership. This generalization disguises significant differences between the composite groups with Indians and East African Asians faring much better than Pakistanis and Bangladeshis. Furthermore, evidence has suggested that Southern Asians incur an "ethnic penalty" in that they require higher qualifications than the indigenous white population to enter comparable occupations. Property has also been shown to be less of an investment for Southern Asians because they are more likely to purchase housing that is of little value and/or is unlikely to retain its worth.

The overall percentage of Southern Asians in the European population is predicted to increase because they have higher rates of fertility than the majority white population and Southern Asian births far outnumber deaths. However, they will remain a very small minority in Europe as even in Britain their number is predicted to increase to and then stabilize at a mere six percent of the overall population.

NADIA JOANNE BRITTON

Further Reading

Anwar, Mohammed, *Between Cultures: Continuity and Change in the Lives of Young Asians*, London: Routledge, 1998

Ballard, Roger, editor, *Desh Pardesh: The South Asian Presence in Britain*, London: Hurst & Co, 1994

Brown, Judith. M, and Rosemary Foot, editors, *Migration: The Asian Experience*, Basingstoke: The MacMillan Press Ltd, 1994

Clarke, Colin, Ceri Peach, and Steven Vertovec, editors, *South Asians Overseas: Migration and Ethnicity*, Cambridge: Cambridge University Press, 1990

Modood, Tariq, *Not Easy Being British: Colour, Culture and Citizenship*, Stoke-on-Trent: Trentham Books, 1992

Werbner, Pnina, *The Migration Process: Capital, Gifts and Offerings among British Pakistanis*, Oxfords: Berg Publishers Ltd, 1990

South Asians in The Americas (Non-U.S.)

Capsule Summary

Location: Canada and the Caribbean
Total Population: 1.7 million; 700,000 in Canada and one million in the Caribbean
Languages: English, Hindi, Urdu, and other languages of South Asia
Religions: Hindu, Muslim, Jain, Sikh, Christian, and other religions of South Asia

South Asian emigration stems from primarily India, Pakistan, and Bangladesh. Before 1947 South Asia was all part of India; Bangladesh was part of Pakistan until it obtained its independence in 1971. The people of South Asian origin in the Americas are part of the 10 million members of the South Asian community living outside their "homeland.". Large-scale emigration

SOUTH ASIANS IN THE AMERICAS (NON-U.S.)

began around 1830 after the abolition of slavery in the Caribbean. The British colonial rulers set up an indentured system which allowed South Asia to provide cheap labor to replace the recently freed slaves. British Guiana started receiving indentured South Asians in 1838; Trinidad, Guadeloupe, and Martinique in 1845; Jamaica in 1854; and Dutch Guiana in 1873.

India was experiencing overcrowded agricultural districts, massive crop failures and the near starvation of whole villages. Indenturing oneself was a way to escape intolerable living conditions. Abuses were rampant. The voyage was under similar conditions as employed for slaves—promises were not kept, living conditions were atrociously bad, and cheating workers out of their wages was common.

Contacts with the homeland were few, but South Asians retained elements of their cultural heritage, that is language, food, religion, celebrations, and music. After 1945, as the South Asian communities became more affluent and travel became much easier, contacts with their homeland intensified: families were united, visits back and forth increased, the government of India encouraged buildings links, and South Asian politicians visited South Asian communities in the Caribbean. Thus there has been a revival of "Indianness" in the 1990s since most originate from what is today India. However, the South Asians in the Caribbean have become active in their countries of residence. For instance, Cheddi Jagan was president of Guyana, Shridath Ramphal was secretary general of the commonwealth, and Hasan Ali served as president of Trinidad and Tobago for seven years.

In Canada, South Asians represent a new type of immigrant—highly educated, professional, entrepreneurial, and transnational in their orientation. South Asians, specifically Sikhs, entered North America via Vancouver in significant numbers in 1903. Forty-three entered in 1904–1905 and 2,623 in 1907–1908. By 1908, the Asian Indian population in Canada was about 5,000, mostly Sikhs residing in Vancouver.

However anti-Asian sentiment quickly developed. Immigration requirements were changed by raising the head tax from $25 to $200, and by requiring an immigrant to be on a continuous voyage from his country of origin, which was not possible from India at that time.

Some Sikhs challenged the regulations by chartering the *Komagata Maru* and setting sail for Vancouver on April 4, 1914. They were denied entry, except for 22 passengers who had proof of return domicile. From 1909 to 1943, only 878 South Asians entered Canada, which did not compensate for the more than 1,000 that left during the economic downturns of the 1920s. Sikhs from Punjab were still the dominate group and remained centered in Vancouver; their concerns became Canada-centered rather than India-centered. They branched out into agriculture and an entrepreneurial class developed. Some owned saw mills while others had smaller businesses. It was a time when the community changed from a group of men doing hard physical labor so they could return to Punjab a *Bara Sahib*, a "big man" or "important person," to a community of families establishing themselves in Canada. *Gurdwaras*, Sikh places of worship, cultural, and religious organizations, were founded. Some maintained their interest in their homeland and supported India's struggle for independence.

Starting with the Immigration Act of 1947 and culminating with the Immigration Act of 1976, the legislation facilitated family reunification, nondiscriminatory admission standards, and fulfilled Canada's humanitarian obligation to refugees. Between 1945 and 1955 1,139 South Asians were admitted, between 1956 and 1962 4,088 entered, and between 1963 and 1967 12,856 came in. With the removal of barriers, 30,501 entered between 1968 and 1972 and 57,411 between 1973 and 1977. By 1996 India ranked fifth in supplying 235,930 or 4.7 percent of Canada's immigrants. The 1967 legislation gave preference to those with education and skills needed in Canada.

South Asia had a ready supply of highly educated medical doctors, engineers, scientist, and managers who quickly entered. They had been educated in a British-oriented system and were familiar with Western ways. The center for South Asians became Toronto and the composition was no longer dominated by Punjabi Sikhs. These new arrivals quickly stepped into mid- and high- level positions, or quickly rose. The benefit to Canada was that it was getting some of the best talent the world had to offer. The benefit to India was that that country was obtaining remittances and technological transfer (but at the same time, losing talent she had invested in educating).

The Canadian South Asian population of the 1990s is more balanced in gender and area of origin. Vancouver was second, until the 1990s when Quebec took over second place. Anti-Asian sentiment and violence broke out in Canada, especially in Toronto and Vancouver in the 1970s, but by the 1990s, South Asians in Canada had become a prosperous minority, enjoying a much higher

1142

level of acceptance than in previous decades. Now their investments and involvements are in both Canada and India and ranges from running an international business to establishing or supporting programs to help the poor and needy.

ARTHUR HELWEG

See also **India; Sikhs; South-Asian Americans (India, Pakistan, Bangladesh)**

Further Reading

Buchignani, Norman, Doreen M. Indra, and Ram Srivastiva, *Continuous Journey: A Social History of South Asians in Canada*, McClelland and Stewart in association with the Multiculturalism Directorate, Dept. of the Secretary of State and the Canadian Govt. Pub. Centre, Supply and Services, Canada, 1985

Chandrasekhar, S., *From India to Canada: A Brief History of Immigration; Problems of Discrimination; Admission and Assimilation*, LaJolla: A Population Review Book, 1986

D'Costa, Ronald, "Socio-Demographic Characteristics of the Population of South Asian Origins in Canada," in *Ethnicity, Identity, Migration: The South Asian Context*, edited by Milton Israel and N.K. Wagle, Toronto: University of Toronto and Centre for South Asian Studies, 1993

Johnston, Hugh, *The Voyage of the Komagata Maru: The Sikh Challenge to Canada's Colour Bar*, Delhi, Bombay, Calcutta, and Madras: Oxford University Press, 1979

Tinker, Hugh, *A New System of Slavery: The Export of Indian Labour Overseas 1830–1920*, London: Oxford University Press, 1974

———, *The Banyan Tree: Overseas Emigrants from India, Pakistan, and Bangladesh*, Oxford, New York, Delhi, and Karachi: Oxford University Press, 1977

Southeast Asian Americans (Vietnam, Laos, Cambodia)

Capsule Summary

Location: United States
Total Population: 1,463,172
Languages: English, French, Khmer, Lao, Vietnamese
Religions: Buddhism, Christianity, Islam, Animism, other

According to the 2000 U.S. Census, there are 1,122,528 Vietnamese-Americans, 171,937 Cambodian-Americans, and 168,707 Lao-Americans living in the United States of America. These 1,463,172 Southeast Asian Americans make up a significant-sized immigrant group in the United States and whose history is a story of unique immigration and adjustment.

The first major influx of immigrants from Southeast Asia occurred in 1975 at the end of the Second Indochinese War between the Democratic Republic of Vietnam (DRV) and the United States. About 130,000 journeyed to the United States after the war ended, and five years later, the number increased to more than 560,000. These Vietnamese, Lao, and Cambodians arrived as refugees and began the struggle in America to survive, eke out a living, and attempt to fit into a new culture. The largest groups of Vietnamese settled in southern California in Westminster, California. This community, located south of Los Angeles in Orange County, became the American capital of the Vietnamese immigrant population. The area has a part of town nicknamed *Little Saigon*, a Vietnamese chamber of commerce, and around 2,000 Vietnamese-owned businesses. According to the 2000 Census, about 146,613 Vietnamese reside in the San Francisco Bay area. The next largest groups of Vietnamese Americans live in the Houston area (63,924) and the Dallas-Ft. Worth area (47,090).

Like the Vietnamese community, Lao and Cambodian ethnic communities sprang up around the United States after 1975 in Texas, Louisiana, Illinois, Washington, Oregon, Virginia, Minnesota, Florida, and Pennsylvania. California has the largest concentration of all Southeast Asian Americans, the only exception being the Hmong, a mountain-dwelling people of Laos and Vietnam, whose largest community is in Minnesota. The largest Cambodian groups live in California (Los Angeles-Orange County-Riverside, 36,233), Massachusetts

SOUTHEAST ASIAN AMERICANS (VIETNAM, LAOS, CAMBODIA)

(Boston area, 17,301) and Washington (Seattle-Tacoma-Bremerton, 12,391). The largest Lao groups reside in California (San Francisco area, 11,545; Sacramento area, 9,814; Los Angeles area, 7,626; San Diego, 7,002), and Minnesota (Minneapolis-St. Paul, 7,576). The Hmong live largely in Minnesota (Minneapolis-St. Paul, 40,707), California (Fresno, 22,456; Sacramento-Yolo, 16,621), and Wisconsin (Milwaukee-Racine, 8,078). Each ethnic group has its own language and culture and lives in relative isolation from the other groups.

The majority of the Vietnamese (among whom were large numbers of ethnic Chinese) came to the United States by American military evacuation in the final days of the Second Indochinese War in 1975. More refugees fled Vietnam as the victorious North Vietnamese forces took control of South Vietnam. Among them were vast numbers of "boat people," who used any sea vessel at their disposal to escape Southeast Asia. Many were first harbored in refugee camps throughout Southeast Asia before immigrating to the United States. While these immigrants were allowed into the United States under various refugee laws, the U.S. government sought the help of volunteer agencies to find American sponsors and to arrange for jobs and housing. The immigrants were then sent to various parts of the country to begin new lives. The government's purpose in this program was to spread them around the country and thus prevent the growth of ethnic colonies like the one that developed in Westminster, California. The plan did not work and, after a period of time isolated from each other, refugee families began to relocate to larger ethnic communities. This second migration resulted in the present settlement and location of the Southeast Asian communities.

These resettled immigrants found life challenging in the United States. While most of the first Southeast Asian refugees had been well-educated urban dwellers, the later arrivals came from rural backgrounds and had limited, if any, education. The Hmong, for example, were largely subsistence farmers without a written language. The new immigrants, like other ethnic immigrant groups from around the world before them, spoke very little English and possessed few skills that would ensure their survival and prosperity in an urban, industrialized setting. Many suffered from physical and psychological traumas that they had experienced before fleeing Southeast Asia. The Vietnamese escaped from oppressive Socialist Republic of Vietnam post-war policies. The Lao and Hmong (who had worked closely

with the U.S. military in the American effort to secure Laos from the North Vietnamese-supported Pathet Lao) escaped systematic repression from the new Lao People's Democratic Republic government. The Cambodians escaped from the genocidal rant of Pol Pot's regime. Their strong work ethnic, strong family ties, emphasis on bettering their lives, and sheer determination have allowed the Southeast Asian Americans to become less dependent upon public aid and to begin to from a new living in America. Members of large Southeast Asian families usually helped one another with living expenses and education costs. Southeast Asia American businesses sprung up in the urban areas where the groups settled. The second generation of Southeast Asian immigrants were able to obtain an education in American schools, thus helping to bridge the cultural gap between themselves and their parents who had immigrated from Vietnam, Cambodia, and Laos. Today, Southeast Asian Americans, while still struggling in some areas of living, have been able to forge a new and successful life in the United States while maintaining the unique culture they brought with them from their homelands.

RICHARD VERRONE

Further Reading

Bass, Thomas A., *Vietnamerica: The War Comes Home*, Soho Press, 1997

Cao, Lan, *Everything You Need to Know about Asian American History*, Plume, 1996

Chang, Robert S., *Disoriented: Asian Americans, Law, and the Nation-State*, New York: University Press, 1999

DeBonis, Steven, *Children of the Enemy: Oral Histories of Vietnamese Amerasians and Their Mothers*, McFarland & Company, 1994

Fong, Timothy P., *The Contemporary Asian American Experience: Beyond the Model Minority*, Prentice Hall, 1998

Freeman, James M., *Changing Identities: Vietnamese Americans, 1975–1995*, Allyn and Bacon, 1996

Hmong Website. <http://www.vstudies.org/>

Kitano, H.H., and Roger Daniels, *Asian Americans: The Emerging Minority*, Prentice, 1988

Morrison, Gayle, *Sky is Falling: An Oral History of the CIA's Evacuation of the Hmong from Laos*, Jefferson, North Carolina: McFarland, 1999

Mote, Sue M., *Hmong and America: Stories of Transition to a Strange Land*, Jefferson, North Carolina: McFarland, 2004

Ong, Aihawa, *Buddha Is Hiding: Refugees, Citizenship, the New America*, University of California Press, 2003

Rutledge, Paul J., *The Vietnamese in America*, Minneapolis: Lerner Publications Co., 1987

Rutledge, Paul J., *The Vietnamese Experience in America (Minorities in Modern America)*, Indiana University Press, 2000

Spain

Capsule Summary

Country Name: Kingdom of Spain
Location: Mainland in Southwestern Europe. Territory includes Canary Islands (in the Atlantic Ocean), Balearic Islands (in the Mediterranean Sea), and the cities of Ceuta and Melilla in Northern Africa
Total Population: 40,217,413 (July 2003)
Form of Government: Parliamentary Monarchy
Ethnic Populations: Spaniards, Catalans, Basques, Galicians, Gypsies
Languages: Spanish (official language of the State), Catalan (official language in the Autonomous Communities of Catalonia, Valencia, and Balearic Islands; also spoken in the Eastern strip of Autonomous Community of Aragon, and in a Northern area of the Autonomous Community of Murcia), Galician (Official language in the Autonomous Community of Galicia; also spoken in western strip of the Autonomous Communities of Asturias and Castile-Leon), Basque (official language of the Basque Autonomous Community; also official language in the Northern area of the Autonomous Community of Navarre), Occitan (spoken in the Aran Valley, in the Autonomous Community of Catalonia), Asturian or Bable (spoken in the Autonomous Community of Asturias), Aragonese or Fabla (spoken in Northern valleys of the Autonomous Community of Aragon), Portuguese (spoken in some villages of the Autonomous Communities of Extremadura and Castile-León), and Bereberic (spoken among the inhabitants of the Autonomous Cities of Ceuta and Melilla)
Religions: Most of the population belongs to the Catholic tradition; there are some minor Protestant, Muslim, and Jewish communities

The Kingdom of Spain occupies most of the Iberian Peninsula and includes the Balearic islands (Mediterranean Sea), the Canary Islands (Atlantic Ocean) and the cities of Ceuta and Melilla on the North African coast. In the past, Spain controlled a vast colonial Empire, which, until the first half of the nineteenth century, included most of Central and South America. The islands of Cuba and Puerto Rico remained under Spanish sovereignty until 1898, as did the Philippines. In Africa, Spain controlled colonies in Equatorial Guinea, the north of Morocco, Ifni, and the Western Sahara. This last colony was abandoned only in 1975.

From the eighth century CE, Christian and Muslim kingdoms fought over the control of the Iberian Peninsula. This phase of history came to an end in 1492 when the Kingdom of Spain occupied most of the Iberian Peninsula and included the Balearic islands (Mediterranean Sea), the Canary Islands (Atlantic), and the Kingdom of Granada was conquered by the Catholic monarchs, who unified the crowns of Castile and Aragon through marriage. The definitive political unity of the state was established in the same period through the colonization of the Canary Islands, the conquest of the Kingdom of Navarre, and the establishment of control over different areas in North Africa.

The process of legal, social, linguistic, and political unification of the Spanish monarchy was consolidated over the course of the following centuries. In the political sphere, institutional differences remained in the territories belonging to the Kingdom of Aragon (Aragon itself, Valencia, the Balearic Islands, and Catalonia), but their autonomy would be suppressed in the eighteenth century following the ascension of the Bourbons to the Spanish throne. The differences observed in the political regime of the Basque Provinces of Biscay, Alava, Guipuzcoa, and Navarre, however, remained intact until the nineteenth century. In the religious sphere, Spanish identity was constructed on the basis of the Catholic faith. This process was aided by the expulsion of the Jews in 1492 (between 500,000 and 800,000 were expelled), and that of the *moriscos* (Muslims who practiced their faith in secret) in 1609 (between 500,000 and 3 million expelled). At the same time Spain became a main bulwark against the Protestant Reformation. In the linguistic sphere, Romance languages dominated almost all of the Iberian Peninsula from the Middle Ages on. Of the pre-Latin languages, only the Basque tongue remained alive in parts of the four northern provinces. The Latin inheritance evolved into different languages in the course of the Medieval period. These were, geographically from west to east, Galician-Portugese, Asturian-Leonese, Castilian, and Catalan. Castilian Spanish was progressively established as the language of the dominant kingdom and as the official language from the sixteenth century on, to the detriment of Latin and the other peninsular languages.

The ideas of liberal constitutionalism began to evolve in Spain in the nineteenth century, together with the development of Spanish political nationalism. These ideas can already be observed in the Constitution proclaimed in Cadiz in 1812. These attempts to politically unify the kingdom came into conflict with the resistance of the Basque Provinces and their claim to maintain their special political regime. The most important aspects of this semi-independent political system would be suppressed by laws enacted in 1839 and 1876, following the First and Third Carlist Wars. However Romanticism and Nationalism were also to develop among the peripheral minorities in the second half of the nineteenth century, creating political and cultural movements which gained rapid ground, especially in the Basque Country and in Catalonia.

The first constitutional attempt to reflect the plurinational nature of the State was carried out during the First Republic (1873) with the drawing up of plans for a federal constitution. This attempt ended in failure after a period of profound crisis. In 1931, following the proclamation of the Second Republic, a system was created to enable some regions to gain autonomy. Catalonia and the Basque Country elected autonomous governments; these, however were suppressed by the military victory of insurgents in the Civil War (1936–1939). The Francoist dictatorship was characterized by a savage repression of national and linguistic differences and by a clear Catholic bias. As a result of the repression, new, left-leaning nationalist groupings sprang up, amongst which the most notable was the Basque separatist movement called *Basque Fatherland and Freedom* (ETA), which has carried out armed struggle from that time until now.

The political transition paved the way for a new constitution in 1978, based on the unbreakable unity of the Spanish Nation (Article 2), but which, at the same time, permits the creation of Autonomous Communities. The most important nationalist movements in Catalonia and other regions joined this constitutional consensus, but this was not true of the Basque Country, where the Constitution was only supported by 30 percent of the electorate, as opposed to 70 percent elsewhere.

Present-day Spain is made up of seventeen Autonomous Communities and two Autonomous Cities (Ceuta and Melilla). The Autonomous Communities wield a considerable level of autonomy. The principal political conflict at this moment is the situation of the Basque Country where the phenomenon of armed struggle continues to be present. Within a population which has a high proportion of immigrants, an important minority proclaim themselves in favor of total independence (between 20 percent and 40 percent of the total population according to different opinion polls) and the majority appears to be favorable to the right to self-determination. While in Catalonia the possibility of an open break from the State does not appear likely, the antagonism between centralist Spanish parties and Basque parties favoring sovereignty does not augur well for a solution to the political conflict in the Basque Country. The two main Spanish parties share their support for the existing constitutional model and the "Basque Question" is clearly the most sensitive subject in Spanish politics.

In linguistic terms, approximately 25 percent of the Spanish population have a mother tongue which is not Castilian. Catalan, which is spoken by some 6 million people (if the Valencian dialect is included), Galician with some 2.5 million speakers, and Basque with 600,000 native speakers in Spanish territory are official languages in their own communities, together with Castilian Spanish, and there are special policies to procure their normalization. The minority Occitan-speaking population of the Aran valley in Catalonia (approximately 4,000 speakers) is also object of special protection, as are, to a more limited extent, the linguistic minorities of Asturias (approximately 250,000 speakers) and Aragon (approximately 8,000) and the Berber-speaking minority in the city of Melilla (approximately 15,000 speakers).

With regard to religious plurality, the Spanish Constitution of 1978 permitted a considerable improvement in the situation of non-Catholics and even the signing of cooperation agreements between the State and the Muslim, Jewish, and Protestant communities. These communities represent very small minorities among Spanish nationals although up to a third of the population of the cities of Ceuta and Melilla is Muslim.

Spain also has a numerous, though dispersed, Gypsy community. Despite the process of assimilation which this community is experiencing, some Gypsies preserve their linguistic differences, although the main difference is in the cultural field. The figures with regard to the size of the Gypsy community are extremely uncertain and vary between 650,000 and 800,000 members. Many problems of coexistence continue to exist and political representation of the Gypsy minority is practically nonexistent at an institutional level.

Lastly, Spain has an increasing number of new minorities due to recent migrations. The immigration phenomenon was practically unknown in Spain until the 1980s. There are currently around 1 million foreigners resident in Spain, of which 200,000 are Moroccans, followed by Europeans and the communities of Peruvians, Dominicans, Chinese, Ecuadorians, and Argentines.

EDUARDO J. RUIZ VIEYTEZ

See also **Basques; Catalans; Occitans**

Further Reading

Artola, Miguel, director, *Historia de España*, Madrid: Alianza editorial, 1994

Barceló, Miquel, director, *Historia de los Pueblos de España*, Barcelona: Argos Vergara, 1984

Conversi, Daniele, *The Basques, The Catalans and Spain*, London: Hurst and Co., 1997

García de Cortazar, Fernando, González Vesga, and Jose Manuel, *Breve Historia de España*, Madrid: Alianza editorial, 1999

Gibbons, John, *Spanish Politics Today*, Manchester: Manchester University Press, 1999

Mar-Molinero, Clare, and Smith Angel, editors, *Nationalism and Nation in the Iberian Peninsula*, Oxford: Berg, 1996

San Román, Teresa, *La diferencia inquietante. Viejas y nuevas estrategias culturales de los gitanos*, Madrid: Siglo Veintiuno de España Editores, 1997

Sellier, Jean, and André Sellier, *Atlas des Peuples d'Europe Occidental*, Paris: La Decouverte, 1995

Tussel, Javier, *Historia de España en el siglo, XX*, Madrid: Taurus, 1999

Sri Lanka

Capsule Summary

Country Name: Democratic Socialist Republic of Sri Lanka (formerly Ceylon)
Location: Island in the Indian Ocean, approximately twenty miles southeast of India
Total Population: 19,742,439 (2003)
Ethnic Populations: Sinhalese (74%), Sri Lankan Tamils (13%), Muslims (7%), Indian Tamils (5%), others (Burghers, Malays, Vaddas, Gypsies, and Parsis) (1%)
Languages: Sinhala, Tamil, English, Malay, Gujarati
Religions: Buddhism (69%), Hinduism (15%), Christianity (8%), Islam (7%), others (such as Zoroastrianism and Bahaism) (1% or less)

The Democratic Socialist Republic of Sri Lanka is an island nation-state located between 5°55' to 9°50' north latitude and 79°42' to 81°52' east longitude in the Indian Ocean. It is separated from India by the Palk Strait. The country is 25,332 square miles (65,610 square kilometers) in size, 270 miles (435 kilometers) long and 140 miles (225 kilometers) wide. Colombo, located on the southwest coast, is the major city. Per capita gross domestic product (GDP) is $3,700 (2002 estimate).

Universal suffrage was introduced to the country's citizens in 1931, with the age of voting established at 18 years or older. The executive branch of government is headed by a president who is elected directly by the voters to a six-year term in office. The president can be re-elected to one addition six-year term in office. The president appoints a prime minister and a cabinet of ministers from among the members of the parliament or legislative branch of government. The parliament comprises 225 members or national representatives. Election of these members to six-year terms, with no limit on the number of terms that can be served in office, is via a proportional representation system. The proportional representation system is intended to facilitate the entry of representatives from smaller ethnic and religious groups into the parliament. The judicial branch of government is headed by a chief justice with other justices of the supreme court, followed by a system of appellant courts, high courts, district courts, and tribunals.

History

Human settlement of the island probably occurred around 500,000 BCE. An indigenous Neolithic technology termed the *Balangoda* culture developed around 5000 BCE. Indo-Aryan settlers seem to have colonized the island from north India in the first millennium BCE. A Sinhalese kingdom based at the north-central city of Anuradhapura developed. Dravidian settlers also began entering the island from south India, probably by the third century BCE. During the second century BCE, Dravidian attempts to control the region of Anuradhapura resulted in Sinhalese counteroffensives, poorly documented events whose historicity has been recast during modern times to serve nationalistic purposes.

The kingdom of Anuradhapura, based on a series of irrigation networks, and with various succeeding dynasties, maintained power despite political and military pressures from dynasties in south India, for around ten centuries. Individual rulers often relied on the support of south Indian rulers and the services of Tamil mercenaries to enforce claims to the throne. Sinhalese kings were drawn into the regional politics of the subcontinent, with invasions and counter invasions, culminating in the Cholas conquering the kingdom of Anuradhapura (circa 1017 CE) and eventually the rest of the island. Chola rulers relocated the administrative capital to the city of Polonnaruwa, further southeast, for strategic reasons. Sinhalese rule was reestablished in the island by 1070 CE. Polonnaruwa developed into a cosmopolitan city during the early eleventh century CE. Conflicts between the Sinhalese rulers and the south Indians coupled with struggles for succession within the Sinhalese ruling families eventually led to the abandonment of Polonnaruwa as the capital city in 1255 CE. A Tamil kingdom arose in the Jaffna peninsula, separated by forests from a new Sinhalese kingdom at Kotte (now located on the outskirts of Colombo) which lasted from the late fourteenth century to the end of the sixteenth century CE. Another important Sinhalese kingdom rose in the central hills of the island, with its capital at the city of Kandy.

During all those centuries, the island had been an entrepôt for international maritime trade. As a result, its Tamil name *Tambapanni* came to be rendered as *Taprobane* by Greeks and Romans. Its Sanskrit name *Serendipa* became the *Serendib* of the Arabs. The Portuguese arrived in the early sixteenth century CE seeking to control the spice trade. Portugal eventually ruled the southwestern coastal region and the Jaffna peninsula of the island, which they referred to as *Ceilao* (from which the name *Ceylon* derives). Under threat of Portuguese incursions into ports such as Trincomalee and Batticaloa on the east coast, the Sinhalese Kandyan kingdom reached agreement with the Dutch promising a monopoly over the spice trade to that European nation in exchange for assistance in expelling the Portuguese. By 1658 CE, Dutch forces had ousted the Portuguese. But, rather than return political control of the coastal regions to the Sinhalese, the Netherlands held on to their conquests. The Kandyan kingdom itself was taken over by a south Indian dynasty through marriage alliances. British forces, also seeking to control the East-West trade routes, expelled the Dutch from Ceylon in 1796 CE. By 1818 CE, the British controlled the entire island, incorporating it

into the Raj. The administrative, economic, legal, political, and transportation systems of modern Ceylon arose under British rule. Ceylon gained independence in 1948, remained part of the British Commonwealth, and was headed by a series of elected Sinhalese prime ministers until 1978 CE when it became a republic. The most serious political conflicts during the postindependence period have centered on relations between the Sinhalese and Tamil communities (see below) and on economic-based insurrections by a Nationalistic Marxist movement called the Janata Vimukti Peramuna (JVP) in 1971 and again in the 1980s CE.

Society

The overall population of Sri Lanka is approximately 19.7 million (2003), with an average annual rate of population growth of 1.3 percent. Infant mortality is 1.6 percent. Life expectancy of women is 75 years, that of men is 70 years. Adult literacy is 92 percent, largely a result of elementary-level through secondary-level education being compulsory and subsidized by the state. University-level education is also subsidized by the state, with entry based on ethic-based proportional ratios.

Ethnically, the population has a majority of Sinhalese (74 percent of the overall population) who claim descent from the north Indian immigrants of the first millennium BCE. They speak, read, and write in the Sinhala language—which is derived from Sanskrit and Prakrit, both Indo-European languages. Early Sinhalese settlers assimilated, culturally and ethnically, various indigenous groups of whom the Vaddas have survived to the present in extremely small numbers. Most Sinhalese (69 percent of the overall population) belong to Theravada Buddhism by confession, ascribing their faith to third-century BCE Indian missionaries. Buddhist monastic dwellings or *viharas* and reliquaries or *dagabas* are a constant presence throughout the country. Partially reflecting its Indian heritage, Sinhalese society has 14 different castes which can determine a person's socioreligious status, societal mobility, and, especially before modern times, profession.

The largest minority group, ethnically, are Sri Lankan Tamils (13 percent of the overall population) also called Jaffna Tamils after the northern city where they are most numerous. They are descendents of immigrants from south India who began arriving from the third century BCE on. Later, during the nineteenth and twentieth centuries CE, under British rule, Tamils from lower and poorer castes of Indian society arrived as laborers to work on tea plantations. Their descendents constitute another Tamil minority in Sri Lanka (5 percent of the overall population). The Tamils speak, read, and write in the Tamil language—which belongs to the Dravidian language family. Most Tamils (15 percent of the overall population) belong to Hinduism by confessional affiliation, that faith having been brought with them from India. Hindu shrines or *devalas* and temples or *kovils* are found in most cities and many towns. The Hindu caste system, with modifications specific to the socioeconomic conditions of Sri Lanka's history, is present among the Tamils and functions in fashions similar to that among the Sinhalese.

Arrival of Portuguese colonizers witnessed the gradual introduction of Catholicism—among the Sinhalese nobility and Sinhalese and Tamil merchants in coastal towns. Catholicism has became the dominant form of Christianity (90 percent of all Sri Lankan Christians). The Dutch colonizers brought Calvinism. Later, Anglicanism was spread by British missionaries. Catholics and Protestants together constitute the third largest religious minority in Sri Lankan society (8 percent of the overall population). Conversion to Christianity by some Sinhalese and Tamils from religious conviction and also owing to socioeconomic benefits gained by converts under colonial rule resulted in modifications to the traditional caste systems. Portuguese, Dutch, and English words were absorbed into the Sinhala and Tamil languages. European names also were adopted, sometimes in conjunction with conversion to Christianity. Yet another legacy of colonialism is that Western-style clothes—shirts and pants for men, dresses for women—were adopted in preference to the more traditional sarong of men and sari of women, especially within urban settings. English became the language of commerce, education, and a designator of membership in the upper social classes by the early twentieth century CE. Use of English as a common medium of communication has remained essential for socioeconomic and internationalist reasons even after the country gained independence—despite attempts by nationalistic Sinhalese from the 1950s through the 1970s CE to eliminate its usage.

Although sporadic political conflicts existed between the Sinhalese and Tamil populations throughout the region's history, there is considerable evidence of long-term ethnic, confessional, and linguistic intermingling. However, recent political conflict, allegedly based on religious and linguistic differences yet having an economic substratum and leading to sectarian riots in 1958, 1977, 1981, and 1983 CE, has culminated in a bloody civil war between Tamil and Sinhalese groups. This conflict is led by the secessionist Liberation Tigers of Tamil Eelam (LTTE) fighting for an independent nation-state based in the northern and eastern regions of the island and the Buddhist clergy opposing any regionally-based devolution of authority and supported by the state and its military.

Arab Moor traders reached the island by the tenth century CE, and their decedents now constitute the second largest minority population group (7 percent of the overall population). Malay traders and workers also reached the island (less than 1 percent of the overall population), now forming an important Muslim group in the southeast coastal area. Largely Sunni Muslims by confession, with smaller Shi'ite groups such as the Isma'ilis (including Da'udi Bohras/Bohoras) who arrived under British rule from India, they all follow the rites prescribed by Islam including devotions at numerous mosques in most main cities and many coastal towns. But the Moors speak Tamil—a legacy of their trading contact with the Tamils—whereas the Isma'ilis utilize Gujarati (the Indian language used by their ancestors), and Malays use their original Austronesian language. Communal customs of Sri Lanka Muslims also reflect, in many ways, a process of cultural assimilation—from food items to wedding dress. Violence against the Muslim minority by the Sinhalese majority occurred during sectarian riots in 1915 CE, quashed forcefully by the British. Some Muslims and Muslim-owned commercial enterprises have also been targets for Sinhala nationalists during attacks aimed at the Tamil community, such as in 1983 CE. During the past decade, rising Muslim political aspirations have led to intercommunal tensions in the eastern and southern provinces of Sri Lanka.

As a legacy of the Portuguese, Dutch, and British colonial periods, descendents of those Europeans have added to the ethnic mix of Sri Lankan society. Commonly referred to as *Burghers* (even though the term should apply in a strict sense only to descendents of Dutch colonists), they speak the English language and practice Christianity (Catholicism and many Protestant sects), while having adopted certain aspects of social caste and food preference from the Sinhalese and Tamil communities. Catholic and Protestant churches are ubiquitous in the cities and larger towns with freedom of worship constant. European-style clothing has always been prevalent among the Burghers. A rise of Sinhalese nationalism in the 1950s CE—resulting in attempts to eliminate the use of the English language and transform

Sri Lankan society from a multicultural one into a Sinhalese culture resulted in large numbers of Burghers emigrating to Europe and Australia in the decades that followed, diminishing both their demographic numbers and their influence within Sri Lanka during the late twentieth and early twenty-first centuries CE.

Another, very small group that owes its presence in Sri Lanka to international economic conditions generated by the British colonial period is the Parsis. The Parsis are descendants of Iranian settlers who migrated to the west coast of India around the tenth century CE, to avoid conversion to Islam after the Arab Muslim conquest of Iran. They practice Zoroastrianism or Mazdaism as a religion, speak Gujarati (picked up by their ancestors in India) and also English (adopted for socioeconomic reasons). Once a community several hundred in number, they too have witnessed a sharp decline in demographic numbers since the 1960s CE as individuals and families have emigrated to the United States, England, Australia, and back to India in search of enhanced educational, economic, and social opportunities. The community does continue to maintain a fire temple and social club in Colombo.

JAMSHEED K. CHOKSY

See also **Buddhists; Hindus; Muslims in South Asia; Netherlands; Parsis; Portugal; Tamils; Zoroastrians**

Further Reading

Bartholomeusz, Tessa J., and Chandra R. de Silva, editors, *Buddhist Fundamentalism and Minority Identities in Sri Lanka*, Albany: State University of New York Press, 1998

De Silva, Daya, and Chandra R. de Silva, *Sri Lanka since Independence: A Reference Guide to the Literature*, New Delhi: Navrang, 1992

De Silva, Kingsley M., *A History of Sri Lanka*, Delhi: Oxford University Press, 1981

Geiger, Wilhelm, *Culture of Ceylon in Medieval Times*, Wiesbaden: Otto Harrassowitz, 1960

Gombrich, Richard F., *Precept and Practice: Traditional Buddhism in the Rural Highlands of Ceylon*, Oxford: Clarendon Press, 1971

Obeyesekere, Gananath, *The Cult of the Goddess Pattini*, Chicago: University of Chicago Press, 1984

Social Scientists Association, *Ethnicity and Social Change in Sri Lanka*, Colombo: Karunaratne, 1984

Tambiah, Stanley J., *Sri Lanka: Ethnic Fratricide and the Dismantling of Democracy*, Chicago: University of Chicago Press, 1986

Wriggins, Howard W., *Ceylon: Dilemmas of a New Nation*, Princeton: Princeton University Press, 1960

Subcommission: Promotion and Protection of Human Rights

Created in 1947 as the Sub-commission on the Prevention of Discrimination and Protection of Minorities, this body was renamed in 1999. It consists of 26 experts acting in their personal capacity, elected by the Commission for Human Rights with due regard for equitable geographical representation. There are six members from African states, six from Asian states, five from Latin American states, three from Eastern European states, and six from the group of West European and Other States. It meets annually in Geneva.

When, in 1948, some delegations to the United Nations (UN) wanted the Universal Declaration on Human Rights to include positive measures for the protection of minorities, they did not have in mind the sorts of groups that have been called minorities in North America. They thought of national minorities of the kind with which the League of Nations (*q.v.*) had been concerned. The General Assembly rejected proposals designed to entitle minorities to preserve their distinctive characteristics. Instead it resolved that the UN "cannot remain indifferent to the fate of minorities" and remitted the issue for closer study in the Sub-Commission.

The UN secretariat in 1949 prepared a memorandum *Definition and Classification of Minorities* which held that a fundamental distinction was to be drawn between (a) minorities whose members desire equality with dominant groups in the sense of nondiscrimination alone, and (b) those whose members desire equality with dominant groups in the sense of nondiscrimination *plus* the recognition of certain special rights and the rendering of certain positive services. It asked, among other things, whether an individual who was not religious could be considered a member of a minority which was defined by a religious faith (like a non-believing Jew). Was an individual free to decide whether he or she was a member of a minority, or could the state decide whether there was a minority and who belonged to it? Were minority rights individual or collective?

In 1951 the Sub-Commission prepared a draft article on the rights of persons belonging to ethnic, religious, and linguistic minorities for inclusion in the International Covenant on Civil and Political Rights. It was later adopted as Article 27 of the Covenant:

> In those States in which ethnic, religious, or linguistic minorities exist, persons belonging to such minorities shall not be denied the right, in community with other members of their group, to enjoy their own culture, to profess and practice their own religion, or to use their own language.

There were further discussions about how the principles embodied in this article were to be implemented, and about how, for these purposes, a minority was to be defined. Proposals on these matters submitted to the Commission on Human Rights by its Sub-Commission were on several occasions referred back for further study. One example was the definition of minority proposed by Francesco Capotorti in 1977:

> A group numerically inferior to the rest of the population of a State, in a nondominant position, whose members—being nationals of the State—possess ethnic, religious or linguistic characteristics differing from those of the rest of the population and show, if only implicitly, a sense of solidarity, directed towards preserving their culture, traditions, religion or language.

In 1985 Jules Deschênes, a Sub-Commission member who had been asked to carry this work forward, submitted a new definition:

> A group of citizens of a State, constituting a numerical minority and in a nondominant position in the State, endowed with ethnic, religious or linguistic characteristics which differ from those of the majority of the population, having a sense of solidarity with one another, motivated, if only implicitly, by a collective will to survive and whose aim is to achieve equality with the majority in fact and in law.

The Declaration on the Rights of Persons Belonging to National or Ethnic, Religious and Linguistic Minorities was adopted by the UN General Assembly in 1992. A working group within the Sub-Commission has continued this line of activity seeking international agreement about principles to be followed in implementation

of the Declaration. As explained in the entry on the Declaration, the Human Rights Committee has expressed an authoritative opinion on the question of whether a government, like that of France, can declare that there are no minorities on its territory, or whether the existence of a minority is a matter of fact to be determined by criteria that are not specified in the Declaration.

Early in 1960 both the Sub-Commission and the Commission on Human Rights noted with deep concern that during the previous year there had been a series of attacks on Jewish burial grounds and places of worship in several European countries, but particularly in what was then the Federal Republic of Germany. The Sub-Commission described them as manifestations of anti-Semitism. The General Assembly, which was also concerned about racial discrimination in non-self-governing territories, condemned "all manifestations and practices of racial, religious and national hatred." When some African delegations argued for a convention against racial discrimination the Assembly decided in favor of a declaration which might later be followed by a convention, and in favor of a separate declaration on religious discrimination. Thus it was that the Sub-Commission drafted what came to be the UN Declaration on the Elimination of All Forms of Racial Discrimination (1963) and the International Convention on the Elimination of All Forms of Racial Discrimination (1965) (see International Conventions).

In 1971 the Sub-Commission was authorized to undertake a study of discrimination against indigenous populations. Since 1982 a Working Group on Indigenous Populations has met annually to review developments and, with the active participation of representatives of indigenous peoples, prepare a draft Declaration on the Rights of Indigenous Peoples. Its draft comprising some 45 articles was agreed in the working group in 1993. In the following year the Sub-Commission transmitted it to the Commission on Human Rights which in turn established its own working group consisting of the representatives of governments. As yet, only a few articles have been agreed. When ready, it will be submitted to the General Assembly.

If the Declaration is agreed it will represent a significant advance on the two ILO conventions, No 107 on Indigenous and Tribal Populations which was adopted and No 169 on Indigenous and Tribal Peoples of 1989. Governments have preferred to refer to these groups as populations rather than as peoples because under international law peoples are entitled to exercise a right to self-determination (q.v.). Many representatives of indigenous peoples insist that their groups are not to be accounted minorities. As the Canadian nomenclature *first nations* recognizes, the indigenous peoples were the original inhabitants of the territory who permitted others to settle on it. In many cases they entered, as equal partners, into treaties with the incomers, so they are not to be likened to minorities within the societies created as a result of settlement.

In the Sub-Commission in 1999 there was a vigorous debate on the report of the Cuban expert who had been appointed, eleven years earlier, to study treaties, conventions, and other arrangements between states and indigenous populations. He distinguished sharply between indigenous peoples and minorities, and claimed that there were no indigenous peoples in Africa or Asia.

In some circumstances migrant workers of a particular national or ethnic origin may be regarded as constituting minorities. In 1973 the Sub-Commission was instructed to study the question. Its report led to the adoption in 1990 of the International Convention on the Protection of the Rights of All Migrant Workers and Members of their Families which will come into force when it has been ratified by 20 states.

MICHAEL BANTON

See also **International Conventions; United Nations and Minorities; United Nations Declaration on Minorities; United Nations Working Group on Indigenous Population**

Further Reading

Banton, Michael, *International Action against Racial Discrimination*, Oxford: Clarendon Press, 1996

Crawford, James, editor, *The Rights of Peoples*, Oxford: Clarendon Press, 1988

Definition and Classification of Minorities (Memorandum submitted by the Secretary-General,. UN document E/CN.4/Sub.2/85. Sales No.: 1950.XIV.3

Hannum, Hurst, *Autonomy, Sovereignty and Self-Determination: The Accommodation of Conflicting Rights*, Philadelphia: University of Pennsylvania Press, 1990

The Indigenous World 1998–99, Copenhagen: IWGIA 1999

Lauren, Paul Gordon, *Power and Prejudice. The Politics and Diplomacy of Racial Discrimination,* Boulder, Colorado: Westview, 1988; 2nd edition, 1996

Thornberry, Patrick, *International Law and the Rights of Minorities*, Oxford: Clarendon Press, 1991

United Nations Action in the Field of Human Rights, 1994, UN document ST/HR/2/Rev.4, Sales No E.94.XIV.11

Sudan

Capsule Summary

Country Name: Jumhuriyat as-Sudan (Republic of Sudan)
Location: The largest country in Africa situated in the Nile Basin between Egypt in the north and the African countries of the Lake Plateau in the south
Total Population: 38,114,160 (July 2003)
Languages: 400 indigenous languages; Arabic is the official language; English is widely used in commerce, education, and government
Religions: Muslim, Christian, and Indigenous

The Sudan is the largest country in Africa, 2,505,813 sq. km. (967, 244 sq. mi.) bordered by Egypt in the north and the Central African Republic, the Democratic Republic of the Congo, Uganda, and Kenya in the south. The eastern frontier is defined by the highlands of Ethiopia and in the west, by Jabal Marra, 3,071 meters (10,073 ft.) and the Sahel and savanna of Chad. Rainfall and the Nile River determine life in the Sudan. North of the capital Khartoum at the confluence of the

Blue and White Niles the deserts (Bayuda, Libyan, and Nubian) stretch 700 kilometers (450 mi.) to the Egyptian border. South from Khartoum to Malakal on the White Nile, 820 kilometers (509 mi.), the *Sahel*, "shore," is a semiarid zone of summer rains that provide vast pasturage for cattle, sheep, and goats. The Upper Nile Basin south of Malakal is well-watered savanna and swamp (*Sudd*) for another 240 kilometers (150 mi.) on the Nile rising to the highlands of the Congo-Nile watershed and the mountains on the Uganda border. Per capita gross domestic product (GDP) is $1,400 (2002 estimate).

In 2001, when the population of Sudan was estimated at 31 million, one-third of the Sudanese were under 18 years of age. Civil war, famine, and rural unrest during the last half of the twentieth century has resulted in the concentration of Sudanese in the urban areas particularly Khartoum, Omdurman, and Khartoum North at the Nile confluence that have absorbed nearly

20 percent of the population by urban sprawl. These cities and towns have not homogenized the Sudanese who still represent some 400 languages. Arabic is the official language and that of commerce, but English is widely used particularly among Sudanese from the South who speak Niger-Kordofanian and Nilo-Saharan languages. The polyglot of languages is confirmed by the diversity of ethnic groups. About 40 percent of the Sudanese regard themselves as Arabs, but they are divided by regional and tribal affiliations. Ethnicity is also confused with religion. Seventy percent of the Sudanese are Muslim, but many (Beja, Nubian, and Fur) are not Arabs. Twenty percent practice traditional religions, particularly in the Southern Sudan, while another ten percent are Christians. Despite the flight to the cities, the economy of the Sudan remains agricultural and pastoral. Sorghum, sesame, and millet are the traditional crops in the rural countryside while cotton remains the principal export from the Gezira and gum Arabic from Darfur and Kordofan in the west. Large herds of livestock roam the plains of the Sudanic Sahel in search of pasture.

Water and, since 1998, oil are the two important natural resources. The control of the Nile waters in the twentieth century enabled the British and Sudanese to develop the island (Gezira) between the Blue and White Niles into a prolific and profitable land for the growing of cotton by Sudanese. The management of the Nile, however, remained a contentious issue as Egypt sought to acquire additional water by the construction in the 1970s of the Jonglei Canal to by-pass loss by evaporation in the *Sudd* at the same time that oil was discovered in the Southern Sudan. These two events coincided in 1983 with the decision by President Jafar Numayri to terminate the autonomous regional government of the South and to impose the Sharia law of Islam upon Southern Sudanese who practiced their traditional religions or were Christians that precipitated the southern insurgency led by Colonel John Garang de Mabior. He organized the Sudan People's Liberation Army (SPLA) which ended water and oil exploration in the Sudan and seized control of the Southern Sudan, one-third of the country. The subsequent bitter civil war became implacable after the coup d'etat on June 30, 1989, by Umar Hasan Ahmad al-Bashir and the National Islamic Front of Hasan al-Turabi. Determined to impose Arabic and Islam throughout the Sudan, al-Bashir escalated the war, despite neither side having the resources to win a mil-

itary victory in the vast and remote lands of the south, which has resulted in the longest sustained conflict in this century at a cost of two million southern Sudanese dead and another four million displaced. The devastation from war has been exacerbated by the years of drought where famine has contributed to the civilian casualties. The massive international humanitarian response to relieve the suffering has been compromised during the past two decades by the intransigence of the Sudan Government, the ambiguous interests of the humanitarian Non-Government Organizations (NGOs), and the internal rivalries within the SPLA and insensitive administration in the areas it controlled.

The many attempts by the Sudan's neighbors (Intergovernmental Authority for Development, IGAD), mediators from America and Europe, and Egyptians and Libyans (ELI) to resolve the deep cultural, economic, and religious differences between the Government of the Sudan and the Southern Sudanese insurgence have failed. After two decades of violence, which has revived the trade in slaves, the massacre of civilian populations, and the destruction of livestock and crops, the development of oil in the South after 1998 has provided the Government of the Sudan with the resources to continue the war with expectations of ultimate victory by the methodical depopulation of those regions of the South to avoid attack by the SPLA where oil is to be found.

Despite international condemnation of the Government of the Sudan for its support for terrorists, its human rights policies, and its scorched-earth tactics in the southern oil fields, peace in the Sudan appears no nearer for the Southern Sudanese in their African environment at the beginning of the twenty-first century than at the independence of the Sudan on January 1, 1956. As a large minority, they cannot be ignored, but their political future remains uncertain when their demands for self-determination are ambiguous between those advocating autonomy in a federal state, the New Sudan, and those demanding an independent Southern Sudan.

ROBERT O. COLLINS

See also **Africa: A Continent of Minorities?**

Further Reading

Holt, P.M., and M.W. Daly, *A History Of The Sudan*, 5th edition, New York: Longman, 1995
Metz, Helen Chapin, editor, *Sudan: A Country Study*, Washington: Library of Congress, 1992

Suriname

Capsule Summary

Location: South America
Total Population: 435,449 (July 2003)
Minority Populations: Amerindian, Chinese, Creole, Hindustani or East Indians, Javanese, Maroons
Languages: Dutch, English, Sranan or Sarnami Hindustani, Javanese, Suriname English-based Creolese or Sranan Tongo (also known as Surinamese or Taki-Taki)
Religions: animist, Hindu, Moravian Brethern and other Protestant, Muslim, Roman Catholic

About the size of Georgia, Suriname—a tropical country hugging the Atlantic between French Guiana and Guyana—is the smallest country in South America. The population of Suriname concentrates mostly along the coast. Almost half the population, about 200,000, lives in the capital, Paramaribo.

Despite the relatively small size of the population, it nevertheless presents a singular ethnic diversity of African, Amerindian, Asian, and European elements. Until 1975 it was a Dutch colony, first settled by the Netherlands in the seventeenth century. The ethnic diversity of Suriname has resulted primarily from policies within the Dutch empire for colonial population transfers to provide under-populated Suriname with a labor supply.

Among the poorer countries of the continent, Suriname's per capita income is approximately $3,500 annually. It remains significantly dependent on the Netherlands for financial support. A growing and dangerous source of income has developed in drugs and arms trading.

The initial interest of the Dutch in Suriname was for the cultivation and trade of sugar. The native population of rival Carib and Arawak groups was, as throughout the Americas, decimated by European diseases. This native population today comprises less than 10,000 people. They are settled along river valleys in the northern, forested interior of the country. Carib-speakers are settled along the parts of the Cappename River in the west and the Maroni River in the east. Other languages of the Carib family, Akurio, Warió, and Warana survived in scattered river-valley areas of the scarcely populated south of the country. Arawak appears in the central northern section of the country

between the Saramacca and Suriname Rivers. Unless evangelized into Christianity, the native population still follows animist or spiritist beliefs.

Labor on the plantations came from African slaves. Their descendants form two distinct ethnic groups today in Suriname. The largest is the Creoles, about a third of the Suriname population. These are descendants of mixed race (usually white and black) ancestors. They speak Guyanese Creole English, also known as Creolese, Surinamese, or Taki-Taki. Since this population is primarily urban, sometimes even termed *town Creoles*, it is among the cities, that one is likely to find speakers of the original colonial and still official national language, Dutch, along with Creole or standard English. Some Spanish is also spoken. The Creole population is primarily Christian, divided among Roman Catholic, Dutch Calvinist, and Moravian Brethern sects.

A second group of African descent is the Maroons, the offspring of slaves who fled plantations during early colonial times. The term *Maroon* is derived from the Spanish *cimarrón*, referring to runaway cattle and hence to individuals who were wild or rebellious. The Maroons established communities in the interior that were oriented to African culture. These enclaves still survive, having an economic base in timber, mining, and river trade. They have maintained a tribal organization, divided into the Aluku (also Boni), Kwinti, Matawai, Ndjuka, Paramaka, and Saramaka. They preserve small pockets of variant English-based Creole languages, Aukan (Maroni River valley), Kwinti (lower Coppename River valley), and Saramaccan (Suriname River valley and Lake Bloomenstein). Their religion has preserved traditional African animist beliefs; however, many have also been converted to Roman Catholicism and the Protestant sect of the Moravian Brethern. Maroons are about ten percent of the population.

The largest minority is the Hindustanis or British Indians. They first arrived in the late nineteenth century as contracted agricultural laborers. Almost a century later, as more than a third of the population, they became the largest minority in the country. They had also become the ethnic and social competitor of the historic Creole population, which had dominated the country. They have differed from the rest of the population because of their language, Caribbean Hindustani, a variant of Hindu, and their Hindu religion. Often speakers also of Dutch, they have entered into small-scale enterprises, and they occupy envied urban, commercial positions.

At about the same time as the British Indians arrived, Javanese from Dutch Indonesia also entered the country as contracted laborers. They now compose almost a fifth of the population, having both rural and urban occupations. Speaking Caribbean Javanese and/or Dutch, their religion is Islam. The different ethnicity, religion, and language of the Creoles and Maroons, Hindustanis, and Javanese make them intensely competitive among each other.

The earliest contracted laborers were from China, and their survivors today compose two percent of the population. Some preserve locally adapted dialects from Hakka (Han), Pundhi (Cantonese), and occasionally Mandarin Chinese. Descendants of the Chinese, who interbred with other ethnic groups, may have the name *Laiap* or *Fanap*.

The aged (over 65 years) in Suriname are a minority of about six percent of the population with life expectancy at just over 71 years. Contrary to the gender balance of other age brackets, women predominate over men among the aged. The minority of those infected with the Human Immunodeficiency Virus (HIV) is just over one percent. Illiterate adults are a minority of less than 10 percent.

EDWARD A. RIEDINGER

See also **Amerindians: (South and Central America); Creole (mixed-origin minorities); Maroons (Bush Negroes)**

Further Reading

African Caribbeans: A Reference Guide, Westport and Connecticut: Greenwood Press, 2003

Dew, Edward M., *The Trouble in Suriname, 1975–1993*, Westport, Connecticut: Praeger, 1994

Hoefte, Rosmarjin, "Suriname," *World Bibliographical Series*, ABC-CLIO, 117, Oxford, England, 1990

Hoefte, Rosmarjin, and Peter Meel, *Twentieth-Century Suriname: Continuities and Discontinuities in a New World Society*, Kingston and Jamaica: Ian Randle Publishers, 2001

Niekerk, Mies van, *Premigration Legacies and Immigrant Social Mobility: The Afro-Surinamese and Indo-Surinamese in the Netherlands*, Lanham, Maryland: Lexington Books, 2002

Price, Richard, and Sally Price, *Equatoria*, New York: Routledge, 1992

Superland, Parsudi, *The Javanese in Suriname: Ethnicity in an Ethnically Plural Society*, Tempe: Arizona State University, Program for Southeast Asian Studies, 1995

Swaziland

Capsule Summary

Location: Southern Africa
Total Population: 1,161,219 (July 2003)
Languages: SiSwati, English
Religions: traditional, Christian

One of the smallest political entities in Africa, Swaziland covers only 17,363 sq. km (6,704 sq. mi). A landlocked country, it is surrounded by South Africa on the north, west, and south, and by Mozambique on the east. On the west the land is high, and there is a steady descent eastwards to the Lebombo Range; the four main rivers flow eastwards. The most densely populated region is the central section. In 2000, when the total population was about 1 million, almost 50 percent were under 15 years of age. Sugar is the main industry and export commodity, though more people were involved in the production of cotton. In the west, where the land is suitable for afforestation, there are now the largest man-made forests in Africa. Though Swaziland once exported iron ore, the deposits have been exhausted. There are large reserves of coal. At the time of independence in 1968, only 40 percent of the land was under Swazi control; since then that proportion has increased: land and mineral concessions have been obtained through negotiation and purchase. Per capita gross domestic product (GDP) is $4,800 (2002 estimate).

Swaziland became a nation in the early nineteenth century under king Sobhuza I. The Swazi people managed to retain their independence against Boer encroachment, but much of their land was lost to individual white farmers and speculators. The country came under Transvaal rule for a while, then became a British High Commission territory following the Anglo-Boer War. King Sobhuza II, who came to the Swazi throne in 1921, sought to recover lands taken over by white settlers and speculators. As the country was led by Britain towards independence in the 1960s, interests around the king formed the Imbokodvo National Movement party, which won all the seats in the new legislature in the pre-independence election in 1967. Independence followed on September 6, 1968, with a constitution that gave the king considerable powers. Sobhuza II ruled for another 14 years after independence, and in that time Swaziland was known for stability and relative prosperity. But the country became increasingly dependent on South Africa, with which it entered a security pact in 1982, the year of Sobhuza's death. Umkhonto we Siswe, the armed wing of the African National Congress of South Africa, found it increasingly difficult to operate from Swaziland, for the South African police frequently entered the territory to capture, and sometimes assassinate, guerrillas. The young Mswati III was crowned as Sobhuza's successor in 1986. Parliament had no real power, and Mswati governed autocratically, with the aid of a small ruling clique. As opposition mounted, and economic growth slowed, his rule became more repressive.

The Swazi did not give up hopes of obtaining land lost in the late nineteenth century, land by the mid-1990s part of the new Mpumalanga province of South Africa, as well as land that would give them access to the sea. A scheme providing for the exchange of land that would provide such access was mooted in the early 1980s, but fell away because of opposition from KwaZulu-Natal. The borders of the early twentieth century therefore remained in place. Relations with Mozambique remained tense in the late 1980s and early 1990s because of the flow of refugees from that country into Swaziland but after peace came to Mozambique relations improved, and by the late 1990s there were plans for joint spatial development initiatives involving the two countries.

At the end of the 1990s, political parties remained illegal in Swaziland, and it was the only country in southern Africa without a multiparty democratic system. There was mounting opposition to the regime, especially from the Swaziland Federation of Trade Unions. But though King Mswati came under increased pressure from within his country and without to liberalize, opposition protest continued to be suppressed. One of the new issues the opposition began to raise at the beginning of the new millennium was the regime's failure to tackle the HIV/AIDS epidemic with sufficient seriousness. There were no exact figures for the extent of infection, but it was estimated that perhaps a fifth of the population was HIV positive. At some point, the democratic forces were likely to challenge the monarchy head-on, but how they might do so was not apparent in early 2001.

CHRISTOPHER SAUNDERS

See also **Africa: A Continent of Minorities?; Mozambique; South Africa**

Further Reading

Booth, A.R., *Swaziland. Tradition and Change in a Southern African Kingdom*, Boulder, Colorado 1983

Davies, R., et al., editors, *The Kingdom of Swaziland: A Profile*, London, 1985

Grotpeter, J., *Historical Dictionary of Swaziland*, Metuchen, 1975

Levin, R., *When the Sleeping Grass Awakens. Land and Power in Swaziland*, Johannesburg, 1997

Matsebula J., *A History of Swaziland*, 2nd edition, Cape Town, 1988

Sweden

Capsule Summary

Location: Eastern part of the Scandinavian Peninsula, Northern Europe
Total Population: 8,878,085 (July 2003)
Languages: Swedish; Finnish, *Mienkäli*, Romany, Saami, Yiddish
Religion: Lutheranism

Sweden is located on the Scandinavian Peninsula. It borders to the Baltic in the south and east, to the North Sea, the Kattegat and the Sound in the southwest, to Norway in the west and Finland in the northeast. In 2000 a bridge opened connecting the city of Malmö in southern Sweden with Copenhagen in Denmark. Sweden has a population of 8.9 million, mainly concentrated to the southern parts of the country. The total area is 173,655 square miles (449,764 square kilometers) giving a population density of 51 persons per square mile (20 per square kilometer). Per capita gross domestic product (GDP) is $26,000 (2002 estimate).

Sweden is a parliamentary democracy and a member of the European Union. It is a monarchy. Today the monarch only serves representational functions. The country is rich in natural resources (iron, minerals, timber) that are the foundations of its industry.

Approximately 80 percent of the population are ethnic Swedes, 11 percent are foreign-born and 8 percent are children of international migrants. Historical, cultural, and territorial minorities make up less than 1 percent of the population.

Swedish used to be the only officially recognized language and Sweden used to be religiously homogeneous, the vast majority belonging to the Lutheran state church. However, many previously accepted facts have changed in recent years. In 1999 five national heritage languages were recognized, and in 2000 the State cut its ties with the Church. Today Islam is the second largest religious denomination in Sweden.

Sweden emerged as a united kingdom in the eleventh century. In the following centuries the Crown extended its rule beyond central Sweden, north along the Gulf of Bothnia and east to the coastal regions of present-day Finland, encroaching upon land used by the indigenous Saami (formerly known as Lapps). The inclusion of what today is Finnish territory led to population exchanges in both directions and the establishment of minorities in both parts of the country. Finnish slash-and-burn peasants were relocated to parts of central Sweden, their descendants maintaining Finnish right up until the twentieth century. Finnish is recognized as a national heritage language.

In Medieval times the Hanseatic League played a vital role for economic and urban development through its trading posts in Stockholm, Visby, and Kalmar. In 1397 Denmark, Norway, and Sweden united in the Kalmar Union with power landing in Danish hands. Swedish peasants revolted in a series of uprisings. In 1527 their elected king Gustav Vasa put an end to Danish supremacy and, using the Reformation, established central control over the provinces. In the sixteenth and seventeenth centuries Sweden became a major European power controlling Baltic and German territories, and incorporating Danish and Norwegian provinces through conquest. Skilled workers from Wallonia developed the iron and steel industry.

The Baltic and German possessions were lost in eighteenth century wars. Sweden's present borders were settled in the Hamina peace treaty in 1809 when Finland was ceded to Russia. Nation-state formation started around the mid-nineteenth century with compulsory school education, railroad construction, and industrialization. Large-scale emigration to North America took place 1850–1930 (over one million emigrants). In 1921 universal suffrage was adopted. The Social Democratic Workers Party soon came into power, leading governments for most of the twentieth century. The welfare state took form in the 1950s and by 1970 Sweden had the highest standard of living in Europe. Labor migration in the 1950s and 1960s and refugee migration thereafter has increased ethnic, religious, and cultural diversity. Sweden defines itself today as a multicultural country.

The largest migrant communities are from Finland, former Yugoslavia, Iran, and Iraq. These countries account for almost half of the foreign-born population. Traditional ethnic minorities are as follows.

Romanies (25,000) have been present in small numbers since the early sixteenth century. The population grew from 3,000 in the 1950s to present numbers through immigration from Finland and Eastern Europe starting in the 1960s. Romanies have suffered centuries of persecution and social exclusion. However, in 1999 Romany was recognized as a national heritage language.

Jews (20,000) have been present since the late seventeenth century. Bans on Jewish immigration prevented earlier settlement. It was not until 1870 that Jews acquired full civic rights. During the early twentieth century Orthodox Jewish immigrants from Eastern Europe more than doubled the Jewish population. After 1945 some Holocaust survivors resettled in Sweden. Although only first generation immigrants were Yiddish speakers, Yiddish is nevertheless recognized as a national heritage language.

Tornedal-Finns (25,000) are a Finnish-speaking border minority. The Hamina peace treaty drew the border in such a way that a Finnish-speaking minority in Sweden was partially isolated from Finns on the other side. Tornedal children were prohibited to communicate in their Finnish dialect, known as *Mienkäli*, as late as in the 1960s. This dialect was recently recognized as a national heritage language.

The *Saami* (17,000 in Sweden) are an aboriginal population inhabiting the mountain regions of Northern Fenno-Scandinavia and the Kola Peninsula. Comparative linguistics, archaeology, and genetics have pieced together a picture of the Saami as possible descendants of hunters and gatherers living in prehistoric Europe before the introduction of agriculture. *Sápmi*, the Saami homeland, is divided between the states of Finland, Norway, Russia, and Sweden. Saami livelihood is linked to reindeer husbandry and the seasonal migration of reindeer herds. Conflicts over land use and land ownership have been persistent and have continued up until this day between the Swedish state and the Saami.

CHARLES WESTIN

See also **Muslims in Europe; Saami; Swedish-Speakers**

Further Reading

Ålund, Aleksandra, and Carl-Ulrik Schierup, *Paradoxes of Multiculturalism: Essays on Swedish Society*, Aldershot, United Kingdom: Avebury, 1991

Jahreskog, Birgitta, editor, *The Sami National Minority in Sweden*, Stockholm, Sweden: Almqvist and Wiksell International, 1982

Magnusson, Lars, *An Economic History of Sweden*, London, United Kingdom: Routledge, 2000

Pred, Allan, *Even in Sweden*, Berkeley: University of California Press, 2000

The Sami People, Oslo, Norway: The Nordic Sami Institute, 1990

Wingstedt, Maria, *Language Ideologies and Minority Language Policies in Sweden: Historical and Contemporary Perspectives*, Stockholm, Sweden: Centre for Research on Bilingualism, Stockholm University, 1998

Swedish-Speakers

Swedish-speakers in the world originate from people that during different historical periods have emigrated from Sweden, located in Northern Europe with a present population of approximately 8.855 million inhabitants. Most of the Swedish emigrants have as groups been short-lived and have not constituted ethnic minorities. Two groups, the Estonian Swedes and the Swedish-speaking Finns, came into existence during the Middle Ages and meet the criteria for being ethnic minorities.

In the course of centuries there have occurred several waves of emigration from Sweden. The largest was the move to North America by almost 1.5 million Swedes between 1850 and 1930. The emigrants from Sweden in modern times, however, have not formed ethnic minorities in the sense of developing into ethnopolitical groups with uniform political aspirations and devoted to the idea of remaining Swedish-speakers. As a rule they have assimilated fairly quickly into the populations of the receiving countries. Swedish-speaking minorities who have preserved their Swedish language and ethnicity through several centuries are found in some of the neighboring countries around the Baltic Sea. They came into existence already in the Middle

Ages. Among them the Estonian Swedes and the Swedish-speaking Finns can be counted among the ethnic minorities of the world. The Estonian Swedes nearly disappeared during the turbulence of World War II, but the Swedish-speaking Finns still form a viable ethnic minority.

Estonian Swedes

The Swedish-speaking population in Estonia, located on the Southern Coast of the Gulf of Finland in the Baltics, is mentioned in historical annals for the first time in the second half of the thirteenth century. It was located on the Estonian coastline, mainly on its islands in the Baltic Sea. The Swedish settlement arose because of migration from Sweden in the west and Finland in the north. The Estonian Swedes were fishermen, small-holders, and coastal skippers. For centuries they experienced injustices and threats from German landlords and Russian authorities. Partly as steps of ethnic defense, the Estonian Swedes initiated many cultural activities and founded Swedish schools, an activity which reached its peak in the early twentieth century. Both elementary schools, training colleges for teachers, secondary grammar schools, and folk high schools with Swedish as the language of instruction were founded. At the end of the 1930s the Swedish-speaking population in Estonia approximated 9,000 individuals. They were strongly hit by World War II, partly because both the Nazi German and the Soviet Russian invaders needed their islands as naval bases. Particularly from the year 1943 on, systematic flights in small carriers over the sea to Sweden were organized, and nearly 8,000 Estonian Swedish-speakers settled in Sweden. At the turn of the millennium there are in Estonia only a few hundred Swedish-speakers, mostly persons of old age.

Swedish-Speaking Finns

Swedish-speakers in Finland constitute just under six percent of the population, or approximately 300,000 individuals. The Swedish-speaking population is mainly concentrated in the coastal areas of western and southwestern Finland and on the Aaland isles in the Baltic Sea. Most of the Swedish-speakers in Finland do not know exactly about their ancestry in Sweden. They are Finns in their national and Swedes in their linguistic identity. In Swedish their designation has been *finlandssvenskarna* and in English different terms such as *Swedish Finns, Swedish-speaking Finns, Finno-Swedes* and *Finland Swedes* have been used, the most common saying being *Swedish-speaking Finns.*

There is no clear consensus amongst historians as regards the time of the first Swedish settlements in Finland. According to some historians, there was already a population movement from the west between the fifth and ninth centuries CE. This can be established with certainty only for the Aaland isles. It is certain, however that Swedish settling occurred in connection with the Swedish crusades during and after the twelfth century. Large parts of Finland's coastal regions were in nearly a thousand years inhabited by a monolingual, Swedish-speaking population. It is only in the twentieth century under the impact of industrialization and urbanization that the language borders between Finnish and Swedish have loosened up and started to disappear. There has been a gradual decline in the proportion of the Swedish-speakers in the population of Finland. It is estimated that the proportion of Swedish-speakers was 17.5 percent in the early seventeenth century, 15 percent in the early nineteenth century, 13 percent in the early twentieth century, and 6 percent at the turn of the millennium. The proportional decline has been due both to a rapid increase in the Finnish-speaking population and to a strong overrepresentation of Swedish-speakers in all big emigration waves, both in the American emigration and in the heavy migration to Sweden after World War II. During the last three decades the proportion of Swedish-speakers has been stabilized around approximately 6 percent.

During former centuries there existed two distinct parts of the Swedish-speaking population in Finland. The larger one was the rural Swedish-speaking population consisting of farmers, fishermen, and coastal skippers; the other was the high status Swedish population which earlier formed the higher estates of bourgeoisie and nobility in the country. Its existence was mainly due to the fact that Finland remained part of the Kingdom of Sweden until 1808. Under the reign of the Swedish King there was mobility of Swedes into the upper estates of Finland and of Finns to Sweden aspiring for better living conditions. The rural coastal Swedish population and the Swedish bourgeoisie in the cities became united in joint civic, cultural, and political activities from around 1900 on as a reaction against the onrush of Finnish-speakers in all walks of life. Swedish was earlier the language of the dominant elite, but today the Swedish-speaking population has by and large a similar occupational and educational structure to that of the national population as a whole.

Finnish and Swedish are, according to the Finnish Constitution, national languages. Finnish citizens have the right to use their mother tongue, Finnish or Swedish, in courts and to obtain documents in their own language. Because of a rapidly increased bilingualism among the Swedish-speakers these rules are often not followed today. The basic unit of Finnish language policy, however, is the primary unit of local government, the commune. The fundamental rule determining the linguistic status of a commune is that it is bilingual if the number of inhabitants who speak the minority language exceeds 8 percent or numbers at least 3,000 people. The majority of the communes in Finland are unilingually Finnish, but there is also a considerable number of bilingual and unilingual Swedish communes with administrative consequences.

The educational needs of the Swedish-speakers in Finland are provided for by schooling with instruction in Swedish on all levels, from kindergarten to the university. There are activities in the Swedish language in all cultural realms. Of particular importance is a vivid Swedish literary production acclaimed both by Swedes in Sweden and Finns in Finland.

ERIK ALLARDT

See also **Estonia; Finns; Sweden**

Further Reading

Allardt, Erik, "Bilingualism in Finland: The Position of Swedish as a Minority Language," in *Language Policy and National Unity*, edited by William R. Beer and James E. Jacob, Totowa, New Jersey: Rowman & Allanheld, 1985

Allardt, Erik and Karl Johan Miemois, "Roots Both in the Centre and the Periphery: The Swedish Speaking Finns," *European Journal of Political Research*, 10 (1982)

Beijar, Kristina, Henrik Ekberg, Susanne Eriksson, and Marika Tandefelt, *Life in Two Languages. The Finnish Experience*, Jyväskylä: Schildts, 1997

McRae, Kenneth D., *Conflict and Compromise in Multilingual Societies: 3, Finland*, Waterloo, Canada: Wilfrid Laurier University Press, 1997

Miljan, Toivo, "Bilingualism in Finland," in *Databook on Finland*, I-II, Ottawa: Royal Commission on Bilingualism, 1966–67

Norrman, Ralf, "The Finland Swedes," in *Indigenous Minority Groups*, edited by John R.G. Jenkins, Waterloo, Canada: Wilfrid Laurier University, 1987

Switzerland

Capsule Summary

Location: Central Europe, east of France, north of Italy
Total Population: 7,318,638 (July 2003)
Ethnic Populations: German (65%), French (18%), Italian (10%), Romansch (1%), other (6%)
Languages: German (official) (63.7%), French (official) (19.2%), Italian (official) (7.6%), Romansch (official) (0.6%), other (8.9%).
Religions: Roman Catholic (46.1%), Protestant (40%), other (5%), none (8.9%) (1990)

Switzerland, a rich mountain country, is located in Central Europe, east of France, north of Italy. It is a confederation of 26 cantons. The government is usually a coalition and the presidency alternates between the seven ministers. Its traditional and strict neutrality has made Swiss politics respected but fairly unknown outside the country, while a high degree of local autonomy and decentralized decision-making referenda complicates the outside perspective.

History

When the Romans conquered the region, which then included the westernmost part of today's Austria, in 15 CE, it was called *Provincia Raetia*, named after an Illirian (or possibly Etruscan) tribe that lived there. The romanization was deep and fundamental, and the Celts who dominated most of the territory were soon totally assimilated. The Romans established a variety of Vulgar Latin as the local vernacular, but in the fifth century Germanic tribes invaded the region and Alemannic German culture and language dominated the central parts of the country. Various nobles and clergymen dominated different parts of the region until three central cantons, Schwyz, Unterwalden, and Uri in 1291 signed a defense treaty to form a confederation (*Eidgenossenschaft*) against the Hapsburg threat to their independence. This was symbolized by the Wilhelm Tell myth. The emblematic Tell represented the free Swiss farmer. Although the ruling aristocracies of the surrounding towns opposed the freedom of the farmers, they came to join the confederation due to external threats. The original cantons were all German-speaking but in the fifteenth and sixteenth centuries French- and Italian-speaking cantons joined the confederation. Others remained associated (*Zugewandte Orte*). When the north became Protestant a delicate political and religious balance arose and had to be maintained.

Not until Napoleon's invasion in 1798 were the cantons were forced (in 1803) to form a country that in the 1848 constitution was stabilized. Swiss neutrality was guaranteed by the Conference of Vienna (1815). Ever since, the decentralized power and the referendum have been distinctive features of Swiss politics.

Society

The German-speaking parts have dominated the country, but although the written language is similar to Standard German the spoken German dialects, *Schwyzertütsch*, are far from standard German, and the feeling of being Swiss is strong among the whole population. The dialects are used both in family and in mass media and official situations. The French dialects differ much less from standard French. Originally the dialect was Franco-provençal (a mixture of French and Provençal), but this dialect is now possibly spoken only by a couple of thousand people in small villages in Jura, Fribourg, and Valais. They are all bilingual. No exact figures are available. This dialect has left an accent and certain words in ordinary Swiss French. Another situation has caused problems—the German taught at French and Italian schools has been standard German and many complain that they cannot understand their fellow countrymen although they have studied German. Recently, courses in Swiss German have begun being taught on television. The Italians share the advantage of the other two groups of having the linguistic and cultural support of a great neighboring country which is not the case for the Romansh speakers of Grisons in the southeast. However, the low number of people speaking Italian outside the cantons Tessin and Grisons increases the tendency of reducing Italian to certain occasions and there is now a discussion of Switzerland being a country of 2.5 languages, where Italian is limited and Romansh disregarded. Many Romansh speakers also suffer from the fact that signs in four languages in many places have substituted Romansh with English as the fourth language. In 1996 Switzerland signed the

European Charter for Regional and Minority Languages and the European Convention for Protection of National Minorities rights and Romansh was given a partly official status. Most cantons are monolingual (four use French and one Italian) which makes the local administration easier. Three are bilingual with German and French (Bern, Fribourg, and Valois, with French being the majority language in the last two) and only one is trilingual (Grisons, where Romansh is spoken in the northwest and southeast, Italian in the south, and German in the rest of the canton). Grisons is therefore the linguistically most complicated canton, and the fact that there is no Romansh-dominated canton makes its situation more delicate. It is a minority language in its own canton while the other languages have at least one where they represent the majority of the speakers. Although Switzerland is a quadrilingual country, very few inhabitants speak more than two languages of which English might be one.

In the 1960s there was a movement for *Jura libre* with the idea of separating Jura from the rest of Canton Bern, which became the case. The separation cannot only be regarded a French-German tension, since most French-speakers in Bern voted against it. It was more a question of a discontent countryside opposing the capital.

Switzerland has also become a major receiver of immigrants who now constitute 19.6 percent of the population. This has had a significant impact on Swiss schools, administration and daily life, but the laws are strict, and immigration has been reduced in recent years. The major Immigrant groups are Spanish, Yugoslav (from the countries that previously formed Yugoslavia), Portuguese, Turkish, and English.

Religious discrepancies have caused conflicts throughout history much more than linguistic differences, but do not separate today. "Swissness" is important, and the Swiss society is considered as being founded on a common intention to stay together without having a common language or church. This intention is based on four communities of essence—German, French, Italian, and Romansh. The French cantons have long been considered *La Suisse romande* with a common language and culture, but recently the feeling has been extended to the other Romance minorities, and the notion of the *Latin Switzerland* as opposed to the predominating German Switzerland has arisen. What this really means is still hard to say.

The Swiss example might seem ideal, but determining whether it is coexistence or a life together is complicated. Domestic migration might change the situation, possibly favoring the two main languages. As most schools only teach one extra language, English is substituting other national languages from the program, which eventually leads to a situation where Swiss citizens will have to use English to communicate with each other in French–German–Italian relations. As the Romansh all live in a bilingual ambiance, English will only be a second "foreign" language in Grisons. Compared to most minority situations in the world, Switzerland remains one of the best, and its example has been used by many East European politicians trying to solve their own minority issues.

Switzerland enjoys a modern economy, low unemployment, and a highly skilled work force. Its gross domestic product (GDP) per capita income ($32,000 in 2002) is greater than most Western European nations. Industries include machinery, chemicals, watches, textiles, and precision instruments. The country did not officially become a member of the United Nations until 2002, and retains a strong commitment to neutrality.

INGMAR SÖHRMAN

See also **Romansh**

Further Reading

Arquint, Jachen, et al., *Die viersprachige Schweiz*, Zürich, Cologne: Benziger, 1982; *La Suisse aux quatre langues*, 1985

Butler, Michael, et al., *The Making of Modern Switzerland 1848–1998*, Basingstoke: Macmillan, and New York: St. Martin's Press, 2000

Cattani, Alfred, and Alfred Häsler, *Minderheiten in der Schweiz: Toleranz auf dem Prüfstand*, Zürich: Neue Zürcher Zeitung, 1984

Keller, Walter, editor, *La Suisse vue par elle-même*, Zürich: Der Alltag and Scalo, 1992

Lüdi, Georges, et al., *Le paysage linguistique de la Suisse*, Bern: Bundesamt, 1997

Syria

Capsule Summary

Country Name: Syrian Arab Republic
Location: Southwest Asia, north of the Levantine region
Total Population: 17,585,540 (July 2002)
Minority Populations: Circassians (e.g., Adygue, Chechen, Daguestani, Kabardians), Armenians, Kurds, Assyrian, Gypsy, Turoyo, Maalula
Languages: Adyghe, Chechen, Bedawi Arabic, Mesopotamian Arabic, Najdi Arabic, North Levantine Arabic, Armenian, Neoaramaic, Azerbaijani, Domari, Kurmandji, Lomavren, Western Neoaramaic
Religions: Sunni Muslim, Alawi Muslim, Ismaili Muslim, Christians, Druze

Syria is located in the north of the Levantine region, bordering Lebanon and the Mediterranen Sea (in the west), Iraq (in the east), Turkey (in the north) and Jordania (in the south). Per capita gross domestic product (GDP) is $3,700 (2002 estimate). The government is a presidential republic with only one legal party, the Baath. The only official language is Standard Arabic.

Islamized at the beginning of the seventh century, the area that is modern-day Syria has had an important geopolitical role, and Damascus was the capital of the Abbasid empire. Syria belonged to the Ottoman empire from 1516 to 1920, when it became a French protectorate. This situation ended with the independence of Syria (1943). Twenty years later, in 1963, a military putsch allowed the Baath to maintain power. During the 1980s, the primary cause of conflict in Syria was domination of political and military posts by the Alawi community to which president Assad belonged. Sunni have posed the most sustained threat to the Baath regime, and the insurrection in the 1980–1982 period was crushed by killing around 25,000 civilians, especially in the cities of Aleppo and Hamah.

The Druze, an ethnoreligious minority, inhabited mountainous areas of southern Syria and also the northeastern hills of Damascus. There are also important groups of Armenians (400,000) throughout the country and in urban centers like Kessaberen. As Arab nationalism has become more important in Syrian political life, Armenians have found themselves under some pressure and have felt increasingly alienated. As a result, they were reported in the 1960s and early 1970s to have emigrated in large numbers.

Small but significant minorities are: Gypsy Domari (15,000 in Syria), spread as nomads from Turkey to India, and speaking an Indoiranian language highly influenced by the Arabic; 40,000 Azerbaijani Turks (called *Turkmen*) of southwestern Syria; and Maalula (30 miles north to Damascus), Turoyo, and Assirian (both in northern Syria), three communities that speak ancient Aramaic languages, thousands of years ago dominants in this area but now spoken by only 60,000 persons.

Besides the minorities just noted, there are two minorities who have had different degrees of integration in Syrian society: the Circassians, immigrants from the south Russian Caucasus who are relatively well-assimilated by the social mainstream, and Kurds, aboriginals of northeastern Syria who are highly marginalized.

By the 1860s the Circassians were forced to migrate to various parts of the Ottoman Empire. Circassians have been Sunni Muslims for the past three or four hundred years. The Circassian population in Syria is around 50,000. At the 1872 migration, the Circassians were settled at Hama, Humus, and the Golan Heights, which were small villages at that time. The second wave of migration in August of 1878 came from the Balkans. The migration wave continued and the Circassian population of Syria at that time climbed up to 70,000. Circassian intellectuals of the 1920s made considerable contributions to vitalize the culture. Syrian administration questioned these intellectuals for political behavior and their schools were shut down along with the Marc newspaper and the Circassian Benevolent Association. At the end of the 1967 Syria-Israel war, the villages of Golan Heights were occupied by Israel and it was another exile for Circassians, who settled in Damascus.

The Kurds of Syria number around 2 milion persons. Their language is prohibited in Syrian schools. They inhabit northern and northwestern Syria: in Kurd Dagh (northwest of Aleppo), in northwest Jazira (between the Tigris and Euphrates) around Jarablus and Ain al-Arab, in northern Jazira around Qamishli, and in northeastern Syria near the borders of Iraq and Turkey. The largest community, in north Jazira, was founded by those who permanently settled inside Syria's borders following the collapse of the Ottoman Empire. The overwhelming proportion of the Kurd population of Jazira, however, were Kurds fleeing from Turkey in the years after 1920.

After Syria's independence, Kurds were purged from the army and in the 1950s an oppression of their ethnic culture started. In 1960–1962, the government's plans to establish Arab farmers in Kurdish regions provoked more than 60,000 Kurds to flee to Damascus, Turkey, and Lebanon. The Baath party in 1963, increased persecution toward the Kurds. One year before, in 1962, more than 120,000 Kurds (20 percent of the Syrian Kurds) lost their Syrian nationality. Kurdish sources say that there are now an estimated 200,000 Kurds in Syria who are officially classified as a special category of *ajanib* (foreigners).

In present times, Syrian-born Kurds with "foreigner" identity cards face tremendous difficulties in their everyday lives. They are not permitted to own land, housing, or businesses. They cannot be employed at government agencies and state-owned enterprises, and cannot practice as doctors or engineers. They are not eligible for food subsidies or admission to public hospitals. They may not legally marry Syrian citizens; if they do, the marriages are not legally recognized for either the citizen or the "foreigner" and both spouses are described as unmarried on their identity cards. Kurds with "foreigner" status do not have the right to vote in elections or referenda, or run for public office. They carry special red identity cards and are not allowed passports to travel outside of Syria.

In September 2002, Syria's minority Kurds demanded President Bashar al-Assad restore citizenship to almost 200,000 of their people left stateless four decades ago. The representative of the Kurdish Democratic Alliance (KDA) said that "we ask the Syrian president to intervene, 40 years after this unjust census, to end the suffering and end the segregation and special laws" against the country's largest non-Arab minority.

JOAN MANUEL CABEZAS LÓPEZ

See also **Armenians; Assyrians; Circassians; Kurds; Roma (Gypsies)**

Further Reading

Abd-Allah, Umar F., *The Islamic Struggle in Syria*, Berkeley: Mizan Press, 1983

Seale, Patrick, *Asad of Syria: The Struggle for the Middle East*, Los Angeles: University of California Press, 1990

Van Dam, Nikolaos, *The Struggle for Power in Syria: Sectarianism, Regionalism, and Tribalism in Politics, 1961–1978*, London: Croom Helm, 1979

T

T'u-Chia

Capsule Summary

Location: China, mainly in the border areas between Hunan, Hubei, Guizhou Provinces, and Chongqing Municipal Prefecture

Population: More than 5.7 million

Languages: Two dialects (southern and northern) belonging to the Chinese-Tibetan language system; these survive only in certain remote villages, however, and most members of the group speak Chinese

Religions: Polytheism; Taoism; shamanism; ancestor worship. Some areas worship the white tiger as a totem

The T'u-chia ethnic group, or *Tujia,* is one of China's 55 ethnic minorities. The name *Tujia* was a term of reference used by others; the group named itself *Bizika,* which means "locally born and grown people." The ethnic origins of the Tujia are debated; there are several conflicting versions. The key difference is their place of origin. One claims the Tujia descended from the Wuman, who moved into the western Hunan from Guizhou Province, while another record says they came from Jiangxi Province in the Tang Dynasty. Increasingly, however, scholars are willing to accept that they originally resided in the western territories of Hunan and Hubei Provinces together with other local ethnic groups who were named *Wulin Barbarian* or *Wuxi Barbarian.* After the Song Dynasty, the Tujia were separately named *Tuding* and *Tumin.* In the 1950s, as part of the government's ethnic identification campaign, Professor Pan Guangdan conducted systematic academic research on their history and culture and traced their origin back to the ancient Ba people. Tujia then received official recognition as an ethnic minority in People's Republic of China (PRC).

Tujia has its own language. It belongs to the Chinese–Tibetan language system, and is divided into two dialects, the southern and the northern, but the writing system has never been found out even up to now. Due to the long-term co-residence with the Han, the Tujia have been largely assimilated and the Chinese language and writing system is mainly used in their daily life and social interactions. Today the Tujia language survives only in the some small remote villages of the northwestern corner of Hunan Province.

The Tujia have long been assimilated in Han culture, but they still keep some of their own traditions and folklore. They have a polytheistic religion that includes Taoism and Shamanism. They also practice ancestor worship. Apart from these, some areas worship the white tiger, which is regarded as its totem. This worship comes from a tale. It says that when the Tujia ancestor Emperor Lin died, his soul left his body and became a white tiger to get into heaven. To remember and honor the Emperor, the Tujia took the white tiger as their ancestor god to worship. This belief can still been found today, as when they make a wooden white tiger and place it in the house shrine. In weddings, a white tiger carpet must be put on the main table in the bridegroom's house to symbolize the worship of the ethnic ancestor.

Besides religious beliefs, the Tujia also have some other special cultural traditions including wedding ritual, dance, and artifacts. One typical wedding ritual is the wedding lament, in which the bride is expected to cry with many tears and loud cries on her wedding day. The wedding lament is not just tears but also includes singing with improvised words and content. Mostly it expresses two main ideas: the debt to the parents and the farewell to all the family and relatives. In the traditional Tujia view, the wedding lament is a symbol of a bride's wisdom and morality.

The most characteristic ritual of Tujia ethnic minority is called, in Tujia language, *Sheba Ri*. In Chinese, *sheba* means "hand-swinging" and *ri* means "to do or perform." This is a public ritual presented for the purpose of praying, which is generally held on the Lunar New Year and the Spring Festival. Now it has developed into an open large-scale social activity involving thousands of people and including dance, singing, socializing, and even some commercial activities such as market exchanges and trading.

The Tujia are well known for their traditional dance, *Maogusi,* which means "Old Grandfather." According to the Tujia epics, this is an old dance to commemorate the achievements of their ancestors. This dance requires at least 15 or s16 performers, and the leading role of the dance is Old Grandfather, while the rest are his sons and daughters or grandsons and granddaughters. All the roles form a big family. During the dance all the performers are required to cover their whole bodies with various grasses and leaves. The dance may last six nights or so, focusing on Tujia social life, including their ancestors' history, war, fishing, farming, and feasting. It is composed of singing, dancing, and speeches: this primitive drama is regarded as the "living fossil" of the Tujia original culture and tradition.

The Tujia are also famous for their ethnic brocade, which are called *Xilan Kapu.* In the Tujia language, *xilan* means "bedcover," and *kapu* means "flower." The brocade is completely handwoven with colorful and symmetrical thread. There are three main themes: scenes of nature, including animals, flowers, grasses; various geometric diagrams; and characteristic designs, such as those for "pleasure," "happiness," or "longevity." Their exquisite workmanship and traditional features make the brocade attractive and famous.

The Tujia live in mountainous areas with plenty of minerals and natural resources, yet the traditional agriculture is still the dominant livelihood of the Tujia. Fishing and simple manufacturing are also important auxiliary industries in some areas. In recent years, the natural scenery and their traditional folklore have attracted more and more tourists. The tourism industry has flourished and become a major source of economic development. For example, Zhangjiejie located in a Tujia dwelling place, has been named the first National Forest Park in China. Some ethnic traditions and folklores are reinvented and elaborated in the process of developing tourism, while at the same time, the tourism industry also changes the traditional ways of life and social interaction.

TIAN HONGLIANG

See also **China**

Further Reading

Dong, Luo, *Ba Feng Tu Yun: Tujia Wenhua Yuanliu Jiexi* [Ba People and Tujia: The Research on Tujia's Origin], Wuhan, Hubei: Wuhan Daxue Chuban She [Wuhan University Press], 1999

Li, Zhongbin, *Keji Jinbu yu Tujia Zu Diqu Jingji Shehui Fazhan* [Technological Improvement and Tujia's Economic and Social Development], Beijing: Minzu Chuban She [Ethnicity Press], 2001

Pan, Naigu, and Naihe Pan, *Pan Guangdan Xuanji* [Selective Works of Pan Guangdan], Beijing: Guangming Ribao Chuban She [Guangming Daily Press], 1999

Shi, Zhiyu, *Negotiating Ethnicity in China: Citizenship as a Response to State*, London and New York: Routeledge, 2002

"Tujia Zu Jianshi Bianxie Zu," in *Tujia Zu Jianshi* [Tujia's Brief History], Changsha: Hunan Renmin Chuban She [Hunan People Press], 1986

Xiang, Bosong, *Tujia Zu Minjian Xinyang yu Wenhua* [Tujia's Folklore and Culture], Beijing: Minzu Chuban She [Ethnicity Press], 2001

T'ung

Capsule Summary

Location: Southern China, mainly in Guizhou, Hunan, and Guangxi provinces
Total Population: 2,960,293 (2000)
Language: T'ung (Kam), belonging to the Tai-Kadai of the Austro-Tai language family; with two dialects (northern and southern), each in turn comprising subdialects
Religions: animism, nature worship, ancestor worship

The T'ung (Dong) are a minority nationality of southern China, living mainly in Guizhou, Hunan, and Guangxi provinces. Based on language, territoriality, common economic pursuits, and common psychological dispositions, the Chinese government classified the T'ung as a minority nationality in the 1950s. In spite of the government's assimilation policies, the T'ung retain their ethnic status as most of them still live in remote valley areas. According to the national census of 2000, the total T'ung population reached 2,960,293. However, since minority group membership may result in political privilege, the current T'ung registry includes many Han people.

Historically, the T'ung have their roots in the ancient Yue nationality, whose ancestors were believed to be the Liao. Through the Tang, Song, Yuan, Ming, and Qing dynasties, the T'ung was variously called the *T'ung people, T'ung barbarian, T'ung Miao, Hole people, Ge-lou*, and the *T'ung family*, among others.

Their language, T'ung (Kam), belongs to the Tai-Kadai of the Austro-Tai language family. There are basically two dialects, northern and southern, each containing more than two subdialects. A written script, based on a modified International Phonetic Alphabet similar to that used in *pinyin*, came into being with the help of the central government in 1958. Long before that, however, the T'ung recorded their life history by carving certain symbols on bamboo. This art has all but disappeared.

Most of the T'ung engage in agriculture and forestry. Their staple food is sticky rice. They also eat a lot of fish. The famed dish of the T'ung is pickled fish (*suan yu*). This food is quite significant in T'ung life. It is not only served to honored guests, it is also required for sacrifices to the deities and for important rites of passage, such as weddings and funerals. Folklore says that a family starts to make pickled fish when a son is born, adding to it every year until he is married. Pickled fish and meat are so greatly relished that they have given rise to the saying, "*T'ung bu li suan*" ("The T'ung cannot be separated from Suan"). Some scholars argue that fish is the T'ung totem. Oil tea, another specialty, is also consumed daily. There are rules of etiquette for serving oil tea to visitors.

The T'ung usually live in the valley close to rivers so bridges are everywhere. Bridges are used not only for transit but are also places where people rest when working. Because of their function and peculiar architectural style, they are called wind-and-rain bridges (*feng yu qiao*). Some are elaborately built and beautifully decorated. Chengyang bridge, located in Sanjiang T'ung Autonomous County of Guangxi Zhuang Autonomous Region, is renowned and has been designated a national cultural legacy. Apart from the wind-and-rain bridges, another distinctive T'ung architectural form is the drum tower (*gulou*). Drum towers represent the pinnacle of the T'ung's architectural work. Like the bridges, the T'ung build the drum towers without using a single nail. The structure is usually decorated with images of fish, shrimp, chicken, and dancing people. Today they are gathering places and centers for social activities such as dancing and singing. Due to their unique style, craftsmanship, design, layout, and functionality, wind-and-rain bridges and drum towers are two obvious cultural symbols of T'ung villages.

Music is another cultural distinction, for the T'ung excel at dancing and singing. The *dage*, (literally, "big song") a style of singing without musical accompaniment, has won worldwide acclaim because the charming polyphony shows exceptional singing skill. To be able to sing is even an important factor in the selection of a mate. The T'ung are also renowned for their folk drama. Although drawn from Han theatrics, T'ung drama is the representative of their arts.

Young men and women are free to choose their mates, unlike traditions among the Han and some minority groups where the decision is left to the parents. In the past, the bride remained at her natal home until becoming pregnant—some times up to three years. This custom is not popular now. When a person dies, the corpse is placed in the ground. As among most Chinese, ancestor worship is practiced.

In their daily religious practices, the T'ung tend toward animistic or natural worship. Benevolent and malevolent spirits exist everywhere in nature. Valleys, rivers, mountains, trees and rocks, bridges and wells all have spiritual significance. Fengshui is commonly practiced. The main deity, *Sak* (grandmother), is female, reflecting the status of women. One view of Sak regards her as she who leads the villagers in their fight against the enemy. Another view, however, considers her to be the highest goddess of the Sak belief. In Guizhou province Sak temples are often built beside drum towers. In Guangxi, where the T'ung also believe in Sak, temples are not popular.

The T'ung people celebrate many feasts throughout the year. The Firecrackers Festival, known as *Sanyuesan*, is celebrated on the third day of the third lunar month. On that day there are various performances, for example, singing competition, blowing lusheng competition, and the T'ung drama performance. Another important festival is T'ong, which usually falls at the beginning of the eleventh month. The T'ong festival is the New Year of the T'ung, and in cities there are big celebrations.

The political organization among the T'ung area was Kuan, which, historically, had different regulations for society, family, spirits, and physical worlds, respectively. Kuan functioned as a sacred law to strengthen internal cohesion and unite people against their enemies.

HOU JINGRONG

See also **China**

Further Readings

Committee of Culture and History Documentary of the Chinese People's Political Consultative Conference (CPPCC), *History of the T'ung (Dongzu Bainian Shilu)*, CPPCC, et al., Beijing: Zhongguo Wenshi Chubanshe, 2000

Rossi, Gai, *The Dong People of China—A Hidden Civilization*, Singapore: Enjoying Asia Books Department of Population, Social Science and Technology Statistics, National Bureau of Statistics (D.P.S.S.T.N.B.S.), PRC, et al., *Tabulation on Nationalities of 2000 Population Census of China (2000 Renkou Pucha Zhongguo Minzu Renkou Ziliao)*, D.P.S.S.T.N.B.S. Beijing: Minzu Chubanshe, 2003

Wang, Shengxian, and Yanhua Luo, editors, *The History and Customs of the T'ung*, Guiyang: Renmin Chubanshe, 1989

Zhang, Weiwen, and Zeng Qingnan, *In Search of China's Minorities*, Beijing: New World Press, 1993

Taiwan

Capsule Summary

Location: Western Pacific, about 100 miles off the southeast coast of China
Total Population: 22.3 million
Ethnic Populations: Hok-lo, Hakka, Mainland Chinese, nine officially recognized groups of indigenous Austronesian peoples
Languages: Mandarin Chinese, Hok-lo, Hakka, various Austronesian languages
Religions: Buddhism, Taoism, Confucianism, Christianity, Islam

Taiwan is officially a province of the People's Republic of China, but it has its own government known as the Republic of China (ROC). It is a small island country about 100 miles (161 kilometers) off the southeast coast of China. Taiwan is approximately 14,000 square miles (36,000 square kilometers) in size, 245 miles (394 kilometers) long, and 90 miles (144 kilometers) wide at the broadest point. The island is bounded to the north by the East China Sea, which separates it from Japan; to the east by the Pacific Ocean; to the south by the Bashi Channel, which separates it from the Philippines; and to the west by the Taiwan Strait, which separates it from China. It has a population of approximately 22.3 million.

History

Until the seventeenth century, Taiwan was inhabited almost exclusively by a number of indigenous groups of Austronesian origin, although it was also visited by Chinese fishers and used as a haven for Japanese and Chinese pirates. The Spanish occupied part of the north of the island from 1626 to 1642. The Dutch had even more ambitious plans for Taiwan, running a trading post and settlement from 1624 to 1662 near what is today the city of Tainan on the Southwest coast. The presence of Spanish and Dutch colonies on the island, and the prospect of work on new sugar plantations, brought an influx of immigrants to Taiwan from nearby China.

In 1661, the Chinese rebel Koxinga, who had hoped to restore the defunct Ming Dynasty, was driven out of China and fled with his armies to Taiwan. They defeated the Dutch and set up a new government on the island, bringing in a new influx of immigrants. The Manchurian Qing Dynasty took over control of Taiwan in 1683, bringing in new waves of both Hok-lo and Hakka immigrants from China. The Hok-lo people, from Southern Fujian Province, tended to settle down in the fertile coastal plains. The Hakka, arriving slightly later from Guangdong and Fujian Provinces, established themselves in the foothills of western Taiwan.

The original Austronesian inhabitants of the western plains largely intermarried with the Chinese. The indigenous populations of the central mountains and east coast remained free from Chinese administrative control during the Qing period, however, and were even able to independently make treaties with Japan. Taiwan remained a part of Fujian Province until 1883, after which it was administered as a separate province.

As a result of the Sino-Japanese War and the Treaty of Shimonoseki, Taiwan became a Japanese colony from 1895 until the conclusion of World War II in 1945. At the conclusion of World War II, Japan was forced to relinquish its colonies in Asia, and Taiwan was placed under ROC control. When China was liberated by the Chinese Communists in 1949, General Chiang Kai-shek (1887-1975) and the KMT (the Nationalists) retreated to Taiwan. The arrival of the KMT on Taiwan brought with it an influx of predominantly Mandarin-speaking immigrants, known as *mainlanders*. Following anti-KMT riots and violent military reprisals in 1947, there have been ethnic tensions of varying intensity between the mainlanders and native Taiwanese.

Contemporary Ethnic Relations

As a result of its history, Taiwan is an ethnically diverse country. Some 70 percent of the population are Hok-lo and about 14 percent are Hakka. Another 14 percent are mainlanders. Austronesian aborigines make up the remaining 2 percent of Taiwan's population. The official language of Taiwan is Mandarin Chinese, but

Hok-lo is the most widely spoken language. The importance of Hok-lo in politics and other forms of public discourse has increased since the lifting of martial law in 1987. Other languages are Hakka and nine Austronesian languages.

The chief religions in Taiwan are Buddhism, Taoism, and Confucianism, but there are also religious minorities of Protestant Christianity, Roman Catholicism, and Islam. Most of the Austronesians identify with either the Presbyterian or Catholic church. Most Muslims in Taiwan are mainlanders, although a small number of native Taiwanese have also converted to Islam. In recent years, there has been a rise in so-called new religions, such as Yi-Guan-Dao, which combines Christianity, Islam, Buddhism, Taoism, and Confucianism into one religion.

Taiwan is well known for its rapid economic development since the 1950s. In 1997, Taiwan had a Gross National Product (GNP) of $284.8 billion, making it the world's twentieth largest economy; in that year its per capita income was $13,198, the twenty-fifth highest in the world. Yet the rewards of economic development have not been evenly distributed among Taiwan's ethnic groups. For the decades immediately following KMT takeover of Taiwan, mainlanders controlled the government and key industries, leaving small-scale industry and petty commerce to the Hok-lo and Hakka "native Taiwanese." Only in recent years has this ethnic division of labor been challenged by the rise of a native Taiwanese middle class and increasing importance of class rather than ethnic divisions among Han Chinese groups.

The nation's Austronesian population remains the least empowered economically. Some aborigines migrate into the cities in search of manual labor, while others remain in relatively impoverished rural areas. Problems of unemployment and poverty still exist, suggesting widespread discrimination against aboriginal peoples. The aboriginal unemployment rate of 7.55 percent, for example, is far higher than the general unemployment rate of 2.84 percent. And median aboriginal salaries remain only 66 percent of their Han Chinese counterparts. In recent years, these and other issues concerning indigenous peoples have been energetically addressed by the Executive Yuan Council of Aboriginal Affairs and a number of autonomous nongovernmental organizations (NGOs).

Taiwan is a parliamentary democracy. The central government consists of a president, vice president, National Assembly, and five constitutionally mandated councils (*yuan*). The Legislative Yuan, the membership of which parallels that of the National Assembly, passes legislation. The Executive Yuan, or cabinet, is headed by a premier and answerable to the Legislative Yuan. The Judicial Yuan is in charge of the judicial system, the Examination Yuan is the civil service commission, and the Control Yuan oversees government administration. Since 1996, the Executive Yuan has included a Council of Aboriginal Affairs responsible for managing affairs concerning the island's indigenous people.

SCOTT SIMON

See also **China; Hakka Chinese; Taiwan's Indigenous Peoples**

Further Reading

Chen, Chung-min, Ying-chang Chuang, and Shu-min Huang, editors, *Ethnicity in Taiwan: Social, Historical and Cultural Perspectives*, Taipei: Academia Sinica Institute of Ethnology, 1994
Government Information Office (ROC), *Republic of China Yearbook*, Taipei: Kwang Hwa Publishers, annual Rubenstein, Murray, editor, *The Other Taiwan: 1945 to the Present*, Armonk, New York: M.E. Sharpe, 1994
———, editor, *Taiwan: A New History*, Armonk, New York: M.E. Sharpe, 1999

Taiwan's Indigenous Peoples

Capsule Summary

Location: Taiwan
Total Population: 381,174 (1.7% of the Taiwanese population)
Languages: nine Austronesian languages (Atayal, Saisiat, Amis, Bunun, Tsou, Rukai, Puyuma, Paiwan, and Da'o)
Religions: Primarily Protestant Christianity and Roman Catholicism

Taiwan's indigenous peoples belong to the Austronesian linguistic family, a language family extending from Madagascar to Easter Island and Hawaii, from Taiwan to New Zealand. A recent theory, based on linguistics and genetic anthropology, suggests that Taiwan may have been the starting point of the entire Austronesian dispersal throughout the Pacific and Indian Oceans after their arrival from southeast China over 6,000 years ago. The study of this migration process, as well as the history of Austronesian settlement in Taiwan, is still in its infancy.

The indigenous peoples of Taiwan's Western plains (*p'ing-p'u tsu*, plains tribes) were of the ethnic groups Luilang, Kavalan, Ketagalan, Taokas, Pazeh, Papora, Babuza, Arikun/Lloa, and Siraya. They have largely intermarried with settlers from China and been assimilated into Chinese culture, although there have been attempts in recent years to revive certain of their cultural practices. There are 11 groups of unassimilated indigenous peoples, primarily located in the central mountains and east coast of Taiwan,

although only nine groups are officially recognized. These ethnic groups and their populations are Atayal (86,042), Saisiat (6,930), Amis (146,165), Bunun (41,691), Tsou (6,838), Rukai (11,595), Puyuma (10,166), Paiwan (67,760), and Da'o (3,987). The Da'o, also known as Yami, live on Orchid Island off the Southeast coast of Taiwan, and probably arrived from the island of Batan in the northern Phillipines about a thousand years ago. In addition, some 30,000 people on the East Coast consider themselves to be Taroko people, although they are classified as Atayal. The approximately 250 Sao (Thao) people near Sun Moon Lake have also not been recognized as an ethnic group because authorities consider their numbers too few to constitute an independent group.

Before 1620, indigenous peoples were the primary occupants of Taiwan, although the island was also visited by pirates and fishermen from China and Japan. In the 1620s, Holland and Spain set up trading posts on the island and started converting the indigenous peoples to Christianity. In 1661, the Chinese rebel Koxinga (Cheng Cheng-kung), who failed in his attempt to restore the Ming Dynasty, retreated to Taiwan and evicted the Dutch. He occupied the Western plains of Taiwan and a small part of the mountainous areas. There were innumerable conflicts between Taiwan's indigenous peoples and waves of Chinese settlers who arrived on the island during the Cheng reign (1661-1683) and Manchu (Ching) rule (1683-1895), but eventually the plains tribes were assimilated into Chinese culture. Nonetheless, the mountains and Eastern plains were still under the effective control of the indigenous peoples as late as 1895.

During the Japanese colonial period (1895-1945), to take control of the island's forests, as well as mineral and other natural resources, the Japanese contained indigenous people into mountain reservations, cutting their traditional territory of 2 million hectares (4.9 million acres) down to 24,000 hectares (59,280 acres). To put down resistance from indigenous peoples, the Japanese launched a number of massacres. In the Five-Year Expedition of 1910 to 1914, over ten thousand Taroko people were killed. During the Wushe Rebellion of 1930, the Japanese massacred all the men, women and children of six Atayal villages. To assimilate indigenous peoples, the Japanese encouraged them to take Japanese names and forced children to learn Japanese in compulsory elementary school education.

After its defeat in World War II, Japan renounced its rights to its colonies in Taiwan and Korea. In 1945, without consulting the island's population, Taiwan was given to the Republic of China (ROC) to be ruled by General Chiang Kai-shek and the Chinese Nationalist Party (Kuomintang, KMT). After the Liberation of China by the Communist Party, the KMT retreated to Taiwan. To consolidate its rule, the KMT government massacred over 20,000 people in the so-called February 28th Incident and imprisoned countless dissidents, including indigenous people, in the 40 years of martial law that followed.

Like their Japanese predecessors, the KMT assumed policies of assimilating indigenous people and reclaiming their lands. Indigenous people were required to take Chinese names and learn Chinese in school. Household registration regulations were composed to forcefully assimilate indigenous people. Upon marriage to a Han Chinese man, for example, an indigenous woman would lose her indigenous legal status. But a Han woman who married an indigenous man would retain her Han Chinese status. Traditional territories, hunting grounds, and ritual sites were nationalized by the government; all lands with development potential were quickly turned over to either the government or Chinese capitalists. Indigenous peoples were relocated in several counties to make room for national parks, industrial zones, and reservoirs. Traditional subsistence activities of hunting, fishing, and slash and burn agriculture were forbidden. Many indigenous people thus flowed into the cities as migrant laborers and prostitutes to make a living. The Da'o homeland of Orchid Island was used to dispose of nuclear waste. To this day, indigenous people still have higher rates of unemployment and poverty than Han Chinese on Taiwan.

In the 1980s, an aboriginal movement began, starting with the foundation of *Gaoshan qing* (Mountain Greenery) newspaper in 1983, and the Alliance of Taiwan Aborigines (ATA) in 1984. After martial law was lifted in 1987, the movement grew in strength and numbers. Several indigenous publications, including *Shan-hai* and *Nandao Shibao*, were started as well as a number of NGOs, some supported by the Presbyterian Church. Since 1991, the ATA and other indigenous groups have been the only Taiwanese NGOs to be recognized by the United Nations. In 1995, indigenous people were finally permitted to use their Austronesian names.

As Taiwan seeks a national identity distinct from China, the small nation has finally become aware of indigenous issues and placed them on the forefront of the national agenda. In 1996, the Executive Yuan set up a Council of Aboriginal Affairs, which has taken a proactive stance on such issues as poverty, unemployment, and land rights. In 1997, legal rights for indigenous peoples were finally included in the ROC constitution. In 2000, the Democratic Progressive Party elected Chen Shui-bian to president and promised to affirm indigenous rights. By 2001, the government was considering the establishment of autonomous regions in areas of high Austronesian population to better protect indigenous rights. Although much progress is still needed, the situation of indigenous people in Taiwan has become arguably better than that of indigenous people in Canada, the United States, and other countries.

SCOTT SIMON

See also **Aborigines; Taiwan**

Further Reading

Allio, Fiorella, "The Austronesian Peoples of Taiwan: Building a Political Platform for Themselves," *China Perspectives* 18 (1998)

Barnes, R.H., Andrew Gray, and Benedict Kingsbury, editors, *Indigenous Peoples of Asia*, Ann Arbor, Michigan: Association for Asian Studies, 1995

Bellwood, Peter, James Fox, and Darrell Tyron, editor, *The Austronesians: Historical and Comparative Perspectives*, Canberra, Australia: Australian National University, 1995

Rubenstein, Murray, editor, *The Other Taiwan: 1945 to the Present*, Armonk, New York: M.E. Sharpe, 1994

———, editor, *Taiwan: A New History*, Armonk, New York: M.E. Sharpe, 1999

Tajikistan

Capsule Summary

Location: Southeastern part of Central Asia (CA)
Total population: 6,863,752 (July 2003)
Languages: Tajiki
Religion: Sunni-Muslims

The main indigenous people of Tajikistan (CAT) are of Iranian origin, contrary to the other predominantly Turkic former Soviet Central Asian (CA) republics. They speak Tajiki, a dialect of *farsi* (Persian language), belonging to the Southwest Iranian language group. Persian settlement in CA dates back to prehistoric times. The total population of Tajikistan was estimated at 6,112,000 in 1997. Tajikistan, like other CA countries, has a multiethnic society. The absolute majority is Sunni-Muslim. In 1991, Tajikistan became independent, and since then a lot of rivalry has been going on between the former communists, Islamic, and democratic forces, resulting in a bloody civil war. In June 1997 a peace agreement was signed between rival groups, but implementation is very slow. Per capita gross domestic product (GDP) is $1,300 (2002).

History

For centuries, forces from different parts of the world made contact with and sometimes ruled over CA. Migrations of Turkic people (sixth century CE and later) influenced Tajikistan's culture. In the seventh and eighth centuries Arabs conquered the region and Islamicised its people. From the thirteenth century, it was ruled or influenced by the Mongol and Timurid empires, the Uzbek Khanate, and Russia/Soviet Union.

Between 1868-1895, Russia gained total control of CA. In 1887 Russia established its frontier with Afghanistan, in 1894 with China. In 1895 Russia signed an agreement with Britain, securing most of the Pamir Mountains to the Russian Empire.

After the Bolshevik Revolution (1917), much of contemporary Tajikistan was included in the Turkestan Autonomous Soviet Socialist Republic and the Bukharan People's Soviet Republic. Basmachi troops, in eastern Bukhara, continued to resist Soviet rule for a few years. As a result of the National Delimination of CA

of 1924-1925 the two parts of Tajikistan formed the Tajik Autonomous Soviet Socialist Republic (TASSR). Until 1929, it was an administrative part of the Uzbek S.S.R. Some 37 percent, of those officially claiming Tajik nationality, were left outside the republic, mainly living in Uzbekistan. In October 1929, the Khojend region, with a mixed Uzbek-Tajik population, was transferred from Uzbekistan to Tajikistan, and Tajikistan gained the status of a full union republic of the Soviet Union (SU). The collapse of the SU led to the somewhat unwilling declaration of independence, establishing a parliamentary republic.

Former Communist Party First Secretary Rakhman Nabiyev emerged as president. An April 1992 power-sharing agreement, giving cabinet posts to the opposition anti-Communist based Tajik Democratic Party (TDP), and the rural-based Islamic Renaissance Party (IRP) unravelled, resulting in civil war. Parliament forced Nabiyev to resign in September 1992, which caused the government to come into the hands of an IRP-led coalition, including TDP and other secular and nationalist groups. In November, acting president Nabiyev handed power to Rakhmonov, leader of the pro-Nabiyev forces in Kulyab. In December, troops (backed by Russian troops) loyal to Rakhmonov regained control and pushed the Islamic-TDP forces to the Afghan border.

A November 6, 1994, referendum, held together with presidential balloting, and boycotted by the opposition, approved Tajikistan's liberal constitution. Official results showed more than 90 percent of voters supporting the constitution. The United Tajik Opposition (UTO), a coalition of nationalist, Islamic, and democratic groups, maintains that this referendum was neither free nor fair. The constitution created a 181-member parliament, elected directly, for a five-year term. It also provides a tripartite division of power with a strong president, empowered to appoint the government, chairman of the National Bank, head of the Constitutional Court, state prosecutor, heads of regional administrations, prime minister, and judges. This president is also head of the executive branch and commander in chief of the armed forces. The constitution also bans discrimination based on nationality, race, gender, and religion.

In the November 6, 1994, presidential elections, official results gave Rakhmonov 58 percent of the vote against Abdumalik Abdullajanov, a former premier from the northern Khojend region. The election law effectively prevented opposition candidates from standing, and the IRP and TDP boycotted the vote. The voting was marred by massive fraud. The opposition also boycotted the parliamentary elections on February 26, and March 12, 1995.

New Parliamentary elections were held on February 25, 2000, with six parties competing, including a coalition of Islamic rebels. President Rahmonov's People Democratic Party received 64.5 percent of the vote, the communists 20 percent, and the IRP 7.5 percent. However, the Islamics were charged with ballot-box stuffing because a turnout of 87 percent was recorded. IRP leader Abdullah Nuri said the results will be accepted and that the peace process is irreversible.

Real political power is highly authoritarian and strongly centralised. Parliament can disband local legislatures and call new elections if local bodies are in violation of national law. However, local strongmen, viewing to control the cotton, metals, and narcotics trade, run large parts of Tajikistan.

Civil War

Political chaos and widespread turmoil overwhelmed the new nation. Communists fought to retain power against an alliance of Islamic, nationalist, and democratic forces (UTO). In the recent civil war an estimated 50,000 people were killed, and thousands were displaced, costing the already devastated economy millions of dollars.

There are two major factions: The Leninabadi (Khojendi) faction, named after the large, rich, northern industrialised province, includes a population with close contacts to Uzbekistan and holds political control over the Communist Party of Tajikistan (CPT) and the Supreme Soviet. The Leninabadi clan (in the north) traditionally enjoyed a clientele relationship with the town of Kuliab in the south, a militant support base for the CPT, of deeply traditional and religious people. When the communists made their parliamentary comeback in November, Emomali Rakhmonov, head of the Executive Committee in Kuliab, was elected as Speaker. This, together with the post of Prime Minister going to a powerful Khojendi man (Abdulmolik Abdullojonov), the Leninabadi faction, once again, established a political monopoly. Although low-scale fighting continued, the government cracked down on the opposition, forcing many of its members to escape the country.

The TDP, IRS, and Laa'li Badakhshon and Rastokhez organisations, draw most of their membership from the Southern (Karategin) Faction, uniting the region under the loose banner of opposition, containing mostly rural people. Their leaders are nationalists from the technocratic rank and file and young members of the Academy of Sciences and the University. The Badakhshanis (Shiite Ismaili sect), seldom occupying high governmental posts, acquired certain defence and security posts, in recent years. The regime possibly tried to gain the trust of these mountainous warriors during the Afghan war.

In December 1996, President Rakhmonov and UTO (disbanded in mid-1999) leader Said Abdullo Nuri signed a cease-fire agreement. The deal met the opposition's longstanding demand to create a National Reconciliation Commission (NRC), to be headed by an opposition representative and composed of all political factions, which would implement peace agreements, repatriate and assist refugees, and introduce legislation for fair parliamentary elections. On June 27, 1997, brokered by Iran and Russia, the two sides signed the Tajik National Peace Accord, formally ending five years of civil war.

Under the terms of the accord, the government was to give 30 percent of the government posts to UTO representatives. A 26-member NRC was established with equal representation from both sides. Nuri became the chairman. The armed forces were to be integrated, banned parties could re-register, amnesty would be given to political prisoners, and prisoners of war would be exchanged. An important agreement was signed in June 1999 for implementing the general agreement on peace.

Tajikistan Society

Tajikistan lies in CA and borders on China, Kyrgyzstan, Uzbekistan, and Afghanistan. There is an autonomous region, Gorno-Badakhshan, in the eastern part of the country. The capital city is Dushanbe and the total area of the country is about 55,250 square miles (143,100 square kilometers). The major cities, in 1989, were Dushanbe with 582,400 inhabitants; Khujand with 164,500; Kulob with 79,300; Qurghonteppa with 58,400; and Urateppa with 47,700.

Of the total population, 3.5 percent was Russian; 25 percent Uzbek; 6 percent Tartar, Kyrgyz, Jew and German, and the rest was Tajik. The sedentary Tajik

TAJIKISTAN

have lost their tribal characteristics and identify themselves with the extended family or village, and region. Hahgayaghi (1995) distinguished four ethnic groups:

1. Pamirs, occupying the western part of Gorno Badakhshan Autonomous Region, speaking a distinct Iranian dialect and belonging to the Ismaili sect;
2. Mountain Tajiks, occupying the high mountain ranges, and having a distinct dialect and culture;
3. Yagnubis, a small community, inhabiting the Yagnub Valley of Fan Darya in Zeravshan, as well as Varzob, and speaking a Soghdian dialect; and
4. Chagatais, of Turkish-Mongol origin, living in Ghorghan Tepeh (and Surkhan Darya in Uzbekistan), who have adopted the Tajik language and culture, though some speak Uzbek.

Tajikistan suffers the lowest gross domestic product (GDP) per capita in the former SU, high population growth rates and widespread poverty. The withdrawal of Soviet material inputs, markets, and subsidies, followed by the infrastructure damage and population displacements as result of civil conflicts, left the national economy in disaster. Between 1990 and 1996, annual average real GDP declined about 16 percent. Since 1997, however, real GDP has been rising at about 4 to 5 percent a year. But the inflation rate stays at a high level (1998, 20 percent; 1999, 24 percent). In 1998, GDP was $1.8 billion, resulting in a GDP per capita of $290.

The main economic sector is agriculture; cotton production accomplishes one third of agricultural output. Aluminium melting is the principal manufacturing activity with one of the world's largest facilities located at Tursunzade. Tajikistan depends entirely on external sources for its ore feedstock. The other important economic activity, being the world's third largest producer,

is hydroelectric power generation. Reliance on a few products makes Tajikistan highly susceptible to trade shocks. Tajikistan has significant resources of gold, silver, antimony, and coal. The main element of Tajikistan's shadow economy, smuggling (mainly narcotics from Afghanistan), is a major cause of concern for Tajikistan and the international community. Tajikistan increased its economic dependence on the countries of the Commonwealth of Independent States (CIS).

Tajikistan is the main gateway to CA for Uzbek Islamic rebels (Islamic Movement of Uzbekistan), based in Afghanistan, and it is the center of wider instabilities in the region. The general fear of the uprising of Islamic fundamentalists forces from Afghanistan, brings CA countries, Russia, and China together.

MEHDI PARVIZI AMINEH

See also **Tajiks**

Further Reading

Amineh, Mehdi Parvizi, *Towards the Control of Oil Resources in the Caspian Region*, New York: St. Martin's Press, 1999
Doerfer, Gerhard, "Turkish-Iranian Language Contacts," in *Encyclopaedia Iranica*, Vol. 5, edited by Eshan Yarshater, Costa Mesa: Mazda Publishers, 1992
Haghayeghi, Mehrdad, *Islam and Politics in Central Asia*, New York: St. Martin's Press, 1995
Hambly, Gavin, editor, *Central Asia*, London: Weidenfeld and Nicolson, 1969
Teeter, Mark H., et al., editors, *A Scholars' Guide to Humanities and Social Sciences in the Soviet Successor States*: The *Academies of Sciences of Russia, Armenia, Azerbaidzhan, Belarus, Estonia, Georgia, Kazakhstan, Kirghizstan, Latvia, Lithuania, Moldova, Tadzhikistan, Turkmenistan, Ukraine, and Uzbekistan*, 2nd edition, Armonk, New York: M.E. Sharpe, 1993
Wheeler, Geoffrey, *The Modern History of Soviet Central Asia*, London: Weidenfeld and Nicolson, 1964

Tajiks

Capsule Summary

Location: Central Asia, mostly in the territory of Tajikistan and Afghanistan
Total Population: approximately 10 million
Language: Tajik
Religion: Muslim, mostly Sunni (Hanafi)

Tajiks is a generic term for speakers of west-Iranian languages in Central Asia and Afghanistan. Their total number is around 10 million but not all of these necessarily call themselves Tajik. The majority of them live in present-day Tajikistan and Afghanistan, but there exists also a large group of Tajik-speakers in Uzbekistan. The

Tajik language belongs to the west-Iranian group and thus ultimately to the large Indo-European family. It is closely related with modern Persian. Often subsumed under the same ethnic category are speakers of east-Iranian languages in the Pamir Mountains, among them the Wakhi, Yaghnobi, and others. This is problematic as these groups do not consider themselves Tajiks and their languages are not comprehensible. They also differ in terms of religious affiliation. While the majority of Tajiks (in the proper sense) are Sunni Muslims of the Hanafi tradition, most of the Pamiri groups are Shiites of the Ismaili branch.

Many Tajiks claim the prestige of being the most ancient group in Central Asia, tracing themselves back to the pre-Turkic (and pre-Islamic) times of the Sogds and other Iranian-speaking populations. Special attention is given to the last Iranian dynasty in Central Asia, the Samanids in the tenth century. There is, of course, some truth to this claim as the Tajiks are the only large Iranian-speaking ethnic group in the region today. Linguistically, however, they are not the heirs of the Sogds (who used an east-Iranian dialect), an honor which would, strictly speaking, have to be attributed to the Pamiri groups.

By the seventh century, the earlier Iranian languages had come under increasing pressure of linguistic assimilation by succeeding waves of Turkic tribes who originated from the northern and eastern steppes. During the same period, Islam arrived in Central Asia. In its course a variation of the Persian language became the prime tongue for administration and literature, the ancestor of modern Tajik. It rapidly replaced the former east-Iranian languages. Turkification, however, continued, and today Iranian speakers are in an almost marginal position in Central Asia. This is a process that continues today and is much bemoaned by Tajik intellectuals who often view themselves as victims.

Feelings of betrayal are due to a large degree to the process of national delimitation during early Soviet times. In spite of their dominant Tajik population (90 percent according to some accounts) the historic cities of Bukhara and Samarkand as well as numerous others were allocated to Uzbekistan. The newly established Republic of Tajikistan was created out of remote mountain areas with little economic potential and little cultural heritage. In Afghanistan, however, Tajik has the status of a state language and as a medium for interethnic communication. Here, Tajiks often occupied key positions in the administration, although state leadership usually lay in the hands of Pashtuns.

The largest concentration of Tajiks today is found in Tajikistan, which became an independent state in 1991. Almost two thirds of the total population of six million are Tajiks, including the Pamiri (approximately 50,000). Tajik-speakers dominate in all provinces—often intermingled with Uzbeks—except for the Autonomous Region Gorno-Badakhshan, which occupies the eastern part of the state. Here, the majority of the population consists of Pamiri and scattered groups of Kyrgyz pastoralists. Tajiks occupy most central positions in society but their dominance is hampered by the fact of strong regional competition, which were partly responsible for the civil war in the 1990s (see the following discussion of the civil war).

In neighboring Uzbekistan, Tajiks live in various proportions in most parts of the country. Official statistics give a figure of slightly more than one million but the actual number may be much higher as many Tajik-speakers are registered as Uzbeks. The provinces of Bukhara and Samarkand probably still have a Tajik majority. Large Tajik populations, often in compact settlements, can also be found in the part of the Ferghana Valley belonging to Uzbekistan, in the central provinces of Tashkent and Dzhizzak, as well as in southern Kashkadarya and Surxandarya. Many Tajiks complain about increasing discrimination and disadvantages in political and economic affairs. Uzbek is the sole state languages and is becoming more and more dominant in the political and educational sphere. On the ground, however, interethnic relations tend to be peaceful.

The Tajik population in Afghanistan is even more difficult to determine. One reason is the long-lasting civil war in this country, which took an enormous toll of human lives among all ethnic groups and forced millions of people to leave the country. A second reason is a weak collective identity among the Tajiks in Afghanistan, which is used only by a part of the linguistic group as an ethnic denominator. Most estimations range between three and four million, only slightly less than the number in Tajikistan. Tajik-speakers settle primarily in northeastern Afghanistan extending south to Kabul. A second center exists in the west of the country, in the province of Herat. Tajiks, under the leadership of Ahmad Shah Masud, were very active in the fight of the Northern Alliance against the Taliban. They used to compose a significant portion of the lower and middle level of the state administration as the state capital Kabul is located in a Tajik-speaking area. Tajik, or Dari, is one of the two state languages and is also a medium of interethnic communication as minority groups speak Tajik rather than Pashtu as a second language.

Very few Tajiks live in other countries like Russia or China (most of these are Pamiri).

In Central Asia, Tajiks have for centuries shared resources and patterns of land usage with the Uzbeks making their living primarily by irrigated agriculture. A large portion of the Tajiks also used to be city dwellers and merchants. Similar to other groups in Central Asia, their economic life has been fundamentally transformed, both during Soviet times and now, with the introduction of a market economy. This affects Tajiks in particular as many of them live in remote areas and were hard struck by the years of civil war.

Tajik society is characterized by strong local identities and the importance of village and neighborhood communities. Kin organization is centered on extended families, and marriage frequently involves relatives. Local proximity often outbalances ethnic boundaries, and regional differences are very pronounced. This was, as mentioned, one main factor in the civil war in Tajikistan. On the other hand, within a given local settings, social relations with Uzbeks and other ethnic groups may be quite intensive and harmonious.

PETER FINKE

See also **Afghansitan; Iranians; Tajikistan; Uzbekistan; Uzbeks**

Further Reading

Atkin, Muriel, "Tajik National Identity," *Iranian Studies*, 26 (1993)

Chvyr, Ludmilla, "Central Asia's Tajiks: Self-Identification and Ethnic Identity," in *State, Religion, and Society in Central Asia*, edited by Vitaly Naumkin, Reading, New York: Ithaca Press, 1993

Djalili, Mohammad-Reza, Frédéric Grare, and Shirin Akiner, *Tajikistan: The Trials of Independence*, Richmond, United Kingdom: Curzon, 1998

Foltz, Richard, "The Tajiks of Uzbekistan," *Central Asian Survey*, 15 (1996)

Roy, Olivier, *The New Central Asia: The Creation of Nations*, New York: New York University Press, 2000

Schoeberlein-Engel, John, *Identity in Central Asia: Construction and Contention in the Conceptions of "Özbek," "Tâjik," "Muslim," "Samarqandi" and Other Groups*, PhD thesis, Harvard University, 1994

Tamil Tigers

The Liberation Tigers of Tamil Eelam (LTTE), commonly referred to as the Tamil Tigers, are a militant rebel group in Sri Lanka. Their violent guerrilla struggle to secure the independence of Eelam, their Tamil homeland, to guarantee minority Tamil rights has left over 60,000 dead in a civil war that has scarred the island nation ethnically, politically, and economically. Led by Vellupillai Prabhakaran, the LTTE engages in a hit-and-run style of jungle warfare. Their willingness to kill innocent civilians and commit political assassinations has labeled them a terrorist organization, both domestically and internationally. Their gains toward autonomy have also made them respected freedom fighters to many.

Though exact numbers are difficult to ascertain, the Tigers have approximately 8,000 to 10,000 active fighting members. How such a small number of combatants have thwarted the Sri Lankan army for so long reflects the strategic genius of Prabhakaran and the complete dedication of each member to the fight for Eelam.

Background

Sri Lankan Tamils are descendants of South India and make up 18 percent of Sri Lanka's population. They predominantly speak the Tamil language and practice Hinduism. Although culturally, ethnically, linguistically, and religiously similar to the 60 million Tamils of South India, the Sri Lankan Tamils have developed their own identity after centuries of established life in North and East Sri Lanka. The Sinhalese, who comprise 74 percent of Sri Lanka, are descendants of the Aryan people of North India, speak Sinhala, and practice Buddhism.

In 1948 Sri Lanka gained independence from Britain. Under British rule, the Tamils excelled at learning English and, as a consequence, held a disproportionately high number of jobs in the government, the nation's largest employer. After independence, the two major Sinhalese political parties contended for elections under the auspices of championing Sinhala as the official language, replacing English. As such, when the Sri Lankan Freedom Party, a Sinhalese political party, was elected, they adopted the Official Language Act No. 33 of 1956, commonly known as the Sinhala Only Act. This made Sinhala the official language, prohibiting English or Tamil from being spoken in the public sphere. Many Tamils soon lost their jobs in the government. Additionally, the Act created a sense of alienation among the Tamils, who feared they were losing language rights simply because they were a minority.

In 1956 the Federal Party, the main Tamil party, organized peaceful Tamil gatherings to protest the Sinhala Only Act, only to be met with Sinhalese violence and an anti-Tamil riot, during which more than 100 Tamils were killed. As a result, Sinhalese and Tamil leaders created the Bandaranaike-Chelvanayakam Pact of 1957, which would have recognized Tamil as a regional language. Due to strong Sinhalese and Buddhist opposition, however, it was never implemented. The Tamils again held peaceful protests in 1958 to obtain the right to use their own language, and once more were met with Sinhalese violence in the form of large-scale anti-Tamil rioting. To make amends, the 1958 Tamil Language (Special Provisions) Act was created in the spirit of granting Tamil language rights, but was never implemented.

Independence also led to discrimination in higher education. Under British rule, the Tamil admission rate was relatively high, which the Sinhalese thought unfair. The government placed quotas on admissions along ethnic lines in a reverse affirmative action. Tamil enrollment decreased significantly.

The government also sponsored Sinhalese colonization of traditional Tamil homelands of the Northern and Eastern provinces under the guise of promoting irrigation projects while development in Tamil areas was unattended. With the influx of Sinhalese, the Tamil majorities of those areas were diluted, making their voices less powerful still, and enraging their community.

At the time of independence the Tamils of Indian descent living in Sri Lanka, brought there by the British in the 1830s to work the tea plantations, were denied citizenship. About half were repatriated to India. While this group, distinct from the Sri Lankan Tamils, is not active in the LTTE, their maltreatment certainly gave

the LTTE another reason to question the motives of the government.

This institutional discrimination which all Tamils in Sri Lanka faced directly led to the emergence of Tamil militancy.

Birth of the LTTE

By 1972 mainstream Tamil politicians called for a federal state, fearing their rights would always be marginalized by the Sinhalese. All major Tamil parties united under one voice as the Tamil United Front, which became the Tamil United Liberation Front (TULF) in 1976 under the leadership of S.J.V. Chelvanayakam, a prominent Tamil politician who earlier fought for Tamil language rights and whose memory is today highly regarded by the LTTE. The TULF won the 1977 election on an Eelam mandate, so popular was the idea of self-rule to most Tamils. But by this time the Tamil youth, many of whom had been denied higher education and faced unemployment, had lost faith that the political process could secure their rights. They began to take up arms and formed several underground groups, thus beginning the militant Tamil movement.

One of these groups was the Tamil New Tigers founded in 1972 by the young Prabhakaran in his home village of Valvettiturai. In 1976 he joined another militant organization, the Liberation Tigers, and soon became its leader. He renamed the organization as the Liberation Tigers of Tamil Eelam, proudly adopting a centuries-old symbol used by the Cholas, ancient Tamil rulers from India. Headquartered in the northern towns of Kilinochchi and Vavuniya, the LTTE first gained notoriety for engaging in bank robbery to secure funds.

Following the emergence of the LTTE and other militant organizations was a series of arrests and detentions of Tamil youth in a crackdown by the government. This provoked an escalation of violence on both sides, leading to another anti-Tamil riot in 1977. In 1979 the Prevention of Terrorism Act passed, which allowed the government to search homes without a warrant, seize property, arrest and detain suspects for 18 months without trial, and admit any statements as evidence in court even if made under duress. In early July 1983 the Emergency Regulation Act passed, which enabled police to cremate the bodies of people shot without establishing identity and without inquiry.

Tensions reached a breaking point on July 23, 1983 when the LTTE ambushed and killed 13 Sinhalese soldiers in retaliation for the murder of Charles Antony, the LTTE's second-in-command. The Sri Lankan government returned the mutilated bodies to Colombo, where the citizens were outraged. Mobs of angry Sinhalese took to the streets carrying voting lists, which contained information regarding people's ethnicities and addresses. They killed hundreds of innocent Tamil citizens, most of them residents of Colombo with no ties to the LTTE. They set fire to Tamil businesses and homes as well, creating thousands of Tamil refugees, many of whom fled to the North and East of Sri Lanka where they survived in wretched, diseased makeshift camps. The police did nothing to stop the violence, nor did the government act to prevent the murders or punish the perpetrators. It was nothing less than a pogrom. After that riot, an unprecedented number of Tamil youth joined the LTTE to fight for Eelam, thus initiating the civil war in Sri Lanka.

By that time, five cohesive Tamil militant movements existed with different ideologies, strategies, and sources of income. Over the course of the war, every group has disappeared except the LTTE, who today serve as the sole negotiating and military voice of Eelam. Intergroup rivalry and fighting only partially explain how the LTTE has become the most influential force shaping the Tamils' future. The LTTE, more than any other Tamil militant movement at the time, is known for its strict discipline which allows it to function so effectively. The Tigers are allowed no drugs, no alcohol, and no casual sex. Marriage is permitted, and Prabhakaran is married with children. Tigers also must renounce family ties to create allegiance to the organization. Tigers who break these rules are punished very harshly and are often condemned to death. Upon joining the organization, Tigers undergo a long period of internment, where they are taught loyalty to their peers and especially to Prabhakaran, their unquestioned leader. This disciplined way of life is a welcomed sacrifice to a committed Tiger, who believes the collective fight for Eelam is more important than the life of an individual. Females also compose a formidable percent of the LTTE and are treated equally as soldiers with a mission. The LTTE includes a special unit called the Black Tigers who are specifically trained to commit suicide bombings, often in public places where innocent Sinhalese civilians are the victims. Members of the LTTE have become infamous for the cyanide capsules they wear around their neck, a chilling reminder that they would rather commit suicide, which they have often done, than face the possibility of betraying the movement during interrogation if captured. Recently, the LTTE has come under international criticism,

especially from the United Nations children's agency, for forcibly recruiting child soldiers as well.

In the early 1980s, the LTTE received training and arms from India's Research and Analysis Wing, equivalent to the Central Intelligence Agency of the United States. The Tigers received financial support from the huge international Tamil diaspora. The many websites dedicated to Eelam were also channels for their funding until the British and American governments stifled their cash flows as part of the war on terror, long before the attack on the World Trade Center on September 11, 2001. With their plethora of propaganda, which includes pamphlets and videos, the LTTE is well equipped to campaign for sympathizers, though civilian Tamil opinion of the LTTE is mixed. While many vocally support the aim of the Tigers, others do not approve of their tactics, and have even been murdered for expressing their dissent. Several Tamil civilians have been shot by Tigers for voting in elections the LTTE has condemned. The LTTE has also murdered pacifist Tamil leaders, such as prominent TULF members Appapillai Amirthalingam and V. Yogeswaran in 1989, who also seek a secure Eelam, but choose to reach a negotiated settlement with the Sinhalese rather than a military solution.

Current Situation

Amid worsening fighting and failed peace negotiations, Indian Prime Minister Rajiv Gandhi and Sri Lankan President J.R. Jayawardene reached an agreement in July 1987 to allow India to send the Indian Peace Keeping Force (IPKF) to intervene in Sri Lanka. The IPKF entered the country as a neutral peacekeeping body to act as a buffer between the Sri Lankan army and the LTTE, and were greeted by the cheers of the Tamil civilians. Their mission was to oversee the disarmament of the LTTE. In their determination to root out militants, however, the IPKF often confused LTTE members with Tamil civilians, and soon both groups faced harassment as if they were the same. The IPKF restricted civilian movement and began committing egregious crimes against Tamil civilians, including robbery, rape, and murder. Their presence soon caused the resentment of all Sri Lankans, who did not want a foreign military on their soil, and by 1990 Sri Lankan President Ranasinghe Premadasa provided arms to the LTTE to fight the IPKF. The LTTE guerrilla campaign was successful. In 1990 the IPKF left Sri Lanka, humiliated, with 1,500 dead Indian soldiers to show for their intervention.

The 1990s brought another decade of violence and instability. In 1991 Prabhakaran engineered the assassination of Rajiv Gandhi during a re-election campaign. After the failure of the IPKF and the murder of Gandhi, the sympathy India had for the LTTE significantly eroded. In 1993 the LTTE assassinated Sri Lankan President Premadasa, the same man who had armed them against India only a few years earlier. In 1994 Chandrika Kumaratunga was elected president of Sri Lanka on a campaign of making peace with the LTTE. After a series of failed peace talks which the LTTE believed were never negotiated in good faith, Kumaratunga herself became a victim of an LTTE attack, losing one eye in a bombing during her re-election campaign in 1999. She was re-elected president. A notable attack that did not target a political leader came in July 2001, when the LTTE killed 14 people during a bombing on the international airport, which destroyed half the fleet of SriLankan Airlines and damaged much of the air force.

The government and the LTTE have not yet been able to agree on terms for peace. As this deadlock became more apparent and the cycle of violence continued, both sides asked Norway to intervene in peace talks in February 2000. They have no military presence in Sri Lanka, only a diplomatic one, and have enjoyed limited success. In February 2002 the Sri Lankan government and the LTTE signed a cease-fire that has lasted for two years, albeit in a precarious manner. Sri Lankan Prime Minister Ranil Wickremesinghe pushes the peace agenda while he is at odds with President Kumaratunga, who has remained skeptical of the LTTE's sincerity regarding a peace accord.

Over the course of its existence the LTTE has shed some of its mystery and become more public. After more than ten years of underground activity, Prabhakaran gave his first interview in 1983 to Indian journalist Anita Pratap, and since then has been willing on occasion to speak publicly. He can even be seen posing for photographs, most predictably every annual Heroes' Day on November 27th, the day after his birthday. Anton Balasingham, the LTTE's lead negotiator and political advisor, often speaks to the press regarding the peace talks and has published extensively on Eelam. S.P. Thamilselvan, head of the political wing of the LTTE, sometimes speaks to the press and gives a face to the potential civilian aspect of the LTTE that will be in control once the war ends. Foreign journalists and civilian visitors alike have access to the areas of the North and East, which are LTTE-run country in all but name. This war has taken a large toll on civilian life and severely damaged the potentially lucrative tourist industry of a country that would otherwise be described as a tropical paradise. It has been conjectured that both sides will simply choose peace because they have tired of fighting. It seems that a settlement will allow the Tamils to gain a large range of regional autonomy while remaining a part of the Sri Lankan nation. Peace is an attractive option that would give Sinhalese and Tamil citizens alike a better life for the first time in decades.

JOSHUA PASTERNAK

See also **Sri Lanka; Tamils**

Further Reading

Hellmann-Rajanayagam, Dagmar, *The Tamil Tigers: Armed Struggle for Identity*, Stuttgart: F. Steiner, 1994

Manogaran, Chelvadurai, *Ethnic Conflict and Reconciliation in Sri Lanka*, Honolulu: University of Hawaii Press, 1987

Manor, James, *Sri Lanka in Change and Crisis*, New York: St. Martin's Press, 1984

Pratap, Anita, *Island of Blood: Frontline Reports from Sri Lanka, Afghanistan and Other South Asian Flashpoints*, New York: Penguin, 2003

Shastri, Amita, "Government Policy and Ethnic Crisis in Sri Lanka," in *Government Policies and Ethnic Relations in Asia and the Pacific*, edited by Michael E. Brown and Sumit Ganguly, Cambridge: MIT Press, 1997

Tamils

Capsule Summary

Location: South India, State of Tamilnadu, Northern Sri Lanka, also Malaysia, Fiji, South Africa; approximately 1.5 million diaspora Tamils located in North America, Australia, United Kingodom, and Germany

Total Population: approximately 60-70 million

Language: Tamil

Religions: Hindu, Muslim, Christian

The Tamils are one of the Dravidian peoples who originally settled in South India and Northern Sri Lanka. In the nineteenth century Tamils from India migrated to other parts of the British colonies, Malaya, Fiji, South Africa and Ceylon, where they worked as labourers and tea pluckers. Ceylonese Tamils, as they were called, migrated primarily to Malaya and Singapore as government servants and planters. The Tamil language is the oldest of the Dravidian family of languages spread all over South India. It is spoken by about 60 to 70 million people. Dravidians are supposed to have been the earliest migrants to the subcontinent. It is, however, not clear where they have come from. One hypothesis is that they originated from Mesopotamia. The Tamils are mostly Hindus with small minorities of Christians (Catholic and Protestant) and Muslims among them. While Tamilnadu is a federal state of the Indian Union, Northern Sri Lanka, the settlement area of the Tamils, is part of the unitary state of Sri Lanka, formerly Ceylon. Tamils constitute an overwhelming majority in the Jaffna peninsula and the rest of the northern Province, called Vanni (up to Vavuniya) and a simple majority in the Northeast, the districts of Batticaloa and Trincomalee. Overall, they make up between 20 and 25 percent of the population. The figures are, however, controversial.

In India, the Tamils are not considered a minority, because the country is made up of a large number of ethnic and linguistic groups, none of whom constitute a majority. Most of these groups are able to administer themselves in linguistically defined states. But the Tamils of Sri Lanka have fought a 20-year civil war against the Sri Lankan government because they felt suppressed and underprivileged by the majority Sinhalese. They could not autonomously administer the regions and provinces where they live, but were governed from the central government in Colombo. While they differ in language and religion from the Sinhalese, these differences are sometimes exaggerated.

History

The history of the Tamils is very ancient. The oldest extant evidence of Tamil classical literature and culture dates from about the beginning of the Common Era, when they lived in small chieftaincies all over South India. The separation into different groups and languages occurred only gradually until the sixteenth century. It is assumed that Dravidians inhabited India before the migration of Aryan-language speaking peoples there. It is still being debated whether the Indus culture was a Dravidian one or something different altogether. The Dravidians gradually retreated into the southern half of the subcontinent below the Dekkhan mountains and probably also reached Ceylon, the Lanka of classical Sanskrit literature. It is a matter of conjecture who the earliest inhabitants of Sri Lanka were, but it seems that the Nagas and Yakkhas, "demon" tribes whom the first "Sinhalese" migrants from modern Bengal encountered, were Dravidian tribes. Rama, the hero of the Indian epic *Ramayana* is supposed to have conquered Ravana, the demon king of Lanka with the help of a monkey army (Dravidian troops). Tamils have reportedly settled in Sri Lanka since very ancient times, but the bulk of them migrated from southern India to the Jaffna peninsula from the eleventh century onwards, in the wake of the Cola conquests. The (Imperial) Colas were a powerful Tamil dynasty from the tenth to the fourteenth centuries, who at the height of their power extended their reach into Sri Lanka and even modern-day Malaysia. The Sinhala rulers had extensive connections to Southern India: commercial, cultural, dynastic, and political, both as allies and enemies. The Colas invaded the country twice, in the eleventh and thirteenth centuries and both times ruled for several decades, though they could never subdue the whole island. A powerful Tamil kingdom emerged in the North from the thirteenth century onwards, which has become known as the kingdom of Jaffna, nominally a fief of first the Colas, then the Pandyas, another South Indian dynasty and then the kingdom of Vijayanagara. It existed until 1620 when the Portuguese defeated it. Jaffna was the last of the maritime kingdoms to be subdued by the Portuguese, only Kandy in the central highlands held out until 1815.

In 1657 the Portuguese were defeated by the Dutch and those in turn by the British in 1795. All of them administered Jaffna as one of the Maritime Provinces, but the British changed the administrative structure in 1833 in the wake of the Colebrooke-Cameron reforms. From then onward, Ceylon was ruled centrally from Colombo. Nevertheless all colonial powers were aware that the Sinhalese and the Tamils were two different groups, and they endeavoured to keep them separate after a fashion:

> Deux Nations differentes semblent dès les tems reculez s'être partegés l'Isle: les Singalais dans l'intérieur sur les Côtes du Sud et de l''ouest, depuis la riviere de Walawe jusgu'a celle de Chilauw, & les Malabares dans les parties du Nord et de l'Est. Ces deux Peuples ont une Religion une langue, & et des Mœurs différentes: Le premier qui *se croit anterieurement arrivé à Ceylon, se prétend originaire de Siam,* en proffesse l'antique Religion Samonéene, & *quoi qu'il occupe un Territoire peu-têtre moins étendu & montagneux il est plus nombreux que les Malabares*: Ceux-ci incontestablement venus de la Presqu'isle de l'Inde suivent le Culte de Brama." [my emphasis, dhr] (Burnand, J., De l'Administration de la Justice dans l'Isle de Ceÿlon, sous le Gouvernement de la Compagnie Hollandoise desJ:Or., from 12.5.1798 (note in the margin: écrit à été pour l'usage de Milors Hobart 1798.)

The British employed a considerable number of Tamils in public service and administration. The Tamils were grateful for the opportunity because Jaffna was an arid zone, which fed its population with difficulty. Whereas the Sinhalese got involved in commerce and trade, Tamils went into government service, education, and the professions. This led later to accusations that Tamils were monopolising these fields. This was a vast exaggeration, however: the Tamils were overrepresented at times in a few departments, but never constituted a majority anywhere. The argument, however, lived on and had a pernicious effect on relations between the two communities after independence.

Until the 1920s, the Tamils considered themselves as one of the *major communities* of the island, not as a minority. This changed with several administrative and constitutional reforms the British introduced, beginning with the Crewe-McCallum reforms 1909/1910, the Manning reforms 1920/1921 until the Donoughmore constitution of 1931 and the Soulbury constitution of 1944 which was the blueprint for the constitution of independent Ceylon. In the Donoughmore constitution, the Tamils were for the first time mentioned as a numerical minority. Even nowadays, the Tamil militants still fight the label *minority* and prefer to be called a nationality or a nation.

Independence and After

The problem of the treatment of the minorities overshadowed the negotiations for a constitution and for independence. It was complicated by the fact that since the nineteenth century, another Tamil minority had been added to the population mix: the Indian Tamils, this time from Tamilnadu proper who were recruited as indentured labor on the coffee and tea plantations by the British. They constituted between 7 and 9 percent of the population, Ceylon Tamils between 10 and 12 percent and Tamil-speaking Muslims about 7 percent. Sinhalese *and* Ceylonese Tamils resented for a number of reasons giving this minority the vote and citizenship in the new country. Shortly after independence on February 4, 1948, therefore, the Indian Tamils were disenfranchised by the ruling United National Party (UNP) under D.S. Senanayake with the consent of the All Ceylon Tamil Congress (ACTC) under G.G. Ponnambalam. A part of the ACTC resented the treatment of the Indian Tamils and split off from it in 1949 under S.J.V. Chelvanayagam to found a new Tamil party: the Federal Party (FP). Over the years, several agreements were concluded with India to deal with the problem of the now stateless Indian Tamils, dividing them by numbers and sending a portion of them back to India (a country many of them had never seen) while granting Ceylonese citizenship to a smaller proportion. Only in very recent years have the Indian Tamils (or Hill Tamils as they are now called) and the Sri Lankan Tamils begun to cooperate to secure the rights of all Tamils.

Already in 1952, Chelvanayagam demanded more autonomy for the Tamil regions, both linguistically and territorially, especially with regard to the newly opened agricultural areas in the Northeast and the Vanni region. This demand intensified after the introduction of the Sinhala Only law in 1956 that made Sinhala the only official language of the country. The SLFP (Sri Lanka Freedom Party) government under S.W.R.D. Bandaranaike introduced this law ostensibly to abolish the prominent place of English in the country, but in reality the law hit the Tamils hardest, because their position in civil service and the professions was now

TAMILS

endangered, unless they renounced their language. Bandaranaike's widow (he himself was assassinated in 1959) Sirima made Sinhala the court language and nationalized the schools in 1960/1961, and in 1971 introduced "standardization" which gave preferential access to tertiary education to the Sinhalese. Coupled with a new constitution in 1972 that renamed the country Sri Lanka, gave Buddhism the foremost place among the religions of the country, and disregarded nearly all demands of the Tamils, this alienated them completely from the state. In the elections of 1977 a coalition of all Tamil parties demanded for the first time no longer autonomy, as hitherto, but a separate state: Tamil Eelam (*Eelam* is an ancient Tamil term for the whole island, besides Ilankai and Lanka). This coalition had first been formed in 1974 under the name TUF (Tamil United Front) and changed to TULF (Tamil United Liberation Front) in 1976. The coalition won the majority of the Tamil vote in 1977. It became the leader of the opposition since the SLFP under Sirima Bandaranaike lost heavily against the UNP under J.R. Jayawardene, who went on to change the constitution and the political system again to introduce an executive presidency. During the civil war, the coalition was more or less marginalized, especially since it was barred from parliament after the riots of 1983. It came, however, into its own again during the election campaign in late 2001 when, under the name Tamil National Alliance (TNA), all Tamil parties cooperated to declare the Liberation Tigers of Tamil Eelam (LTTE) the sole representative of the Tamils. Having been banned as a terrorist organization in Sri Lanka in 1998, the LTTE could not and would not take part in the elections, but the ban was lifted after the cease-fire. The LTTE has now revived its political wing; whether it will field candidates in eventual new elections, remains to be seen.

Civil War

Unlike the Indian Tamils, the Sri Lankan Tamils could neither be disenfranchised nor sent to an assumed home: they were Ceylonese. Resentment against them built up because of their assumed educational and economic privileges. Riots against the Tamils in 1958 (in the wake of a futile attempt by Bandaranaike and Chelvanayagam to come to a solution: the Banda-Chelva Pact), 1961, and 1977 hardened positions on both sides. Shortly after 1972, the first militant resistance had formed, emerging out of

the students' wing of the TULF. The LTTE (who still refers to Chelvanayagam as the founding father) was formed in 1976, the leadership fell to its charismatic member V. Prabhakaran (1954) in 1978. Full militancy developed only after the promulgation of the Prevention of Terrorism Act in 1979 that enabled arbitrary arrests, house searches, and torture by police and army of young Tamil males.

The full-blown civil war dates from 1983 when in July of that year severe anti-Tamil riots started in Colombo, some say instigated by government agencies. The riots shocked the world, and from then on, the LTTE went from strength to strength. The government could not subdue the young people fighting for their own country and rights despite employing extreme measures. Security searches, torture, economic embargoes, and army occupation affected the general population, not the Tigers. Many Tamils fled the increasing repression, and the Tamil diaspora that developed overseas, kept support for the Tigers alive.

In 1987, the Indians brokered an accord between Sri Lanka and India that could have put an end to the conflict and gave the Tamils autonomous rights within a united Sri Lanka. Peace lasted, however, only a few months. After that, the Indian Peace-Keeping Force was embroiled in a severe war of attrition with the Tigers, and in 1990, the IPKF left, leaving the Tamil areas to the LTTE. Soon after, what has become known as Eelam War II broke out, and it lasted with no decisive successes on either side until 1994 when Chandrika Kumaratunga and her People's Alliance (PA) won the parliamentary and presidential elections on the promise to put an end to the war. Even this cease-fire was short-lived; the Tigers broke off negotiations in April, and in late 1995 a determined military campaign delivered Jaffna, until then under the control of the Tigers, into the hands of the Sinhala army. Nearly the whole population fled into the Vanni. The success was short-lived. The Tigers regrouped to strike back from the Vanni where they had retreated. While for two years the army command assured the world that the Tamil areas were 98 percent secured, the Tamils struck with devastating effect in May 2000 when they took heavily fortified Elephant Pass, the only land access to the Jaffna peninsula. Their march stopped shortly before Jaffna when Sri Lanka flew in heavy equipment from abroad.

Until 1991, the Tigers could hope for refuge and help from South India, this assistance ceased, however, when an alleged LTTE suicide bomber blew up

Rajiv Gandhi in Sriperumbudur near Madras. By then, the Tigers had become known for spectacular attacks on military and economic targets, often by suicide bombers. In 1992, they were banned as a terrorist organization by India and, in the late 1990s, by the United States and the United Kingdom as well. After they struck the military airport at Katunayake in August 2001 to devastating effect, the Sri Lankan business community demanded negotiations. The government requested Norway to facilitate talks. This was, however, only a half-hearted effort. A vote of no confidence forced new parliamentary elections less than a year after the victory of the PA in late 2000, and in December 2001, the UNP won under Ranil Wickremesinghe who became Prime Minister. Since then, an uneasy cohabitation has prevailed between the PA executive President and the cabinet. On February 22, 2002, Wickremesinghe managed to negotiate a cease-fire with the LTTE who had unilaterally kept a truce since Christmas 2001. It was supervised by a Scandinavian-led *Sri Lanka Monitoring Mission* (SLMM). Several rounds of peace talks began. Most important in the cease-fire agreement was the clause that both sides would retain the areas under their control. This has given the LTTE a sort of statelet in the Vanni where they hold sway, though Jaffna is still under army occupation.

The cease-fire has held to date, though in April of 2003, the LTTE withdrew from the peace talks because it claimed they were not conducted sincerely nor with a view to help the war-afflicted economy of the Northeast. In November 2003 President Chandrika took three important ministries under her own control, sidelining the Prime Minister. Shortly before, the Tigers had outlined their ideas of a federal set-up in Sri Lanka in their Interim Self-Governing Authority (ISGA) proposal. Chandrika had been unhappy with the cease-fire, which she considered too lenient towards the LTTE and felt marginalized by events. Her liberating stroke, however, went awry: internationally, it was generally denounced, and talks between both big parties on how to deal with the political crisis and the problem of the Tamils have not led to any conclusions. In his customary Heroes' Day Speech on November 27, 2003 Prabhakaran denounced the inability of the Sinhala parties to cooperate. This, he said, was extremely bad for the Tamils who did not know whether an agreement concluded with one party would be honoured by the next. If this state of affairs did not change, he said, the renunciation of the demand for independence for Tamil Eelam would have to be reconsidered.

Economy and Society

The Tamil areas of Sri Lanka remained agricultural until the twentieth century. Property units were comparatively small and landowners had to work the land side-by-side with agricultural labor. Well into colonial times, trade relations with India were important, until government policies put an end to them in the 1970s. Smuggling, however, remained rampant. A growing population necessitated a shift in economic orientation, and Tamils took up education, government service, and the professions. After independence, few industries were located in the Tamil areas, though they are supposed to be rich in some resources: ilmenite, for example. Drilling for oil in the Gulf of Mannar has begun. Since the war, many Tamils have relocated to the West and Australia where, again, they engage mainly in the professions and government service. The militants, however, have started successful economic enterprises, which are also alleged to finance their military endeavours. In the course of the war, Jaffna and, to some extent, the Vanni have become "remittance economies" relying on funds from overseas. This has distorted the economy considerably and it has only slowly begun to revive. However, while Jaffna recuperates after a fashion, the LTTE-controlled Vanni remains on a subsistence level because neither development funds nor foreign aid reach the area.

Hinduism in Tamil Sri Lanka is of the Saivite variety, that is, Siva is considered the highest God, but the veneration of a mother goddess, Amman, is also popular. Hindu society is traditionally tolerant, and especially in Sri Lanka, syncretistic forms of religion are well established. More important than religion is the caste allegiance of the people and the adherence to a "Tamil way of life," however defined. Religious conflict in the area has been rare, whereas caste conflicts did occur until the 1960s.

The Tigers take pains to emphasise that theirs is not a religious conflict: the movement boasts members of all religions except Buddhism. They do not object to Buddhism as such, but to the exclusionary claims of Sinhala Buddhism. Their demands are rather centred on language, territory, and citizens' rights. Today, this perspective also includes the Hill Tamils, yet there remains the problem of the Muslims. In the beginning, Chelvanayagam claimed to speak for all Tamil-speaking peoples, which included Muslims, and originally, a good number of Muslims participated in the Tamil movement. In their blueprint for an independent state, the Tigers had even made special provisions for Muslims. In the course of the war, however, relations deteriorated, particularly in the East, because the Muslims increasingly cooperated with the Sinhalese army. Fifty thousand Muslims were expelled from Jaffna in 1990 for security reasons. Though the Muslims are Tamil-speaking, they do not consider themselves Tamils. They do not identify with the Sinhala-speaking Muslims of the Southwest either. They are in between, demanding privileges and possibly an autonomous region of their own. This complicates the peace talks considerably.

Tamil society has generally been conservative and more caste conscious than the more liberal Sinhala society. The highest, and most numerous, caste are the land-owning Vellalar, corresponding to the Goigama on the Sinhala side. Among the militants, however, the Karaiyar, a fishing and soldier caste, were more important, because Prabhakaran is a Karaiyar. They carried on trade with India and became smugglers on its interdiction. They also made up the armies and generals of the Jaffna kings. The Karaiyar are largely Catholic.

The militants have undertaken to effect a reform of society alongside the fight for independence. They want to abolish caste, and to some extent, the caste system has been eroded through war and migration, though it remains to be seen how durable this will turn out to be. By recruiting women in considerable numbers and forbidding the taking and giving of dowry, they have also enhanced women's self-confidence and independence. Women have been prominent among the so-called suicide Tigers. The Karaiyar have man-

aged to present themselves as the guardians of Tamil culture and society while simultaneously changing this society and making inroads into Vellalar dominance. They achieved this by referring back to the glorious, heroic age of classical literature and tradition.

DAGMAR HELLMANN-RAJANAYAGAM

See also **India; Sri Lanka; Tamil Tigers**

Further Reading

Hellmann-Rajanayagam, Dagmar, *The Tigers—Armed Struggle for Identity*, Heidelberg, 1993
———, editor, *Peace Initiatives Towards Reconciliation and Nation Building in Sri Lanka. An International Perspective*, proceedings of the Workshop July 13-15, 2001, Bangi, Malaysia, Kuala Lumpur, 2002
Manogaran, Ch., and B. Pfaffenberger, editors, *The Sri Lankan Tamil Ethnicity and Identity*, Hawaii, 1994
Narayan Swamy, M.R., *Tigers of Lanka: From Boys to Guerillas*, 3rd edition, Colombo, 2002
———, *Inside an Elusive Mind: Prabhakaran, The First Profile of the World's Most Ruthless Guerilla Leader*, Delhi, 2003
Pathmanathan, S., *The Kingdom of Jaffna, Part I. (circa AD. 1250–1450)*, Colombo, 1978
Pfaffenberger, Bryan, *Caste in Tamil Culture: The Foundations of Sudra Domination in Tamil Sri Lanka*, Bombay, 1982
Pratap, Anita, *Island of Blood: Frontline Reports from Sri Lanka, Afghanistan and other South Asian Flashpoints*, New Delhi, 2001
Seifert, Frank-Florian, *Das Selbstbestimmungsrecht der Sri Lanka-Tamilen zwischen Sezession und Integration*, Stuttgart, 2000
Silva, C.R. de, *Sri Lanka—A History*, New Delhi, 1987
Silva, K.M. de, *A History of Sri Lanka*, London, 1981
Somasundaram, Daya, *Charred Minds: The Psychological Impact of War on Sri Lankan Tamils*, New Delhi, 1998
Spencer, Jonathan, editor, *History and the Roots of Conflict*, London, 1990

Tanzania

Capsule Summary

Country Name: United Republic of Tanzania
Total Population: 35,922,454 (July 2003)
Ethnic Divisions and Languages Spoken: approximately 130 ethnic groups, each with own language. Important native African groups are Chagga, Gogo, Ha, Haya, Hehe, Makonde, Nyamwezi, and Sukuma, though the coastal lingua franca Swahili is the national language. The languages of the Asian minorities are Gujarati and Kachchi. English and Omani Arabic are important second languages.
Religion: Christian (40 %), Muslim (33 %), traditional beliefs and other (27 %)

Tanzania lies in eastern Africa and comprises mainland Tanganyika and the island of Zanzibar. It has a population of approximately 36 million, and is a presidential-parliamentary democracy. There are well over 100 different African peoples in Tanzania, mostly Bantu-speaking. The largest among them are the Chagga, Gogo, Haya, and Sukuma with a population of over 1 million each. Swahili, however, is the national language. There are also several non-Bantu peoples, of which the Iraq^w (400,000 speakers) and Masai (150,000 speakers) are the largest. The ethnonyms of Tanzania correspond to the language names. Non-African minorities include Indians (Gujarati and Kachchi-speaking), and English native speakers. Per capita gross domestic product (GDP) is $600 (2002).

Arab traders began to visit the East African coast in the first millennium CE. The Portuguese reached the region in 1497 and controlled it until the seventeenth century, when the Sultan of Oman took power. In 1885, Tanganyika became German East Africa, and after World War I it was administered by Britain.

It is believed that Zanzibar's contacts to the Middle East region are also very ancient. The Portuguese made it one of their tributaries in 1503; at the end of the seventeenth century the Portuguese were driven from the region by Omani forces. The Omani Sultan of Zanzibar declared himself independent from Oman in 1861, but lost much of his sovereignty in 1890, when Zanzibar became a British protectorate. Tanganyika achieved its independence on December 9, 1961 from Britain, while Zanzibar underwent a revolution on December 10, 1963. On April 26, 1964 the two countries merged into the United Republic of Tanzania, governed as a one-party state by President Julius K. Nyerere, chairman of the Party of the Revolution (*Chama cha Mapinduzi,* CCM).

During Nyerere's rule, Tanzania was one of the few African countries that remained relatively undisturbed from ethnic, racial, and religious conflicts. After his resignation, the stability began to disintegrate slowly. Nyerere had propagated an African socialism that would combine the predominantly rural peasantry with modern socialist statecraft; priority was given to the development of the agricultural sector through so-called *Ujamaa*, a kind of *kolkhoz* system. Since the population was mainly dispersed on small plots of land, peasants were forced to move from their traditional homes to newly constructed settlements to promote efficient agricultural production. This model never achieved the intended economic results, but the potentially divisive array of social groups and the stress on Swahili as a national language at the cost of other indigenous languages achieved a high degree of ethnic cohesion. The *Ujamaa* experience, both in its

development and in its life-setting in the villages has also been a source of positive encounters for Muslims and Christians. After the retirement of Nyerere in 1985, Ali Hassan Mwinyi, a Muslim and former president of Zanzibar, became his successor.

In May of 1992 the monopoly of the CCM was abolished in favor of a multiparty system. Soon after the establishment of new parties, ethnic and religious tensions made the differentiation of ethnic, racial, and religious minorities and majorities an issue. While there is virtually no tension between African ethnic groups and still no state repression based on ethnicity, this is no longer so in regard to non-African minorities. In January of 1993 the leader of the Democratic Party (DP), Mtikila, ruthlessly utilizing deep-seated African resentments against the Asian residents, and stirred up prejudice against the Asian Tanzanians, mostly Indians from Gujarat, by accusing them of economically exploiting the poor, African "indigenous" majority for their own benefit.

The Asian families in Tanzania form a wealthy class of traders; especially in the second half of the nineteenth century, the influx of manpower and capital from India made the Indians the dominant economic power in Tanganyika and Zanzibar, financing large trade caravans into the interior and lending considerable amounts of money to the Sultans of Zanzibar in exchange for privileges. The Indians maintained much of this economic domination untill today, making them a scapegoat for any economic hardship of the poorer African majority. Indians and other Asian minorities maintain strong transnational links to their countries of origin which has led to doubts about their loyalty to Tanzania; moreover they are frequently accused of sectarianism and offensive religious practices.

The CCM tried to prevent any debate relating to this, and to protect the Indians, since they are the financial backbone not only of Tanzania but also of the CCM. Financial aid by Indian businessmen became decisive in the 1995 election of Benjamin Mkapa, the CCM candidate for President. However, violence immediately followed Mtikila's campaign of prejudice, and some Indian Tanzanians were attacked by DP supporters. Later in 1993, after the police had removed peddlers from the streets of Dar es Salaam's Kariakoo quarter, these violently responded by looting Asian shops.

Fissures also appeared in the country's Muslim-Christian relations. As early as 1984, separatist tendencies on Zanzibar Island and Pemba worried the government in Dar es Salaam. In particular, the oppositional Civic United Front (CUF) advocated a secession, and is an organ of Muslim groups who do not believe that their political, social, and religious interests are adequately represented within the Union. The presidential elections on Zanzibar in 1995 and 2000 brought victory to Salmin Amour and his CCM. However, the elections of 2000 are especially regarded by independent observers as tainted by fraud. Subsequently, several anonymous Muslim groups threatened the mainland with terrorist bombings.

Muslim-Christian fissures are also noticeable on the mainland, where the Muslims are a formidable minority. Religiously motivated riots took place in Dar es Salaam, especially during 1998. Apparently as reaction to the arrest of Muslim fundamentalists, several lives were lost in the uproar of Muslim groups. Observers noted a growing dissatisfaction of African Muslims in regard to their continuing discrimination in virtually all sectors of life, and a latent mixture of social problems and religious animosities. The central government continues to arrest Islamic leaders and to combat any tendency to enforce Islamic principles in public life, for example by prohibiting Muslim girls from wearing veils in school.

REINHARD KLEIN-ARENDT

See also **Africa: A Continent of Minorities?; Gujaratis; Muslims in Africa**

Further Reading

Kahigi, Kulikoyela, Yared Kihore, and Maarten Mous, editors, *Lugha za Tanzania. Languages of Tanzania*, Leiden: CNWS Studies, 2000

Kaiser, Paul J., "Structural Adjustment and the Fragile Nation: The Demise of Social Unity in Tanzania," *The Journal of Modern African Studies*, 34, no.2 (1996)

Rasmussen, Lissi, *Christian-Muslim Relations in Africa: The Cases of Northern Nigeria and Tanzania Compared*, New York: Saint Martin's Press, 1993

Trimingham, John Spencer, *Islam in East Africa*, Oxford: Clarendon Press, 1964

Voigt-Graf, Carmen, *Asian Communities in Tanzania: A Journey through Past and Present Times*, Hamburg: Institute of African Affairs, 1998

Tatars

Capsule Summary

Location: Crimean Peninsula (Ukraine) and Uzbekistan
Population in Territories of Former Soviet Union: 400,000
Languages: Crimean Tatar (a Kipchak Turkic language) and Russian
Religion: (Sunni) Muslim

The Crimean Tatars are a Turkic-speaking, Sunni Muslim people who trace their origins to the Crimean peninsula (now southern Ukraine). While the Crimean Tatars have traditionally been described as descendents of the Golden Horde, their formation as an ethnic group is much more complicated. The Crimean Tatars have pre-Mongol origins in the ancient peoples of the Crimean peninsula. The Crimean Tatars therefore consider themselves one of the three indigenous peoples of the peninsula, along with the *Karaim* and *Krymchaki*. In addition to residing in the historic homeland of Crimea (where a population of 270,000 composes 11.9 percent of the total population) and places of former exile such as Uzbekistan, there are large populations of Crimean Tatars in Turkey where they number over five million, Bulgaria (10,000), Romania (40,000), the United States (6,000), and Germany (unknown).

Ethnogenesis

Geography played a formative role in the ethnogenesis of the Crimean Tatars. By offering three very different ecosystems of the steppe, mountain, and coast, the physical geography of the Crimean region clearly shaped not only the means of subsistence of the peoples, but also the interaction between them. The northern two thirds of the Crimean peninsula is an extension of the Eurasian steppe and nomadic groups migrating from the east such as the Scythians, Sarmatians, Huns, Khazars, Pechenegs, Kipchaks, and Mongols were attracted to the excellent pasture it offered their herds. This land is far from limitless, however, and many of these nomadic tribes were forced to seek refuge in the Crimean mountains by the stronger nomadic groups that arrived after them. There was both assimilation and adaptation as the groups pushed southward and westward in successive waves.

On the other side of the Crimean mountains, the coastal region experienced a similar dynamic with a different ethnic composition. Primarily European peoples arrived from the Black Sea via the Bosporus, including Greeks, Genoese, Venetians, Armenians, and Turks. Highlighting this pattern, Kudusov suggests that by the fifth century, the steppe, mountain, and coast were already three distinctive territorial-economic zones. He stresses that the mountains were not just a shelter from invaders of the steppe, but a unique cradle for the formation of the indigenous peoples, including the Crimean Tatars (Kudusov 1995).

History

The Tatar-Mongol invasion of Crimea in the thirteenth century represents a turning point in this dynamic. When the clans within the Horde began pulling apart in the fifteenth century, independent khanates established themselves in the peripheral regions. The Crimean Khanate was one such khanate, and possessed all the characteristics of a fully developed, premodern state. It claimed descent from Chingis Khan, but these *Tatars* as they were called, assimilated with the indigenous and European groups already living in Crimea. As a result of the assimilation, a Crimean version of the Tatar ethnic group developed that was quite distinct from the Kazan, Astrakhan, and other Tatars. The region is far from homogenous, however, and subethnic differences between the Tatars of different regions have persisted. Today, Crimean Tatars divide themselves into three subgroups based on the territorial-economic zones.

It was under the Khanate that all three geographic regions came under one rule for the first time. Haci Giray established an independent khanate in the 1440s. The Crimean Khanate is noted for its legal system based on a combination of Islamic law, traditional Tatar law, and Ottoman law, as well as the unique system of power sharing that meant it was not an autocracy. Although the Crimean Khanate was under Ottoman influence for much of its history, it was an important state from the early sixteenth to the end of the seventeenth centuries.

The Crimean khanate remained an important power in eastern Europe until 1783 when Crimea was annexed to Russia by Empress Catherine II. The Crimean peninsula offered the czarist regime warm water ports that could enhance the economic, political, and cultural ties of Russia with Europe; fertile soils capable of growing products for export as well as feeding Russians in the interior; and a secured southern border that would magnify Russia's military potential vis a vis Turkey. Command of the region would also bring Russia one step closer to realizing the dream of becoming the "Third Rome" after Constantinopol. All of this depended on controlling, removing, or eliminating the Crimean Tatar people, who as Muslim Turks were believed to be potentially disloyal subjects. The czars considered a proposal for their removal but it was not carried out.

The colonial period witnessed one of the most dramatic out-migrations in European history. The Crimean Tatar population left in a series of waves, culminating in a mass migration after the Crimean War of 1853-1856. According to some sources, this wave may have reached 200,000 of the 300,000 Tatars then living in Crimea. The Russian appropriation of the Tatars' land and the oppressive conditions of the new regime are two of the factors that made the Tatars willing to leave. The presence of linguistic, religious, and cultural kin across the Bosporus in Turkey provided added incentive.

As destructive as it was for Tatar society as a whole, the Russian colonial period created conditions in which a new Crimean Tatar intelligentsia arose that was capable of formulating a nationalist project. Ismail Bey Gaspirali or Gasprinski (1851-1914), who founded and edited the newspaper *Terjuman*, was among the influential thinkers along these lines. The early twentieth century was a tumultuous time in which the nationalist ideas began to spread. In December 1917, the nationalist party *Milli Firk*a gained ascendancy in a self-proclaimed independent Tatar state under the leadership of Çelebi Cihan. However, it was quickly extinguished by the Bolsheviks in January, 1918.

Having installed Bela Kun, the Soviet regime called upon Ibrahimov for advice on how to quell rising dissent. His recommendation was to make Crimea into an autonomous republic. This was not what the Communist government in Crimea wanted, but central authorities nevertheless pushed for changes. Lenin recognized that if he was to win the loyalty of minority groups, concessions would be needed and he instituted a Soviet nationalities policy that, on paper at least, allowed for the right of succession of national minorities. The Soviet Committee of Nationalities announced the formation of the Crimean Autonomous Soviet Socialist Republic on October 18, 1921. It was led by Veli Ibrahimov.

The Crimean Autonomous Soviet Socialist Republic represents a fleeting Golden Age before this status was revoked and Crimea, along with the rest of the USSR, was plunged into mass repression of intellectuals and clergy, state-sanctioned famine, and forced collectivization of agriculture. Because the traditional Arabic script of the Crimean Tatars was changed to Latin script from 1926-1927 and then from Latin to Cyrillic in 1936, it became increasingly difficult for Crimean Tatars to learn their language and history or perpetuate cultural traditions.

The Crimean Tatars experienced Russianization followed by Sovietization, leaving them with ravaged cultural institutions and as much as 50 percent of the population eliminated by World War II. So it is not surprising the Crimean Tatars initially viewed the Nazi invasion as a sign of hope. Once the Germans established their administration in Crimea, however, it became apparent that although they had been allowed some religious freedoms during the occupation, the Nazis could be as oppressive in their rule as the Soviets.

Tatar collaboration with the German regime is one of the most controversial topics in Soviet history. The Crimean Tatars were charged with engaging in punitive expeditions against the Soviet partisans; participating in the German self-defense battalions; and providing intelligence services for the German and Romanian occupation. However, it has since been recognized that Crimean Tatar participation in the German battalions was not necessarily voluntary, often being secured at gunpoint. It must also be added that severe hunger and disease in the Soviet ranks led people of all nationalities to desert and join the Germans. According to Pohl, the total number of Tatars assisting the Germans reached 20,000 or ten percent of the population. Regardless of the role they played, the Tatars were slated for German removal because they stood in the way of the plan to establish a German Riviera. In the wake of the Allied victory, it would be left to a victorious Stalin to carry out the act.

While the Soviet regime ostensibly deported the Tatars for their activities during the war, other nationalities collaborated on an equal or greater scale and it has become increasingly clear that it was not the real reason for Stalin's order. Rather, Stalin's domestic policy with regard to the Tatars was derived from his foreign policy and macroeconomic concerns. Stalin wanted complete control of Crimea because it formed an important part of the Soviet military strategy. Specifically, the Soviet Union planned to gain access to the Dardanelles and acquire territory in Turkey. The Crimean Tatars, who had ethnic kin in Turkey, were once again viewed as potentially disloyal. The Soviet authorities also wanted to continue to develop Crimea as a health resort area for the Soviet Union, particularly for the benefit of party officials.

The Crimean Tatar contribution to the Soviet war effort has been minimized by Soviet historians, although Tatars joined both the Soviet partisans fighting in the Crimean forests and the Red Army sent to the front. Whereas official sources suggest 20,000 Crimean Tatars fought in the Red Army, unofficial Tatar sources suggest the figure is over 50,000. As a result of their exceptional patriotism, eight Crimean Tatars received the order of Hero of the Soviet Union. The extent of the Tatars' anti-Soviet behavior is a topic of ongoing dispute.

Deportation

In the early morning hours of May 18, 1944 armed secret police officers (members of the People's Comissariat for Internal Affairs, NKVD) knocked on the doors of the Crimean Tatars and told them to get ready. They were taken by car and truck to central collection points where they were loaded onto trains used for livestock. Since most of the able-bodied men were still at the front, the majority of deportees consisted of women, children, and the elderly. In all, 191,044 were loaded onto the cattle cars bound for the Ural Mountains and Soviet Central Asia, primarily Uzbekistan. They traveled for several weeks in extreme conditions. Not only were they deprived of food and sanitation, the Crimean Tatars were not allowed to give the dead a Muslim burial. Rather, the dead were unceremoniously thrown out of the trains. When they arrived, the Tatars were interned under forced-labor conditions in what is referred to as the "special settlement" system. In the first three years, according to conservative NKVD estimates, approximately 22 percent of the population perished from infectious diseases, malnutrition, and dehydration. According to Crimean Tatar accounts, however, the losses are much higher, consisting of 46 percent or approximately half the population.

Following their departure from Crimea, place names were changed, graves were desecrated, and books in the Tatar language and architecture destroyed to eradicate indications of their presence. The first public announcement of the event did not come until two years later when *Izvestiia* published a decree explaining the abolition of the Crimean Autonomous Soviet Socialist Republic and its reconstitution as an entity of lower political status. It labeled the Crimean Tatars as "traitors" to the Soviet Union. This became part of the ascribed identity of the group and a representation against which ethnic self-consciousness and identity formed.

In 1956, the special settlement system was dismantled and many of the Crimean Tatars in the Urals relocated to Central Asia to be closer to Crimean Tatar kin and other Muslims. In the same year, Khrushchev delivered his famous XX Party Congress address denouncing Stalin. All the deported groups were rehabilitated at this time except for the Crimean Tatars, Meskhetian Turks, and Volga Germans.

A decree absolving the Tatars of mass treason was not issued until 1967. This sparked many Tatar families to try to return to Crimea, but authorities in Moscow had stipulated that while they were free to move about, they should not be allowed to obtain a *propiska* (residence permit) or become employed in Crimea. Most of the families who tried to settle in Crimea at this time were re-deported. The decree also failed to acknowledge the Tatars as a bona fide nationality, referring to them only as "Tatars formerly residing in Crimea." They were not successful in returning on a mass scale until the late 1980s and early 1990s.

Crimean Tatar National Movement

The exiled people's efforts were initially devoted to physical survival, but in the mid-1950s, veterans and elders began to write letters to the authorities asking to be returned. They believed that the issue of return could be resolved only if the central leadership were convinced of their loyalty to the Soviet State. By the 1960s, however, a growing number of activists were discouraged by the lack of results of the letter writing campaign. This ushered in a phase in which movement organizers began to channel the goals and strategies of the movement along more radical democratic lines. They were especially inspired by the Crimean history they discovered. Their research not only suggested they had been wrongfully deported, but reminded them of their history as a politically powerful and culturally developed state.

Beginning in the summer of 1965, there was an almost uninterrupted presence of Crimean Tatar delegates in Moscow. Among other activities, they produced leaflets now known as *samizdat* literature. The information bulletins were part of the movement organization that Crimean Tatars developed. One of its most important characteristics was that it was decentralized, composed of initiative groups with activists willing to go to Moscow, and supporters who participated more quietly from home by donating money to support the delegation, signing and circulating petitions, and supporting the families of imprisoned activists. While the leadership role in formulating the movement's position was taken primarily by activists, they drew on sentiment pools that were already in existence: the Crimean Tatars actively remembered the homeland and dreamed of return.

As a result of the Tatars' agitation to return, major repressive blows were dealt by the Soviet authorities. Crimean Tatars suspected of disloyalty to the Soviet Union were arrested, tried, and imprisoned. Even as the Soviet regime attempted to portray the activists as petty thieves, and sometimes imprisoned them with regular, as opposed to political, criminals, the Crimean Tatars built their movement along peaceful, democratic lines as a movement for human and national rights.

A pivotal moment in the National Movement came in 1978 when a Crimean Tatar man named Musa Mamut protested their condition. He had been denied registration at his home and imprisoned for "violation of the passport regime." Upon returning from prison, he was again threatened with imprisonment. Mamut decided he preferred death to losing the freedom to live in his homeland. So when the authorities came to take him for questioning, he immolated himself in front of his home. After his death, Mamut became a martyr and a model.

As agitation for repatriation gained credence in the places of exile, the authorities waged a corresponding battle to dissuade the Tatars. This included a plan to resettle them not in Crimea but in a specially created autonomous region in Central Asia called Mubarek. They were promised housing, jobs, and cultural institutions of their own. The Committee for State Security (*Komitet Gosudarstvennoy Bezopasnosti,* KGB) succeeded in recruiting some prominent Tatars, but it failed to gain broad-based support. The complete lack of historical ties to that area, plus a complete void in the collective memory of the people meant that for the Crimean Tatars, Mubarek held little appeal.

In April 1987, the first All-Union conference of representatives of the National Movement's initiative groups was held in Tashkent, and the delegates decided to appeal to Gorbachev. When they failed to get the desired response, another conference was held at which it was decided to send a delegation to Moscow to press their demands. In July 1987, over 2,000 Crimean Tatars, from all parts of the Soviet Union held a series of highly visible demonstrations in Moscow. Their protest registered in the international news and sparked numerous letters on their behalf from other dissidents. In addition to sweeping the Tatars out of Red Square, the authorities published a Soviet News Agency (TASS) announcement stating they had created an official government commission to resolve the Crimean Tatar issue. The TASS announcement also brought up the Tatars' behavior during World War II, and stated they had incinerated fellow citizens in ovens. These allegations provoked outrage among the Crimean Tatars who renewed their commitment to the National Movement. In an increasingly widespread movement, Tatars gave up hope that the Soviet government would facilitate their repatriation.

Changes brought about by *glasnost* and *perestroika* also emboldened the Crimean Tatars to formalize their already existing political organization. In the early stages of the movement, there were three factions: the Central Initiative Group with Mustafa Dzhemilev at its head, the Fergana Group lead by Yuri Osmanov, and the Samarkand Group lead by Rolan Kadiev. The three branches coalesced into two social movement organizations beginning with the National Movement of Crimean Tatars (NDKT), created in 1987. The NDKT's conservative approach of advocating on behalf of the Crimean Tatars' return while operating according to the Party protocols was not endorsed by all. Therefore, in 1989, more radical Crimean Tatars organized the Organization of the Crimean Tatar National Movement (OKND) to pursue a more aggressive platform. They held that to be successful, they would have to internationalize their efforts. The leader of the NDKT, Yuri Osmanov, was assassinated in 1993 and while the organization continues to issue sharp criticism of the OKND, it is far less powerful than the later organization. Also in 1989, a commission under the leadership of Yanaev recommended the full political rehabilitation of the Crimean Tatars and the cancellation of any acts that were of a repressive or discriminatory nature.

In the 1990s the Crimean Tatars became increasingly politically organized. In June, 1991 the Second Kurultai or Congress was convened in Simferopol (named after the first Congress that took place among early nationalists in 1917). The Kurultai elected 33 people by secret ballot to serve in the *Mejlis*, the authoritative political body or plenipotentiary committee of the Crimean Tatar people. The *Mejlis* declared the sovereignty of the Crimean Tatar people, adopted a national anthem and a national flag. The Kurultai also elected a chairman or president, Mustafa Dzhemilev.

Repatriation

The Crimean Tatars began repatriating on a massive scale beginning in the late 1980s and continuing into the early 1990s. The population of Crimean Tatars in Crimea rapidly reached 250,000 and leveled off at 270,000 where it remains as of this writing. There are believed to be between 30,000 and 100,000 remaining in places of former exile in Central Asia.

While the vast majority of the Tatars remaining in Central Asia still hope to return, political and economic conditions prevent them. A flooded real estate market makes it difficult for Tatars to sell their homes in Central Asia and rampant inflation in Ukraine makes it close to impossible to construct or purchase new ones. New border and customs regulations complicate relocation.

Those who repatriated also faced difficult conditions. Even though the central authorities no longer had any objections, local officials initially opposed their return, fearing it could lead to ethnic unrest and stretch already limited resources. Since all Tatar property had been confiscated and redistributed to others in 1944, the Tatars faced the task of starting over for the second time in a 50-year time span. Given that their former homes were occupied by new residents, and given the unwillingness of the local authorities to help them find or build housing, the Tatars squatted on vacant land. Tatars occupied unused state land on the outskirts of cities and towns and built temporary shelters or lived in the cargo containers that had brought their belongings. Officials ordered the destruction of the squatters' settlements with bulldozers, but each time, the Crimean Tatars began to rebuild. There were also instances in which the Tatars threatened to immolate themselves in response to the security forces' attempts to remove them. As a result of the Tatars' determination, negotiations took place and the settlements were eventually legalized. Today, the settlements still lack basic infrastructure such as plumbing and paved roads. While some Tatars live in beautifully completed homes, many have been unable to finish construction.

Despite the successful repatriation of over half the population, the Crimean Tatars' struggle for full repatriation and a full restoration of their rights is not complete. Battles for representation in the Crimean legislature as well as disagreements about suffrage and citizenship have characterized the last decade. The present state of affairs represents a deterioration from the situation beginning in the mid-1990s when the Crimean Tatars held a quota of 14 seats in the Crimean Parliament. In 1998, there was a series of mass demonstrations protesting the Crimean Tatars lack of voting rights (linked to citizenship) in what is now the Autonomous Republic of Crimea (ARC). The citizenship issue has been largely resolved but the issue of representation remains complicated by the Tatars minority status. As of 2001, the Crimean Tatars still compose only 11 to 12 percent of the population. One of the more significant political victories came in 1998 when two prominent Tatar political leaders, Mustafa Dzhemilev and Refat Chubarov, were elected to the Ukrainian Upper Parliament. Complicating the political difficulties has been the increasing criminalization of the Ukrainian economy and the proliferation of criminal groupings.

The Crimean Tatars' primary objectives are government-sponsored return of the Crimean Tatar people to Crimea; full restoration of their rights and property; recognition of the Crimean Tatar *Mejlis* as the official representative body; and representation of the Crimean Tatars in the Crimean Parliament. In addition to a full political rehabilitation and repatriation to the homeland, the Crimean Tatars are engaged in revitalizing their religion, language, and culture. The Crimean Tatars adopted Islam during the tenth through twelfth centuries and it became the state religion under the Crimean Khanate. During the Soviet period, they experienced pressure to become secularized like other peoples. This was especially intense for the Crimean Tatars because of the Soviet regime's fear of Islamic fundamentalism. During the Stalin era, hundreds of mosques were closed, clergy were executed, and marking the Muslim holidays was not permitted. Because the alphabet had been changed, many Tatars lost the ability to read the *suras* or verses in their Qur'an. Crimean Tatars nevertheless resisted the repression of religion, and at the moment of deportation many Tatar families thought to take their copies of the Qur'an if nothing else.

Once in exile, there was little hope for the outward observance of religion. In spite of the prohibition, elders continued to say prayers in exile and the presence of other Muslim peoples reinforced what Muslim identity was left. Following the break up of the Soviet Union, Islam has experienced tremendous resurgence. The Crimean Tatars are part of this, although they are by no means fundamentalist and their spiritual life is more accurately a synthesis of pre-Islamic and Islamic beliefs and practices. The holidays, for example, are oriented around traditional Muslim holidays, the lunar calendar, seasonal changes, and events in the farming lives of Crimean Tatars. Two of the largest holidays observed by Tatars are *Oraza bairam* and *Kurban bairam* (holiday of sacrifice). Tatars also mark the anniversary of the 1944 deportation. Religion is also manifest in rites of passage such as circumcision. An increasing number of couples go to a *mullah* at the time of marriage in addition to completing the Soviet secularized registry. Wakes or *pominki* for remembrance of the dead, and fasting during the month of Ramadan are also important spiritual observances.

Aside from renewing their religious traditions, the Crimean Tatars have been struggling to restore other cultural traditions. A primary focus of concern and activity is language. Music and dance have also received attention. After over 50 years of exile, programs to renew the arts including embroidery with gold and silver thread, fine jewelry making in the filigreed Tatar style, and the weaving of kilims or carpets, have begun.

As a result of their tumultuous history, the Crimean Tatars are now spread out not only through the former Soviet Union, but Turkey (where there are believed to be 5 million) Bulgaria, Rumania, and the United States.

GRETA UEHLING

See also **Ukraine; Uzbekistan**

Further Reading

Aleksandrov, Grigorii Matveevich, *Fakel nad Krymom* [Torch Over Crimea], Bahçesaray: Avdet, 1991
Allworth, Edward, editor, *Tatars of the Crimea*, Durham: Duke University Press, 1988; revised edition, 1998
Cemiloglu, (Dzhemilev), Mustafa, "A History of the Crimean Tatar National Liberation Movement: A Sociopolitical Perspective," in *Crimea: Dynamics, Challenges, and Prospects*, edited by Maria Drohobycky, Lanham Maryland: Rowman and Littlefield, 1995
Chervonnaia, Svetlana Mikailovna, and Mikhail Guboglo, *Krymskotatarskoe Natsional'noe Dvizhenie (1991–1993) Tom 1* [The Crimean Tatar National Movement (1991–1993) Volume 1], Moskva: Rossiskaia Akademiia Nauk, Tsentr Po Izucheniiu Mezhnatsional'nykh Otnoshenii [Moscow: Russian Academy of Sciences Center for the Study of International Relations], 1992

Conquest, Robert, *The Nation Killers: The Soviet Deportation of Nationalities*, New York: Khronika, 1970

Dzhemilev, Reshat, editor, *Zhivoi Fakel* [Human Torch], New York: Crimea Foundation, 1986

Fisher, Alan, *The Crimean Tatars*, Stanford: Hoover Institution Press, 1978

International Organization for Migration (IOM), *Profile and Migration Intentions of Crimean Tatars Living in Uzbekistan*, Geneva: Technical Cooperation Centre for Europe and Central Asia, 1997

Karpat, Kemal H., "The Crimean Emigration of 1856-1862 and the Settlement and Urban Development of Dobruca," in *Turco-Tatar Past, Soviet Present*, edited by Ch. Lemercier-Quelquejay, G. Veinstein, and S.E. Wimbush, Paris: Editions De L'Ecole Des Hautes Etudes en Sciences Sociales, 1986

Kudusov, Eric, "Etnogenez korenogo naseleniia Kryma [Ethnogenesis of the Indigenous Populations of the Crimea]," *Kasavet*, 24, no. 1 (1995)

Nekrich, Alexander, *Nakazannye Narody* [The Punished Peoples], New York: Khronika, 1978

Pohl, J. Otto, *Ethnic Cleansing in the USSR, 1937-1949*, Westport, Connecticut: Greenwood Press, 1999

Poliakov, Vladimir, *Krym: sud'by narodov i liudei* [Crimea: Fate of Nationalities and Peoples], Simferopol: International Renaissance Foundation, 1998

Sevdiar, Memet, *Etudy ob etnogeneze Krymskikh Tatar* [Studies on the Ethnogenesis of Crimean Tatars], New York: Crimea Foundation, 1997

Uehling, Greta, "The Crimean Tatar National Movement: Social Memory and Collective Action," in *Globalizations and Social Movements*, edited by John Guidry, Michael Kennedy, and Mayer N. Zald, Ann Arbor: University of Michigan Press, 2000

Zemskov, N., "Spetsposelentsy iz Kryma: 1944–1956 [Special Settlers from Crimea 1944-1956]," *Krymskie Muzei*, 1, no. 94, Simferopol: Tavria (1995)

Thailand

Capsule Summary

Location: Southeast Asia peninsula, bordered by Burma to the West and Northwest, by Laos to the North, by Cambodia to the Southeast, and by the Gulf of Thailand and Malaysia to the South

Total Population: 64,265,276 (July 2003)

Per Capita GDP: $7,000 (2002)

Minority Populations: Thai (32%); Thai-Lao (30%); Northern Thai (17%); Chinese (11%); Malay (4%), Khmer (1%); Hilltribes (2%)

Languages: Thai, Lao, Malay, Chinese (chiefly Taechiw), Mon, Khmer, Karen, Hmong, Kuy, and other Tai languages, such as Tai Yai, Tai Nuea, Phuthai, and Saek

Religions: Theravada Buddhism (94%), Islam (4%), Christianity (less than 1%), Confucianism, Hinduism, Sikhism, Animism

Thailand is a medium-sized country in mainland Southeast Asia, with a population of around 63 million. The present borders of Thailand are the result of various rather arbitrary treaties; Siam (as Thailand was formerly known) was composed of a patchwork quilt of small kingdoms, sewn together to create a buffer zone between British and French imperial designs. In the late nineteenth century, the absolute monarchy created a modern nation-state characterized by strong central authority. Since 1932, Thailand has been a constitutional monarchy, alternating between military and parliamentary rule. The parliamentary system has been consolidated since the end of the last military regime in 1992. However, centralization of power remains a key feature of the Thai political order, and minorities have generally been subordinated to rule by Bangkok.

Thai (Bangkok Thai, Central Thai, Standard Thai, Siamese) is the national language used as the medium of mass media and instruction throughout the country. It belongs to the southwestern branch of the Tai family, a subgroup of Tai-Kadai. Regional dialects include Northern Thai (Kam Muang or Lanna), Northeastern Thai (Isan or Lao), and Southern Thai (Paktai). Other languages spoken in Thailand are Chinese (mainly Taechiw, Hainan, and Guangdong dialects), Mon, Khmer, Vietnamese, and a number of "hilltribe" languages. The latter consist of three different linguistic groups: Tibeto-Burman (including Karen and Loloish languages such as Akha, Lahu, Lisu, Mpi, Bisu, and Ugong), Hmong-Mien (Hmong and Yao), and Mon-Khmer (for example, Htin, Kuy (Suay), and Khmu). Other Tai languages spoken in scattered communities mainly in the north and along the Thai-Lao border include Tai Yai (Shan), Tai Lue, Phuthai, Puan, and Saek. Except for Bangkok Thais, most people in Thailand are bilingual and speak Bangkok Thai as a second or third language.

Regional Minorities

Contrary to popular conceptions, ethnic Thais do not constitute a majority of the population. Northeasterners (Khon Isan), who are culturally and ethnically Lao, form the largest minority group. Historically speaking, the area known as Isan was part of the Lao Kingdom in the fifteenth century. Isan remains the most economically deprived part of Thailand. Many Isan people are poor farmers; large numbers find seasonal or long-term unskilled employment in and around Bangkok, mainly in the industrial, construction, or service sectors. Northern Thailand, with its center in Chiang Mai, is populated mainly by Northern Thais (Khon Muang) and other ethnic groups generally known as "hilltribe" people (Chao khao). Northern Thais are ethnically distinct from central Thais and constitute an important minority group, but this distinction has been successfully downplayed by the Thai state. There have been extensive interactions and, recently, conflicts over land use between northern lowlanders and highlanders. The very term *hilltribe* is controversial, evoking an official view of these peoples as primitive and peripheral.

The 14 provinces of the south are home to Malay Muslims (Khon Paktai) who speak the Southern Thai dialect and the Jawi dialect of Malay. There are also some Malay Muslims in Bangkok and the North. Strong ethnic identities exist among these regional minorities; Malays in particular often feel they are economically and culturally marginalized by dominant Buddhist Thais. Resettlement programs and spontaneous migration have seen large numbers of Buddhist Thais move to the South, competing for employment and resources with Malay Muslims.

Other minority groups in the north are Tai-speaking communities such as Tai Yai and Tai Lue, who still maintain their traditional ways of life and keep close ties with their kin in upper Burma and Yunnan. Like other peripheral minority groups, they live on the fringe of Thai society and feel socially and economically inferior to ethnic Thais. Some Tai-speakers such as Tai Dam (Black Tai) and Saek are relatively recent migrants from China and the Indochinese Peninsula.

Migrant Minorities

The Chinese (overseas Chinese) form the second largest minority group in Thailand. Economically motivated, they migrated to Thailand in the beginning of the twentieth century and have established themselves and assumed a leading position in some areas of the Thai economy. They are concentrated in the greater Bangkok metropolitan area, and in urban centers throughout the country. While in the first half of the twentieth century the Chinese were regarded as politically suspect and barred from government employment, today's Thailand-born Chinese are Thai citizens, speak Thai as their mother tongue and are not subject to the same kind of racial discrimination as their forefathers. The younger generations of Chinese often have virtually no knowledge of the Chinese language. Compared with other minority groups, the Chinese have been the most successful economically and politically: many have joined the civil service and have obtained important administrative and political positions. Most recent Thai prime ministers have been Chinese, for example. The Chinese have also intermarried extensively with Thais, so that in urban areas of Thailand the distinctions between Chinese and Thai have become extremely blurred.

Another group of Chinese migrants in Thailand is known as the Haw (Yunnanese Chinese). They are Muslim refugees who fled the Chinese Revolution and settled mainly in the North, particularly in Chiang Mai, Chiang Rai, Lampang, and Lamphun.

South Asian migrants from India and what is now Bangladesh entered Thailand in the late nineteenth century. Most of them settled initially in Bangkok, typically engaging in the textile and tailoring business, but later diversifying into a broader range of business and professional occupations. In the South they are concentrated mainly in Songkhla and in the North in Chiang Mai and Chiang Rai. As Hindus, Sikhs, or Muslims, South Asian migrants have accommodated to Buddhism-based Thai culture but still retain their religious traditions. Two smaller groups of Muslim immigrants in Bangkok and the central plains are Indonesian businessmen and Cham refugees. The latter are descendants of the ancient kingdom of Champa who entered Thailand from Cambodia as a result of wars in the nineteenth century.

Mon (Raman) immigrants who fled Burma during the sixteenth to eighteenth century came to settle in the North and the central plains. The Khmer in Thailand can be divided into two groups: long-term residents since the Ayutthaya period in the fifteenth century, and refugees from the civil strife in Cambodia from 1975 to 1979. Like ethnic Thais, both Mons and Khmers are Theravada Buddhists and were traditionally wet-rice cultivators, but the former have become specialized in pottery and brick making. Another group of political immigrants is the Vietnamese who entered Thailand from the late eighteenth century until after the consolidation of North Vietnamese rule in 1975. They are concentrated mainly in Bangkok and the Northeast.

Highland Minorities

A survey in 1995 by the Tribal Research Institute lists a total of approximately 700,000 "hilltribe" people (*chao khao*) in scattered communities in Thailand's 20 northern and northwestern provinces. They belong to six officially-recognized tribes, namely Karen (Yang), Hmong (Miao), Lahu, Akha (Ikaw), Mian (Yao), and Htin (Maal, Pray). Among these, Karens and Hmongs form the largest groups. Other peripheral highland minorities include Lisu, Lua (Lawa), Khmu, Mlabri (Phi Tong Luang), and Paluang, recent arrivals from Burma. The term *Lua* used by the Thai refers to several different linguistic and ethnic subgroups such as the Ugong (Lua of Kanchanaburi, Suphanburi, and Uthai Thani) and the Bisu (Lua of Chiang Rai). Living at the periphery of the Thai nation-state, highland minorities have been regarded as agents of forest destruction, land encroachers, and narcotics traffickers. The Hmong uprising in 1967 marked the beginning of an official discourse about the Hmong and other highland minorities as security threats to the Thai nation. Though most of the highlanders have been living within the area of what is today Thailand for centuries, they are not recognized as full citizens and are often represented as illegal aliens by officials and the media.

Creation of Thainess

There are two contrasting perspectives regarding minorities politics in Thailand. The official view, constantly found in statements from both civil and military government sources, is that Thailand is an ethnically homogeneous country and minorities are well assimilated to the mainstream culture. The revisionist view is that Thailand is a plural, heterogenous society in which one ethnic group, the Thai, has sought to ensure its political, cultural, and social dominance. According to scholars who subscribe to the latter view, ethnicity is defined along hegemonic lines, as evidenced by policies and practices adopted with the aim of eradicating or suppressing diversity.

Thai governments have encouraged all minority groups to assimilate and become loyal citizens. This resulted in uniform linguistic and educational policies urging all non-Thais to speak and become literate in Standard Thai, a codified speech based on the

language used by the elite and upper class in Bangkok. Many development projects which brought administrators and officials from Bangkok to regional areas were also put into practice. To promote nationalism among regional and highland minorities, such terms as *Thai-Muslim, Thai-Isan, Lanna-Thai,* and *Highland-Thai* were created and reinforced. The assimilation policies evinced different responses from different regional minorities. While Northern and Northeastern Thais welcomed these policies to the extent that they were still allowed to maintain their own cultural identities, Southerners or Malays were more reluctant to assimilate and were inclined to view the assimilation policy as a form of internal colonialism by the dominant group.

Problems and Prospects

Although violent ethnic conflicts in Thailand were minimal, minorities—particularly economically less powerful groups—have been subject to popular contempt and official mistrust. Derogatory terms were used by ethnic Thais to refer to other non-Thai groups: *Jek* for the Chinese, *Khaek* for South Asian migrants and Malays, *Yuan* for the Vietnamese, *Maew* for Hmong, and *Lao* for Isan people. As a term of reference, *Lao* has a pejorative meaning, referring to a person who is provincial, ignorant, and often uneducated. Regional areas were perceived by Bangkok officials as primitive and dirty places occupied by those who did not understand Thai. In addition, some minority groups such as Malays and the Vietnamese were, at one time, labelled as threats to the nation because of their alleged associations with separatist movements and the Communist Party of Thailand. Recently, Hmong refugees have also been under the government's close monitor, for fear that they are involved in leftist insurgency in Lao PDR.

The turn of the twenty-first century has seen an improvement on the minorities issue in Thailand, with the implementation of policies that put more emphasis on minority rights and respect of local cultures. Since the end of the communist insurgency, members of minority groups have been able to speak more openly about their origins and cultures. Still, a number of basic but challenging problems face the Thai government today. To cite just two examples: most highland minorities (two thirds of the highland population) are still denied citizenship and face threats to their land tenure and tensions between Malay Muslims and Sino-Thai officials and businesspeople are evident in places such as the Southern province of Pattani. The plain fact is that the majority of Thai citizens are not ethnically Thai, yet the Thai state remains in denial concerning this crucial issue, doubtless fearing that to acknowledge the multiethnic character of Thai society will further exacerbate some longstanding tensions.

KRISADAWAN HONGLADAROM AND DUNCAN MCCARGO

See also **Hmong; Khmer; Lao-Tai**

Further Reading

Bradley, David, "Identity: The Persistence of Minority Groups," in *Highlanders of Thailand*, edited by John McKinnon, Oxford: Oxford University Press, 1983

Foster, Brian L., "Ethnic Identity of the Mons in Thailand," *Journal of the Siam Society*, 61 (1973)

Hewison, Kevin, "Minorities in Thailand," Paper Presented at the Workshop on Locating Power: Democracy, Opposition and Participation in Thailand, Asia Research Centre on Social Political and Economic Change, Murdoch University, October 6-7, 1994

Keyes, Charles, *Isan: Regionalism in Northeastern Thailand*, Data Paper No. 65, Ithaca: Southeast Asia Program, Department of Asian Studies, Cornell University, 1967

Keyes, Charles F., editor, *Ethnic Adaptation and Identity: The Karen on the Thai Frontier with Burma*, Philadelphia: Institue for the Study of Human Issues, 1979

McKinnon, John, editor, *Highlanders of Thailand*, Oxford: Oxford University Press, 1983

Scupin, Raymond, "Thailand as a Plural Society: Ethnic Interaction in a Buddhist Kingdom, *Crossroads*, 2, no. 3, 1986

Skinner, William G., *Chinese Society in Thailand: An Analytical History*, Ithaca: Cornell University Press, 1957

Thongchai, Winichakul, *Siam Mapped: A History of the Geo-Body of a Nation*, Honolulu: University of Hawaii Press, 1994

Turton, Andrew, editor, *Civility and Savagery: Social Identity in Thai States*, Richmond: Curzon, 2000

Wijeyewardene, Gehan, "Thailand and the Tai Versions of Ethnic Identity," in *Ethnic Groups Across National Boundaries in Mainland Southeast Asia*, edited by Gehan Wijeyewardene, Singapore: Social Issues in Southeast Asia, Institute of Southeast Asian Studies, 1990

Tharu

Capsule Summary

Location: Tarai plains of Nepal and adjacent districts in India
Total Population: 1.2 million in Nepal, similar numbers in India (1991 Census)
Language: Tharu
Religion: Predominantly Hindu

The Tharu are an indigenous group of people inhabiting the Tarai region in the southern lowlands of Nepal. With the exception of Tharu populations in the Indian districts of Uttar Pradesh, the largest in Nainital district and other concentrations in Bihar, in West Champaran, the Tharus are represented as one of the largest ethnic minorities in Nepal. There are approximately 1.2 million Tharus distributed amongst 22 districts in the Nepalese Tarai (HMG, 1991). The Tharu are often described as one people. However, many subgroups exist, amongst the largest: Kochila Tharu in the eastern Tarai; Chitwaniya Tharu in the central Tarai; and Dangaura Tharu, Kathariya Tharu, and Rana

Tharu in the western Tarai. The distribution of Tharu populations in the Tarai are found in the following districts from east to west: Jhapa district: 9,600; Morang district: 60,391; Sunsari district: 75,079; Udayapur district: 18,369; Saptari district: 61,640; Siraha district: 20,617; (central) Dhanusha district: 1,697; Mahottari district: 7,522; Sarlahi district: 15,359; Rautahat district: 21,821; Bara district: 49,389; Parsa district: 32,701; Chitwan district: 45,392; (west) Nawalparasi district: 73,494; Rupandehi district: 55,803; Kapilbastu district: 43,709; Dang-deukhuri district: 111,574; Surkhet district: 4,941; Banke district: 45,564; Bardiya district: 153,322; Kailali district: 206,933; and Kanchanpur district: 70,544 (HMG, 1991).

The Tharu are made up of a number of localized groups that are linguistically and culturally different. Tharu groups differ in language, dress, social organization, social customs, material culture, and religious rituals. Although most Tharus are Hindu, Tharus living in the eastern parts of the Tarai are predominantly

Hinduized and have Brahman priests; whereas Tharus in the far western Tarai are much less so, and follow non-Brahmanical ritual practices. Over time the domination of Hindu peoples from India and Nepal have influenced Tharu festivals and rituals. The homelands of the Tharu are now a mixture of many ethnic cultures following the internal migration of hill populations to the south of Nepal. This demographic shift has dramatically influenced Tharu traditions, land ownership patterns, and agricultural practices.

The origins of the Tharu have been a matter of speculation amongst anthropologists and historians for decades. Diverse accounts have classified Tharu origins on the meanings of the word *Tharu* and more so on the environments in which it was thought the people came from and settled to. One point commonly accepted is that they remain the indigenous peoples of the Tarai. Some assume that the Tharu entered the Tarai as one group at a particular time and settled in one location from which they spread across the entire length of the Tarai, each group being effected by different social, economic, and political developments of a particular region, thus shaping their unique identity. However, it remains uncertain as to when this movement of people took place and whether they were one people or many different people moving from many regions at different times, contributing to the cultural diversity found in the Tharu population today.

Historically, the lowlands of the Tarai were mainly settled by malaria-resistant Tharus. The earliest record of settlement dates back to theeleventh century. At the end of the nineteenth century, the feudal Rana Regime encouraged migration from India in an attempt to develop the Tarai. The Tharus, however, dominated, cultivating the malaria-infested forests and yielding valuable revenues for the State. The Tharus' extensive knowledge of forest resources became vulnerable when the government introduced malaria eradication programs during the 1950s and encouraged migration from the hill districts of Nepal. After 1960, with the eradication of malaria, the forested lands of the Tarai became the destination for large-scale migration. Large areas of forests were cleared for new settlers and Tharu populations became outnumbered. Many uneducated Tharus lost land through the fraudulent actions of hill migrants. The worst case being in western Tarai where a new class of bonded labor was formed known as the *Kamaiya* system. New hill migrants also brought with them their farming methods and spread them throughout the region, successfully

transforming the Tharus' sociocultural traditions and economy. Now the Tharu are considered a minority in their own land. The population increase has been seen as a systematic endeavour by the State to ethnically transform the Tarai. The destruction of forests by highways, the continuing spread of agriculture, and the Timber industry establishment in the Tarai region has impacted the ritual activities of the Tharu as forest shrines were destroyed and worship rituals were abandoned. During the 1960s, forest preservation further contributed to the displacement of some Tharu communities, coinciding with land reform policies that shifted Tharu patterns of land ownership, destroying their seminomadic way of life.

All of the Tharu subgroups have developed distinct identities with their surroundings. The identity of a Tharu village is completely merged with the forest. The forest for the Tharu is an essential part of their economy, their spirituality, and their cultural identity. The Tharu people highly revere the forest as a place where gods and spirits dwell and believe that when forests are destroyed the forest gods abandon the area. The patriarchal family forms the basic unit of production in Tharu society. In the past the Tharu used to live in extended families, however nuclear families are now increasing. Social and conomic transformations in Tharu society brought about by forest clearing, hill migration, land reform, and political unification have played a crucial role in shaping the Tharu ethnic identity.

Paharization, Hinduization, and *Nepalization* are terms that describe the efforts by the Nepal State to ethnically transform the Tarai. The systematic resettling of hill people to the Tarai, a process called *paharization*; has aimed to secure Nepal's national structure against immigrants from India. The political ideology of Nepal of adopting high caste Hindu symbols has sought to *Hinduize* tribal groups. *Nepalization* has sought to bring the use of a common language amongst ethnic groups in Nepal as the basis of integration and affirming a national identity. The effect of the state's objective of national integration has politically and culturally unified the Tharu, as Tharu groups have become more politically active and aware of their cultural identities and boundaries. The Tharu Welfare Society was the first Tharu social organization in Nepal, which formed in 1949. It initially focused on cultural activities but now promotes socioeconomic development as a response to the Tharus' losing land to migrants from the hills. Other nongovernment organizations such as Backwards Society Education (BASE) and The Nepal Indigenous Development

Society (NIDS) have also sought to empower the people for education and economic improvement.

JOANNE MCLEAN AND SHUKAI CHAUDHARI

See also **Hindus; India; Nepal**

Further Reading

Dhakal, Suresh, Janak Rai, Dambar Chemchong, Dhruba Maharjan, Pranita Pradhan, Jagat Maharjan, and Shreeram Chaudhary, *Issues and Experiences: Kamaiya System, Kanara Andolan and Tharus in Bardiya*, Kathmandu: Society for Participatory Cultural Education (SPACE), 2000

HMG, Central Bureau of Statistics, *Population Census 1991 (2048)*, Nepal, 1991

Guneratne, Arjun, "Modernization, the State, and the Construction of a Tharu Identity in Nepal," *The Journal of Asian Studies*, 57, no.3, 1998

Guneratne, Arjun, "The Shaman and the Priest: Ghosts, Death & Ritual Specialists in Tharu Society," *Himalayan Research Bulletin*, 19, no.2, 2000

Krauskopff, Gisele, "The Anthropology of the Tharus: An Annotated Bibliography," *Kailash: A Journal of Himalayan Studies*, 17, no. 3 & 4, 1995

Krauskopff, Gisele, and Pamela Meyer Deuel, editors, *The Kings of the Nepal and the Tharu of the Tarai*, Los Angeles, California: Rusca Press, 2000

McLean, Joanne, "Conservation and the impact of relocation on the Tharus of Chitwan, Nepal," *Himalayan Research Bulletin*, 19, no.2, 2000

Mueller-Boeker, Ulrike, *The Chitwan Tharus in Southern Nepal: An Ethnoecological Approach*, Kathmandu: Nepal Research Centre Publications, 1999

Skar, Harold O, editor, *Nepal: Tharu and Tarai Neighbours*, Kathmandu: Bibliotheca Himalayica/EMR, 1998

Srivastava, S, *The Tharus: A Study in Cultural Dynamics*, Agra: Agra University Press, 1958

Tibetans

Capsule Summary

Location: Tibet Autonomous Region and Tibetan Autonomous Prefectures in the People's Republic of China (henceforth Tibet); Tibet-Himalayan borderlands; exile communities in India, Nepal, Bhutan, and western countries

Total Population: approximately 5 million (4.5 million in Tibet); 500,000 along the Himalayan borderlands; 100,000 in exile

Minority Populations: Qiang (e.g., Gyalrong, Minyak, Pumi), Monguor (Tu), Salar, Hui, Naxi (Nakhi), Lisu, Yi, Mongolian, Han

Languages: Lhasa Tibetan, various Tibetan dialects, Mandarin Chinese and regional dialects of Chinese, Qiangic languages, Tibeto-Burman languages, Mongolian languages

Religions: Tibetan (Tantric/Vajarayana) Buddhism, Bon, Islam

Since about the 1960s, the names Tibet and Tibetans have captured global attention. Apart from political conundrums, the Tibetans have come to be known through their religious and cultural legacies. Presently, the Tibetans constitute one of China's 56 minority nationalities in the Tibet Autonomous Region and various autonomous prefectures in four surrounding provinces, namely Qinghai, Gansu, Sichuan, and Yunnan. Another group of ethnic Tibetans known as Bhotias or Bhutias (from *Bhot*, the Indian name for Tibet) are minorities along the Tibet-Himalayan borders in Nepal

and India. Despite being citizens of these two countries, the Bhotias speak Tibetan languages as their mother tongues, share Tibetan culture, and practice Tibetan religions (Buddhism and Bon). In the wake of the Chinese occupation of Tibet in 1959, the legal status of Tibet and its relationship to China has been hotly debated. These, together with the preservation of Tibetan culture and identity, are the challenges it faces in the modern world.

Geographical Location and Way of Life

Tibet borders Nepal and Bhutan to the south, India to the south and west, China proper to the east, and Chinese Turkestan to the north. Although its area is more than 15 times the size of England, its population in Tibet proper (i.e., Tibet Autonomous Region) is only two million. As the label "the roof of the world" suggests, most of its land lies over 2,500 meters above sea level and the Tibetans are known as those who live at the highest altitudes of any human population. Tied to the geographical conditions, their economic life centers around three principal activities: animal husbandry, agriculture, and long-distance trade. The nomads who inhabit the uncultivable plains and pastures in the north and northeast tend yaks, yak-cow hybrids, goats, and sheep. The settled, valley-dwelling people in the south and southeast grow barley and in lower areas wheat, buckwheat, corn, and potatoes. Many of the southeasterners, so-called Khampas, lead lives as seminomads, farming in the valley and at the same time grazing livestock on the highlands. The Tibetans of all regions are also involved in long-distance trade as another mode of subsistence. Traveling to villages and towns, the nomads exchange salt, wool, skins, and other animal products with the farmers for barley, their main staple food, or trade with other low-land traders for tea and manufactured goods. As pilgrimage is highly valued in Tibetan society, they often combine it with trade. The result of these trading and pilgrimage journeys enables them to maintain close contact with other Tibetan populations and with other ethnic groups who reside in Tibetan areas. Apart from these activities, small industries based on specialization in crafts are engaged in by some marginal groups. These groups as well as foreign merchants and artisans (e.g., Kashmiri, Newar) who possess no land, are usually considered the lower class of the society. Following the Chinese occupation of Tibet, a large number of Tibetans became refugees, and hence have no connection with land. This has had a great impact on Tibetan society as a whole and the idea of class as associated with occupation and land possession is irrelevant to the modern life in exile.

Historical and Political Background

At the beginning of the Tang dynasty's rule of China, Tibet was called *Tubo* and by other subsequent terms such as *Tibbat* or *Tubbat* in Arabic and *Tibet* in Western languages. The country was traditionally divided into four regions: Western Tibet (Tö Ngari), Central Tibet (Ü-tsang), Eastern Tibet (Kham), and Northeastern Tibet (Amdo). Although most of what is known about Tibetan history focuses only on the Yarlung dynasty and the Lhasa state of Central Tibet, semi-independent kingdoms and principalities existed in various parts of the Tibetan plateau. There were, for example, the kingdoms of Ngari and Ladakh in Western Tibet, Derge in Kham, and Coni in Amdo. After the fall of the Qing dynasty at the turn of the twentieth century, Tibet saw many conflicts with China. Their native rulers were gradually suppressed and the whole country came under Chinese control in the wake of the Lhasa uprising in 1959. Presently, Central Tibet, together with Western Tibet, is under the administration of Tibet

Autonomous Region (*Xizang*) and the Tibetan race is called *Zangzu*, a new Chinese term for "Tibetan nationality." Divided into various autonomous prefectures, the area of Amdo occupies the bulk of Qinghai, the southwestern edge of Gansu, and the northernmost grasslands of Sichuan. The Kham region consists of autonomous prefectures in western Sichuan, the eastern portion of the Tibet Autonomous Region, northwestern Qinghai, and northwestern Yunnan.

The Notion of "Ethnic Tibet"

Contrary to popular belief, Tibet was never inhabited by a homogeneous population; it has always been multiethnic and multicultural. The *Qiang* (Chinese ancient term covering all the nomads of the regions west of China) were reported to be one of the first groups who dwelled in Tibetan areas. Their descendants (e.g., Minyak, Gyalrong, Pumi) have lived along the Sino-Tibetan borderlands and maintained relations with the Tibetans of Amdo and Kham. Presently, they speak Amdo koiné and Kham koiné as well as local Chinese dialects as lingua franca. Such Qiang groups as the Pumi and Baima are officially classified as being of Tibetan nationality, despite the fact that they speak non-Tibetan languages. The issue of ethnic classification in Tibet is a complicated one. There has been much discussion on the notion "Tibetan-ness": whether it should cover non-Tibetan speaking populations like the Qiang who share Tibetan culture and religion, or whether the notion should be measured on a purely linguistic ground.

During the period of the Tibetan Empire (seventh to ninth centuries), other non-Tibetan groups in Tibet included the Yüeh-chih of Indo-European stock, the Dards in Western Tibet, the Tuyuhun (Turco-Mongols), as well as the Hor of Mongol origin.

Today, non-Tibetan minorities in Tibet include the Hui (Chinese Muslims), Salar (Turkic Muslims), and Monguor (Tibetanized Mongols) in Qinghai and Gansu; Tibeto-Burman speaking groups (e.g., Naxi, Lisu, Yi) in Sichuan and Yunnan; and Monpa in southern TAR. In addition, Han Chinese, who are a minority in Tibet but form a majority of the Chinese nation state, have become one of the most salient groups of non-Tibetans in urban Tibetan, areas particularly in TAR. Many of the non-Tibetan minorities speak local Tibetan dialects and some are literate in Tibetan. Moreover, they practice Bon, Tibet's indigenous religion, Buddhism, or folk religion which incorporates certain elements of both.

Ethnic complexity in Tibet is augmented by the fact that there is great diversity among the Tibetans themselves. This results in a multitude of mutually unintelligible dialects, a variety of ritual practices, as well as strong regionalism and prejudices, such as those of the Lhasans against regional groups, particularly the Khampas.

Tibetans of the Southern Himalayas

Along the high Indo-Tibetan borderlands in Himachal Pradesh and Jammu and Kashmir lie several enclaves inhabited by Tibetan Buddhists. They include Ladakh, Spiti, Zangskar, and Lahul, which were traditionally part of Western Tibet. The most studied group of these is the Ladakhis, who numbered about 100,000 in 1990. Despite having lived together with the Muslims of Kashmir in a Hindu country, a good number of the Ladakhis still follow Tibetan Buddhism and certain indigenous territorial cults. As in other Tibetan areas, multilingualism is a fact of life. Ladakhi children grow up speaking at least three languages: Ladakhi Tibetan as their mother tongue; Urdu, the offical language of Kashmir; and Hindi, the national language learned from school.

Another Himalayan Tibetan-speaking population, though small in number, is in Sikkim in India. Sikkim was formerly dominated by the Lepchas (Rong), a Tibeto-Burman-speaking people who were later converted to Buddhism. The Tibetans from Central Tibet and Eastern Tibet migrated to Sikkim in the sixteenth century and formed a Tibetan polity there. Later on it became a British protectorate and finally part of the Indian Union. However, Nepali immigrants began coming to Sikkim in the midnineteenth century and now Nepalis and those of Nepalese descent make up over 70 percent of the population.

Sharing a similar history of settlement with the Sikkimese, the Bhutanese migrated from Tibet in the sixteenth century. Before the arrival of Tibetan immigrants, Bhutan was inhabited by many non-Tibetan groups who lived in lowland village clusters. Descendants of the Tibetans settled in the mountainous areas and became the ruling class of this Buddhist state. As in Sikkim, Bhutan's population today includes a significant proportion of Nepalis, mainly due to Nepali migration to Bhutan at the beginning of the twentieth century.

The Bhotias also reside in the far North of Nepal, from West to East. They consist of many hill communities such as the Mugum, Limirong, the Loba of Mustang, Dolpo, Nupri, Tsum, Jirel, Sherpa, and Lhomi. They are ethnically Tibetans and their lands were part of Tibet, though they were mostly self-governing with little influence from Nepalese or Tibetan authorities. Except for the Sherpas who depend on tourism, these Himalayan-Tibetan groups trade salt and animal products from Tibet for grain and manufactured goods from India. They also participate in agriculture and pastoralism.

The Balti and Purik Tibetans of Pakistan are Islamicized, though they still speak Tibetan as their mother tongue. When compared with other Tibetan-speaking populations in the Southern Himalayas, little anthropological work has been done on them.

Tibetan Refugees and Construction of Tibetan Identity

In 1959, about 70,000 Tibetans followed their political and spiritual leader, the 14th Dalai Lama, in fleeing Tibet and resettling in exile communities in Nepal, India, Bhutan, and subsequently in several Western countries such as the United States and Switzerland. Their population has since grown to around 100,000.

The Tibetan government in exile under the administration of the Dalai Lama was established in Dharamsala in North India. They were granted a large degree of autonomy from the government of India in running their internal affairs, which include schooling and managing welfare programs largely supported by Western organizations. A number of schools for Tibetan refugee children were set up both in India and Nepal by the Tibetan government. These schools play a crucial role in the development of ethnic pride and identity among these children.

The refugees have also attempted to preserve their major teaching lineages and cultural values. Several monasteries, including Buddhist colleges, have been built in exile communities. Efforts have also been made to disseminate Buddhist teachings to the Western world. This has resulted in the establishment of various religious centers in the United States and other countries, the translation of Buddhist and Bon teachings into English and other Western languages, and the writing of Tibetan autobiographies for Western audiences.

Although the Tibetan diaspora has made Tibet and Tibetans better known in the global community, it has also brought along several social and political problems. The Tibetan cause has come to be seriously debated within the Tibetan community. Some have openly expressed their dissatisfaction with the Dalai Lama's China policy, which they consider too compromising. Over the last decade, the general discourse among Tibetan exiles seems to have shifted from the need to regain political independence to what one should do to prosper in exile. Socially, the youngsters are developing new identities that are more cosmopolitan and Westernized. This has created conflict with the older generation and accentuated the gap between the Tibetans in exile and those in the homeland, some of whom are greatly Sinicized.

KRISADAWAN HONGLADAROM

See also **Bhutan; China; Hui; India; Nepal; Yi**

Further Reading

Bell, Charles, *The People of Tibet*, Delhi: Motilal Banarsidass, 1992 (1928)

Carrasco, Pedro, *Land and Polity in Tibet*, Seattle, 1959

Diehl, Keila, *Echoes from Dharamsala: Music in the Life of a Tibetan Refugee Community*, Berkeley: University of California Press, 2002

Driem, George van, *Languages of the Himalayas*, Volumes 1 and 2, Leiden: Brill, 2001

Huber, Toni, *Amdo Tibetans in Transition. Society and Culture in the Post-Mao Era*, Leiden: Brill, 2002

Klieger, P. Christiaan, editor, *Tibet, Self, and the Tibetan Diaspora, Voices of Difference*, Leiden: Brill, 2002

Samuel, Geoffrey, *Civilized Shamans: Buddhism in Tibetan Societies*, Washington: Smithsonian Press, 1993

Tigre

Capsule Summary

Location: Northwest Eritrea, along the border with Sudan

Total Population: about 690,000 (including some 200,000 in Sudan as refugees)

Languages: Tigre (Khasa), To-Bedawi

Religion: Islam (95%), Christianity (5%), both mixed with traditional cults

Tigre is the name of a South Semitic language spoken by a large group of indigenous peoples in Northwest Eritrea, which should not be confused with the *Tigrinya*, the name of another language of people who live in the Eritrean and North Ethiopian (Tigray) highlands. Both languages derive from the old Ge'ez language, now only retained as the language of Orthodox Christian Church liturgy and scholarly texts. The Tigre live in the northwestern lowlands of Eritrea, partly spilling over into Sudan, and form about 30 percent of the total Eritrean population. The main Tigre groups are the Beni Amer, Beit Asgede, Ad Shaikh, Mensa, Beit Juk, and Marya.

The Tigre do not form one unified ethnic group but are territorially and socially diverse, based on different kinship and clan formations. They are also characterized by divergent customary law traditions. Until recently they had "tribal federations" (a political designation), the best known of which is that of the Beni Amer. The latter also have a traditional paramount chief called the *diglal*.

At present, almost all the Tigre are Muslims (except part of the Mensa), and among them Sufi orders (Qadiriyya and Mirghaniyya) are important. Until the middle of the nineteenth century, most of the Tigre-speaking groups were Christian, owing to their connections with the Ethiopian imperial state and the influx of Christian highlanders who, over the centuries, settled in the areas as nominal lords over the Tigre peoples. (For example, the Bet Asgede are said to descend from a Christian man from the highland region of Akkele Guzay.) The Tigre country still has several ruins of old Christian churches.

Most Tigre are pastoralist people, tending herds of camels, sheep, goats, and also some cattle and donkeys, but many have become peasant cultivators, traders, and civil servants. When Eritrea was an Italian colony (1890-1941) many Tigre served as soldiers in the colonial army, serving in both Ethiopia and in Libya.

The traditional social structure and ethnic or tribal relations of the Tigre groups was exceedingly complex, and is still not entirely understood. One cannot speak of clear ethnic groups here, because the ethnic, linguistic, territorial, and clan lines overlap and fuse in Tigre group formation, leading to a peculiar hierarchy.

For instance, some Beni Amer speak Tigre (Semitic), others To-Bedawi (a Cushitic language). Among the Tigre there were various alliances and federations based on either clan lines or territorial contiguity, as well as an encompassing lord-vassal structure (defining labor tribute, intermarriage patterns, political loyalty, etc.). The word *tigre* itself means "commoner," "vassal," or "serf." Their lords, who lived among them and mixed with them, were referred to as *nabtab*, or also called *shumagalle* or *shumagulle* (perhaps derived from the Tigrinya/Amharic word for "elder") and became a kind of hereditary aristocratic class. The proportion was on average about one lord to ten vassals. In their turn, the Tigre themselves had slaves. Between these classes, a sort of ritual and economic division of labor as well as rules regulating intermarriage and food consumption existed. Starting essentially under British rule since 1941, this hierarchy has largely dissolved and is no longer socially visible, although a consciousness of who belonged to what stratum is retained and often plays a role in choice of marriage partners.

Both under Italian colonialism and in present-day Eritrea, the Tigre remained on the sideline of national politics and economic life. Their harsh natural environment and the mobile pastoral lifestyle made them marginal in several respects. They entered the political scene only in the period of the British mandate in Eritrea (1941-1952), when a large Tigre gathering in 1947 formulated a demand to abolish the lord-vassal relationship throughout the area. This was formally done in 1949. Later, many Tigre entered as rebels into the Eritrean Liberation Front (ELF) fighting against Ethiopian rule (from 1962 on), and in the course of the armed struggle the remaining traditional obligations under this system were scrapped. During the years of guerrilla struggle, the Tigre were involved in the Muslim-dominated ELF, but after its rival, the Eritrean Peoples' Liberation Front (EPLF), replaced the ELF in the late 1970s as the main contender for power, the Tigre lost influence. However, the period of the liberation struggle was one of important social changes, as the radical EPLF, after bringing areas under its control, aimed at far-reaching social change in the domains of gender relations, customary law, marriage, education, and traditional customs like folk healing and ritual.

Like other groups in independent Eritrea after 1991, the Tigre have undergone some amount of cultural construction, in that the group, despite its heterogeneous and fluid composition, was designated as one nationality. This ascribing of an official identity will probably put an end to earlier processes of boundary crossing and assimilation among them—common in the absence of state authority—and perhaps will give rise to collective struggles on the basis of this new group identity. To give one example of a new opposition: under the current regime the Beni Amer who speak the Beja language (To-Bedawi) are not seen as part of the Tigre but as a separate group, the Hidarib.

The Tigre have a rich but largely unknown culture and oral tradition (history, poetry, songs, epics). The first and most impressive documentation of these traditional forms was made by early twentieth-century scholars like the great Orientalist E. Littmann and Swedish missionaries like K. Rodén and R. Sundström, while later the ELF and the EPLF also did their own collection of Tigre oral traditions. Since independence in 1991, several books and teaching materials in Tigre have appeared. While there are studies of the Tigre language, modern anthropological or historical studies on the Tigre peoples are lacking. Thus, it is difficult to describe contemporary Tigre society, but it seems likely that in the context of the Eritrean liberation struggle and of the independence period after 1991, social and cultural change among the Tigre has been quite dramatic.

JON ABBINK

See also **Eritrea; Sudan**

Further Reading

Höfner, Maria, "'Überlieferungen bei Tigre-Stämmen', I. 'Ad Shek," *Annales d'Éthiopie* 4, (1961)

Nadel, Siegfried F., "Notes on Beni Amer Society," *Sudan Notes and Records*, 26, no. 1 (1954)

Shack, William A., "Tigre: Beni Amer, Bilen and Related Peoples," in *The Central Ethiopians*, London: International African Institute, 1974

Trimingham, John Spencer, *Islam in Ethiopia*, London: Geoffrey Cumberlege/Oxford University Press, 1952

Tiruchelvam, Neelan (Tamil-Sri Lankan)

Dr. Neelan Tiruchelvam was a leading scholar and activist in the fields of minority rights, constitutional law, democracy, peace and conflict transformation. He was held in equally high esteem in his native Sri Lanka and internationally for his lifelong dedication to nonviolent and constitutional solutions to human rights problems.

Born the son of a Tamil lawyer and cabinet minister, Tiruchelvam was himself a distinguished lawyer and politician. Both he and his wife Sithie graduated in the 1960s from the faculty of law of the University of Ceylon. In the 1970s, following mass killings and other human rights violations by government forces, he was among those who helped establish the Sri Lankan civil and human rights movement. With the imposition of the 1978 Constitution by the Jayawardene regime, he and others continued to argue for political accommodation in a climate of increasing polarization between a repressive state and Tamil extremism.

A senior partner with the law firm of Tiruchelvam Associates, throughout the 1970s and 1980s Tiruchelvam held academic posts at home and in the United Sates, including a fellowship at Yale and a lectureship at Harvard. In 1981, with his fellow Sri Lankan K.M. de Silva, he participated in a Ford Foundation-sponsored conference in Trincomalee on ethnic conflict, following which in 1982 they established the International Centre for Ethnic Studies (ICES) for the promotion of ethnic reconciliation and conflict resolution. At about the same time Tiruchelvam founded the Law and Society Trust (LST), and he remained a director of ICES and board member of the LST for the rest of his life. Both organizations attracted researchers and activists to Colombo from all over the world; both also promoted work on gender issues, which Tiruchelvam strongly supported.

At home, from 1978 onwards Tiruchelvam held a succession of official appointments, including membership of the Presidential Law Commission and the Presidential Commission on Democratic Decentralisation and Devolution (DDC); his minority dissenting report was subsequently acted on and accepted for the framing of the DDC legislation. His parliamentary career began as an MP for the moderate Tamil United Liberation Front (TULF) in 1983. After the anti-Tamil pogrom in 1983, Tiruchelvam and his TULF colleagues were expelled from parliament by the Jayawardene government for not taking the oath of allegiance to the unitary status of the Sri Lankan constitution. He returned to Parliament in 1994 and remained a TULF MP for the rest of his life. Constantly involved in seeking solutions to Sri Lanka's intercommunal conflict, he was one of the originators of the 1987 Indo-Sri Lankan Accord and played a key role in the 1995 reform and devolution program of the Chandrika Kumaratunga government.

Abroad, Tiruchelvam served as a member of international observer and expert missions to Pakistan, Chile, Hungary, Bangladesh, Nepal, Kazakhstan, Ethiopia, and South Africa. He was the first speaker from the floor at the opening session of the UN Working Group on Minorities in Geneva in 1995 and inaugurated a lecture series in Geneva that took place each year just before the Working Group. Having joined the Council of the London-based non-governmental organization Minority Rights Group (MRG) International in 1994, he was elected Chair of its Council in April of 1999.

In 1999 Tiruchelvam was the leading Tamil politician involved in framing the draft constitution of the Chandrika Bandaranaike administration, especially its proposals on devolution. At the time of his death the same year, he was working on an equal opportunity law seeking to end social and gender discrimination. Tiruchelvam was killed by a suicide bomber in Colombo on July 29, 1999, only weeks before he was due to leave for Harvard to teach law and human rights. The Liberation Tamil Tigers of Eelam are widely held to have been responsible, and he had known for some time that his life was in danger. On his death, UN Secretary-General Kofi Annan, UN High Commissioner for Human Rights Mary Robinson, and US President Bill Clinton were among the many who expressed shock and dismay and paid tribute to his life and work.

Tiruchelvam was described after his death as "the main political link between Sri Lanka's Sinhala, Tamil, and Muslim communities; the bond that held together

Sri Lanka's human rights community and a key link between Sri Lanka and the international community," and as "the foremost democratic political thinker the Sri Lankan Tamil society has ever produced" (ICES, *Neelan Tiruchelvam 1944-1999: Sri Lankan Visionary and World Citizen - Selected Tributes*, 2000, pp. 1, 5). He had frequently observed the connections between inappropriate conceptions of development and the violation of human rights. In one of his last speeches, made in Delhi in 1999, he said: "The real challenge is to enable us to construct a future which acknowledges the diversity of the people of the world and provides for a plurality of belonging to the world, the nation, and the community."

Biography

Born in Colombo, Sri Lanka (then Ceylon), January 31, 1944. Educated at the University of Ceylon Law Faculty, LLB 1966, and Harvard University Law School LLM, 1970, SJD 1973; Fullbright Fellowship, 1969-1971. Academic appointments: University of Ceylon 1967-1968; Examiner in Law, Ceylon Civil and Foreign Service Examination, 1968-1969; Fellow in Law and Modernization, Yale Law School, 1971-1973; Visiting Reader, Sri Lanka Law College, 1973-1974; Associate Director, Law and Development Division, 1978-1980, and Member, Board of Management, 1978-1983, Marga Institute, Colombo; Visiting Fellow, 1986-1987, and Lecturer in Law, 1988-1989, Harvard Law School. Legal, political and nongovernmental work in Sri Lanka: Member of Ceylon Bar, 1968; Member, Board of Management, Sri Lanka Foundation, 1978-1983; Member, Sri Lankan Law Commission 1978-1983; Member, Presidential Commission on Democratic Decentralization and Devolution, 1979-1980; Legal Consultant, Greater Colombo Economic Commission, 1979-1980; Member, Committee on Privatisation, 1979-1981, and Committee on Investment Protection Agreements, 1979-1983; Member, Minister of Justice Panel of Consultants; Member, Presidential Commission on Devolution; Senior Partner, Tiruchelvam Associates; Member, Board of Trustees, Law and Society Trust; Director, International Centre for Ethnic Studies. International appointments: Executive Director, Asian Council for Law and Development, 1978-1985; Member, International Observer Missions to Pakistan and Chile, 1988; Member, Non-Governmental Mission from SAARC Countries, Parliamentary Elections in Pakistan (1988, 1997), Bangladesh (1991), Nepal (1991); member of other international missions: Hungary (1990), Nepal (1990), Kazakhstan (1992), Ethiopia (1992), South Africa (1993); numerous other major international seminars, consultations, and conferences; Council Member, Minority Rights Group International, 1994-1999, and Council Chair, 1999. Publications: *Ideology of Popular Justice: A Socio-Legal Inquiry*, 1982; *Ethical Dilemmas of Development in Asia*, co-edited with Godfrey Gunetilleka and Radhika Coomaraswamy, 1982; *Judiciary in Plural Societies*, coedited with Radhika Coomaraswamy, 1987; numerous articles and papers in scholarly publications; posthumous: *Selected Writings: Human Rights, Constitutionalism, Diversity and Pluralism*, 2000; *Transcending the Bitter Legacy: Selected Parliamentary Speeches*, edited by Lisa M. Kois, 2000. Died in Colombo, Sri Lanka, on July 29, 1999.

Selected Works

Ideology of Popular Justice: A Socio-Legal Inquiry, Vikas, 1982
Ethical Dilemmas of Development in Asia, coedited with Godfrey Gunetilleka and Radhika Coomaraswamy, Lexington Books/D.C. Heath, 1982
Judiciary in Plural Societies, coedited with Radhika Coomaraswamy, Pinter, 1987
"Sri Lanka's Ethnic Conflict and Preventive Action: The Role of NGOs," in *Vigilance and Vengeance: NGOs Preventing Ethnic Conflict in Divided Societies*, edited by Robert I. Rotberg, Washington, DC: Brookings Institution Press, 1996
"Civil Society and Ethnic Conflict in Sri Lanka," in *History and Politics: Millennial Perspectives: Essays in Honour of Kingsley de Silva*, Colombo: Law and Society Trust, 1999
"Development and the Protection of Human Rights," presentation to the Council of Europe, 1993, in *Nethra* (ICES), special issue *Mourning and Honouring Neelan Tiruchelvam*, vol. 3, no. 4, July-Sep 1999, pp. 27-39
"Devolution and the Elusive Quest for Peace in Sri Lanka," in *Creating Peace in Sri Lanka: Civil War and Reconciliation*, edited by Robert I. Rothberg, Washington, DC: Brookings Institution Press, 1999
"The Ethnic and Cultural Dimensions of Human Rights Policy," address to the European Parliament's Committee on Development and Cooperation, 1993, in *Nethra* (ICES), special issue *Mourning and Honouring Neelan Tiruchelvam*, vol. 3, no. 4, July-Sep 1999, pp. 59-64
"The Politics of Federalism and Diversity in Sri Lanka," in *Autonomy and Ethnicity: Negotiating Competing Claims in Multi-Ethnic States*, edited by Yash Ghai, Cambridge: Cambridge University Press, 2000
Selected Writings: Human Rights, Constitutionalism, Diversity and Pluralism, Colombo: ICES, 2000
Transcending the Bitter Legacy: Selected Parliamentary Speeches, edited by Lisa M. Kois: Colombo, ICES, 2000

MILES LITVINOFF

See also **Minority Rights Group International; Sri Lanka; Subcommission: Promotion and Protection of Human Rights; Tamil Tigers; Tamils; United Nations Declaration on Minorities; United Nations Working Group on Minorities**

Further Reading

Eide, Asbjorn, "Good Governance in Ethnically Heterogeneous Societies," Neelan Tiruchelvam Commemoration Lecture Series, 1, Colombo: ICES, 2001
Fernando, Basil, "The Challenge of Dr. Neelan Tiruchelvam's Life, Work and Ideas," *Human Rights Solidarity* (Asian Human Rights Commission), 10, no. 12, (December 2000)
Ignatieff, Michael, "Nationalism and Self-Determination: Is There an Alternative to Violence?" Neelan Tiruchelvam Millennium Lecture 2, Colombo: ICES, 2001

International Centre for Ethnic Studies Home Page. 9 June 2004
<http://www.icescmb.slt.lk>

Steiner, Henry J., Robert Clark, Stanley Tambiah, Roberto Unger, Clarence Dias, and Mithran Tiruchelvam, "Neelan Tiruchelvam 1944-1999," Memorial Address, Cambridge, Massachusetts: Harvard Law School, 2000

Neelan Tiruchelvam 1944–1999: Sri Lankan Visionary and World Citizen—Selected Tributes, Colombo: ICES, 2000

Nethra (ICES), special issue *Mourning and Honouring Neelan Tiruchelvam,* 3, no. 4, July-Sep 1999

Nissan, Elizabeth, *Sri Lanka: A Bitter Harvest,* London: MRG report, 1996; revised edition, 2001

van der Stoel, Max, "Human Rights, the Prevention of Conflict and the International Protection of Minorities: A Contemporary Paradigm for Contemporary Challenges," Address in Memory of Dr. Neelan Tiruchelvam, Warsaw: Organization for Security and Cooperation in Europe, 1999

Tofa

Capsule Summary

Location: South central Siberia, on the territory of Irkutsk Administrative Region, Russian Federation
Total Population: approximately 600-700
Language: Tofa (Tofalar)
Religion: animist

The Tofa (also known as *tofalar,* formerly *karagas*), were formerly hunters and reindeer-herders of the south Siberian *taiga* (forested mountains). Once practicers of animistic religion and dwellers in bark-covered teepees, they now live in log cabins in three mountain villages. Still, the Tofa may be the least documented among native Siberian peoples. Early travelers who visited the Tofa reported a few limited details of their physical appearance, pastoralist lifestyle, and material culture. Some evidence for the practice of shamanism was collected, including ribbon-bedecked shamans' costumes and deer-hide drums now on display in Russian museums. The Tofa were forcibly settled in the 1930s. Since that time, language shift, cultural decline, and Russification have proceeded apace. Though the Tofa still maintain a distinct culture and ethnic identity, they find themselves under increasing pressure to abandon their language, land, and traditions. The Tofa language is now seriously endangered and spoken fluently only by elderly persons.

The Tofa share a close cultural and linguistic affinity with two other small, isolated, and endangered groups of nomadic and seminomadic reindeer herders. The nearest of these are the Todzhu, reindeer herders of northern Tuva. The Todzhu speak a language quite closely related to Tofa. Another closely related group is the Tuha (also known as Dukha or Tsaatan), nomadic reindeer herders of northwestern Mongolia, who number fewer than 200 persons. The Tofa, Todzhu, and the Tuha form a common culture area, strikingly similar to each other in terms of language, folklore, nomadism, animism, and reindeer ecology. These three peoples represent the southernmost extreme of reindeer pastoralism in the world.

South-Siberian reindeer herders differ from the large-scale reindeer (caribou) ranchers of Scandinavia, Alaska, Canada, and northern Siberia, who live in tundra areas and raise large herds of reindeer for meat. The Tofa, by contrast, use reindeer primarily for their milk products, and as pack and riding animals, while wild game is the principal source of food. This unusual combination of hunting and herding shaped the Tofa religion, customs, language, and worldview.

Tofalaria, as the ancestral Tofa territory is called in Russian, is located in the foothills of the Sayan Mountains in western Irkutsk administrative region along the border with the Republic of Tuva. It contains three remote villages: *Alygdzher, Nerkha,* and *Gutara.* The 1989 Soviet census recorded 731 Tofa persons, but intermarriage with Russians and others is common and many Tofa are of mixed ancestry. The Tofa were recognized in 1926 as a "small-numbering people," a special ethnic status in the Soviet Union. However, they failed to meet the minimum population standard needed to receive an officially sanctioned orthography. Efforts at writing or publishing were prohibited until 1989, when Russian scholars developed an alphabet based on Cyrillic letters and published a primer to teach schoolchildren. The writing system has not been widely accepted and few adult Tofa-speakers read it. The language is currently spoken fluently by only about 30 persons. No children in the community are learning or using Tofa as their first language; on a scale of language endangerment it is thus considered moribund and likely to disappear in the coming decades. Contact among native speakers from different villages is sporadic, as travel between the three villages is increasingly difficult. All speakers now use Russian for daily communication, even at home.

Tofa belongs to the northern (or northeastern) branch of the Turkic family, making it a distant cousin of Turkish. It also shows considerable Mongolian influence and borrowing of words from an earlier, now extinct language, probably of the Yeniseyan family. Tofa boasts a rich legacy of legends, stories, and songs. As of 2001, a few elderly people were still able to sing songs or recite traditional stories like the following one, a Tofa creation myth:

How the earth was created
In the very beginning there were no people,
there was nothing at all.
There was only the first duck,
she was flying along.
Having settled down for the night,
the duck laid an egg.
Her egg broke.
The liquid of her egg poured out.
From it, a lake was formed,
and the egg's shell became earth.
That is how the earth was created.

For indigenous people such as the Tofa, whose entire culture developed around the productive activities of hunting, fishing, gathering, and reindeer breeding, the native language reflects an intimate knowledge of the land and natural resources. The Tofa way of life depends on complex knowledge of the land and its resources, which in turn depends on rights of access to that land and its resources. A variety of political, social, economic, and institutional pressures, particularly during the Soviet period, eroded this connection to the land. Soviet collectivization was followed by the introduction of the *sovkhoz* (state farm), forced settlement of mobile reindeer herders, the introduction of boarding schools for children, and the establishment of village-based fur-processing and sewing enterprises to employ the wives of herders. The emphasis on so-called production nomadism was a major blow to the south-Siberian reindeer herders' way of life. These changes also undermined family structures by which language and culture should be transmitted from one generation to the next. By the late 1940s, the state had banned shamans (traditional healers and religious practitioners), forbid the use of the language, sent many children off to boarding schools, and conscripted young men to fight Nazi Germany on the western front of World War II. Following decades brought an influx of Russian settlers, leaving the Tofa outnumbered in their own titular territory.

In the face of all this, the Tofa struggled to continue to hunt, herd, practice animism, maintain a separate ethnic identity, retain their language, and pass on cultural knowledge to their children. They can claim modest success in some of these areas. Many Tofa still engage in traditional activities of hunting, fishing, and gathering of berries, pine nuts, and medicinal plants. A smaller number engage in animistic religious practices that include making offerings of tea, food, and vodka to the local spirits that are believed to reside in mountains, rivers, and campfires. Fewer than half a dozen Tofa men still practice reindeer herding, and the number of deer had declined to well under 1,000 head in the year 2001. As the last speakers of Tofa grow old, the death of the language in the next two decades becomes a great likelihood. With it, much of the cultural legacy may also come to an end. Left behind is a community that has forgotten its own creation story.

K. DAVID HARRISON

See also **Mongolia; Siberian Indigenous Peoples; Tuvans**

Further Reading

Forsyth, J., *A History of the Peoples of Siberia*, Cambridge: Cambridge University Press, 1992
Vainstein, S.I., *Nomads of South Siberia*, translated by M. Colenso, Cambridge: Cambridge University Press, 1980

Togo

Capsule Summary

Location: West Africa, between Ghana and Benin
Total Population: 5,429,299 (July 2003)
Languages: Ewe, Kabye, French, Kotokoli, Moba, Tchamba, Fulbe, and many others
Religions: Traditional animism, Christianity, Islam

Togo is a multiethnic state in West Africa with an area of 56,000 square kilometers (21,620 square miles), lying along the Gulf of Benin, sandwiched between Ghana, Benin, and Burkina Faso. The per capita gross domestic product (GDP) is $1,400 (2002). French is the official language, though Ewe, Mina, and other minority languages are spoken beyond their ethnic boundaries. The system of government is multiparty and quasi-democratic, in that the President was reelected for a five-year term in 1998 in fraudulent elections. In 2001 President Eyadema (of the Kabye ethnic group) continued as Africa's longest serving dictator. No one ethnic grouping or religious tradition forms a majority in Togo. In 2000, when there were some 5 million Togolese (according to an unofficial UN estimate), the collective Ewe subgroups represented up to 40 percent, the Kabye collective (including Kabre, Losso, Lama, Logba, and Nawdm) up to 25 percent, with other significant populations of between 18 and 30 different ethnolinguistic groups constituting less than 3 percent. Classification however, is contentious, and the Summer Institute of Linguistics' Ethnologue lists 43 languages for Togo. Migrant populations of Yoruba, Lebanese, and Europeans are less than 0.1 percent.

The population of the central mountains is perhaps the oldest in Togo, with recent archeological research dating the presence of the Tchamba, Bago and Bassari peoples as far back as the ninth century. Northern Mossi kingdoms date back to the thirteenth century. Ewe migration narratives from Nigeria and archaeological finds in the region of Notse put the earliest appearance of Ewe speakers at about 1600. Other research suggests the Kabye and others were the last to settle in the Kara region coming perhaps from Kete-Krachi in Ghana as recently as 250 years ago. Parts of north Togo were for a long time under the influence of Islamic kingdoms, such as that of Umar Tal of the nineteenth century.

European presence began in the fifteenth century and became permanent from the sixteenth. Though Danish, Dutch, Spanish, British, Germans, and French all sailed the coastal region, the Portuguese were the first to establish local economic control. For the next three centuries the area that is Togo today was sandwiched between the two powerful slave-trading kingdoms of Ashanti and Dahomey and consequently Togolese ethnic groups were over-represented in the trans-Atlantic slave trade. During the same period, a growing trans-Sahara Arabic trade in slaves, kola, and gold, moved south through Togo.

Missionaries arrived in the mid-1800s and set up schools and churches in the Ewe region of Ho (present-day Ghana), Kpalime, and Agou. The first indigenous language that was standardized and published was Ewe. The Germans annexed Togo as a *Schutzgebiet* (protectorate) in 1884. Initially treaties applied only to the coastal region, though over the next 15 years the German colonial administrators moved their capital from Zebe to Lomé and extended control north as far as present day Burkina Faso. Extension was a brutal military process and fierce resistance came from the Kotokoli, the Kabye, and Konkomba. Once occupation was complete, a system of roads and railroads were built by German money and forced labor, primarily consisting of northern and central ethnic minorities.

British, French, and African troops invaded and captured German Togoland in 1914. For the duration of the war, British troops controlled much of the Ewe region, also reuniting the Konkomba kingdoms. The League of Nations mandates officially began in 1922, with one third under British control, and two thirds under the administration of France. The Ewe subgroups were further divided by the border, while the Konkomba regained unity under their capital Yendi. Many smaller groups such as the Akposso were severed from their farmlands. During the mandate, the French forced large numbers of Kabye to settle in the central and south regions, officially to combat overcrowding, but really to provide cheap labor reserves for plantations and industrialization. During the same period, the capital grew rapidly and all of Togo's ethnic groups and religions gained a foothold in the historically Ewe region. With independence, British Togoland joined the Republic of Ghana and French Togoland became the independent Republique Togolaise.

With independence the Ewe subgroups, with greater literacy and economic resources, were overrepresented in government and administration. Northern groups, such as the Kabye and Kotokoli, however, represented over 80 percent of the armed forces. This ethnically biased distribution of political and military capital set the stage for Black Africa's first coup d'etat. A second coup in 1967 saw a Kabye leader become president. The president then oversaw a program of redistribution of these resources, as large numbers of northerners entered the political and administrative arena, in turn redirecting a substantial percentage north. During the late 1970s, taking his lead from Mobutu, the former dictator of Zaire, Eyadema launched a program of *authenticité* which essentialized ethnic identities, but further exacerbated the north-south division.

Ethnic tensions have occasionally flared into violence in modern Togo, though official and unofficial political propaganda and the stated platform of political parties greatly exaggerates existing cleavages. During the 1991-1992 revolution hundreds of thousands of Kabye fled north to escape political violence in the south. At the same time southerners fled to Ghana and Benin. Southerners, almost exclusively Ewe-speakers, continue to be exposed to brutality and harassment. Among the southern groups, especially the Ewe, Christianity in various guises pervades. The Moba, Mossi, Kotokoli, and Tchamba are heavily Islamicized. Traditional and animist religions remain powerful in all communities, especially outside urban centers.

Besides the Ewe and Kabye minorities, the Moba (eight percent) and Kotokoli/Temba (ten percent) are the largest subgroupings. The Moba distinguish themselves from the Konkomba, however, as do the Bassari and Tchamba from the Kotokoli. The following minority ethnolinguistic groups also represent three percent or less of the population: Adele (also known as Bidire, Bedere, Gidire, Gadre); Akebou (Kebu, Kabu); Akposo; Anii (Bassila, Winji-Winji); Anufo (Tchokossi); Anyanga; Ashanti; Bago; Delo (Nrtubo); Dendi; Fon-Gbe; Fulbe (Fulani); Gurma (Gourmantche); Hausa; Ife (Ana, Baate); Kambole; Kpessi; Mahi; N'Gam-Gam; Mamprusi; Mossi (More); Sola (Soruba, Miyobe, Bijobe); Tamberma (Batammmaraba, Somba, Tamari); Yanga; and the mixed-race descendants of returned slaves known commonly as *Brazilians*.

BENJAMIN N. LAWRANCE

See also **Ewe**

Further Reading

Bouraima, Nouridine, and Yves Marguerat, *La population du Togo en 1981: Premières observations sur les résultats provisoires du recensement de novembre 1981*, Lomé: République togolaise, Ministère du plan, de l'industrie et de la réforme administrative, Direction de la statistique, 1983

Cornevin, Robert, *Histoire du Togo*, 3rd edition, Paris: Berger-Levrault, 1969

Decalo, Samuel, *Historical Dictionary of Togo*, 3rd edition, Baltimore and London: Scarecrow Press, 1996

Delval, Raymond, *Les Musulmans au Togo*, Paris: Publications orientalistes de France, Centre de hautes études sur l'Afrique et l'Asie modernes, 1980

Grimes, Barbara, editor, *Ethnologue*, 13th Edition, Summer Institute of Linguistics, 1996

Marguerat, Yves, *Population, migrations, urbanisation au Togo et en Afrique noire: Articles et documents (1981–1993)*, Lomé: Presses de l'Université du Bénin, 1994

Piot, Charles, *Remotely Global: Village Modernity in West Africa*, Chicago: Chicago University Press, 1999

Toraja

Capsule Summary

Location: Indonesia, southwestern and central Sulawesi
Total Population: approximately 414,000
Religions: Christian, Muslim, traditional beliefs

Languages: Austronesian, Western Malay-Polynesian, Sulawesi, Toraja-Sa'dan (Bare'e)

The Toraja of South Sulawesi are one of Indonesia's minority tribes who have successfully created a national and international reputation. Toraja prominence has emerged largely through tourism, due to their attractive villages surrounded by rice fields and mountains and their unique funeral ceremonies involving pig and water buffalo sacrifices.

According to the 2002 census, there are 414,436 Toraja, including 361,010 Christians who are 78 percent Protestant and 12 percent Catholic, as well as 33,332 Muslims and 20,094 practitioners of a traditional religion known as *Aluk To Dolo,* or "way of the ancestors."

The arrival of Dutch missionaries at the turn of twentieth century, the establishment of mission schools and churches, the influx of post-World War II Protestant missionaries, and the establishment of a strong local religious leadership base have all helped create a predominately Christian Toraja population in the midst of a national Islamic majority.

In spite of the Indonesian economic crisis of the late twentieth century, and the decline of Western tourism to predominately Islamic countries in the wake of September 11, 2001, the area's economy continues to benefit from foreign and domestic tourists. The tourism industry highlights the most striking aspects of Toraja culture, such as elaborate funeral rituals, effigies of the dead, cliff-side tombs, and carved Toraja houses. A dramatic increase in tourism occurred over a 20-year period, starting in 1973 when approximately 400 foreign tourists visited. In 1994, the region had 53,700 foreign visitors and 205,000 domestic visitors. Local economies have also benefited from traveling Toraja laborers seeking employment opportunities on Sulawesi, other Indonesian islands, and even in the international marketplace, and who then bring their savings back to Tana Toraja ("Torajaland"). Torajaland also provides opportunities for laborers from other areas to work in local businesses and gain employment on Toraja work projects.

For much of the population of Tana Toraja, life follows the familiar patterns of the past. Many still make their living from wet rice agriculture, coffee planting, small garden plots, and poultry and swine farming. Torajan society recognizes a hierarchy based on age, descent, occupation, and wealth. There were once three basic ranks: 'the aristocracy, commoners, and serfs or slaves. Today slavery is illegal and the ranks are becoming blurred as each succeeding generation chips away at the distinctive characteristics that separated the ranks. Nevertheless, in some social gatherings and ritual ceremonies, rank from generations past may determine the way people interact with each other.

The Toraja have strong emotional, economic, and political ties to a number of different groups. The most basic tie is the family (*rarabuku*), viewed as relations of blood (*rara*) and bone (*buku*). Starting with the nuclear family (parents and children), Toraja *rarabuku* relationships extend bilaterally, through the mother and the father, and in extended kinship directions. Toraja also have close affiliations in another group, the ancestral house or *tongkonan,* which contrasts with the ordinary house or *banua.* Toraja houses (*tongkonan* and *banua*) provide more than shelter. They are important kinship points of reference through which one traces familial ties. Toraja people may be vague about genealogical links with distant relations, but they can invariably trace the locale where their parents and grandparents were born, and are usually able to recognize their relations or link with others through a particular *tongkonan.*

The *tongkonan,* then, consists of a group of people who determine descent from a common ancestor. Men and women are equally present and participate in ceremonies, rituals, and the decision making of the various groups. Husband and wife, or brother and sister, are expected to combine resources and help each other meet the expense of participating in rituals held by either side, a custom called *bassi sirengge.* Contributions to family ceremonies on both sides should ideally be kept roughly in balance. This effectively limits people's claims over ownership of the *tongkonan* and keeps up the ritual obligations of belonging to not only several houses or people, but to all people who belong to the *tongkonan.*

The Toraja have two main ritual categories, linked to the sun and smoke. *Rambu Tuka* rituals are associated with the rising sun and ascending smoke, in the north and east, and include rites connected with fertility and abundance. In this category are rituals for rice planting and harvest, life cycle stages such as birth and marriage, personal house and some health issues, and community renewal activities. Pigs and chickens are sacrificed. *Rambu Solo* rituals are paired with the setting sun and descending smoke, the south and the west, and consist mainly of the mortuary feasts where water buffalo and pigs are killed as offerings to the ancestors.

Funerals are a key depiction of Toraja custom and a major draw for the tourist industry. They are also opportunities for Toraja people to solidify their relationships in their kinship groups. Elaborate contributions to a funeral, for example, provide individuals a place to prove not only their devotion to a deceased parent, but also create a forum to launch a claim for a share of that parent's land. The amount of land an individual inherits from the deceased might depend on the number of buffalo that person presented for killing at the funeral. Thus, feasting at funerals is highly competitive because claims to descent are based not only on blood relationships, but also on the social recognition of the relationship through public displays. The feasting, however, also puts in motion a complex distribution of the meat which depends on one's status in a particular *tongkonan* and activates an elaborate network of debts and obligations that is passed on to succeeding generations.

Displays of wealth at funerals have special meanings for non-Christian, traditionalist Torajans. They believe that life in the afterworld follows the pattern of life on earth, and that the souls of sacrificed animals will follow their owners to the afterworld (*Puya*, "the land of souls") which is under the earth. Expensive death feasts are seen as the way for the deceased to reach *Puya* and the judge Pong Lalongdong. Following that encounter, the deceased may ascend a mountain up to heaven and join ancestors as stars who protect people and rice crops. For Christians who follow Biblical teachings on salvation, death, and the afterlife, the funeral feasts are more social functions than spiritual realities. In an effort to bring clarity for Christians who participate in the funeral ceremonies, the Gereja Toraja, the largest Protestant organization in Tana Toraja, published a 267-page volume on the ceremonies entitled, *Christian Perceptions of Rambu Solo*.

Many years ago, Christians full of new religious zeal, anxious to separate from the old ways, destroyed their ancestral *tongkonan* houses, causing ruptures in social relations with kin who were outraged at the desecration of their traditional homes. The Christian church rationale for the destruction was the explicit connection between *tongkonan* structures and spirit rituals. For example, when *tongkonan* structures are renewed, their distinctively shaped roofs are replaced, and members of the social group gather for a ritual in which trancelike dances are used to call the spirits for help. Elaborate carvings with spirit associations decorated many structures. However, over the years, rather than destroy *tongkonans*, some Torajas have started to Christianize the house carvings, incorporating different motifs such as the cross. Instead of appeals to the spirits in a house dedication, Christians call on God to bless the house and ask the Holy Spirit to empower present and future generations.

SARAH MANAPA

See also **Indonesia**

Further Reading

Adams, Kathleen M., "Making-up the Toraja? The Appropriation of Tourism, Anthropology, and Museums for Politics in Upland Sulawesi, Indonesia," *Ethnology*, 34 (1995)

Cohen, Margot, "Funeral Rights," *Far Eastern Economic Review*, 161, no. 3 (1998)

Hollan, D., and J. C. Wellenkamp, *Contentment and Suffering: Culture and Experience in Toraja*, New York: Columbia University Press, 1993

Tangdilintin, L.T., and M. Syafei, *Toraja: An Introduction to a Unique Culture*, Rantepao, Ujung Pandang: Lepongan Bulan Foundation, 1975

Waterson, Roxana, "Entertaining a Dangerous Guest: Sacrifice and Play in the Ma'pakorong Ritual of the Sa'dan Toraja," *Oceania*, 66, no. 2 (1995)

Torres Strait Islanders

Capsule Summary

Location: Torres Strait, Queensland, Australia, located between mainland Australia and Papua New Guinea

Total Population: Approximately 30 000, of whom 6 000 live in Torres Strait

Languages: English, Meriam Mer, Kala Kaway Ya, Kalaw Lagaw Ya., Torres Strait Creole

Religion: Christian

One of Australia's two indigenous groups, Torres Strait Islanders are a seafaring people who inhabit the islands between southern Papua New Guinea and northeast mainland Australia, in the state of Queensland. The majority of Torres Strait Islanders now live in the Queensland cities of Cairns, Townsville, Brisbane, Mackay, and Rockhampton. The Torres Strait islands, comprising over 100, are divided into four groups, with the inhabited ones being the top western islands comprising Boigu, Dauan, and Saibai Islands; the eastern islands comprising Stephen (Ugar), Murray (Mer), and Darnley (Erub) Islands; the central and near western islands comprising Badu, Mabuiag, Moa, Yam, Coconut (Waraber), Sue (Poruma), and Yorke (Masig) Islands; and the inner islands comprising Prince of Wales (Muralag), Hammond (Kiriri), Thursday, and Horn (Narupai) Islands. There are also two significant mainland islander communities, Bamaga and Seisia, which are located on northern Cape York Peninsula at the southern end of Torres Strait. Thursday Island is the commercial and administrative centre.

Melanesian in origin, the population was enriched by a significant influx of Pacific Islanders, Japanese, Malays, Filipinos, Indians, Chinese, and Singhalese in the late nineteenth century. The language of the eastern Torres Strait is Meriam Mer, which is related to the Papuan language groups. Kala Lagaw Ya, which is related to Aboriginal languages, is the central islands language, while Kalaw Kawaw Ya, a dialect of Kala Lagaw Ya, is the language of the top western islands. Kalaw Kawaw Ya is still widely spoken, but the others are considered to be endangered. Torres Strait Creole is the lingua franca, with English being used for official purposes.

The first European explorer to sail into the area was the Spanish navigator Luis Vaez de Torres, in 1606, but it was not until the early nineteenth century, when the strait became an important navigation route for ships traveling from the Australian colonies to Great Britain, that interaction with islanders increased.

The discovery of commercial quantities of beche-de-mer and pearl shell in the 1860s led to a rapid influx of fishing interests and the beginning of colonial occupation. The introduction of Christianity by the London Missionary Society (LMS) in 1871 also had a profound impact. The colony of Queensland moved swiftly to bring the islands under its control, annexing the northern ones. In 1877 Thursday Island was established as the commercial and administrative center.

The impact of European expansion into the Torres Strait was dramatic. Islanders were decimated by introduced diseases, and Christianity was propagated and adopted. Pacific Islanders and other foreigners who crewed the fishing boats settled and married local women, while many islanders now had to work on the boats to pay for European goods and dowries.

Under the benevolent Government Resident John Douglas, (1885-1904), the power of the LMS was curbed and elected councils formed to advise the European teacher-supervisors who administered the island communities. Following Douglas' death, Islanders were brought under the same restrictive legislation applying to Australian Aborigines. They were forced to endure a form of internal colonialism which treated them as a separate race who would gain little by participation in Australian life.

Resentment over restrictive conditions in the Torres Strait fishing industry culminated in the Maritime Strike of 1936, the first organized Islander challenge to European authority. During World War II the Islanders played a vital role against the Japanese, when over 700 men enlisted in the Torres Strait Light Infantry Battalion. This was recognized, a gradual lessening of state government restrictions resulted. The post war period was also characterized by extensive migration to mainland Queensland, primarily in search of improved employment opportunities and living conditions.

With Commonwealth involvement in Torres Strait affairs from the 1970s, the period of internal colonialism ended. The Mabo native title decision of 1992, recognizing Torres Strait Islander occupation prior to British colonization, was followed by further successful land and sea claims. In 1994 the Torres Strait Regional Authority (TSRA), a Commonwealth statutory authority, was established, and there is an ongoing campaign for self-determination and autonomy.

Traditional Torres Strait society was a rich and complex culture, revolving around the oceans and the seasons. There was an extensive trade and bartering system between the inhabited islands and with the mainland peoples of New Guinea and Cape York. A warring people, interisland conflict and raids were an ongoing occurrence, with ritual cannibalism of enemies practiced. Religion and sorcery were all pervasive and powerful, providing the framework for the conduct and regulation of society. Hunters and fishermen, they lived on a diet of dugong, turtle, and fish, as well as fruit and vegetables from their gardens.

In 1871 the London Missionary Society established a mission on Darnley Island. This seminal event, known as the *Coming of the Light*, is celebrated and commemorated annually on July 1. While Islanders embraced Christianity, they have retained their traditional stories and beliefs. Unlike Australian Aborigines, they were not displaced or removed from their homelands, and have maintained close and enduring ties with the sea, continuing to utilize and exploit its resources.

The introduction and assimilation of Pacific Islanders and other non-Europeans into Torres Strait society has resulted in a vibrant and unique culture. Known as *Ailen Kustom,* it is a source of pride, unity, and strength, bonding Torres Strait Islanders throughout the region and the mainland. Communal feastings, where turtle and dugong are eaten, are a regular occurrence, followed by traditional singing and dancing. Torres Strait Islander art and sculpture is also very distinctive, with many artists combining traditional motifs and forms with contemporary styles.

JEREMY HODES

See also **Australia; Melanesians; Papua New Guinea**

Further Reading

Beckett, Jeremy, *Torres Strait Islanders: Custom and Colonialism*, Cambridge: Cambridge University Press, 1987
Ganter, Regina, *The Pearl-Shellers of Torres Strait: Resource Use, Development and Decline, 1860s–1960s*, Melbourne: Melbourne University Press, 1994
Haddon, Alfred Cort, editor, *Reports of the Cambridge Anthropological Expedition to the Torres Straits*, 6 vols., New York: Johnson Reprint, 1971
Mullins, Steve, *Torres Strait: A History of Colonial Occupation and Culture Contact, 1864–1897*, Rockhampton: Central Queensland University Press, 1994
Sharp, Noni, *Stars of Tagai: The Torres Strait Islanders*, Canberra: Aboriginal Studies Press, 1993
Singe, John, *The Torres Strait: People and History*, Brisbane: University of Queensland Press, 1989
Wilson, Lindsay, *Thathilgaw Emeret Lu: A Handbook of Traditional Torres Strait Islands Material Culture*, Brisbane: Dept. of Education, 1988
———, *Kerkar Lu: Contemporary Artefacts of the Torres Strait Islanders*, Brisbane: Department of Education, 1993

Travelers (Irish Nomads)

Location: Ireland
Total Population: 25,000 in Ireland, more than 25,000 of Traveler heritage elsewhere in the world
Languages: English and *Shelta,* an English-Irish creole
Religion: Roman Catholic

Travelers are a minority ethnic group of Ireland distinctly separate from mainstream Irish society possessing its own traditions and social customs, most notable of which is a historical tradition of itinerancy. Although the Travelers are Ireland's largest ethnic minority group, they compose less than one percent of the population of Ireland, with approximately 23,000 people in the Republic of Ireland and 1,500 in Northern Ireland. Approximately 15,000 Irish Travelers have migrated to Britain, 10,000 to the United States, and smaller numbers to Australia, New Zealand, South Africa, and Canada. Until recent times Irish Travelers were referred to as *tinkers*, a word derived from the Irish word *tinceard* (meaning "tinsmith"), in reference to their occupation as tinsmiths and metalworkers. The name *tinker* is now generally used only as a derogatory term.

Irish Travelers have existed for centuries in Ireland, but their origins are unknown and highly debated. Because of the similarities of their nomadic lifestyles, in the past researchers incorrectly identified Travelers as related to Romani Gypsies. However, the Romani population in Ireland is quite small, there is no genetic evidence that the two ethnic groups are related, and most modern research concludes that Irish Travelers are indigenous to Ireland. Theories abound as to the origins of the Travelers' nomadic lifestyle and worldview. Some believe that they are residual members of an ancient class of wandering poets, or the descendents of medieval craftspeople who traveled the Irish countryside making goods in exchange for food and lodgings. Others believe that Travelers are the descendants of landed gentry pushed off their property by the English during different times of social and political turmoil. A third theory postulates that Travelers are the descendents of those who were left homeless as a result of the Great Irish Famine of the 1840s and 1850s. In all likelihood each of these factors have played some part in the establishment of the Traveler community.

During the course of Irish history, hundreds of thousands of settled Irish were forced out of their homes due to poverty, but not all became Irish Travelers—many were able to resettle when times were better, while others emigrated to America, England, Canada, or Australia. However, those who chose the life of the road gradually developed their own ethnic identity focusing upon a common adaptation to nomadism. Because Irish Travelers generally did not own land or pursue stable wage employment, they were forced to be resourceful and pursue subsistence by performing a variety of jobs and services for members of the settled community. The dominant trade of most Travelers was tinsmithing, but depending upon the season they also traded horses and donkeys, cleaned chimneys, worked as seasonal laborers and farmhands, or peddled wares. Women Travelers were also known by the settled community for their storytelling and fortune-telling abilities. During the harsh winter months some Travelers, particularly women and children, resorted to scavenging and begging. Prior to the late 1800s, most Travelers journeyed by foot and carried their goods on their backs or in pushcarts. After the 1870s many Travelers used tents or horse-drawn carts. The barrel top wagon was introduced into Ireland after World War I, and in the following decade Traveler caravans became more common. Travelers usually journeyed within a small area of the country, camping along the outskirts of towns and villages. The average length of stay in a village or town was generally a week or two, but this depended on the length of time work was available, the relationship between the settled community and the Traveler group, and the weather.

The nuclear family was the basic social unit in traditional Traveler society. Travelers journeyed in small groups, usually consisting of two to four closely related nuclear families, because larger bands would have more difficulties finding adequate work or resources from settled communities. However, Travelers considered themselves to be members of a much larger extended family. Social events such as weddings, funerals, and fairs allowed the occasion for extended families to act as a collective, where they sang and danced, shared stories and news, and chose suitable marriage partners for their children. Most Travelers married other Travelers, but in the event that a Traveler married an outsider, the settled person was never accepted as a true Traveler, even if he or she conformed to the Traveler lifestyle. Traveler families are larger than the settled population, and are devoutly religious Roman Catholics. A unique feature of Traveler culture was the use of a creole language called *Shelta* or the *Cant,* comprised of a mixture of Irish Gaelic and English. *Shelta* was first devised as a means of maintaining secrecy and to disguise their speech in front of non-Travelers. Today, *Shelta* is mainly used as a method of reinforcing community ties. Although English is the primary language of most Travelers, *Shelta* is still taught to Traveler children from birth.

After World War II the need for most of the Travelers' traditional crafts and skills was eliminated as a result of improved technology, industrialization, and agricultural mechanization. Consequently, many Travelers were forced to migrate to urban areas in search of new sources of income. Dublin became a favored location for Traveler migration from the 1960s because of governmental efforts to assimilate Travelers into mainstream Irish culture by providing them with money, housing, and supplies. Today a few Travelers still travel across the country in caravans or on foot, but most have now adapted to a more settled lifestyle. Less than half live in regular homes or housing projects, while the rest live in mobile homes or trailers parked on the side of the road, in empty lots, or in fields.

Despite governmental efforts, the quality of life of the Traveler community has generally not improved during the latter part of the twentieth century. Aside from those living in homes or housing projects, most Travelers do not have access to running water, heat, or electricity. Health care and education are not accessible to many Travelers, and as a result, infant mortality is three times higher than the national average, life expectancy is at least ten years shorter than the settled population, and ninety percent of travelers are illiterate. Much of the settled community considers the Traveler community to be responsible for their own plight and their encampments to be eyesores and health hazards. Travelers are often the victims of racism, are frequently barred from schools, dances, and pubs, and are sometimes targeted by pickets and mob attacks. However, in recent years advocacy groups, often led by Travelers themselves, have become more active in their efforts to generate support to improve the living conditions of the Traveler community.

ERIN STAPLETON-CORCORAN

See also **Ireland**

Further Reading

Gmelch, George, *The Irish Tinkers: The Urbanization of an Itinerant People*. Prospect Heights, Illinois: Waveland Press, 1985

Gmelch, Sharon, *Nan: The Life of an Irish Travelling Woman*, Prospect Heights, Illinois: Waveland Press, 1986

Helleiner, Jane, *Irish Travellers: Racism and the Politics of Culture*, Toronto: University of Toronto Press, 2000

Mary McCann, Séamas Ó Síocháin, and Joseph Ruane, editors, *Irish Travellers: Culture & Ethnicity*, Belfast: Institute of Irish Studies, 1984

Oppersdorff, Mathias, *People of the Road; The Irish Travellers*, Syracuse, New York: Syracuse University Press, 1997

Ó Riain, Seán, *Solidarity with Travellers: A Story of Settled People Making a Stand for Travellers*, Dublin: Roadside Books, 2000

Tribes: India (Adivasis/Scheduled Tribes)

The tribal communities in India consist of a large number and a great variety of ethnic groups with different linguistic, racial, religious, and occupational characteristics. The tribal groups are spread over the entire country. A classification of the tribes based on any of the racial or ethnic criteria has not been very successful because of the complexity, diversity, intermixing, migration, and different dialects of the tribal people. However, extensive research has been conducted on some of the tribes in India out of administrative necessity by the British from the nineteenth century on and out of scholarly and academic interest and humanitarian reasons after India gained complete independence from the British in 1948. The number of tribes and subgroups, according to one of the studies conducted by Anthropological Survey of India was 461 tribal groups including subgroups (Singh, 1998). However, the government has recognized 573 communities as Scheduled Tribes (Heitzman and Worden, 1996) and the number has varied over time (Singh, 1998). The official listing published by the Central Government of India is subject to change due to additions or deletions because of the lack of clear-cut criteria for identification, classification, and distinction of the tribal groups and people. The 1931 census estimated them to be 22 million, in 1941 the figure was 10 million, and in 1961 it was 30 million.

The issue of identification of tribes has also been significantly politicized in India in recent years because of the benefits associated with such a classification. The Banjaras of Andhra Pradesh are classified as a Scheduled Tribe but not in the neighboring state of Maharashtra (Heitzman and Worden, 1996). The total number of the tribal population according to the Indian Census of 1991 was estimated to be 68 million or approximately 8.1 percent of the total population. The number of tribal refugees moving in and out of the country from Bangladesh, Burma, and China and the migration of the tribal people into cities makes it extremely difficult to get an accurate count. It is estimated that the current tribal population in India is around 80 million, thus making it the largest tribal population of any country in the world. It constitutes about a quarter of the world's indigenous population.

The Scheduled Tribes have in the past traditionally stayed in isolated or separated regions and some of them included forests and hills. Most of the tribes have been in contact with the Hindus for more than 2000 years.

However, the tribal groups are quite varied and heterogeneous. No typical description of the tribal groups would be individually applicable to the different groups spread throughout India. In the case of literacy, for example, it can be stated that the general level of literacy in the tribes is considerably lower than the rest of the Indian population. The literacy rates, as per the 1991 census was 30 percent for the Scheduled Tribes, compared to 52 percent for the national average. However, the literacy rates in the tribal groups range as high as 80 percent or more to lower than 10 percent of the population. Similarly, the percentage of tribal population in different parts of the country varies quite significantly, from a high of 90 percent of the population in the northern states such as Arunachal Pradesh, Meghalaya, Mizoram and Nagaland, to less than 2 percent of the population in the states of Kerala, Tamilnadu, and Uttar Pradesh. Similarly, the stereotypical characterization of all the tribal communities as a nomadic, forest-based, hunting, food-gathering, and foraging would be misleading, though the economy of some tribal groups are still forest-based and dependent on the resources of the forests. Currently, many tribal members have taken up different occupations. They work in areas outside their own village or territory, have entered into government service or work for private businesses and industries. The tribes also vary in terms of their population size, ranging from 7 million for the Gonds to less than a hundred Chaimals (Heitzman and Worden, 1996). Again, for example, though the majority of the tribal community is egalitarian, there are large tribes like the Gonds that are highly stratified and hierarchical (Heitzman and Worden, 1996).

Though most of these groups consider themselves as Hindus, Muslims, Buddhists, or Christians, some of the tribes have incorporated beliefs and practices from more than one religion and some other tribes observe native religious rituals and practices. Many tribal groups have their own local deities. In some other tribes, it would not be uncommon to have a Hindu priest conducting a marriage ceremony. The tribal beliefs and rituals are quite varied. For example, they range from nonhunting groups to headhunting practiced by some Naga groups in the nineteenth century. The variations among these groups are reflected in the nature and composition of the family, marital customs and practices, and the diets of the tribal groups. The proselytizing of the tribes to Christianity has been viewed with alarm by the Indian government. There is also an ongoing effort, supported by some groups in the population to eliminate the converted groups from the list of Scheduled Tribes. The nomenclature, terms of identification of tribes and tribal groups in India have changed many times over a period of time. There is no general agreement among the anthropologists, administrators, and the general population in India about the term *tribe* (Ghurye, 1959). Though the names of the individual tribes were commonly known all over India, the term *tribe* with a common identity that encompassed all the different individual tribes was not used prior to the British colonial rule in India. The terms *caste* and *tribe* were used interchangeably in the nineteenth century. In the 1901 census, the term *tribe* was designated to groups that practiced animism. It was changed later to the practice of tribal religion and in the 1931 census the term *primitive tribe* was used (Xaxa, 2003). In the nineteenth century, the British administrators also used a stereotypical term, *criminal tribes*, to identify the tribes that were reputed for criminal behavior, and the term was later dropped. The term *Scheduled Tribes* was introduced by the British in 1935, again for administrative purposes. The term

continued to be used even after India gained independence from the British. The term, *Scheduled Tribes*, has a legal connotation now, which refers to the tribes that are listed in the official government documents under article 342. Only the groups thus included in the list can claim the special benefits and advantages provided by the Central and the State governments. The tribal groups are now generally using the term *Adivasis* as the preferred term to describe themselves, though the Government of India has contested that designation because many of the tribes have migrated from their original inhabitations or residential areas. The term *Adivasis* has multiple connotations that mean original inhabitants, the first group of dwellers, aborigines, or indigenous people. The terms *Adivasis* and *Scheduled Tribes* are used here synonymously.

Traditionally, the tribal groups have had a low social standing in India because of many negative stereotypes, such as uncivilized, forest dwelling, and uneducated. Most of the tribes were also supposed to belong to the lower castes. Many efforts are being made to remove the stigma and improve their economic status and social standing. One such effort is the reservation of seats, which is an affirmative system based on quotas. The Scheduled Tribes (along with the Scheduled Castes, another list published by the government) were granted reserved seats in the legislature, educational institutions, and government service. The purpose of the quota system was to compensate for the injustices of the past by providing educational, political, and economic opportunities that were denied to the tribal population for many centuries. It was considered as a matter of social justice because the tribes were historically disadvantaged. This arrangement has raised many questions (Galanter, 1984). The reservations were a form of affirmative action system that actually specified quotas intended to last for 10 years after the Indian constitution was adopted in 1950, but the reservation system has been renewed again and again for 10 years each time. The system is in operation even today, more than 50 years since the adoption of the constitution, and the advisability of such an arrangement is being questioned. In spite of all the regulations and the quota system, the Scheduled Tribes are underrepresented in the Class I category, the upper most level of the government.

Changes and Challenges

Currently, the tradition of peaceful coexistence among the tribal groups and the other communities in India has been continued with some significant exceptions. Cases of mass murder or intertribal warfare have been relatively rare. However, most of the tribal groups continue to be subject to prejudice, discrimination, exploitation, and atrocities. The Indian papers routinely report these incidents. There has been a continuous wave of protest movements by the tribal groups in India. The protests arise from a number of concerns and can be classified into five major categories, namely, tribal identity and related cultural issues, social acceptance and equality, political power, economic opportunity, social justice and human rights. The changing Indian landscape has brought many opportunities as well as problems. Tribal identity has so far shown remarkable resilience in the face of all types of changes, including linguistic assimilation or dissolution of the dialects used by the tribes. It is very hard to continue with the past traditions and beliefs against the onslaught of popular media through the TV, influx of a large number of refugees in the northeastern part of India, and introduction of other technological innovations. New occupations, transportation, communication, and new technologies have intruded on the old system. However, the beautiful works of art, woodcarvings, simple musical instruments, and spectacular costumes of the tribal people are uniformly admired, and their rich contributions to the Indian society and culture are widely acknowledged. Social acceptance and equality revolves around the issues of prejudice, discrimination, and lower social status in the caste hierarchy. The rights of self-determination, self-government, and autonomy are crucial to the survival of minority groups.

Tribal people in India had enjoyed autonomy until the sixteenth century and they are demanding some form of autonomy again. They were also involved in uprisings against the British rulers from the eighteenth century on (Vidyarthi and Rai, 1977). The tribal groups have demanded autonomy to avoid being a small minority, ignored and exploited by others. The insurgency in Nagaland has revolved around these issues for more than 50 years. Two other states were carved out through violent acts of rebellion, skirmishes, and violent actions.

In most cases, in spite of the reservation system, political power is exercised by the elite groups. Even in those states with tribal members in political control, officials from nontribal groups run the bureaucratic system. Economic opportunities revolve around issues of employment and sustainable economic development. Poverty levels for the tribal groups are more than

twice the national average rates. When new mining or forest industry is introduced in a tribal area, most of the economic benefits accrue to the new people who migrate to that area and not to the tribal people in that area. When a new dam is built, the tribal groups are relocated to different parts of the country that are not suitable or hospitable to them, and many of them return to the vicinity of their former areas much poorer and more handicapped than before. Traditionally, most of the tribes have relied on the land, forests, and rivers for their sustenance. Economic development reduces the access of the tribal people to these resources. Exploitation by moneylenders and a judiciary that is partial to the landlords and the police are other examples. The tribal people often have communal ownership of land and individual property ownership is not commonly practiced by them. They do not necessarily have papers or documents to prove their ownership. Tribes are generally self-sufficient and an increasing dependence on trade brings many hardships, resulting in land and forest alienation. The rate of unemployment and underemployment is extremely high among the tribal people. Child labor still exists in spite of efforts to minimize it and ban it in hazardous occupations. The issue of social justice and human rights has gained urgency because of atrocities committed by the citizenry, police, or army, including imprisonment, torture, and violence against male and female members of the tribe. Though special officers have been appointed by the government to prevent and check for atrocities against the Scheduled Tribes and Scheduled Castes, such appointments have not stopped the violence against the Scheduled Tribes.

A number of programs (schemes) have been undertaken by the central government and state governments to improve the economic and educational conditions. These include, for example, subsidy and loan programs, irrigation including bored well schemes, animal husbandry, subsidy for trade, learning of vocational skills and agriculture. The governments have set up other projects, such as the Integrated Tribal Development Projects, Tribal Research Institutes, cooperative banks, The Central Sector Scheme, National Scheduled Tribes Financial Development Corporations, and a large number of welfare schemes. In addition, there are also a very large number of nongovernmental or semigovernmental organizations to help the tribal groups. There are also many other projects initiated by the tribal groups. Clearly the outcomes are mixed. The efforts of the government have succeeded in some areas but clearly failed in other areas. The poverty level, unemployment, and low level of literacy in general, are clear indications of the areas where they have failed. There is a strong need for adult education in the tribal areas. In the schools, for example, good teachers avoid the tribal areas or each school is run by a single teacher. There is also a high dropout rate or low attendance because the books are not in the tribal language or are irrelevant to the experiences of the children and the schools are often inaccessible.

However, there are significant changes in the political composition of some states. An overwhelming majority of the tribal population in some of the newly created states in India has resulted in the reservation of most of the state legislative assembly seats for Scheduled Tribes. In 1987, 59 of 60 seats in Arunachal Pradesh, 39 of 40 in Mizoram, and 55 of 60 in Nagaland were reserved for the Scheduled Tribes (Research, Reference, and Training Division, 2002). Such a proviso is likely to significantly alter the balance of power between the Scheduled Tribes and the rest of the population in some of these states, by allowing the Scheduled Tribes to avoid competition with the non-tribal groups. It is important to see if the safeguards for the Scheduled Tribes based on the founding fathers' views will work in this case (Saxena, 1981).

It is too early to predict the long-term outcome of these changes, but they deserve a close scrutiny.

SUBHASH SONNAD

See also **India; Untouchables (Harijans/Dalits/Scheduled Castes)**

Further Reading

Galanter, Marc, *Competing Equalities: Law and the Backward Classes in India*, Bombay: Oxford University Press, 1984

Ghurye, G.S., *The Scheduled Tribes*, Bombay: Bombay Popular Book Depot, 1959

Heitzman, James, and Robert L. Worden, editors, *India, a Country Study*, Washington DC: Federal Research Division, 1996

Research, Reference and Training Division India 2002, *A Reference Annual*, New Delhi, Ministry of Information and Broadcasting, Government of India, 2002

Saxena H.S., *Safeguards for Scheduled Castes and Tribes: Founding Fathers' Views*, New Delhi: Uppal Publishing House, 1981

Singh, K.S., editor, *People of India National Series Volume III: The Scheduled Tribes*, Calcutta, India: Oxford University Press, 1998

Vidyarthi, L.P., and B.K. Rai, *The Tribal Culture of India*, Colombia, Missouri: South Asia Books, 1977

Xaxa, Virginius. "Tribes in India," in *Oxford India Companion to Sociology and Social Anthropology*, edited by Veena Das, New Delhi: Oxford University Press, 2003

Trimble, David (Northern Ireland)

David Trimble is one of the most significant figures in current Northern Irish politics, though his past activities suggest that he was a seemingly unlikely candidate to assume the critical role that began when he became the leader of the Ulster Unionist Party (UUP) in 1995. He had been a barrister and lecturer in law at Queen's University in Belfast since 1968. He was not very active in politics through the early years of his career, but following the British government's decision to dissolve the Northern Irish Parliament in 1972 in the wake of IRA and Protestant paramilitary violence, he became disenchanted with the course of politics, which led to his involvement in the controversial Vanguard movement in the 1970s. Vanguard, or the Vanguard Unionist Progressive Party (VUUP), was a far-right Northern Irish

group that broke away from the UUP. Vanguard was founded in March 1973 by Protestant hardliner, William Craig. The group advocated the full independence of Northern Ireland from the United Kingdom and resisted both violent and nonviolent Catholic efforts at securing increased civil and economic rights. The party also called for the forced dispersal of the Irish Republican Army (IRA) and a reversal of all previous reform undertaken by Brian Faulkner and his UUP predecessors.

In interviews with one of his most recent biographers, Henry McDonald, Trimble wrote off his involvement in the Vanguard party to youthful inexperience, noting that he was only 29 during the strike period following the meetings at Sunningdale between representatives of the Irish and British governments. These meetings were the first of many called in an effort to stem the tide of violence in Northern Ireland. Some historians take Trimble at his word that his involvement in the party was nothing more than a youthful flirtation with radical right-wing politics, yet Trimble was one of the leaders of the damaging 1974 strikes that followed the Sunningdale meetings that attempted substantial political reforms, including the granting of civil rights to Northern Irish Catholics. Trimble remained active in the party until it fell apart amidst internal squabbles in 1978.

Trimble rejoined the UUP and at first seemed content to continue a nonpolitical career as a law professor. In the late 1980s, however, he gradually began to establish himself within the UUP, associating himself with the block that sought to have political autonomy for Northern Ireland. In 1990, he was elected to Parliament for the constituency of Upper Bann. With a burgeoning reputation in the party, he then went on to become a member of the UUP delegation at another round of multiparty peace talks in 1991.

In 1995, his hard-line, pro-Protestant stance in the controversy surrounding the stand-off at Drumcree near the town of Portdadown over a disputed parade by local members of the Orange Order, the largest Protestant organization in Northern Ireland, only cemented his reputation as a staunch opponent of reform. His uncompromising stand helped him to win the UUP leadership in September of 1995. In one of those rich ironies of which history is so fond, Trimble then became the UUP point person in the peace talks that had begun in 1993 with the issuing of the Anglo-Irish Agreement. The former hardliner of Drumcree seemed to sense that the audience for Northern Irish politics was becoming increasingly international. Pressure was coming from Ireland, England, and the United States with greater urgency than ever before.

With all the knowledge and skill of an expert lawyer, Trimble went to work on forging the peace, working especially closely with the Northern Irish Catholic politician, John Hume. Multiparty talks concluded with the Good Friday, or Belfast, Agreement on April 10, 1998. He backed the deal despite the opposition of more than half his Parliamentary colleagues, though later won more support for his approach from the party. The Agreement called for wide-ranging reform in Northern Ireland, including electoral reform, antidiscrimination laws, job-creation plans, and the comprehensive reorganization of the RUC, often viewed with suspicion by Catholics and

accused of collusion with Protestant paramilitaries. The significance of the Agreement was bolstered when Trimble and John Hume shared the 1998 Nobel Peace Prize for their joint efforts to bring peace and stability to Northern Ireland.

Although Protestant Unionist opponents regard him as the man who sold out to their longstanding republican enemies, and nationalist critics have little faith in his willingness to fully recognize their rights, most observers agree that the Good Friday Agreement could not have been done without Trimble. Only he had the negotiating skills and the command of the issues to broker a deal, and only he possessed the political clout among Protestants to grant it legitimacy. Trimble served as First Minister in Northern Ireland from 1998 through 2003, a term in which he often fought more with his own party than with politicians from the SDLP or Sinn Féin.

On the heels of electoral losses in November 2003, the UUP's influence has waned, with important members switching to the more conservative, anti-Catholic Democratic Unionist Party, a development that led Peter Robinson, deputy leader of the DUP, to boast that "Unionism is under new management." Regardless of his party's, or his own political fate, Trimble has earned an important and distinguished place in the history of Northern Ireland—he and John Hume brought the embattled province closer to peace than any who had tried before them.

Biography

William David Trimble. Born: October 15, 1944 in Bangor, County Down Northern Ireland. Educated at Bangor Grammar School and Queen's University Belfast, graduated LL.B (1st class) in 1968, qualified as a Barrister at Law, 1969. Lecturer in Law, Queen's University, 1968-1977, Senior Lecturer, 1977-1989. Head of Department, Commercial and Property Law, 1981-89. Convention Member for South Belfast, Vanguard Unionist party, 1975-1976. Member, Devolution Group, 1979-84. Vice Chairman, Lagan Valley Unionist Association, Ulster Unionist Party (UUP), 1983-1985, Chairman, 1985. Founder and Chairman, Ulster Society, 1985-1990; Chairman, Lisburn Ulster Club 1985-1986. Chairman UUP Legal Committee, 1989-1995. Honorary Secretary of the Ulster Unionist Council, 1990-1996. Chairman, Constitutional Development Committee, 1985. Member of Parliament at Westminster (London), 1990-Present. Leader, UUP, 1995. Winner, with John Hume, Nobel Peace Prize, 1998. First Minister, Northern Ireland Assembly, 1998-2001, 2002-Present.

JOHN H. DAVIS

See also **Catholics in Northern Ireland; Hume, John (Northern Ireland Catholic); Northern Ireland**

Further Reading

Cochrane, Feargal, *Unionist Politics and the Politics of Unionism since the Anglo-Irish Agreement*, Cork: Cork University Press, 2001

Hennessey, Thomas, *The Northern Ireland Peace Process: Ending the Troubles*, London: Gill & Macmillan, 2000
McDonald, Henry, *Trimble,* London: Bloomsbury, 2001
McKay, Susan, *Northern Protestants: An Unsettled People*, Belfast: Blackstaff Press, 2000
Mulholland, Marc, *The Longest War: Northern Ireland's Troubled History*, Oxford: Oxford University Press, 2002

Tuareg

Capsule Summary

Location: Sahara Desert region of West Africa, especially northern Mali and central Niger
Total Population: approximately 1 to 2 million
Language: Tamacheq
Religion: Muslim

The Tuareg are a desert-dwelling people spread across a vast expanse of North and Western Africa, but now centered primarily in the western Sahara Desert and the Sahelian region of West Africa in the modern-day nations of Mail and Niger. Initially desert traders, camel herders, and warriors, many Tuareg are now merchants and agriculturalists in the southern desert side region of West Africa. Many have become security guards as well as leather and ornamental sword artisans for the tourist industry. Because of their widespread dispersion in several countries, including Mauritania, Algeria, Mali, Niger, and Libya, exact popu-lation figures are impossible to calculate. Estimates range from approximately 1 to 2 million Tuareg throughout North and West Africa. They are a minority in every country where they reside. In West African countries, they also constitute a distinguishable racial minority, being of Arab-Berber descent. They are often discriminated against and treated as outsiders by indigenous West African groups. In the 1990s, there were several serious Tuareg uprisings in northern Mali and northern Niger seeking economic development and greater autonomy from the black African-dominated governments. The Tuareg speak the Tamacheq language and are Muslims.

Precolonial History

The Tuareg claim descent from the Berbers of North Africa and are believed to have migrated southward into the Sahara Desert during the Arab invasions of North Africa in the seventh century. Beginning in about the tenth century, the nomadic, camel-herding Tuareg started to migrate even further southward from the central Sahara into the desert-side regions of West Africa, especially the region of modern-day Mali and Niger. Owing to increasingly difficult conditions in the Sahara, these migrations continued over the centuries, placing the majority of the Tuareg population along the southern edge of the desert where there was better pasture and increased trade with savanna peoples. The Tuareg quickly dominated most of the trans-Saharan trade networks and links between the desert and savanna regions of West Africa.

The Tuareg formed several political confederations, called *kels*, in both the desert and desert-side regions. The confederations ranged from a few hundred people to several thousand. At the lowest level was the camp, consisting of a few families and their dependents. Groups of camps formed a section or *tauchit*, headed by a noble-born, elder male chief. The sections formed together to form the confederation, or *kel*, which was headed by a commonly recognized leader. Regardless of their confederation or their primary location, the Tuareg embraced Islam and spoke the Tamacheq language. They also considered themselves superior to other ethnic groups in West Africa because of their Arab-Berber origins.

Two important confederations emerged in the southern desert edge in the fourteenth and fifteenth centuries. The Kel Eway and Kel Gress in the savanna combined their traditional camel pastoralist and trading occupations with agriculture. They also raided neighboring farming people for crops and slaves. The slaves of the Tuareg were used to farm in the savanna and also served as porters in the trans-Saharan and other trades. Some of these raids gave the Tuareg control over several small savanna states which paid tribute to the Tuareg in slaves and agricultural goods. The Tuareg acquired a reputation for being fierce desert warriors and ruthless raiders.

By the fifteenth and sixteenth centuries, Tuareg society consisted of a complex hierarchy of numerous social groups, ranging from the Tuareg nobles to various levels of servile dependents. The nobles consisted of fair-skinned nomads who prided themselves on their North African origins. Some aristocratic nobles with large numbers of dependents were comparable to managers of large firms. These aristocrats invested in trade, agriculture, animal husbandry, and other economic pursuits while overseeing a large labor force of servile dependents. They also invested in raids, both on caravans and sedentary peoples. Other castes among the Tuareg included tribute-paying clients and then various strata of slaves, depending partly on how recently they were captured and partly on their loyalty to the nobility.

The Tuareg maintained a complex relationship with their servile dependents and recognized numerous levels of dependency which were usually rather fluid. For example, later generation slaves, or *iklan*, received considerably better treatment than newly captured peoples. They were often fairly well integrated into Tuareg society and could be freed either through self-redemption or manumission by their master. They then improved their status to that of freed slaves who could amass considerable wealth and improve their status. The *iklan* generally cultivated grains and vegetables on their owners' lands, and sometimes accompanied trade caravans into and across the Sahara Desert. Although always subordinate to the nobles and never fully accepted as pure Tuaregs, the *iklan* and other servile dependents were generally considered as junior members of the noble family, and played an important role in the Tuareg economy. Through loyalty and marriage, servile dependents could improve their status and condition. Hence the Tuareg people have always been a very diverse mixture of Arab, Berber, and West African.

Desert-dwelling Tuareg confederations also raided sedentary communities along the desert edge for agricultural goods and captives. These slaves were then transported into the desert where they worked in the salt mines or on the oases. Their treatment was much harsher than the slaves of the savanna confederations and they were frequently sold to other Tuareg groups in the desert. Many captives were also sold into the trans-Saharan trade and exported to North Africa and

the Middle East. Desert and desert-side confederations also exchanged slaves, camels, salt, and agricultural products. Raiding of caravans and travelers as well as of rival confederations was also an important economic activity of the Tuareg.

By the sixteenth century, Tuareg confederations had established control over numerous trans- Saharan trade routes linking West and North Africa. They also took control over several important trading centers such as Gao, Timbuktu, and Djenne, all in modern-day Mali. However, the Tuareg never established a strong centralized state. Numerous *kels* did join together to set up the sultanate of Agadez, headquartered in modern-day Niger, to regulate trade and arbitrate conflicts among the different confederations without threatening the power or autonomy of any of the individual *kels*. Despite the sultanate of Agadez, however, confederations in the region continued to attack one another's caravans and communities.

Colonial and Recent History

The arrival of the French in the region in the late nineteenth century seriously disrupted the economy and society of the Tuareg. While other groups were often easily conquered by colonial armies, the Tuareg fiercely resisted European occupation. In return, the government of French West Africa began a concerted campaign to subdue the Tuareg and then to force them to settle in agricultural villages. Throughout the early years of the twentieth century, when virtually all other groups in the region had been colonized, Tuareg resistance continued. Several confederations, notably the Kel Gress and Kel Eway, mounted uncoordinated attacks, preventing French subjugation of the Agadez region until about 1916. Desert-dwelling confederations remained independent even longer, repelling all French attempts at conquest until well into the 1920s. Eventually, however, all the confederations were subjugated under European rule.

Once under colonial rule, the Tuareg suffered significant setbacks. The abolition of slavery caused enormous upheaval among the Tuareg and their servile dependents, depriving the nobles of their primary source of labor and their dependents of security and work. Many dependents negotiated new relationships with their former masters. Others became refugees, forcing their former owners to become agriculturalists. The colonial administration also imposed high taxes on trans-Saharan trade and confiscated large numbers of camels from the Tuareg for use in their own military campaigns. These harsh measures resulted in a series of rebellions in the 1910s and 1920s that were brutally crushed by the French. The rebellions and their suppression caused further economic decline, destroying much farmland, wells, and crops. Some Tuareg subsequently fled the French colonies for Libya or Nigeria.

At independence, the Tuareg formed a significant minority in the countries of Mali and Niger which were dominated by West African peoples. In the 1970s, both Mali and Niger started mining for uranium in areas traditionally claimed by the Tuareg. The massive Sahelian droughts of the 1970s and 1980s also caused serious economic disruption for the Tuareg. A series of attacks on towns for supplies were brutally crushed by the military governments of Mali and Niger. Many Taureg fled into neighboring countries where they were usually treated harshly by the local peoples. Other Tuaregs left the desert permanently and moved into towns along the desert edge. The Tuareg have never been easily assimilated into West African societies and have often faced discrimination.

Ethnic Conflicts

In the 1990s, Tuareg uprisings in both northern Mali and Niger have been brutally suppressed. Thousands of Tuaregs have died and many more have fled into Burkina Faso, Algeria, Mauritania, and Libya. The violence has been fueled by disputes over land and trade routes but more importantly by what the Tuareg feel is their exclusion from the political affairs of the nations where they reside and economic discrimination both at the national and local levels. Some radical groups called for the formation of an independent all-Tuareg Saharan Republic carved out of Mali and Niger. Not surprisingly, the national governments quickly and brutally suppressed the rebellions which were poorly organized and not well-coordinated. In mid-1994, the signing of an agreement between the new civilian government of Mali and the Unified Movements and Fronts of Azawad, the leading dissident Tuareg group, granted limited autonomy to the region. It also provided for some economic development. The rebels agreed to a cease-fire and withdrew their call for an independent Tuareg nation. In Niger, a similar agreement between the main rebel group, the Organization of Armed Resistance, and the government was signed in 1995. It also provided for some limited autonomy as well as economic development in return for an end to calls of independence and the cessation of attacks. After the agreements, some refugees returned to the area. The violence has subsided considerably but there are sporadic outbreaks of violence between Tuareg and government forces. Talks continue but progress on economic development has been very slow, especially as Mali and Niger are among the poorest countries in the world and have scant resources.

Society

Tuareg society today is vastly different from that of precolonial times. Colonialism and then independence have had a greater impact on the Tuareg than that on most other West African groups. The decline and virtual disappearance of trans-Saharan trade as well as the abolition of slavery deeply undermined the Tuareg economy. The replacement of camels by automobiles as the primary vehicles crossing the Sahara desert and the loss of most camel herds during the droughts of the 1970s and 1980s removed a central element of Tuareg identity. The enormous environmental problems in the desert and desert-side regions, especially rapid desertification, likewise affected the Tuareg, many of whom became refugees seeking wage employment. Many Tuareg now make their living selling leather goods and ornamental swords to tourists in cities such as Timbuktu, Bamako, and Niamey. Others have become security guards for homes and businesses as well as joining police and military forces, relying on their reputation as fierce warriors and soldiers. The traditional social strata continues to exist, but largely in name only. Many Tuareg now speak West African languages, having abandoned Tamacheq. Given recent history and discrimination, it is unclear how long Tuareg customs and identity can survive.

ANDREW F. CLARK

See also **Berbers; Burkina Faso; Mali**

Further Reading

Baier, Stephen, *An Economic History of Central Niger*, Oxford: Clarendon Press, 1980

Baier, S., and Paul Lovejoy, "The Tuareg of the Central Sudan," in *Slavery in Africa*, edited by S. Miers and I Kopytoff, Madison, 1977

Briggs, L.C., *Tribes of the Sahara*, Cambridge: Harvard University Press, 1960

Charlick, Robert, *Niger: Personal Rule and Survival in the Sahel*, Boulder: Westview Press, 1991

Fugelstad, Finn, *A History of Niger 1850–1960*, Cambridge: University Press, 1983

Imperato, Pascal, *Mali: A Search for Direction*, Boulder: Westview Press, 1989

Keenan, Jeremy, *The Tuareg People of Ahaggar*, New York: St. Martin's Press, 1977

Norris, Henry, *The Tauregs*, Warminster: Aris and Philips, 1975

Turkey

Capsule Summary

Location: Southeastern Europe and southwestern Asia
Total Population: 68,109,469 (July 2003)
Language: Turkish (official), Kurdish, Arabic, Armenian, Greek
Religions: Muslim (99.8%) (mostly Sunni), other (0.2%) (mostly Christian and Jew)

The Republic of Turkey is located in southeastern Europe and southwestern Asia, bordering the Black Sea, between Bulgaria and Georgia, and bordering the Aegean Sea and the Mediterranean Sea, between Greece and Syria. The lands of Turkey are located at a point where the three continents making up the old world, Asia, Africa, and Europe, are closest to each other, and straddle the point where Europe and Asia meet. The surface area of Turkey, including the lakes, is 814,578 square kilometers (314,503 square miles). It is much larger than many European countries or even Texas in the US. Out of the total land, 97 percent is in Asia and this part is called Anatolia or Asia Minor; 3 percent is in Europe and is called Thrace. Although 97 percent of Turkey is located in Asia, in many respects it is accepted as a European country and as a result, Turkey takes its place in nearly all European contests and associations. Because of its geographical location the mainland of Anatolia has always found favor throughout history, and is the birthplace of many great civilizations. It has also been prominent as a center of commerce because of its land connections to three continents and the sea surrounding it on three sides.

The total population is approximately 68 million. Turkey is a parliamentary democracy. There are many languages spoken in the country and ethnically 80 percent of the population is Turkish, and 20 percent is estimated to be Kurdish. The second language is Kurdish, which is followed by Arabic, Armenian, Greek, and others. Per capita gross domestic product (GDP) is $7,300 (2002 estimate).

History

The Republic of Turkey, founded in 1923, has its roots in two historical sources deep in the depths of the past. One of these resources inherited by modern Turkey is the successful history of the Turks over more than 4,000 years. The other is the fact that Turks have been settled in Anatolia since the eleventh century.

According to the historical records of China, the earliest known Turks lived in Dzungaria, to the north of East Turkestan in 2000 BCE. During the 1500s BCE, the Turks scattered, becoming nomads and warrior tribes, and settling in the regions of Altai and the Tien Shan Mountains. Political, military, and climatic changes in this region from the second century on caused the nomadic tribes to establish settled civilizations along the edges of the steppes. The Huns settled in Central Asia and Europe; the Akhuns in Afghanistan and north India; the Oghuz in Iran and Anatolia; the Bulgars in the Balkans and on the banks of the Volga; the Sabars in Caucasia; the Pecheneks, Kipchaks, and Uzs in Eastern Europe and the Balkans; and the Uigurs in inner Asia. Thus, between the second century BCE. and the twentieth century CE the original Turkish tribes scattered themselves over an area of 18 million square kilometers (7 million square miles), and founded several states and empires. Meanwhile Anatolia, where Eastern and Western civilizations meet, nourished the most ancient civilizations of the world. The Hattis were the oldest known people of Anatolia; they attained a high level of civilization in 2500 BCE. The Hittite, who entered Anatolia via the Caucasus mountains, integrated with the Hattis and established the first social and political organization in Anatolia. The Hurrians, Luwians, Urartians, Phyrigians, Lydians, Carians, Lycians, Ionians, and Byzantines all established great civilizations here. Eventually, the Turks created three great states on this soil.

It was the Seljuks of Oghuz Turks who opened the doors of Anatolia for the Turks. They established a powerful empire in western Asia in 990 CE. In 1071 the Seljuk Emperor Alparslan reached the frontiers of Anatolia and defeated the Byzantine emperor, Romanus IV Diogenes at Malazgirt in Eastern Anatolia.

The Anatolian Seljuk State was based at Konya and owned a flowering civilization, but it was short-lived because of the attacks of the Mongols who defeated it fatally at the Battle of Erzincan in 1243. After this defeat, Anatolia broke up into several principalities. One of these, the Ottoman Turks, eventually reunited the other principalities previously under Seljuk domination and reestablished the unity of Anatolia.

Thus, they founded one of the largest and longest-lived empires of history and created a civilization and culture which reached its apogee in the sixteenth and seventeenth centuries under a succession of brilliant rulers, including Mehmet II, the Conqueror of Istanbul; Süleyman I, known in Europe as "the Magnificent"; and Murad IV, Conqueror of Baghdad and Yerevan. These sultans were not only brilliant generals and statesmen, but also highly educated men who wrote poetry and composed music within the Ottoman Court tradition and were generous patrons to the visual arts. From the end of seventeenth century, however, the Ottoman Empire went into a gradual decline, which culminated with the end of World War I.

During the war, the empire suffered a loss of 3.5 million casualties and, defeated by the Allies, signed an armistice at Mondros on October 30, 1918. Following this armistice, the Ottomans were forced to sign the Sevres Treaty on August 10, 1920, which aimed at dividing the lands of the empire. At this defining moment of history, under the leadership of Mustafa Kemal Atatürk, the Turkish nation waged the War of Independence, against the foreign powers to be able to live as a free, sovereign, and independent country. The War of Independence started on May 19, 1919 and ended by the proclamation of the Republic of Turkey on October 23, 1923. After the victory, the Turkish Grand National Assembly in Ankara abolished the office of the Sultan on November 1, 1922, thus ending 631 years of Ottoman rule in the world. The revolutionary reforms that Mustafa Kemal Atatürk put into force during his presidency of 15 years following the founding of the Republic were aimed at transforming the country into a constitutional, modern state.

In 1945 Turkey joined the UN, and in 1952 it became a member of NATO. In 1974 in response to threats from Greece, Turkey intervened militarily in Cyprus to protect Turkish Cypriots; approximately 37 percent of the northern part of the island remains under Turkish Cypriot control. Relations between the two countries have remained strained, and only the Turkish government recognizes the Turkish Republic of Northern Cyprus (proclaimed in 1985). Settlement talks with the United Nations were underway in the 1990s but remain unresolved.

In 1984 Kurdistan separatists staged an insurgency in southeast Turkey, using terrorist tactics in their attempts to create an independent state. The Marxist-Leninist Kurdistan Workers' Party (PKK) has observed a unilateral cease-fire since September of 1999, although clashes and violence has continued between the PKK militants and the Turkish military.

Society

About 98 percent of the Turkish population is Muslim. However, everyone in Turkey has freedom of religion and belief. Because the country is secular, no one can be forced to participate in religious ceremonies or rites against their will and no blame can be attached to anyone because of their beliefs. The first phases in the introduction of secularism were the abolition of the Caliphate and the Ministry of Sheria and Pious Foundations on March 4, 1924, followed by the introduction of separate educational and judicial systems, the hat reform, the closure of dervish retreats and religious sects, the acceptance of a Sunday weekend holiday rather than the Moslem Friday, and finally, the adoption of the principle of secularism in the constitution in 1937. In secular Turkey, all religious affairs are administered by a central government organization affiliated to the Prime Ministry, namely the Department of Religious Affairs.

The Republic has introduced universal principles of law to Turkey. In this context, the idea that all citizens are equal and free without any discrimination based on race, language, and religion, establishes the basis of the Republican Covenant, which ensures social unity. Democracy, which enables citizens to express their thoughts freely and to participate in political process; and the rule of law, which makes it possible for them to live free from fear and oppression, are products of the social contract of the Republic.

TUNCAY BABALI

See also **Turks**

Further Reading

Cem, Ismail, *Turkey in the 21st Century*, Rustem, 2001
Kedourie, Sylvia, editor, *Seventy-Five Years of the Turkish Republic*, London, 2000
Kinross, Lord, *The Ottoman Centuries*, New York, 1977
Kirisci, Kemal, and Gareth M. Winrow, *The Kurdish Question and Turkey*, London, 1999
Lewis, Bernard, *The Emergence of Modern Turkey*, London, 1961
———, "Why Turkey is the Only Muslim Democracy?" *Middle East Quarterly* (March 1994)
Mantran, Robert, *Histoire de l'Empire Ottomane*, Paris, 1989
Oymen, Onur, *Turkish Challenge*, Cambridge University Press, 2000

Turkmen

Capsule Summary

Location: Central Asia, Southwest Asia, northern Iran, northern Afghanistan, southern Siberia, western China
Total Population: approximately 6 million
Language: Turkoman
Religion: Muslim

Turkmen (ethnonyms: Turcoman, Turkoman, or Turkomen) have an ethnic origin that may be traced to the Oghuz, a loose confederation of Turkic-speaking tribes which coalesced in the south and west of present-day Mongolia in the seventh and eighth centuries CE. They maintain the theory of a mythical common ancestor, Oghyz Khan, from whom emerged 22 to 24 original tribes that gave rise to the Turkmen. Within the subsequent century, the Oghuz migrated west into the steppe areas north and west of the Aral Sea and along three Central Asian rivers, the Syr Darya, Murgab, and Amu Darya.

The term Turkmen was applied initially during the tenth century CE to those Oghuz who became Muslims. Following the Mongol invasions, most Oghuz were converted to Islam. The Turkmen are Sunni Muslims and relatively few are Shia Muslims. Although their religious history since the thirteenth century shows a strong adherence to Islam, such as daily prayers, fasting, and pilgrimages, the Turkmen tribes and clans have separate cemeteries and saint's shrines. Shamanistic elements such as the evil eye and curing ceremonies are retained, especially in nomadic, rather than sedentary, populations. Tribal identity and affiliations remain significant in maintaining social relations and in politics. In the pre-Soviet era, traditionally among more than a dozen tribal groupings, the Teke, Yomut, and Ersari were the largest demographically, and clan affiliations remain strong in their patriarchal, patrilineal, and patrilocal extended family society. Most marriages are arranged and involve a *kalong* (bride price) and often-simulated bride capture, but without forced marriages. Behavior and social norms derive from *Asat* (customary law), *Sherigat* (Islamic law), and *Edep* (rules of appropriate behavior and etiquette). Each Turkmen tribe and clan have rich oral traditions (legends and tales) that describe and define tribal genesis and genealogy thereby playing a crucial role in the providing a sense of identity.

The Turkmen language, Turkoman, belongs to the family of Turkic languages spoken in Eastern Europe (Bashkir, Chuvas, and Tatar), the Caucasus (Azeri or Azerbaijani and Kumuk), Southwest Asia (Azeri and Turkish), Central Asia (Kazak, Kyrgyz, and Uzbeki), Southern Siberia (Khakas, Tuva, and Yakut), and China (Kazak and Uygur). In general, Turkmen residing in Iran speak Persian Dari while the more urban Turkmen of Turkmenistan, because of long Russian and Soviet influence, speak Russian. Prior to 1869, before Russian and Soviet presence, the Turkmen wrote in Chaghatai written in Arabic script but this was replaced by Latin, and later by Cyrillic script; in the mid-1990s Latin script was reintroduced. However, in Afghanistan the Turkmen have continued to read and write in Arabic script.

Demographically in 2001 the Turkmen numbered about 6 million and lived mainly in Turkmenistan and in neighboring parts of Central Asia, Iran, and Afghanistan. The Republic of Turkmenistan, the former Turkistan Autonomous Soviet Socialist Republic established in 1918, became independent on October 27, 1991, consists of 488,100 sq km (188,450 sq mi) and in 2000 had a population of 4,518,000 (40 percent aged 14 or younger) of which 77 percent (3,480,000) are ethnically Turkmen, 9.2 Uzbek, 6.7 Russian, and 2.0 Kazakh, with other ethnic groups comprising the remaining 5.1 percent. Approximately 186,000 Turkomen live in the other polities of the Commonwealth of Independent States or CIS (Kazakstan, 4,000; Kyrgystan, 10,000; Tajikistan, 22,000; and Uzbekistan 120,000) and in the Russian Federation (approximately 30,000, with 12,000 of these in the Stavropol region of southwest Russia). An estimated 2,496,000 Turkmen lived in Afghanistan in 1978 but more precise recent census information is unavailable, although an estimate of 700,000 was suggested in 1997. There are about 850,000 Turkmen in northern Iran, especially in the Transcaspian region of northern Iran, and in northwestern and northeastern Afghanistan where they are minorities among Pushtun and Hazara. Smaller groups, generally fewer than 10,000, inhabit areas in

Iraq, Syria, and Turkey where they experience minority discrimination, particularly in Turkey since 1958. The demographic estimates of Turkmen in China and Siberia suggest fewer than 40,000.

Traditionally a pastoral nomadic people, the Turkmen raised sheep, goats, cattle, camels, horses, cattle, and donkeys, but many Turkmen in Turkmenistan under Soviet rule adopted wheat and cotton agriculture (frequently augmented by irrigation systems) and livestock breeding, necessitating a sedentary way of life. However, some Turkmen in the other regions retain a nomadic pastoral lifestyle, emphasizing transhumance sheep and goat herding. Wool and cotton processing is done by women who weave a variety of items including traditionally patterned carpets, storage bags, door coverings, horse and camel trappings, ornaments for felt *gara* (often called *yurts*), and carpets. Many so-called Oriental or Bukharan wool carpets are actually made by Turkmen women, often assisted by children, and are prized by Western collectors as well as other Central Asians who purchase them as an investment and hedge against inflation.

CHARLES C. KOLB

See also **Afghanistan; China; Iran; Turkmenistan**

Further Reading

Bacon, Elizabeth, *Central Asians under Russian Rule: A Study in Culture Change*, Ithaca, New York: Cornell University Press, 1980

Barthold, W., *Turkestan down to the Mongol Invasion*, 4th edition, London: Gibb Memorial Trust, 1977

Curtis, E. Glenn, editor, *Kazakhstan, Kyrgyzstan, Tajikistan, Turkmenistan, and Uzbekistan: Country Studies*, Washington, DC: Federal Research Division, Library of Congress, U.S. Government Printing Office, 1997

Dupree, Louis, *Afghanistan*, revised edition, Princeton: Princeton University Press, 1980

Ember, Melvin, and Carol Ember, editors, *Countries and Their Cultures*, New York: Macmillan Reference, under the auspices of the Human Relations Area Files (Yale University), 2001

Encyclopedia Iranica, Vol. 5, Costa Mesa, California: Mazda, 1990

Gall, Timothy L., editor, *Worldmark Encyclopedia of Cultures and Daily Life, Volume 3: Asia and Oceania*, Detroit: Gale, 1998

Katz, Zev, editor, *Handbook of Major Soviet Nationalities*, New York: Free Press, 1975

Krader, Lawrence, *Peoples of Central Asia*, Uralic and Altaic Series, Vol. 26, 2nd edition, Bloomington: Indiana University and The Hague, The Netherlands: Mouton, 1966

Litvinoff, Miles, director, *World Directory of Minorities*, London: Minority Rights Group International, 1997

Mandelbaum, Michael, editor, *Central Asia and the World: Kazakhstan, Uzbekistan, Tajikistan, Kyrgyzstan, and Turkmenistan*, New York: Council on Foreign Relations Press, 1994

Meyer, Karl E., and Shareen Blair Brysac, *Tournament of Shadows: The Great Game and the Race for Empire in Central Asia*, Washington, DC: Counterpoint, 1999

Saray, Mehmet, *The Turkmens in the Age of Imperialism: A Study of the Turkmen People and Their Incorporation into the Russian Empire*, Ankara: Turkish Historical Society, 1989

"Turkmenistan," in *The CIA World Factbook 2000.* <http://www.odci.gov/cia/publications/factbook.af.html>

Turkmenistan

Capsule Summary

Location: South western Central Asia
Total Population: 4,775,544 (July 2003)
Ethnic Population: Turkmen (77%), Uzbek (9.2%), Russian (6.7%), Kazakh (2%), other (5.1%) (1995)
Languages: Turkmen (72%), Russian (12%), Uzbek (9%), other (7%)
Religions: Muslim (89%), Eastern Orthodox (9%), unknown (2%)

Turkmenistan is one of the former Soviet Central Asian (CA) states. Turkmen are predominantly of Turkic origin and speak Turkmen. Turkmen settlement in CA dates probably back to the eleventh century CE. The total population of Turkmenistan is about 4.8 million. Turkmenistan, like other CA countries, is a multiethnic society. The absolute majority of Turkmen, are Muslims. In 1991, Turkmenistan became independent from the Soviet Union.

Turkmenistan borders Kazakhstan, Uzbekistan, Afghanistan, Iran and the Caspian Sea. The capital city is Ashgabat and the country's total area is 488,100 square kilometers (188,500 square miles). About nine-tenths of the countryside is desert. The Karakum desert is one of the biggest in the world. The major cities of Turkmenistan in 1991 were: Ashgabat with 416,400 inhabitants; Chärjew with 166,400; Dashhowuz with 117,000; Mary with 94,900; and Nebitdag with 89,100 inhabitants.

History

Until about the eighteenth century, the Turkmen were mainly ruled by the Seljuqs and the Mongols. Before the conquering by the Russian Empire, the Turkmen were a nomadic, pastoral people organized by tribes.

In the early 1700s, Russia launched invasions into the area, mostly unsuccessful. Complete control of the Turkmen by the Russians was reached in 1881; they were included in the governorate-general of Turkistan. After the Bolshevik Revolution, the region came under Soviet control in 1918. At that time, however, nationalist forces established an independent government. They were immediately defeated by the Red Army in 1920. Soviet forces formed an autonomous Turkmen region in 1921 and eventually, in 1924, created the Turkmen Soviet Socialist Republic (SSR), as a result of the National Delimination of CA from the Turkmen *oblast* and the Turkmen districts of the former Khorezmian and Bukharan republics. The Turkmen S.S.R. became part of the Soviet Union in 1925.

In 1990, a resolution claiming sovereignty passed through the parliament of the Turkmen S.S.R., resulting in independence, due to the collapse of the Soviet Union. The Turkmen Communist Party (TCP) was renamed the Democratic Party of Turkmenistan (DPT), and they kept ruling the country. Turkmenistan's first constitution, as an independent republic, was implemented in May 1992.

The office of president was established in Turkmenistan in 1990. The new constitution increased the powers of the president: the president is head of state, head of the Council of Ministers with the option of appointing a prime minister at any time, and supreme commander of the armed forces. The president must be directly elected for a five-year term with a maximum of two consecutive terms. However, in 1994 the legislature voted to extend President Saparmurad Niyazov's term of office until 2002, and voters endorsed the decision in a nationwide referendum.

Turkmenistan's constitution provided a new legislature, a 50-member body called the *Majlis* (Assembly). However, the 175-seat Supreme Soviet elected in 1990 was allowed to serve out its term, and elections to the new Majlis were delayed until 1994. Members of the Majlis are directly elected and serve a five-year term.

The Khalq Maslakhaty (People's Council), a supervisory organ, is authorized to perform some duties normally engaged by the legislature. It is the most powerful governmental body, debating and approving some legislation, reviewing possible constitutional amendments, and holding the power to vote an expression of "no confidence" against the president. The Khalk Maslakhaty is headed by the president of the republic.

The judicial system of Turkmenistan includes a Supreme Court, the highest court in the nation, and a Supreme Economic Court. The Supreme Economic Court rules on contract disputes, conflicts between businesses, and other commercial and taxation issues. Under the 1992 constitution, the president of Turkmenistan appoints and removes all judges.

A multiparty system does not exist, and most candidates run unopposed elections. The only political organization is the DPT and it retained its position as the republic's only legal party. Head of the DPT is President Niyazov, the only standing party in the legislative elections of 1994. In late 1992 Niyazov announced, as a first step toward establishing a multiparty system, that the Peasants' Party, founded that year by an agrarian-interest faction in the Majlis, would eventually be permitted to register. As of early 1998, however, the party was not yet registered, forcing the opposition to go underground, and some opposition leaders went in exile.

Niyazov's style of leadership has been increasingly authoritarian, and he developed a cult of personality, naming himself *Turkmenbashi* (Leader of the Turkmens). Political freedom is routinely suppressed and Niyazov's government controls the media. Censorship is widespread because freedom of the press is not guaranteed in the constitution. The government sought to prevent the development of a politicized Islamic movement and maintained control over the Islamic establishment, which publicly supports Niyazov.

In 1992 the government began developing a national defense force, based on former Soviet military units that were still stationed in the country. Under an agreement with Russia and Turkey, Turkmenistan's armed forces have to operate under joint Turkmen-Russian command, with Turkish military advisers, until they are fully developed. The republic has an army of 14,000 troops and an air force of 3,000.

Society

Like other CA countries, Turkmenistan is multiethnic. Since independence, the Muslim population has significantly increased, accounting for 60 percent of the total population in 1959, and 77 percent in 1992. Between 1959 and 1979 CA's population has almost doubled from 22,978 million to 40,167,000 million. Population growth in Turkmenistan was 2.4 percent.

Turkmenistan is the most ethnically homogeneous of the CA republics; of the total population of 4,731,000, 77 percent are Turkmen, 9.2 percent Uzbek, 6.7 percent Russians; 2 percent Kazakh; 5 percent Tartars, and the rest are Ukrainians, Armenians, Karakalpaks, and others.

Contrary to other former Soviet republics, Turkmenistan has not experienced a massive emigration of minorities since independence. This is mainly because there is no fanatical nationalism among the Turkmen majority. Instead, Turkmens have retained centuries-old tribal allegiances that are stronger than their sense of nationhood, and tribal-based hostilities are far more marked than interethnic tensions. No tribal unrest has been developed against the government, which has cautiously avoided obvious favoritism toward any one tribe and generally worked to suppress tribal identification. The three largest Turkmen tribes are the Tekke in the central part of the country, the Ersary in the southeast, and the Yomud in the west.

Turkmen belongs to the Oghuz branch of Turkic languages of Khorasani Turkish language. Turkmen was made the official language of the Turkmen SSR in 1990. Under Turkmenistan's 1992 constitution, Russian lost its official status as the language of interethnic communication.

Turkmen and other CA people are traditionally Sunni Muslims of the Hanafi school, which was introduced gradually, during the Arab invasions of the seventh and eighth centuries. The Soviet policymakers sought to suppress religion in general and Islam especially, because of its potential for creating coherent resistance to Soviet rule. After independence, many Turkmen and other CAs have revived their Islamic heritage. Sunnites account for about 87 percent of Turkmenistan's population. Sufism, or Islamic mysticism, is also prevalent in the republic. Some of the country's ethnic minorities—notably Russians, Ukrainians, and Armenians—are Eastern Orthodox Christians, while the Azerbaijani minority is Shi'ite Muslim.

Turkmenistan was the second poorest country of CA during the Soviet era, after Tajikistan. Turkmenistan's main products are oil and natural gas. Turkmenistan had a gross domestic product (GDP) per capita income of $6,700 in 2002. Other important Turkmen products are silk, cotton, wool fibers and fabrics, carpets, sheep, horses, and camels. Turkmenistan has one of the world's major natural gas reserves and numbers third among the regional states in oil reserves. According to recent investigation, the country's reserves may be as high as 34 billion barrels of oil and about 159 trillion cubic feet of natural gas reserves. After independence, policymakers tried to formulate ambitious national development plans, the backing of which would be determined by the country's ability to monetize its oil and gas reserves. Thus Turkmenistan has been called the "Central Asian Kuwait". All countries that currently are delivered oil and gas by Turkmenistan are in debt to Turkmenistan. In response, Turkmenistan periodically threatened and at times actually terminated transport of gas to several of these countries.

Turkmenistan is actively canvassing numerous alternatives to expand its critical hydrocarbon revenue base, by increasing gas sales to the CIS, offering offshore Caspian areas to foreign investors, expanding the relationship with Iran in both oil and gas, and initiating deliveries of natural gas to Pakistan.

Ultimately, however, the success of the proposed Trans-Caspian gas pipeline and the Baku to Ceyhan oil pipeline will largely determine Turkmenistan's ability to fully realize the value of its hydrocarbon reserves.

MEHDI PARVIZI AMINEH

See also **Armenians; Karakalpaks; Kazaks; Turkmen; Ukrainians; Uzbeks**

Further Reading

Amineh, Mehdi Parvizi, Towards the Control of Oil Resources in the Caspian Region, New York: St. Martinís Press, 1999

Doerfer, Gerhard, "Turkish-Iranian Language Contacts," in *Encyclopaedia Iranica*, Vol. 5, edited by Eshan Yarshater, Costa Mesa: Mazda Publishers, 1992

Goetz, Roland, *Turkmenistan: Informationen ueber eine unbekannte Republik*, Koeln: Bundesinstitut fuer ostwissenschaftliche und internationale Studien, 1995

Haghayeghi, Mehrdad, *Islam and Politics in Central Asia*, New York: St. Martin's Press, 1995

Hambly, Gavin, editor, *Central Asia*, London: Weidenfeld and Nicolson, 1969

Wheeler, Geoffrey, *The Modern History of Soviet Central Asia*, London: Weidenfeld and Nicolson, 1964

Turks

Capsule Summary

Location: Balkans, Moldova, Western Europe
Total Population: between 3 and 4 million
Language: Predominantly Turkish
Religion: Predominantly Muslim

In looking at the situation of Turks as minority communities, key questions are how a Turk is defined, which groups are regarded by Turkey as their "kin," and which groups view Turkey as their kin-state. Turkish belongs to the Altaic linguistic family, and the foundation of the Turkish Republic in the 1920s from the ruins of the Ottoman Empire saw large numbers of Turkish-speakers who previously had been part of the Ottoman Empire left outside the new state. In addition many non-Turkish-speaking Muslims also identified with or were seen by others as being Turks due to their religious affiliation.

The Ottoman Empire was an empire ruled by Islamic precepts for most of its existence. In line with these, the empire was, until attempted changes beginning with the Tanzimat reforms in the mid-nineteenth century, divided not along ethnolinguistic lines but by religious affiliation—the *millet* system. As such all Muslims were seen as equal first-class citizens and the elite was multiethnic. Until the end of the nineteenth century, the concept of being a *Turk* as used in modern parlance was alien to the Ottoman elites, who saw themselves as Ottomans rather than Turks. The latter had the connotation of being uneducated peasants. The early twentieth century saw the growth of a distinct Turkish nationalism within the empire. Initially led by Turkic speaking émigrés from Russia, this movement gained momentum and became important during the Young Turk regimes of 1908-1918. The steady collapse of the Ottoman Empire both fueled this movement and raised the new idea of a union of all ethnic Turkic groups in one state—the dream of *Turan* stretching from the Balkans to China. World War I gave a fleeting hope that this dream could be accomplished. However, defeat of the Ottoman Empire saw an end to such fantasies. The new rulers led by Mustafa Kemal (Ataturk) resolutely turned their backs on any notions of Turan or expansion from the Anatolian core

which was now designated as the indivisible territory of "the Turkish nation." But who were "the Turkish nation"? After some ambivalence, Kemal (despite his own origins from Macedonia) essentially defined the Turkish nation as constituting the Muslim population of Anatolia. Greek Orthodox Christians were expelled en masse and exchanged with Muslims from Greece. Religion was the criterion: Turkish-speaking Christians were sent to Greece while non-Turkish-speaking Muslims were sent to Turkey. The Muslim community of Western Thrace and the Orthodox community in Istanbul and two islands were exempted from this population exchange.

Thus despite the strong territorial model for Kemalist nationalism based on common citizenship (as reflected in Article 66 of the current Constitution which states: "Everyone bound to the Turkish state through the bond of citizenship is a Turk") there were, from the start, elements of both perceived aliens within and kin outside. The conscious policy of propagating a cohesive sense of national identity and creating a widespread national consciousness in Turkey saw a great emphasis on the ethnic Turks and their language at the expense of other groups like the Kurds, whose separate identity and language were denied. However, despite Kemal's insistence on abandoning the dream of Turan, summed up in his slogan "Peace at home, peace in the world," the new state-propagated nationalism strongly stressed Central Asia as the Turks original fatherland as well as the affinity with other Turkic peoples. This has led to a retention of the sense of kin in Central Asia. Combined with this is the religious factor which has seen many Balkan Muslims who are not ethnic Turks look to Turkey as a potential kin-state.

The collapse of the Soviet Union created hitherto unknown opportunities for contact with Turkic-speaking groups in Central Asia. Whether these people can be included under the rubric of *Turks* is debatable. Certainly, the pan-Turkist currents within and without Turkey view the Turkic-speaking peoples of Central Asia as kin and ultimately look towards union with them. However, the long years under Soviet rule which included the deliberate attempt at creating new nations like the Uzbeks, and Turcomen, has resulted in these Turkic-speaking peoples having a separate national consciousness, and there is acceptance (outside pan-Turkist circles) that while there are many shared cultural values resulting from shared religious linguistic and historical factors, the Uzbeks, for example, are a separate people from the Turks of Turkey. In the Balkans, however, this does not appear to be the case. Probably due to the communities there being minorities within the essentially Orthodox Christian states (Albania of course is the exception), which were also remnants of the Ottoman Empire, there has remained on both sides a strong identification of themselves as Turks rather than Turkic peoples. The crucial aspect here appears to be that of a minority. Where the perceived kin outside Turkey constitute a majority and have built up or been encouraged to build up a separate national consciousness (for example the Uzbeks or the Azeris), then Turkey and Turks perceive their case differently from that of minorities—especially minorities within essentially Christian states. If they were once part of the Ottoman Empire then this is further amplified. However, the point about being Muslim minorities within non-Muslims states is not exclusive. The Turkic minorities in Iraq for example are also felt to fall within the category of Turkey's kin abroad, of which Turkey sees itself as a possible protector. Also, of late, the authorities have also come to regard the Christian Turkic people of Moldova, the Gagauz, as falling within this category.

For these reasons, concentration is given to the communities in the Balkans, both ethnic Turks and other Muslims, who look to Turkey as a kin-state and to how Turkey has responded. These communities include those in Cyprus, Bulgaria, Greece, Moldova, Romania, and former Yugoslavia. Also considered is the situation of the large numbers of Turkish citizens who have settled in western Europe, especially Germany, to find work or seek asylum.

Remnants of the Ottoman Empire in the Balkans

Sizeable Islamic groups, both ethnically and nonethnically Turkish, remained in all the successor states which emerged from the collapse of Ottoman rule in the Balkans. With the exception of Albania, all the new states were "Christian" in character, and the presence of sizeable Muslim minorities within the new states was often seen as problematic. These minorities were often viewed as mere remnants of the Ottoman Empire, which were expected to disappear.

Greece

The Muslim community in Western Thrace amply illustrates the problems of trying to differentiate groups who look to Turkey as a kin-state by ethnicity or religion alone. In the population exchanges between Greece and Turkey in 1924, religion, not ethnicity or language, was the criterion. As a result many Muslim Slavs (Pomaks) and Roma (Gypsies) in Western Thrace remained, especially in villages in the Rhodope mountains. Since the 1920s there has been a steady and continuing emigration of Turkish-speakers to Turkey; some 250,000 have emigrated.

In theory, the rights of the 120,000 or so in the Muslim community of Western Thrace were, and remain, guaranteed under Article 45 of the Lausanne Treaty of July 24, 1923. In the initial postwar period there was a rare rapprochement between Greece and Turkey, the traditional enemy, then seen as an ally in NATO against what was perceived as a more serious threat from Communist Bulgaria. The latter might have tried to use the Bulgarian-speaking Pomaks as a fifth column. As a result the Pomaks were actively encouraged to become Turks and compulsory Turkish education was introduced for them. However, the authorities soon reverted to the traditional anti-Turkish line and the traditional denial of any ethnic minorities within Greece. Worried at the rise of ethnic-Turkish assertiveness in the region, which has seen serious intercommunal rioting, the Greek authorities now appear to be trying to reverse this.

A slight relaxation of some of the more petty measures against the Muslim population occurred as a result of an agreement in January of 1990 between the then Prime Minister Mitsotakis and opposition leader Andreas Papandreou after the initial disturbances in Komotini in January of that year. This agreement foresaw an economic improvement in the area with some concessions to the minority along with a greater state presence and the settlement of Greeks from the former USSR to strengthen the Greek presence. The agreement also included attempts to split the Muslim community into it component parts and divide the Pomaks and Roma from the ethnic Turks. This policy, which has seen attempts to portray the Pomaks as the pre-Slav inhabitants of Thrace who, as such, are "closer" to the Greeks than the Turks, has been an abject failure. The Pomak community continues to strongly identify itself with the Turkish community and is in the process of becoming solidly Turkicized.

The education system is crucial due to its role in propagating shared cultural values. In 1968 a special teacher training center for Turks was set up in Thessalonika, whereas before teachers had come from Turkey. The Greek authorities appear to have tried to keep contacts with the kin-state as small as possible. One aspect of this is the insistence on calling them *Muslims*, not *Turks*. The training of "native" teachers, who, the Turks claim teach an outdated, backward curriculum with little contact with developments in Turkey, appears to have been a key part of this. Despite the 1968 Greek-Turkish protocol on education, severe problems of adequate textbooks for the Turks in Western Thrace remain, with accusations that the Greek authorities deliberately hold back books sent from Turkey. The implementation in 1985 of the May 1984 law that the entrance exams to the two secondary Turkish minority schools in Komotini and Xanthi (there are some 300 primary schools) as well as graduation exams have to be in Greek resulted in a dramatic decline in the numbers of pupils—from 227 in Xanthi and 305 in Komotini in 1983-1984, to 85 and 42 respectively in 1986-1987.

Greece's continuing refusal to officially recognize the existence of ethnic minorities within its borders has resulted in official distrust of community leaders like elected mufti Mehmet Emin Aga who openly identify themselves as Turks. At the end of the 1980s even elected MPs who ran on an explicitly Turkish platform were prosecuted and sentenced to terms of imprisonment which were commuted to large fines. Mehmet Aga was nominated to office by the Muslim (previously predominantly Pomak) community of Xanthi on August 17, 1990 and served as official mufti until he was ousted and replaced by a government appointee following a new law—law No. 1920 of December 24, 1990 which replaced existing legislation dating from 1920 on the appointment of muftis. He carried on as unofficial mufti and has suffered a number of prosecutions for usurping the title of mufti. At the latest, held at the Lamia city court near Athens (some 600 km or 373 mi from Xanthi) on May 28, 1998, he was sentenced to a further six months imprisonment, making the total until then 79 months of which he has served six and paid fines to commute others. Mehmet Aga appealed to the courts against his dismissal immediately after he was ousted but that case has yet to be heard.

Cyprus

In Cyprus, Turkey, along with Greece and the UK, was a guarantor power and public opinion in Turkey was outraged at what were perceived as Greek threats against the Turkish population on the island during the 1960s. Finally in 1974, using Article 4 of the Cyprus Treaty of Guarantee as a justification for unilateral intervention, the Ecevit government sent the Turkish army in and effected massive population transfers. This had massive popular backing in Turkey. The invasion eventually resulted in the setting up in 1983 of the ethnically homogeneous Turkish Republic of Northern Cyprus (TRNC), which is unrecognized by the international community.

Cyprus has remained partitioned, and despite repeated efforts by the international community there has been little progress towards a settlement. In effect the Turks of TRNC are a majority within their own internationally unrecognized state. In 1996 TRNCs population was 200,587 of whom 164,460 (82 percent) were citizens of TRNC. However, large numbers of Cypriot Turks have emigrated and been replaced by Turks from Turkey who made up 15 percent in 1996, so much so that some see the Cypriot Turks as a minority within TRNC, and there have been reports of alienation between the two communities.

Bulgaria

In Bulgaria, ethnic Turks are concentrated in the south around Kardzhali and in the northeast around Razgrad. Emigration of Turks to Turkey continued in the interwar period. During the 1920s and 1930s, Turkish schools, especially primary schools, were closed. The advent of dictatorship in 1934 saw a further deterioration with bans on the use of the new Latin script and the reinstatement of the Arabic script for all Turkish publications. This was an apparent attempt to dissuade mother-tongue expression—the Arabic script being both difficult to learn and inappropriate for Turkish—and to hinder links with Ataturk's Turkey which had changed its script.

The postwar period saw a change. The traditional pattern of emigration to Turkey resumed in 1950-1951. However, beginning in the 1950s, the Zhivkov regime, over a long period, pursued a repressive forced assimilatory policy, which was progressively applied to all the country's major minority populations with the exceptions, for propaganda reasons, of the small Jewish and Armenian minorities. This policy came to a head with the massive violent campaign against the ethnic Turkish minority, some 10 percent of the population, in late 1984. The Turkish state and public reacted with outrage and Turkey declared willingness to open her borders. In 1989 the Zhivkov regime, panicking at the rising tide of organized discontent among the Turks to the policy of ethnic denial, allowed the Turks to leave and some 300,000 fled. However, despite the return of perhaps half of those from the original great exodus of 1989, emigration to Turkey continued, spurred on by a severe decline in the economy of many minority regions, especially tobacco-growing ones in the south.

Unlike most other post-Communist countries, the Bulgarian Constitution makes no mention of collective minority rights, nor do they appear in any legislation. On the contrary, the constitution bans everything that might be interpreted as collective political rights for minorities. Territorial autonomy is prohibited, as are political parties based on ethnic or religious grounds. The Law on Parties furthermore stipulates that all parties must execute their activities in the Bulgarian language. Despite these hurdles, the Movement for Rights and Freedom (DPS), essentially an ethnic Turkish party led by Ahmed Dogan, has been allowed to operate, and in the October 1991 elections it gained 24 MPs (out of a total of 240), over 650 village mayors, 1,000 councillors, and 20 municipal mayors. It played a significant role in the early 1990s as a third force between the Union of Democratic Forces (SDS) and the former Communist Bulgarian Socialist Party (BSP). However, the DPS became faced with splits (five deputies left the parliamentary faction in 1994) and erosion of support due in part to emigration and in part to supporting unpopular economic policies in these coalition governments. In the December 1994 elections the party won 15 MPs with 5.4 percent of the vote. In the April 1997 elections, to be sure to clear the 4 percent electoral hurdle, it entered as the senior partner of a coalition, the Alliance for National Salvation, comprised of small center-right parties and monarchists. The Alliance gained 7.6 percent of the vote and 19 seats.

Former Yugoslavia

The Turks in former Yugoslavia numbered 101,292 as per the census of 1981. However, their number, as reflected in censuses, has fluctuated wildly. The census of 1948 gave 95,940 Turks while that of 1953 recorded 203,938, yet by the next census seven years later the number was only 131,481. These big fluctuations were due to external events. In the immediate postwar period, the Turks were seen as suspect due to friendship between Turkey and the West. As a

result, many Turks declared themselves to be Albanians in the 1948 census. However, by 1953, following the break with Albania after the Tito-Stalin split, the Albanians were now seen as suspect and so now many Albanians and Muslim Slavs declared themselves to be Turks—of the 203,938 in the 1953 census, 32,392 gave Macedonian as their native tongue and 27,086 gave Albanian.

The period from 1953 to 1966 also saw extensive emigration to Turkey of many Turks from Yugoslavia—some 80,000 according to figures from Yugoslavia's statistical yearbooks, or over 150,000 according to some Turkish sources. However, some of these emigrants were unable to speak any Turkish and were in fact either Muslim Albanians or Slavs who were claiming to be Turks to escape from communist Yugoslavia.

Macedonia

Most Turks in former Yugoslavia lived in Macedonia. In the 1971 census there were 108,552 declared Turks in Macedonia, and by the census of 1981 the number had dropped to 86,690. Such a decline was the more surprising given the high birthrate of ethnic Turks. It appeared that many who previously had declared themselves to be Turks were now calling themselves Muslims while others were declaring themselves to be Albanians or Roma. In the April 1991 census the figure had risen slightly to 97,416. The communist authorities, worried at the rise of Albanian nationalism, asserted that many Turks in Macedonia had been Albanianized under pressure from the large nationalistic Albanian community.

Similarly to the Albanians, the Turks were a recognized nationality of former Yugoslavia, and in Macedonia were allowed many educational and cultural rights from the outset, including primary and secondary schools, television and radio programs and a newspaper, as well as various cultural organizations, and these have continued in independent Macedonia.

As elsewhere in the Balkans, the situation is confused by the presence of Muslim Slavs (*Torbeshi* in Macedonia) some of whom self-identify with Turks. In 1992 a number of Torbeshi in the Debar region requested schooling in Turkish, not Macedonian—a request the authorities turned down eliciting protests from the main post-Communist Turkish political organization, the Democratic Party of Turks in Macedonia (DPTM). However, it does seem that many of the Torbeshi, are identifying with the ethnic Turkish community despite not speaking Turkish. This is further illustrated by the choice in 1998 of a DPTM mayor in the Torbeshi district of Zupa near Debar and a DPTM deputy to parliament. However, the community remains small.

Romania and Moldova

Some 80,000 Turks (Tartars) live in Romania where they are recognized as official minorities and represented in parliament. More territorially compact are the 140,000 Gagauzi in Moldova. The breakup of the USSR saw the proclamation of a breakaway republic of the Gagauzi regions in September 1990, but, unlike that of Moldovan Transnistria with its large Russian-Ukrainian population, the Gagauz regions were reincorporated into the state and a law of 1994 gave local autonomy to the five areas where the Gagauz predominate, the largest of which is centered on Comrat.

Turkish Gastarbeiter of Germany and other West European states

By far the largest number of Turks living abroad, about two million, live in Germany, and the Turkish community there is arguably the most important of such groups of Turkish citizens abroad. There have been a number of studies of this and other Turkish guestworker communities abroad. All these studies look at the problems of national identity of the Turkish guestworkers when they settle permanently in the host country. This is especially problematic in Germany, the classic model for ethnic nationalism, because the state jealously guards what it considers as "pure" German culture from perceived alien influence. It is further amplified in the cases of children born in Germany (or in other host countries) to Turkish parents residing there. Half of the Turks in Germany have lived there for almost 20 years. Unlike other immigrant groups (Spaniards, Greeks, etc.) they show little sign of wanting to return to their original homeland. Studies confirm that while Islam is of crucial importance to Turkish immigrants in retaining their "otherness" in host countries, there is little inter-Islamic solidarity with other Muslim groups. For Turks abroad, Islam is primarily a badge of their Turkish national identity. Despite this, there appeared to be little sign that either first-generation or second-generation Turks would take advantage of opportunities for naturaliation. It would appear that for the Turks, giving up their "Turkishness" and completely adopting German culture was and remains a block.

However, this remains a complex issue. Some who are born in Germany are losing their Turkish identity.

On the other hand others, especially those who are deliberately taken to stay for lengths of time in Turkey, are not. If the latter remain too long outside of the mother country, the problems of fully reintegrating into Turkish culture in Turkey become greater.

A crucial development in the strengthening of Turkish identity in Germany has been the rise of radical German nationalism and consequent attacks on immigrants, most notably the firebomb attacks on Turkish hostels in Moen and Solingen in November of 1992 and April of 1993 respectively. Following these outrages, numbers of Turks took to the streets of Germany chanting slogans like "Turkey Turkey über alles" and "Allah is great" and a number of clashes occurred between Turks and Germans.

Of course many of these immigrants are not ethnically Turkish, many are of Kurdish origin and many of these are politically active Kurdish nationalists who are unable to operate openly in Turkey itself. There are perhaps 400,000 Kurds from Turkey in Germany of whom it is estimated that over 90 percent either support or are intimidated to support the Kurdistan Workers Party (PKK) which has been fighting the Turkish state since 1984. Similarly, in Britain, the main Turkish center in London, the Halk Evi in Stoke Newington, was taken over by PKK militants in the late 1980s. In Britain the Turkish community is further split by the presence of the large Turkish-Cypriot community who predate the mass arrival of Turks and Kurds in the 1980s. In Germany there have been rival demonstrations between Kurds and Turks over the treatment of Kurds in Turkey. In common with other groups, nationalism appears to be strong in the Kurdish diaspora and the conflict within Turkey is mirrored outside. The massacres in Kurdistan appear to be playing a crucial role in reinforcing Kurdish identity among Turkey's Kurds abroad. While this can perhaps be overstressed, there does appear to be a difference between the greater solidarity and political activism of the Kurds abroad compared with the Turks.

The communications revolution has also had profound effects. On the one hand it has meant that a country like Greece or Bulgaria is no longer able to isolate itself from the outside world and pursue policies of forced assimilation against minorities, which include Turks and other Muslims. On the other hand, Turkish citizens in Western Europe can now easily tune into domestic Turkish television. This has greatly aided a retention of national identity. For men, especially, the role of football, both supporting Turkish football teams and watching the matches on television, plays an important role. While private television plays a similar role for women, traditional Turkish attitudes towards women remain. Indeed, the claim by traditionalist that second-generation Turks in Germany do not know how to behave "correctly" usually refers to the attitudes and actions of the women. Many Turkish women in Europe live dual lives: modern, twentieth-century ones in the morning when they go out, but traditional ones of strict male control when they return home. This dual roles put a great deal of strain on many women, as well as on their male partners—the latter feel constrained to act in traditional modes even when living in societies where these modes do not apply.

Like Muslims living in Orthodox Christian states in the Balkans, Islam has been and continues to be a crucial element of identification for many Turkish citizens in Western Europe. In many host countries, the Islamic organiation of Turkish migrants functions as an ethnic interest group, making claims and demands which transcend purely religious ones. Here the situation varies from country to country. The organization of the religious life of Turkish citizens abroad, as foreseen in Article 62 of the Turkish Constitution, is mainly channeled through the Turkish Directorate of Religious Affairs (called the *Diyanet* for short). The Diyanet advocates a unity which is primarily Turkish, with nationalist ideals like patriotism, love of the fatherland, and martyrdom propagated as Islamic values. Ataturk's secular state-building nationalism is dressed up in Islamic clothes. However, in the 1970s oppositional Muslim groups began to be active in setting up mosques and prayer rooms and expounding a competing Islamic ideology. Followers of Nakşuibendi Sheikh Suleyman Hilmi Tunahan (who died in 1960) set up a network of Turkish Islamic centers in Western Europe. In the late 1970s and early 1980s, the Milli Gorus movement, set up by radical Islamists against the official Diyanet position, also gained strong support among migrants. A radical wing split off in 1983 and openly attacked the secular Republic of Turkey as well as the Diyanet, which was portrayed as the "Directorate of Treachery Affairs" (*Hiyanet*).

Faced with this challenge, the Diyanet responded by greatly expanding its own network. In addition, the Turkish authorities set up semiofficial representatives of the Diyanet in various European countries to administer many mosques for Turks. Such an organization in the Netherlands, for example, is the Islamic Foundation, which is formally linked to the Diyanet in its statutes. The Islamic Foundation runs some 70 percent of the 160 Turkish mosques in the Netherlands. In Germany there is another Diyanet, the DITB, which similarly controls between half and two thirds of Germany's Turkish mosques. Similar organizations exist in Belgium and other West European countries. This has seen the Diyanet-linked organization controlling the majority of mosques in Germany and the Netherlands, where Turks are the dominant Islamic community. In Belgium their influence is somewhat checked by the position of the Islamic Cultural Centre in Brussels, which is controlled by the World Muslim League.

Thus, the Diyanet is a major force among Turkish Muslims in Western Europe. However the rival Islamic organizations remain as serious competitors. In the late 1970s and early 1980s the Diyanet attacked the Islamic Cultural Centres of the Suleymancs in Germany and the Netherlands for being extremist and illegal. The latter countered by accusing the Diyanet of attempting to stifle independent development of Turkish Islamic communities, and of intervention by Turkey in the internal affairs of other states. Some form of modus vivendi appears to have taken place between the Diyanet and most other Turkish Muslim groups, although tensions remain. The rise in Turkey of a radical Islam critical of the official Diyanet line is mirrored in Turkish communities outside. Criticism has also come from non-Muslims who view the strong "official" Turkish nationalist content in the Diyanet—loyalty to the Turkish flag and deep emotion at the Turkish national anthem and the like—as hindering integration into the European host society and running counter to perceived ideas of a European Islam.

Of course, these considerations only apply to Turkish Sunni Muslims. The Alevi Turks are estimated to have made up a disproportional high percentage of guestworkers in the 1960s and 1970s. In addition, Alevis have since the birth of the republic traditionally tended to support parties of the left, and there was a sizeable emigration of radical left-wingers from Turkey following the military coup of 1980. Such people, fleeing severe persecution from within Turkey by the military rulers, were also not sympathetic to Sunni Islamic models of Turkish identity, preferring radical Marxist models based on class rather than national issues. Alevis were also prominent among these groups of Turks abroad, and, similarly to the rise of Sunnism, there has been something of an Alevi revival, including the religious aspect. This has occurred both within Turkey, and among the guestworkers in Western Europe, with a rise in interest and growth of Alevi associations in cities like Berlin.

Conclusion

A major difference is evident in the feelings of national attachment between those groups in the Balkans and the groups of Turkish guestworkers living in Western Europe. In the former, the communities appear in little danger of becoming assimilated into the (Christian) majorities. In this, the *millet* heritage of the Ottoman Empire lives on. While the Balkan states have had considerable success in assimilating fellow Orthodox Christian groups into the majority, the Muslims have proved far harder to assimilate. Moreover, in many parts of the Balkans there is a process of attraction towards the majority Muslim group of smaller Muslim groups like the Pomaks. In the Eastern Balkans, the ethnic-Turkish mass is the main group exerting this attraction, while in the West there is also the Muslim Albanian one as a rival. Thus, far from appearing endangered in terms of national identity, the Turks in the Balkans seem to be becoming more assertive and actually assimilating other groups themselves. In Western Europe this process is not so marked. Many second-generation Turks are becoming assimilated into the host society. They are looking less and less to Turkey as a kin-state and more to the states in which they reside, highlighting the difference between long-standing communities and more recent immigrants.

HUGH POULTON

See also **Bulgaria; Cyprus; Germany; Greece; Macedonia; Moldova; Romania; Turkey; Yugoslavia**

Further Reading

Antes, Peter, and Klaus Kreiser, *Muslims in German—German Muslims? Questions of Identity, Muslims in Europe*, Research paper No 28, Birmingham: Centre for the Study of Islam and Christian Muslim Relations, Selly Oak Colleges, December 1985

Basµgoz, Ihan, and Norman Furniss, editors, *Turkish Workers in Europe: An Interdisciplinary Study*, Indiana: Indiana University Turkish Studies, 1985

Kocturk, Tahire, *A Matter of Honour: Experiences of Turkish Women Immigrants*, London: Zed, 1992

Poulton, Hugh, *Top Hat Grey Wolf and Crescent: Turkish Nationalism and the Turkish Republic*, London: Hurst and New York: New York University Press, 1997

————, and Suha Taji-Farouki, editors, *Muslim Identity and the Balkan State*, London: Hurst and New York: New York University Press, 1997

Slomp, Jan, Ge Speelman, and Willem de Wit, *Muslims in the Netherlands, (Muslims in Europe, Research Paper no 37)*, Birmingham: Centre for the Study of Islam and Christian Muslim Relations, Selly Oak Colleges, March 1988

Soysal, Yasmin, "Workers in Europe: Interactions with the Host Society," in *Turkey and the West*, edited by M. Heper, O. Metin, and H. Kramer, London: I. B. Tauris, 1993

Tutsi

Capsule Summary

Location: Central Africa (concentrated in Rwanda, Burundi, Congo)

Total Population: 3,267,000 (1998, *Minorities at Risk* project, University of Maryland)

Major Languages: Kinyarwanda (also English, French)

Major Religions: Roman Catholic, Protestant, Muslim

The Tutsis are a small ethnic group living in Central Africa. They are concentrated in Rwanda, Burundi and Congo, and make up approximately 14 percent of the total population in Rwanda and Burundi and 2 percent in Congo. There are also Tutsis, some of whom are refugees, living in Uganda, Tanzania, Europe, and North America. Their native language is *Kinyarwanda* or *Kirundi*, but many Tutsis also speak other African languages (e.g., *Swahili* or *Lingala*), English, and/or French. Since 1990, major conflicts in Rwanda, Burundi, and Congo have resulted in the deaths of over a million Tutsis. The conflicts in Burundi and Congo continue while the situation in Rwanda has stabilized. Though the Tutsis are small minorities in each country in which they reside, they have historically been a powerful and privileged minority. They have had serious conflicts with the Hutus of Rwanda and Burundi who make up approximately 85 percent of the population in each country, and with various Bantu groups in eastern Congo. Their history and current position within these countries cannot be understood outside of their relationships with these other ethnic groups.

History

Simple explanations of the differences between Tutsis and Hutus cannot capture the complexity of their historical and current relationships in Rwanda, Burundi, and Congo. Tutsis are generally described as pastoralists (cattle herders) while the Hutu were mainly agriculturalists (farmers). This simplistic differentiation, however, did not hold true in all cases. For example, Hutu sometimes owned cattle or cared for Tutsi cattle and were tied to their owners through a patron-client system. Catharine Newbury describes a patron-client relationship as an "instrumental friendship between two persons of relatively unequal socioeconomic status. The relationship usually involves the exchange of protection and/or benefits from the person of higher status (the patron) for general loyalty and service from the lower-status person (the client)" (Newbury, *The Cohesion of Oppression: Clientship and Ethnicity in Rwanda, 1860-1960,* 1988, p. 16). Thus, the main distinction between the two groups historically was based in economics, not ethnicity, and status was the principal determinant of rank and privilege (Lemarchand, 1994). Even the widely cited population figures for the two groups in Rwanda and Burundi (85 percent Hutu, 14 percent Tutsi) are based on estimates from the 1930s and do not reflect the mass killings that have taken place in both countries since 1959 or the fact that a substantial number of people in both countries are of mixed origins.

Distinctions between Tutsi and Hutu were to some degree created rather than being a product of primordial or biological differences. Speaking about Burundi, Alphonse Rugambarara explains that modern day "use of the terms Hutu and Tutsi reflects a deliberate effort to create and maintain a Tutsi ideology and a Hutu ideology . . . These two ideologies, born in the womb of the political class shortly before independence, have created and maintained this so-called ethnic consciousness, which may not have come into being had the experience of politics been lived and defined differently. . . . Behind the problem of definition (of ethnic categories) lies a problem of perception" (Rugambarara, 1990, p. 37, as quoted by Lemarchand, *Burundi: Ethnocide as Discourse and Practice,* 1994, p. 14).

In both Burundi and Rwanda, ethnic identity has developed so that social relations in what were once very complex, stratified societies have been simplified to a social system of mutually opposed and rigid ethnic categories. Those who argue for the distinctiveness of each group of people promote the idea that Hutu and Tutsi are physically and occupationally distinct peoples and that the differences are self-evident. This argument ignores that the groups speak the same language and share a common culture, that Tutsis could fall on hard times and move into the Hutu category and that Hutus who acquired wealth could move into the Tutsi category, and that the groups have intermarried over time. The transformation of ethnic identity into more rigid categories in both countries took place within the context of colonialism, though assigning blame to the deterioration of Hutu-Tutsi relations solely to the Belgium colonizers would also be a simplification of the situation.

Ethnic Relations in Burundi

It is a mistake to assume that the political and social structures of precolonial Burundi and precolonial Rwanda were the same. Though there were similarities, they cannot be treated as identical cases. The hierarchy of status in Burundi began with the King, followed by the princely class (*ganwa*), the Tutsis, the Hutus, and the Twa. Within each class, there was also a hierarchy of status. For example, Tutsi-Banyaruguru held higher status than the Tutsi-Hima. Like in Rwanda, Hutus and Tutsis could gain or lose status over time, yet there was a lot more rivalry within the princely class in Burundi than in Rwanda (Lemarchand, 1994). On the eve of the colonial period, the Burundi kingdom was fragmented into four regions. The king and his sons controlled two regions, other princes a third, and semi-autonomous chiefs of Hutu or Tutsi origins the fourth. Because there was a great deal of rivalry within the princely class, Tutsi leaders had to expend a great deal of effort in consolidating their support among both the lower class Hutu and Tutsi. In fact, the monarchy in Burundi was dependent on Hutu elements for its legitimacy and was not associated with Tutsi supremacy (Lemarchand, 1994).

The Belgians took over the territory in 1917 following Germany's defeat in World War I. Beginning in 1929, Belgium instituted a policy of bringing together a number of previously independent chiefdoms under a single prince. The number of chiefdoms declined from 133 in 1929 to 35 in 1945 (Lemarchand, 1994). The king's sons fared best under this arrangement.

Prior to independence, two parties, Unity and National Progress Party (UPRONA) and the Democratic Christian Party (PDC), emerged as strong contenders to take over the leadership of the country. In 1961, the Prime Minister designate, a popular prince, was assassinated, allegedly by PDC supporters. In 1962, the UN agreed to the partition of Rwanda and Burundi, and Burundi became independent on July 1, 1962. For several years, the king attempted to consolidate his power by appointing both Hutu and Tutsi to positions within the government. However, the Hutu prime minister was assassinated in January 1965 and the king was overthrown in November 1965. In 1966, the Tutsi-dominated military abolished the kingdom for good. The military ruled the country until 1993 when democratic elections were held and Melchoir Ndadaye, a Hutu, gained the presidency.

In 1972, Hutu rebels attempted a coup and attacked Tutsi civilians. The military retaliated and killed some 80,000 to 100,000 Hutus. Educated Hutus were specifically targeted in an attempt to incapacitate future Hutu rebel activities. Many Hutu fled to Tanzania following the slaughter. Lemarchand suggests that after the genocide of 1972 in Burundi, ethnicity emerged as a different phenomenon "in which memories of martyrdom emerge as a central feature of the social construction of identity" (Lemarchand, *Burundi: Ethnocide as Discourse and Practice,* 1994, p. xiv). Whereas in Rwanda, the Tutsis emerged as a martyred people after the 1994 genocide, in Burundi, it was the Hutu who were the victims of the minority Tutsi who held the power.

Several coups occurred throughout the 1970s, and political parties were not allowed to function. In response to disorganized rural violence in 1988, the military again massacred large numbers of Hutus (5000-20,000). In 1991, the Party for the Liberation of the Hutu People (*Palipehutu*), which was founded in the 1980s, launched attacks in northern towns in the hope of provoking a general Hutu uprising. Palipehutu forces continued to launch attacks over the course of the following two years. Under pressure to democratize, President Pierre Buyoya agreed to multiparty elections in 1993. As stated above, a Hutu was elected president. He was assassinated by members of the military after only several months in office. This assassination provoked a cycle of violence in the country that it has yet to recover from. There was a brief respite from the violence in January of 1994 when the Catholic Church brokered a settlement. The Hutu dominated Front for Democracy in Burundi (FRODEBU) and the Tutsi dominated UPRONA agreed to share power, and Hutu Cyprien Ntaryamira became President. Unfortunately, he and Rwanda's president Habyarimana were assassinated in April of 1994 while flying into Kigali.

Relations between Hutus and Tutsis in Burundi have been destructive since the events of 1994. After Ntaryamira was killed, another power-sharing arrangement was agreed to, and Hutu Slyvestre Ntibantunganya took power. He was unable to quell the violence in the country, and was overthrown in a coup in 1996. Former president Pierre Buyoya, a Tutsi, regained power, and continued to rule in early 2001. An estimated 200,000 people had been killed in Burundi in the early 1990s, and fighting continued into the twenty-first century. The southern region of the country is the home base of Hutu rebels, and attacks against civilians and the government are frequent occurrences. In addition, Hutu rebels have bases in eastern Congo, so the Burundian government also has a stake in the ongoing Congo war. Though Burundi did not experience genocide like neighboring Rwanda after the assassination of both countries' presidents in 1994, the situation in Burundi is much less stable than in Rwanda in early 2001. Ethnic relations between the Hutu and Tutsi will continue to deteriorate as long as the ideology of ethnic hatred continues to find resonance among the people.

Ethnic Relations in Rwanda

Prior to German colonization in 1899, Rwanda was a Tutsi kingdom. The Belgians took over the territories of Rwanda and Burundi in 1917. The Tutsi kingdom was a highly stratified social system based on inequalities between and within the Hutu and Tutsi groups. Also important in defining one's social status was one's region of origin. With the growth of the Belgian colonial system, power over land, cattle, and people became concentrated in the hands of Tutsi elites, so relations between the ethnic groups deteriorated. The changes in the land tenure system (the right to land ownership or usage) further altered relations between the two groups. The patron-client ties which had bound them before the advent of colonialism became less reciprocal and more exploitative, and Hutus began to become discontented with the power arrangements in the country.

As the colonial era was drawing to a close, Tutsi elites agitated for immediate independence while the Hutu elites demanded a transition period in which educated Hutu leaders would take power followed by full independence. The Belgians who had been supporting the Tutsis decided to back the majority Hutus rather than the Tutsis at independence. The result was further entrenchment of a Hutu power ideology. During 1959-1961, radical Hutu leaders carried out a mass killing of the Tutsi. Some 20,000 to 100,000 were killed and hundreds of thousands fled to Uganda, Burundi, Tanzania, and Congo (Kimonyo, 2000).

Because Tutsis retained control after independence in neighboring Burundi, much of Rwanda's recent history has been influenced by events there. For example, the 1972 massacre of Hutus in Burundi triggered a slaughter of Tutsis in 1972-1973 in Rwanda. To restore order in Rwanda, the military took over in July of 1973 and Major General Juvenal Habyarimana became head of state. From this time until the end of the genocide in 1994, the Rwandan government was dominated by Northern Hutus, particularly from the Gisenyi region. Habyarimana's authoritarian rule alienated not only the Tutsis but also Hutu elites from other regions.

In 1987, Rwandan Tutsis living in Uganda, many of whom were in the Ugandan military, established the Rwandan Patriotic Front (RPF). The RPF invaded Rwanda in October of 1990 in an attempt to force Habyarimana out of power. Over the course of the following two years, the RPF kept military pressure on the Rwandan government. Because of pressure from external forces to democratize, a depressed economy and the threat of the RPF, Habyarimana agreed to peace talks. Between August 1993 and January 1994, the government and RPF agreed to two power-sharing arrangements in which the RPF was to gain a certain number of cabinet positions and integrate its soldiers into the Armed Forces of Rwanda (FAR). Extremist Hutus within the government of Rwanda were vehemently opposed to any power-sharing arrangement with the RPF, and clashes broke out between different factions of the government.

In April or 1994, extremist Hutu forces launched a genocide against the Tutsis and moderate Hutus after Habyarimana's plane, carrying himself and the president of Burundi, was shot down over Kigali. Within 100 days, some 800,000 people, mostly Tutsis, were killed. The genocide was systematic, led by a few radicals but carried out by the Hutu masses. The RPF eventually worked its way to Kigali and took over the country in July. After the RPF took over, some 2 million Hutus, some of whom were killers, fled to eastern Congo out of fear of retaliation from the new Tutsi government. The RPF rounded up genocide suspects, and today some 120,000 people are in jail awaiting trial on genocide-related crimes. Most of the refugees had returned to Rwanda by the end of 1997. Genocidal forces continued to operate within Rwanda until 1998, but since that time, the government has been able to guarantee security throughout the country. The government, dominated by Tutsis since the RFP ended the

genocide, remains concerned that thousands of radical Hutus who committed the genocide (*Interahamwe*) continue to operate in eastern Congo and are supported by the Congolese government. It therefore maintains a presence in the Congo, which in early 2001 was embroiled in a civil war.

Relations between the Hutu and Tutsi in Rwanda are stable, though tensions remain below the surface. Since few people in the country were untouched in one way or another by the genocide, it is difficult to imagine that Hutus and Tutsis will soon be able to reconcile their differences and unify as a nation. However, the government has been engaged for several years in promoting peace, stability, national reconciliation, and healing. The success of these efforts will depend on a number of issues: economic prosperity, the war in neighboring Congo, the success of *gacaca* trials (a traditional system of justice based in local communities) of genocide suspects, and the efforts of the government to be inclusive of all groups. After the success of the RFP in overthrowing the genocide forces in 1994, thousands of Tutsis who had been living outside the country, many of whom had never lived in Rwanda, returned there. In addition to Hutu-Tutsi tensions in general, tensions between Tutsi newcomers and Tutsis who survived the genocide exist. The newcomers mostly speak English whereas the rest of the country is French-speaking, are generally highly educated, and are in control of the government. The future of the country hinges on their ability to bridge the existing social gaps in the country and promoting the welfare of all Rwandans.

Ethnic Relations in Congo

Congolese Tutsi (known as the *Banyamulenge*) and Congolese Hutus have long been considered foreigners by other ethnic groups in their country and discriminated against as a collective group (together the *Banyarwandans*). Some Congolese Hutus and Tutsis were refugees, but others are natives of the area or Rwandans brought to Congo (then Zaire) by the Belgians in the mid-twentieth century to work the fields. Most of the land occupied by the *Banyarwandans* in eastern Congo traditionally belonged to local chiefs who rented it to them on terms and taxes imposed by the chiefs. Under the rule of Mobutu Sese Seko (1965-1997), the *Banyarwandans* were not considered citizens of Congo. Though they were formally granted citizenship rights in 1972, in practice they have had no voting rights and no representation.

In 1993, the *Banyamulenge* began organizing against perceived injustices, especially paying taxes to local chiefs, and for the first time distinctions between Congolese Hutus and Congolese Tutsis were made by "native" Congolese. Tensions between livestock farmers, the *Banyamulenge*, and indigenous crop farmers in the area exploded in several villages in northern Kivu. Between March of 1993 and January of 1994, over 10,000 people, mostly *Banyamulenge*, were reportedly killed, and over 250,000 were displaced. Shortly before the fighting began, the local governor was said to have been encouraging "native" groups to attack the *Banyamulenge*.

In 1996, a rebellion led by the *Banyamulenge* broke out in eastern Congo. They had been subject to growing discrimination after the influx into Congo of approximately 2 million Rwandan refugees following the 1994 genocide. The *Banyamulenge* rebels received support from Rwanda, Uganda, and other Congolese. Within less than a year, the rebels overthrew Mobutu, and installed Laurent Kabila (a Congolese *Luba*) as president. Kabila renamed the country the Democratic Republic of Congo (DRC) and included many Rwandan and Congolese Tutsis in his administration. This led to renewed resentment against the Tutsis by other Congolese who considered them "foreigners."

After a short time in power, Kabila ordered all Rwandans out of the country and then allied himself with his former allies' enemies, the *Interahamwe* (Rwandan Hutus responsible for the 1994 genocide). The Rwandan and Ugandan governments, mainly for security reasons, in turn launched a second rebellion in eastern Congo in late 1998. Kabila's government had allowed rebels from Rwanda (Interahamwe) and Uganda (Allied Democratic Forces) to operate bases in Congolese soil from which they launched invasions into their respective countries. The rebellion continues into early 2001 with Ugandan and Rwandan troops and their Congolese allies (led by *Banyamulenge*) controlling much of the east and north of the country, and Kabila's government controlling much of the west and south. Kabila himself was assassinated on January 16, 2001 by one of his security guards. His son Joseph was installed as president shortly thereafter.

The international community has attempted to broker peace since the second rebellion began. A cease-fire agreement, the Lusaka Peace Accords, was signed by all parties in July 1999. However, the Accords did little to end the fighting. Angola, Namibia, and Zimbabwe are allies of the government in the war. Numerous rebel groups are also active in the war. Among the rebel groups that have launched raids from the DRC into their own countries are the *Interahamwe* from Rwanda, Hutu rebels from Burundi, members of the Allied Democratic Forces from Uganda, and UNITA rebels from Angola. As many as 1.7 million people have died as a result of the wars in the DRC since 1996. Until the war in Congo is resolved, ethnic relations will continue to deteriorate in the Congo, and even after its resolution, there are no guarantees that the Tutsi will be more secure living in their native land.

ANNE M. PITSCH

See also **Burundi; Congo; Rwanda; Tanzania; Uganda**

Further Reading

Gourevitch, Philip, *We Wish to Inform You that Tomorrow We Will be Killed with Our Families: Stories from Rwanda*, New York: Farrar, Straus, and Giroux, 1998

Gurr, Ted Robert, Principal Investigator, *Minorities at Risk Project*, <www.bsos.umd.edu/cidcm/mar>

Kimonyo, Jean Paul, "Causes of the Rwandan Genocide and Beyond," in the conference Paper *Conflict and Peace-making in the Great Lakes Region*, Entebbe, Uganda, 2000. Paper available from the Center for Conflict Management at the National University of Rwanda.

Lemarchand, René, *Rwanda and Burundi*, New York: Praeger Publishers, 1970

———, *Burundi: Ethnocide as Discourse and Practice*, Cambridge University Press, 1994

Newbury, Catherine, *The Cohesion of Oppression: Clientship and Ethnicity in Rwanda, 1860–1960*, New York: Columbia University Press, 1988

Prendergast, John, and David Smock, *Reconstructing Peace in the Congo*, Washington, DC: The United States Institute of Peace, August 1999

Uvin, Peter, "Ethnicity and Power in Burundi and Rwanda," *Comparative Politics*, 31, no. 3 (April 1999)

Weiss, Herbert, *War and Peace in the Democratic Republic of the Congo*, Uppsala, Sweden: Nordiska Afrikaninstitutet, 2000

Young, Crawford, *Politics in the Congo: Decolonization and Independence*, Princeton: Princeton University Press, 1965

Tutu, Desmond (South African)

Desmond Mpilo Tutu (born 1931), a leading figure in the resistance to apartheid in the 1970s and 1980s, was in the mid-1990s appointed chair of South Africa's Truth and Reconciliation Commission.

Tutu was born in Klerksdorp, west of Johannesburg. He wanted to study medicine, but his Methodist parents could not afford the fees to send him to medical school. He was educated at a Swedish mission school, then an Anglican institution, before going to a teacher-training college in Pretoria. He taught for four years, then resigned when the Bantu Education Act took control of schools from churches. He then studied for the Anglican (Church of England) priesthood at St Peter's Theological College in Rosettenville, Johannesburg, where he came under the influence of Father Trevor Huddleston of the Community of the Resurrection, a fierce critic of apartheid. For Tutu, entering the church was a way to serve his people.

After being ordained in 1961, he won a scholarship to study at King's College, London, and he worked as a part-time curate at St. Albans from 1962 to 1967. He returned to South Africa in 1967 to become chaplain at Fort Hare University in Alice. After lecturing in Lesotho he worked for the World Council of Churches' Theological Education Fund in London. In 1975 he returned permanently to South Africa when he was appointed dean of Johannesburg, the first black person to hold such a major post in the Anglican church in South Africa. He refused to ask for government permission to live in the deanery in a white suburb, and instead went to live within Johannesburg's major black township, Soweto.

In May 1976, some weeks before the Soweto Uprising began, he warned the government of rising tensions, but his warning was disregarded. He was encouraged by Father Aelred Stubbs, his mentor, to meet young black consciousness activists, and when the police murdered Steve Biko, the black consciousness leader, he was invited to speak at his funeral. Rising rapidly in the church, he became bishop of Lesotho, then general secretary of the South African Council of Churches (SACC), which represented some twenty member churches, from 1978 to 1985. He worked to strengthen the Council's contacts with the African National Congress in exile.

He was briefly bishop of Johannesburg before being named archbishop of Cape Town, the head of the church in South Africa, Namibia, Swaziland, and Lesotho, in 1986.

In the 1980s he played a significant role in the mobilizing of international opposition to apartheid. That role, and the courage he showed in South Africa in being an outspoken critic of apartheid, was recognized by the award to him of the Nobel Peace Prize in 1984. He was not only an exceptionally powerful orator; he combined this with great political skills and moral leadership. Charismatic, and with a strong sense of humor, he filled a leadership gap in the 1980s in the black community in South Africa. He spoke out with passion on the evil of apartheid and the justice of the fight against it. Yet he could also be a conciliator. In the mid-1980s he was denounced and demonized by most of the white community for his support for sanctions against South Africa, yet at the same time he often intervened to prevent clashes between security forces and protestors in the townships during the state of emergency.

Tutu spoke in prophetic terms of South Africans as "the rainbow people of God." He led a march in Cape Town in September 1989 against police violence, the first such march for many decades and an important moment in the transition to a new order. After the release of Nelson Mandela in 1990, he began withdrawing from an active political role, though one of his proudest moments came in 1994 when he introduced Mandela to the people of Cape Town after he had been elected president of South Africa. In the following years, he remained an influential figure, promoting the idea of the "rainbow nation," and commentating on events with both wit and seriousness. He denounced high salaries for members of parliament and the "gravy train," and the growth of the country's arms industry.

In 1995, on the eve of his retirement as Archbishop of Cape Town at the age of sixty-five, he was appointed head of the Truth and Reconciliation Commission. This was set up to investigate gross human rights violations in the period from 1960 to the advent of the new democratic order, and to provide for the granting of amnesty to those who made full disclosure. He presided over many meetings of the human rights violations committee, at which victims gave testimony, and on occasion wept at what he heard. He resisted attempts by the African National Congress at the last moment to prevent the publication of the Commission's report, and in October 1998 he proudly handed over the five-volume report to President Mandela. He was critical when the government did not grant the financial reparations recommended by the Commission. While busy with the Commission, he was diagnosed with prostrate cancer, and went to the United States for treatment. After the Commission ended its work, he spent two years in the United States before returning to South Africa. It was expected that the Commission would reassemble in 2001 to complete a final report, after the amnesty hearings had been completed.

Biography

Desmond Mpilo Tutu, South Africa's most prominent church leader. Born October 7, 1931 in Klerksdorp, Transvaal, South Africa. Ordained into Anglican priesthood, 1961; Dean of Johannesburg, Bishop of Lesotho, Secretary of the South African Council of Churches, Archbishop of Cape Town. Awarded the Nobel Peace Prize, 1984. Advocated the imposition of sanctions against apartheid in South Africa. President of All Africa Conference of Churches, 1987. Head of the Truth and Reconciliation Commission, 1995; delivered Truth and Reconciliation Commission's report to President Mandela, October of 1998. Married (to Leah Tutu); four adult children.

Has received more than 100 honorary degrees from universities around the world.

Selected Works

Hope and Suffering: Sermons and Speeches, 1983
The Words of Desmond Tutu, edited by N.Tutu, 1989
Crying in the Wilderness: the Struggle for Justice in South Africa, Grand Rapids, Mich., 1982; London, 1990
The Rainbow People of God. South Africa's Victory over Apartheid, edited by J.Allen, 1994
No Future Without Forgiveness, 1999

CHRISTOPHER SAUNDERS

See also **South Africa**

Further Reading

Battle, M., *Reconciliation: The Ubuntu Theology of Desmond Tutu*, 1997
Boraine, A., *A Country Unmasked*, Cape Town, 2000
Borer, T.A., *Challenging the State. Churches as Political Actors in South Africa 1984–1994*, Notre Dame, 1998
du Boulay, S., *Tutu : Voice of the Voiceless*, Harmondsworth, 1989
Graybill, L., *Religion and Resistance Politics in South Africa*, Westport, Connecticut: 1995
Mungazi, D.A., *In the Footsteps of the Masters: Desmond M. Tutu and Abel T. Muzorewa*, Westport, Connecticut: 2000
Tlhagale, B. and I. Mosala, editors, *Hammering Swords into Ploughshares: Essays in Honour of Archbishop Mpilo Desmond Tutu*, Johannesburg, 1986
Truth and Reconciliation Commission, *Report*, 5 vols., Johannesburg, 1998

Tuvans

Capsule Summary

Location: South central Siberia, Russian Federation
Total Population: approximately 300,000
Language: Tuvan (Tyvan)
Religions: animist, Buddhist

Tuvans occupy a land of vast, rolling steppes and forested mountains in a southern Siberia region of the Russian Federation, located just along the northern border of Mongolia. Smaller, scattered communities of nomadic Tuvans also inhabit Central and Western Mongolia, Russia proper, and the People's Republic of China. While many Tuvans are urbanized, a large percentage still practice an age-old livelihood of herding sheep, goats, camels, yaks, and horses along circuitous, seasonal migration routes across the grassy plains.

Tuvan applied arts are uniquely adapted to the available natural materials and the needs of a nomadic life. The paragon of Tuvan engineering is the ergonomic nomads' dwelling known in English as a *yurt* and in Tuvan as *ög*. Made of felt, wood and leather, yurts are collapsible and can be quickly disassembled and moved by truck, horse, or camel to a new campsite. Ornately fashioned saddles, bridles, and riding crops—essential tools for any herdsman—are hung on display just inside the yurt's entrance.

In recent years Tuvans have won worldwide renown for their vocal artistry. In a unique style of singing—called *overtone* or *throat* singing—the singer manipulates individual resonant harmonics of the vocal tract to create melodies. Sound is of central importance to Tuvan art and aesthetics. Natural sound produced by the elements, wind, water, and animals may be embellished, improvised, and echoed in Tuvan singing and instrumental music. The *byzanchy*, a two-stringed bowed fiddle, can imitate the sound of a horse whinnying, trotting, and galloping.

As practicing animists, Tuvans venerate natural springs, rivers, mountains, mountain passes, and other topographic features. Animism is based upon belief in spirits or spiritual forces thought to inhabit features of the natural environment (mountains, hills, rivers, springs, trees, fire), certain animals (bears, birds, foxes), and even some human-made objects (various types of totems, drums, and shrines). In addition to these grounded or local spirits, the Tuvan belief system includes a pantheon of sky gods and sky spirits, referred to under the general term *Kurbustug* ("sky deity") and believed to reside in the nine layers of heaven. There are also malevolent spirits thought to reside under the ground.

The practice of animism is facilitated by, but not dependent on, a class of self-named practitioners known as shamans (called *ham* in Tuvan). Shamans may diagnose illnesses, read fortunes, give advice on good or bad days for certain activities, purify homes, communicate with the deceased, and perform various rites, including healing rituals. The shaman's essential accoutrement is the *küzüngü*, a flat brass disc about three inches in diameter with a bunch of ribbons or strips of cloth tied to it. Shamans may also optionally possess a drum (*düngür*), a ribbon-bedecked robe, and other tools and totem objects. A shaman traditionally had to possess his or her own unique songs or invocations, known as *algysh*. These were believed to be the product of direct visions or inspirations from the spirit world. In one example of a song, a female shaman employs imitations of animal sounds to summon her animal helper spirits. She calls upon them to assist her in an out-of-body flight to other worlds.

The practice of animism coexists with Tuva's other main religion, the *yellow faith*, a variety of Buddhism brought to Tuva in the sixteenth century by Tibetan monks. His holiness the XIVth Dalai Lama of Tibet remains a much-venerated spiritual leader for Tuvans. His portrait may be found hanging in the yurts of most Tuvan nomads. With the political liberalizations of *perestroika* in the 1990s, Tuvans entered a period of greater freedom to practice their long-suppressed Buddhist faith. This was accompanied by an intense renewal of interest in religion, including animism, Buddhism, and newly imported creeds. In 1999, an essentially political coalition enthroned Aganak Hertek, a young novice aged 18 who had been in training with Tibetan lamas for less than two years, as the head lama (*kamby lama*) of all Tuva. While only men can be lamas, Tuvans' unique interpretation of Buddhist practice allows them to marry and raise a family, in contrast to traditional Tibetan Buddhism, which requires that lamas remain celibate.

The Tuvan language (*tyva dyl*) belongs to the eastern branch of the Turkic language family, along with Sakha (Yakut) and Uighur. The standardized Tuvan language was codified between 1928 and 1950. Based on a geographically central dialect, it was close to the language spoken by most Tuvans. Dialects spoken on the periphery of Tuva differ considerably. These include the dialect of the former reindeer herding *Todzhu* people of northeastern Tuva, the strongly Mongolian influenced dialects of the southeast, and mountain dialects of Western Tuva. Unique characteristics of Tuvan include a pitch accent system and widespread vowel harmony.

The first Tuvan alphabet was developed in the early 1930s by a Tuvan Buddhist monk named Mongush Lopsan-Chimit. In the 1930s and 1940s a number of Tuvans became literate using primers written in this alphabet. After 1945, on the heels of a brutal Stalinist repression of Tuvan intellectuals, a modified Cyrillic (Russian) alphabet was imposed. Literacy is now nearly universal in Tuva, due to compulsory schooling. Though many books are available in Tuvan, few outsiders ever learn the language and only small portions of the literature have yet been translated.

K. DAVID HARRISON

See also **China; Mongolia; Siberian Indigenous Peoples**

Further Reading

Anderson, Gregory D.S., and K. David Harrison, *Tyvan* München: Lincom Europa, 1999

Forsyth, J., *A History of the Peoples of Siberia*, Cambridge: Cambridge University Press, 1992

Kenin-Lopsan, Mongush, *Shamanic Songs and Myths of Tuva*, Budapest: Society for Transoceanic Research, 1993

Levin, Theodore C., and Michael E. Edgerton, "The Throat-Singers of Tuva," *Scientific American*, 281, no. 3 (September 1999)

Vainstein, S.I., *Nomads of South Siberia*, translated by M. Colenso, Cambridge: Cambridge University Press, 1980

Twa

Capsule Summary

Locations: Rwanda, Burundi, Eastern Democratic Republic of Congo (DRC), and Southwestern Uganda
Total Population: 70,000-87,000
Languages: Banyarwanda, Kirundi, Kirega, and others
Religions: Traditional religious practices and Christianity

The stem *-twa* is used as an ethnonym by agricultural peoples over most of Sub-Saharan Africa to refer to peoples who are in almost every case hunter-gatherers and former hunter-gatherers; they are recognized as the original inhabitants of the area they occupy and as people who have very low status. *Twa* is applied to Pygmies in Central Africa, to Bushmen in Southern Africa, and to other hunter-gatherers in other parts of Africa. Geographical references are necessary to distinguish different groups. The Twa Pygmies of the Great Lakes inhabit parts of southwestern Uganda, eastern DRC, Rwanda, and Burundi. All Twa in the region recognize their shared descent from the first hunter-gatherer inhabitants of the mountainous area they still occupy despite speaking different languages today.

The Twa live dispersed over approximately 100,000 square kilometers (38,610 square kilometers). Their total population is estimated to be 69,500 to 87,000; 30,000 to 40,000 in Burundi, 16,000 in DRC, 20,000 to 27,000 in Rwanda, and 3,500 to 4,000 in Uganda. The highest population densities occur in mountainous areas around Lake Edward, Lake Kivu, and Lake Tanganyika. The Twa are a minority numerically and politically, making up between 0.02 and 0.7 percent of the total population in the various countries they occupy.

In most of their traditional territory, the Twa have been forced to abandon their forest-based hunter-gatherer lifestyle. This began centuries ago in Uganda, Rwanda, and Burundi. Here, highly organized precolonial kingdoms dominated by extensive agricultural and pastoral economies had cleared swathes of forest by the early twentieth century.

In these areas many Twa were unable to depend on hunting and gathering. Culturally indisposed to farming and other subsistence strategies requiring long-term investments, many Twa chose economic activities with more-or-less immediate returns on labor. They became woodcrafters, tinkers, blacksmiths, potters, day laborers, bards, performers, and some groups served at the royal courts.

With the forests destroyed, immigrants no longer depended on the Twa for access to the forest and its produce. The Twa became dependent on the farmers for food and land. As Twa lost the autonomy the forest provided, their neighbors' perception of them became more negative, discrimination more marked, and exploitation easier. While maintaining their own values and distinctive lifestyle, these Twa adopted aspects of the languages and religious practices of their neighbors. They share clan names and marriage practices and hold critical roles in chieftaincy and earth-fertility rituals.

The Kivu region of DRC has a more diverse history, with a greater variety of linguistic groups, political structures and population migrations. Lowland forest remains across the region today, Twa here have better access to forest. This has resulted in greater economic independence and more effective resistance to certain types of domination by their neighbors.

Throughout the region the Twa became incorporated into the locally dominant society at the very lowest level. Their low status, small numbers, and the dispersal of their communities have contributed to their extreme political weakness and the serious difficulties they have in asserting their rights and resisting expropriation and violence.

Foresters, Fisher Folk, and Potters

Due to the alienation of the Twa from their forests, they have become a diverse community. Today Twa distinguish themselves into three main groups according to their dominant economic practices: foresters, fisher folk, and potters.

Less than seven thousand Twa have access to forest today. They are known as *Impunyu*. Most live on the borders of forest and agricultural areas but use the forest daily. They are known to live in Uganda (Bwindi, Mgahinga, and Echuya forests), Rwanda (Gishwati forest, Parc des Volcans, and Nyungwe forest), and in many areas of Kivu province DRC. *Impunyu* are seminomadic, spending extended periods in favored campsites both in and outside forest areas. Groups are small, rarely exceeding 50 people, and often based around members of a particular clan. *Impunyu* obtain essential foods by hunting a variety of small and medium-sized mammals and collecting tubers, leaves, fruit, honey, and fungi according to season. Additionally they trade forest produce with farmers for goods, food, or cash; transform forest produce into craftwork to sell; or hire out their labor. Each clan collectively owns an area of forest, which is recognized as theirs by other Twa and identified by certain named valleys, rivers, hills, and trees. Traditional religion is based on the forest, performing rituals at sacred caves, hills, valleys, swamps, or trees. Even when these sacred sites are inside national parks, *Impunyu* continue to visit them secretly.

Little is known about the small groups of fisher folk. The majority live around Lake Kivu and on Idjwi Island in DRC and some live on the shores of Lake Tanganyika and Lake Rweru. Their numbers are unknown but are unlikely to exceed 3,000-4,000 people. As fisher folk they trade fish for food and money; as craft workers, men make canoes and paddles and women make baskets, mats, and fish traps. Some do a little pottery and many have small farms. Like other Twa they are considered the first inhabitants of their areas and are required to participate in important chiefly rituals.

Most contemporary Twa, around 60,000 to 76,000 people, are potters. As immigrant farmers and pastoralists steadily destroyed their forest habitat many Twa turned to pottery for an income. In many areas pottery has replaced hunting as a symbol of Twa identity.

That a woman's task came to symbolize the collective identity of the Twa reflects the increasing importance of women to the group's livelihood. Today women are the focus of family life. Marriages are generally unstable and many women have had several husbands. Children usually stay with their mother. When mothers are ill or unable to work the family becomes very vulnerable. Without forest for hunting or land to farm, men's role in supporting their family has diminished. So too has their self-esteem and social value. Many women complain of men's alcoholism and domestic violence.

In the 1970s industrially produced jerricans, basins, bowls, plates, and the like became widely popular. This competition forced Twa to keep their prices static and attractively cheap. As a result of inflation the real income gained from pottery fell. Additionally, access to clay has become increasingly difficult as land pressure has encouraged farmers to reclaim clay marshes for cultivation. In general as pressure on a local resource increases, the Twa are the first to be denied access to it.

Today those Twa still making pottery may become financially poorer by continuing. The time, effort, and resources invested in producing pots and taking them to market can exceed the financial returns gained from selling them. The collapse of the Twa's craft economy has forced them into increasingly marginal subsistence strategies, like casual day labor and begging. In 1993, begging was a major activity for 70 percent of Rwandan Twa. Some children, especially those living near urban centers, start begging at four or five years of age. They have more success than their elders.

Discrimination

In addition to their increasing poverty and marginalization, the Twa are discriminated against by mainstream society. This discrimination is similar to that experienced by other hunter-gatherers in Sub-Saharan Africa and is typically manifested as negative stereotyping, the denial of their rights, segregation, and land dispossession.

Twa are claimed to be backward, childish, dirty, ignorant, immoral, and stupid. In myths and chiefly rituals the Twa's hunting life is portrayed as decadent, immoral, and depraved. In these and other ways the Twa are stereotyped as not fully human or socialized beings. Such attitudes have a profound effect on the

Twa's status in wider society. Their rights as first inhabitants are conveniently denied because they are not considered as real people.

The denial of their rights includes, notably, their rights to land, but also other rights such as the right to represent and speak for themselves, or to practice their traditional economy. This is a major problem for *Impunyu*, who are actively prevented from hunting and gathering in the remaining forest on their ancestral lands. In other cases, Twa tenants are denied the right to freedom of movement and association, and landlords claim their labor and other capacities. In many areas Twa will have difficulty in obtaining justice through local courts unless they are represented by non-Twa.

Other people will not eat or drink with Twa, will not marry them, will not allow them to approach too closely, to sit on the same seat, or to touch cooking and eating implements. They must live apart from others, not draw water from wells at the same time as others, remain on the margins of public spaces, and when selling goods in markets must sit away from other sellers.

The Twa have been dispossessed of almost all their traditional lands and rarely enjoy security of tenure for what remains. This chronic landlessness results from the absence of historical recognition, in customary or statute law, for hunting and gathering to confer rights over land. The recent establishment of conservation areas demonstrate the enduring nature of this. Following evictions from the Kahuzi-Biega National Park in DRC during the 1970s and 1980s, or more recently in 1990s Uganda when Bwindi and Mgahinga forest reserves were established, compensation was paid to those who had transformed forest into farmland and habitations, but not to *Impunyu* who depended entirely on the forest. Similar events occurred in Gishwati Forest, the Parc des Volcans, and Nyungwe Forest in Rwanda.

The Twa are one of the most disadvantaged groups in the Great Lakes in terms of land ownership. Surveys of Rwandan Twa in 1995 and 1997 showed that only 1.6 percent had enough land to feed their families. In 2002, only 22 percent of Twa households in Cyangugu province, Rwanda, had agricultural land. In a recent national survey, 80 percent of Rwandan households owned some farmland.

Genocide and War in the Great Lakes

During the recent wars in the Great Lakes, all belligerents held negative stereotypes of the Twa. Consequently, Twa are vulnerable to attack from either side or of being coerced to take up arms. Security in the region is extremely poor; different armed groups intermittently attack civilians or steal food and property. Like their neighbors, the Twa suffer greatly during wars. But, in contrast to many of their neighbors they have fewer resources to fall back on during a crisis, the marginal areas they occupy are popular with armed groups seeking to avoid detection, and their lack of political patronage and extreme poverty makes them vulnerable to manipulation.

The Rwandan Genocide of 1994 offers a tragic example of the consequences of intense conflict between powerful groups on a marginalized and despised minority. During three months after April 6, 1994, mass killings resulted in the deaths of nearly one million, mostly Tutsi, Rwandans, around 14 percent of the population. The Twa only made up between 0.3 to 0.4 percent of the Rwandan population, yet it is estimated that up to 30 percent of Rwandan Twa died or were killed during the genocide and ensuing war. The majority of victims were Twa children and men. Men were often accused of participating by both sides during the conflict. Very poor children are extremely vulnerable to the perils of war and life as refugees. The burden of rebuilding homes and caring for the remaining children fell mostly upon women.

Seeking Representation

Despite their extensive marginalization, in 1991 some Twa succeeded in setting up the first representative organizations of Twa people. The Association Pour la Promotion des Batwa in Rwanda and the Programme d'Intégration et de Développment du Peuple Pygmée au Kivu in DRC were founded to promote Twa human rights, and to assist Twa to improve their standard of living.

The courage and persistence of these associations has inspired the formation of other Twa groups, most recently in Burundi and Uganda. The Twa are now embarked on a process which enables them to represent themselves at local, national, and international levels. They are now aware of, and participating in, the international movement supporting minority and indigenous rights. Indeed their example has helped stimulate the emergence of a regional network of forest, hunter-gatherer organizations across Central Africa.

JEROME LEWIS

See also **Burundi; Congo; Rwanda; Uganda**

Further Reading

Barume, Kwokwo, *Heading towards Extinction? The Expulsion of the Twa from the Kahuzi-Biega National Park, Democratic Republic of Congo*, Copenhagen: Forest Peoples' Program and IWGIA, 2000

De Carolis, Antonio, "Changements socio-economiques et degradation culturelle chez les pygmoides Ba-Twa du Burundi," *Africa (Roma)*, 32, no 2 (1977)

Jackson, Dorothy, "Some Recent International Initiatives in Equatorial Africa and Their Impacts on Forest Peoples," in *Central African Hunter-Gatherers in a Multidisciplinary Perspective: Challenging Elusiveness*, edited by K. Biesbrouck, S. Elders, and G. Rossel, CNWS, Universiteit Leiden, 1999

———, *Twa Women, Twa Rights in the Great Lakes*, Minority Rights Group Report, London: Minority Rights Group International, 2003

Kagabo, J.H., and V. Mudandagizi, "Complainte des gens d'argile, les Twa du Rwanda," in *Cahiers des Etudes Africaines*, 14, no. 1, Cahier No. 53 (1974)

Lewis, Jerome, *The Batwa Pygmies of the Great Lakes Region*, Minority Rights Group Report, London: Minority Rights Group International, 2000

Lewis, Jerome, and Judy Knight, *The Twa of Rwanda. Assessment of the Situation of the Twa and Promotion of Twa Rights in Post-War Rwanda*, World Rainforest Movement and International Work Group for Indigenous Affairs, 1995

Schadeberg, Thilo, "Batwa: The Bantu Name for the Invisible People," in *Central African Hunter-Gatherers in a Multidisciplinary Perspective: Challenging Elusiveness*, edited by K. Biesbrouck, S. Elders, and G. Rossel, CNWS, Universiteit Leiden, 1999

Wæhle, Espen, "The Twa of Rwanda: Survival and Defence of Human Rights," in *Central African Hunter-Gatherers in a Multidisciplinary Perspective: Challenging Elusiveness*, edited by K. Biesbrouck, S. Elders, and G. Rossel, CNWS, Universiteit Leiden, 1999

Woodburn, James, "Indigenous Discrimination: The Ideological Basis for Local Discrimination against Hunter-Gatherer Minorities in Sub-Saharan Africa," *Ethnic and Racial Studies*, 20, no. 2 (1997)

Woodburn, James, "Egalitarian Societies," *Man, the Journal of the Royal Anthropological Institute*, 17, no. 3 (1982)

Tyrolese German-Speakers

Capsule Summary

Location: Alps region of Europe, in the county called South Tirol, officially Trentino Trentino-Alto Adige, which makes up part of the northern border region of Italy with Austria
Total Population: approximately 280,000
Language: German
Religion: Catholic; Protestants were outlawed by the Hapsburgs

South Tyrol, or Tirol, is approximately the Trentino-Alto Adige county of current Italy; its main river, the Adige, flows from the Alps into the gulf of Venice. Its northern neighbors are two Austrian counties, North Tirol and East Tirol, which are famous ski and holiday areas with Innsbruck as a capital. North and South Tirol are linked by one of the busiest mountain passes of Europe, the Brenner. South Tirol stretches from this pass down to the Dolomites ridge. The county is bordered by Switzerland to the west, and to the south and east are Milan, Venice, and Trieste on the Adriatic Sea. The county's capital is Bolzano (*Bozen* in Tirolese); the other main towns are Bressanone (*Brixen*), Merano (*Meran*), and Trento. The northern part of the region is mainly inhabited by Tirolese German-speakers; the southern part has an Italian majority population.

For many centuries the whole Tirol was part of Austria. One aim of the Italian national movement—which led to the unification of the Italian states and the formation of modern Italy—was to take possession of parts of the Austrian empire inhabited mainly by Italians. The end of World War I, which found Italy on the winning side and Austria on the losing side, offered an opportunity to do so. The peace treaty of Saint-Germain in 1919 did not respect the ethnic border (contrary to expectations based on principles proclaimed by President Wilson of the United States). Thus the new border went deep inside Austrian German-inhabited territory, cutting Tirol in two: the larger, sunnier, and more fertile part (South Tirol; 16,200 square km or 6,255 square mi) was seized by Italy; the colder northern part (12,647 square km or 4,883 square mi) was left to Austria. By then 92 percent of South Tirol's inhabitants were native German-speakers, 3 percent spoke Italian, and 4 percent spoke Ladin—a neo-Latin language, also called *Rhetoroman*, used by some 30,000 people across Switzerland and Italy. Later, the South Tirol region called Alto (Upper) Adige was united with the Italian-majority region of Trentino for purposes of both administration and assimilation.

These developments were the main starting points for a long-lasting conflict between the Italian majority and the German minority, and a major source of tension between Austria and Italy. But there were also other considerations worthy of note.

The free country of Tirol, the "land of the mountains," was named after the fortress of Tirol in the Meran region. It obtained its independence from Meinhard II, a German duke; but it became a Hapsburg territory through a marriage between a Hapsburg—Rudolf—and Meinhard's daughter. This region, an important passageway for merchants, adventurers, artists, craftsmen, missionaries, and knights, tried to preserve its freedom and later its autonomy. Its unification with other Hapsburg territories was strongly opposed by its people. There was no serfdom; the Tirolese *Bergjäger* ("mountain hunter") battalions were fierce and devoted fighters. Tirol always had some kind of local government, and for centuries its constitution was one of the most democratic in Europe.

Tirol fought several times with the French and the Bavarians. In 1805, following Austria's third defeat, Tirol was annexed to Napoleon's ally, Bavaria, which abolished the privileges of pageantry, closed the Catholic monasteries, and introduced compulsory inoculation against smallpox. Although the Tirolese had been loyal to the Hapsburgs, in 1809 Emperor (Kaiser) Franz I of Austria betrayed Tirol, yielding to the demand of the French for the sake of peace and, as a guarantee, marrying his daughter Marie Louise to Napoleon. The name *Tirol* and some Tirolese laws were also abolished; as a result, the Tirolese undertook a fight for freedom against the Napoleonic order. Their troops, led by Andreas Hofer, were badly equipped and after three victories were eventually defeated. Hofer himself was betrayed, and after a mock trial the French executed him in Mantua, Italy; but he would become a legend and a symbol of the south Tirolese separatist movement. In 1813, following Napoleon's defeat, Tirol again became part of Austria.

In 1848, when bourgeois democratic revolutions broke out across Europe, the kaiser took refuge in Tirol. In the Reichsrat, the Austrian parliament of that time, the Italian nationalist and revolutionary Giuseppe Mazzini spoke in favor of a separation of the Italian-inhabited region of Austria; this would-be Italian state was to include South Tirol up to the Brenner Pass. After debates that lasted for decades, however, the territorial claim was rejected by the Reichsrat in 1902.

In 1915, in a secret contract signed in London, the Entente powers promised Italy a large stretch of land, including South Tirol. Italy saw its chance and entered World War I on the side of the Entente. The armistices of late fall 1918 found the Austrian and Italian troops at a standstill, with an equilibrium of forces. However, the peace treaty of 1919 created a small Austria and a large number of Austrian-German minorities in the successor states.

Shortly after the takeover, Italy came under the fascist regime of Benito Mussolini. In 1922 the Italian fascists tried to deal with the question of the German minority by abolishing the German language, German schooling, and German culture, and by colonizing the territory with a large number of native Italian-speakers. They assumed that this ethnic inundation would resolve the issue in a natural way—that some of the Germans would be assimilated and the others, who could not consider themselves Italian, would have no option except to emigrate. Accordingly, the fascist administration heavily penalized those who tried to teach the German language, sentencing them to prison, deporting them to southern Italy, or sending them to concentration camps located on various islands. All the former teachers of German, as well as clerks who had served under the Austro-Hungarian emperor, were removed from their posts or relocated in purely Italian regions. In 1923, names created by Italian nationalists were introduced to replace the traditional German names of the settlements. In 1925, Italian was declared the only official language and every publicly displayed German name was taken down. (However, the Catholic church of Tirol continued teaching in German, in "catacomb" schools.) By 1935 Mussolini saw an advantage in centering industry in the Tirol to facilitate the colonization of the region. The Lancia works, based in Turin (Torino), established production sites there, but the South Tirolese were excluded from employment. Instead, the workforce was recruited from mainland Italy, and these "industrial colonists" were housed in apartments built especially for them. All these measures gave rise to an Italian-speaking territory under Tirolese control.

In 1938 there was an expectation that the Tirol would soon be annexed by Austria and subsequently by Germany. Mussolini was angered by the prospect of a German annexation of Austria (Anschluss), but he simply concentrated his troops in the Brenner Pass, ready to hinder any plan to annex the Tirol. Hitler, who was looking for allies and was grateful that Mussolini did not, ultimately, oppose the Anschluss, sacrificed the South Tirolese and the related territorial claim. Shortly afterward, Hitler proposed that all Germans should be removed from South Tirol and settled elsewhere in the German Reich, where there would be a promise of better standards of living. Nazi propagandists declared that those who wanted to stay were traitors, and the leaders of the South Tirolese community proclaimed, similarly, "We lived together; we will stay together." This move was in fact the first of numerous population shifts that Europe would experience during and after World War II. The threats and the difficulties of the past twenty years—a period when the proportion of Italians had risen from 3 percent to 24 percent—induced the German-speaking majority to acquiesce in the "order of the epoch": 210,000 chose to leave and only 37,000 chose to stay. The evacuation went on until 1941. Some 70,000 people left for the newly conquered lands in Eastern Poland and Yugoslavia, but all of them, along with the native German population (*Volkdeutsch*) of those regions, were forced to leave after the end of World War II.

In 1946 Austria tried to validate its old border claim against Italy, since that claim now did not seem at all hopeless: Italy was one of the losers and had been an important ally of Hitler, whereas Austria had positioned itself as Hitler's first victim; and all across Austria, hundreds of thousands of people demonstrated to regain South Tirol. The issue of exerting influence on Italy in the future was of far greater importance for the winners than the settlement of this dispute. However, Austria's attempts were not totally fruitless. In a bilateral agreement with Italy, minority rights were established. These included education in the mother tongue and the equal status of the Italian and German languages in public offices, documents, and geographical denominations. The South Tirolese could now take back their original German names; many had been forced to adopt Italian names to have access to state jobs, pensions, and housing. The agreement also ensured proportional minority representation in the public services; minority regions were promised their own parliamentary assembly and executive powers; and Rome acknowledged the right of Vienna to represent the South Tirolese internationally.

The Italian parliament established self-government in the South Tirol in 1948, but with a significant alteration: the overwhelmingly German county of Bozen was united with the Italian-majority Trentino (the Italian Tirol), and as a result the region was guaranteed an Italian majority. The implementation of the agreement was delayed, but after 1955, when Austria received independent and neutral status, Rome attempted further colonization.

Austria put the question on the agenda of the United Nations, which in 1960 adopted a resolution stating that the issue should be solved peacefully—thereby implicitly recognizing that Austria had a right to representation in the South Tirolese community. The radicals then lost patience and, instead of waiting any longer for a peaceful solution, began a series of bombings in Italy. This terrorist campaign brought the Italian government to the negotiating table, and a committee was set up to investigate the radicals' demands. The plan that emerged described in detail the minority rights that were being sought and granted Austria an indirect right of veto. In 1972, the new constitution of the regional self-government came into being; thereafter the most important demand—proportional representation in all public posts, from firemen to school directors—was gradually met. The region became very prosperous, while Italy was eroded by successive crises. However, at the point when everything seemd to be settled, the fragile peace was jeopardized because the Italian majority began to resist the concessions. For instance, the Italians protested the implications of putting the German language on an equal footing with Italian in public administration. Italian railway and customs officers coming to the Tirol from the south did not necessarily want to learn German as adults. Moreover, such officers could expect to spend only a few years in the region, since personnel were frequently rotated to forestall corruption. The Tirolese had also demanded equal footing for their language in the courts and in the police force, and this objective too was strongly opposed by the the local Italians. The Tirolese parliament in Bozen—where the conservative people's Party of South Tirol, the Südtirolese Volkspartei (SVP), enjoyed a comfortable absolute majority—did adopt the measures that the German-speakers demanded, but approval failed to come from Rome. Even though Germans formed a majority in the parliament, the strongest Italian party was the neofascist party, which vehemently opposed any extension of rights regarding the use of the German language.

As of this writing, the dispute had not been resolved. Evidently, Italian fascism might lead to German nationalism as a reaction, and vice versa; evidently, too, a great deal of care and tolerance would have to be exercised by everyone, on both sides of the issue, if a resolution was to be found.

The Tirolese are very proud of themselves as a group, are lovers of freedom, and are intense patriots.

LASZLO KOCSIS

See also **Austria; Germans; Italians; Population Shifts**

Further Reading

Filla, Wilhelm, "National Minorities in Austria," in *Austria: A Study in Modern Achievement*, edited by Jim Sweeney and Josef Weidenholzer, Aldershot, United Kingdom: Avebury, 1988

Osmaczyk, Edmund Jan, "Austria-Italy Dispute," in *Encyclopedia of the United Nations and International Agreements*, Vol. 1, 3rd edition, edited by Anthony Mango, New York, Routledge, 2003

———, "Upper Adige," *Encyclopedia of the United Nations and International Agreements*, Vol. 4, edited by Anthony Mango, New York, Routledge, 2003

Wolff, Stefan, editor, *German Minorities in Europe: Ethnic Identity and National Belonging*, Oxford: Berghahn, 2000

Tyvans, *See* Tuvans

U

Udmurts

Capsule Summary

Country Name: Udmurts
Location: Udmurtia, the eastern part of the Russian plain, the European part of the Ural region, between the Kama River and its tributary, the Vyatka River
Total Population: 1,636,000 (2003). Russians (58%), Udmurts (31%), Tartars (7%); remainder represent more than 100 ethnic groups of the Russian Federation and the former Soviet Union
Languages: Udmurt (dialects: North Udmurt and South Udmurt), Russian as a second language, Tartar
Religions: Russian Orthodox, Protestantism, Old Believers, indigenous religion, Islam, secular

Udmurts, formerly known as Votyaks, are an ethnic group living mainly in Russia's Udmurt Republic (Udmurtia), a sovereign republic whose capital city is Izhevsk. Udmurtia has a land area of 16,255 square miles (42,100 square kilometers), and is located in the forested foothills of the Ural Mountains, between the Kama and Vyatka Rivers, 823 miles (1,325 kilometers) northeast of Moscow. The language of Udmurtia is called Udmurt (Votyak), and is spoken by 750,000 native speakers of whom about 500,000 live in the Udmurt Republic and 16,000 live in Kazakstan. The Udmurt language belongs to the so-called Permian branch of the Finno-Ugric Subgroup of the Uralic family of languages. Its alphabet is based on the Cyrillic with several non-Russian letters.

Udmurts refer to themselves as *udmurt, vudmurt, odmort, udmort, ukmort* (plural, *-joz* is added, e.g., *udmurtjoz*). The name for the Udmurts in the Russian language is *Votyak*, which the Udmurts consider disparaging; its use is outdated. As of 2003 the population of Udmurtia was 1,636,000; 70 percent is rural and 30 percent, urban. There are approximately 750,000 ethnic Udmurts who live all over the world, with the greatest numbers living in the Perm Province, Bashkortostan, Tatarstan, in the provinces of Kirov and Yekaterinburg of the Russian Federation, and in the Mari Republic. Occasional Udmurt settlements exist in Siberia, Kazakstan, and the Far East.

History

In the ancient times Udmurts lived in the territory of the present-day Kirov region of Russia and Tatarstan. Escaping from interethnic conflicts and attempts of violent Christianization that increased after the conquest of the Kazan Khanate, the Udmurts moved further to the East and North. The first Russian settlers came to the area in the twelfth and thirteenth centuries. The north of Udmurtia became a part of the developing Russian state. By 1557, after the capture of Kazan by Ivan the Terrible, Udmurtia was fully incorporated into Russia.

Since 1740, czarist Russia took drastic measures to convert the Udmurt people to Russian Orthodox Christianity. As a result the first purely Udmurt settlements were founded, and the first Udmurt grammar, dictionaries, biblical translations, and literary works were published. Under Russian domination, industrialization began with the establishment of factories for copper and ironworks between the years 1756 to 1761. In 1780 the first settlements acquired the status of a city—district centers Glazov and Sarapul. The second half of the nineteenth century was marked by the rapid development of industry and culture in Udmurtia. Many private factories, workshops, banks, partnerships, gymnasiums, industrial colleges, theaters, and libraries were opened.

The growth of national consciousness among Udmurts emerged after the 1917 Revolution and led to the establishment of the Udmurt autonomy. The Votyak (Udmurt) Autonomous Region was proclaimed on February 27, 1921. From 1934 to 1991, the region was known as the Udmurt Autonomous Soviet Socialist Republic (UASSR); after the dissolution of the Union of Soviet Socialist Republics (USSR) in 1991, UASSR was changed to the Udmurtia Republic, a member of the Russian Federation. During the 1930s the Udmurts suffered forced collectivization and relocation under the Soviet regime, and by 1937 tens of thousands of Udmurts were deported. Udmurtia underwent substantial industrial development as part of the industrialization of the Ural Mountains area during World War II. Large production facilities together with their employees were evacuated to the Udmurt territory, greatly increasing the proportion of immigrants, mainly Russians, in the population.

During the Cold War era, large numbers of Udmurts migrated to secure work on construction projects in Volgograd, Sverdlovsk (Yekaterinburg), and Siberia or migrated to Kazakstan and the Ukraine. Between 1971 and 1988, over 1,000 Udmurt villages were abandoned and their inhabitants, forced to relocate.

Ethnicity and Language

The Udmurts are one of the oldest eastern-Finnish people in the northwest woodland Urals. According to Russian sources from the fourteenth to early nineteenth centuries, the Udmurts were referred to as "ari", "arsk people", "chud otezkaya", and "votyaki". Udmurts' self-designations have included "udmurts" or "udmorts". The majority of Udmurts (67 percent) live in Udmurtia. More than one-third of the remainder reside in groups and are dispersed outside this area, mostly in Bashkortostan, Tatarstan, Mari El, in the Perm, Ekaterinburg, and Kirov regions, in Kazakstan, Siberia, and the Far East.

By their language Udmurts belong to the Finno-Ugric community of nations like Komi, Mari, Mordvanians, Estonians, Finns, Karelians, Saami, Hungarians, Khanty, and Mansi. The closest linguistic relatives of Udmurts are the Komi (who reside in the Komi Republic and elswhere), and the most distant are Hungarians, the Khanty, and the Mansi. The written Udmurt was developed in the eighteenth century (the first Udmurt grammar was published in 1775) on the basis of the Cyrillic alphabet. The Udmurt literature and language have been studied not only in Udmurtia and Russia, but also in Hungary, Finland, Estonia, Germany, France, the United States and many other countries where a great number of experts are carrying out research in Udmurt studies. Anthropologists relate Udmurts to the Urals branch of the large European race which has some features of the Mongolian race. The origin of the Udmurts is connected with autochtonous tribes of the Vyatsko-Kamski region, representatives of the Ananian archaeological culture of the eighth to third centuries BCE. They were contemporaries and ethnocultural partners of the Scythes and Sarmats, the peoples of Central Asia and the Caucasus, as well as of some other nations that inhabited more distant areas at that period of time. Udmurts maintained brisk trade with India and Egypt. The first illustrations of the Udmurt people and their life appeared in the Russian chronicles in the fourteenth century. Udmurts paid tribute to the Volga Bulgaria, the Golden Horde (Mongol rulers led by Batu Khan, grandson of Genghis Khan), and the Kazan Khanate. By the end of the fifteenth century (after the conquest of Vyatka), the northern group, and in the middle of the sixteenth century (after the fall of Kazan), the southern group of Udmurts entered the Russian Centralized State.

Culture and Religion

The Udmurts were historically dependent upon forests, which sustained a great impact on their industry, households, their spiritual and material cultures. They were farmers since the Bronze Age. Udmurts cultivated mainly rye as well as oats, barley, millet, hemp, flax, and later on wheat, buckwheat, potatoes, and corn. Forestlands required constant fertilizing, therefore cattle-breeding was an important sector of agriculture. Udmurts prized domestic handicrafts and works: men processed wood, leather, wool, and women sewed, wove, and embroidered. Udmurts also hunted and traded mostly fur-bearing animals, squirrels in particular, fish, and honey. The Udmurt word *kondon* ("money") translates as "price of a squirrel," as squirrel skin was the trade equivalent at that time.

Udmurtia represents a significant portion of the industrial area of Urals, wheree growth was stimulated by many industries that were moved from Western Russia to the less vulnerable Urals region during World War II. Today engineering, steel milling, metallurgy, lumbering, and machine building remain important industries. Songs are of specific interest in the Udmurt folklore. The Udmurt people live on the border of Europe and Asia, the Great Woods and the Great Steppe, the Turkic-Moslem and the Slavic-Christian worlds—an old contact zone of many different cultures. Nevertheless, for many centuries the Udmurts have succeeded in retaining their culture and language. Moreover, being within the limits of their historical lands and geographically placed in the center of the Finno-Ugric nation system, the Udmurts preserved (probably due to slow historical development, an archaic way of life) an entire layer of their ethnocultural complex deriving from the Finno-Ugric Unity period.

Due to a rich historical network of culture and art establishments as well as the works of Udmurt writers, composers, architects, artists, designers, and theatrical performers, professional and folk art developd steadily and remarkably in the Udmurt Republic. This characterizes not only Udmurt art but also that of the Russians, Tatars, Mari, and other people.

Udmurt *belles lettres* have a tradition lasting two centuries that began with ecclesiastical texts. From the first classic writers Grigori Vereshagin and Kuzebai Gerd, and creative works of prominent writers of realism such as T. Arhipov, G. Krasilnikov, M. Petrov, a national literature emerged. Theatrical art has no such similar tradition, although companies formed in the Russian and Udmurt theaters in Izhevsk, Opera and Ballet Theater of the Udmurt Republic as well as theaters in Glazov and Sarapul.

Today, in the Udmurt Republic there are eight professional theaters, five state creative musical groups, the Philharmonic Society, and a state circus, currently under reconstruction. In addition there are over ten state and several dozens of public museua that record and preserve the history and culture of the country and its people.

Udmurtia is a multinational region where 21 religions are represented. There are 161 religious organizations, 121 of which are registered as legal entities. The Russian Orthodox Church of Moscow Patriarchy is the largest denomination in Udmurtia. In addition there are also two congregations of Old Believers—a schismatic group of the Russian Orthodox Church—who maintain prayer houses and two churches. Protestantism is the second largest denomination in Udmurtia. It began in the nineteenth century. Presently there are 47 communities of different Protestant denominations, the largest being Pentecostal, Baptists, and Charismatics. Unlike believers of other denominations, the Protestants actively collaborate with religious centers in the United States, Finland, Sweden, Canada, and other countries. Muslim organizations comprise less than 10 percent of the all functioning communities in the region. There are 14 Muslim groups under the Spiritual Directorate of the Udmurt Muslims, which is led by Mufti Gabdulla Mukhametshin. New mosques were built in the cities of Izhevsk and Sarapul in 1995, followed by an active period of mosque building in smaller Muslim communities during the last few years. The chief mosque in Izhevsk has a Muslim school where students learn the Koran and the Arabic language. Muslim organizations have business links with Islamic countries of the Middle East.

In ancient times Udmurts worshiped nature and pagan gods as part of their indigenous beliefs and practices. Their beliefs were elucidated in Udmurt folklore, myths, legends, and fairy tales. Some of the original religious structures and sites where priests prayed and worshipped remain today in some Udmurt villages. Contemporary religious life in Udmurtia is quite diverse. The church and government aim to unite their efforts in improving the ethical standards, education, and lifestyle of the people especially in terms of treating social ills. Local government takes an active part in the construction and restoration of places of worship. Religious literature is published in Russian as well as in the native languages spoken in Udmurtia. Spiritual musical festivals and other events with government sponsorship are held regularly.

MARAT AKCHURIN

See also **Russia; Udmurts**

Further Reading

Winkler, Eberhard, *Udmurt*, München: Lincom, 2001

Uganda

Capsule Summary

Country Name: Republic of Uganda
Location: Eastern Africa
Total Population: 25,632,794 (July 2003)
Ethnic Populations: Baganda (17%), Ankole (8%), Basoga (8%), Iteso (8%), Bakiga (7%), Langi (6%), Rwanda (6%), Bagisu (5%), Acholi (4%), Lugbara (4%), Batoro (3%), Bunyoro (3%), Alur (2%), Bagwere (2%), Bakonjo (2%), Jopodhola (2%), Karamojong (2%), Rundi (2%), non-African (European, Asian, Arab) (1%), other (8%)
Languages: Numerous, including Luganda, Swahili, English (official)
Religions: Roman Catholic (33%), Protestant (33%), Muslim (16%), indigenous beliefs (18%), Other (Hindu, Jewish)

Uganda is a landlocked, medium-sized East African country located on the equator and bordered by Rwanda, Congo, Sudan, Kenya, and Lake Victoria. The land encompasses jungle, plain, savannah, volcanoes, mountainous terrain, lush fertile lands, tropical swamps, lakes, and forests and thus supports a diversity of occupations including agriculture, livestock, pastoralism, and inland fishing.

Ugandans can be classified into several broad groups: the Bantu-speaking majority, who live in the central, southern, and western parts of the country; and non-Bantu speakers who occupy the eastern, northern, and northwestern portions of the country (Nilotic and Central Sudanic peoples). The Bantu include the large and historically highly centralized kingdom of Buganda, the smaller western Ugandan kingdoms of Bunyoro, Nkore and Toro, and the Busoga states to the east of Buganda. The peoples in the Nilotic and Central Sudanic category include the Iteso, Langi, Acholi, Alur, Karamojong, Jie, Madi, and Lugbara in the north and a number of other smaller societies in the eastern part of the country.

The Bantu form the majority and include the Baganda, the largest single ethnic group, who constitute 18 percent of the population. The people of the southwest comprise 30 percent of the population, divided into five major ethnic groups: the Banyankole and Bahima, 10 percent; the Bakiga, 8 percent; the Banyarwanda, 6 percent; the Bunyoro, 3 percent; and the Batoro, 3 percent. Peoples of the north, largely Nilotic, comprise the next largest group and include the Langi, 6 percent and the Acholi, 4 percent. In the northwest are the Lugbara, 4 percent. The Karamojong, 2 percent, occupy the considerably drier, largely pastoral territory in the northeast. Europeans, Asians, Arabs, and refugees and displaced persons from Sudan, Congo, Rwanda, and Burundi comprise about 1 percent of the population with other groups accounting for the remainder.

Society

Uganda is a nation forged out of diversity. More than 40 distinct societies are found within its postcolonial borders, many with their own homelands, language, cultural practices, and religious beliefs. Uganda's peoples are usually classified based on linguistic differences; most people speak languages that originate from the Nilotic, Sudanic, or Bantu language groups. The Nile River provides a natural boundary between the Nilotic and Sudanic speaking peoples of the north, and the Bantu speakers of the more populous south. Ugandans are thus born into social and linguistic diversity and many Ugandans speak up to ten languages and dialects, whereas English (and to a lesser extent Swahili) are used as lingua franca to transcend regional and linguistic differences.

Uganda's ethnic and cultural diversity is a noticeable feature of Kampala, the verdant political and economic capital. The city sits near Lake Victoria within the traditional lands of the Baganda, who despite being Uganda's largest ethnic group, only account for half of Kampala's estimated 2 million population and 17 percent of the national population. Kampala's remaining population come from all over Uganda and East Africa (especially post-1994 Rwanda); thus, even Uganda's largest ethnic groups often find themselves as minorities with regard to the nation as a whole. However, to put this in perspective, Uganda's smallest ethnic groups, such as the Batwa forest pygmies and the Bayudaya, Uganda's Jewish people, only number a few thousand.

Uganda's recent population growth has been considerable, increasing from an estimated 16.6 million in 1991 to nearly 25 million in 2002. Around 20 percent live in towns and cities with the remaining 80 percent living in villages and rural areas. Agriculture is Uganda's main economic sector and coffee is its principal export. Per capita income (GDP) in 2002 was $1,200. The majority of Ugandan families, whether living in rural or urban areas, fetch water from wells and cook on open charcoal fires. Houses are often made from wattling, wood, breeze-blocks, and mud that is mixed with straw and turned into bricks in kilns. In many rural areas people live a subsistence lifestyle and share similar working practices based on agriculture and livestock. As such there are notable commonalities among Uganda's ethnic groups, particularly with regard to the ways people orient themselves toward social relationships, work, time, religion, and nature. However, closer examination often reveals different perceptions of the person, religion, spiritual influence, misfortune, and illness. These are especially marked amongst the pastoral, nomadic, and cattle rearing populations, such as the Karamojong, whose distinctive social and cultural practices are sometimes seen at odds with Uganda's program of "modernization." Likewise, the Batwa forest pygmies, who were displaced from their traditional forests, find it difficult to integrate into contemporary Ugandan society.

When considering the diversity of Uganda's ethnic groups, it is important to focus upon people's religious practices that present empirical starting points with which to begin understanding the different populations. Religious identity also provides an effective way for Ugandans themselves to understand each other within such a diverse field of cultural identity and complex rules of status, age, and gender. Around 85 percent of people identify themselves as Anglican or Catholic with the remainder mostly being Muslim. Over the past 100 years these world religions have steadily become incorporated into Ugandan culture and play an essential part in social and political life. Nevertheless, these are grounded within even stronger substrate of traditional cosmologies and accordant beliefs.

History

Uganda is a poor tropical country with a minimal health budget, high mortality rates and low life expectancy. Furthermore, since Uganda's independence in 1962, Ugandans have lived through the regimes of Idi Amin (1971–79), Milton Obote (1966–71 and 1979–85), and wars (1978–79 and 1980–85). During those years they were subject to undisciplined armies used to harassment, thieving, and killing. Different ethnic groups were often targeted, most visibly in 1972, when Amin expelled the Ugandan-Asian population. The economy disintegrated alongside state institutions, health services, and schools. The seeds for change were sown during Amin's last years, when he invaded Tanzania and charged the already volatile political climate. In late 1978, Tanzanian forces invaded Uganda and ousted Amin; Milton Obote came to power for a second time, but was overthrown in 1985 by Yoweri Museveni's National Resistance Army.

Museveni's first act was to suspend political parties, arguing that these were rooted in tribal allegiances that were responsible for Uganda's history of armed conflict and instability. Museveni, heavily influenced by Julius Nyerere (neighboring Tanzania's "founding father"), instituted the one-party National Resistance Movement System. Under the "Movement System" parties still exist but cannot campaign for office, recruit members, or raise funds. Instead a government is formed that in theory represents Uganda's diverse population. The Government has the extremely difficult task of remaking a society destabilized by colonialism, war, and HIV/AIDS. The Movement System has brought relative stability to southern parts of the country and invited back the Asian families expelled by Amin. Nevertheless, Uganda's future remains unclear as wars and conflict continue to destabilize the western and northern borders that are predominantly populated by minority peoples. Western donors are placing increasing pressure to institute western style democracy that the Government believes will allow old ethnic tensions to resurface, and in the June 2000 referendum, Ugandans themselves voted to continue the Movement System.

Recently, the government is drawing criticism for its intolerant attitude toward the media and opposing political groups. Charges of corruption, intimidation, and cronyism are becoming more widespread. Under the National Resistance Movement, Uganda has made enormous strides over the last 20 years especially women's rights, primary education, and the fight against HIV/AIDS, but what the next 20 years may hold remains uncertain.

ANDREW IRVING

See also **Bantu**

Further Reading

Baker, Wairama, *The Marginalization of Minorities*, Uganda: The Minority Rights Group, 2001

Frank, Marion, *Aids-Education through Theatre: Case Studies from Uganda*, Bayreuth: University of Bayreuth, 1995

Gifford, Paul, *African Christianity: Its Public Role*, Bloomington: Indiana University Press, 1998

Hansen, Holger Bernt, and Michael Twaddle, editors, *Developing Uganda*, Ohio University Press, 1998

Knighton, Ben, *Karamojong Traditional Religion: Dying Tradition or Living Faith*, Ashgate Publishing, 2003

Parkin, David, *Neighbours and Nationals in an African City Ward*, London: Routledge, 1969

Sempebwa, Joshua, *African Traditional Moral Norms and Their Implication for Christianity: A Case Study of Ganda Ethics*, St. Augustin: Steyler Vertez, 1983

Tripp, Aili Mari, *Women and Politics in Uganda*, University of Wisconsin Press, 2000

Turnbull, Colin, *The Mountain People*, Touchstone Books, 1987

Twaddle, Michael, *Kakungulu and the Creation of Uganda, 1868–1928*, Swallow Press, 1993

Whyte, Susan Reynolds, *Questioning Misfortune: The Pragmatics of Uncertainty in Eastern Uganda*, Cambridge and New York: Cambridge University Press, 1997

Ukraine

Capsule Summary

Country Name: Ukraine (formerly Ukrainian Soviet Socialist Republic)
Location: Eastern Europe
Total Population: 48,055,439 (2003)
Language: Ukrainian
Religions: Ukrainian Orthodox–Moscow Patriarchate, Ukrainian Orthodox–Kiev Patriarchate, Ukrainian Autocephalous Orthodox, Ukrainian Catholic (Uniate), Protestant, Jewish, Muslims

Ukraine is located in Eastern Europe, bordering Belarus in the north, Poland in the northwest, Slovakia and Hungary in the west, Romania and Moldova in the southwest, the Russian Federation in the east and northeast, and Turkey, across the Black Sea, in the south. The country has a land area of 603,700 square kilometers (233,000 square miles) and is the third largest country in the Commonwealth of Independent States.

The population of Ukraine is estimated at 48,055,439 (2003). It is predominantly urban with around 70 percent of the people living in cities and towns. The country's capital city, Kiev (Kyyiv), is home to 2,611,000 people (2001), or 6 percent of the population. Ukraine has a negative population growth rate of –0.69 percent, and it is estimated that the population could decline to 45,000,000 by 2020. Ukraine has a relatively high population density, of around 80 people per square kilometer (206 people per square mile).

Ukraine is a unitary republic, and the form of government is presidential democracy. The government succeeded the independent government that existed between the years of 1917 to 1920, after gaining independence from the Russian Empire (Russia acquired then Ukrainian land from Rzeczpospolita [the Polish-Lithuanian Union] and Turkey [The Ottoman Empire]). In 1920 it became a part of the Soviet state, and in 1924 it became one of the founding members of the Soviet Union. The country was among the first Soviet Republics to declare its independence from the Union of Soviet Socialist Republics (USSR) on August 24, 1991. On June 28, 1996, the country adopted its new Constitution. The *Verkhovna Rada* (Parliament) is a unicameral 450-member national legislative body. The president is the head of state and elected by popular vote for a five-year term with a maximum of two terms. The president nominates the prime minister, who must be approved by the *Verkhovna Rada*. Since independence a number of political parties, ranging from radical nationalist groups and liberal Democrats to conservatives and hard line Communists, have appeared in the country. According to the new Election Law, 225 seats are proportionally allocated to those political organizations that gain 4 percent or more of the total votes. Despite some tensions between the Ukrainians and Russians, the largest ethnic minority, and emergence of several extreme right and nationalist organizations, there have never been military conflicts or confrontations during the post-Soviet era.

Ukraine is a multi-ethnic country. Ethnic Ukrainians, who are ethnically and linguistically close to the

Russians and Belarusians, make up 77.8 percent of the country's population (2001). Ethnic Russians make up the largest minority, about 17.3 percent of the population, while ethnic Belarusians, 0.6 percent, Moldovans, 0.5 percent, Crimean Tatars, 0.5 percent and various other groups make up the remaining 3.3 percent of the population. The current ethnic structure was formed during the twentieth century. The Soviet government encouraged migration from various parts of the Soviet Union to the Ukraine and emigration of the Ukrainians (sometimes forcibly) to other parts of the USSR. The Ukraine lost between 3 and 8 million people in famines in the 1920s and 1930s and between 5 and 8 million people during World War II and Nazi occupation. However, unlike some other Soviet republics, Ukraine experienced a smaller-scale immigration of Russians and other nationalities from the USSR. As a result, throughout the Soviet era, the number of Ukrainians in the republic remained roughly the same, at around 75 to 80 percent. Since independence in 1991, between 500,000 and 1,000,000 Ukrainian residents opted to leave the country, mainly for Russia and the Organisation for Economic Co-operation and Development (OECD) countries. In addition various estimates indicate that between 500,000 and 1,000,000 people moved temporarily both legally and illegally to Russia and other European countries in search of seasonal and other jobs.

During the Soviet era, the central government in Moscow promoted Russian as the lingua franca in education, the mass media, and everyday life. According to the 1989 census, around 56.2 percent of ethnic Ukrainians said that they could speak Russian fluently. The Ukrainian language was made the official language of the country in 1990 and it became the language of instruction in educational institutions and government administration. However, the Ukrainian Law on Citizenship granted citizenship to all people who lived in Ukraine, without the language restrictions seen in Estonia or Latvia. Russian is still widely used in the country as the lingua franca, although it is less common in the western Ukraine. The younger generation prefers to learn English or German.

In the 1990s the Ukraine, like neighboring Poland and Russia, witnessed a growing interest in religion, viewed as a part of its strengthening national identity. The majority of ethnic Ukrainians (80 percent) and Russians belong to the Russian Orthodox Church. In the 1990s there was a split in the Orthodox Church in the Ukraine and a group of the Orthodox clergy established the Kiev Patriarchate, which is independent from the Moscow Patriarchate. A considerable group of Ukrainians (mainly in the western Ukraine) belong to the Ukrainian Catholic (Uniate) church. However, despite the growth of religious practice and the existing tensions between the followers of the Kiev Patriarchate, the Moscow Patriarchate, and the Ukrainian Catholic (Uniate) church, religion does not play an important role in everyday political life of the Ukraine. The Muslim population of the country is represented mostly by the Crimean Tatars who live mainly in the Crimea that has a status of Autonomous Republic. A small radical group of the Crimean Tatars demand independence of Crimea from the Ukraine. There are also other small religious communities whose religious practices are generally tolerated.

After 1991, Ukraine experienced major economic changes attempting to reform the economy that largely relied on agriculture and manufacturing. These reforms were based on three mechanisms: rapid mass-privatization, price liberalization, and currency reforms. The Ukrainian government privatized a significant proportion of enterprises in the industrial and agricultural sectors between 1992 and 2000. The Ukraine also introduced its currency—Hryvna (Hryvnia), which remained volatile in the late 1990s and early 2000s.

Ukraine's GDP per capita is among the lowest in Eastern Europe (in purchasing power parity), at around $4,500 (2002). Throughout the 1990s, the country experienced economic difficulties and despite significant economic changes, it underwent a steep economic recession. Economic output declined by around 50 percent between 1991 and 2001, although accelerated economic recovery was registered between 2001 and 2004. The unemployment rate remains at over 3.8 percent of the labor force (1999), affecting mainly industrial workers, rural people, and women with children. Independent experts put the real unemployment numbers at about 18 percent on par with neighboring Poland, but there is no strong evidence that poverty is correlated with any particular ethnic group. In 2003 the United Nations Development Programme's (UNDP) Human Development Index (HDI) placed the Ukraine in seventy-fifth place, significantly behind Poland, Romania and Russia, and Dominica, but ahead of Kazakstan, Suriname, and Jamaica.

RAFIS ABAZOV

See also **Ukrainians; Russia; Russians; Belorusians**

Further Reading

Magocsi, Paul Robert, *A History of Ukraine*, Seattle: University of Washington Press, 1996

———, *Historical Atlas of Central Europe (History of East Central Europe, Vol. 1, 1)*, Seattle: University of Washington Press, 2002

Miler, Alexei, *The Ukrainian Question: The Russian Empire and Nationalism in the Nineteenth Century*, Budapest: Central European University Press, 2003

Motyl, Alexander J., *Revolutions, Nations, Empires*, New York: Columbia University Press, 1999

Petersen, Roger, *Resistance and Rebellion: Lessons from Eastern Europe (Studies in Rationality and Social Change)*, Cambridge: Cambridge University Press, 2001

Snyder, Timothy, *The Reconstruction of Nations: Poland, Ukraine, Lithuania, Belarus, 1569–1999*, New Haven, Connecticut: Yale University Press, 2003

Ukrainian Government Web Site. <http://www.kmu.gov.ua/control/>

Ukrainian Parliament Web Site. <http://www.rada.kiev.ua/>

The Ukrainian President's Office Home Page. <http://www.president.gov.ua/>

Whitmore, Sarah, *State Building in Ukraine: The Ukrainian Parliament, 1990–2003*, London: Routledge, 2004

Wilson, Andrew, *The Ukrainians: Unexpected Nation*, 2nd edition, New Haven, Connecticut: Yale University Press, 2002

Ukrainians

Capsule Summary

Location: mostly in the territory of Ukraine, in Eastern Europe
Population: 45 million
Languages: Ukrainian (official); Russian (most common)
Religions: Orthodox/Pravoslav, Greek Catholic, atheist

History of Ukraine

The territory of Ukraine was part of the "migration highway" for a large number of tribes from the steppes of Eurasia. Between the fifth and seventh centuries CE, Slavs started to descend from their native land in the north, the Pripjaty swamps, and spread toward south and east. Later the successive waves of migration brought the Avars, Bulgarians, Hungarians, Petchenegs, and Cumans. In 901 CE, the Vikings/Varegs of Rurik founded the first principality—the Rus of Kiev, to secure their established trading routes down the Dniepr River. The rulers were later assimilated by the Slav majority and between the years 969 to 971, Prince Sviatoslav went to war with Byzantium. Under the reign of St. Vladimir, the state flourished; the period between 1019 and 1054 was the highpoint of the Kievan Rus, under the rule of Wise Yaroslav. In the tenth and eleventh centuries Kiev Rus became the largest and most powerful state in Europe.

In 1223 the Mongols of Dzinghis khan won a great victory over the Russians at the Khalka River, and later in 1241 the Mongol tatars of Bhathu khan destroyed Kiev and devastated the whole country and much of central-eastern Europe. In the decades that followed Lithuanian and Polish attacks resulted in the conquest of the western part of the territory by Lithuania, during the twelfth and fourteenth centuries. Galicia was controlled by Poland in 1349, while the southern and eastern parts of the territory were under Tatar control.

An uprising against the Tatars broke out in Rostov in 1262 and the unsuccessful struggle made the Russian principality to stretch far up north in the colder forest region, which was not suitable for the horseback-warriors of the steppes. The effort paid off and had finally culminated in the victory of D. Ivan Donskoy over the Tatars at Kulikovo, near Moscow in the year 1380. Thus the principality of Moscow became the most powerful Russian principality and Russia became synonymous with Moscow and its politics. The former center of power, the state of Kiev, from then on lies on the southwestern border region and became known as the principality on the border or U-krayina.

In 1385, the Polish-Lithuanian union strengthened its grip on the country, and many fled to the east where they were mixed with a blend of steppe warriors, who remained from the migrating people and formed the Cossack people on the Don. The Cossacks were renowned for their fighting abilities and nonetheless for their cruelty, and became the elite forces of the Russian czarist army. They were used to fight in all of the wars, mainly those fought against the Ottoman empire and the Tatar states, like the Crimean khaganat.

In the fifteenth century the south of the country was conquered by the Ottomans, but in the sixteenth century the bigger part of the country came under Polish rule. Thus much of it became part of Poland in 1569 by the Union treaty of Lublin, while three other principalities were annexed by the state of Moscow.

Between the years of 1648 to 1654, a great popular uprising led by hatman Bogdan Hmelnitskiy liberated most of Ukraine from the Polish rule. After the victory of 1654, the reunification treaty of Ukraine with Russia was decided by the rulers' council: the Rada from Pereyaslav. A Polish-Russian war followed it between 1654 to 1667, and Poland lost all its Ukrainian territories including the town of Kiev, Galicia, and Bukovina.

During successive Russian-Turkish wars that were successful, Russia gradually seized the Black Sea region of what is now Ukraine between 1735 to 1739, annexed the Crimea in 1783, and finally reached the southern seas and established its Black Sea fleet between 1787 to 1792.

The Rise of the Ukrainian National Movement

The development of the Ukrainian national identity started at the dawn of the 1848 European national democratic revolution. In 1846, a Ukrainian secret society, The Brothers of Cirill and Method, was born in Kiev to boost the wakening of the national conscience. One of its cofounders, N. Kostomarov, wrote a book entitled the "Existence of the Ukrainian people," according to which the basis of democratic principles are found in the Cossack and religious communities' traditions. The other founder, one of the greatest Ukrainian national poets of all times, Taras Sevchenko, protested the deep Russian czarist oppression. For this he was sentenced to lifelong service in the Russian army, as an ordinary soldier.

The Ukrainian and Belarusian intellectuals did not dream of an independent homeland at this time, but desired a federal county status within the Russian empire. For westerners they seemed to be pretty much the same people and for the Russians they simply didn't exist. Thus the first Russian census of 1897 found a population of 11,921,086 in the Ukrainian district. No distinction was made among Pravoslavs—they were simply considered Russians.

The Russian government from St. Petersburg tried to suppress the Ukrainian language and culture, banning everything which could have maintained the national identity of these people. In 1863 the home secretary, P. Valuyev, ordered the censors not to allow the editing of manuals or any kind of books in Ukrainian, mostly those which may be of interest to a potentially large number of people. He had considered Ukrainians nonexisting, as simply the western component of the Great Russian nation. Although this decree was abolished years later in 1876, the Czar Alexander II had forbidden the edition or import of Ukrainian books, with the exception of belletristic works, which remained in force until 1906.

In Austria-Hungary the situation of the Ukrainians was much better, especially after the 1867 compromise, when a constitutional monarchy was set up. Regional parliaments were elected, and two of them were based in the Ukrainian majority regions of Galicia and Bukowina. Thus Austria became the stronghold of Ukrainian culture and nationalism, and the former Habsburg territories of western Ukraine retainedthis role within the Ukrainian society, ever since.

In 1900, a brochure "The Independent Ukraine," was published in *Lemberg/L'viv*, which served as a program for the creation of the first Ukrainian national party—the Ukrainian Revolutionary Party. The brochure stated that Ukraine stretches from the Carpathians to the Caucasus, suggesting the might of the Kievian Rus principality. The party was dissolved two years later, and the majority of its members entered the social-democratic movement, leaving nationalism for the future. This didn't mean, however, that Ukrainian nationalism ceased to exist. In 1911 a paramilitary national organization "the Society of the Sitch-gunners" was created.

In 1914 as World War I broke out, the Russian governor of Kiev banned all Ukrainian newspapers and all authorized forms of Ukrainian cultural and national life. After the Russian army had penetrated Austria in early 1915, and occupied most of Galicia and Poland, the great prince promised the unification of Poland under the Czarist flag, but the Ukrainian question didn't exist for him. The Ukrainian nationalists suffered merciless persecution by the invading troops, and many fled to the west or were tortured and exiled to Siberia. The rift between the Ukrainian national movements from Austria and Russia persisted until 1917. When the socialist revolution broke out in the hinterland, Ukrainians formed their central council, the Rada, which also acted as a kind of government. On June 13, 1917, the council publicized their declaration known as the I. Universal (declaration) of the Ukrainian Central Rada. Its president, M. Hrushevskiy, proclaimed the maintenance of the territorial unity with Russia but on an equal footing with the Ukrainian Peoples Republic, whose borders were determined.

By the end of November 1920 the civil war ended and the red army had conquered Ukraine, which became a soviet republic. The peasant masses followed the Bolshevik leaders. The peasant uprisings led to brutal punishment; the Bolshevik regime with its agricultural policy and ideological class struggle was responsible for the great famines (1921–22) and (1929–33). Millions of peasants died or were sent to Gulag (system of forced labor camps) by Stalin.

The national movement turned into a nationalist/communist one.

The political cleansing that followed, from 1929 onwards, became permanent, especially among minority Ukrainian party activists.

On June 22, 1941, the German conquest started and covered the entire Ukraine. They seized Kiev on September 8, and Hitler established his headquarter in Vinnitsa. Prior to that more than 10,000 people were killed by the retreating soviets in 1941. The underground Organization of the Ukrainian Nationalists (OUN) continued its activity during the short Soviet occupation and started to cooperate with the Germans, forming an SS battalion, the Galitshina.

Ukraine was seen also as part of the German vital space and was therefore under civilian administration. According to the secret Nazi plan, the population should form a great work force in order to build up a German empire, and subsequently the number of the Slavs was to be reduced by starvation, forced labor, and colonization of German population. Few people, however, enjoyed greater rights and cultural autonomy. Thus many anti-Soviet people, such as the Tatars from Crimea and Cossacks joined them from the entire region. Stalin punished them after the war by moving them to Kazakstan and Siberia. The death camps set up for Jews, communists, and other antisocial elements took some one million lives in Ukraine and Belarus. Ukrainian nationalist gangs also took part in the roundup and mass murders.

In July 1944, the OUN formed the Ukrainian insurgent popular army, UPA, waiting for the British to stop the Soviet advance and spread eastwards, its sphere of influence. The UPA's aim was to protect the western Ukrainian population from Soviet deportations and vengeance. The population supported the insurgents and the fight went on until Stalin's death. The UPA has spread its activity over the whole of Ukraine, in the Slovak mountain range and across the border into east Poland. So in 1947, the Soviet Union, Czechoslovakia, and Poland signed an agreement to overcome the " bandits." Altogether, some 300,000 people were subjected to mass arrests, deportations, and exiles to Siberia. The process was fostered by forced collectivization, and eastern Ukrainian teachers were brought to convert the

people. The Greek Catholic church was banned after their refusal to unite with the Pravoslav church. The uprising continued well into the 1950s, in spite of many calls for cease-fire and promise of amnesty by the soviet authorities. The problem was finally solved by forced industrialization, which brought a large number of Russian settlers to the region. The leaders were either killed in combat (Suhovits) or executed (Ohrimovits). The final and tragic end was the assassination by KGB agents of the two OUN leaders L. Rebet and S. Bandera, in West Germany in 1959.

To the estimated five million Ukrainian victims of the World War and after, including civilians and Jews, former Soviet citizens recovered from the Western allies were added. After the war the Stalinist regime sought vengeance and asked for the repatriation of all the former soviet citizens who fled to the West. This included many Ukrainians and other minorities as well the war prisoners, deserters, young conscripts, czarist sympathizers, white army veterans—everybody who wasn't a Soviet citizen. By this he wanted to avoid western emigration, dissolve the existing one, and liquidate everybody who might pose a potential threat to the regime

In 1946 when the worst drought ever came upon war-torn central-eastern Europe, the Ukrainian peasants were forced to give to the soviet state 7.2 million tones of grain—far exceeding their production capacities. The next year, due to lack of seeds for sowing, Ukraine, already devastated by war, experienced a cruel famine reaching even to cannibalism. The famine was used to punish the non-Russian, non-proletar citizens who dared to question soviet supremacy. Reprisals continued until Stalin's death in 1953, although the accent was shifted more and more toward cultural resistance. The Ukrainian Nikita Khruschev became Stalin's successor and uncovered Stalin's atrocities.

In 1985 Mikhail Gorbachev launched an irreversible process of democratization which soon led to the disintegration of the USSR. On October 9, 1990, the pluralist party system was introduced, and as the communist putsch did not succeed in August 1991, the Communist Party of the Soviet Union was suspended and its Central Committee decided to dissolve itself. On August 24, 1991, Ukraine proclaimed its independence strengthened by the December 1 referendum. L. Kravtchuk became the first president. Days after, the three presidents met in secret and decided to dissolve the Soviet Union and create on December 8, the Commonwealth of Independent States (CIS), based on a Federation between the Slavic states of Russia, Belarus, and Ukraine.

The Ukrainian Society

The society is divided along many rifts. The first and major one is between the nationalists, the militant Ukrainians of the West, the partially Russified town dwellers, the younger generation, and the population from the East where a very large 11 million Russian minority forms a compact majority along the actual Russian border. The Russian past, the presence of the 21 percent Russian minority, the Russian and Soviet imperial legacy, ane the continuing communist tradition cast a dark shadow on Ukraine's national and cultural identity. The other rift involves the use of languages. Ukrainian is the only official language, although Russian is the most common language. The Russian, and later Soviet, school system was very successful in promoting this so called "common language." The Soviets avoided calling it official language. A great number of Ukrainians have undecided nationality; they oscillate between Ukrainian and Russian, and the choice is even more difficult when the two nations are abutted. Linguistically, their common Slavic vocabulary is about 80 percent similar.

The aggressive Ukrainization, especially in the terms of language usage, eventually may produce the splitting of the country if the Ukrainians are not tolerantof the Russian speakers. The western Ukrainians see the source of all the troubles in Russia and want to join the West while the easterners want closer ties with Russia, due to emotional and traditional economic ties.

Other rifts exist between the faithful and the atheists, and between the resurgent Greek Catholics and the state Orthodox/Pravoslav religion. Moreover, some Orthodox recognize the patriarch in Moscow, though others recognize the patriarch in Kiev. The nation is in the process of forming, and the development of strong regional identities is inevitable.

Crimea

Crimea could be a promising example of problem-solving regarding national minorities and regional autonomy, but also the main testing ground for the young Ukrainian democracy and the desired ethnic linguistic, cultural, and religious tolerance.

Crimea was colonized by the Russians after the annexation in 1787 of the Crimean kaghanat. Today it has a Russian majority, a strong Ukrainian minority, and Tatars make up only 10 percent of the 2.5 million people.

Crimea was added to Ukraine in the 1950s during an administrative reorganization when the Soviets could not imagine that the empire might dissolve and Ukraine would be separated from Russia. The Russian majority does not want to loose soviet era dominance and wants to secure this stronghold for Russia inclusively for the Black Sea fleet. After the Ukrainian independence, the Crimean parliament proclaimed independence from Ukraine. The move was also fueled by the bitter dispute over the ownership of the strategic peninsula that the Russians fought for a long time. Today Crimea is an autonomous republic with Ukrainian and Russian flags representing a fragile compromise.

Minorities in Ukraine

Ukraine is a country with a large minority population that includes some 46 different communities. The most prominent are the 11.5 million (21 percent of the entire population) Russians living mainly in the Eastern Russian border area. There are 200,000 Hungarians in the Zakarpatskaya border region with Hungary, making up for 19 percent of the population; 200,000 ethnic Romanians in N. Bukowina (23 percent of Cernovtsi region); 170,000 Poles in the Vinnitsa region; and 250,000 (10 percent of the population) Tatars in Crimea. The Belarusians, Germans, and Jews are in smaller numbers, although Jews and Germans formed a significant minority in the past. Ruthenians, the main population of Zakarpatskaya, are more of a religious and historical minority that never belonged to Ukraine or Russia before 1946. It was part of Hungary for 1000 years and of Czechoslovakia for 20 years.

Laszlo Kocsis

See also **Ukraine; Belarusians, Russia; Russians; Germany; Germans**

Further Reading

Britannica Book of the Year, 1991
The Fluctuating Ethnic and Religious Composition of the Carpathian/Balkan Range, Szekelyudvarhely: Haaz Press, 1996
Shoup, P.S., *The East European and Soviet Data,* Handbook, Columbia University Press, 1981
Heller, M., and A. Nekrits, *The History of the Soviet Union,* London, Overseas Publications Interchange Ltd, 1992
Heller, M., *The History of the Russian Empire,* Budapest, Osiris, 1996
Pandi, L., compiler, *Central Europe 1763–1993,* collection of maps, Osiris, Budapest, 1997
The Times Atlas for World History, London, 1992

Ulster Irish

Capsule Summary

Location: Province of Ulster (Northern Ireland and Republic of Ireland)
Total Population: 1,051,000
Languages: English, Irish (Gaelic), Scots/Hiberno
Religions: Protestantism, Catholicism

In the general context of the total Irish population on the island of Ireland (3,924,140 in 2003), the Ulster Irish are a minority. The term Ulster Irish is tautological. Historically, Ulster is a province of nine counties: Donegal, Fermanagh, Tyrone, Armagh, Down, Antrim, Cavan, Monaghan, and Derry (Londonderry) created from Coleraine, small areas of Donegal, and north Tyrone in the seventeenth century. In the Plantation of Ulster the following counties were escheated or forfeited to the British Crown: Armagh, Cavan, Donegal, Fermanagh, Londonderry, and Tyrone following the "Flight of the Earls" in 1607. The British government favored a cautious settlement to include grants of land to native peoples. By 1630, nearly 7,000 British settlers, largely from the Lowlands of Scotland, had migrated to these counties, most to escape poverty. There had been a long tradition of Gaelic lords employing Scottish mercenaries, and hereditary families of soldiers like the MacSweeneys and the MacDonnells were absorbed into Gaelic Ulster society. Monaghan was excluded from plantation because under Elizabeth I's government, the greater lords of the areas had been dispossessed in favor of lesser lords who were made freeholders of the lands they occupied. Cavan was largely planted by Englishmen who had been local garrison commanders. The grants of land were often made in compensation for arrears of payment for military services during the 1590s—hence the origin of such Ulster military families as the Brookes, the Blaneys, the Bretts, and the Bagenals.

However the various plans for the settlement of Ulster did not live up to expectations and the rate of migration was slow. A growing number were also Presbyterians so that in addition to Catholics, both Gaelic and Old English, and Protestant or Church of Ireland—the new Protestant element of Presbyterianism was added to the religious mix in Ulster. By the 1630s settlers were beginning to arrive on their own initiative rather than being brought over from the undertaker's home region ("undertaker" was the plantation technical term for one who undertook to plant an allocated area of forefeited lands in Ulster). Not all stayed on the lands of their original grants as internal migration developed when tenants sought easier tenures and better land. In this way distinct English, Scottish, and Irish localities began to emerge.

In 1600 there were only five major urban centers—Newry, Carrickfergus, Derry, Armagh, and Downpatrick. By 1613 there were 36 incorporated boroughs returning Protestant members to the Irish Parliament. Although dispossession of lands was not as severe as once thought to be the case, the Irish suffered a loss of status because many Irish often remained on ancestral lands as tenants. Likewise native Irish holding church or termon lands lost out to the new landlords, the Protestant bishops. From 1537 to 1870, the Church of Ireland was the established state church whose Head was the English monarch.

Despite the general decline in their fortunes, the native Ulster Irish continued to look to their ancestral lords for leadership in their growing antipathies to the new landlords, as attacks on the settler communities erupted. In October 1641, Sir Phelim O'Neill led a serious rebellion against the principal fortified positions; it is estimated that about one-fifth of the Protestant population of Armagh was killed, and there were retaliatory massacres of Ulster Irish Catholics in Antrim, Down, and Fermanagh. Many wild exaggerations of genocide and barbarity in the 1640s have been countered by the more sober accounts of modern historians, but clearly an anti-Catholic culture grew up and persisted virtually until the present "Troubles." As history itself became politicized into slogans or rallying cries such as "Remember 1641" and "Remember 1690," notable conflicts such as those at Derry and Derry Walls, Aughrim Enniskillen, and the Boyne were commemorated as Protestant victories. The Ulster rebellion of 1641 soon merged into the general Irish Rebellion of 1641 to 1653 and therefore into the English Civil War and the advent of Oliver Cromwell.

Events in the seventeenth century led to a siege mentality among the Protestant Ulster Irish. The idea of heroic endurance against a barbarous infidel was a mentality that was fuelled by hell-fire preachers, pamphleteers, ballad-makers and biased accounts of the rebellion such as that of Sir John Temple. The general ethos that Ulster was Protestant, was loyal to the English Crown, and was politically Unionist had its roots in the events of the seventeenth century. However, by the late seventeenth century, the Presbyterians had become the most anti-Catholic, and so too had the Ulster Irish word for Scot (*Albanach*), synonymous with Protestant. By the eighteenth century the most Gaelic province of Ireland had in fact become the most anglicized of them all, developing an increasing Protestant majority. It pursued a more industrialized future, which in economic terms in the early twentieth century began to differentiate the province from the rest of Ireland. Nevertheless, the assumption in the late twentieth century that Ulster was predominantly Protestant can be challenged as intermarriages began to occur at every social level; in fact, by the second half of the nineteenth century Catholics were in a small majority. When the island of Ireland was partitioned in 1922, Catholics comprised 43.7 percent of the population. Ulster then as a province was also divided into the six counties of Tyrone, Fermanagh, Armagh, Londonderry, Antrim, and Down thus forming the new state of Northern Ireland. The three Ulster counties of Cavan, Monaghan, and Donegal were added to the twenty-six counties or Eire, which was renamed the Republic of Ireland in 1949. The reasons for that particular division and the various consequent injustices due to separating some communities from the south and others from the north, such as the 25 percent Protestants of Donegal and the Catholic majority of the City of Derry, helped to give rise to and aggravate the present Troubles. In the 1991 census Catholics were 38 percent of the Northern Irish population. Few Catholics today would admit to a cultural or political Ulster identity rather than seeing themselves as a minority within a majority in Ireland. Though Protestants see themselves as the majority in Northern Ireland, they would of course be a minority in a united Ireland; hence there is a problem of a "double minority" in Ireland. The label "Ulster" is generally rejected by Catholic nationalists except for All Ireland sporting events in Gaelic Athletic Games and in Rugby Union Football fixtures and in which of course there is no longer any sectarian bias. Those

who stress the separate nature of the north of Ireland, such assome geographers and demographers, would claim that Ulster's physical characteristics have played a part in its cultural identity. Undeniably, factors such as the proximity to Scotland; the historic plantations; the waterways of the Lower Bann, Lough Neagh, and the Upper Bann rivers (which make for an east-west divide); the waterways of the Erne loughs and rivers; and the east-west line formed by the drumlin hills from Fermanagh to Down create a physical divide from the south of Ireland. West of the Bann rivers remained strongly Gaelic likewise Fermanagh and South Tyrone. However, parts of the provinces of North Leinster and North Connaught, like the modern counties of Louth and Sligo, had a common historical and cultural experience with that of Ulster. Linguists likewise are now showing in contradistinction to the revival of the Gaelic language in the North that there was also a Scots/Hiberno language with its distinctive dialects.

Within these boundaries—cultural, physical, political and religious, and considering the various qualifications that can be made, one can make a case for an identifiable Ulster Irish minority, but it is far from being a fixed or immutable minority. Over the centuries, especially when the emigration of Ulster Scots to colonial America during the eighteenth century is considered, they have proved to be a far from insignificant minority in the history and development of North America.

JOHN MCGURK

See also **Catholics in Northern Ireland; Ireland**

Further Reading

Bardon, Jonathan, *A History of Ulster*, London, 1992

Buckland, Patrick, *A Factory of Grievances: Devolved Government in Northern Ireland; 1921–1939*, Dublin, 1979

Connolly, S.J., editor, *The Oxford Companion to Irish History*, Oxford, 1998

Dickson, R.J., *Ulster Emigration to Colonial America*, Belfast, 1976

Elliott, Marianne, *The Catholics of Ulster, a History*, Penguin, 2000

Lee, J.J., *Ireland 1912–1985*, Cambridge, 1989

Maxwell, M. Percival, *The Scottish Migration to Ulster in the Reign of James I*, London and New York, 1973

O'Connor, Fionnuala, *In Search of a State*, Belfast, 1993

Stewart, A.T.Q., *The Narrow Ground: Aspects of Ulster*, London, 1977

United Arab Emirates

Capsule Summary

Country Name: *Al Imarat al Arabiyah al Muttahidah* (United Arab Emirates)
Location: Middle East, between Saudi Arabia and Oman
Total Population: 2,484,818 (including 1,606,079 non citizens) (2003)
Language: Arabic (official), Persian, English, Hindi, Urdu
Religions: Muslim 96% (Shi'a 16%), Christian, Hindu, and other (4%)

The United Arab Emirates (UAE) is located on the Arabian Peninsular in the Middle East, bordering Oman in the East, Saudi Arabia in the southwest, Qatar in the north-west, and Iran is across the Persian Gulf on the north. The country has a land area of 82,880 square kilometers (32,000 square miles) and it is slightly smaller than the state of South Carolina in the United States.

The population of the United Arab Emirates was 2,484,800 people in 2003. Some other estimates put it at 3,440,000 that includesall undocumented workers and expatriate community. It is predominantly urban with around 70 percent of the people living in cities and towns. The capital city, Abu Dhabi (also Abu Zaby), is home to about 700,000 people (2004), or 35 percent of the population. The UAE has a high population growth rate of 1.57 percent, and it is estimated that the population will double by 2030. It has a relatively high population density of around 29 people per square kilometer (74 people per square mile).

The UAE is a federal state, which consists of seven emirates. In this political system, certain authorities are reserved for the UAE's federal government and other powers are reserved for member emirates. The government's structure was established according to the 1971 provisional Constitution. Between the late nineteenth and mid-twentieth centuries, the country was under British protection, and its population largely relied on subsistence economy. In the 1950s major oil fields were discovered and the inflow of petrodollars radically changed the economic and social environment in the country. Through series of negotiations with the British, the country obtained its independence peacefully on December 2, 1971. In December 1971, UAE adopted

its provisional Constitution, which was extended several times before it became permanent in 1996. The president is the head of state and elected by rulers of the seven emirates. The president nominates the prime minister and the Council of Ministers, who must be approved by the Council of rulers. The rulers also appoint 40 members of the Federal National Council for a two-year term.

The UAE is a multiethnic country. Representatives of several local Arab tribes, who are ethnically and linguistically close to the Arabs of the Arabian Peninsula, make up 20 percent of the country's population. The Arabs from other countries (mainly Jordanians, Palestinians, and Egyptians), and Iranians make up around 23 percent of the population. Representatives of South Asia and South East Asia (mainly Bangladeshis, Indians, Pakistanis, Sri Lankans, and Filipinos) make up 50 percent. Various other groups together make up the remaining 8 percent of the population. The current ethnic structure was formed after the 1950s, when the government encouraged migration from various parts of the Middle East and Asian countries for jobs in the booming oil, petrochemical, and service sectors. In the 1990s there was inflow of people from the newly independent communist countries. However, most of these people are not citizens and have no political rights though they have been living in the country for decades. Nevertheless, members of the native and immigrant communities havecoexisted peacefully. There are no interethnic conflicts, although some tensions exist between various social groups.

Arabic is the official language of the country. However, many communities preserve their native languages and their members speak Persian, Hindi, Urdu, and other languages at the family and community levels. English is widely used in the business community, in services (especially tourism), financial, and banking sectors. The government encourages study and usage of foreign languages, since it promotes the UAE as a business and commercial *entrepôt* in the Middle East, tries to diversify its economy, and to attract new technologiesto the country.

In the late 1990s, the UAE, like neighboring Saudi Arabia and some other Middle Eastern countries, saw a growing radicalization of various Islamic groups. Islam is the official religion of the country and the majority of the UAE's population (96 percent) is Muslim. There are very small communities of Christians and Hindus. Their religious practices are generally tolerated. Militant Islamic groups did not play a prominent role after September 11, 2001, terrorist attacks on the United States, and the beginning of the U.S.–led wars in Afghanistan and Iraq, although some radical Islamic groups are very vocal in the local political and religious debates and in the mass media.

The UAE's GDP per capita income is among the highest in the Middle East at $22,100. The country largely relies on export of its crude oil and petrochemical production, but in the 1990s, it significantly diversified its economy and developed new sectors, such as banking, finance, tourism and hospitality business, and other industries (especially garment). Despite macroeconomic stability and success in structural changes, the economy proved to be vulnerable to external shocks due to volatility of oil prices in the international market in the late 1990s and early 2000. In 2003 the UNDP's Human Development Index (HDI) placed the United Arab Emirates in forty-eighth place, behind Lithuania, Kuwait and Croatia, but ahead of the Bahamas and Latvia.

RAFIS ABAZOV

See also **Saudi Arabia; Arabs: Palestinians; Immigrant Workers in Arab States**

Further Reading

Clements, Frank A., compiler, *United Arab Emirates*, revised edition, World Bibliographical Series, vol. 43, Oxford, England, 1998

Cordesman, Anthony H., *Bahrain, Oman, Qatar, and the UAE: Challenges of Security*, Boulder, Colorado: Westiew Press, 1997

Fasano, Ugo, et al., editors, *United Arab Emirates: Selected Issues and Statistical Appendix*, Washington, DC: International Monetary Fund, 2003

Federal National Council. <www.almajles.gov.ae>

Khalifah, Anid-Amar, *The United Arab Emirates Socio-Economic Development and Its Foreign Manpower Requirements*, Genèva: Institut universitaire de hautes études internationales, 1988

Lienhardt, Peter, *Shaikhdoms of Eastern Arabia*, New York: Palgrave, 2001

Ministry of Education and Youth. <http://education.gov.ae/>

Ministry of Planning. <http://www.uae.gov.ae/mop/Ehome.htm>

Said Zahlan, Rosemarie, and Roger Owen, *The Making of the Modern Gulf States: Kuwait, Bahrain, Quatar, the United Arab Emirates and Oman*, Ithaca, 1999

United Arab Emirates, Central Statistical Department, *Annual Statistical Abstract*, Abu Dhabi (Annual Publication)

United Arab Emirates' Government. <www.uae.gov.ae>

United Arab Emirates Yearbook, London: Trident Press, (Annual Publication)

United Kingdom

Capsule Summary

Country Name: United Kingdom
Location: Western Europe, islands including the northern one-sixth of the island of Ireland between the North Atlantic Ocean and the North Sea
Total Population: 60,094,648 (2003)
Ethnic Populations: Approximately 4 million
Languages: English, Welsh (about 26% of the population of Wales), Scottish form of Gaelic (about 60,000 in Scotland). Ethnic languages: predominantly English, and Urdu, Bengali, and Sylheti
Religions: Anglican and Roman Catholic 40 million, Muslim 1.5 million, Presbyterian 800,000, Methodist 760,000, Sikh 500,000, Hindu 500,000, Jewish 350,000

The United Kingdom (UK) comprises Britain (England, Wales, and Scotland) and Northern Ireland.

Geographically, it faces the northwestern edge of the continent of Europe.

The form of government in the UK is a constitutional monarchy. There are three branches of the government: the executive, the legislative, and the judicial. The executive branch is composed of the Head of State (a hereditary monarch), the Head of Government (the Prime Minister and leader of the majority in the House of Commons), and a Cabinet (appointed by the Prime Minister). Since February 6, 1952, the Head of State has been Queen Elizabeth II. Since May 2, 1997, the leader of the Labor party, Tony Blair, has been Prime Minister. The legislative branch consists of the House of Lords and the House of Commons. There have been calls for reform of the appointment process for the House of Lords, which at the present time, is primarily hereditary. The 659 members of the House of Commons (Members of Parliament) are elected by popular vote.

In 1998, elections were held for a Northern Ireland Parliament. Transfer of power from London to Northern Ireland took place at the end of 1999, but was revoked in 2000, when disputes between existing parties and paramilitary organizations persisted. In 1999, elections for a new Scottish Parliament and a new Welsh Assembly were held, devolving power from Westminster. The Judicial branch is part of the House of Lords.

Society and Ethnicity

The latest Census was taken in April 2001, the results of which will provide the most accurate population count and other up-to-date demographic information. The current population is approximately 60 million, with more than 4 million belonging to minority ethnic communities. There are minority groups in the UK who are not British, but are considered white (such as Turkish, Greek, French, Italian, Spanish, Portuguese, and German). The British usage of the term *minority ethnic* refers to groups such as African, African Caribbean, South Asian, Chinese, or of Irish origin, who are British but socially designated as nonwhite and thus experience discrimination. In the 1980s, these groups were subsumed under the political banner of "Black." Minority ethnic is used rather than the more common "ethnic minority" in order to acknowledge the sociological and anthropological facts that all individuals whetherhite or nonwhite have an ethnicity.

More recent estimates from the 1997 Labour Force Survey indicate that minority ethnic individuals now account for 6.4 percent of the population, the majority of whom live in England. Based on the results of this survey, the ethnic composition of the United Kingdom is as follows: 93.79 percent white (British: English, Scottish, Welsh, Irish, and Other white), 1.6 percent Indian, 1.0 percent Pakistani, 0.4 percent Bangladeshi, 0.3 percent Chinese, 0.3 percent Other Asian, 0.5 percent Black Other, 0.6 percent Black African, 0.9 percent Black Caribbean, and 0.6 percent unspecified.

For the first time, the latest 2001 Census form included a Mixed category. This should provide useful information about the number of individuals who identify themselves as belonging to a mixed race, that is having one Black African, Black Caribbean or Asian parent and one white parent. Thirty-nine percent of children under the age of 16 years with a Black Caribbean mother or father have a white mother or father, suggesting this group is the fastest growing ethnic group. This is reflected in the increase in inter-racial unions within minority ethnic communities. Among British-born Caribbeans, 25 percent of all men with a partner live with a white woman and 14 percent of Caribbean women with a partner live with a white man. Among those who identified as Black Other, more than 50 percent of the men and almost half of the women, who were living with a partner, had a white partner. Among South Asian men, 8 percent of Indian men, 6 percent of Pakistani men, and 3 percent of Bangladeshi men, had white partners; 4 percent of Indian women, 1.3 percent of Pakistani women and a statistically insignificant percentage of Bangladeshi women in couples had white partners. Twenty-five percent of Chinese women and 13 percent of Chinese men had white partners.English is the first language for most residents of the United Kingdom including members of minority ethnic communities. The publication, *Ethnic Minorities in Britain* reported that with the exception of Caribbeans, nearly all minority ethnic individuals speak another language at home. For the South Asian (Indian, Pakistani, Bangladeshi) communities these include: Punjabi, Urdu, Bengali, Sylheti, Hindi, and Gujerati. Urdu, spoken by Pakistanis, and Bengali and Sylheti, the community languages for Bangladeshis, are mentioned as primary minority ethnic languages, because if given the choice, members of these communities are most likely to use these in preference to English. Chinese in Britain also speak a number of languages and dialects, of which Cantonese is the most common. In addition to English, Black Africans speak both a variation of English known as Pidgin English as well as the languages of their particular ethnic group, such as Igbo, Yoruba, Hausa (Nigerians), or Fante (Ghanaians). Black Caribbeans all speak English, but also use variations of English and other African and European languages, which are known as Creole or Patois. With the more recent arrival of refugees and asylum seekers from Sierra Leone, Somalia, Angola, Congo, Sri Lanka, Afghanistan, and Iraq, other languages including French, Somali, Portuguese, and Arabic could be added to the list of languages spoken in minority ethnic communities.

Religion is one way to differentiate minority ethnic communities from their White British counterparts as most members of minority ethnic communities have a different religion than White British and Irish people and they tend to be more religious. The exceptions to this are Black Caribbeans and Black Africans who, if practicing, tend to be Christian. Pakistanis and Bangladeshis are predominantly Muslim. Indians are either Hindu or Sikh. Religious Chinese are either Christian or Buddhist.

Historical Presence of Minority Ethnic Communities

Depending on the starting point, one could argue that everyone residing in the United Kingdom has origins elsewhere. This may include descendants of the invading Romans, Saxons, Vikings, and Normans or at various times during the nineteenth and twentieth centuries, of the thousands of refugees who fled persecution or famine in France, Ireland, Russia, and elsewhere. As Peter Fryer points out in *Staying Power* and Ron Ramdin reinforces in *Reimaging Britain*, there has been a continuous minority ethnic (African and Asian) presence in Britain for the past 500 years. There were African soldiers in the Roman imperial army, which occupied the British Isles for 350 years. In the sixteenth century, African slaves, then known as "blackmoores," were brought to England as servants for Queen Elizabeth I. Indians from northern India had reached England by the beginning of the sixteenth century and were to be found at the court of James IV of Scotland.

The relatively small number of Africans and Asians who worked as servants and performers would continue to increase; first African and then Asian labor became integral to British economic expansion through trade (slaves, cotton, tobacco, and sugar) and subsequently industry, during the Industrial Revolution. As a result of these commercial enterprises, in the seventeenth and eighteenth centuries, more African people, in particular, were involuntarily brought to Britain as slaves and servants. British employees of the East India Company, who had employed Indian servants while residing in India, brought Indians with them to Britain. This period gave way to the abolitionist movement which counted among its opponents to slavery "Free Black" (emancipated slaves) writers, such as Phyllis Wheatley, Ignatius Sancho, and Olaudah Equiano. Their efforts along with those of other Free Blacks as well as white members of the British Anti-Slavery Movement resulted in the abolition of slavery by Acts of the British Parliament in 1834. In the last third of the nineteenth century until the end of World War I, the expansion of the British Empire followed so that by the beginning of World War II, the British counted 25 percent of the world's population as

their colonial subjects. The colonization process entailed imposing a British way of life on predominantly nonwhite people. The rise of British Imperialism coincided with the emergence of scientific racism.

As a result of British trade with and colonization of Africa, the Caribbean, and Asia, many Africans and Asians worked on British ships, which operated from the port cities of Bristol, Liverpool (in England), and Cardiff (in Wales) that are home to the earliest Black settlers. In World War I, Africans, African Caribbeans, and Asians fought for the British. Many seamen chose to stay on in the multiracial communities of Tiger Bay now known as Butetown in Cardiff, and in Liverpool. In 1919, there were enough Black people in Britain to provoke what were described as race riots in these two cities as well as Glasgow (in Scotland) where many Asians had settled.

Africans, African Caribbeans, and Asians were also conscripted to fight in World War II. When the war ended and the British economy demanded a cheap-workforce, recruits, mostly from the Caribbean, were invited to fill posts, such as those in the National Health Service and in transport. This latest period of immigration lasted from 1948 to 1962 and heralded the beginnings of increased racial and ethnic tensions. This conflict manifested itself as prejudice against migrant communities, such as discrimination in employment and housing. In 1958 riots in two cities of London, Nottingham and Notting Hill, highlighted the extent of what became known as Britain's "colour problem." The Immigration Act of 1962, the 1964 White Paper on immigration policy, and the Race Relations Act of 1968 among other legislations only fueled debates between conservative opponents of African, African Caribbean, and Asian immigration, assimilation and integration, and the more liberal advocates of racial tolerance which was later referred to as "multiculturalism."

By the early 1970s, most British territories were no longer under colonial rule. The persistent discrimination against Black immigrants and their British-born children and grandchildren inspired historian Ron Ramdin to coin the phrase "Empire-Within." At the same time, UK's industries were in economic decline. In 1979, Margaret Thatcher, the leader of the Conservative Party at the time, won the general election on the strengths of a platform that promised increases in output and reduction in public expenditure and unemployment. Thatcherism emphasized British enterprise at the expense of the most disadvantaged members of society and to the advantage of "Yuppies" (Young

Upwardly Mobile Professionals). In the 1980s, social deprivation and racial injustice (such as the Deptford fire in which 13 young black people died) coupled with police harassment of minority ethnic youth, and conflicts between working class British-born Black youth and working class white racists, contributed to a series of rebellions in almost every city with a sizeable Black presence. Twenty years later, this cycle has repeated itself in the form of uprisings in four Northern formerly industrial English towns and cities, particularly Oldham near Manchester, Burnley, Bradford, and Leeds. The issues are once again those of class, generation, and economic and social deprivation. The groups involved are primarily young Pakistani and Bangladeshi men who are fighting against young white working class men, many of whom are thought to be members of or sympathetic to right-wing extremist organizations such as the British National Front and the National Party.

Minority Ethnic Communities in the Present

In the twenty-first century, the existence of disadvantage and the persistence of resistance are what create political unity and discord among minority ethnic communities even though the terms of reference have changed (Indian, Pakistani, and Bangladeshi communities now prefer the term Asian as opposed to Black which is now generally used to describe people of African and African Caribbean descent). Diversity and innovation are the two terms that characterize the positive contributions minority ethnic communities have made and continue to make to British society. These are evident in all sectors from slave, colonial and industrial economies and the war efforts in the past, and more recently in politics, business, education, the arts (literature, music, dance, theater, film), sport, and cuisine.

A leading trading power and financial center, the national GDP is divided among agriculture (1.4 percent); industry (24.9 percent); and services (73.7 percent). The United Kingdom has large coal, natural gas, and oil reserves, and services, particularly banking, insurance, and business, which account by far for the largest proportion of GDP while industry continues to decline in importance. The GDP per capita income was $25,500 in 2002. The economy of the United Kingdom is one of the strongest in Europe as inflation, interest rates, and unemployment remain low.

JAYNE IFEKWUNIGWE

See also **English; India; Ireland; Wales**

Further Reading

Cohen, Phil, editor, *New Ethnicities, Old Racisms*, London: Zed, 1999

Commission on the Future of Multi-Ethnic Britain, *The Future of Multi-Ethnic Britain: The Parekh Report*, London: Profile Books, 2000

Fryer, Peter, *Staying Power: The History of Black People in Britain*, London: Pluto, 1984

Hesse, Barnor, editor, *Un/Settled Multiculturalisms*, London: Zed, 2000

Modood, Tariq, et al., *Ethnic Minorities in Britain: Diversity and Disadvantage*, London: Policy Studies Institute, 1997

Owusu, Kwesi, editor, *Black British Culture and Society*, New York and London: Routledge, 2000

Phoenix, Ann, and Charlie Owen, "From Miscegenation to Hybridity: Mixed Relationships and Mixed Parentage in Profile," in *Hybridity and Its Discontents: Politics, Science and Culture*, edited by Avtar Brah and Annie Coombes, New York and London: Routledge, 2000

Ramdin, Ron, *Reimaging Britain: 500 Years of Black and Asian History*, London: Pluto, 1999

United Nations and Minorities

Early Years

In the years immediately following the establishment of the United Nations, minority rights were not an explicit concern of policymakers and those who drafted the foundation documents of contemporary human rights law. There is no specific reference to minorities in either the United Nations (UN) Charter or the Universal Declaration of Human Rights (UDHR). The minority issue was not neglected but was expressed through universal principles of respect for human rights without distinction as to "race, sex, language or religion" (articles 1 (3), 13, 55c, and 76c of the UN Charter). Human rights were set to characterize the UN age. The approach was centred on the individual (although society, community, and family also figure in the UDHR), the concern was global, and the promise was limitless. The great leveller of nondiscrimination would make attention to the rights of particular groups supererogatory. The key was the development and consolidation of secure national identities, essentially monolithic, homogeneous, constrained, and stable. Nation-building momentum increased with the addition of new States to United Nations membership. Many of the States were conglomerates with vast territories and complex demographics. They would either stand whole or fall apart. Hence the urge to build nations from the arcane geometries of the colonial powers, whose former colonial boundaries would only be defensible as boundaries of new States if their populations were stamped with the stamp of unity. In the UN Charter, the approach was sanctified by the principle of the sovereign equality of States, noninterference in the domestic affairs of States, and the principle of self-determination. This last principle became a right of the whole "people" in a colonial territory to immediate independence, together with a guarantee of territorial integrity, at least against the machinations of colonial powers pursuing divide and rule policies.

But there were other straws in the wind. The protection of minorities was listed among the terms of reference of the UN Commission on Human Rights which established a subordinate body—the Sub-Commission on Prevention of Discrimination and Protection of Minorities [the Sub-Commission] at its first session in 1947. The Sub-Commission (UN Doc. E/CN.4/52, section V) explained the differences between nondiscrimination and minority rights:

1. Prevention of discrimination is the prevention of any action which denies to individuals or groups of people equality of treatment which they may wish.
2. Protection of minorities is the protection of nondominant groups, which, while wishing in general for equality of treatment with the majority, wish for a measure of differential treatment in order to preserve basic characteristics . . . differential treatment of such groups or individuals belonging to such groups is justified when it is exercise in the interest of their contentment and the welfare of the community as a whole.

Even though the UN Charter and the UDHR did not engage directly with minority rights, General Assembly resolution 217C(III), passed on the same day as the UDHR, declared that the United Nations could not remain indifferent to the fate of minorities. There was a crossover between the drafting of the UDHR and the drafting of the Genocide Convention, both finalized in 1948. It seems clear that the omission of any article on cultural genocide from the Convention affected the UDHR. The prohibition of cultural genocide was unacceptable to those who drafted the Convention partly because it might have retarded nation-building processes. Nevertheless, the effect of the Convention on minority rights was equivocal— genocide was a crime of group destruction—in the words of the General Assembly resolution 96(I), it was "a denial of the right of existence of entire human groups"—and such a concept was important for future reflections of the international community on culture and ethnicity. Somewhere in all this, minority rights were locked into Cold War arguments. Soviet and Yugoslav ideas and drafts kept alive a certain scepticism about the claims of the individual rights model to solve all contemporary problems relating to ethnicity.

Eliminating Racial Discrimination; Protecting Minority Rights

From the 1970s, approaches to the ethnic question were changing. The International Covenants came into force in 1976. Liberals were becoming more curious about minority rights, digressing on individual and collective rights, looking afresh at neglected aspects of political community. The doctrine of Apartheid exercised a pernicious influence on the understanding of minority rights. The subtleties of differentiating between State-imposed racial segregation and group demands for a measure of separate recognition in cultural spheres in order to guarantee cultural existence and survival were often lost. The universal rights/nondiscrimination package was coming to appear as insufficiently nuanced for every group everywhere. Nevertheless, the principle of nondiscrimination has remained an essential factor in the totality of international efforts to address the situation of minorities. Although the *International Convention on the Elimination of All Forms of Racial Discrimination* does not employ the term "minority," it addresses manifold forms of "ethnic" disadvantage in prohibiting discrimination (any distinction, exclusion, restriction, or preference) based on "race, colour, descent, or national or ethnic origin," which "has the purpose or effect of nullifying or impairing the recognition, enjoyment or exercise, on an equal footing, of human rights and fundamental freedoms in the political, economic, social, cultural or any other field of public life." The Convention provides that special measures for individual or group advancement shall not be regarded as discrimination provided that they do not "lead to the maintenance of separate rights for different racial groups" and are not continued "after the objectives for which they have been taken have been achieved". Such special measures are mandatory in appropriate circumstances. The Convention covers discrimination in economic and social rights as well as civil and political rights, and contains provisions prohibiting State and private action in the area of racial discrimination, a provision on racial segregation and apartheid, as well as addresses the issues of remedies for discrimination and general antiracism education. In practice, the Committee on the Elimination of Racial Discrimination [CERD] has been greatly concerned with the protection of minority and indigenous rights, and, *inter alia*, has issued general recommendations on indigenous peoples and on the Roma. CERD is generally sceptical of State claims that they have no minorities: In *General Recommendation XXIV* (1999) CERD stated that in cases where "States Parties recognize the presence on their territory of some national or ethnic groups or indigenous peoples, while disregarding others," the Committee recommends that "criteria should be uniformly applied to all groups, in particular the number of persons concerned, and their being of a race, language, or culture different from the majority or from other groups within the population." CERD is also sceptical of claims that because interethnic harmony prevails in the country concerned, there is no need for anti-discrimination legislation. It seems fair to say that CERD has become more minority-sensitive over the years since the coming into force of the Convention.

The explicit reference to minorities in Article 27 of the International Covenant on Civil and Political Rights (ICCPR) and the elaboration of this norm by the Human Rights Committee has played a key role in developing the contemporary consciousness of minority rights:

> In those States where ethnic, religious or linguistic minorities exist, persons belonging to such minorities shall not be denied the right, in community with the other members of their group, to enjoy their own culture, to profess and practise their own religion, or to use their own language.

The function of the phrases relating to States "in which . . . minorities exist" appears to be twofold.

First, it is clear that many States at the time of drafting considered that they had no minorities and the phrase recognises this. On the other hand, the phrase delineates a collective aspect of existence. The group or communal dimension of existence has informed deliberations on the meaning and application of Article 27.

In *Lovelace v. Canada,* the Human Rights Committee stressed the role of the "community" in relation to a woman denied membership under Canada's Indian Act in an Indian Band because of marriage to a non-Indian, observing that "Persons who are born and brought up on a reserve, who have kept ties with their community and wish to maintain these ties must normally be considered as belonging to that minority." The Human Rights Committee has also indicated that in the enjoyment of rights under Article 27, the right of individuals to participate in aspects of community life may be restricted, but only if legislation reflects the legitimate aim of minority group survival and well-being, and the restriction on the right of an individual is not disproportionate to that aim. As the Committee observed in *Lovelace v. Canada*:

> Whatever may be the merits of the Indian Act in other respects, it does not seem . . . that to deny Sandra Lovelace the right to reside on a reserve is reasonable, or necessary to preserve the identity of the tribe. The Committee therefore concludes that to prevent her recognition as belonging to the band is an unjustifiable denial of her rights under Article 27 . . . read in the context of the other provisions referred to.

The collective aspect of minority rights is also addressed in *Lubicon Lake Band v Canada* where threats to the "way of life and culture of the . . . Band" *as such* were referred to by the Human Rights Committee. The Committee issued a *General Comment* (No. 23) on Article 27 in 1994, which summarises its experience in the application of the article. Inter alia, the Comment takes great pains to separate the rights of members of minorities from the right of self-determination. The term "autonomy" is absent from the Comment, as is any definition of "minority" though the Comment stresses that citizenship or permanent residence in the State concerned are not requirements for minority "existence." On the other hand, a territorial element appears in paragraphs specifically implicating indigenous peoples:

> One or other aspect of the rights of individuals protected under that article [27] - for example, to enjoy a particular culture - may consist in a way of life which is closely associated with territory and use of its resources. This may particularly be true of members of indigenous communities constituting a minority.

This insight was amplified in another paragraph:

culture manifests itself in many forms, including a particular way of life associated with the use of land resources, especially in the case of indigenous peoples. That right may include such traditional activities as fishing or hunting and the right to live in reserves protected by law. The enjoyment of those rights may require positive legal measures of protection and measures to ensure the effective participation of members of minority communities in decisions, which affect them.

The General Comment in effect distinguishes claims in the nature of territorial autonomy from the issue of ways of life and utilization of land resources. Ways of life and cultural connection are not automatically equated with control of territories. Nevertheless, the notion of a site, area, or place associated with a particular culture guide us toward its protection under instruments on minority rights. When the mechanics of a particular culture revolve around a relationship with a specific territory, this must be accounted for in the calculus of rights.

"Lift-Off"

By the end of the 1980s, the concern with political decolonization in Africa and Asia had largely ebbed away and the focus shifted on to economy and development. The unravelling of the Soviet Union and Yugoslavia revealed discrete peoples, with sharply differentiated identities. Identity and culture emerged as key postmodern themes, overriding consciousness of class as the authentic mediator of social relations. The politics of ethnicity and nationalism were the surrogate bodies, the carriers of the new consciousness into social action. Liberal theory woke up to a world of shattered communities and found that history had not ended. As new entities revealed themselves like a series of Russian dolls, international organizations moved to "do something about" minorities. Regional activity was notable in Europe, through the work of the Organization for Security and Cooperation in Europe (OSCE) and the Council of Europe. At the global level, the International Labour Organization (ILO) produced Convention 169 on Indigenous and tribal peoples in 1989, and the UN Convention on the Rights of the Child made explicit reference to minority or indigenous issues, including the following article (30):

In those States in which ethnic, religious or linguistic minorities or persons of indigenous origin exist, a child belonging to such a minority or who is indigenous

shall not be denied the right, in community with other members of his or her group, to enjoy his or her own culture, to profess and practise his or her own religion, or to use his or her own language.

Besides applying the Article 27 of the International Covenant on Civil and Political Rights (ICCPR) norm to children, the provision employs gender-neutral language and brings together minorities and indigenous peoples. Following in the train of the post-Cold War developments, the *Declaration on the Rights of Persons belonging to National or Ethnic, Religious and Linguistic Minorities* [UNDM] was proclaimed by the UN General Assembly on 18 December 1992. For the time being (see below on the World Conference against Racism), the Declaration represents the broad UN position on minority rights. Despite the paragraph in its preamble claiming inspiration from Article 27 of the ICCPR, the Declaration represents a fresh start and is not simply an expansion of the ICCPR. The text required 14 years to emerge from the bowels of the UN. The drafters of the instrument were aware of distinctions between individual and collective rights, which in the UNDM are consistently for "persons belonging to" minorities, and not "minorities" as such. However, Article 1.1. of the Declaration transcends the tentative phrasing of Article 27 and explicitly describes identity and existence as fundamental attributes of *groups*. The obligation to protect such existence and identity is set out as *mandatory*. The Declaration does not offer a definition of minority, which raises the question (among many others) of whether citizenship of the State in question is a requirement for minority "status." The *Commentary* on the Declaration by the Chairperson of the Working Group on Minorities (Eide, in UN Doc. E/CN.4/Sub.2/AC.5/2001/2) suggests (paras. 10 and 11) that "While citizenship as such should not be a distinguishing criterion which excludes some persons or groups from enjoying minority rights under the Declaration, other factors can be relevant in distinguishing the rights that can be demanded by different minorities." Those who live compactly together in a part of the State territory may be entitled to rights regarding the use of language, and street and place names which are different from those who are dispersed, and may in some circumstances be entitled to some kind of autonomy. Those who have been established for a long time in the territory may have stronger rights. The best approach appears to be to avoid making an absolute distinction between "new" and "old" minorities. These are very controversial propositions; while many States supported these views, others insisted that, as with Article 27 of the ICCPR, minority rights are not predicated upon the holding of a particular citizenship.

A limited range of rights is set out in Article 2, which begins by replacing the "shall not be denied the right" of Article 27 with the positive "have the right." The Declaration makes an important textual departure from Article 27 in its wide-ranging specification of participation rights—minority rights "to participate effectively in cultural, religious, social, economic and public life," and the right to participate effectively in decisions affecting them. Modalities of participation remain unspecified but the development of mediating organizations to facilitate participation is legitimate since the article also sets out a right to establish and maintain associations. The "own associations" right is supplemented by rights to establish and maintain free and peaceful contacts including "contacts across frontiers with citizens of other States to whom they (the members of minorities) are related by national or ethnic, religious or linguistic ties." Article 3 mitigates the "individualism" of the Declaration by envisaging the exercise of rights individually *as well as in community*" with other members of the group— in case States should be tempted to "decide" that culture, religion, etc., are to be carried on only in private. Eide makes the salient observation (*Commentary*, para. 53) that "This principle [in Article 3] is important, because Governments or persons belonging to majorities are often tolerant of persons of other national or ethnic origins until such time as the latter assert their own identity, language and traditions. It is often only when they assert their identity as persons belonging to a group that discrimination or persecution starts".

The measures set out in Article 4 in qualified language confront important aspects of group life. Mandatory language extends to members of minorities the promise that they may "fully and effectively" exercise all their human rights without discrimination and on basis of equality. Measures are not defined, but the term is appropriate to cover both legislative and non-legislative measures. Article 4.2. provides that States must facilitate the expression and development of minority culture, traditions and customs, etc., "except where specific practices are in violation of national law and international standards." The qualification specifically addresses the objection sometimes placed against minorities and indigenous peoples, that group traditions may incorporate *practices* inconsistent with human rights. This, however, raises but does not dispose

issues of distinguishing or severing the links between cultural practices on the one hand, and cultures and cultural values, on the other, with the objective of limiting the first, while validating the second. The provisions in Article 4 on learning and instruction in mother tongue are qualified and ambiguous: "States should take appropriate measures so that, wherever possible, persons belonging to minorities may have adequate opportunities to learn their mother tongue or to have instruction in their mother tongue." The intended contrast in the Declaration's references to "instruction in" and "learning" mother tongue is between learning through the medium of one's own language, and being taught the rudiments of that language. The important point is the validation of mother tongue education, though linguistic "purism" is not encouraged. While mother tongue education is legitimated, this does not dispense with the need to learn the official or State language. Article 4 states in its fourth paragraph:

> States should, where appropriate, take measures in the field of education, in order to encourage knowledge of the history, traditions, language and culture of the minorities existing within their territory. Persons belonging to minorities should have adequate opportunities to gain knowledge of the society as a whole.

This is aimed at promoting self-knowledge on the part of minorities, and their awareness of the wider world, while informing society at large of the cultural and other contributions of minorities to the nation as a whole. Accordingly, the culture, history, traditions, etc., of minority groups should be the subject of positive valuations and not of distorted representations which produce low self-esteem in the groups and negative stereotypes in the wider community. Reciprocally, minority doctrines of ethnic exclusiveness are discouraged. Eide comments that the provision suggests the need for "both multicultural and intercultural education. Multicultural education involved educational policies and practices which meet the separate educational needs of groups in society belonging to different cultural traditions, while intercultural education involved ... policies and practices whereby persons belonging to different cultures ... learn to interact constructively with each other". His *Commentary* (para. 69) observes that,

> Formation of more or less involuntary ghettos where the different groups live in their own world without knowledge of, or tolerance for, persons belonging to other parts of the national society would be a violation of the purpose and spirit of the Declaration.

It is also asserted (para. 68) that the Declaration is against tendencies "towards fundamentalist or closed religious or ethnic groups." Much depends on what one means by a "ghetto," on what counts as a "closed" society, and which societies are "fundamentalist."

Articles 5, 6, and 7 set out important elements of development and cooperation in the matter of minority rights. Article 8 sets minority rights in their universal context and "balances" their exercise with the rights of others, implying that measures for minorities are generally compatible with equality, while strongly suggesting that they should not be pushed too far to the detriment of others. Article 8.4—"Nothing in the present Declaration may be construed as permitting any activity contrary to the purposes and principles of the United Nations, including sovereign equality, territorial integrity and political independence of States"—connects with the fear of some States that minority rights may lead to self-determination. To the extent that a secessionist threat exists, it must be in virtue of other principles of international law, and this applies equally to the converse argument that the Declaration "protects" territorial integrity from valid claims to self-determination. Article 9 points to contributions from the United Nations to the realization of the purposes of the text. The language is such as to implicate all organs of the UN system.

Working Group on Minorities

The specific follow-up to the Declaration proceeded slowly. The Commission on Human Rights, adopted resolution 1995/24 on March 3, 1995 authorizing the Sub-Commission to establish a Working Group on Minorities. The mandate of the Working Group is entrusted to (a) review the promotion and practical realization of the Declaration, (b) examine possible solutions to problems involving minorities, and (c) recommend further measures, as appropriate, for the promotion and protection of the rights of persons belonging to minorities. The Working Group met for the seventh time in 2001, and now enjoys an "indefinite" mandate. It provides a framework within which NGOs, members of minority groups or associations, academics, governments, and international agencies may meet to discuss issues of concern and attempt to seek solutions to problems. According to the *United Nations Guide for Minorities* (pamphlet no. 2, 2), the hope is that the meetings and dialogue will lead to greater understanding of minority issues

and mutual tolerance among minorities, and between minorities and governments. A considerable number of valuable papers were prepared for the sessions and seminars were organized, the results of which have been discussed at the meetings. The Working Group focuses to a significant extent on conceptual clarification of the minority question—analyzing concepts and issues such as existence, recognition, definition, self-determination, autonomy, language rights, education, etc. The Working Group has adopted flexible arrangements to encourage participation in its sessions by all those interested in and able to contribute to its work.

Overview and Prospects

A notable feature of contemporary developments is the manner in which minority rights elements have been "mainstreamed" into the work of the United Nations. The UN treaty-bodies and the Charter-based organs increasingly incorporate, elaborate, and refine aspects of minority rights. The Commission on Human Rights and the Sub-Commission, the special rapporteurs and working groups, the procedures for dealing with mass violations, the individual communications procedures, etc., have all sharpened their awareness of minority and indigenous issues. Questions of minority and indigenous rights also arise in connection with development, health, environment, and intellectual property. It should not be forgotten that individual members of minorities are entitled to all human rights, and not simply those which make specific reference to "minority". It appears probable nonetheless that further steps may be taken by the UN to promote specific minority rights. There is discussion on prospects for a Convention on minorities stemming from the preparatory work for the World Conference against Racism. The proposal from the Geneva Expert seminar on racism, refugees, and multiethnic States: That the World Conference should recommend "that the United Nations elaborate an international instrument of a binding character defining the rights and obligations of persons belonging to minorities," appears as paragraph 79 of the UN Secretariat's "Elements for a draft Declaration and Programme for the World Conference." The emergence of the Special Rapporteur for indigenous peoples may well bring forth proposals for an analogous institution for minorities.

Taking the ensemble of general human rights and specific minority rights, the international community has elaborated a complex set of norms and procedures to underpin the rights of individual members of minority and support the existence of groups. Thus far, minority rights have largely eschewed group rights, and instead chosen "individual rights exercised in community with others" as the appropriate methodology— only in the case of indigenous peoples have clearer "group rights" been articulated. Minority rights in UN instruments do not define *minority* but generally refer to "national or ethnic, religious and linguistic" minorities; other groups may be categorised simply as "vulnerable communities." "Rights of minorities" are thus understood as rights in the field of existence, identity, language, education, participation, and development; they do not approach the wilder shores of self-determination or autonomy, though the absence of an international definition of "peoples" blurs distinctions between rights of peoples and those of minorities. Minority rights endeavour to protect groups from discrimination, and provide a defense for personal and group expressions of identity and the development and flourishing of such identities in a globalizing world.

PATRICK THORNBERRY

See also **United Nations Declaration on Minorities; United Nations Working Group on Indigenous Populations; United Nations Working Group on Minorities; Apartheid; Human Rights; Minorities and Language; Minority Rights Group International**

Further Reading

Capotorti, Francesco, *Study on the Rights of Persons Belonging to Ethnic, Religious and Linguistic Minorities* New York: United Nations, 1991

Hannum, Hurst, "The Rights of Persons Belonging to Minorities," in *Human Rights: Concepts and Standards,* edited by Janusz Symonides, Ashgate and UNESCO, 2000

Phillips, Alan, and Allan Rosas, editors, *Universal Minority Rights*, London and Abo: Minority Rights Group and Abo Akademi University, 1995

Rehman, Javaid, *The Weaknesses in the International Protection of Human Rights*, The Hague: Kluwer Law International, 2000

Spiliopoulou-Akermark, Athanasia, *Justifications of Minority Protection in International Law*, Uppsala: Justus Forlag, 1997

Thornberry, Patrick, *International Law and the Rights of Minorities*, Oxford: Clarendon Press, 1991

United Nations Declaration on Minorities

By way of introduction to the more detailed analysis of the United Nations Declaration on the Rights of Persons Belonging to National or Ethnic, Religious, and Linguistic Minorities, some general remarks do provide a fairly good indication about its importance as well as general tendency. In this way, the subsequent article-by-article analysis can proceed against the background of this general framework, contributing to a balanced assessment.

Capotorti had already urged in his well known 1979 study regarding Article 27 of ICCPR that a Declaration should be developed, which elaborates the principles of that article, by way of guidelines for the states. However, the Declaration does contain provisions that go beyond Article 27 and arguably reflect an evolution of views in the United Nations (UN) since 1966.

The 1992 UN Declaration is the end product of 14 years of diligent work by the special Working Group,

established by the UN Commission on Human Rights on recommendation of the UN Sub-Commission. The Declaration is the first international instrument exclusively devoted to the protection of minority rights, albeit it is not legally binding on UN member states. It does have a certain value as it is solemnly adopted by a resolution in the General Assembly. Furthermore, UN bodies themselves are obliged to respect the norms contained in it.

Whereas Article 27 of ICCPR only refers to ethnic, religious, or linguistic minorities, the UN Declaration on Minority Rights has apparently attempted to transcend the discussion regarding the respective scope of "national" and "ethnic." The Declaration should thus be interpreted so that the members of the four categories of minorities are able to rely on it.

Although the Declaration contains some more elaborate standards in comparison to Article 27, these are still rather vague and furthermore, formulated in such a cautious way that states can easily argue that they comply. The use of formulations like "wherever possible," "when appropriate," and "adequate opportunities" inevitably concede a wide margin of appreciation to the states. The Declaration arguably intends to strike a balance between a progressive attitude regarding minority protection, attempting to provide a set of explicit minority rights, and the states' preference to define minority rights sufficiently broadly so as not to hamper their freedom of action.

The Declaration recognizes explicitly the right to identity of minorities, unlike Article 27 of ICCPR. It is furthermore important that Article 1, para. 2 and Article 4, para. 2 point to the existence of a state obligation to take special measures, which are designed to maintain and promote the separate minority identity.

Article 2 enshrines in its second and third paragraphs, an introduction at the level of international law, of the right for members of minorities to effective participation not only in the cultural, religious, and social but also in the economic and public, even political life of the state. Although the latter does not amount to granting some kind of right to autonomy for minorities, their members should at least have an effective say in decisions, which are closely related to their lives, identity, and future.

Group rights in the sense of rights attributed to a group as such, are clearly and deliberately avoided in the Declaration. The rights of the Declaration can nevertheless be exercised collectively by the members of a minority "in community," reflecting a certain recognition of the group dimension of the minority reality.

Article 4 of the Declaration reflects in its first and second paragraphs the two pillars of a full blown system of minority protection, namely the prohibition of discrimination in combination with the fundamental rights and freedoms of the members of minorities on the one hand, and "special" minority rights on the other hand.

Article 4, para. 3 concerns education in and/or of the mother tongue for members of minorities, while para. 4 underlines the possibility to improve, through the education system, the mutual understanding and respect between members of the minority and the rest of the population.

Although the UN Declaration on Minority Rights is significant in that it clarifies the content of Article 27 of ICCPR and furthermore points to the existence of positive state obligations regarding minorities, it cannot be denied that it is burdened by several deficiencies. Little or no content is given to the right to enjoy one's own culture or to the right to profess and practice one's own religion. The members' of minorities right to use their own language is also meagerly developed since only a qualified reference is made to native language education while nothing is spelled out about the crucial issue of language use in the communication between members of minorities and the public authorities, nor about the right of minorities to use their own language in private and public media.

Overall, the careful, cautious formulation of the provisions in combination with the weak normative value of the Declaration presumably entails that the actual level of minority protection since the adoption of the Declaration is mainly determined by the good will of the states.

It can thus justifiably be said that there is still a strong need for further standard setting as well as for effective implementation mechanisms. In this regard, the decision of the UN Commission on Human Rights to authorize the Sub-Commission to establish a Working Group on Minorities to promote the protection of minorities and the implementation of the UN Declaration on Minority Rights is to be welcomed.

KRISTIN HENRARD

See also **United Nations and Minorities; United Nations Working Groups on Minorities; Human Rights; Minorities and Language; Minority Rights Group International**

Further Reading

Capotorti, Francesco, *Study on the Rights of Persons Belonging to National or Ethnic, Religious and Linguistic Minorities*, New York: United Nations, 1979

Eide, Asbjorn, *Commentary to the Declaration on the Rights of Persons Belonging to National or Ethnic, Religious and Linguistic Minorities*, UN Doc. E/CN.4/Sub.2/AC.5/1998/WP.1, May 13, 1998

Pejic, J., "Minority Rights in International Law," *Human Rights Quarterly* (1997)

Packer, John, "On the Content of Minority Rights," in *Universal Minority Rights*, edited by Allen Phillips and Allan Rosas, Abo/Turku: Abo Akademi Tryckeri, 1995

Phillips, Allen, and Allan Rosas, editors, *The United Nations Minority Rights Declaration*, Abo/Turku: Abo Akademi Tryckeri, 1993

Thornberry, Patrick, "The UN Declaration on the Rights of Persons Belonging to National or Ethnic, Religious and Linguistic Minorities: Background, Analysis, Observations and an Update," in *Universal Minority Rights*, edited by Allen Phillips and Allan Rosas, Abo/Turku: Abo Akademi Tryckeri, 1997

Spiliopoulou-Akermark, Annastasia, *Justifications of Minority Protection in International Law*, London: Kluwer, 1997

United Nations Working Group on Indigenous Populations

The United Nations (UN) Working Group on Indigenous Populations is a subsidiary organ of the Sub-Commission on the Promotion and Protection of Human Rights (previously the Sub-Commission on Prevention of Discrimination and Protection of Minorities). It was established in 1982 by the UN Economic and Social Council (ECOSOC), to assist the Sub-Commission. The Working Group reviews developments pertaining to the rights of indigenous peoples and promotes international standards concerning their rights and facilitates dialogue between governments and indigenous peoples. The Working Group has five members chosen from the Sub-Commission. Each member represents one of the five geographic regions of Africa, Asia, Eastern Europe, Latin America, and Western Europe. The Working Group meets annually, one or two weeks before the Sub-Commission in Geneva.

Background of the Working Group

Indigenous peoples are considered, among the world's minorities, as one of the most disadvantaged groups. Indigenous peoples are also referred to as "first peoples," tribal peoples, aboriginals, and autochthons. There are about 5,000 indigenous groups made up of 300 million people, living in over 70 countries on five continents.

Indigenous peoples are excluded from decision-making processes, are marginalized, exploited, forcefully assimilated, and subjected to repression, torture, and murder when they stand up to defend their rights. Infear of persecution, indigenous peoples often become refugees and sometimes even have to hide their identity, abandoning their languages, traditional customs, and clothing.

In 1970 the UN Sub-Commission on the Prevention of Discrimination and Protection of Minorities commissioned an extensive study of the problem of discrimination against indigenous populations. José R. Martinet Cobo acted as Special Reporter for the study. In 1981 he first submitted a report to the Sub-Commission, but much of the information was outdated and incomplete. The study and the interest it generated led in 1982 to the creation of the Working Group of Indigenous Populations. In 2000 ECOSOC established the Permanent Forum on Indigenous Issues as a subsidiary organ. It is a forum composed of 16 experts representing an equal number of government and indigenous experts. The forum advises ECOSOC, helps to coordinate UN activities, and discusses indigenous concerns relating to development, culture, the environment, health, and human rights.

Additionally, the United Nations Development Program (UNDP), the United Nations Children's Fund (UNICEF), the International Fund for Agricultural Development (IFAD), and the United Nations Educational, Scientific, and Cultural Organization (UNESCO) have programs that are directed at specific indigenous groups that work to improve health and literacy and to combat environmental degradation of their native lands.

Role of the Working Group

The Working Group has two main tasks:

1. Review national developments pertaining to the promotion and protection of the human rights and fundamental freedoms of indigenous peoples; and
2. Develop international standards concerning the rights of indigenous peoples, taking account of both the similarities and differences in their situations and aspirations throughout the world.

In reviewing national developments, the Working group receives and analyzes written information submitted by governments, specialized agencies, other organs of the UN, international and regional intergovernmental organizations, non-governmental bodies, and the indigenous peoples themselves.

The Working Group is not authorized to review specific allegations of human rights violations. It also cannot make decisions about particular cases. Instead, Working Group participants should push issues through the UN system into the Sub-Commission, then the Commission on Human Rights and so forth.

Working Methods

The Working Group provides a framework within which all representatives of indigenous peoples, their communities and organizations, meet representatives of the Working Group to discuss issues of concern and attempt to seek solutions to problems. In the Commission on Human Rights and the Sub-Commission, the Commission and Sub-Commission Members, Government Observers, and representatives of Non-Governmental Organizations (NGOs) with consultative status may speak, but in the Working Group, all indigenous persons are allowed to take part in discussions.

The Chariperson-Rapporteur visits countries for first hand information and provides information on UN activities in the field of indigenous peoples' rights to identify issues which need to be taken up in standard setting.

The Draft Declaration on the Rights of Indigenous Peoples

The Working Group started to prepare a draft declaration on the rights of indigenous peoples in 1985, taking into account the comments and suggestions of participants in its sessions, particularly representatives of indigenous peoples and governments.

In July 1993, at its eleventh session, the Working Group agreed on the final text of the draft declaration, which was then submitted to the Sub-Commission.

The Commission on Human Rights in 1995 established an open-ended intersessional working group to consider the text submitted by the Sub-Commission and to elaborate a draft declaration for consideration and adoption by the general Assembly within the International Decade of the World's Indigenous People (1995–2004). The General Assembly has affirmed that the adoption of such declaration is a major objective of the decade. The official goal of this draft declaration is to provide a minimum standard for the protection of the rights of indigenous peoples throughout the world.

The draft declaration on the rights of indigenous peoples represents one of the most important developments in the promotion and protection of the basic rights and fundamental freedoms of indigenous peoples.

MEHDI PARVIZI AMINEH

See also **Indigenous Peoples; United Nations Working Group on Indigenous Peoples United Nations Working Group on Minorities**

Further Reading

United Nations Draft Declaration on the Rights of Indigenous Peoples, Commission on Human Rights, *Sub-Commission on Prevention of Discrimination and Protection of Minorities, Forty-Fifth session, 1993*
———, *Discrimination against Indigenous Peoples, Report of the Working Group on Indigenous Populations on its Eleventh Session, 1993*

United Nations Working Group on Minorities

The United Nations (UN) Working Group on Minorities is a subsidiary organ of the Sub-Commission on the Promotion and Protection of Human Rights (previously the Sub-Commission on Prevention of Discrimination and Protection of Minorities). It was established in 1995 by the Sub-Commission. The Working Group recommends practical measures for the promotion and protection of the rights of persons that belong to minorities. It is composed of five experts who are members of the Sub-Commission, representing each of the five geographic regions of Africa, Asia, Eastern Europe, Latin America, and Western Europe. The Working Group meets once a year in May in Geneva for five working days. It prepares a formal report submitted to and discussed by the Sub-Commission meeting each August. The report is also made available as a background document for the Commission on Human Rights.

Background of the Working Group

In almost all states there exist minority groups that because of their own ethnic, linguistic, or religious identities differ from the majority population. Minorities seek recognition by their governments, secure their rights of identity, speak their own language, enjoy their own culture, and participate in public and political life. The protection of minority rights until recently did not get the same level of attention at the UN as that of other rights. As ethnic, racial, and religious tensions have escalated in recent years, all too often as a result of violations of minority rights, the interest in issues that affect minorities has grown.

The protection of the human rights of members of ethnic, religious, or linguistic minorities is specifically protected in the International Covenant on Civil and Political Rights (ICCPR) and more generally in the Principle of Non-Discrimination which forms the basis for all UN human rights law. In 1992 the General Assembly adopted the Declaration on the Rights of Persons Belonging to National or Ethnic, Religious and Linguistic Minorities giving the work of the UN a new impetus.

To ensure more effective protection of the rights of persons belonging to minorities, the Sub-Commission on Promotion and Protection of Human Rights established the Working Group in 1995.

Role of the Working Group

The three main tasks of the Working Group are:

1. Review the promotion and practical realization of the Minorities Declaration.
2. Examine possible solutions to problems involving minorities, including the promotion of mutual understanding between and among minorities and governments.
3. Recommend further measures, as appropriate, for the promotion and protection of the rights of persons belonging to national or ethnic, religious and linguistic minorities.

The agenda of the Working Group includes a wide range of subjects. It reviews the constitutions and legislations of nation states and examines the extent to which they have realized the Minorities Declaration, or effective protection of the rights of persons belonging to national ethnic minorities. Other topics include language rights, intercultural and multicultural education, and the right to participate in political and public life.

Working Methods

The Working Group provides a framework within which nongovernmental organizations (NGOs), members of minority groups or associations, academics,

governments, and international agencies meet to discuss issues of concern and attempt to seek solutions to problems. When the Working Group presents information about the situation of minorities in a specific country, the country's representative may respond. Recommendations proposed by participants (not always members of the Working Group) are set forth in the annual report to the Sub-Commission. The Sub-Commission may forward suggestions for the promotion and protection of minority rights to the Commission on Human Rights and the Economic and Social Council (ECOSOC).

The Working Group also organizes series of seminars together with national institutions and nongovernmental organizations on topics related to the Minorities Declaration. The reports of these seminars serve as a basis for further discussion during the sessions of the Working Group.

Prospects

Minority problems are often related to the existence of structures or systems that have the effect of either perpetuating the marginalization of minority communities from decision-making or of unfairly benefiting majority populations or dominant groups in the economic, social, and political life of the country.

The fact that minority problems are appreciated has led to recommendations for the protection of the identity of minorities and respect for diversity. Acceptance of diversity by the majority or dominant groups often requires that they better understand the culture, customs, language, and history of minority communities. This, in turn, has led to the recommendation that curricula and programs of intercultural and human rights should be developed. Social, economic, and political inequalities between communities and groups have also been identified as a root cause of conflict. As a consequence, equality, social justice, and fair representation, as called for under minority rights protection and promotion, are increasingly perceived as a conflict prevention measure. Thus, discussions and documents adopted by different UN forums support the approach of the Working Group through advocating the establishment of mechanisms for dialogue and arrangements for participation to address the exclusion and marginalization of minority communities. The Working Group is gaining ground as a more important focus for UN activities regarding minority issues. Some major aspects of the issues discussed in its meetings are multicultural and intercultural education, recognition of the existence of minorities, participation in public life, including thorough autonomy and integrative measures, inclusive development, and conflict prevention.

MEHDI PARVIZI AMINEH

See also **Minorities and Language; United Nations Declaration on Minorities; United Nations Working Group on Indigenous Populations**

Further Reading

United Nations Declaration on the Rights of Persons Belonging to National or Ethnic, Religious and Linguistic Minorities, Office of the High Commissioner for Human Rights, 1992

United Nations Guide for Minorities, Office of the High Commissioner for Human Rights, 2001

Untouchables (Harijans/Dalits/Scheduled Castes)

Capsule Summary

Location: India, Pakistan, Sri Lanka, Nepal, and Bangladesh
Total Population: 205 million (in India)
Religion: Hindu, Buddhism, Christianity

According to India's caste system, an *untouchable, dalit,* or *achuta* is a person outside of and beneath the four castes (the Hindu system of hereditary classes). Untouchables have historically been the focus of intense discrimination, racism, and abuse by the police as well as members of higher-caste groups that enjoy the state's protection. They have been denied access to land and jobs, discriminated against, socially shunned, as well as killed, beaten, and raped. People who worked in lowly, unwanted, and unclean occupations (often involving the killing of animals) were seen as "polluting peoples" and were therefore considered "untouchable." The Untouchables held virtually no rights in Indian society, although their treatment could vary from region to region. Various human rights groups, organizations, governments, and figures such as Mohandas Karamchand Gandhi, Bhimrao Ramji Ambedkar, and Jyotirao Phule took up the cause of the *dalits* in the twentieth century.

Harijan—meaning "Children of God"—was a polite form for the *untouchables* coined by Gandhi (Hari is another name for Vishnu, a Hindu God). Untouchables generally considered this term to be condescending and prefer the name *dalit*, variously translated as "crushed," "stepped on," "broken," or "oppressed". *Scheduled castes* (meaning socially and educationally backward groups) was a term introduced in the Government of India Act in 1935 by the British, a designation constitutionally recognized when India

gained independence in 1947. *Dalit* was adopted as the official term in Indian government documents in 1990. The history of the caste system originally referred to as the *Varnasrama* dharma or social system in India is ancient. The Indus Valley civilization started to decline in 2000 BCE when the Aryans or Indo-Aryans—descendants of the Indo-Europeans—entered the northwest of India in 1500 BCE. The caste system is believed to have been established by the Aryans (Arya means pure or good in Sanskrit) as the result of encounters between the Aryans and Dravidians, the residents of India. Religious Vedic (literally meaning "law") scriptures were composed from about 700 BCE onward. These scriptures introduced an administrative system based on four *varnas* ("colors" in Sanskrit) that are believed to have emerged from Mana, a primordial being. These *varna* designations are translated as the source of the Indian castes. According to the religious text, *Manusmriti* ("Laws of Manu") written circa 200 CE, the four castes were based on four *varnas*—Brahmins (white, the priests and teachers); Kshatriyas (red, the rulers and warriors); Vaishyas (yellow, the merchants and craftsmen); and Shudras (black, the workers or laborers). Each *varna* is characterized by appropriate rules of conduct including rules regarding marriage, eating, and physical proximity, and is further subdivided into many *jatis* or communities. A fifth group described the people who are *achuta*, or untouchable. Untouchables are therefore outcasts and outside of the caste system due to their perception as being impure and even subhuman. The conflict between pollution and purity, which dates to the ancient scriptures, governed all social interaction among castes. The Shudras and the untouchables were denied the social and economic rights enjoyed by those who belonged to the first three castes, who were also seen as "twice born," referring to their natural birth and to their ceremonial entrance into society later in life.

Although in India, the *jat* (community) could refer to any community that shares religion, language, origin, or similar geographical background, the use of the term *caste* first by Portuguese colonialists and later by the British reflects a distortion of the original word's meaning. Moreover, in the ancient scriptures the *Varnasrama* system divided society into four occupational and spiritual orders of life. Some scholars argue that the corruption of this system over time, especially under British colonialism, contributed to the unfortunate situation of the Untouchables in the modern age.

The Untouchable movement has two centuries of history. The role of Christian missionaries during colonial rule is significant, although skeptics and conservative Hindus opposed this on the grounds of forceful conversion. By 1850s, shamed or inspired local Hindu reformers emerged, notably Jyotirao Phule (1827–1890). Called "The Other Mahatma" (a reference to Gandhi) by *Dalit* intellectuals, Phule also led the farmers' movement, the women's movement, and a nonBrahmin-oriented environmental movement. During the reign of the British Raj, the period of British rule over the Indian subcontinent (1858–1947), the caste (or *jat*) system emerged as a controversial issue in the eyes of both Indians and Westerners. For instance Sir Herbert Risley published *The Tribes and Castes of Bengal* in 1892, a text in which he described a comprehensive classification of the races of India into seven types. Some scholars have argued that the Western view of the Indian system was interpreted and overlaid with racial (and often racist) theories, the effects of colonialism, and a cultural misunderstanding of Indian cultural realities. For example, the four colors (from "white" to "black" as "pure" and "impure") were interpreted in racial terms. It would seem that the castes grew more rigid and inflexible in modernity (and under British rule). Moreover, while the classification of Indian groups did not translate into racial groups, per se, "untouchability" has been attacked under the purview, and rightly so, of racial discrimination.

The British government provided reservations (special provisions equivalent to affirmative action principles in the United States) for Muslims by declaring communal electorates (established via the Government of India Act, 1919). Similar reservations were lobbied for lower-caste Hindus by the leaders from the Depressed classes, as they were called at the time. The Indian National Congress Party, headed by Gandhi, opposed such reservations on caste grounds, as they amounted to a divide-and-rule strategy by the British Raj when taken alongside the separate electorates for Muslims. Ambedkar—a *Dalit* himself and a leader from the Untouchable community—represented the interests of the untouchables, or Depressed classes as they were often called during this time. Gandhi believed that untouchability represented a perversion of the *varna* laws and that plight of the *dalits* would be lessened by a change of heart and beliefs among Hindus. He declared that untouchability represented no part in Hinduism as a religion or spiritual teaching. While Gandhi's sincerity in abolishing untouchability led to many initiatives such as the *Harijan Sevak Sangh* (a welfare association), some *dalits* found it condescending as the movement operated within the ambit of the Hindu religion. Ambedkar was a beneficiary of a Hindu reformer, the Maharaja of Baroda, and later became the head of the Indian Constitutional Committee. He argued that the Untouchables could not have freedom without the destruction of the caste system. Ambedkar preferred the term *dalits* and argued that the position of the untouchables could never be improved as long as they remained within the domain of Hinduism. He turned to the revival of Buddhism among *dalits* (converting himself later in life) as he viewed Buddhism as more tolerant to lower-caste groups.

The *Dalit* movement in India emerged at the same time as Indian nationalism and Marxism. Many historians and thinkers tended to articulate the caste discrimination from a Marxist perspective—an approach rejected by Ambedkar and other *dalit* intellectuals. The latter argue that caste discrimination is embedded within religion, and is deeper than "class," which is defined in terms of holding or not holding the means of production, or private property. As a result, Phule tried to formulate a new, theistic religion; Periyar (or Thanthai) E.V. Ramasamy promoted atheism and rationalism; Ambedkar turned to Buddhism; others in the Tamil Nadu state of India's non-Brahman movement tried to claim Saivism as an independent religion. Despite widespread conversion in the postindependence era to Christianity, the plight of the *dalits* continued. During the 1900s, the *dalit* movement grew under the leadership of Ramaswamy, a former Congress party member who renounced party membership on the grounds of its Brahmanical supremacy and began a non-Brahmanical movement. The non-Brahman movements of western and southern India during the colonial period were the most powerful expressions of a pan-Indian upsurge that sought to confront and destroy the millennia-old caste hierarchy. The huge success of Ramaswamy's movement led to more equitable conditions among castes, primarily in the southern (the so-called Dravidian) states. In the north, however, discrimination still deeply divides society, with many organizations claiming to assert the superiority and privilege of the Brahmin caste and the subjugation of the *dalit*s.

Three years after Independence, the Indian Constitution officially banned the practice of untouchability. Article 17 states that "Untouchability is abolished and its practice in any form is forbidden. The enforcement of any disability arising out of untouchability shall be an offence punishable in accordance with law."

While the law declares that it is one of the fundamental rights of every citizen not to be discriminated on grounds of caste, nowhere in the Constitution is "untouchability" defined. Nonetheless, while the Indian caste system is an example where culture overrules politics, the overall status of *dalit*s has improved since. A recent report by Human Rights Watch points out that two *Dalit* women are raped every day. The only *dalit* president of India, K.R. Narayan, in his address to the nation on Republic Day (2000), said: "Untouchability has been abolished...but it is ingrained in the attitudes of people and nurtured by the caste system." The Union Government of India has introduced the reservation system—as recommended by the Mandal Commission in 1990—that improved access for *dalit*s to educational institutions and public sector employment.

The cause of the *dalit*s has emerged in international politics as well. The *Dalit* caucus at the World Conference against Racism in Durban, 2003, raised international awareness about caste discrimination. The United Nations Human Rights Commissioner Mary Robinson, South African President Thabo Mbeki, and Cuban leader Fidel Castro publicly stated that the time had come for the *Dalit*s to win justice. The official position of the Indian government remained that the Durban conference was not the right platform for raising this issue.

MURALI SHANMUGAVELAN

See also **Ambedkar, Bhimrao Ramji (*Dalit*); Gandhi, Mohandas Karamchand (India); India**

Further Reading

Ambedkar, B.R, *Annihilation of Caste*, Jullundur City: Bheem Patrika Publications, 1968
Beteille, Andrew, *Caste, Class and Power: Changing Patterns of Stratification in a Tanjore Village*, Delhi: Oxford University Press, 1996
Dalit Media Network, *A Dalit President Speaks*, Chennai: Dalit Media Network Press, 2000
Human Rights Watch, *Broken People*, New York: Human Rights Watch Press, 1999
Iliah, Kancha, *Why I Am Not a Hindu?* Calcutta: Stree Publications, 2001
Omvedt, Gail, *Dalits and the Democratic Revolution; Dr. Ambedkar and the Dalit Movement in Colonial India*, Delhi: Sage Publications, 1994
Sathiyamurthy, T.V., *Region, Religion, Caste, Gender and Culture in Contemporary India—Vol. 3*, Madras: Oxford University Press, 1996
Smith, Brian K., *The Laws of Manu*, Delhi: Penguin Classics, 1991
Thapar, Romila, *A History of India, Volume One*, London: Penguin Books, 1966

Uruguay

Capsule Summary

Location: South America
Total Population: 3,413,329 (July 2003)
Ethnic Populations: white (88%), mestizo (8%), black (4%), Amerindian, practically nonexistent
Languages: Spanish, Italian, German, Portuguese, Russian
Religions: Roman Catholic (66%) (less than half of the adult population attends church regularly), Protestant (2%), Jewish (1%), non professing or other (31%) (includes Mennonite, Jewish)

Among the smallest countries in South America, Uruguay has one of the region's most democratic governments. Known at one time for its prosperity and equitable distribution of national wealth, the country has in recent decades suffered from economic stagnation. The population is culturally homogenous. The language spoken is Spanish and the vast majority is white, descended primarily from Spanish, Italian, and

Portuguese immigrants. There are small *mestizo* (mixed race) and black communities. Roman Catholicism is the largest religion, with the nominal adherence of two-thirds of the population. Nearly a third of the population has no religious affiliation. The evangelical Protestant, Mennonite, and Jewish religions each has several tens of thousands of adherents. Per capita GDP is $26.82 billion (2002).

About the size of the state of Missouri, Uruguay is bordered on the north by Brazil. From this border, the land gently descends as a hilly plateau in the northern half of the country and then as a rolling plain in the southern half. The western border of the country is the Uruguay River; and the eastern, the Atlantic Ocean. The capital is the ocean port of Montevideo lying midway on the country's southern Atlantic coast. Nearly half of the country's population is concentrated in the metropolitan region of Montevideo. Uruguay is separated from Argentina not only by the Uruguay River but also by the wide delta of the Rio de la Plata.

Uruguay did not exist during the colonial period, before the nineteenth century. It was a buffer area between Argentina, a Spanish colony and Brazil, Portuguese. Uruguay's leveled, well-watered land attracted ranchers and farmers from both regions. However, Spanish settlement dominated. There was a small indigenous population that was, however, decimated during the advance of the European settlers, leaving no native minority today.

War broke out for possession of the Uruguay territory between the newly independent countries of Argentina and Brazil at the beginning of the nineteenth century. To avoid the continuation of this regional power competition, Uruguay was established as a separate country, to act as a buffer between the two larger rivals. Caught between two huge neighbors, Uruguayans have proven fierce in defending their independence but been modest so as not to provoke the rancor of either.

The Portuguese introduced slavery into Uruguay. By the end of the eighteenth century, almost a fourth of the population was of African origin. Through intermarriages between blacks and whites, a *mestizo* or mixed racial group developed. By the end of the twentieth century, nearly six percent of Uruguayans identified themselves as "black." Afro-Uruguayans have a higher rate of unemployment in the country, are paid less, and are more likely to be engaged in manual labor.

Although the Indian population has disappeared, a mixed breed or *mestizo* still survives, primarily in the rural interior. This population does not comprise more than ten percent and has no indigenous language. All such languages are now extinct.

Racial and national identity is of great importance in Uruguay due to the European ethnic character of the country. Predominantly white, Spanish, and Catholic in character, its elites engaged in constant political battles and warfare during the nineteenth century. However, toward the end of that period, the country became increasingly prosperous due to its agricultural and meat exports to the industrial regions of Europe. To guarantee peace for continued economic development, Uruguay created one of the earliest and most advanced welfare states, which guaranteed fair wages and working conditions, health care, education, and retirement benefits. At this time waves of European immigrants flocked to Uruguay, as they were doing also to the United States, Argentina, and Brazil. They came to Uruguay primarily from Spain and Italy, with some from Russia and Germany, bringing the small Jewish population of the country. During the height of immigration, nearly half of the country's population was foreign born. Today a third of the population is of Italian descent. Uruguay has one of the lowest rates of illiteracy in Latin America. Strong government support for education and the arts has produced an intense literary and cultural life in the country, giving the culture of the small country an exceptional worldwide presence. Uruguayans also identify with their traditional frontier and cowboy or *gaucho* culture.

While Uruguay has a fairly solid and homogeneous national culture, economic problems during the latter part of the twentieth century produced a resurgence of critical political divisions. Traditionally, ranchers and business elites, professionals and the middle class, and small farmers and blue-collar workers have divided into two major parties: the Colorado (Red) and the Blanco (White). The former has dominated Uruguayan history since the nineteenth century. However, as income from Uruguay's exports began to decline in the last half of the twentieth century and as it became more and more difficult thereby to meet the costs of the country's welfare state, political rivalries intensified. Guerilla warfare emerged and military repression followed during the 1970s. The Colorado and Blanco parties have now alternated more frequently in power.

However, political stability has not restored Uruguay's economic prosperity. In the last decades of the twentieth century, the most significant minority in Uruguay was the one that was leaving it: the young. Generations of young Uruguayans were unable to find employment in their country. Often well-educated, they left Uruguay to try their fortunes in Europe or, occasionally, the United States, where they face competition with people of other nationalities displaced by the forces of globalization. Population growth in Uruguay is less than one percent a year, and the population steadily aging and graying.

EDWARD A. RIEDINGER

See also **Amerindians: South and Central America; Portugal**

Further Reading

Devoto, Fernando, *L'emigrazione italiana e la formazione dell'Uruguay modernoI*, Turin: Edizioni della Fondazione Giovanni Agnelli, 1993

Finch, Martin Henry John, and Alicia Casas de Barrán, *Uruguay*, World Bibliographical Series, 102, Oxford, England: Clio Press, 1989

Hudson, Rex A., and Sandra W. Meditz, *Uruguay: A Country Study*, 2nd edition, Area Handbook Series, Washington, DC: Federal Research Division, Library of Congress, 1992

Lewis, Marvin A., *Afro-Uruguayan Literature: Post-Colonial Perspectives*, Lewisberg, Pennsylvania: Bucknell University Press, 2003

Sosnowski, Saul, and Louise B. Popkin, editors, *Repression, Exile, and Democracy: Uruguayan Culture*, Durham, North Carolina: Duke University Press, 1995

Soutelo Vázquez, Raúl, *De América para a casa: Correspondencia familiar de emigrantes galegos no Brasil, Venezuela e Uruguai, 1916–1969*, Santiago de Compostela, Spain: Consello da Cultura Galega, 2001

Spedding, Alison, and Aljandrina da Luz, "Bolivia and Uruguay," in *No Longer Invisible: Afro-Latin Americans Today*, edited by Minority Rights Group, London: Minority Rights Publications, 1995

Willis, Jean L., *Historical Dictionary of Uruguay*, Latin American Historical Dictionaries, 11, Metuchen, New Jersey: Scarecrow Press, 1974

Uygurs (Uigurs)

Capsule Summary

Location: China, Kazakstan, Kyrgyzstan, Uzbekistan, Turkmenistan, Tajikistan, Mongolia, Turkey, Pakistan, Saudi Arabia, Taiwan, Germany, United States
Total Population: 10 million
Language: Uighur
Religion: Sunni Islam

The Uygurs (Uighurs) are the largest Muslim group of China (8.4 million). Most of them live within Xinjiang, an autonomous region of northwestern China. Half a century ago, they were still the most numerous ethnic group in Xinjiang, comprising almost 80 percent of the population. Today they are less than half of Xinjiang's inhabitants due to the large influx of Han Chinese settlers. Scattered groups of Uighurs are living elsewhere in China. An isolated group of Uighurs live in Taoyuan and Changde districts of the Hunan province. They are said to date back to emigrants during medieval times.

Minorities of the Uighur diaspora can also be found in Kazakstan (210,000); Kyrgyzstan (37,000); Uzbekistan (37,000); Tajikistan (3,600); Turkmenistan (1,200); Mongolia (1,000); Afghanistan (3,000); Pakistan (7,000); Saudi Arabia (6,000); Taiwan (200); and Turkey (500). Smaller groups of post–World War II emigrants are found in Germany and United States. Recent refugees from contemporary Kazakstan and China are living in most western countries.

History

Throughout history several Uighur empires were founded in Central Asia. As early as 744 CE, a Uighur empire was established at Karakorum in present-day Mongolia. It was conquered in 840 CE by the ancient Kirghiz. A Uighur empire re-emerged in Turpan between the years 844 to 932 CE. A third, primarily Buddhist Uighur kingdom, was re-established near Turpan and Kucha in Jungaria in 932 CE. In the thirteenth century, the Buddhist Uighur Kingdom submitted to Genghis Khan's Mongol Empire. During the rule of his successors, the Turkic people of northwestern China converted to Islam.

However, despite official historiography attempts to establish links between these former Uighur empires, the historical ties remain unproven. Turkic oasis-dwellers have been living in Kashgaria since early medieval times. During the seventeenth century they were ruled by Oirat Mongols, but after the conquest by Qing dynasty conquest in 1758, their territory became integrated as the "Western Regions."

During the nineteenth century several Islamic insurrections occurred in the territory. In 1865 Yakub Bek proclaimed himself, with the support of the Kokand Khanate, the Emir of Kashgaria. He ruled the greater part of Kashgaria and parts of Jungaria for few years. In 1877 Kashgaria was recaptured by the Qing army. A final consolidation of the territory took place, as it became the Chinese province of Xinjiang in 1884. Many Uighurs settled in Russia at that time.

Until the beginning of the twentieth century, the sedentary oasis-dwellers—mostly peasants, traders, and townsmen—were known as Sarts by the nomads and outsiders. The Turkic language was called Eastern Turki by western scholars. The Chinese categorized them as *chantou* ("turban heads"). The oasis-dwellers identified themselves according to places of residence, such as Kashgarlyk, Turpanlyk, Yarkantlyk, Khotanlyk, etc. Uighurs are by tradition agriculturalists, caravan men, and traders. They also carry on old craft traditions.

Most of the Uighurs in the post-Soviet Central Asian republics are descendants of immigrants and refugees from Xinjiang. They moved during time of war and unrest in China, in the 1880s, 1940s, and early 1960s. Many of them have kept ties with relatives in Xinjiang through kinship. Whereas the Uighurs of the Ferghana Valley of Uzbekistan are assimilated into Uzbek culture, the Uighurs in Kazakstan and Kyrgyzstan have successfully developed their identities as minority groups within the new states.

Construction of a National Identity

At an all-Uighur meeting in Tashkent, Uzbekistan, in 1921, a group of Turkic refugees from China formally requested that the name Uighur should be used as their proper national identification. The Soviet government accepted this and in the Soviet Census of 1926, the ethnonym, Uighur appears along with those of other Central Asian Turkic peoples. However, the Taranchis and the Kashgarlyks were still listed separately in the 1926 census.

During the 1930s and the 1940s a new sense of united Uighur identity was also fostered in Xinjiang, in part through the policy of Soviet-backed Sheng Shicai, who encouraged cultural activities among the various ethnic groups living within Xinjiang. Toward the end of Sheng's ascendancy in Xinjiang and in the period of Nationalist control in Xinjiang, which followed until 1949, the Uighur as a people developed a national consciousness that was to manifest itself politically in the founding of an East Turkistan Republic in 1944.

After 1949, guided by Soviet advice, the new Communist regime of China continued the use of the name Uighur. The first decades of Maoist rule suppressed the Uighur cultural activities and religious institutions. The so-called Cultural Revolution destroyed a lot of the cultural heritage of the locals in Xinjiang. However, from the early 1980s, a new policy was implemented, and since then, many aspects of Uighur culture, including the language and literature have been allowed to prosper. Uighur intellectuals have themselves been involved in this new cultural Uighur nation-building as historians, linguists, and scholars.

Included in the modern Uighur category are several small ethnic groups which are all culturally and ethnically distinct from each other. In the Maralbashi and in the Merkit areas, live the Dolans, a group of semi-nomadic cattle breeders. Another distinct group are the Lopliks, who once lived as fishermen and gatherers around Lop Nor and the Konche River. Only few Lopliks still live in the traditional area. In Ili valley live small remnants of the so-called Ili Turks, who still speak a separate Turkish language. A small ethnic group living as itinerant musicians, circumcisers, and craftsmen are the 5,000 Abdals or Aynu in southern Xinjiang. For census purposes all these small ethnic groups are today included among the Uighurs.

Recent Change

The creation of separate states in former Soviet Central Asia has brought changes to the Uighurs, not only in Kazakstan, Kyrgyzstan, and Uzbekistan, but also in Xinjiang. Although there is now little prospect of confrontation with Russia or Kazakstan, the China still maintains large ground and air forces and most of its nuclear ballistic missiles in Xinjiang.

Strong anti-Han and anti-Communist government sentiments are prevalent in contemporary Xinjiang. However, the conflicts, bombings, and riots that took place in the last few years are probably more due to the high unemployment, the backward economic situation, harsh Chinese policy, interreligious conflicts and the huge influx of Han Chinese into the region. Also, the environmental devastation and groundwater contamination caused by the nuclear tests contribute to local hostility to the Han Chinese presence.

Even though Uighur mobilization in contemporary Xinjiang most certainly has been inspired by the changes that have restructured Central Asia in the last decade, the independence movement is probably stronger among groups in exile than within Xinjiang. A large number of Uighur exile organizations were founded in Europe and North America in recent years. There is a lot of information and propaganda about the current situation for the Uighurs in Xinjiang and elsewhere on the Internet, which gives an impression of a large separatist movement going on in Xinjiang. However, the actual separatists among the Uighurs in China are few in number. The political activities toward China, of the Uighur groups in Kazakstan and Kyrgyzstan, have created some worries between Beijing and the new leaders of these Central Asian republics.

Uighurs are by tradition Sunni Muslims of the Hanafi school. A few Sufi orders are active among them. Religion was suppressed during the Bolshevik and Maoist regimes. Since the mid-1980s, religious practice has been allowed and Islam is becoming more visible and important within the Uighur society. Religious holidays are widely celebrated and many Uighurs take part in the pilgrimage to Mecca.

Language

The Uighur language belongs to the southeastern Turkic branch and is closely related to Uzbek and Salar. There are couple of major dialect groups: the northern dialects spoken north of Tian Shan that include the Taranchi dialect of Ili, and the southern dialects in Kashgaria. The Lop dialect is seen as a third dialect within contemporary Uighur, although it is probably more related to Kyrgyz than Uighur. The language is used not only by the Uighurs, but also as a regional lingua franca among other ethnic minorities in Xinjiang.

The literary language was developed during the twentieth century. The Taranchi dialect, spoken in northwestern Xinjiang, was made the standard form and is still used today. However, in southern Xinjiang,

where the majority of the Uighurs live, a number of local dialects continue to be spoken. Uighur language has traditionally been written in the Arabic script. During a brief period in the 1970s, a pinyin-based Latin script was in use among the Uighurs in China. The Uighurs in former Soviet Union developed their literary language independent of their relatives in China. They followed the same development as other Turkic people in Soviet Central Asia. In the 1920s, Arabic script was used, just to be replaced by a Latin script in 1928. However, due to Stalinist politics in the late 1930s, a Cyrillic script was introduced for the Uighurs, which is still the script used in Kazakstan and Kyrgyzstan.

INGVAR SVANBERG

See also **China; Afghanistan; Kazakstan; Kyrgyzstan; Mongolia; Pakistan; Saudi Arabia; Taiwan; Tajikistan; Turkey; Turkmenistan; Uzbekistan**

Further Reading

Benson, Linda, *The Ili Rebellion: The Moslem Challenge to Chinese Authority in Xinjiang 1944–1949*, Armonk, New York: M. E. Sharpe, 1990
Gladney, Dru C., "Relational Alternity: Constructing Dungan (Hui), Uygur, and Kazakh Identities across China, Central Asia, and Turkey," *History and Anthropology*, 9, no. 2 (1996)
Jarring, Gunnar, *Agriculture and Horticulture in Central Asia in the Early Years of the Twentieth Century with an Excursus on Fishing*, Stockholm: Almqvist & Wiksell International, 1996
Rudelson, Justin, *Oasis Identies: Uyghur Nationalism along China's Silk Road*, New York: Colombia University Press, 1997
Rudelson, Justin Ben Adam, "China," in *Islam Outside the Arab World*, edited by David Westerlund and Ingvar Svanberg, Richmond: Curzon, 1999
Starr, S. Frederick, editor, *Xinjiang: China's Muslim Frontier*, New York: M. E. Sharpe, 2003
Svanberg, Ingvar, "Ethnic Categorizations and Cultural Diversity in Xinjiang: The Dolans along the Yarkand River," *Central Asiatic Journal*, 40, no. 2 (1996)

Uzbekistan

Capsule Summary

Country Name: Republic of Uzbekistan
Location: Central Asia, north of Afghanistan
Total Population: 25,981,647 (July 2003)
Minority Populations: Russians, Tajiks, Kazaks, Tatars, Karakalpaks, Koreans, Kyrgyz, Ukrainans, Turkmens, Jews, and numerous other groups
Languages: Uzbek (state language) (74.3%), Russian (14.2%), Tajik (4.4%), other (7.1%)
Religions: Muslim (88%) (mostly Sunnis), Eastern Orthodox (9%), other (3%) (including Jews)

Uzbekistan is a state in the heart of Central Asia that achieved its independence after the dissolution of the Soviet Union in 1991. It encompasses 447,000 square kilometers (277,765.8 square miles) and borders Kazakstan to the north, Kyrgyzstan and Tajikistan to the east and southeast, Turkmenistan to the southwest, and Afghanistan to the south. The total population is 25 million. The majority are Uzbeks (officially 70 percent). The largest minorities are Russians, Tajiks, and Kazaks. The name Uzbek derives from a Mongol ruler in the fourteenth century. Per capita GDP is $2,600 (2002).

History

The territory of present-day Uzbekistan has been for a long time inhabited by sedentary agriculturalists who subsisted on the water that drained from the Pamir and the Alatau mountain ranges. The population always concentrated on a few oases while most of the territory, as the Qyzyl-Qum desert in the western part, is only usable for livestock rearing.

Until the sixth century CE, the population was largely Iranian-speaking. For many centuries, the east-Iranian Sogds inhabited most of the agricultural regions in Central Asia. They founded several small fiefdoms but did not unite into one political entity. With the arrival of the first Turkic-speaking tribes in the sixty and seventh centuries the situation began to change. Since then a slow but steady process of Turkification transformed the ethnic configuration of Central Asia. Around the same time, the Islamization of this part of the world began. In this process, Persian became the court language and replaced the earlier east-Iranian

languages. The period of the Mongol empire during the thirteenth and fourteenth centuries supported both Turkification and Islamization.

During the late fourteenth and fifteenth centuries, the territory of Uzbekistan was the centre of another great empire, that of Timur Lenk (the Lame). It covered much of adjacent areas in Central Asia and the Middle East and lasted for about 150 years. Finally, Timur's successors were expelled by other Turkic tribes who arrived from the northern steppes. These groups called themselves Uzbeks. In the following centuries the Uzbeks founded three independent states, the Khanates of Khiva and Kokand, and the Emirate of Bukhara. All three were subsequently incorporated into the Russian Empire during the later part of nineteenth century. In 1924 the Uzbek Soviet Socialist Republic was founded within the Soviet Union. Like other republics, it was firmly embedded within the state structure and centrally planned economy, although since the 1950s, formal political leadership was largely in the hands of Uzbeks.

Postindependence

Uzbekistan was one of the last Soviet Republics to declare its independence on August 31, 1991. Since that time, the country is ruled by President Islam Karimov and opposition to his regime has been rigorously suppressed. The government officially is a presidential democracy, although most elections do not meet international standards. Like other post-Soviet states Uzbekistan is in a process of nation building in which historical figures—like the medieval ruler Timur Lenk—and symbols are evoked to create a sense of commonality among its citizens. Many members of minority groups complain about the language policy and lack of political participation.

The economy of Uzbekistan is still largely based on agriculture. During Soviet times cotton became almost a national product. This had devastating ecological consequences such as the drying of the Aral Sea. Since independence the amount of land devoted for grain cultivation has gradually increased to make the country less dependent on imports. Economic reforms are very slow in Uzbekistan, which impede foreign investment to a large degree. Most agricultural as well as industrial production is still organized by central planning. The standard of living of the population has deteriorated significantly since the Soviet period. The annual GDP per capita income is $2,500.

The exact numbers for ethnic minorities in Uzbekistan are difficult to obtain. The largest group used to be Russians who accounted for 1.5 million in 1989. Since then their number has dropped below one million because many of them left for Russia. Most Russians settle in urban areas, particularly in Tashkent, Navoyi, and in the city of Ferghana. The same is true for other European immigrants as Ukrainians or Germans. The largest of the autochthonous groups, officially, are the Kazaks who today outnumber Russians. They settled primarily in the Tashkent region, in Karakalpakistan, and in the Qyzyl-Qum desert between Khiva and Bukhara. Especially the Kazaks in Tashkent have lived there for centuries and today many of them have become Uzbekized. The third group is the Tajiks who officially number one million. However, the number of Tajik-speakers is much higher, probably around three million, as many of them declared, or were forced to declare themselves Uzbeks. In the cities of Bukhara and Samarkand, they form the overwhelming majority of the population.

Tatars, including the Crimean Tatars who were deported during World War II, made up more than 500,000 before 1990 but their numbers have significantly decreased in recent years as many of them accompanied the Russians who migrated to Russia. Karakalpaks settled predominantly in the Autonomous Republic in the far west of Uzbekistan that bears their name. They number approximately half a million. In addition to that, smaller numbers of Kyrgyz (230,000) and Turkmens (150,000) are also found; most of them live near the border of the respective country. Other groups include Koreans (150,000) who were also victims of the Stalinist deportation, and Central Asian Jews. The latter had numbered around 100,000 during Soviet times but most of them

left the country since. Smaller minorities include Meskhetian Turks (who were also deported from the Caucasus), Armenians, Central Asian Gypsies, and many others.

Many members of minority groups complain about increasing disadvantages connected with their ethnic affiliations. Mostly affected by this policy are the Russians and Tajiks. The former often lost their privileged economic and political positions with the fall of the previous regime; the latter are particularly vulnerable because they are culturally (but not linguistically) very close to the Uzbeks. Many individuals are unable to tell their respective affiliation because their ancestry is of mixed origin and they master both languages equally well. In comparison to other states in the region, the pressure on other ethnic groups in Uzbekistan is not of competition but of assimilation. Differences are played down and common cultural patterns magnified. At the same time, a strong tendency towards linguistic Uzbekization exists. Minorities are welcome to join the state but will have to sacrifice some of their distinctiveness for that.

PETER FINKE

See also **Diaspora, Jewish; Kyrgyz; Russians; Tajiks; Tatars; Turkmen; Uzbeks; Uygurs (Uigurs)**

Further Reading

Capisani, Giampaolo, *The Handbook of Central Asia: A Comprehensive Survey of the New Republics*, London: Tauris, 2000
Critchlow, James, *Nationalism in Uzbekistan: A Soviet Republic's Road to Sovereignty*, Boulder, Colorado: Westview Press, 1991
Fane, Daria, "Ethnicity and Regionalism in Uzbekistan: Maintaining Stability through Authoritarian Control," in *Ethnic Conflict in the Post-Soviet World: Case Studies and Analysis*, edited by Leokadia Drobizheva, Armonk, New York: Sharpe, 1996
Ilkhamov, Alisher, "Shirkats, Dekhqon Farmers and Others: Farm Restructuring in Uzbekistan," *Central Asian Survey*, 17, no. 4 (1998)
Yalcin, Resul, *The Rebirth of Uzbekistan: Politics, Economy and Society in the Post-Soviet Era*, Reading, New York: Ithaca Press, 2002

Uzbeks

Capsule Summary

Location: Central Asia, mostly in the territory of Uzbekistan
Total Population: approximately 25 million
Language: Uzbek
Religion: Muslim, mostly Sunni (Hanafi)

The Uzbeks are Turkic-speaking Muslims living in Central Asia. The majority of Uzbeks live in the territory of Uzbekistan, but there are sizeable Uzbek minorities in all neighboring states. The Uzbek language belongs to the southeastern (or Uygur) branch of the Turkic languages most closely related to Uygur, which is spoken primarily in the Autonomous Region of Xinjiang, China. It is somewhat more distantly related with other Turkic languages in the region, namely Kazak, Kyrgyz, Turkmen, and Karakalpak. In contrast, the Tajiks, with whom the Uzbeks often live in close vicinity, as well as Russians and other European immigrants, speak Indo-European languages. The vast majority of Uzbeks are Sunni Muslims of the Hanafi tradition. Uzbekistan in its present form was created during the early period of the Soviet Union, but there exists a long history of statehood in the region. In 1991, with the disintegration of the Soviet Union, Uzbekistan declared its independence.

History

Until the sixth and seventh centuries Central Asia was primarily inhabited by Iranian-speaking groups, sedentary agriculturalists as well as pastoral nomads. Since that time Turkic tribes started to enter the region and gradually adopted the way of life of the previous inhabitants. This was a process that lasted for more than 1,000 years and is still going on in some parts of Uzbekistan. The ethnic history of Uzbeks is thus made up of several groups: a) the descendants of the Iranian population who adopted the Turkic way of life, b) early Turkic tribes that arrived before the Mongol invasion, and c) later Turkic tribes that arrived during or after the Mongol invasion.

Among the latter, of prime importance is the tribal group that actually gave their name to the present ethnic group, the Uzbeks. The name originally derives from a descendant of Genghis Khan. Uzbek Khan had ruled in the steppes of present-day Kazakstan during the fourteenth century. Later, the tribal confederation that he headed split into two groups, the ancestors of the modern Uzbeks and Kazaks. In the year 1500, a successor of Uzbek Khan, Shaybani Khan, led the Uzbek part of this confederation south to conquer the fertile region of Mawarannahr, the land between the two rivers, Amu Darya and Syr Darya (also called Transoxania, the land beyond the Oxus). He ousted the descendants of another great ruler in the history of Central Asia, Timur Lenk (Timur the Lame), out of Central Asia into Afghanistan and India where they founded the Moghul empire. Timur himself, although he claimed to be partly of Mongol origin, had been a member of one of the earlier Turkic tribes mentioned above. In present-day Uzbekistan, he is turned into the most important figure in the history of Uzbek statehood.

Shaybani Khan and his successors ruled the sedentary regions of Central Asia, which roughly correspond to present-day Uzbekistan and Tajikistan, from the city of Bukhara. During the following centuries two entities broke off forming independent states, the Khanates of Khiva and Kokand. When the Russian Empire expanded southward during the 1860s and 1870s, they met with little resistance from the three Uzbek states who frequently fought each other. While the Khanate of Kokand was firmly integrated into the administrative structure of the colonial state, Bukhara and Khiva attained the status of vassals.

The submission to the new Soviet state met with fierce resistance by some groups within Central Asia, among them many Uzbeks. The so-called Basmachi could only be subdued after several years of violent clashes, which took the character of a civil war. Occasional fighting continued until the late 1930s. At that time, the territory of Central Asia had already been divided into five separate republics. Uzbeks as the largest and most centrally located group often ended up on different sides of the border. Because of their number and strategic position, they were to some degree favored by the early Soviet regime compared to other indigenous ethnic groups.

Areas of Uzbek Settlement

Uzbeks live primarily in present-day Uzbekistan and in contiguous areas in neighboring states. These areas are not the product of recent migrations but of the way boundaries were drawn between the republics during the early Soviet period. In addition, Uzbeks are found in other parts of the former Soviet Union, as well as in China, Saudi-Arabia, Turkey, and other places. The latter are descendants of former refugees who fled Central Asia in colonial Russian or early Soviet times.

The majority of Uzbeks live in the state that bears their name, Uzbekistan. According to official statistics, more than 70 percent of the country's population, or 19 million individuals, are Uzbeks. This number may be somewhat overestimated as many members of minority groups, particularly Tajiks, are registered as Uzbeks. Within Uzbekistan, Uzbeks form the majority in all provinces except for the westernmost region, the Autonomous Republic of Karakalpakistan. Not surprisingly, their political and economic status within the country is not subject to any discrimination. Uzbek is the sole state language and is becoming increasingly dominant in political and educational spheres.

Uzbeks also form the largest minority in neighboring Tajikistan, approximately 1.5 million or 25 percent of the population. Most of them live in the northern Sughd (formerly, Leninabad) province, which occupies the portion of the Ferghana valley that belongs to Tajikistan. Other Uzbeks live in Hissar, Kurgan-Tube, and Khatlon regions of western and southwestern Tajikistan, close to the border with Uzbekistan. In economic terms, Uzbeks live up to or above the national average as most of them settled in the more developed parts of the country. Their political representation is limited. Uzbek is not recognized as an official state language, although school instruction in Uzbek does exist. Several organizations have been founded to promote the interests of the Uzbeks in Tajikistan, but so far little resentment against the government has been heard of. Uzbeks remained largely unaffected by the civil war in the early and mid-1990s.

In Kyrgyzstan, Uzbeks make up about 14 percent of the population (or 650,000 people). This makes them the largest autochthonous minority in the country, third only to the Kyrgyz and Russians. They settle almost exclusively in the border region of Uzbekistan, in the southern provinces of Osh and Jalalabad. Here, they often form a local majority, especially in the urban areas. The two provinces are separated from the rest of the country by mountain ranges, which are impassable during most of the winter. In 1990, violent clashes broke out between Uzbeks and Kyrgyz in and around the city of Osh, killing hundreds. Today, the situation is relatively calm. In fact, both groups express a feeling of neglect by the central government in Bishkek. As in other republics, the Uzbeks in Kyrgyzstan suffer from severe restrictions on the crossing of new state boundaries primarily imposed by the government of Uzbekistan. In the past, marriages across the border had been very common. As a result, members of one family often live on both sides of the state line and today face difficulties visiting each other. Within Kyrgyzstan, Uzbek is used for school instruction but does not have the status of an official language. In local and national parliaments as well as governmental positions, there are few Uzbek representatives than their overall number would suggest.

Kazakstan is probably the most diverse state in Central Asia with officially more than 140 ethnic groups (nationalities). Uzbeks form a relatively small minority of 2.5 percent (or 400,000) of the population. Most of them live in South Kazakstan province with Chimkent as the center. Here, Uzbeks form the majority in some areas near the border with Uzbekistan. This region is believed to be more traditional and religious than other parts of Kazakstan because of the large Uzbek minority. Similar to the above-mentioned countries, Uzbek is not an official state language but locally used for school instruction. Uzbeks are rarely found in senior political positions. They are often accused, however, as is the case also in Kyrgyzstan, of controlling local trade.

According to various sources, the number of Uzbeks in Turkmenistan is 8 or 9 percent (or 400,000) of the population. The majority of them settled in the northern provinces of Lebap (capital city is Turkmenabad, formerly Charjew) and Dashhowuz along the border with Uzbekistan. Especially the cities in this area are predominantly populated by Uzbeks. Minority rights in Turkmenistan are probably worse than in any other Central Asian state and this affects the Uzbeks in particular. Tightened border controls, preference given to Turkmens in political and economic spheres, and attempts to culturally assimilate minorities are particular issues in this respect.

The case of Afghanistan is different from others because this area has not been directly affected by the process of creating artificial nations in Soviet times. The Uzbeks were one of the major ethnic groups in the north of the country for centuries. Today, the majority of them are settled in the provinces of Kunduz and Mazar-i Sharif. Estimates vary, but it is believed that the total number is around 1.5 millions or five to six percent of the population. In recent years, Uzbeks became known as one of the key elements in the Northern Alliance against the Taliban, under the leadership of General Dostum. As other minorities, Uzbeks suffer from centuries of domination and land appropriation by Pashtuns, the ethnic group that dominates Afghanistan.

Uzbek Society and Identity

The fertile areas of Mawarannahr were the center for agriculture in Central Asia. This is conducted in oases of different sizes and often at a significant distance from each other, separated by large tracks of land only to be used for extensive pastoralism. As mentioned earlier, the Uzbeks mainly consist of Iranian-speakers who adopted the Turkic way of life, and Turkic tribes who abandoned their nomadic way of life. For centuries, an ecologically sustainable and socially acceptable water management was the key issue to be solved within society. Local communities therefore were more important than pastoral nomads who gave prominence to genealogical ties. During socialist times, agriculture in Central Asia was collectivized and firmly integrated into the state structure. In many agricultural areas cotton was developed into a quasi-monoculture that had disastrous effects on the regional climate (such as the drying of the Aral Sea). Today, the region is faced with the challenge of transforming to a market-driven economy.

Uzbek society reflects the mixed ethnic heritage of the people. While most former Iranian-speakers probably never had a tribal structure, some of the previously Turkic tribes lost theirs in the course of time. Other groups retain some tribal identity. Overall, however, Uzbek social organization is more characterized by the importance of extended families and village communities. Marriage patterns strongly reflect the sedentary character of the society. Men are clearly dominant in Uzbek society. There are strong preferences for large families, which was reinforced during Soviet times with medals and financial rewards for women who gave multiple births. The traditional political order has been fundamentally transformed around the local administration and members of the communist party during the socialist period. Today former elites are often seen in crucial positions and are able to control human and other resources.

Within the localized patterns, ethnic differences play lesser role than expected. In many parts of the Uzbek-populated world, there exists a very close relationship with other ethnic groups, especially with Tajiks. In Bukhara or Samarkand province, many people think of themselves as "one people with two languages." Common cultural patterns and frequent intermarriage account for this. Bilingualism is almost universal, although the two languages are mutually unintelligible. On the other hand, distinctiveness toward Kazaks and Kyrgyz—linguistically much closer—is strongly pronounced. Here, the traditional opposition between sedentary and nomadic ways of life seems of great importance.

PETER FINKE

See also **Afghanistan; Kazaks; Kazakstan; Kyrgyzstan; Tajikistan; Tajiks; Turkmenistan; Uzbekistan**

Further Reading

Allworth, Edward, *The Modern Uzbeks: From the Fourteenth Century to the Present: A Cultural History*, Stanford, California: Stanford University Press, 1990

Baldauf, Ingeborg, "Some Thoughts on the Making of the Uzbek Nation," *Cahiers du Monde Russe et Soviétique*, 32 (1991)

Fierman, William, *Language Planning and National Development: The Uzbek Experience*, New York: Mouton de Gruyter, 1991

Manz, Beatrice, *Central Asia in Historical Perspective*, Boulder, Colorado: Westview Press, 1994

Rasuly-Paleczek, Gabriele, "Ethnic Identity versus Nationalism: The Uzbeks of North-Eastern Afghanistan and the Afghan State," in *Post-Soviet Central Asia*, edited by Touraj Atabaki and John O'Kane, London: Tauris, 1998

Roy, Olivier, *The New Central Asia: The Creation of Nations*, New York: New York University Press, 2000

Schoeberlein-Engel, John, *Identity in Central Asia: Construction and Contention in the Conceptions of "Özbek," "Tâjik," "Muslim," "Samarqandi," and other groups*, PhD thesis, Harvard University, 1994

Subtelny, Maria, "The Symbiosis of Turk and Tajik," in *Central Asia in Historical Perspective*, edited by Beatrice Manz, Boulder, Colorado: Westview Press, 1994

V

Vanuatu

Capsule Summary

Country Name: Republic of Vanuatu
Location: Oceania, group of islands in the South Pacific Ocean
Total Population: 199,414 (July 2003)
Languages: English, French, pidgin (known as Bislama or Bichelama), plus more than 100 local languages
Religions: Christian, indigenous beliefs, and Jon Frum Cargo cult

Formerly known as the New Hebrides, Vanuatu is an archipelago nation in Melanesia consisting of 12 large and 60 smaller islands. The 450-mile-long (724.05-kilometer-long) nation has a population of 175,000 people, among whom over 100 distinct languages are spoken. The capital, Port Vila, is on Efate Island. In 2002 the per capita GDP was US$2,900.

Human settlement in Vanuatu dates from at least 2,500 BCE. Its traditional social organization is based upon patriarchal extended families that aim to acquire wealth, traditionally measured in the number of pigs and wives owned by each adult male. Women were traditionally viewed as inferior, contaminating, and even dangerous and were rarely educated or independent of males. Separation of the sexes within households was common, and women were excluded from traditional ceremonies and rituals. Tensions between coastal clans and those from the inland, or bush, areas were evident, and shifting alliances among the clans made warfare a central social experience. *Kastom*, a mélange of indigenous arts, practices, and beliefs defined males' daily lives, whereas women traditionally performed household and family chores including the provision and preparation of food.

Portuguese explorers first visited the New Hebrides in 1606, but the archipelago only became an object of European imperial competition in the 1870s. The Great Powers wanted the islands as a whaling base and as a source of laborers. Europeans regarded Hebrideans as savages, and in the late nineteenth century, 100,000 natives were coerced into indenture contracts, a process known as *blackbirding*. They were placed on ships, sent to Australia, Fiji, and New Caledonia, and put to work on roads, mines, and plantations.

Natives made scattered attacks on European missionaries, officials, and planters. British and French warships responded, sometimes by shelling coastal villages in reprisal. To control indigenous rebels and to stem further German expansionism in the South Pacific, Britain and France established a joint military administration over the archipelago in 1887. In 1906, the two Powers consolidated their control by establishing a unique and awkward civilian government for the islands known as the Condominium.

French companies aggressively acquired land and developed commercial copra plantations. British planters were less successful, and by the mid-1930s, French residents outnumbered the British ten to one. By 1940,

French growers had imported over 20,000 indentured Vietnamese workers to the New Hebrides from Indochina. On the eve of World War II, 1,500 white Europeans lived amongst 65,000 Melanesians in the New Hebrides.

The Condominium reserved virtually all civil and political rights to European expatriates. A single colonial officer, known as the Native Advocate, was assigned to represent indigenous persons. The growth of capitalism, the cash economy, and Christianity reinforced traditional differences between coastal and bush people, preventing the development of unified resistance to colonial occupation. Even so, after hundreds of Melanesians were press-ganged into labor cohorts and shipped to France to aid Allied forces during World War I, Britain and France introduced a threadbare "native administration" that offered basic protections for native peoples. Neither Great Power invested in infrastructure development or in the welfare of the local population, for fear of losing such investments to its Condominium partner. As late as the 1950s, the interiors of several large islands gave little evidence of European occupation or administration, and significant elements of precontact culture remained intact.

Although the principal island battlegrounds of World War II lie to the north, important Allied bases were built on Espiritu Santo and Efate Islands. Postwar liberalization in Britain and radical politics in metropolitan France briefly accelerated progress toward decolonization. Forced labor was outlawed and greater government participation for natives, including limited franchise rights, was permitted. In the 1960s, France curtailed such developments for its own strategic reasons, forcing Britain to delay advances toward independence for the New Hebrides as well.

Native grievances against continued colonial governance coalesced around the issue of land ownership. French interests controlled 40 percent of the islands' land area. A nationalist movement developed during the 1960s known as the *Nagriamel*, focusing on native land claims. It was followed by formation of the New Hebrides National Party. These organizations used the land alienation issue to unify indigenous people of difference cultural and linguistic heritage. Widespread familiarity with the English and French languages aided cohesion, as did the use of *bislama*, a form of modified English developed by indentured laborers who returned to the New Hebrides after working on overseas plantations. Political pressures from nationalists forced France to allow the formation of a national assembly based on universal suffrage in 1974. A poorly coordinated effort to exempt Espiritu Santo from the New Hebrides was quelled, and the nation achieved independence as the constitutional democracy of Vanuatu in 1980.

Kastom emerged as a keystone of postindependence political culture, managed and defined by an all-male National Council of Chiefs. Ethnic and cultural tensions persisted within the diverse population. The Melanesian majority controls most government offices, and although the constitution prohibits discrimination, the Eurasian, Chinese, and Vietnamese minorities face prejudice. Most land now belongs to native islanders, and national laws forbid land sales to noncitizens.

Despite their voting rights, women continue to be largely excluded from public life. In 1991, however, the Vanuatu Cultural Center initiated a project to identify and support women's skill in the production of *pandanus*, or plaited mats. The program highlighted women's economic contributions while also displaying their overlooked role in preserving *kastom*.

The 1990s in Vanuatu were characterized by political instability and economic malaise. An attempt by a paramilitary police force to overthrow the government in 1996 was thwarted, and in 1997, the government agreed to a stringent economic restructuring program promulgated by the Asian Development Bank. Around 80 percent of the population remains tied to subsistence agriculture, although small fishing and mining industries provide some employment opportunities. Vanuatu regularly has substantial balance of payments deficits. It imports food items, cars, televisions, and other manufactured goods from Australia, New Zealand, and the United States. The chief consumers are coastal residents, especially those in Port Vila, who increasingly emulate Westernized lifestyles. This phenomenon deepens the traditional divide between bush clans and coastal people.

LAURA M. CALKINS

Further Reading

Aldrich, Robert, *France and the South Pacific Since 1940*, Honolulu: University of Hawaii Press, 1993

Asian Development Bank, *Vanuatu: Performance, Policy, and Reform Issues*, Manila: Pacific Island Economic Report, Asian Development Bank, 1997

Bolton, Lissant, *Unfolding the Moon: Enacting Women's Kastom in Vanuatu*, Honolulu: University of Hawaii Press, 2003

Bonnemaison, Joel, editor, *Arts of Vanuatu*, Honolulu: University of Hawaii Press, 1996

Rodman, Margaret, *Masters of Tradition: Consequences of Customary Land Tenure in Longana, Vanuatu*, Vancouver: University of British Columbia Press, 1987

Rodman, Margaret, *Houses Far From Home: British Colonial Space in the New Hebrides*, Honolulu: University of Hawaii Press, 2001

Shineberg, Dorothy, *The People Trade: Pacific Island Laborers and New Caledonia, 1865–1930*, Honolulu: University of Hawaii Press, 1999

Tan, Ling Hui, *Vanuatu: Recent Economic Developments*, Washington, D.C.: International Monetary Fund, 1996

Venezuela

Capsule Summary

Country Name: Bolivarian Republic of Venezuela (*República Bolivariana de Venezuela*)
Location: Northern coast of South America, bordering the Caribbean Sea and the North Atlantic Ocean, between Colombia, Brazil, and Guyana
Total population: 26,008,481 million (2004)
Languages: Spanish (official) and several indigenous languages
Religion: Nominally Roman Catholic 96 percent, Protestant 2 percent, other 2 percent, also Maria Lionza Cult, Protestantism, and Santeria

The Bolivarian Republic of Venezuela is located on the northern coast of South America, bounded by the Caribbean Sea and the Atlantic Ocean to the north, Brazil to the south, Colombia to the west and southwest, and Guyana to the east. Venezuela's total population is estimated at 26 million and largely comprises *mestizos,* people of mixed ethnicity, who represent two-thirds of the country's inhabitants. The Afro-Venezuelan minority is estimated at 10 percent, although there is no official data about this group. The indigenous population is approximated at half a million people, and the immigrant population of 1.5 million come mainly from Colombia, Italy, Portugal, and Spain. The official languages are Spanish, at the national level, and some 38 indigenous languages, official only in the states where indigenous peoples live.

About 85 percent of the country's population lives in large cities alongside the Caribbean coast, and more than half live below the poverty line. Venezuela was ruled by military strongmen for most of the first part of the twentieth century, but democratically elected governments have been in power since 1959. Today, Venezuela is among the five largest oil producers in the world, and oil exports account for about one third of the national GDP, estimated to be $131 billion (2002). The per capita income was $5,400 in 2002.

Before the arrival of the Spaniards in the late fifteenth century, Venezuela was populated by a great diversity of indigenous societies belonging predominantly to the Carib, Arawak, and Chibcha linguistic families. Most of the country's inland territory belonged to what has been called the Orinoco cultural area, currently characterized by its low demographic concentration, dispersed and highly mobile settlement pattern, and a remarkable absence of social institutions and central authority. However, there is archaeological evidence that higher levels of concentration and coordination between settlements existed in precolonial times. The western part of the country was populated by indigenous societies with more hierarchical and centralized forms of organization, in the Andes and western coasts. The arrival of the Spaniards marked the beginning of the extinction for most indigenous groups of the northern coasts and navigable rivers; they were subjugated by the dominant society and decimated by war and disease.

The low concentration of indigenous people in the center of the territory sparked the introduction of African slaves in the seventeenth century, who supplied the labor demands of the booming cacao economy. Most of the black slaves were of Bantu origin, brought from Central Africa and the Antilles, and, by the end of the century, the black population and its descendants had already transformed the coasts of the country into a predominantly mestizo area. At this time, the remaining indigenous population retreated to remoter areas in the south, east, and northwest of the country, or were assimilated into the majority society.

During the war of independence from 1810 to 1824, the indigenous, black population was loyal neither to the royalists nor to republicans; they constantly changed sides according to their interests. José Tomás Boves, a white Spanish royalist, defeated the republican revolt led by Simon Bolivar in 1813 with an army of mestizos and liberated blacks, who tormented republican cities under the slogan "death to the whites!" Later, Bolivar realized the importance of recruiting blacks, Indians, and the majority mestizo population to his side and in 1816 proposed freedom of slaves and incorporated mestizos and blacks into his army. Although slavery was not abolished until 1854, the inclusion of nonwhites in the republican army shattered the old colonial social order.

After independence, Venezuela was governed by local leaders (*caudillos*) of varied ethnic origins who formed a kind of federation of chiefdoms. This contributed to racial interbreeding and reinforced the predominantly mixed blood composition of the country. By the end of the nineteenth century, however, military strongmen influenced by European notions of race awakened latent interracial and ethnic tensions. Thus, during the first half of the twentieth century, political authorities supported and promoted European immigration, primarily from Spain, Portugal, and Italy, aimed at "improving" the ethnic composition of the country. After 1935, with the liberalization of the political system, the mestizo majority gained political and economic power, allowing people of all races to have access to positions of power. This tendency was reinforced with the beginning of democratically elected governments in 1959.

The relative social mobility created what Wright (1990) called "the myth of racial democracy," the mistaken idea that Venezuela is a society which has achieved racial equality due to its preeminently mixed blood constitution and the presence of black people in positions of power. In reality, most blacks still live in poor, rural, and isolated enclaves scattered alongside the northern coasts of the country, and minority groups are subject to subtle but severe forms of discrimination. However, nonwhites have more participation in economic and social institutions in Venezuela than in most other South American countries, with the exception of Surinam and Guyana. This is not the case for the Indian population, which has been denied access to political or economic power and has been subject to inhuman treatment until recently. Until 1999, indigenous peoples were governed by a 1915 Missions' Law, which deprived them from the most basic legal and civil rights while promoting their integration into national society.

From 1998, President Hugo Chavez, mestizo himself, has led a leftwing government whose style has sparked latent racial and class tensions in the country. In 1999, progressive laws protecting minority groups were incorporated into the constitution, laws which included the country's recognition of the Indians' rights to cultural and linguistic distinctiveness, as well as to their ancestral lands. However, the application of new laws has been difficult due to political instability and economic crisis.

Today, Venezuela is a heterogeneous society where aspects of Indian, European, and African origin are combined. The Maria Lionza Cult is an example of the cultural syncretism that characterizes most of its society. The worship of Maria Lionza, an Indian Goddess with European facial features, originates in the mountains of Sorte, in Yaracuy, a cacao-growing region in which racial and cultural mixing began in the sixteenth century. Apart from the Indian Goddess, the cult includes veneration of African deities, historic characters, and Catholic icons. Aspects of the three predominant cultures are also combined in food, music, and other aspects of the everyday life.

GERMÁN FREIRE

Further readings

Berglund, Susan, and Humberto Hernández, *Los de afuera: un estudio analítico del proceso migratorio en Venezuela 1936–1985*, Caracas: CEPAM, 1985

Coppens, Walter, editor, *Los Aborígenes de Venezuela*, Caracas: Fundación La Salle de Ciencias Naturales, Instituto Caribe de Antropología y Sociología, four volumes, 1980–1998

Wright, Winthrop, *Café con Leche: Race, Class, and National Image in Venezuela*, Austin: University of Texas Press, 1990

Vietnam

Capsule Summary

Country Name: Socialist Republic of Vietnam
Location: in various parts of Vietnam, particularly the highland areas in the north bordering on China, and in the northwest and west, bordering on Laos and Cambodia
Total Population: 81,624,716 (July 2003)
Languages: Vietnamese (official), English (increasingly favored as a second language), French, Chinese, and Khmer; mountain area languages (Mon-Khmer and Malayo-Polynesian) more than fifty different languages belonging to three language families subdivided in eight language groups
Religion: Buddhist, Hoa Hao, Cao Dai, Christian (predominantly Roman Catholic, some Protestant), indigenous beliefs, Muslim

Vietnam is located in Southeastern Asia, bordering the Gulf of Thailand, Gulf of Tonkin, and South China Sea, alongside China, Laos, and Cambodia. According to the current official ethnic classification, Vietnam has 54 recognized ethnic groups, including the majority Kinh (or Viet) people. The Kinh numbered 67,500,000 in 2001. Large minorities include lowland groups like the Hoa (ethnic Chinese, mainly in Ho Chi Minh City), the Khmer (in the Mekong Delta), and the Cham in the Mekong Delta and the south-central provinces of Ninh Thuan and Binh Thuan. Most ethnic minority groups, however, can be found in the midlands and highlands of Vietnam, which comprises three-fourths of the territory. In the northern Highlands—north and west of the Red River Delta—the Tay, Thai, Nung, Muong, HMong (Meo) and Dao (Yao) exist, which all have over 500,000 members. In the Central Highlands and the Truong Son Range (Annam Cordillera) separating (as well as bridging) Vietnam, Laos, and Cambodia, important indigenous groups are the Giarai (Jarai, Jorai), Ede (Rhadé), Bana (Bahnar), Hre, Coho (Koho), Raglai, Mnong, and Xtieng (Stieng) with over 50,000 people. Many of these groups are straddling Vietnam's borders with China, Laos, or Cambodia, whereas other groups like the Hmong migrated southward into Vietnam, Laos, Thailand and Myanmar in the course of the last centuries.

During the last millennium Vietnam has expanded its territory from its base in the Red River Delta in the north to the lowlands of the central and southern parts of what is now Vietnam, incorporating Cham and Khmer populations and territories in the process.

Vietnam's western borders with Laos and Cambodia became fixed under French colonial rule, creating the political space for a westward movement of the majority Kinh people into the highlands. The development of the modern nation-state with its fixed borders thus created the category of ethnic minorities.

Since the colonial era, each political regime embarked on a process of ethnic classification, with differing outcomes. The former South-Vietnamese regime used a racial category (*sac-toc*) to distinguish ethnic minorities from the majority Kinh, while the current Communist regime uses a term (*dan toc*), which refers to both nation and ethnicity in a way reminiscent of the "national minorities" of the former Soviet-Union and China. Today's official ethnic classification is predicated on linguistic differentiation. Vietnam's minorities belong to three different language families (sub-divided into eight language groups). Most languages are mutually unintelligible, and many ethnic groups have subgroups speaking different dialects and even languages. Some Vietnamese linguists estimate that the actual number of languages spoken in Vietnam may be more than 100.

Even though ethnic categories seem fixed, with each person having an ethnic label indicated on her or his identity card, recent research has suggested that many such identities and ethnonyms are relatively recent constructions. However, today such constructions have hardened into relatively fixed notions about the ethnic groups to which people belong.

With over 50 different ethnic groups, it is impossible to generalize about minority culture and lifestyles. One group (Hoa, or ethnic Chinese) is primarily urban and oriented toward trade and services, whereas some other lowland groups are related to historical civilizations based on wet-rice cultivation (Cham, Khmer). Some upland groups (Tay, Nung, Thai) have traditionally been wet-rice farmers in valley bottoms, whereas other groups (Ede, Giarai, Mnong) have tended to rely on rotational shifting cultivation. Some small groups in the Annam Cordillera (Chut, Ruc, Arem) until recently lived subsisted primarily on hunting and gathering. In actual practice, however, there was and is considerable difference between various local groups of one ethnicity. For instance, some Hmong communities have terraced wet-rice fields, while other groups plant corn on permanent rain-fed fields, have poppy plantations and orchards, or practice itinerant shifting cultivation. Most upland ethnic communities combine various farming and livelihood strategies, and agricultural distinctions have begun to blur with the influx of lowlanders, the increase in population density, and the growing pressure on the natural resources.

Kinship systems and gender relations vary widely. Some Austronesian and Austroasiatic speaking groups in the Central Highlands are matrilineal with strong extended families, whereas other ethnic groups have patrilineal or cognatic kinship systems. Although men are dominant in all ethnic groups, women's positions varies widely, depending on their political, ritual, and household status. In some groups, women can be heads of households, have title to land and assets, or represent their units to the outside world, whereas in other groups their position tends to be confined to a subservient role. The overlay on customary practices of statutory law based on Western concepts and rooted in a mixture of patriarchal Kinh culture and socialist ideology has mixed effects on gender relations. It extends formal legal rights to land, protection, and education to women, often undermining social support systems provided by extended families and their traditional land rights.

Religious beliefs and practices range from Buddhism (Khmer, Hoa, Thai), Islam, and Hinduism (Cham) to animist beliefs, ancestor worship, and shamanism (most other groups). Although Catholicism is widespread among the Bana group, some of the animist groups in both the Northern and Central Highlands (Hmong, Ede, Giarai) are converting to evangelical Christianity in large numbers—a movement that the present authorities are actively trying to counter. Some of the larger groups had scripts that were used in ritual, religious, or political contexts, but for most groups scripts have been developed more recently or are nonexistent. Traditional polities were often feudal (in the North) or had decentralized, "big man"-type of political systems, but most ethnic polities recognized the overlordship of larger lowland states. In general, communities that lived at higher elevations paid respect to stronger, more populous and more tightly organized communities in the valleys or coastal lowlands.

History

The region came under the influence of the Chinese during the first century BCE, and Vietnam remained under Chinese control until the tenth century CE.

France occupied Vietnam as the colony of Indochina from the 1880s until 1945. The French were defeated in 1954 by forces under the leadership of nationalist Ho Chi Minh, notably in the Battle of Dien Bien Phu. Although the upland ethnic minorities were only brought into the orbit of the modern state by the end of the nineteenth and the beginning of the twentieth century, they bore the brunt of Vietnam's successive wars for national liberation, evidenced by the fact that the biggest, decisive battles (Dien Bien Phu and An Khe, 1954; Banmethuot 1975) took place in minority upland areas. Revolutionary guerrillas sought to wean local minority populations from the colonial regimes in the strategic highlands, while the French, Americans and Chinese sought to turn minorities against Vietnam's revolutionaries during the First (1946–54), Second (1961–1975), and Third (1978–79) Indochina War.

At the 1954 Geneva Conference in Switzerland, Vietnam was partitioned, ostensibly temporarily, into Northern and Southern zones, with a general election to be held in June 1956. The partition forced about 2 million North Vietnamese to migrate to the South as the communist north began to implement radical land reforms.

These divide-and-rule tactics have left enduring scars in the relations within and between some ethnic communities and with the state. Relations have been tense, especially in the Central Highlands when an autonomy movement of Central Highland minorities (known as Montagnards or Degar) formerly associated with the U.S. Special Forces fought a low-intensity guerrilla war for their own homeland. After 1975 the reunified Vietnamese state moved quickly to try to take control of the strategic borders in upland areas by trying to "settle down" ethnic minority communities in stable villages, and bringing large numbers of ethnic Kinh people from densely populated lowland areas to "New Economic Zones" in the uplands. After 1990 the Central Highlands—the coffee belt of Vietnam—became a target of migration, resulting in massive deforestation, a severe risk of land degradation, and appropriation by newcomers of land that indigenous minorities consider theirs. In February and March 2001, the loss of land rights, harassment of evangelical groups, and contacts with the political leadership of the "Degar" diaspora sparked massive demonstrations that took the authorities by surprise.

The Vietnamese government holds an inclusive concept of the nation-state in the sense that people from all ethnic groups hold Vietnamese citizenship and have equal rights before the law in a multi-ethnic country. In a unique and unprecedented move, an ethnic Tay person was elected as Secretary-General of the

Communist Party in April 2001. At the same time, the state and party predicated their policies on strong views about "backward" cultures, superstitions, and "wanton destruction of the forest" through shifting cultivation, all seemingly requiring outside interventions. Today, the resulting development effort often proactively undermines local cultural practices to be replaced by supposedly more advanced and scientific practices that often resemble Kinh lowland lifestyles.

Vietnam is a poor, densely populated country with a 2002 GDP per capita income of only $2,300. The ravages of years of war and the loss of Soviet financial support post-1991 have adversely affected the economy. GDP growth of 8.5 percent in 1997 dropped to 6 percent in 1998 and 5 percent in 1999. Growth then rose to 6 percent to 7 percent between 2000 and 2002, despite the global recession. Regardless of the massive investments by the state and foreign donors in the highlands through health, education, resettlement, and reforestation projects, all quantitative and qualitative data suggest that ethnic minorities in Vietnam—often residing in remote areas—tend to be the poorest segment of the population and are comparatively underserved by the state in terms of education, health, and other services. A United States–Vietnam Bilateral Trade Agreement came into effect in 2001 and was expected to significantly increase Vietnam's exports to the United States.

OSCAR SALEMINK

See also **Cambodia; Khmer; Laos; Vietnamese**

Further reading

Condominas, Georges, *We Have Eaten the Forest: The Story of a Montagnard Village in the Central Highlands of Vietnam*, New York: Hill and Wang, 1977

Dang Nghiem Van, *The Sedang in Vietnam*, Hanoi: National Center for Social Sciences and Humanities/UNESCO, 1998

Dang Nghiem Van, *Ethnological and Religious Problems in Vietnam*, Hanoi: Social Sciences Publishing House, 1998

Dang Nghiem Van, Chu Thai Son, and Luu Hung, *Ethnic Minorities in Vietnam*, Hanoi: The Gioi Publishers, 2000

General Statistics Office, *Data and Results from the 3% Sample of the Population and Housing Census, 1/4/1999*, CD-ROM, Hanoi: Central Data Processing Centre, 2000

Hemmet, Christine, *Montagnards des Pays d'Indochine dans les Collections du Musée de l'Homme*, Boulogne-Billancourt: Editions Sépia, 1995

Hickey, Gerald, *Sons of the Mountains. Ethnohistory of the Vietnamese Central Highlands to 1954*, New Haven: Yale University Press, 1982

Hickey, Gerald, *Free in the Forest, Ethnohistory of the Vietnamese Central Highlands to 1954–1975*, New Haven: Yale University Press, 1982

Jamieson, Neil L., Le Trong Cuc, and A. Terry Rambo, *The Development Crisis in Vietnam's Mountains*, Honolulu: East-West Center Special Reports # 6, 1998

Michaud, Jean, editor, *Turbulent Times and Enduring Peoples: Mountain Minorities in the South-East Asian Massif*, Richmond, Surrey: Curzon Press, 2000

Nguyen Tu Chi, *La Cosmologie Muong*, Paris: l'Harmattan, 1997

Rambo, A. Terry, Robert R. Reed, Le Trong Cuc, and Michael R. DiGregorio, editors, *The Challenges of Highland Development in Vietnam*, Honolulu: East-West Center Program on Environment, 1995

Salemink, Oscar, *The Ethnography of Vietnam's Central Highlanders: A Historical Contextualization, 1850–1990*, Richmond, Surrey: Curzon Press; Honolulu: University of Hawaii Press (Anthropology of Asia Series), 2003

Salemink, Oscar, editor, *Viet Nam's Cultural Diversity: Approaches to Preservation*, Paris: UNESCO, 1999

Taylor, K.W., On Being Muonged, *Asian Ethnicity* 2, no. 1, 2001

Van de Walle, Dominique, and Dileni Gunewardena, "Sources of Ethnic Inequality in Viet Nam," *Journal of Development Economics*, 65, 2001

Vietnamese

Capsule Summary

Location: Vietnam, North America, Europe, Australia, Southeast Asia
Language: Vietnamese
Population: 80 million
Religion: Buddhism, Taoism, Confucianism, Christianity, Ancestor worship, Animism, Hoa Hao, Cao Dai

The Vietnamese live as a minority in many countries in the world. They can be defined as those who trace origins or heritage to Vietnam. The term *Vietnamese* often refers to citizens of the nation-state of Vietnam, but it is also commonly used to describe the majority ethnic group, which composes more than 80 percent of the population of that country, otherwise known as the Kinh. Although Vietnam is ethnically diverse, many people from other ethnic backgrounds have been assimilated, becoming *Vietnamese* in ethnicity as well as citizenship. As to those who live beyond Vietnam's borders, constituting a minority, the term can refer either to people from Vietnam, regardless of ethnicity, or, more narrowly, to the ethnic Kinh.

Vietnamese identity is tied up with the question of origins or roots. Many who consider themselves Vietnamese trace their origins to the Red River delta in what is now northern Vietnam. In some calculations, an identifiably Vietnamese state existed in the delta 4 or 5 millennia ago. Covering only a small proportion of today's Vietnam, the Red River delta was ethnically diverse, its society matrifocal and its political system decentralized. Rice was grown but not the wet-rice agriculture grown today. Sea and land routes connected it with societies as far away as India and China.

One of the pivotal moments in the history of the Vietnamese people came with the annexation of the Red River delta by an expansionist China in the second century BCE and its administration for 1 millennium as a Chinese province. The country was controlled by administrators and colonized by Chinese settlers, whose administrative legacy left profound traces, as did their philosophical and religious systems, cultural orientation, and linguistic impact. During this time, contacts with the world beyond the middle kingdom also took place as doctrines such as Buddhism expanded in influence. At various points during this long period of domination, the locals repeatedly rebelled against Chinese authority, eventually gaining independence in 939 CE.

Over the next millennium, China remained a dangerous neighbor and a source of further cultural influences. However, the Vietnamese themselves became extremely successful in expanding down the Indochinese peninsula, fighting and then swallowing the kingdom of Champa and taking over a large proportion of Cambodia. These peoples and those in the highlands became minorities in a Vietnamese polity, and many were assimilated; however, their culture, social relations, and economic systems also enriched the Vietnamese and oriented them toward the Southeast Asian world. Although many who live in the regions colonized by Vietnam in the last thousand years now look back to the Red River delta as a font of identity, many have a more complex, hybridized, or localized sense of their origins.

The process of expansion and consolidation of central rule was interrupted by French colonization of the country. The country was reshaped, although unevenly, by the impact of the French in terms of language, culture, economy, and political systems, and new horizons to Europe were opened. The French divided the country, and not even after the French withdrew was political unity regained. The wars of decolonization and postcolonial rivalry were extremely destructive and impacted in many spheres. Postcolonial Vietnam comprised two states, one in the socialist orbit, the other capitalist, who battled each other in the name of opposing visions of what it means to be Vietnamese. This divisive episode oriented the Vietnamese toward new conceptual horizons. To this day, the legacy of these colonial and postcolonial conflicts is strong.

The war terminated in April 1975 when communist troops took over the southern regime's capital, Saigon. Many of those with affiliations to the Saigon regime managed to escape abroad. The massive exodus of refugees, which occurred in the late 1970s, grabbed media headlines around the world, making the Vietnamese a high-profile minority. The refugee exodus comprised a large number of ethnic Chinese, urbanites, intellectuals, southerners, and residents of coastal provinces, fleeing economic stagnation and persecution by the new regime on political, ethnic, social, and religious grounds.

The bulk of the "Boat People" settled in countries such as the United States, Canada, and Australia, which were relatively wealthy multicultural nations with long traditions of migration and yet are also home to significant social divides and racial and cultural tensions. Europe, particularly France, also took many refugees. For most Vietnamese, the adjustment period was long and hard. Most had to learn a new language, struggle with unfamiliar cultural contexts, and come to terms with changed economic and social circumstances. Community organizations, religious institutions such as churches and temples, and traditional social associations have aided the process of settlement. A substantial number of Vietnamese have done well in business, the professions, industry, agriculture, and fishing. Like members of many other migrant communities, the second generation adapted to their homeland better than the first, but many also face a large generation gap. As Vietnam has opened up and liberalized its economic system, Vietnamese from these countries have returned to visit their relatives, invest in the construction of domestic residences and businesses, donate to charities and the refurbishment of religious buildings, and provide an important source of new ideas and cultural forms in the homeland.

Other less-prominent Vietnamese minorities live elsewhere in the world. One significant group lives in Cambodia, where they practice fishing, trade, agriculture, and artisanal and professional work. Although they have long been in the country, many were killed or driven into exile during the Lon Nol, and Khmer Rouge periods. Another wave entered the country after the Vietnamese army occupied the country; however, they are still subject to prejudice and mistrust. Vietnamese also live in neighboring China, Laos, Thailand, and other Asian countries. Another important group are those who studied or worked in former East Bloc countries, who stayed on after the fall of Communism in Europe.

PHILIP TAYLOR

See also **Vietnam**

Further Reading

Elliott, Duong Van Mai, *The Sacred Willow: Four Generations in the Life of a Vietnamese Family*, Oxford University Press, 1999
Jameison, Neil, *Understanding Vietnam*, Berkeley: University of California Press, 1993
Marr, David G., *Vietnamese Tradition on Trial 1920–1945*, Berkeley: University of California Press, 1981
Templer, Robert, *Shadows and Wind a View of Modern Vietnam*, New York: Penguin, 1999
Thomas, Mandy, *Dreams in the Shadows: Vietnamese-Australian lives in transition*, St Leonards, New South Wales, Australia: Allen and Unwin, 1999

Vlachs

Capsule Summary

Location: Eastern Europe, including Moldova, Ukraine, Romania, Serbia and Montenegro, and Hungary
Total Population: approximately 15 million
Languages: Romanian, other dialects
Religions: Christianity (Orthodox and Catholicism)

The Vlachs consist of four distinct groups: The biggest one is the Rumun/Romanian, Daco-Rumanian, followed by the Arumuns/Kutzovlachs, the Meglenovlachs, and the Istrovlachs. The last three groups form minorities in their native lands in the Balkans.

Northern Vlach (Romanian) is spoken north of the Danube and in Serbia's Timok valley. Kutzovlach is spoken by a few hundred thousand in Macedonia, Albania, Greece, and the Meglenovlachs who live north of Thessaloniki, Greece, but are in the process of assimilation. Istrovlach is spoken by a couple of thousands on the Istrian peninsula of Croatia and Slovenia.

According to the latest official statistics from the region there are 14,724,400 Vlachs (97.6 percent of the total population) in Walachia and Western Moldova (proper Romania), 5,684,142 (73.6 percent) in Transylvania, 2,797,226 (64.5 percent) in Eastern Moldova (Moldavia), some 350,000 in Ukraine in the Balti, Tsernowits, and Odessa districts, of whom there are 29,485 in the Zakarpatskaya region, 38,941 (1.93 percent) in the Voyvodina district, 21,179 (0.365 percent) in Central Serbia, and 10,740 (0.1 percent) in Hungary.

Significant communities had virtually disappeared from Central Serbia and Macedonia (159,632 [5.3%]), Voivodina (67,679 [4.5%]), Bulgaria (64,000 [1.3%]), and Albania (10,000) during the decades following World War I peace treaties. In the meantime, due to the sharp increase of the Romanian territories, the number of communities has doubled and sharply increased in the new territories of Transylvania—from 53.1 percent to 73.6 percent—while in Moldavia the percentage has remained almost the same due to the equal rate of increase of the other cohabiting nationalities of the Soviet Union.

The origin of the Vlachs is a historical puzzle. *Vlach* means shepherd in Albanian, and the first communities appeared in the Albanian-Macedonian border region, where the mixed origin population was subdued by long Roman and Slavic influence. They adopted Christianity from the Greek Byzantium, through the Bulgarian Empire whose capital and religious center was in the Ohrid-lake district, by that time. A great number of names contained Vlach, such as Vlahorini and Vlahinye, in the Central Serbian-Macedonian-Albanian region as well as early medieval documents.

As Bulgaria later came under the rule of the Empire of Byzantium and the hardships of the population increased, in 1187 Peter and Assan proclaimed the Bulgarian-Vlach empire. As the Bulgarian empire stretched northwards, it spilled across the Danube into the scarcely populated areas of the Walachian plains, swept out many times by the migrating people. The shepherds coming from the overpopulated and poor, ragged lands of the Balkans had found an ideal settling place and a new home. Thus, the common empire became increasingly Bulgarian as the Vlachs emigrated north across the Danube, and the land between it and the Carpathian Mountains became known as Walachia. Following the mountain trails on the "highway of the Carpathians," they reached up north to the Beskides of Ukraine and into the northern hills of Cumania-Moldova.

Their first state was organized by the Cumans, in Walachia, during the fourteenth century, but the Cumans and other nationalities were gradually absorbed by the Vlach-Slav majority. During the centuries of the Turkish conquest, the majority of the population fled north across the Carpathians into Transylvania-Hungary to escape wars and their feudal lords, the Fanariots. The Greek merchants from the district of Fanar in Istanbul, who bought from the sultan the right to reign, were always in great hurry and exploited the population. Their average rule lasted less than one year, during a period of almost two centuries, leading to mass exodus to the northwest. The Russian Turkish war of 1877 finally brought to an end Turkish sovereignty, the country now called Romania had achieved its independence.

World War II found Romania participating with over 1 million troops to boost Hitler's effort to subdue Russia. As the war seemed to be lost and the Soviet army made a decisive stroke well into Romania, the nation turned against its former allies. The Russian army took advantage of this, and the final period of the war saw Romanian troops alongside the Russians, engaged in fierce fighting with the German and Hungarian troops. The 1947 Paris peace treaty, although considering Romania as a former enemy, put the 52.1 percent Hungarian-populated Eastern and Northern Transylvania under Romanian sovereignty again.

A Hungarian autonomous region was created in 1952 and was abolished in 1968 by N. Ceauşescu. The dictator pursued colonization of the recaptured territories, forced collectivization, and industrialization of the entire country, faithfully following the Stalinist hard-line until its end. Its secret police, the Securitate, of the size of an army, was the most fearsome in Central Europe. The society was reduced to silence, due not only to the oppression of minorities and intellectuals but also due to the nationalist course and satisfaction offered by the opportunities for the ethnic Romanian peasants in the more developed urban areas of Transylvania.

The general oppression, starvation, and the shortage of basic utilities however led to the Christmas 1989, antidictatorial uprising that had turned into a bloody anticommunist revolution, the last one in the former communist satellite countries of the Union of Soviet Socialist Republics (USSR). Although Stalinist dictator Ceausescu was overthrown, the regime's building blocks (i.e., the party bureaucracy, the secret police, and other oppressing structures), although formally abolished, remained in fact untouched. This legacy explains why the social and economic reforms are slow, in spite of the political change.

The Vlach societies are of Balkan tradition. The only difference is that part of the Transylvanian Vlach society acquired some central European culture due to its cohabitation in the Austro-Hungarian territories. The Moldavian Vlach society acquired an eastern Slavic and Turkic culture; the Walachian society and all of the other groups from the Balkans acquired Byzantian, Greek Orthodox, southern Slavic, and Turkish culture. In the late nineteenth and twentieth centuries, Italian, German, and mainly French culture continued this row.

In the main Vlach-populated area, that of current Romania and Moldavia, there are significant rifts along geographical, historical, cultural, and linguistic lines. After independence in 1991 due to Romanian pressure, the Kishinev parliament adopted the abolition of the Cyrillic alphabet and the declaration of Moldavian as the official language. In fact, the Romanians understand and want to witness the introduction of the closely related Romanian language, but part of the Vlach population and the Slav, Gagauz Turkish minority strongly oppose it.

All the Vlachs were using the Cyrillic alphabet until the period between 1848 and 1859, when the Greek Catholic Vlachs of Transylvania demanded the introduction of the Latin alphabet. They also wanted to be called Roman (Romîn) and to be considered the direct descendents of the late settlers of the Roman Empire, which had a colony in the region called Dacia between 106 and 271 CE. This served as a basis for the so-called Daco-Romanian continuity theory, which affirms that the Romanians, as the direct descendents of the Romans and of the conquered Dacians-Thracians, had permanently and continuously inhabited the actual area of Romania and had since always formed a majority. The theory founded the presumed historical rights upon the actual territory, and, from a historical hypothesis, became a tool serving political purposes.

LASZLO KOCSIS

Further Reading

Barta, G., B. Köpeczi, et al., *Akadémiai kiadó* [History of Transylvania], Budapest, 1994

Boia, L., *History and Myth in the Romanian Conscience* [in Romanian], Ed. Humanitas, Bucharest, 1997

du Nay, André, *The Origins of the Romanians*, Toronto; Buffalo, Matthias Corvinus Publishing, 1996

Pándi, L., *Köztes Europa* [Europa in Between], Osiris, Budapest, 1997, collection of maps

Philippide, Al., *Originea românilor*, 2 vols, Iassy, 1923–27

Rosetti Al., and B. Cazacu, *Istoria limbii romane* [History of the Romanian language], Ed. Academiei RSR, Bucharest, 1969

Rösler, R., *Romanische studien.Untersuchung zur älteren Geschicte Rumäniens*, Leipzig, 1871

W

Wales

Capsule Summary

Location: United Kingdom, main island west of England
Total population: 3 million
Languages: Welsh, English
Religion: Christian

At just over 8,000 square miles (20,720 square kilometers), the principality of Wales is a small European country and home to nearly 3 million people, of whom one in six lives in the capital, Cardiff. It is bounded on the north by the Irish Sea, on the east by England, on the south by Bristol Channel, and on the west by St. George's Channel. For most of the last millennium, the destiny of Wales has been inextricably linked with that of its larger neighbor, England.

In 1039, Gruffudd ap Llywelyn united the ancient kingdoms of the entire country for the first and only time; his quarter-century reign is remembered as a time of rare tranquility in Welsh history. Norman and English encroachments into Wales led to several wars during the twelfth and thirteenth centuries, and increasingly the Welsh lost ground and were forced into desperate rebellion. The most famous, perhaps, was that led by Owain Glyndwr, who defeated the English and united Wales under his rule in 1400. Several envoys from European states attended his crowning, and his parliaments met in Machynlleth and Harlech. Within a few years, however, Wales began to suffer a number of military setbacks. By 1410 it could no longer claim to be an independent state. Since that date, Wales has been firmly under the control of successive English administrations. Although full union with England had been practically achieved by the 1284 Statute of Rhuddlan, the constitutional position was formalized in 1536 by the Act of Union, the preamble of which stated its intention "to extirpate all and singular the sinister usages and customs" differing from those of England. The document, arguably the most important in Welsh history, also declared, "Wales shall stand and continue for ever from henceforth incorporated, united and annexed to and with his Realm of England."

Welsh Society

Today, the country can be divided into three parts; Welsh-speaking Wales (the mainly coastal regions stretching from the northwest counties to Carmarthenshire); Welsh Wales (the people of the former mining valleys of South Wales who feel Welsh but do not speak the national language); and British Wales (the remainder of the country, where most of the people are either English-born or work in neighboring English cities like Bristol and Liverpool).

Welsh, one of the oldest living languages in Europe, provides the bedrock of the country's national identity. Welsh is a Celtic language. Cornish and Breton are sister tongues while Manx, Irish, and Scots Gaelic could more accurately be described as distant linguistic relatives. To the foreigner, Welsh can be difficult on the ear and a strain on the eye. The village of *Llanfairpwllgwyngyllgogerychwyrndrobwyllllantisiliogogogoch* is but one example of linguistic challenges to the foreign visitor to Welsh-speaking Wales (it translates as "the Church of Mary in a white hollow by a hazel tree near a rapid whirlpool by the church of St. Tisilio by a red cave").

With English rule came successive attempts to destroy the Welsh language. A British Government Commission of Inquiry into the state of education in Wales reported in 1847 that "the Welsh language is a vast drawback to Wales and a manifold barrier to the moral progress and commercial prosperity of the people. It is not easy to over-estimate its evil effects." One Commissioner did make reference to the often brutal methods which were used to discourage children from speaking their native tongue:

> My attention was attracted to a piece of wood suspended by a string round a boy's neck, and on the wood were the words 'Welsh stick'. This, I was told, was a stigma for speaking Welsh. But, in fact, his only alternative was to speak Welsh or say nothing. He did not understand English and there is no system in exercise of interpretation.

These acts were complemented by the English media, which constantly portrayed Welsh in a negative light. In 1866 the influential London *Times* newspaper described the language as "the curse of Wales," while in 1885 it claimed that the "low social and educational condition (of Wales) is due to the prevalence of the Welsh language."

Despite Government efforts to extirpate the use of Welsh, the state of the language was still strong entering the twentieth century. The 1901 census indicated that of a population of 2,012,876, some 929,824 spoke Welsh of whom almost 300,000 were monoglots. In addition, 25 weekly newspapers and 28 monthly magazines were published entirely in Welsh, while in the last decade of the nineteenth century almost 10,000 new book titles appeared in the national language.

The Welsh Language Society (*Cymdeithas yr Iaith Gymraeg*) was formed in 1962 after a radio lecture given by Saunders Lewis in which he identified television as "the Chief Assassin of the Welsh language." During the 1979 election campaign, Conservative Party leader Margaret Thatcher attempted to woo Welsh voters with the promise of a new television station in the Welsh language. When she appeared to distance herself from this proposal after becoming

Prime Minster, the leader of Plaid Cymru, Gwynfor Evans, threatened to go on a hunger strike. His threat had the desired result, and on November 2, 1982, Sianal Pedwar Cymru (S4C) came into being. Today about 20 percent of the people of Wales are native Welsh speakers, while a further 15 percent are proficient in the language. The efforts of nationalists and the countervailing forces of Anglicization (particularly television and literature) will probably balance each other out in the coming decades, and it is unlikely that there will be any dramatic increase or decrease in usage of the Welsh language in Wales.

Politics

Unlike the Irish, who utilized the extension of the franchise and the introduction of the secret ballot in the nineteenth century to organize a nationalist party to fight their case in Westminster, the Welsh have traditionally channeled their efforts into the major opposition parties of the United Kingdom. Since 1922, the Labor Party has been the largest party in Wales and has taken over the position formerly held by the Liberal Party. Wales has produced its share of British leaders, of which David Lloyd George, Aneurin Bevan, and Neil Kinnock are the best known.

In August 1925, a new nationalist party, *Plaid Cymru* (Party of Wales), was established. Initially composed of a small coterie of idealists and a subject of ridicule in some quarters, the party was to develop into the most important Welsh political movement of the twentieth century. Though most Welsh nationalists confined their activities to the constitutional sphere, a minority dedicated themselves to more radical agitation. In 1952, a small republican group called *Y Gweriniaethwyr* attempted to blow up a pipeline taking water from Claerwan in Wales to the English city of Birmingham. Two years later, a similar attempt was made to blow up the Fron Aqueduct transporting water to Birmingham from the Elan Valley. This was the first act of a new group, *Mudiad Amfddiffyn Cymru* (Movement for the Defense of Wales), which embarked on a series of minor attacks during the 1950s. After the arrest of key leaders in 1963, MAC disappeared as mysteriously as it had emerged. It was replaced by the Free Wales Army that managed to capture media headlines throughout the 1960s.

These military activities were on a very small scale and involved only a handful of individuals. Most Welsh nationalist sentiment was directed into a reinvigorated *Plaid Cymru* whose basic aims promoted cultural and political nationalism, decentralized socialism, and membership in the United Nations. The party made a breakthrough with the election on July 14, 1966 of Gwynfor Evans as the member of the British parliament for Carmarthean. Representation at Westminster was increased to three in 1974 before dropping to two in 1979. The party retained these seats in 1983 and doubled its parliamentary representation to four seats in the 1992 and 1997 elections.

Increased Autonomy

Plaid Cymru believed their hour had come in 1979 when a reluctant British administration was coaxed into holding a referendum on the issue of whether powers held by the Welsh Secretary of State should be devolved to a local administration in Cardiff. The Government stipulated that 40 percent of the registered electorate would have to cast their votes affirmatively for the proposal if it was to become law. Though nationalists opposed the proposal for its timidity, many secretly believed that its implementation would be a step in the right direction. Only 59.1 percent of the electorate turned out on March 1, 1979, however, and of those only 20 percent voted in favor of the Assembly.

The election in 1997 of a Labor Government committed to constitutional reform reawakened hopes for devolution for Wales. A new Assembly composed of 60 members (40 elected by the British first past the post system and the remainder by proportional representation) was proposed for Wales. The responsibilities of the Welsh Office were to be transferred to the Assembly though the position of a Secretary of State for Wales would remain, acting as a bridge to Westminster.

Many of the factors which had militated against the establishment of an assembly in 1979 continued to impede progress toward increased autonomy for Wales. Of the 2.25 million people eligible to vote, over half a million had been born outside Wales. Most of these were from England, felt little attachment to Welsh language or culture, and had no desire to see the link to London weakened. In this sense, they were not unlike the Anglophone minority in Quebec. Many more suspected that a local assembly, which would be deprived of most governmental powers and responsibilities, would be a mere talking shop and be a source of prestigious jobs for the local Labor "Taffia" (Welsh Mafia). However, there were many factors that had changed since the 1979 referendum and made ratification more likely. Seventeen years of

Conservative rule accentuated the feeling in Wales that they were being ruled by a distant and hostile administration that had little time for Welsh concerns. Second, the "yes" campaign received substantial support from influential newspapers like the Liverpool Daily Post (read mainly in the North) and the Western Mail (read mainly in the South). Third, in contrast with the indifference of the Conservative Government in 1979, the Blair-led Labor administration put their full support behind the proposals and embarked on an intensive publicity drive. Finally, a simple majority of the vote was required for ratification, a far more attainable threshold than that set by the Conservatives two decades earlier. Despite these changes in the political climate of Wales, barely half the electorate (51.3 percent) mustered sufficient enthusiasm to cast their vote, of which a tiny majority (50.3 percent) endorsed the proposal for an assembly.

It is highly unlikely that Wales will develop into an independent state during the next century. Many Welsh people could accurately be described as cultural nationalists who are increasingly pinning their hopes on a Europe of the regions. Unlike the Irish and the Scots, the Welsh have for many years directed their efforts into preserving their nation as opposed to creating a state. While the establishment of a parliament in Edinburgh with tax-raising powers has aroused fears that the Scots may act as a catalyst for the break-up of the United Kingdom, few believe, except perhaps the most optimistic nationalists, that the Cardiff Assembly has the potential to create such a constitutional crisis. Indeed, the British Government hopes that an Assembly with limited powers and firmly entrenched within the United Kingdom constitutional framework strikes a balance between the desires of nationalists and unionists alike and may mollify nationalist demands for greater political freedom.

In the absence of political institutions, Welsh identity has tended to rest on the less tangible, but arguably more emotive, symbols of nationhood. The Welsh national flag is a red dragon, the heraldic symbol of Wales, on a green and white background, and the use of the dragon to symbolize Wales goes back to the middle of the first millennium. Saint David or Dewi (d. 589) is the Patron Saint of Wales (indeed the country provided the Irish with St. Patrick) and March 1 is St. David's Day.

DONNACHA Ó BEACHÁIN

See also **Ireland; United Kingdom**

Further Reading

Davies, John, *A History of Wales*, London: Penguin, 1994

Davies, John, *Plaid Cymru*, Cardiff: Welsh Academic Press, 2000

Dunkerley, Andrew, and Andrew Thompson, editors, *Wales Today*, Cardiff: University of Wales Press, 1998

Evans, Gwnfor, *Fighting for Wales*, Talybont: Y Lolfa, 1990

Jenkins, Geraint H., and J. Beverley Smith, editors, *Politics and Society in Wales 1840–1922*, Cardiff: University of Wales Press, 1988

Morgan, Kenneth O., *Modern Wales: Politics, Places and People*, Cardiff: University of Wales Press, 1995

Walloons

Capsule Summary

Location: Western Europe, primarily the southern provinces of Belgium
Total Population: approximately 3.5 million
Language: French
Religions: Roman Catholic; Protestant

Walloons are the French-speaking people of Belgium, and they call themselves *Wallons* (with only one *o* in French). Today, Walloons belong to the second most important language community in Belgium, after the Flemings (*Vlaams*), who speak Flemish, a language in the same family as the Dutch spoken in the Netherlands. Belgium has over 10 million inhabitants. Flemish is spoken by more than half of the population in Belgium (by the Flemings); about one third of all Belgians speak French (that is, the Walloons). There is also a small German-speaking community (about 4 percent of the population) in the extreme east of Belgium, thinly grouped along the German border.

There are less than 4 million Walloons, who live mostly in cities such as Brussels (in French, *Bruxelles*), Liège, Mons, Namur, Charleroi, and in rural regions such as the Ardennes. Walloons speak the same French language as in France, with no noticeable difference, although the French-speaking community of Belgium uses some specific words that are unknown in France: for instance, to indicate the number *90*, Walloons would say *nonante* instead of *quatre-vingt-dix*. There are also six local romance dialects located in small regions just south of Brussels: three dialects of Wallon, Rouchi (Picard), Gaumais, and Champenois.

Although located on the Flemish-speaking side, Brussels, as the capital, is officially bilingual. Since the Gilson Bill (1963), there are officially four linguistic zones in Belgium. The Flemish-speaking Flanders (in Flemish, *Vlaanderen*) and the French-speaking *Wallonie* (in English, *Wallonia*) are the two main regions, and both are fiercely monolingual. There are also the bilingual Brussels-capital sector and the German-speaking region. These artificial divisions can hide exceptional situations of minority groups in each opposite region, with mixed communities here and there, plus various linguistic conflicts in many Belgian provinces. These linguistic forces and proportions can vary through place and time.

Even if Walloons, as a sociolinguistic group, are concentrated in more than half of Belgium's territory, mainly in Southern provinces, one cannot actually "see" that linguistic frontier on the Belgian map. There is no *Wallonie* region written as such on most common maps. One can only recognize the names of cities: Antwerpen (in English: Antwerp), Ieper, and Ghent are in the Flanders zone, but in French, these cities are named Anvers, Ypres, and Gand. That linguistic border between Flemish- and French-speaking zones can be seen as a somewhat imaginary line, more or less like a parallel line from west to east, just south of Brussels and north of Liège. In English, many Belgian cities are named and spelled in their Flemish version, and rarely in their French form.

Most Belgians are Catholics. Belgium is a clear example of two important linguistic communities living in two distinct parts of a country, two opposite groups whose main difference is not racial, ethnic, or religious, but rather linguistic. As for *Québécois* within Canada, it is clear that although Walloons are a minority within Belgium, these French-speaking groups are a majority in their own region, in this case Wallonia.

The people of Belgium existed even before the time of the Roman occupation (57 BCE). Christianized by the seventh century, Belgium had once been occupied by the Germans and then the Spanish, and it was, at different times, a part of the Hapsburg Empire (Austria), France, and The Netherlands. After Napoleon's defeat at the Battle of Waterloo, not far from Brussels, in 1815, Belgium was integrated into the United Kingdom of the Netherlands until 1830.

Flemish as a language has not always been dominant in Belgium. When that new country became independent in October 1830, Belgium's only official language was to be French. This new linguistic and cultural identity would help the Belgians make clear their independence from the previous Dutch control. In the mid nineteenth century, political elites in Flanders were bilingual and spoke French. It was not until 1898 that Flemish was recognized as an official language along with French. The gradual disappearance of the French presence in Flanders, and the refusal of bilingualism by Flemish-speaking citizens, caused Walloons to initiate their own movement. Walloons felt like foreigners while traveling in a monolingual Flanders. The man behind the Walloon movement, the Walloon politician Jules Destrée (1863–1936), wrote in 1923: "It is the bilinguism of Flemish cities that make us feel that we are in Belgium . . . . If French was banned in Flanders, we would be foreigners, as in Rotterdam or Utrecht." (Kesteloot 1993, 13).

Destrée was among the first Belgians to comprehend the links between language and nation, and to understand the Belgian dichotomy: "Without going to the extreme of the Flamingants [sic] when they say [in Flemish] "De taal is gansch het volk" (language makes a people), we may admit that language is not the only the means of expressing ideas but often contributes to the formation of them." This 1916 statement by Destrée was quoted by scholar Chantal Kesteloot, who studied the question of whether Walloons could be a specific and distinct nation (Kesteloot 1993, 13).

From 1842, a Flemish nationalist movement agitated in favor of having the Flemish language taught in Flanders schools and at the University of Ghent. The French majority responded with various patriotic movements. First, there was a literary circle named the *Société liégeoise de littérature wallonne* (1856), and there was also, most importantly, the *Mouvement wallon* (1886). This was followed by various groups, among them the *Assemblée wallonne* (1912), the *Mouvement populaire wallon* (in the 1960s), and a political party, the *Rassemblement wallon* (1968). Another movement, the *Rattachistes*, is still active, and is made up of Walloons who want Wallonia to separate from Belgium in order to become, once again, a part of France.

Since the 1950s Flanders has been dominant in Belgium economically, socially, demographically, and politically. One of the possible reasons for this development is the fact that traditional commerce from coal mines has been much less profitable for Walloons in the last few decades, while petroleum and gas refineries are more prosperous in the Flanders zone, which has direct access to the North Sea. The city of Brussels, which was once exclusively Francophone, is now a bilingual metropolis.

YVES LABERGE

See also **Belgium**

Further Reading

Delforge, Paul, Philippe Destatte and Micheline Libon, *Encyclopédie du Mouvement wallon*, 3 volumes, Charleroi: Éditions de Institut Jules-Destrée, 2001

Destrée, Jules, *Belgium and the Principle of Nationality*, Westminster: The Council for Study of International Relations, N° 5, 1916

Kesteloot, Chantal, *Mouvement wallon et identité nationale*, N° 1392, Bruxelles, Centre de recherche et d'information sociopolitiques (CRISP), series "Courrier hebdomadaire", 1993

Washington, Booker T. (African-American)

Born a slave in Virginia, Booker Taliaferro Washington (1856–1915) rose to become the most powerful and influential African American leader of the late nineteenth and early twentieth centuries. Washington was publicly known as an accommodationist to white supremacy while emphasizing racial pride, solidarity, and self-help for the black community. He advocated, among other things, industrial education and economic nationalism. Though his actions were lauded by members of both races, there were many who criticized his general philosophy and his way of combating the race problem of the day. Despite his complicated legacy, Washington's long-range goals were fundamentally the same as those of his rivals. He was a pragmatic leader at a time of increased restrictions and violence directed toward the African-American community.

Soon after the Civil War, Washington's mother Jane moved him and his three siblings to Malden, West Virginia, where a young Booker T. worked in the salt and coal mines. Despite his busy work schedule, Washington struggled to gain an education by studying and taking classes around his job obligations. In 1872, he left Malden for Hampton, Virginia to seek admission to Hampton Normal and Agricultural Institute. The principal of Hampton Institute, General Samuel Chapman Armstrong, combined the missionary method of education with that of industrial training. He believed that the means for black advancement was through hard work, accumulation of capital and land, and the creation of stable families and communities. Armstrong preached that blacks should remain in the South and eschew politics and the agitation for political rights. He theorized that African Americans would gain equality in an indefinite future, through their economic success and proved worthiness.

After graduating from Hampton in 1875, Washington ventured back to Malden to teach and later briefly to attend a Baptist Seminary. In 1879, however, he returned to Hampton to teach for a couple of years before founding Tuskegee Normal and Industrial Institute in Alabama in 1881. Taking Hampton's model to Tuskegee, Washington built an all black institute that taught self-determination and quickly equaled other black institutions of the day. It emphasized industrial education designed for economic independence in an area dominated by sharecropping. The school became larger than the town, as it bought surrounding farmland and sold it at low rates to create a community of land and homeowners. The Institute and its surrounding community became the model black town. It was the example of Washington's vision of a self-reliant community turning segregation into autonomous development. In addition to his efforts at Tuskegee, Washington created the National Negro Business League in 1900, which was formed to stimulate self-help and racial solidarity as it encouraged the development of African American businesses.

Washington's move toward *the* black leader took him beyond the grounds of Tuskegee. On September 18, 1895, he gave a speech, the Atlanta Compromise, at the Cotton States and International Exposition in Atlanta. In the address, Washington expressed his belief that if left alone blacks could prosper and give something to the nation as a whole. In an attempt to disarm southern whites, Washington declared that agitation for social equality was not where African Americans needed to put their energies and that in "purely social" matters the races could "be as separate as the fingers, yet one as the hand in all things essential to mutual progress." In return for this relinquishing of the demand for immediate civil and political rights, Washington called on whites to remove any barriers to black economic advancement and become mutual partners in uplifting the South and the nation.

After his Atlanta Exposition address, Washington became the negotiator between the races. Andrew Carnegie and other white philanthropists gave money to uplift the race, and Washington allocated the funds to areas that he saw fit, such as black businesses, other black schools and, unbeknownst to the donors and virtually everyone else, to civil rights test cases. Washington also became the principal black advisor of both Presidents Theodore Roosevelt and William H. Taft. It is through these contacts and positions, and those in the black community, that Washington built what was called the Tuskegee Machine, a tangled web of patronage that had influence in many black newspapers, businesses, social and political sectors at the turn of the century.

Of course, not all blacks agreed with Washington's publicly known racial philosophy. The largest outcry against his bossism and conservatism came in connection with his perceived control over the press. A group, led by William Monroe Trotter and W.E.B. Du Bois, which became known as the radicals, believed that Washington's "hush money" prevented an alternative approach to the race problem from getting national attention. This group pushed for full political and civil rights, emphasized liberal education over industrial training and desired unfettered expression of their ideas.

Around the turn of the century, the radicals began challenging Washington from within the Afro-American Council. In 1903, Du Bois openly criticized Washington's methods in his volume, *The Souls of Black Folk*. In the same year Trotter, the editor of the *Boston Guardian*, was arrested for disorderly conduct as he openly challenged Washington in what became known as the Boston Riot. Two years later Du Bois, Trotter, and others formed their own organization, the Niagara Movement, dedicated to persistent agitation for civil rights, voting rights, equal education, and general human rights. Washington attempted to infiltrate the new group, as he would the National Association for the Advancement of Colored People (NAACP) when it organized in 1909.

Washington's concessions to the white South failed to achieve his stated goal, as Southerners did not stop at all things "purely social" in the process of creating the Jim Crow system. He was also unable to get any president to speak out against lynching or the growing segregation laws. Furthermore, the secrecy around some of his actions and his ruthless attack on some of his critics has left many individuals uncertain about his legacy. Washington, however, created the largest black school in the Jim Crow South, he preached self-reliance and economic independence, and he built the National Negro Business League to promote such action at a time when African Americans were being lynched by the hundreds each year and black civil and political rights were ruthlessly denied. He was a pragmatic leader who carved something out of a horrendous situation, and his ideas influenced, among others, Marcus Garvey, the Nation of Islam, and Malcolm X. Booker T. Washington died in Tuskegee, "the city that he built," on November 14, 1915.

Biography

Booker Taliaferro Washington. Born in the spring of 1856 near Franklin County, Virginia. Studied at Hampton Normal and Agricultural Institute, Hampton, Virginia. Taught school in Malden, West Virginia, Hampton Normal and Agricultural Institute, and Tuskegee Normal and Industrial Institute, Tuskegee, Alabama. Addressed Atlanta Exposition on September 18, 1895. Founder, Tuskegee Normal and Industrial Institute, 1881, and National Negro Business League, 1900. Died in Tuskegee, Alabama on November 14, 1915.

SHAWN LEIGH ALEXANDER

See also **Du Bois, W.E.B.; Farrakhan, Louis; Garvey, Marcus; Malcolm X; Muhammad, Elijah; National Association for the Advancement of Colored People (NAACP)**

Selected Works

The Booker T. Washington Papers, edited by Louis R. Harlan and Raymond Smock, 14 vols., 1972–1989
The Future of the American Negro, 1899; reprint, 1969
The Story of My Life and Work, 1900; reprint, 1969
A New Negro for a New Century, 1900; reprint, 1969
Up from Slavery: An Autobiography, 1901
The Negro Problem: A Series of Articles by Representative American Negroes of To-Day, 1903; reprint, 1969
Frederick Douglass, 1907
The Negro in Business, 1907; reprint, 1971
The Negro in the South, His Economic Progress in Relation to His Moral and Religious Development; Being the William Levi Bull Lectures for the Year 1907, (with W.E.B. Du Bois), 1907
The Story of the Negro: The Rise of the Race from Slavery, 2 vols., 1909; reprint, 1969
The Man Farthest Down: A Record of Observation and Study in Europe, 1912
My Larger Education: Being Chapters from My Experience, 1969

Further Reading

Du Bois, W.E.B, *The Souls of Black Folk*, edited by David W. Blight and Robert Gooding-Williams, Boston: Bedford Books, 1997
Harlan, Louis R., *Booker T. Washington: The Making of a Black Leader, 1856–1901*, New York: Oxford University Press, 1972
———, *Booker T. Washington: The Wizard of Tuskegee, 1901–1915*, New York: Oxford University Press, 1983
———, and Raymond Smock, *Booker T. Washington in Perspective: Essays of Louis R. Harlan*, Jackson: University Press of Mississippi, 1988
Meier, August, *Negro Thought in America, 1880–1915: Racial Ideologies in the Age of Booker T. Washington*, Ann Arbor: University of Michigan Press, 1963
———, and Elliott M. Rudwick, *Along the Color Line, Explorations in the Black Experience: [Essays]*, Urbana: University of Illinois Press, 1976

Welsh *See* **Wales**

White Australia Policy (1901–1973)

White Australia is the unofficial term that has gained wide currency to portray public attitudes to, and government policies for, policies of restrictive immigration. These policies, originating in the mid-nineteenth century, were driven mainly by the desire of the early Australian colonial settlers to maintain an exclusive white settlement particularly when confronted with the economic imperatives of the need for nonwhite labor in several colonies. The need for labor in the flourishing pastoral Australian economy, mainly of wool and wheat production, drove some pastoralists to seek cheap coolie laborers from India as early as the 1820s. This initial foray into nonwhite labor migration was soon to be followed by the first waves of Asian migrant labor in the mid nineteenth century. This was mostly as contract indentured labor and included Melanesians (*Kanakas*) working in the sugar plantations of Queensland and Chinese laborers in the Victorian goldfields.

Throughout the 1850s and 1860s there was a large influx of Chinese laborers which at one time reached about 12 percent of the work force in Victoria. Unlike the early indentured labor, based on a legal contract between worker and employer, the mid nineteenth century Asian labor was on a credit ticket system of unfree labor. Consequently, the economic bond was no longer between employer and imported labor, but between the latter and brokers overseas who had complete control over the services of imported labor. This system of unfree coolie labor heightened economic competition with Australia's native labor, which was no longer reliant on the transportation of convict labor.

The increased presence of coolie labor led to public agitation focused on local labor protection. Hence, the demand for maintaining adequate living standards of native Australian workers by preventing the importation of cheap Asian labor. Hostility to Chinese labor expansion, resulting in racial riots, mob violence, and lynching, led to the introduction of the first statutory acts relating to restrictive legislation in the colonies of

Victoria (1855), South Australia (1858), and New South Wales (1861). This early legislation was complemented by other measures discriminating against Asians already legally resident in Australia with regard to working conditions and wages. Queensland presented itself somewhat differently on the question of restrictive legislation (introduced only in 1877) because it was argued that nonwhite labor (mostly Kanakas) was necessary for the tropical working environment of the sugar industry, and to a lesser extent, in pearling and *bêche-de-mer* fishing.

By the late 1880s and throughout the 1890s anti-Asian attitudes, though focused mainly on Chinese immigration, were the universal complaint of the working class (unions, and political parties representing the working class) and the common concern of nearly all colonial governments. The economic defense of anti-Chinese immigration policies, based on the grounds of security, justice, and equity for native Australian workers was, in addition, heavily tinged by distinctly racist arguments. Much of this reasoning was framed in the language of the nineteenth century doctrines of racial superiority and social Darwinism. Accordingly, the Chinese, as a race, were "inferior" because of their inherited characteristics, their moral depravity, proneness to crime, and corruption. Moreover, they were likely to pollute the purity of an unmixed nation, which was considered the indisputable condition of unity and social cohesion.

These anti-Chinese sentiments based on both economic and racist grounds became the core of the pursuit of a White Australia. Importantly, these sentiments were directed not just against Asian immigration, but against all other non-European groups. By the late 1890s, there were a series of colonial laws restricting Chinese immigration, barring them from specified occupations and denying citizenship. Admittedly, these restrictive measures proved problematic for some Asian groups, such as the Indians and the Japanese.

The Japanese, for instance, stood out as a more advanced nation in the late nineteenth century, especially after the Sino-Japanese war of 1894 and the defeat of Russia in 1905, and they were not considered in the same light as the Chinese. The Indians, on the other hand, were a part of the British Empire and were considered to be entitled to the benefits and privileges of being British subjects.

The opposition to nonwhite immigration, focused primarily on the Chinese, existed alongside the ingrained hostility of Australian settlers toward indigenous Australians, the Aboriginal people, who were mostly confined to reserves or treated as protected persons. As a result, this broad-ranging racial ideology became a defining element in shaping a sense of Australian identity and was a significant factor in determining the type of citizenship and the desired identity in the kind of society a future Australian nation would embrace. The desire for an *Australian* nationhood was manifest in the 1890s as the quest for full independence from Britain and release from the shackles of colonial controls. According to Alexander Deakin, one of the leading figures in the movement for establishing an Australian Federation comprised of the six British colonies to constitute the Australian nation, "the unity of Australia was nothing if that did not imply a united race." In short, Australian nationalism was driven by the twin demands of complete sovereignty and the need for racial and cultural homogeneity.

Not surprisingly, one of the first policy initiatives of the newly established Federation of States was to enact the racial exclusion legislation of 1901, *The Immigration Restriction Act* (I.R. Act), with the specific purpose of safeguarding the "unmixed nation." To avoid overt suggestions of discrimination on grounds of race or any direct reference to color, the criteria for exclusion were based on a *dictation test* (sometimes known as the Natal test) relating to a European language (later amended to "any prescribed language"). The formal legislative basis for racial exclusion in Australia rests on the 1901 I.R. Act as well as *The Pacific Island Labourers Act* of 1901, which specifically referred to the use of Melanesian labor (the *Kanakas*) in the Queensland sugar industry. These early statutes served to confirm a blanket opposition to *all* non-European immigration. The main objective was to instill a sense of national identity, linking race, nation, and color.

The logic and rationale of these discriminatory policies soon became the emblem of Australian national identity and remained a dominant influence on all other policies, particularly during the first five decades after Federation. However, the post–World War II period which witnessed Australia's growing maturity as an economically affluent independent nation was severely constrained by an underlying sense of national insecurity. This insecurity arose largely from the dilemma of the nation as an historically white European nation located among hordes of "aliens," the peoples of the Asia-Pacific region, represented by the popular slogan, "yellow peril." It was this sense of unease that provided the main grounds for justifying Australia's continued adherence to policies of racial discrimination and controlled immigration. Furthermore, the sentiments of a White Australia had a profound influence in shaping the nature and form of external affairs and defense policies.

However, the dominant ideology of a White Australia which had been such a powerful and determining influence on all aspects of public policy and social life was severely challenged by the impact of a whole range of issues relating to domestic and external affairs in the post–World War II period. Notably, events such as growing trade relations with Japan, mass migration allowing for non British immigrants, the emergence of a more cosmopolitan middle class, and the overseas experience of countries such as the United States and Canada with more relaxed immigration policies, all contributed to a weakening of traditional Australian attitudes and orthodox policies about immigration.

These issues and concerns were destined to markedly change the nature and characteristics of Australian society and its institutions. Above all, the relaxation of immigration policies, allowing for the entry of non British immigrants, following the mass migration policies of the post-war period, transformed Australia from a parochial, monocultural society consisting mainly of British settlers to a cosmopolitan, polyethnic, multicultural society, all of which challenged the credibility of traditional attitudes and policies toward Asian and other non European immigration. This led to pockets of agitation for immigration reform stemming mainly from the growing number of middle class intellectuals.

A significant policy shift in 1958, which led to the migration of part Europeans (those of mixed race), was followed by a further relaxation in the 1960s permitting the immigration of well-qualified Asians. By the 1970s there was, overall, a noticeable change in public attitudes and moves within the main political parties toward weakening the opposition to total exclusion of non-Europeans. These moves for reform by the critics of the

White Australia policy and political leaders culminated with the abrogation of the *Immigration Restriction Act of 1901*, with bipartisan support in 1972, by the reformist Whitlam Labor government (1972–75).

Since the removal of the White Australia policy from the statute book there has been a steady but highly regulated inflow of Asian immigrants to Australia, and this includes refugee immigrants as well as other, voluntary settlers. Thus, Australia now shares with other immigrant settler societies, like Canada and the United States, a substantial number of business and professional immigrant settlers of Asian origin. The Asian component in the total population now constitutes about 4–5 percent of the population and has led to a backlash creating isolated but influential anti-Asian immigration movements, reminiscent of the 1890s. However, official policy and overall community attitudes, as revealed by polling and attitudinal studies, remain firmly committed to the basic principles underlying a nondiscriminatory immigration policy.

LAKSIRI JAYASURIYA

See also **Australia**

Further Reading

Brawley, S., *The White Peril: Foreign Relations and Asian Immigration to Australasia and North America*, Sydney: University of New South Wales Press, 1995
Jayasuriya, L., and PooKong Kee, *The Asianization of Australia? Some Facts about the Myths*, Carlton: Melbourne University Press, 1999
London, H.I., *Non-White Immigration and the 'White Australia' Policy*, New York: New York University Press, 1970
Willard, M., *History of the White Australia Policy to 1920*, Carlton: Melbourne University Press, 1967
Yarwood, A.T., *History of the White Australia Policy*, Melbourne: Melbourne University Press, 1974

Wolof

Capsule Summary

Location: West African coast, mostly in Senegal, Mauritania, and Gambia
Total Population: about 2.8 million
Neighboring Peoples: Lebu, Fulani, Serer
Language: Wolof
Religion: Islam

The Wolof (Ouolof, Yallof, Walaf, Waro-Waro) are a large ethnic group living mostly in the West African countries of Senegal (where 2.62 million Wolof represent 36 percent of the population), Mauritania (10,000) and Gambia. In Senegal, the main Wolof areas are the Baol, the Jambur, the Siin, and Dakar.

The Wolof area is subject to desertification, so many of the Wolof subsistence farmers have settled in cities. In recent years, many of the Wolof have spread out in the Ivory Coast and Europe (France, Spain, and Italy) to find better jobs. In France the Wolof total about 35,000.

History

Beginning in the eleventh century, the Wolof forefathers migrated from Mali in the northwestern coastal Senegal area, from the left bank of Senegal River, to Cape Vert.

Oral family histories indicate that at least some of the first settlers in the area were of Fulbe origin. Moreover, some traits of the Fulbe and Wolof languages point to the assumption of a common origin. Much Wolof history has been preserved in oral epic poems. It is assumed that the Wolof descend from the legendary wise man Ndiandiane Ndiaye, who became the king of the Waalo and the Jolof after having emerged from the waters of the Senegal river.

According to oral traditions and the reports of Arabian historians, Wolof history probably dates back to about the twelfth or thirteenth centuries. By the end of the 1300s, the Jolof domain had grown into a large empire of separate, self-governing states (Kajoor, Baol, Sine, Saloum). By the 1500s, the empire had split into four major Wolof kingdoms: Waalo, Jolof, Kajoor, and Baol.

Until the eighteenth century, Wolof rulers played a key part in the slave trade, directing slave raids and selling captured individuals from inland populations to the Europeans established on Gorée Island off the coast of modern day Dakar.

During the nineteenth century, the French took up the systematic conquest of the Senegal river basin. Since then, Wolof history coincides with the history of Senegal.

Traditional Society

The Wolof were ruled by headmen, the *laman*, who were from high ranking lineages based on the length of time that they had resided in the area. These local chiefs were usually appointed by the king and paid their allegiance to him by maintaining order in the hinterlands and collecting taxes and tributes. The Jolof monarchical regime encouraged the creation of a rigorous social stratification in which social status is determined by birth. The social structure was organized in classes and castes. The classes were the aristocracy (*garni*), the freeborn class (*goor* or *jambur*: mainly common subsistent farmers), and the slaves (*jaam*). Besides, society was divided into caste-like categories, characterized by endogamy, which refer to the division of labor The *geer* comprised high-ranking noblemen and subsistence farmers; the *gnegno* comprised the artisans (considered a low class in Wolof society), and the bards, *gewel*.

This stratified social order continues to influence present day society. For instance, intermarriage between castes is a very rare occurrence; many individuals who belong to the slave caste work as tenant farmers of the owners of their ancestors. There is a complex code of behavior based on social status. A person belonging to the upper class is expected to maintain the highest social standards.

This unequal and dominating system, produced by an ancient centralized political structure, blends very well with the family structure, because this is also hereditary and based on blood links.

Family

The Wolof family structure is based on the tenets of hierarchy and solidarity. The hierarchy is expressed through the predominance of the men over the women and of the elderly over the young. The solidarity of the extended family *mbokk* (this word derives from *bokk* which means "to have in common" [to share]) made up of the families of brothers of the same father, produces the resources necessary for the sustenance of the various groups.

The agnatic (paternal) lineage (*bokk askan*) has great social weight. It determines the inheritability of

social conditions (the belonging to a caste and inheritance rights to assets and status), it determines also the social virtues of honor (*daraja*) and reputation (*bayre*) which, in Wolof culture, belong more to the family than to the individual.

The patrilineal lineage governs marriage as well. The bride reaches the bridegroom's home (*eggale*) after giving her dowry (*waajtay*). The Wolof prefer cousins as marriage partners. The adoption of marriage, preferably between cousins of the agnatic (paternal) lineage (*askan*) or the uterine (maternal) lineage (*xeet*) and of the dowry, renders the matrimonial choice, which occurs within the framework of a complex exchange system, compliant. The paternal uncle (*baay-bu-ndaw*, "little father") has the same social position as the father: he may marry the widow. The maternal uncle (*ndey-ju-goor*, "male mother") may educate the offspring. This complementary structure of the family system however is jeopardized by the changes that have occurred especially in the economic relationships. The monetary economy has produced a breakdown in the family web and the birth of individualism. Family solidarity and cooperation are thus made more difficult.

Religion

Islamic expansion caused by the Fulbe in the nineteenth century has determined the predominance of the patrilineal lineage. Today its consolidation in brotherhoods takes care of the need for solidarity relationships.

The Wolof belong to Islamic Sufi brotherhoods, like the *Tijaniyya* and the *Mouridiyya*. However, some pre-Islamic beliefs are still held, particularly by the women. They believe that both good and evil spirits (*djinn, rabb*), as well as witchcraft (*ndëmm*) exist in each village.

Language

Wolof is the main African language of Senegal and Coastal Gambia, where 7 million people speak it (including second language speakers).

The Fula-Wolof language belongs to the Niger-Congo family, Western Sudanic subgroup; West Atlantic branch. It has several dialects: Baol, Cayor, Dyolof (Djolof, Jolof), and Jander. The language of communication and trade during the colonial era, Wolof has become an unofficial lingua franca, which facilitates interethnic exchange. This has been brought about equally by the swift urbanization in the "melting pot" of Dakar and by the wise stewardship of ethnic groups by President Senghor.

Massimo Repetti

See also **Gambia, The; Mauritania; Senegal**

Further Reading

Bara-Diop, Abdoulaye, *La société Wolof. Les systèmes d'iné-galité et de domination*, Paris: Karthala, 1981

Bara-Diop, Abdoulaye, *La famille Wolof*, Paris: Karthala, 1987
Belcher, Stephen, *Epic Traditions of Africa*, Bloomington: Indiana University Press, 1999
Clark, Andrew, *Frontier to Backwater: Economy and Society in the Upper Senegal Valley, 1850–1920*, Lanham and Oxford: University Press of America, 1999
Ly, Bubacar, *L'honneur et les valeurs morales dans les sociétés ouolof et toucouleur du Sénégal*, Paris: Université de Paris V, 1966
McNee, Lisa, *Selfish Gifts: Senegalese Women's Autobiographical Discourses*, New York: State University of New York Press, 2000

Wright, Richard (African-American)

Richard Wright's contribution to African-American letters is so vast and long-lasting that calling it a contribution is an error. Without him, there would be no contemporary African-American literature as we recognize it today. His work has had enormous influence on the writers who followed him and on American thinking about the African-American experience. Wright's most important work, *Native Son,* and the later critical arguments that ensued, laid the groundwork for much that has since been thought, said, and written about race in America.

Born and raised in the Deep South in the early years of the twentieth century and living later in Chicago and New York City, Wright shared the pattern of life of many African Americans of the time. As a child he lived through the worst Jim Crow had to offer, enduring economic hardship and white supremacist society. As a young adult he took part in the great migration from South to North made by so many African Americans during and after World War I who were looking to leave this situation behind and to find work in the North. While in Chicago he became involved in the causes of the worker and the African American, joining the Communist Party. Moving to New York, he took part in the political and cultural life of the Harlem whose earlier cultural ferment, the Harlem Renaissance, had been so important to African-American life. Wright's life and times—his experiences and the experiences of those around him—greatly informed his work. The things he saw and the people he knew were

reflected in the things he said about the world. In turn, the things he said about the world were so powerful that the world came to reflect them as well.

Wright's first published work—essays, stories, and poems—came out of his time in Chicago and involvement with the John Reed Society and the Communist Party and reflected the social concerns of those groups. In particular, Wright's commitment to use literature to effect social change can be traced to these beginnings. His first book, *Uncle Tom's Children,* consists of four long stories that combine class consciousness and race consciousness to tell stories of white racism. Published in 1938, it was well received, winning the *Story* magazine prize for work submitted by an author associated with the Federal Writers' Project. The success of *Uncle Tom's Children* allowed him the time to concentrate on his next book. In its writing, Wright was determined not to repeat what he saw as his first book's sympathetic picture of suffering, and to write a book too "hard and deep" for tears. That book, *Native Son,* appeared in 1940, and with it appeared a new kind of African-American literature.

Native Son was an enormous literary and commercial success, selling over 200,000 copies in its first three weeks of publication. It confronted the reality of race in America in a way no book before it had, with an anger no African-American writer had dared to express. The novel tells the story of Bigger Thomas, a young black man painted into a corner by difficult circumstances and bad luck. *Native Son* told

Bigger's story through literary naturalism's determinist eye, adapting naturalism's sense of the inevitable results of environmental pressure on individuals to a subject on which it had not previously been trained, the lives of African Americans. This story of life in Chicago's slums was thus hailed as a masterpiece of the social protest novel (and was in fact based in part on actual events), and earned Wright comparisons to masters of the genre such as Theodore Dreiser, John Steinbeck, and even Fyodor Dostoyevsky, and praise from writers such as Ralph Ellison and critics such as Malcolm Cowley.

Bigger's story is told in three parts, "Fear," "Flight," and "Fate." The movement of the three sections emphasizes the sense of the inevitability of Bigger's fate. Hired away from a street gang to be the driver for a rich white family, Bigger succumbs to the pressures of the situation, accidentally smothers the family's drunk daughter in fear that he will be discovered in her bedroom after helping her to bed, and in a panic cuts off her head and burns her body in the furnace. His fake blackmail note fails to keep him out of suspicion, as the daughter's remains are found in the furnace, and Bigger takes flight with his girlfriend. Thinking that her presence might slow him down and lead to his capture, Bigger kills her as well, but is nonetheless captured. The last third of the book details the different reactions to Bigger's crimes, including his lawyer's explanation of the effects of racism on Bigger's psyche, and Bigger's ultimate measure of existential self-knowledge before he goes to the chair. From the book's opening with the black rat that Bigger confronts in his apartment, which turns on his family when it is cornered, to the rat skittering across the abandoned apartment in which he hides before he is caught, the novel never abandons its naturalist imperative: to show how an individual is subject to the pressure of his or her environment. Wright's achievement in the novel is to extend the pressures the social novel considers beyond class to race, to show the ultimately psychological effects of racism on African Americans.

Wright adapted *Native Son* for the stage in 1941, and also in that year published *Twelve Million Black Voices: A Folk History of the Negro in the United States,* a study in words and photographs of African-American life from the slave ships of the Middle Passage to the plantations of the South to the cities of the North. In 1945, Wright published *Black Boy: A Record of Childhood and Youth.* The autobiography described not just white racism but also its divisive effects on African-American communities; it was, like *Native Son,* a critical and commercial success.

Wright wrote many more novels and nonfiction works while still in America and while living as an expatriate in Paris after World War II. In these years, his work was informed by his evolving thinking on race, his repudiation of Communism, his increasing fascination with existentialist philosophy, and his contact with the ideas of negritude and other new ideas emerging from Africa. However, none of the writing that he produced had anything approaching the impact of his earlier work.

Wright's reputation endures, resting largely on *Native Son.* It suffered some at the hands of James Baldwin, who, in a 1948 essay entitled "Everybody's Protest Novel," criticized the novel for being, in his eyes, not great art but reductive protest fiction along the lines, ironically enough, of Harriet Beecher Stowe's 1852 antislavery novel. Wright also lost his position as the pre-eminent African-American writer to Ralph Ellison, when Ellison's more experimental and artistically complex *Invisible Man* appeared in 1952. However, while his aesthetic reputation may have dimmed somewhat, Wright is still recognized for the impact of his work and the power of his greatest novel.

Biography

Born Richard Nathaniel Wright in Roxie, Mississippi, September 4, 1908. Studied at Howe Institute, Memphis, Tennessee; Seventh-day Adventist school, public Jim Hill and Smith-Robertson Junior High schools, Jackson, Mississippi. United States Postal Service worker, Chicago, Illinois, 1928–30; Harlem editor of the *Daily Worker,* 1937; cofounder, *New Challenge,* 1937; member of editorial board, *New Masses,* 1938–1944; researcher, Federal Writers' Project, 1935–39. O'Henry award for "Fire and Cloud," 1938; Guggenheim Fellowship, 1939. Died in Paris, France, November 28, 1960.

Selected Works

"Blueprint for Negro Writing," *New Challenge,* Fall, 1937
Uncle Tom's Children: Four Novellas, 1938
"Portrait of Harlem," *New York Panorama,* 1938
Native Son, 1940
Uncle Tom's Children: Five Long Stories, 1940
"How 'Bigger' Was Born," *Saturday Review,* June 1, 1940
Native Son (The Biography of a Young American): A Play in Ten Scenes, With Paul Green, 1941
Bright and Morning Star, 1941
12 Million Black Voices, with photo-direction by Edwin Rosskam, 1941
"Not My People's War," *New Masses,* June 17, 1941

"I Tried to Be a Communist," *Atlantic Monthly*, August-September, 1944, later collected in *The God That Failed*, edited by Richard Crossman, 1949
Black Boy: A Record of Childhood and Youth, 1945
Cinque Uomini, 1951
The Outsider, 1953
Savage Holiday, 1954
Black Power: A Record of Reaction in a Land of Pathos, 1954
The Color Curtain: A Report on the Bandung Conference, 1956
Pagan Spain, 1957
White Man, Listen!, 1957
The Long Dream, 1957
Eight Men, 1961
Lawd Today, 1963
American Hunger, 1977
Richard Wright Reader, 1978
Early Works: Lawd Today!, Uncle Tom's Children, Native Son, 1991
Later Works: Black Boy (American Hunger), The Outsider, 1991
SAMUEL COHEN

Further Reading

Baker, Houston A., Jr., editor, *Twentieth Century Interpretations of Native Son*, Englewood Cliffs, New Jersey: Prentice-Hall, 1972

Baldwin, James, "Everybody's Protest Novel," in *Notes of a Native Son*, Boston: Beacon, 1955
Ellison, Ralph, "Richard Wright's Blues," in *Shadow and Act*, New York: Random House, 1964
Fabre, Michel, *The Unfinished Quest of Richard Wright*, New York: Morrow, 1973; Urbana: University of Illinois Press, 1993
Gates, Henry Louis, Jr., and K.A. Appiah, editors, *Richard Wright: Critical Perspectives Past and Present*, New York: Amistead, 1993
Gayle, Addison, *Richard Wright: Ordeal of a Native Son*, New York: Doubleday, 1990
Howe, Irving, "Black Boys and Native Sons," in *A World More Attractive*, New York: Horizon
Kinnamon, Kenneth, editor, *New Essays on Native Son*, New York: Cambridge University Press, 1990
Miller, Eugene E., *Voice of a Native Son: The Poetics of Richard Wright*, Jackson: University Press of Mississippi, 1990
Rampersad, Arnold, editor, *Richard Wright: A Collection of Critical Essays*, Englewood Cliffs, New Jersey: Prentice Hall, 1995
Walker, Margaret, *Richard Wright: Daemonic Genius*, New York: Amistad, 1988

Y

Yakut, *See* Sakha (Yakut)

Yanomami

Capsule Summary

Location: southeastern Venezuela (Atabapo and Rio Negro departments in Amazonas state) and northwestern Brazil (the states of Roraima and Amazonas)
Total Population: approximately 25,000
Language: Yanomami (possibly linked to Macro-Pano-Tacanan)
Religion: Yanomami

The Yanomami, who are perhaps the most well-known "primitive" people in the world, are the largest group of people surviving in the Americas with a non-Western language and lifestyle. Widely dispersed over a vast and rugged Amazonian territory, they sustain themselves by hunting, gathering, and tropical forest horticulture. They are politically decentralized and live in as many as 200 seminomadic communes, most of which shelter between 20 and 150 people. Living mainly in Venezuela, but also in Brazil, the Yanomami have been increasingly imperiled since 1987 by an influx of gold miners.

The Yanomami are exceptional among Amazonian peoples in several respects. They speak a language that is not clearly related to neighboring languages; they lack a gene that is almost universally found among other indigenous Americans; and they are the only horticulturists in the region who grow plantains as their staple crop. In other respects, too, the Yanomami are plainly "marginal" Amazonians: They travel mainly on foot rather than by canoe; they traditionally live in remote highlands rather than in river valleys; they hunt with exceptionally long bows; and they ritually burn and consume the bones of their dead.

Yanomami cultural difference is rooted in both the recent and distant past. They originally migrated to the highlands, like a belt of other peoples on the fringe of the central rainforest, because they were driven away from the rivers by mightier farming and trading peoples: Carib-speakers to the north and Arawak-speakers to the south. Ultimately, this flight to higher ground spared the Yanomami the fate of their neighbors, who by 1750 had been decimated by European slave traders. Subsequently, the Yanomami expanded slowly into the now depopulated lowlands, where they entered the zone of European influence.

The Yanomami, who may have originated as a single tribe, first began to break into distinct subgroups about 700 years ago when the Sanemá subgroup branched off. (*Sanemá*, like Yanomami, means "people.") Near the start of the eighteenth century, after Europeans had arrived, the Ninam spun off, and a century later the Yanomam gravitated away from the Yanomamo. These groups differ considerably in size. In the early 1980s there were roughly 12,000 Yanomamo, 5,000 Yanomam, 3,000 Sanemá, and 850 Ninam.

All subgroups speak distinctive but mutually intelligible dialects of a single language and all share many cultural traits. Each group, meanwhile, is further subdivided into smaller branches—for instance, the Xilixana branch of the central Ninam and the Aica branch of the southern Ninam.

Most Yanomami live in circular communal structures known as *shabonos,* with open-air plazas in the middle ringed by gardens and forest. *Shabonos* are usually occupied for a few years, until the commune moves elsewhere in search of fresh gardens and hunting territory. Few communes grow larger than 150 members, and when they do, they tend to bifurcate. When this happens, each half builds a *shabono* of its own.

Interaction between neighboring communes is intense, with frequent individual visits and periodic intercommunal celebrations of family and trade ties. Although these celebrations occasionally turn violent, they are also a vital mechanism of solidarity.

Every family lives in a space of its own on the rim of a *shabono*. Typical families include a husband and a wife—occasionally multiple wives or, in rare instances, multiple husbands, children, and elderly or single relatives. Every wife has a hearth of her own, and everyone sleeps in hammocks. Gardens and peach palms are owned by adult men. Men hunt and women prepare cassava.

Yanomami culture is profoundly male dominated. Women are not consulted about their marriages, and wives are always at risk of being beaten by their husbands. Shamans, whose mission is to ward off evil spirits, are invariably men.

Communes usually consist of two or more "factions," each of which is led by a group of male relatives (a patriarch and his brothers, sons, and cousins) whose wives and children count as junior members. Among the Sanemá, who are far less reluctant than other Yanomami to name the dead, there is also clear evidence of lasting, named, male-descended clans with members dispersed across several communes. This dispersal reflects that, in general, men and women who share male ancestors are not allowed to marry and therefore must seek spouses outside their own factions—or, indeed, outside their own communes.

The "ideal" Yanomami commune would consist of two factions with balanced numbers of intermarrying men and women. In such a situation no one would ever have to leave his or her birth commune. Because there are seldom enough potential mates in any given commune, however, the Yanomami often marry into other communes. Once married, the groom is obliged to perform extensive bride service for his wife's parents, often for many years. In most cases, this entails matrilocal residence, in which the groom lives with his wife's family, creating a filament of connection among families, factions, and communes; but it also forces young men to leave their homes.

Thus, when men obtain especially coveted trade goods, they often trade them to other communes for wives, without agreeing to move or perform bride service. In the past, unequal exchanges of this type were rare, but they have become common since the 1950s, when Euro-Americans began to bring large quantities of industrial products into the region. Steel axes, especially, appeal to the Yanomami, who use them to enhance the productivity of their horticulture. The influx of steel, however, has had disruptive effects on Yanomami culture. Communes compete fiercely over access to Euro-American goods, since privileged access to a prime source of goods—such as a mission or anthropological camp—enables a commune to obtain a stream of wives and laborers from poorer communes by exchange. The inequality this generates, in turn, spurs fierce intercommunal feuds.

Thus weakened by internal strife, the Yanomami are also endangered by violence from gold-seekers. Recently they have advocated energetically on their own behalf, with support from groups like Survival International.

DAVID NORMAN SMITH

See also **Brazil; Venezuela**

Further Reading

Early, John D., and John F. Peters, *The Xilixana Yanomami of the Amazon: History, Social Structure, and Population Dynamics*, Gainesville: University Press of Florida, 2000

Ferguson, R. Brian, *Yanomami Warfare: A Political History*, Santa Fe, New Mexico: School of American Research Press, 1995

Peters, John F., *Life among the Yanomami: The Story of Change among the Xilixana on the Mucajai River in Brazil*, Peterborough, Ontario: Broadview Press, 1998

Ramos, Alcida Rita, *Sanumá Memories: Yanomami Ethnography in Times of Crisis*, London and Madison: University of Wisconsin Press, 1995

Shapiro, Judith Rae, *Sex Roles and Social Structure among the Yanomama Indians of Northern Brazil*, Ann Arbor: University of Michigan, 1980

Smole, William J., *The Yanoama Indians: A Cultural Geography*, Austin and London: University of Texas Press, 1976

Yao

Capsule Summary

Location: Malawi, Tanzania, and Mozambique (in eastern and southeastern Africa)
Total Population: approximately 1.6 million
Language: Yao, Chewa
Religion: Muslim (80%), Christian and other religions (20%)

The Yao are an ethnic group living in eastern and southeastern Africa. Their total population amounts to 1.6 million, of which 1 million live in Malawi around the southeastern tip of Lake Malawi and 400,000 in southern Tanzania. Another 200,000 (some estimate even 500,000) can be found in Mozambique to the south and west of the confluence of the Lugenda and Ruvuma rivers. The latter region is their area of common origin. The Yao are historically and politically one of the most important ethnic groups in Malawi, although ChiYao speakers have a share of only 13.8 percent of the total number of speakers in Malawi. In Tanzania and Mozambique they are hardly visible. Their main occupations and economy are based on agriculture (maize, rice, and manioc) and fishing.

Their language, ChiYao, is a Bantu language and is roughly mutually intelligible with the other neighboring Bantu languages. It is not recognized anywhere as an official language, and it is confined to village and family communication.

Since the 1830s, the Yao steadily migrated from Mozambique into southern Malawi, mainly into the Shire River region. This migration was initially caused by slave raids of the Lolo and Makua (Bantu peoples living to the south of the Yao). In the 1860s, a severe drought and subsequent famine drove Yao immigrants from the lower Shire valley further into the highlands of southern Malawi. The original inhabitants, the Mang'anja, were subdued and ransacked by the invaders. However, the similarities of custom between them and the Mang'anja made accommodation possible, and many Mang'anja remained or soon returned.

At least from the seventeenth century on, the Yao made their living partly by long-distance trade, which even reached the East African Coast. They exchanged iron products, tobacco, and salt mainly for cloth. When the demand in slaves and ivory grew in the eighteenth and nineteenth centuries, many Yao willingly switched to slave and ivory trade and received cloth and firearms from Arab slavers in exchange. This resulted in the creation of Yao chiefdoms who hunted slaves among the surrounding peoples and among each other. The Yao tradition of trade is reflected today in their small-scale trade and migrant labor.

Today around 80 percent of the Yao are Muslims because, at the height of the slave trade in the 1870s, many Arab traders started to live with the Yao; the Islamization of the Yao subsequently proceeded rapidly and continued until the 1920s. The reasons for Islamization included the wish to achieve the same social status as the Arabs and, in particular, the opposition against British missionaries and administrators trying to end the slave trade. Furthermore, Islam better fitted the needs of the Yao chiefs, because it stressed the unity of secular and religious power to their advantage.

The Yao chiefdoms were, for the most part, not united when the British arrived in the region and could not organize a coordinated resistance, although several Yao chiefs fiercely resisted the British occupation. However, in 1896, the British pacified the Yao and banned the slave trade. Because of their military traditions, the Yao later played an important role in the police and the armed forces of the British Nyasaland Protectorate.

During the rule of Hastings Kamuzu Banda and his Malawi Congress Party (MCP) from 1964 to 1994, the "Chewa-ization" of independent Malawi was pushed forward. Banda himself belonged to the Chewa (Nyanja), the largest Malawian people. This Chewaization followed ethnical stereotypes: Chewa were often said to be unambitious and easy to control, while the Yao, among other Malawian peoples, were said to be proud and warlike. Since Banda's aim was to secure a compliant base of support against those who would challenge his authority, he secured that support from the Chewa but not from the Yao. Banda bought the loyalty of the Chewa by pumping money into the central region of Malawi, their main settlement area, and by the Chewa-ization of the Malawian national identity through language policy and historiography. In 1968, ChiChewa was made the only official African language in Malawi, with Yao and Tumbuka banned from official use.

Throughout his presidency, Banda identified the Yao minority with "anti-Christian" Islam and with resistance to western education and modernization. During the Cabinet Crisis of 1964, the Yao allied themselves with Henry Chipembere, who was the leader of ministers rebelling against Banda's pretensions to absolute rule. Chipembere was also a member of Parliament for Mangochi, a predominantly Yao district. The apparent support of the Yao for anti-Banda sentiments only seemed to confirm to him his belief that they had maintained their resistance to change.

The first democratic multiparty elections in Malawi took place in May 1994. The ruling MCP and President Banda were ousted, and Bakili Muluzi was elected, a Yao Muslim and leader of the United Democratic Front (UDF). Votes for the three most important candidates appeared to be driven by group loyalty, with Banda finding his base of support among the Chewa, Chihana (chairman of the Alliance for Democracy, AFORD) among the Tumbuka, and Muluzi among the Yao as well as other Southerners. Muluzi's Yao support, however, accounts for only three of the ten districts that he won. Ethnic support for Muluzi was only significant as non-Chewa southern districts consistently voted in opposition to the MCP, even when it meant that the candidate was not of their own people. Muluzi simply was the most visible politician of a most visible people, and he was not a Chewa.

In June 1999, Muluzi was reelected as president and prevailed against an MCP-AFORD coalition. However, the election was contended by the opposition coalition to have been rigged by the UDF. Violent reactions of MCP and AFORD supporters followed, mainly in opposition strongholds of northern Malawi. MCP supporters destroyed ten mosques, and the mob targeted Muslims to articulate protest against Muluzi. During this turmoil deep-seated prejudices against the Muslim minority came to light that apparently lay in the identification of Muslims with ruthless trade practices, in particular the slave trade in the nineteenth century.

REINHARD KLEIN-ARENDT

See also **Bantu; Gujaratis; Malawi; Mozambique; Tanzania**

Further Reading

Alpers, Edward A., *Ivory & Slaves in East Central Africa*, London: Heinemann, 1975

Augustini, Günter, *Die Yao-Gesellschaft in Malawi*, Saarbrücken: Verlag der SSIP-Schriften, 1974

Kaspin, Deborah, "The Politics of Ethnicity in Malawi's Democratic Transition," *The Journal of Modern African Studies*, 33, no. 4 (1995)

Mitchell, J. Clyde, *The Yao Village*, Manchester: Manchester University Press, 1956

Thorold, Alan, "Metamorphoses of the Yao Muslims," in *Muslim Identity and Social Change in Sub-Saharan Africa*, edited by Louis Brenner, London: Hurst, 1993

Vail, Leroy, and Landeg White, "Tribalism in the Political History of Malawi," in *The Creation of Tribalism in Southern Africa*, edited by Leroy Vail, London, Berkeley, and Los Angeles: James Currey, 1989

Yemen

Capsule Summary

Country Name: Republic of Yemen
Location: Middle East, between Oman and Saudi Arabia
Total Population: 19,349,881 (July 2003)
Minority Populations: Mahra, Socotrans, Bedouin, and Jews
Languages: Arabic (official), Mahri, and Socotri
Religion: Muslim including Shaf'i (Sunni) and Zaydi (Shi'a), small numbers of Jewish, Christian, and Hindu

The Republic of Yemen, at the southern tip of the Arabian Peninsula, was formed in 1990 by the unification of the Yemen Arab Republic (North Yemen) and the People's Democratic Republic of Yemen (South Yemen). North Yemen gained its independence from the Ottoman Empire in 1918, while Aden, and later the sultanates of the Hadramawt, formed a British protectorate until independence in 1967. Although the population of 17 million is almost entirely Moslem, the majority of northern Yemenis are Zaydite while the southerners are Sunni. The united country has a heterogeneous population with, in addition to several minorities defined on an ethnic basis, a large number of tribal groups in the north. Yemen is one of the poorest countries in the Arab world; per capita GDP in 2002 was US$800.

The majority of Yemeni Moslems are Sunni, following the Shafi'i school. The south and east have always enjoyed a degree of independence, but for many centuries Sunni Moslems of the central highlands (principally concentrated south of Yarim, and particularly in Ibb and Ta'izz) as well as those of the Tihama (the western coastal plain) were subject to the authority of the Zaydite Imamate that ruled northern Yemen until the establishment of a republic in 1962.

In a united Yemen, the Sunni population of the highlands can no longer be considered a minority, although it is true that if their religious beliefs set them apart from their Zaydite neighbors, so, too, their culture differs from that of their coreligionists both of the Tihama and of the Hadramawt. The latter region has traditionally been a center for Shafi'i religious learning as well as for commercial activity and has received cultural influences from East Africa and Indonesia.

The people of the Tihama, Sunni Moslems numbering about 2 million, are culturally distinct from the highlanders. There are strong African influences, a result of voluntary migrations from the Eritrean and Somali coasts and of slavery, and these influences are evident both in social structures and in their material culture: housing and clothing styles are very different from those of the highlands and women are often not veiled. The Tihama has also been most subject to foreign influences because it was ruled by the Ottoman Empire for a longer period than the rest of Yemen and it also had contacts with European powers. Nevertheless, despite its unique cultural identity, the Tihama is strongly Yemeni and has invariably formed part of the dominant political unit: Zabid was the site of the first capital of an independent Islamic Yemeni state. The tribes of the Tihama are the only Sunni tribes in Yemen. They are referred to collectively as the Zaraniq.

Approximately 35 percent of Yemenis are Zaydites and may be divided into two groups: the sedentary agriculturalists of the more fertile and better watered areas of the highlands, and the nomadic groups of the dryer and less hospitable north east. The distinction between the groups is not clear-cut, because many nomadic groups practice some agriculture whereas many sedentary groups are also pastoralists. The various peoples can be grouped into three tribal confederations, although the word *confederation* implies a stability that is somewhat illusory. North of San'a, the Hasid and the Bakil confederations are the two principal divisions of the Hamdan group, while the Madhhij confederation includes the tribes of the Ma'rib region. Contrary to popular belief, most Yemeni tribes are not nomadic, although tribal identity is more important among nomadic tribes than among sedentary tribes, among whom territorial-based affiliations are often strong.

The *sada* (singular: *sayyid*) are a nontribal Zaydite aristocracy, numbering about 50,000. Historically they depended upon tribal Yemenis for protection and served the Imamate as functionaries. Although their influence has declined in recent years, they are still present in the north, particularly in Sa'da.

Approximately two percent of the population are Ismaili. Formerly found in the west, both in the highlands and on the coast, their numbers have diminished in recent years and they are found today in the hills west of San'a. There are several Ismaili tribal groups.

There is no longer a Yemeni Christian community; Christians, like Hindus, are immigrants of recent origin. Until the mid-twentieth century there were some 60,000 Yemeni Jews. In 1949–50 almost 50,000 Yemenis were airlifted to Israel in Operation Magic Carpet. Most of the remainder have immigrated since, while others have converted to Islam, and today there may be fewer than a thousand Jews in the country, living mostly in rural areas in the north. The Jewish contribution to Yemeni material culture has been significant, particularly as artisans and specifically as jewelers; a few traditional Jewish houses remain standing in the former Jewish quarter of San'a.

The Bedouin are nomadic tribes that range across the deserts and semideserts of the Arabian peninsula. Some 700,000 Bedouin (about four percent of the population) include north-central Yemen, particularly the areas north and west of Wadi Hadramawt extending to the Saudi Arabian border, within their territory. Unlike the nomadic Zaydite tribes, the Bedouin are true nomads, and are Sunni, although their religious practices diverge from Sunni orthodoxy in several respects. The Marxist regime of the former South Yemen encouraged the Bedouin to settle, but since unification, many have resumed their nomadic lifestyle.

Two distinct ethnic minorities live in southern Yemen. In the Far East, and occupying a territory that straddles the Omani frontier, are the Mahra people, numbering some 250,000. The Mahra follow both nomadic and sedentary lifestyles: like the Bedouin, many were forced to settle by the Marxist regime; similarly, many are again adopting the nomadic lifestyle best suited to the region, herding sheep, goats, or camels. Mahra in coastal areas are skilled fishermen. Some 60,000 Mahra still speak a South Arabian language, Mahri, related to the now extinct pre-Arabic languages of Yemen, although Arabic is the mother tongue of most Mahra. Arabic-speaking nomadic Mahra are often assimilated to the Bedouin.

The Yemeni island of Socotra, population 80,000, lies 500 kilometers (310 miles) south of the coast of Al Mahra, closer to Somalia than Yemen. The population of the coast, the Sahriyah, are descended from Mahra, Arab, Indian, African, and Greek immigrants, are Sunni Moslem, and speak Mahri or Arabic; the aboriginal Socotran population, known as Bedu or Joboliyah and now largely confined to the inland areas of the island, seem to be related to the original inhabitants of South Arabia and speak Socotri, a South Arabian language. The Socotrans practiced Nestorian Christianity in historical times; conversion to Sunni Islam was not finally completed until the seventeenth century; as recently as the nineteenth century, Socotrans prayed in Socotri and with their backs to Mecca.

IAIN WALKER

See also **Ismailis; Oman; Saudi Arabia**

Further Reading

Burrowes, Robert, *Historical Dictionary of Yemen*, Lanham, Maryland: Scarecrow Press, 1995
Doe, Brian, *Socotra: Island of Tranquility*, London: Immel Publishing, 1992
Dresch, Paul, *Tribes, Government, and History in Yemen*, Oxford: Clarendon Press, 1989
Leveau, Rémy, Franck Mermier, and Udo Steinbach, editors, *Le Yémen Contemporain*, Paris: Karthala, 1999
Naumkin, V.V., *Island of the Phoenix: An Ethnographic Study of the People of Socotra*, Reading: Ithaca Press, 1993
Parfitt, Tudor, *The Road to Redemption: The Jews of the Yemen 1900–1950,* Leiden: Brill, 1996
Pridham, B.R., editor, *Economy, Society and Culture in Contemporary Yemen*, London and Dover, New Hampshire: Croom Helm; Exeter, Devon: Centre for Arab Gulf Studies, University of Exeter, 1985
Rouaud, Alain, *Les Yemen et Leurs Populations*, Bruxelles: Editions Complexes, 1979
Stone, Francine, editor, *Studies on the Tihamah*, London: Longman, 1985
Tobi, Yosef, *The Jews of Yemen: Studies in Their History and Culture*, Leiden and Boston: Brill, 1999

Yi

Capsule Summary

Location: Mainly in Sichuan, Yunnan, and Guizhou provinces, southwest of China
Total Population: 6,578,524
Language: Six different Yi languages
Religion: Various

The Yi are one of 55 ethnic minorities officially recognized by the Peoples Republic of China in the 1950s. Although their population of 6,578,524 represents 0.57 percent of the total population, they are the sixth largest among the minority groups in China. The Yi live mainly in Sichuan, Yunnan, Guizhou, and Guangxi provinces. Members of the Yi in each area are quite different, with their own unique languages, customs, and social systems. Yi languages belong to the Tibetan-Burmese subbranch of the Chinese Tibetan language family. Yi speak at least six varieties of language, each of which is unintelligible between each group. The Yi currently use two different written scripts. The old Yi script is syllabic and has recently undergone some minor modification. It is currently used in Liangshan (Cool Mountain) areas in Sichuan and Yunnan. The Latin-based Yi script was created by the government in the 1950s. This script is currently used for literary classes in Yunnan.

History

The Yi are indigenous to Yunnan and Sichuan. Based on historical records the Yi are related to the ancient Di and Qiang people in west China. During the period between the second century BCE and the early Christian era, the ancient Yi centered their activities around the areas of Dianchi in Yunnan and Qiongdou in Sichuan. After the third century the ancient Yi extended their activities to northeastern and southern Yunnan, northwestern Guizhou, and northwestern Guangxi. They were known as Yi in the eastern Han (25–220), Wei (220–265), and Jin (265–420) dynasties. After the Jin dynasty the Yi were known as Cuan, or Wumans. Since the Yuan dynasty they were referred to as *Luoluo* (or *lolo*), which came from one of the tribes of Luluman. In the early Han dynasty, the Kingdom of Dian was set up in the area around the Dianchi Lake in Yunnan. The chief of the Yi was the King of Dian. Around the eighth century, a kingdom of Nanzhao was established in the northern Ailao Mountain and Erhai areas, with the Yis as the main group. Bai, Naxi, and other groups were included. In 937 Nanzhao was superseded by the Kingdom of Dali. In the thirteenth century, the Kingdom of Dali was conquered by the Mongols of the Yuan dynasty. The Yuan set up regional prefectural and county governments and military and civil administration in Yunnan, Guizhou, and Sichuan, appointing hereditary headman Yi *tusi* to rule the local peoples. The Qing dynasty subsequently abolished the *tusi* system and appointed administration officials.

Yi living in the Greater Liangshan Mountain (Cool Mountain) area in Sichuan and the Lesser Liangshan area in Yunnan retained a slavery-based society until the late 1950s. In this society there were four different classes: black Yi (Nuohuo), white Yi (Qunuo), and two different ranks of slaves (Ajia and Xiaxi). The black Yi, the highest ranked and slave-owning class, made up 7 percent of the total Yi population. They owned 60 to 70 percent of the arable land and a large amount of other means of production. The black Yi were determined by blood lineage and marriages with people of the other three ranks were forbidden. The white Yi made up 50 percent of the population. They were controlled by the black Yi as subjects under the slave system, although they could not be sold and killed by their slave-owners at will. The white Yi lived within the areas governed by the black Yi slave-owners, had no freedom of migration, nor could they leave the areas without the permission of their masters. They had to pay some fees to their masters when they wanted to sell their land. They enjoyed relative independence economically, however, and could control Ajia and Xiaxi, who were inferior to them. Ajia, one rank of slaves, made up one third of the population. They could be freely sold, bought, and killed by the black Yi and white Yi slave-owners. Xiaxi was the lowest rank, making up 10 percent of the population. They had no freedom and were treated as domestic animals.

After the founding of the Peoples Republic of China (PRC), Yi was officially recognized as one of the ethnic minorities in the PRC; the name Luoluo was replaced, because the written characters of Luoluo contain an insulting meaning. Whether the Yi, as recognized by the government, form one single ethnic group or several groups is still a matter of debate among Western and Chinese scholars.

There have been several Yi autonomous prefectures and counties set up since the 1950s; each of these prefectures reflects the existence of a majority Yi group in that region. These autonomous groups include the Liangshan Yi autonomous prefecture, Mabian and Ebian Yi autonomous counties in Sichuan, the Chuxiong Yi autonomous prefecture, Eshan, Lunan, Ninglang, Nanjian, Jingdong, and Yangbi autonomous counties in Yunnan, and Weining Yi-Hui-Miao autonomous county in Guizhou.

Theoretically, in these Yi autonomous areas, Yi and Han should be used as the official languages in local government. Schools should also have bilingual teaching programs for Yi children, but in practice, this is not always the case. In Sichuan, since the 1980s, however, the Yi language has been actively promoted as a medium of instruction and as a subject of the school curriculum from primary schools to the tertiary colleges in the Liangshan Yi autonomous prefecture. This prefectural government publishes school textbooks in the Yi language and a Yi language newspaper, entitled *Lingshan News*, published weekly. Yi living in urban areas have adopted the Han customs, culture, and language.

In the rural areas, Yi still maintain their culture, customs, and language peculiar to that particular Yi group. The majority of Yi women do not have equal status with men and have no right to inherit family property. Most Yi girls rarely finish primary schools and marry at a young age. In many places, married women stay at their parents' home until their first child is born. The Yi weddings include frolic episodes of "kidnapping the bride" and fighting between the bride and the groom as part of the ceremony, to add to the joyous atmosphere. The slavery system in the Liangshan areas was not abolished until the spring of 1958 when democratic reform took place. The reforms abolished slavery and all privileges of the slave-owners, confiscated or requisitioned land, cattle, farm tools, houses, and grain from the slave-owners, and distributed them among the slaves and poor people.

LINDA TSUNG

See also **China**

Further Reading

Harrell, S., "The History of the History of the Yi," in *Cultural Encounters on China's Ethnic Frontiers*, edited by S. Harrell, Hong Kong: Hong Kong University Press, 1994
Lin, Y.H., *The Great Change in Liangshan Yi*, Beijing: Commercial Press, 1995
Ma, Y., *China's Minority Nationalities*, Beijing: Foreign Language Press, 1989

Yoruba

Capsule Summary

Location: southwestern Nigeria, southeastern Benin, and north-eastern part of Togo
Total Population: approximately 30 million
Language: Yoruba
Religion: Christianity, Islam, and traditional Yoruba religions

The Yoruba are an ethnic group living in Nigeria, Benin, and Togo, with smaller communities found further afield, in Sierra Leone, Brazil, and Cuba. There are approximately 30 million Yoruba. The majority of the Yoruba people, over 25 million, live in the southwestern part of modern Nigeria, where they form the second largest ethnic group and represent 18 percent of that country's population. A substantial number of the Yoruba people also live in the southeastern part of the Republic of Benin and the northeastern part of Togo. Chief Yoruba cities are Lagos, Ibadan, Abeokuta, Akure, Ilorin, Ogbomosho, Oyo, and Ife.

In Nigeria, Benin and Togo originally formed what was known as the Yoruba Empire, before the Europeans colonized Africa and partitioned the continent. Some Yoruba population is also found in other parts of Nigeria and other parts of West Africa such as Sierra Leone, Ghana, and Liberia. As a result of the transatlantic slave trade, many Yoruba descendants exist in Brazil, Cuba, Trinidad, Tobago, and other parts of the Caribbean Islands. Their language, Yoruba, is the second most widely spoken language in Nigeria. It is a member of the Defoid language family, which is a constituent member of the Benue Congo phylum. Within Defoid, Yoruba's closest relatives are Igala and Isekiri in Nigeria, Tsabe and Idaitsa in the Republic of Benin, and Ana and Ife-Togo in Togo Republic.

The majority of Yoruba people are Christians, with the Church of Nigeria (Anglican), Catholic, Pentecostal, Methodist, and indigenous churches having the largest memberships. Moslems make up about a quarter of the Yoruba population, with the traditional Yoruba religion accounting for the rest.

History

It is difficult to determine how far back the Yoruba people have been in their homeland because efforts to write down the Yoruba language did not begin until sometime in the early nineteenth century. Even though the Yoruba people were highly skilled in other human endeavors, they did not develop the art of writing and therefore kept no written records. They relied upon memory, for the most part, to preserve their records in the form of oral traditions. However, there has been much speculation regarding the origins of the Yoruba people. The Yoruba people themselves have traditionally attempted to answer the question of their origin in their oral traditions. Many scholars have used these oral traditions to reconstruct early Yoruba history. One of the major problems with basing a people's origin on oral traditions is the imperfection of oral traditions. For example, oral traditions give satisfying answers that are not intended for disputation or critical examination. Oral traditions must be accepted in the same way that matters of faith are accepted by followers.

Using empirical and scientific research, many scholars have suggested that the Yoruba people migrated to where they are currently located from Egypt, eastern Sudan, or the "lost continent" of Atlantis. As a result of noted similarities to Jewish customs, some earlier writers have identified Yoruba as one of the ten "lost tribes" of Israel. Yoruba who have converted to Islam generally claim Mecca as their point of origin. However, new and more scientific sources such as archaeology and linguistics have disproved the popular theories that link the origin of the Yoruba people to Arabia, Egypt, Sudan, or Meroe. These theories were found to have no valid bases. Based on strong linguistic evidence, it is now claimed that the Yoruba people or their immediate ancestors moved from the Niger-Benue confluence area to the place that has now become their homeland. This claim rests largely on the classification of African languages by Joseph Greenberg and supported by some other linguists.

Society and Ethnicity

Linguists have classified the Yoruba language as relating to other languages such as Igbo, Edo, Nupe, Idoma, Igala, and so on. The Niger-Benue confluence is established as the original home of this group of languages.

Because there is enough evidence to believe that this is true, then the speakers of these languages must originate from the home base of the languages they speak. Through this linguistic evidence, linguists also established that the Yoruba language separated as a distinct one from the sister languages at least three or four thousand years ago, that is, from 2,000 or 1,000 BCE. This means that the Yoruba people had emerged as a distinct language group any time from about 2,000 to about 1,000 BCE. Ile-Ife became the first Yoruba settlement to become prominent soon after the people acquired distinctiveness as a separate language group.

Traditionally, the Yoruba people began their life as fruit gatherers, because they lived in an area where vegetation was forest and wooded grassland. Aside from the different Nigerian federal and state jobs currently available for Yoruba men and women, the Yoruba economy is based on farming, craft specialization, and trade. Hunting, fishing, animal husbandry, and the gathering of wild foods are practiced. Chickens, guinea fowl, pigeons, ducks, and turkeys are kept as domestic fowl; and goats, sheep, pigs, horses, dogs, cats, rabbits, and guinea pigs are also domesticated for the Yoruba people. Wild birds and game are hunted in the forests and in the open grasslands. Fish and shrimp are caught in the larger rivers, the lagoon, and along the ocean. Professional hunters and anglers sell their fresh catch through traders in the market or dry it for sale in areas where fish and game are not plentiful.

The Yoruba practice a form of social organization in which the lineage, ebí or idílé, is basic. The lineage is composed of several kindred nuclear families. It is an extended family, consisting of father, mother, and children of the nuclear generation or first generation and their offspring up to as many generations as possible. It is assumed that the evolution of the lineage began as far back as when the Yoruba people emerged as a distinct group. The lineage is an important and an indispensable fabric of Yoruba society, with the focus and center of each descent group within the society playing a major role in the social, political, economic, religious, judicial, and intellectual aspects of Yoruba life. The lineage is the basis of an individual's identity and membership in the society and for his political and social rights. It is the focus of strongest allegiance, and authority is symbolized and to some extent exercised by a lineage head chosen on consideration of age and genealogical proximity.

Women played and continue to play a major role in the economic, political, religious, and social lives of the Yoruba people. As there were traditional women in different leadership positions such as queens, market leaders, and religious leaders, so are there many Yoruba women leaders in today's Nigerian federal, state, and local offices. Despite that the Yoruba society is still very much a polygamous one, women have ways of influencing what goes on politically, at home, and in the society.

The Yoruba people traditionally had a monarchical system of government in which an Oba (king) became the embodiment of the state. The Oba had supreme authority in the state and his word was taken as law; his attributes are Oba, Aláse, and Èkejì Òrìsà (king, ruler, and second in command to the gods). Traditionally, the Oba's palace was usually the most impressive in the community and located in the center of the settlement or town, which formed the capital of his domain. Even though the Oba was treated as second in command to the gods, in practice, he or she was not an absolute ruler. He governed his state with the advice and active involvement of a council of chiefs. These chiefs were representatives of lineages and other interest groups in the society, creating a system of effective check and balances. After the Yoruba land was colonized by the British, the Yoruba kings lost some of their political power. They are no longer as politically powerful as they were before colonization.

In the traditional Yoruba system of government, there was no separation of powers in the sense that the same body, namely, the Oba and his chiefs, performed the legislative, executive, and judicial functions. The members of the governing body were usually concerned with the welfare and happiness of the people. This is why the judicial system was governed more by concern for humanity rather than by justice for its own sake. In the Yoruba judicial system, the underlying motive was reconciliation of the disputants to promote societal harmony.

It was because of this principle of reconciliation and societal harmony that there were no isolated courts in the Yoruba land traditionally. The three tier courts were within the precincts of the compound head for the lineage, the house of the ward chief for the ward, and in the palace of the Oba, for the town or kingdom. Similarly, there were no isolated prison houses. Offenders who were imprisoned stayed in the abode of the compound head, the ward chief, or in the palace of the Oba. Because this principle of humaneness and reconciliation was largely absent from the Western-type judicial system introduced in the colonial period, the Yoruba people hated the colonial courts, including the so-called Native Courts. This also explains why many Yoruba people outside the educated elite indulged in their continued patronage of the traditional courts, even when forbidden, during the colonial period. Many of them still find arbitration in the traditional setting more satisfying even up to this day.

Another enduring aspect of the Yoruba society is their traditional religion. Religion played and continues to play a major role in most aspects of their lives, both private and public. Their cosmology or their worldview, as well as their concept of life, have influenced the development of religious attitudes among them. Religion forms the foundation and all-governing principles of life for them. As far as they are concerned, the full responsibility of all the affairs of life belongs to the Deity; their own part is to do as they are ordered (by the Deity) through the priests and diviners whom they believe to be the interpreters of the will of the Deity. As a result of the slave trade, the Yoruba who became slaves in Cuba, Brazil, and the Caribbean Islands brought their gods, beliefs, and traditional folklore. Syncretism is the factor that facilitated the preservation of Yoruba religious belief in the Americas. This syncretism between the Yoruba òrìsà and the Catholic saints in Brazil, Cuba, Haiti, and Trinidad permitted the Yoruba to continue the cult of their gods in secret, under the cover of Christianity. In this way, the survival of Yoruba gods was perpetuated in the diaspora.

Yoruba as a Minority

Among ethnicities in Nigeria, a strong correlation exists between religious differences and ethnic and regional diversity. Since Olusegun Obasanjo was sworn in as Nigerian president in May 1999, communal conflicts have increased in number and intensity, causing hundreds of deaths and displacing thousands. Muslims in the north and Christians in the south of Nigeria have experienced ethnic and religious tensions for quite some time. The emergence of increasingly militant groups such as the Oodua People's Congress (OPC), a pro-Yoruba organization, Ijaw youth groups in the Niger Delta, and the Arewa People´s Congress (APC, formed to protect the interests of the Hausa-Fulani in the north) have contributed to the communal conflicts.

According to a 2002 International Religious Freedom Report published by the U.S. Department of State, the most significant incident occurred between September 7 and 13, 2001, when 2,300 persons were killed in ethno-religious violence in Jos in Central Nigeria. Approximately 80 percent of the victims were Hausa Muslims, who constitute a significant minority in Jos. Christians of different groups were reported to have attacked each other, and Yoruba Muslims reportedly attacked Hausa Muslims. According to the Nigerian Red Cross, approximately 11,600 people were displaced internally. The military was able to restore stability and the conflict appeared to have been primarily ethnic and secondarily religious.

ANTONIA FOLARIN SCHLEICHER

See also **Fulani; Hausa; Nigeria**

Further Reading

Alade, Charles Adenrele, "Aspects of Yoruba Culture in the Diaspora," in *Culture and Society in Yorubaland*, edited by Deji Ogunremi, and Biodun Adediran, Rex Charles, 1998

Atanda, J. Adebowale, "The Yoruba People: Their Origin, Culture, and Civilization," in *The Yoruba History, Culture and Language*, edited by Olatunde O. Olatunji, John of Printers Limited, 1996

Bascom, William, *The Yoruba of Southwestern Nigeria*, Wayland Press, 1984

"Nigeria: International Religious Freedom Report 2002," U.S. Department of State. http://www.state.gov/g/drl/rls/irf/ 2002/ 14073.htm

Yugoslavia

Capsule Summary

Country Name: Federal Republic of Yugoslavia (abolished in 2003)
Total Population: 10.6 million
Minorities: Albanians (16%); Montenegrins (5%); Hungarians (3%); Muslims (3%); Roma (1%); Croats, Slovaks, Macedonians, Romanians, Bulgarians, Ruthenes, Vlachs, Turks, and Slovenes (all under 1%)
Languages: Serbo-Croation, Albanian, and Hungarian
Religions: Eastern Orthodox Christianity, Islam, and Catholicism

The Federal Republic of Yugoslavia (and from 1945 to 1992 Socialist Federal Republic of Yugoslavia) is located in southeastern Europe, between Croatia, Bosnia and Herzegovina, Albania, Macedonia, Bulgaria, Romania, and Hungary. The country is mountainous with few lowland plains. After a decade of war, the economy of Yugoslavia is weak and struggling. The estimated per capita GDP is $1,800.

The government of Yugoslavia is in transition. Until the 1991, Yugoslavia consisted of six subsidiary republics. As a result of the civil wars that began in 1991, only two republics remain: Serbia and Montenegro. Each republic has its own president and unicameral parliament and both send representatives to a bicameral Federal Assembly, the rest of whose members are chosen by elections. The president of Yugoslavia is chosen by the Federal Assembly. Because Serbia is so much larger than Montenegro (approximately 10 million to 600,000), Serbia tends to dominate the politics of Yugoslavia.

Although theoretically a democracy, the democratic processes in Yugoslavia have been deeply flawed. Strongman Slobodan Milosevic dominated the Republic until his ouster from power in October 2000, and under his tenure, normal democratic practices were subverted by corruption, police intimidation, and assassination. With the election of President Vojislav Kostunica, and the arrest of Milosevic, Yugoslavia may be on the road toward real democracy.

History

Yugoslavia's complex ethnicity stems from its turbulent history. In approximately the sixth century CE, Slavic peoples migrated into southeastern Europe. These peoples, although originally sharing a common ethnic and linguistic heritage, became separated into sharply differentiated groups. During the late Middle Ages two empires collided and fought over the region: the Habsburg Empire, later called the Austro-Hungarian Empire, and the Ottoman Turkish Empire.

In the north, the areas occupied by the Habsburg Empire adopted Catholicism and the Latin alphabet. The Slavic peoples in this area—Slovenes and Croats—drew their cultural roots from central Europe. In the southern lands occupied by the Ottoman Empire, most of the Slavic peoples—Serbs, Montenegrins, and Macedonians—remained loyal to Eastern Orthodox Christianity. Some southern Slavs, however, were converted to Islam by the Ottomans and developed their own culture and traditions. In addition to the various kinds of Slavs, the region was also settled by Albanians, Hungarians, and Roma (Gypsies).

In the nineteenth century, the Serbians and Montenegrins were able to free themselves from Ottoman control and establish independent states. The northern Slavs remained under Habsburg rule until the coming of World War I, when the Austro-Hungarian Empire was destroyed. Yugoslavia was created in 1918 when the Slavic parts of the collapsed Austro-Hungarian Empire were merged with the Kingdom of Serbia to form a new kingdom, which became known as the Kingdom of Yugoslavia.

The new Yugoslavian state had a complex ethnic makeup. Most of the population was Slavic, but made up of different Slavic subgroups. In the northwest, Slovenes and Croats were mostly Catholic and used the Latin alphabet. In the south, the Serbs and Montenegrins were mostly Eastern Orthodox and used the Cyrillic alphabet. The only thing they had in common was the Yugoslavian king and tenuous ethnic connection. This patchwork kingdom was destroyed by World War II (1939–1945) and the invasion of the German army (1941).

Nazi rule did terrible damage to Yugoslavia and helped to exacerbate ethnic conflicts. The Nazis supported a fascist Croatian puppet government that was responsible for the murder of hundreds of thousands of Serbs, Jews, and Gypsies. A resistant movement was formed that included Yugoslavians from all ethnic groups. After the end of that war, the Communist resistance leader Joseph Tito built a new Yugoslavian government, making himself its Communist dictator. Tito's government attempted to limit ethnic nationalism, which it saw as being contradictory to the internationalist principles of Communism. The government created by Tito had six republics—Serbia, Montenegro, Croatia, Macedonia, Slovenia, and Bosnia and Herzegovina—which were supposed to share power. The ethnic groups in these countries were deeply divided, and it was only Tito's dictatorial control that kept the country together.

After Tito's death in 1980, Yugoslavia began a slow disintegration. Nationalist Serbs, led by former Communist leader Slobodan Milosevic, demanded more power for Serbs in Yugoslavia's federal government. Milosevic and his followers orchestrated the persecution of the Albanian and Hungarian minorities living inside Serbia. Nationalists in other republics, fearing Serb power, began to demand more rights for their ethnic groups.

In 1991 the country broke apart. Slovenia and Croatia declared their independence, followed by Macedonia and Bosnia and Herzegovina. All that was left of Yugoslavia was the republics of Serbia and Montenegro.

From 1992 to 1995, ethnic fighting raged across Bosnia and Croatia. Yugoslavian troops (meaning primarily Serbian troops), under the direction of Milosevic, supported the efforts of Serb minorities to establish control over wide sections of those two countries. It was during this period that Serb forces in Bosnia were responsible for using policies called *ethnic cleansing*, to clear areas of other ethnic groups. Ethnic cleansing was essentially a combination of terrorism backed by occasional mass murders. It was a form of genocide.

Even before the fighting began in Bosnia, Milosevic had organized the persecution of ethnic minorities within Serbia itself. Most victimized were the ethnic Albanians, most of whom lived in the Serbian province of Kosovo. The province had been semiautonomous before Milosevic came to power, but many Serbs resented Albanian domination of the provincial government. While most Kosovars were ethnic Albanians, Kosovo itself was the site of many famous Serbian battlefields and religious shrines. For this reason, nationalist Serbs were reluctant to let it go. Milosevic's 1989 decision to forcibly take over the Kosovar government was popular with most nationalist Serbs. Albanians suffered under Serbian rule for ten years. Resistance by some Albanians led to escalating violence. In 1998, Milosevic began moving large numbers of regular and paramilitary troops into the province to suppress Albanian resistance. These troops attacked Albanian villages and many foreign observers feared that Milosevic and his supporters wanted to ethnically cleanse Kosovo of its Albanian population.

When international political pressure failed to stop Serbian forces, the United States and its North Atlantic Treaty Organization (NATO) allies launched a bombing campaign against Yugoslavia in an attempt to force Milosevic to allow outside troops to enter Kosovo and protect the Albanians. In spite of intense bombardment, or perhaps because of it, Serbian forces increased their attacks on Albanian villages; unknown numbers of civilians were murdered and tens of thousands of Albanians fled from Kosovo. Finally, in June 1999, Milosevic agreed to accept NATO's terms. Serbian forces withdrew from Kosovo and were replaced by NATO soldiers. Kosovo became, in effect, an independent country under NATO protection. Most of the Kosovar refugees returned to the province.

With Yugoslavia suffering from the economic fallout of Milosevic's wars, the president became steadily less popular. On September 24, 2000, Milosevic was defeated in an election by opposition leader Vojislav Kostunica. After 2 weeks of mass demonstrations, Milosevic accepted the results of the election and stepped down as president. Milosevic had come to power because of the popularity of his policies of persecuting ethnic minorities in Yugoslavia. His defeat seemed to mark an end of such policies. In 2001, Yugoslavian police arrested Milosevic for his crimes and in July he was sent to The Hague to stand trial before an international tribunal for his crimes against humanity, the central one being his support for ethnic cleansing against the Albanian minority of Kosovo and the Bosnian Muslim population of Bosnia.

Minorities

The nationalist character of the Yugoslavian government during the late 1980s and 1990s led to the large-scale mistreatment of minorities. In the post-Milosevic era, these abuses have begun to disappear, but the Yugoslavian government remains strongly influenced by nationalist sentiments and minorities still suffer as a result.

The largest minority in Yugoslavia are the Albanians. Making up approximately 16 percent of the population, most of them live in Kosovo. While a minority in Serbia as a whole, the Albanians make up the majority of Kosovo's population, perhaps as much as 90 percent. The great majority of Albanians are Muslims, but significant minorities belong to different Christian churches. Although their native language is Albanian, many speak Serbo-Croatian.

Until 1989, Kosovo was largely self-governed as an independent province under loose Serbian authority. Milosevic inaugurated a ten-year period of Serb control. The Albanian language was displaced by Serbo-Croatian in secondary schools and its presence at the university level was greatly reduced. Albanians lost positions in government and suffered economically. Serbian police and military units used brutal tactics to repress Albanian protests.

With the June 1999 arrival of NATO troops, Serbia's police were replaced by NATO peacekeepers. Albanians began to slowly take over the reigns of provincial government. Kosovo now operates as an independent political entity and the Albanians, formerly a minority within Serbia, now function as a majority in Kosovo.

Within Kosovo, the Serbs themselves are a minority, one that is suffering some persecution at the hands of the once-abused Albanians. During the ten years of Serb control of Kosovo, some Albanian politicians (most famously, Ibrahim Rugova) advocated nonviolent resistance. Now that the Serbs no longer run the government, many of these politicians advocate respecting the rights of the Serbs still living in Kosovo. Militant Albanian leaders, however, are less forgiving, and many support or encourage attacks on the Serb minority in Kosovo. Serbs have been beaten and killed, their houses burned. NATO troops in Kosovo try to prevent such crimes but lack sufficient numbers to maintain tight control over the whole province. Because of this violence, thousands of Serbs have left Kosovo, moving to Serbia proper. There has even been persecution of non-Albanian Muslims by Albanian nationalists who count nationalist unity as more important than religious unity.

Hungarians make up a sizable minority in Serbia, most of them living in the province of Vojvodina, which is located in northern Serbia. Most Hungarians in Serbia are Catholics. Vojvodina, like Kosovo, was organized as a semiautonomous province under Serbian control. With the rise to power of Miloservic, Vojvodina lost its independence and a new government was put into place that emphasized Serbian nationalist policies.

As a result, the government worked to regulate more tightly Hungarian news-papers and television shows and to put some limitations on Hungarian schools, of which there are many in the province. Nevertheless, the Hungarians in Vojvodina never suffered the kind of persecution endured by Albanians in Kosovo.

Montenegrins also make up a minority within Yugoslavia. Most Montenegrins live in the Republic of Montenegro, where they make up approximately two thirds of the population. Ethnically and linguistically, Montenegrins are very close to Serbs. Some Montenegrins, particularly those who are Orthodox Christians, consider themselves Serbian. Because Montenegro is a full partner in the Yugoslavian state, the Montenegrins never suffered persecution from the Serb majority (which, in Montenegro itself, made up a minority of the population). The other minorities in Montenegro were also free from persecution. During the 1990s, the Montenegrin leadership distanced itself from Milosevic and his policies. During the Kosovo conflict, Montenegro opened its doors to thousands of Albanian refugees.

There is also a substantial population of non-Albanian Muslims in Yugoslavia. More than 300,000 live in Serbia and Montenegro (almost all of them in areas bordering Bosnia). Ethnically they are Slavic—they are descendents of Serbs and Montenegrins who converted to Islam during the long period of Ottoman rule—but, as in Bosnia, they have developed a culture that has diverged from the Serbo-Montenegran majority. During the Bosnian war, the Muslims of Serbia suffered persecution, and there were reports that some Muslim towns were ethnically cleansed by Serbian paramilitary forces. Persecution decreased after 1995 and has been reduced even further after the ouster of Milosevic in 2000. Many Slavic Muslims wish to secede from Yugoslavia and join Bosnia, a policy unlikely to be supported even by the post-Milosevic Yugoslavian government.

Other sizable minority groups include the Roma (Gypsies), Croats, and Slovaks. The Roma live primarily in Serbia's cities and have their own ethnic solidarity associations. Human rights groups accuse the Yugoslavian government of ignoring persecution of the Roma in schools, housing, and employment. As in other European countries, popular prejudice against the Roma is common. Croats and Slovaks mostly live in Vojvodina. During the breakup of Yugoslavia these minorities suffered persecution and ethnic cleansing at the hands of paramilitaries and government forces. This persecution lessened in the late 1990s. There is a small Jewish population (approximately 3,000), most of whom live in Belgrade.

CARL SKUTSCH

See also **Bosnia and Herzegovina; Bulgaria; Croatia; Macedonia; Macedonians; Serbs; Slovenia; Vlachs; Yugoslavs (Southern Slavs)**

Further Reading

Allcock, John, *Explaining Yugoslavia*, New York: Columbia University Press, 2000
Malcolm, Noel, *Kosovo: A Short History*, New York: Harper Collins, 1999
Silber, Laura, and Allan Little, *Yugoslavia: Death of a Nation*, New York: Penguin Books, 1997

Yugoslavs (Southern Slavs)

Capsule Summary

Location: Republics of former Yugoslavia
Total Population: not available
Languages: Serbian, Croatian, and Bosnian
Religions: Eastern Orthodox, Catholic, and Moslem

South Slav is a common name for a group of Slav tribes, alongside the Eastern and Western ones. These tribes evolved into the current Bulgarians, Serbs, Croats, Slovenes, and Montenegrins, and those Islamized during the Middle Ages, the Bosnians (Boshniaks). Being often subject to foreign rule, they sought methods of emancipation, including reunification with other adjacent peoples, as a part of the Slavophile project. It proved to be utopian and too difficult to be implemented, first, because of internal conflict and lack of consent between the people themselves, and, second, because of obstruction by the "great powers." After the breakdown of the Ottoman and Austro-Hungarian empires, a Serbia-dominated multinational Kingdom of the Serbs, Croats, and Slovenes was founded (1918)—later (1929–1941) called the Kingdom of Yugoslavia. The three main peoples—Serbs, Croats, and Slovenes—were anticipated to form one people, but domination of the Serbs prevented this. After World War II, Yugoslavia (1945–1991) consisted of six republics—Bosnia and Herzegovina, Croatia, Macedonia, Montenegro, Serbia, and Slovenia. However, the supranational entity, the Yugoslavs, remained marginal and almost disappeared with the federation's breakdown.

History

Southern Slavs, the Bulgarians, Serbs, Croats, and Slovenes, were separated, centuries ago, by the Magyars from their northern linguistic kinsmen, the Western and Eastern Slavs. Among the Yugoslavs, both religion and language are sources of division: the Croats and Slovenes are Catholics, and the Serbs are mostly Eastern Orthodox. Moreover, under the term *Serb*, such diverse peoples as the Serbs Proper, the Montenegrins, the Bosnians, the Herzegovinians, and the Dalmatians are often included. The Bosnians and Herzegovinians include large minorities of Moslems and Catholics, and the latter are particularly numerous in Dalmatia on the Adriatic coast.

The Serbs founded a kingdom, after their invasion from the north in the seventh century, in the area drained by the headwaters of the Lim and White Drim rivers. During the twelfth century, Serbs expanded southward to Kosovo, and during the period of their efflorescence, into Albania, Macedonia, and Thessaly in Greece. The so-called Old Serbia arose as an important kingdom during the thirteenth and fourteenth centuries. Arrival of the Ottoman Turks in the latter part of the fourteenth century terminated this period of expansion, and many of the Serbs fled northward while others became "Turkicized" and "Albanicized." After the flight of the Serbs from the plain of Kosovo, this region was soon colonized by Albanians, who still remain there. Under foreign domination—Bulgarians and Serbs under the Ottoman Empire, and Slovenes, Croats, and part of Serbs under the Austro-Hungarian Empire—were further divided. Only in the nineteenth century, an idea of a state emerged in which all South Slavs would live together—while the concepts and designs of unification remained radically different. A Croat philologist, Ljudevit Gaj, founded in the 1930s an "Illyrian movement" that envisaged a union of the Habsburg Slavs with the Serbs in an "Illyrian" state—initially within the Austro-Hungarian Empire. Serbs, however, achieved a quasi-independent status and thus attracted hopes of the subjacent Slavs elsewhere. The aspired position as the dominant people of Yugoslavia has only been won through centuries of retrenchment and struggle; they strived to "Slavicize" and "Serbicize" by force the minorities within their boundaries. Bulgaria, which was far less enthusiastic in joining such an alliance, later became a rival of Serbia, and after being confronted with its Western neighbor in a series of wars, preserved a cool and adversary attitude toward both Serbia and the whole of Yugoslavia.

Founded in 1918 after the breakdown of the Ottoman and Austro-Hungarian empires, a Serbia-dominated Kingdom of the Serbs, Croats, and Slovenes—and later (1929–1941) the Kingdom of Yugoslavia—included nearly all of the three South Slavic peoples mentioned, but also hundreds of thousands of Magyars, Bulgarians, and Albanians, among the subject minorities. The three main peoples—Serbs, Croats and Slovenes—were anticipated to form one people. Renaming the country "Yugoslavia" ten years later revealed an even firmer unitarist policy. This country's administrative structure was rearranged without any reference to the original ethnic or national composition. This design failed following the Nazi occupation in 1941 and the ferocious civil war that involved the Croatian fascist-type Ustasa, Serbian Chetniks, and a multinational Communist-led guerilla troops under the leadership of Josip Broz Tito. He solved the nationality question and in the 1945 founded the Federal People's Republic of Yugoslavia (after 1963, the Socialist Federal Republic of Yugoslavia). It consisted, first, in the construction of "Yugoslavism" ("Yugoslaviahood") as a supranational identity, and, second, in the establishment of a sophisticated constitutional system to ensure equal representation and power sharing of all national groups. This Yugoslavia consisted of six republics—Bosnia and Herzegovina, Croatia, Macedonia, Montenegro, Serbia, and Slovenia. In each of these—with the exception of Bosnia and Herzegovina (Bosnian Moslems were guaranteed the status of nation in 1968)—a particular nation comprised a clear numerical majority. Thus, Macedonians, a subject of assimilation in the Kingdom of Yugoslavia as "Southern Serbs," were elevated to the level of a separate nation, and hence authorized by their own parastate. The six republics enjoyed a high degree of internal autonomy, endorsed by a complicated federal system. In addition to the nations and nationalities, the constitutional system also acknowledged the self-declared Yugoslavs—people who did not consider themselves to belong to any of the designated categories, but most often were children of interethnic marriages, or those who desired to hide their connection to unpopular ethnicities such as Moslem or Bulgarian. Across the censuses, the percentage that was Yugoslav remained relatively low (1.7 percent in 1961, 1.3 percent in 1971, 5.4 percent in 1981, and 3.0 percent in 1991). The concept of "Yugoslavhood" lost its plausibility and prestige with the demise of the federal political organs, the collapse of Yugoslavia, and the rise of nationalism in the newly established independent republics (for example, in the Federal Republic of Yugoslavia they were slightly more than 3 percent, that is, less than a national minority, such as the Hungarians).

STEPHAN E. NIKOLOV

See also **Bosnia and Herzegovina; Croatia; Croats; Macedonia; Macedonians; Serbs; Slovenia**

Further Reading

Djokic, Dejan, editor, *Yugoslavism: Histories of a Failed Idea*, London: C. Hurst & Co., 2003

Godina, Vesna V., "The Outbreak of Nationalism on Former Yugoslav Territory: A Historical Perspective on the Problem of Supranational Identity," *Nations and Nationalism*, 4, no. 3 (1998)

Meier, Viktor, *Yugoslavia: A History of its Demise*, London: Routledge, 1999

Pavkovic, Alexander, "From Yugoslavism to Serbism: The Serb National Idea 1986-1996," *Nations and Nationalism*, 4, no. 4 (1998)

Udovicki, Jasminka, and James Ridgeway, editors, *Burn This House: The Making and Unmaking of Yugoslavia*, Durham and London: Duke University Press, 1997

Wachtel, Andrew Baruch, *Making a Nation, Breaking a Nation: Literature and Cultural Politics in Yugoslavia*, Stanford, California: Stanford University Press, 1998

Z

Zambia

Capsule Summary

Country Name: Republic of Zambia
Total Population: 10,307,333 (July 2003)
Languages: English (official), major vernaculars: Bemba, Kaonda, Lozi, Lunda, Luvale, Nyanja, Tonga, and about 70 other indigenous languages
Religions: Christian 50 percent to 75 percent, Muslim and Hindu 24 percent to 49 percent, indigenous beliefs 1 percent

The Republic of Zambia lies in southeastern Africa, has a population of just over 10 million, and is a presidential-parliamentary democracy. Its border countries include Angola, Democratic Republic of the Congo, Malawi, Mozambique, Namibia, Tanzania, and Zimbabwe. Approximately 40 ethnic groups live in Zambia and speak their own languages. The most important African groups are the Bemba (2 million), Lozi (473,000), Nsenga (427,000), Nyanja (989,000), and Tonga (990,000), as well as the Lala-Bisa.

There are nearly 40 African peoples in total, all Bantu. The *ethnonyms* of Zambia correspond to the language names. Non-African minorities include Asians (mostly Gujarati-speaking Indians), and English native speakers. The language of the Indian minority is mainly Gujarati. English is the official language and an important second language. The GDP per capita was $880 in 1999.

Zambia was inhabited between 1 and 2 million years ago, although present-day ancestors (the prima-rily Bantu-speaking population) did not settle in the area until the seventeenth and eighteenth centuries. Zambia was under the jurisdiction of the British South Africa Company from 1889 to 1924, when it became a British Protectorate called Northern Rhodesia. During the 1920s and 1930s, advances in mining spurred development and immigration. On October 24, 1964, it became the independent nation of Zambia. From 1964 to 1991, Zambia was ruled as a one-party state by Kenneth Kaunda and his United National Independence Party (UNIP). The current president (chief of state) is Levy Mwanawasa (since January 2, 2002).

With a soaring debt and inflation rate in 1991, and subsequent domestic pressure, President Kaunda was forced to allow Zambia to move towards multiparty democracy. National elections on October 31, 1991 brought a stunning defeat to Kaunda. Frederick Chiluba, chairman of the Movement for Multiparty Democracy (MMD), announced sweeping economic reforms, including privatization. From the beginning, however, his government showed strong tendencies toward abuse of power, corruption, and a disastrous economical policy. In particular, this prepared the breeding ground for the emergence of latent problems regarding ethnic minorities.

During 1995, ethnic turmoil occurred in several southern Zambian cities. Africans looted and burned shops and industrial estates of wealthy Indians after two Indians had been accused of involvement in ritual murders of several African children. Numerous Indians temporarily left their homes for Lusaka and Zimbabwe. The reason for the harassment of the Asians lay in the desperate social situation of many African Zambians, but deep-rooted ethnic stereotypes justified the encroachments in the minds of many Zambians.

Asians had migrated to Zambia in the nineteenth and twentieth centuries, mostly from Gujarat where they successfully engaged in large-scale trade. With this success, and a tendency to confine themselves in relations to their own ethnic group, Asian immigrants soon raised the animosity of the African majority, which was shared by whites during colonial times. Asians were accused of exploiting the country, of transferring their profits abroad, and of forming a trading network totally closed to Africans, denying any chance for Africans to participate in the economic growth. This antipathy found further expression in contempt for Indian cultural practices and habitats, which were regarded as depraved and disgusting.

Racist attitudes were also manifested during the parliamentary debate in respect to the constitutional amendment in 1996. One passage of the amendment decreed that both parents of a candidate for Zambian presidency must be Zambian citizens by birth or descent, apparently to prohibit Kaunda (whose father was born in Malawi) from a renewed candidature. In the course of the debate on who should be regarded as Zambian, the Asian and European minorities were targets of racist tirades by several members of parliament. This resulted even in the resignation of the non-African ministers Zukas and Patel from their posts.

The second major ethnic problem Zambia faces is the explosive situation in its Western Province, sometimes called *Barotseland*. It is chiefly inhabited by the Lozi minority. Their traditional kingdom comprised the Western Province, the Caprivi region of Namibia, and northern Botswana in precolonial times. During 1995, the situation in the region worsened and temporarily slipped from the control of the government. On the occasion of a congress, 3,000 traditional authorities showed sympathy for a possible separation of the Western Province from the rest of Zambia. In addition, they protested the possible introduction of a new land law by the government, which took away control over land distribution from the traditional chiefs.

During 1998, the so far relatively unknown Barotse Patriotic Front (BPF), under its leader Imasiku Mutangelwa, threatened to separate from the rest of Zambia, distributing pamphlets and writing a letter to Chiluba. A warning from the Minister of Defense was answered by the BPF with militant rhetoric. Even more alarming were newly established connections between the BPF and secessionists of the bordering Caprivi.

In 1999, separatist agitation in the Caprivi by Lozi politicians and Namibian refugees (who had fled to Botswana from repression by the Namibian police) increased. Politicians from the Western Province tried to put Lozi unity on the political agenda. While the BPF further advocated secession from Zambia, the chairman of the oppositional party, Agenda for Zambia (AZ), Mbikusita-Lewanika, called for a plebiscite concerning the status of the Western Province in Zambia. Both the BPF and the AZ referred to the right of self-determination of the Lozi. This, in their opinion, was guaranteed by the Barotseland treaty of 1964 in which the Western Province was made part of Zambia.

After renewed violent clashes between Lozi separatists and the Zambian Armed Forces in August 1999, Mutangelwa publicly declared his sympathy for the secessionists and called on all Lozi to support the struggle. The government gave the order to the police to interrogate Mutangelwa, whereupon he fled to the residence of the South African ambassador in Lusaka and asked for political asylum in South Africa. This was denied, and Mutangelwa was surrendered to the Zambian police.

Presently, the idea of secession does not seem to find broad support, neither among the traditional and the younger elite of the Lozi, nor among the rural population of the Western Province. Thus, local elections and parliamentary by-elections have not produced a satisfactory result for the secessionists.

Despite progress in privatization of government-owned copper mines, Zambia's economy remains one of the poorest in the world, with a GDP per capita income of only $800 in 2002. Copper represents 50 percent of all exports, although other industries include construction, foodstuffs, beverages, chemicals, textiles, fertilizer, and horticulture. Agriculture employs 85 percent of the population; products include corn, tobacco, peanuts, cotton, and sugarcane.

REINHARD KLEIN-ARENDT

See also **Bantu, Gujaratis**

Further Reading

Chipungu, Samuel N., *Guardians in Their Time. Experiences of Zambians under Colonial Rule 1890–1964*, London and Basingstoke: MacMillan Press, 1992

Osei-Hwedie, Bertha Z., "The Role of Ethnicity in Multi-Party Politics in Malawi and Zambia," *Journal of Contemporary African Studies*, 16, no.2 (1998)

Phiri, Bizeck J., "Decolonization and Multi-Racial Liberalism in Northern Rhodesia: A Reassessment," *Zambia Journal of History*, 5 (1992)

Power, Joey, "Race, Class, Ethnicity, and Anglo-Indian Trade Rivalry in Colonial Malawi, 1910–1945," *The International Journal of African Historical Studies*, 26, no.3 (1993)

Sichone, Owen B., and N.R. Simutanyi, "The Ethnic and Regional Questions, Ethnic Nationalism and the State in Zambia: The Case of Barotseland 1964–1994," in *Democracy in Zambia: Challenges for the Third Republic*, edited by Owen B. Sichone and Bornwell C. Chikulo, Harare, Zimbabwe: SAPES Books, 1996

Zana, Leila (Kurd)

Leila Zana has been a leading figure in the struggle for recognition and rights of the Kurds in Turkey. She was born on May 3, 1961, in the environs of Diyarbakr, the main Kurdish city in Turkey, to a poor, traditional Kurdish family. She has four sisters and a brother. Her conservative father made her leave elementary school after a year and half and arranged her marriage to her cousin Mehdi Zana, a prominent radical Kurdish politician more than 20 years her senior. They were married in 1975.

Although her husband was a leading Kurdish politician, political and family life were clearly separated, and her political awakening did not come about until 1980, when he was sentenced to ten years' imprisonment for political activity. With her husband in prison, she began to discover her own identity and began learning Turkish properly—previously she spoke only Kurdish—to educate herself politically. The situation of the Kurds in Turkey since the founding of the republic was characterised by nonrecognition on the part of the state, enforced by the military, although during a few periods (such as the 1960s and the time of this writing) the repression was not quite so forthright. The 1980s, following the military coup of 1980, were a period of intense repression directed against all manifestations of a separate Kurdish identity. Leila Zana was politiczed by her own self-education and by her visits to her husband in prison, where he suffered torture after his arrest. In 1984, she began political activity with hunger strikes and demonstrations outside the prison.

In July 1988, she was arrested with 83 others in connection with disturbances outside the prison when relatives were refused permission to visit the prisoners, and some were beaten. She was held for 50 days on charges of "incitement" and was tortured, receiving beatings and electric shocks. Her first imprisonment reinforced her growing politicization and heightened her awareness of the subservient position of women in both Turkish and Kurdish society, and on her release she became a leading spokeswoman for the Kurdish cause in Turkey. On October 20, 1991 she was elected to parliament as a member of the People's Labor Party (HEP), which gained some 70 percent of the vote in the southeast, openly declaring, "We are going to parliament to be the voice of Kurdish liberation." She became the first Kurdish woman parliamentary deputy.

There had been a number of attempts to set up legal Kurdish political parties in Turkey. HEP was formed in 1990 by seven members of parliament who had been expelled from the Social Democratic Populist Party (SHP, at that time the main left-of-center political party in Turkey) for attending a conference in Paris in November 1989 on the Kurdish situation. These seven, along with three other SHP deputies, established HEP on June 7, 1990. However, SHP reabsorbed HEP just before the elections of October 1991 in a deal that allowed the Kurdish members to stand under the SHP umbrella, and which bolstered SHP's showing in Kurdish areas. The tensions inherent in this deal became apparent almost immediately afterward when several of the new deputies, led by Leila Zana, attempted to take the parliamentary oath (which declares allegiance to Turkey as an indivisible state) in Kurdish rather than Turkish, causing pandemonium among the outraged Turkish deputies. The next day she was forced to leave SHP, and with others she helped reestablish HEP in 1992.

HEP was formally closed by the authorities in 1993, allegedly because it "functioned against the indivisible integrity of the state and of the nation, and became the focal point of illegal political activities." However, on May 7, 1993, 18 Kurdish deputies, again with Leila Zana prominent, helped form the Democracy Party (DEP).

DEP was similarly banned on June 16, 1994, and this ban allowed Leila Zana and 12 former DEP deputies whose parliamentary immunity had been lifted on March 2 to be charged with treason. Six of these had already fled abroad, to Belgium.

The trial of the remaining seven DEP deputies, including Leila Zana, and an independent deputy ended on December 8, 1994. Under Article 125 of the penal code, all of them had been accused of betraying the state and trying to destroy Turkey's territorial integrity because of their alleged links with the Kurdistan Workers' Party (PKK, a radical Kurdish opposition group led by Abdullah Öcalan; in 1984 it had begun armed resistance to the Turkish state in which 30,000 people were subsequently killed). The severest sentences were given to Leila Zana, Hatip Dicle, Ahmet Turk, Orhan Dogan, and Selim Sadak who each received 15 years and remained imprisoned at the time of this writing.

The trial caused much international censure. The European Parliament, on September 29, 1994, decided to suspend all contacts with the Turkish Parliament as well as to recommend that the proposed customs union with Turkey be suspended in protest. The final sentences produced further international protest, and international human rights groups called for the prisoners' release. After the trial, the imprisoned former DEP deputies revealed that they had been sent by the late President Turgut Ozal to meet Abdullah Öcalan, claiming that this visit had been part of an attempt to stop the bloodshed in the southeast region.

Since then, Leila Zana's reputation as one of the leading Kurdish figures in Turkey has continued to grow, and for many she embodies the indomitable Kurdish spirit. Although it is understood that at times the Turkish authorities would have liked to release her and avoid the adverse international publicity her continued detention attracts, she reportedly refuses to accept release unless her imprisoned colleagues are also freed.

Biography

Leila Zana. Born May 3, 1961 in Diyarbakr in southeast Turkey. Married at age 14 to a leading Kurdish radical politician, Mehdi Zana. Mother of two children. Arrested in 1988 during a demonstration against torture of prisoners and detained for two months. Elected to parliament in 1991 as the first Kurdish woman deputy. Arrested March 4, 1994 and sentenced to 15 years' imprisonment for treason. Awarded the Sakharov Prize for Freedom of Thought in 1995. At the time of this writing, remains in detention in a prison in Ankara.

Selected Works

Writings from Prison, French edition 1996, English 2000

HUGH POULTON

See also **Kurds; Turkey**

Further Reading

Institut Kurde de Paris, *The Kurdish Deputies: Prisoners of Conscience,* Paris: May 1995

Poulton, Hugh, *Top Hat, Grey Wolf, and Crescent: Turkish Nationalism and the Turkish Republic*, London: Hurst; New York: New York University Press, 1997

Zhuang (Chuang)

Capsule Summary

Location: South and southeast of the Popular Republic of China, mostly in Guangxi province.
Total Population: Approximately 18 million
Language: Zhuang
Religion: Animist

The ethnic label *Zhuang* was created by the Han people, and has been employed since the Qing dynasty (1644–1911) to describe various Thai ethnic groups whose members call themselves Bu Nong, Bu Tai, Bu Ban, Bu Tho, Bu Man, Bu Lao, or Khun Tho. In 2000, there were about 18 million Zhuang, 70 percent of them living in Guangxi (The others are scattered throughout Yunnan and Guizhou provinces.). Demographically, they rank second among the 56 "nationalities" (*minzu*) of China, far behind the Han. Their language idiom, Zhuang, belongs to the Austro-Thai branch of the Thai-kadai family. It includes two languages, the northern and the southern, both embracing several dialects. The Zhuang language is composed of 23 initial consonants and 78 vowels and final consonants. It is one of the most complicated tonal languages in the world, with six main tones and two split ones. The influence of various Chinese idioms (mainly Hakka and Cantonese) is noteworthy, especially within the ancient ideographic script. In 1957, the State Board of China instituted a Romanized alphabet for the Zhuang, adorned with some Cyrillic characters and Arab numerals used to discriminate the tones. In March 1958, the same State Board, taking into account that the Zhuang populate about 60 percent of the Guangxi territory, proclaimed the province as a Zhuang Autonomous Region.

Various hypotheses have been put forward concerning the origin of the Zhuang. A majority of Chinese historians think that they are descended from the Bai Yue ("the Hundred Viets") who peopled the present Zhuang area after the defeat of the Yue confederacy in 333 BCE. Others surmise that they stem from the intermixing of Yue and Drang peoples, the latter coming from Szechuan.

The Zhuang territory first came under the administration of China's central authority in 221 BCE, when the emperor Qin Shi Huang established a presence there. However, during the Han dynasty, the Chinese were mainly preoccupied with the border areas. Consequently, the heart of the Zhuang country, located between the You and Zuo tributaries of the Si river, escaped their control. It is only under the Tang (618–908) that the Empire strengthened its authority over the region. Military governors ruled the mountainous or remote areas and a heavy regime of taxation was imposed. From this period onward, the immigration of Han settlers was encouraged, and their arrival entailed an increasing competition with the local peasantry for the control of land. The Zhuang rebelled against this state of affairs, first in 756 and later in 822. The situation grew increasingly complicated in 966, when the southern part of the Zhuang territory was annexed by the newly created Dai Co Viet kingdom (which would eventually become Vietnam).

After a century of triangular wars between Chinese, Viet, and Thai, the latter were forced to accept their distribution on both sides of a frontier corresponding approximately to the present Sino-Viet border. In China, the Song Dynasty applied the system of indirect administration, later known as *tu si*, the main purpose of which was to reduce the revolts of the Man ("the southern barbarians") by delegating to them minor functions of government, notably the authority on the smallest territorial units, as the last links in a long hierarchical chain. The *tu si* were chosen by the central authority, the title was hereditary, and their heirs had to attend Chinese school, a commitment whose implicit aim was to quicken the process of "Sinocization" of the natives.

Under the Yuan (1279–1368) and the Ming (1368–1644), the system of "military settlements" (*tun tian*) was extended to the southern fringes of the empire. According to this policy, Han peasant-soldiers were sent in great numbers to the Far South to clear new land, to pacify the area, and to protect the frontier. Although many of these soldiers married local women, they were considered to be invaders by the Zhuang aristocracy, who organized several revolts during the fifteenth century. The imperial bureaucracy reacted by the reform of the *gai tu gui liu* ("abolition of chiefdoms, return to central power"). This new policy, combined with the strengthening of the military settlements and a series of natural disasters, pushed many Zhuang to flee during the next centuries toward Vietnam, where they were absorbed by the Nung, a closely related Thai group. Another reaction was a massive involvement of the Zhuang in the Taiping revolt (1850), whose leader was a Hakka living in Guangxi. After the defeat, the insurgents moved to Tonkin where, organized in a movement named Yellow Flags, they fought against the French. The Zhuang also contributed to the Revolution of 1911 by becoming key members of the Tong Meng Hui, an activist group Sun Yat-sen formed to promote his cause. During the next decades, many rallied to the Communists, and the first pro-Communist organization was founded in Guangxi in 1925.

Despite centuries of fierce resistance to the Chinese administration, the Zhuang never succeeded in promoting their own cause and gaining real autonomy. On the contrary, they were taken over by the Communists, and because of the infiltration of Han elements into their territory, their language and culture has been subjected to a deep Chinese influence. Today, Zhuang people are primarily plains dwellers growing wet-rice and maize alongside the Han peasantry. Their way of life is in many respects impossible to distinguish from that of the Han. Their method of social stratification, which in times past was characterized by the feudal tripartite (nobility, commoners, and slaves), was abolished by the Communists in 1949.

BERNARD FORMOSO

See also **China**

Further Reading

Barlow, John G. "The Zhuang Minority Peoples of the Sino-Vietnamese Frontier in the Song Period," *Journal of Southeast Asian Studies,* Vol. XVIII-2, 1987

Cauquelin, Josiane, "Les Zhuang," *Péninsule*, 29, 1994

Eberhard, Wolfram, *China's Minorities: Yesterday and Today*, Belmont, California: Wadsworth Publishing Company, 1982

Zimbabwe

Capsule Summary

Country Name: Republic of Zimbabwe
Location: Southern Africa
Total Population: 12,576,742 (July 2002)
Languages: English (official), Shona, Sindebele (the language of the Ndebele, sometimes called Ndebele), numerous but minor tribal dialects
Religions: syncretic (part Christian, part indigenous beliefs) 50 percent, Christian 25 percent, indigenous beliefs 24 percent, Muslim and other 1 percent

The Republic of Zimbabwe is a land-locked country of 390,757 sq. kms (150,872 sq. miles) bounded on the north and northwest by Zambia, on the southwest by Botswana, on the east by Mozambique and on the south by South Africa. Land more than 1,200 meters (3,937 feet) above sea level runs across the country from southwest to northeast; land below 900 meters (2952.75 feet) lies along the Zambezi basin in the north, and the Limpopo and Sabi basins in the south and southeast. The eastern highlands is the most mountainous area. Most mineral deposits, including gold and iron ore, are found on the highland and adjacent midlevel; no oil has been found, but there are substantial deposits of coal.

In 2002 the population was just over 12.5 million, although this number remains unstable and reflects the excess mortality rate due to AIDS. Represented ethnic groups in Zimbabwe are African 98 percent (Shona 82 percent, Ndebele 14 percent, other 2 percent), mixed and Asian 1 percent, white less than 1 percent. A relatively small number of white farmers and companies engage in commercial farming. Resettlement of Africans and occupation of white farms have been encouraged by the state. In the early 1990s, white commercial farmers owned more than 40 percent of all farming land and produced about 80 percent of the country's cash crops. Most rural African households live in poverty on communal lands, most of which suffers from overpopulation and overstocking. Per capita income (GDP) was $2,100 in 2002.

History

The earliest inhabitants of the area date from Bantu-speaking peoples in the fifth century CE. Until 1979, Zimbabwe was known as Rhodesia; it gained independence from the United Kingdom in 1980. The colony of southern Rhodesia was established by the British South African (BSA) Company in 1890. The BSA Company had hoped for extensive gold deposits, but these were not found. When BSA Company administration ended in 1923, the British government allowed the white settlers to choose either to join South Africa or take over the administration themselves. They voted to remain separate and developed their own racially segregated society, only nominally under British authority. The most important piece of segregationist legislation was the Land Apportionment Act of 1930, which divided the country unequally into two parts and restricted African access to all the better land. African males had to migrate from the rural areas to the towns, farms, and mines to work, to pay the required taxes. Few blacks got the vote, and so the white settlers were able to arrange things to suit their interests. By the late 1950s, the white population had increased to over 200,000; many of the recent immigrants quickly became relatively prosperous. As Africans resented their subordination, strikes and protests mounted and nationalist parties were born.

Meanwhile Southern Rhodesia became the major constituent of a Central African Federation founded in 1953. This broke up in the early 1960s, and white voters in 1962 returned a white supremacist party to power, the Rhodesian Front (RF). When Britain refused to consider independence for Southern Rhodesia under the existing minority-rule constitution, the RF made

Ian Smith prime minister, and in November 1965 he declared unilateral independence (UDI). Britain and other countries imposed economic sanctions, but they proved ineffective for many years. The British government tried to negotiate a new settlement, but when the opinion of the African majority was tested, it was found that the compromise deal was unacceptable. From 1972, guerrilla war intensified, and, within a few years, large areas of the country had effectively been liberated. It was the impossibility of winning the guerrilla war in the long run, as well as increased international pressure, that brought down the Smith regime.

The African nationalist movement split in 1963 into the Zimbabwe African People's Union (ZAPU) led by Joshua Nkomo and the Zimbabwe African National Union (ZANU), led first by Ndabaningi Sithole and then by Robert Mugabe. In the war, Mugabe's forces were mainly based in Mozambique, Nkomo's in Zambia. A crucial development was the withdrawal of South African government support for the Smith regime in 1976; the South African prime minister, John Vorster, realized that the independence of Mozambique in 1975 had altered the regional balance of power and made it impossible for Smith to win the war. Smith then attempted an internal settlement, and Bishop Abel Muzorewa took over as prime minister. But in 1979, with the war having reached a stalemate, all parties agreed to attend a conference at Lancaster House in London, chaired by the British, and it drew up a constitution for an independent Zimbabwe and provided for a mechanism of transition. The British appointed a governor to rule for a brief period, in which an election was held; Zanu-PF, as Mugabe's party was called, won overwhelmingly. The British then withdrew, and the country became independent with Mugabe the new prime minister. He has been the country's only ruler (as president since 1987) and has dominated the country's political system since independence.

To the surprise of most whites, Mugabe preached reconciliation and dropped his radical, socialist goals. He was constrained in what he could do by the Lancaster House constitution: For a period, whites were to have a disproportionate political role in the house of assembly. The vague assurances about a fund to assist in land redistribution came to little. The war had been fought to regain land, and the importance of the commercial farming sector made the problem a difficult one to deal with. Mugabe soon had to face a dissident movement in Matabeleland, where opposition was ruthlessly crushed and the security forces committed massive abuses of human rights. There was increasing talk of the advantages of a one-party state. The reservation of seats for whites was abolished in 1987, and at the end of that year, Mugabe became executive president. He now included Joshua Nkomo, his old rival, in his government. Unemployment began to rise, and students and others voiced protest against the regime. Although in 1991 the government adopted a structural adjustment program, the economy continued to decline. In 1996, Mugabe was sworn in for a third term as president, but he and his government were increasingly attacked for corruption and arrogance. After funds set aside to assist war veterans were used by members of the government, veterans were given a large payout in 1997, which the country could not afford. After food riots in 1998, Mugabe announced that farmers would no longer receive compensation for confiscated land, and a list was published of properties to be taken over; members of the ruling elite were some of the first beneficiaries. In early 2000, Mugabe held a referendum on constitutional changes, which he lost. He then gave free rein to so-called war veterans to occupy farms. A number of white farmers were killed as the police stood by. In the parliamentary election in June, the Movement for Democratic Change came close to winning a majority of seats, despite intimidation. Mugabe then continued supporting the land invaders, ignoring the rule of law, and when the media and the judiciary challenged this, he took steps to muzzle both. The Zimbabwean dollar declined even further, inflation sky-rocketed, and the economy began to look very sick. Yet other countries continued relations with the Mugabe government, unsure how best to act to help force him out.

CHRISTOPHER SAUNDERS

See also **Zambia**

Further Reading

de Waal, V., *The Politics of Reconciliation: Zimbabwe's First Decade*, London, 1990

Herbst, J., *State Politics in Zimbabwe*, Berkeley, 1990

Rasmussen R., and S. Rubert, *Historical Dictionary of Zimbabwe*, Metuchen, New Jersey, 2nd edition, 1991

Stoneman S., and L. Cliffe, *Zimbabwe: Politics, Economics and Society*, London, 1989

Sylvester C., *Zimbabwe: the Terrain of Contradictory Development*, Boulder, Colorado, 1991

Tamarkin, M., *The Making of Zimbabwe*, London, 1990

Verrier, A., *The Road to Zimbabwe, 1890–1980*, London, 1986

Zoroastrians

Capsule Summary

Name: Zoroastrians (Zardoshti) or Mazdayasna

Location: Minority communities worldwide. Largest communities in India, Iran, Canada, United States, England, and Pakistan. Much smaller communities in Australia, Hong Kong, Russia, Singapore, South Africa, Sri Lanka, and Tajikistan

Total Population: Approximately 155,000 worldwide

Languages: Mainly Gujarati, Farsi (New Persian), and English

Religion: Zoroastrianism or Mazdaism

General

Zoroastrians (also Zardoshti) are followers of a religion called Zoroastrianism. Zoroastrianism, or Mazdaism, a faith that eventually came to trace its tenets to words attributed by tradition to an eponymous individual named Zarathushtra (also Zardosht), developed into a major religion in ancient and medieval Iran. During that period it influenced Hellenistic, Jewish, Christian, and Muslim beliefs, praxes, and societies—especially in the Middle East. After the Arab conquest of Iran in the seventh to eighth centuries CE, the number of Zoroastrians declined gradually through conversion to Islam. Zoroastrian communities have survived not only in Iran but also on the Indian subcontinent, where they are called the Parsis, and more recently in several countries around the world. Zoroastrians generally refer to themselves as Mazdayasna, "Mazdeans" or "worshipers of Mazda," a term that acknowledges their reverence for a divinity called Ahura Mazda, "wise lord" or "deity of wisdom," rather than by the designation as Zoroastrians given to them by Europeans.

History

Probably originating in Central Asia, the Zoroastrian or Mazdean community spread its beliefs and practices among other Proto-Iranian groups during the second and first millennia BCE. Members of the community, including their priests known as magi, settled on the Iranian plateau by the ninth century BCE. Zoroastrianism became an important faith in the Achaemenian Empire (550–330 BCE) and the Parthian kingdom (247 BCE–224 CE). Zoroastrians formed the demographic majority, and Zoroastrianism was the official faith of the

Sasanian Empire (224–651 CE). Zoroastrians were also numerous in western Central Asia during Late Antiquity and the early Middle Ages as merchants, farmers, pastoralists, and soldiers. Other religious communities, like Jews and Christians, in Iran during those centuries were regarded as official minorities. Contact with Jews and Christians transmitted Zoroastrian apocalyptical and eschatological notions to members of those two communities. In turn, Zoroastrians partially assimilated the Jewish and Christian concepts of prophethood and monotheism.

After the Arab conquest of Iran, conversion to Islam gradually occurred and reached its zenith by the middle of the ninth century CE. Muslim authorities initially restricted conversion to maintain steady revenue from the *jizya*, "poll tax," which was levied from each non-Muslim, but later enforced the espousing of Islam. The threat of absorption into an increasingly large Muslim community reinforced the Zoroastrian tendency toward cultural preservation, and as the community grew smaller, this tendency increased. Eventually, many Zoroastrians withdrew from all major forms of interaction with Muslims and sought refuge in the thinly populated regions of central Iran at towns like Yazd and Kerman. Surviving the asperities of time, their descendants continued the faith and its practices, despite having to pay the poll tax to the Muslims for remaining Zoroastrian. Finally, in 1854 CE, Parsi Zoroastrians of India were able to send an emissary to the Qajar court in Iran to intercede on behalf of the Iranian Zoroastrians—as a result, the poll tax was abolished shortly thereafter. During the twentieth century CE, a brief period of respite from economic hardship and pressure to adopt Islam was experienced under the Pahlavi dynasty, which promoted Zoroastrians to positions of authority, encouraged the expression of Zoroastrian religious and cultural practices, and glorified Iran's pre-Islamic past. The advent of the Islamic Republic of Iran, in 1979 CE, has witnessed a return to strict socioreligious minority status for Zoroastrians under the new Muslim constitution of Iran.

Several groups of Zoroastrians had emigrated from Iran in earlier centuries to avoid persecution by Muslims and conversion to Islam. Some noble families and their retainers relocated to China via Central Asia. Their descendents survived there, even building fire temples, and, despite proscription in 845 CE, until the thirteenth century. Other groups moved to the Caucasus and the Russian steppe with limited success. On the other hand, the Parsis or Indian Zoroastrians, descendants of émigrés who migrated to the western coast of India around the tenth century CE, have flourished.

Society

There were nearly 60,000 Zoroastrians in Iran in 1966 CE. By 1984 CE, the population had declined considerably. Despite inflated figures in recent censuses that put the community's numbers around 90,000, a figure officially revised downward several times thereafter to around 45,000, the number of Zoroastrians continues to decline in the twenty-first century. This decline is the result of several factors: conversion to Bahaism is one, increased attempts to enforce conversion to Islam is another, and the war between Iran and Iraq during the 1980s forced many Zoroastrians youths to emigrate—to escape military conscription—finding refuge in the United States and Canada where they number approximately 3,000 and in Europe where they number around 2,000. Although officially recognized as a minority and represented in national settings, Zoroastrians in Iran are often offered very limited protection from their Muslim neighbors by the current Islamic revolutionary regime that governs the country. Nonetheless, Zoroastrians continue to survive not only in the central Iranian city of Yazd which has been their stronghold for several centuries, but also in Tehran, the country's capital, at the cities of Shiraz and Isfahan, and even in Khorramshahr, which is close to the Iraq-Iran border. Among the Iranian Zoroastrians, like their counterparts the Parsis or Indian Zoroastrians, the religion's tenets are taught to the children, basic rituals continue to be practiced by priests and laity, and clerical and lay organizations remain vigorously active within the community. Unlike the Parsis, Iranian Zoroastrians accept converts to the community, although they do not proselytize for fear of retribution from the majority Shi'ite Muslim community.

The Parsis presently number about 76,400 in India and 2,800 in Pakistan. They have also experienced globalization due to economic and social factors in the nineteenth and twentieth centuries. As a result, other demographically important groups of Parsis reside in Canada and the United States where they number approximately 8,000, and in England and Scotland where they number around 4,000. Even smaller groups ranging from a few thousand individuals to a few hundred or less are located in regions of Africa, Asia, Australia, and Europe.

During medieval and premodern times, Zoroastrians also resettled in very small numbers within areas of the Eurasian steppe—which may have been the original homeland of the community and its religion during the second and/or first millennia BCE. As a result, demographically insignificant communities are still present in countries such as Russia and Tajikistan.

JAMSHEED K. CHOKSY

See also **Parsis**

Further Reading

Boyce, Mary, *A Persian Stronghold of Zoroastrianism*, Oxford: Claredon Press, 1977
———, *Zoroastrians: Their Religious Beliefs and Practices,* London: Routledge and Kegan Paul, 1979, reprinted 1988
———, *A History of Zoroastrianism*, Vol. 2, Leiden: E.J. Brill, 1982
———, *A History of Zoroastrianism*, Vol. 1, Leiden: E.J. Brill, 2nd edition, 1989
Boyce, Mary, and Frantz Grenet, *A History of Zoroastrianism*, Vol. 3, Leiden: E.J. Brill, 1991
Choksy, Jamsheed K., *Conflict and Cooperation: Zoroastrian Subalterns and Muslim Elites in Medieval Iranian Society*, New York: Columbia University Press, 1997
———, "Zoroastrianism," in *How Different Religions View Death and Afterlife*, edited by C.J. Johnson and M.G. McGee, Philadelphia: Charles Press, 2nd edition, 1998
Duchesne-Guillemin, Jacques, *Symbols and Values in Zoroastrianism: Their Survival and Renewal*, New York: Harper and Row, 1966
Hinnells, John, *Zoroastrians in Britain*, Oxford, England: Clarendon Press, 1996
Humbach, Helmut, edited and translated, *The Gathas of Zarathushtra and the Other Old Avestan Texts*, 2 vols., Heidelberg, Germany: Carl Winter, 1991
Davoud, Pour-e, *Introduction to the Holy Gathas*, Bombay: Fort Printing Press, 1927
Mistree, Khojeste, *Zoroastrianism: An Ethnic Perspective*, Bombay, India: Zoroastrian Studies, 1982
Soroushian, Jamshid S., *History of the Zoroastrians of Kerman*, Kerman, Iran: N.p., 1992 (in Farsi)
Writer, Rashna, *Contemporary Zoroastrians: An Unstructured Nation*, Lanham, Maryland: University Press of America, 1994
Zaehner, Robert C., *The Dawn and Twilight of Zoroastrianism*, London: Weidenfeld and Nicolson, 1961

Index

C

opposition to colonialism, 414
outspokenness and radicalism (1950s), 414
professional life, 413
racism and, 413
The Souls of Black Folk (1903), 413
Dukhobors
extremist group of, 416–417
general information, 416
language, 416
non-recognition of state power, 416
religion, 416
in Russia, 417
Sons of Freedom, 417
and spiritual Christians, 416
and Tolstoy, Leo, 416
in United States, 417
Dutch East India Company, 610
Dutch Guiana, and South Asians, 1142
Dutch Reformed Church, founding of, 308

E

Easter Island
and Chile, 284
Euronesians in, 446
and Rapa-Nui, 284
Eastern Samoa, Euronesians in, 446
East Indians, in Cuba, 350
East Timor
culture, 420
economy, 420
ethnic groups, 419–420
fight for independence, 611
general information, 419
history of, 419
independence (1974), 420
independence (1994), 420
and Indonesia, 419–420, 615
Indonesian invasion (1975), 420
Indonesian occupation, 420
international aid, 420
language, 419, 420
Portuguese colonization, 419–420
and Ramos-Horta, José, 1002–1003
refugees, 420
religion, 419, 420
Tetum in, 419–420
Economic and Social Council (ECOSOC), 567
Ecuador
economy, 421, 422–423
ethnicity and society, 422
general information, 421
history of, 421–422
independence movement, 422
independence from Spain (1822), 423
indigenous groups, political activity of, 422
Quechua, 990–992
religion, 421
and Spain, 421
Education rights
historical and political aspects, 424
Indian social system and, 424
national and international law and, 423
nondiscriminatory treatment at, 423
origin and evolution of, 424
preservation of power and, 424–425

social position and, 424
women and, 424
World Declaration on Education for All, 423–424
Egypt
Bedouins in, 426
Berbers in, 426
early Christians in, 306
Coptic Christians and, 331–333, 426
desert monasticism, 426
ethnicities and minorities, 426
general information, 425
history of, 425–426
Islamic resurgence in the 1970s, 426–427
language, 425
Nubians in, 426
religion, 425
religious minorities in, 427
and Sudan, 1153
zabbaleen, 426–427
Eleutherian Adventurers, 172
El Salvador
Amerindians in, 427
economy, 428
general information, 427
history of, 427–428
language, 428
Lenca in, 428
Pipíl in, 428
political repression of minorities (1930s), 428
religion, 428
and Spain, 427
and U.S., 427, 428
Emancipation Proclamation, 319
England, *see also* Great Britain
and United Kingdom, 1263
English, the
Celts and, 430
as ethnic minority, 429
general information, 429
as highly hybridized people, 430
history of, 429
language, 429, 430
and Normans, 430
and Northern Ireland, 429
and other nations, 429
political culture, 430
religion, 429
reverse migration, 430
and Scotland, 429
and Wales, 429
Environmental racism
defined, 431
social structure and, 431–433
test of, 431
Epirus, 63
Equal opportunity
analysis of policies for, 434
definitions, 432–433
difference principle, 433
equal access, 433
equal treatment, 433
principle of merit, 433
types of equality, 433
Equatorial Guinea
and Annobonés, 107–108
Bubi in, 241–243

F

INDEX

INDEX

O

P

3